Personal Finance

2d Edition

Ike Mathur

Professor of Finance
Southern Illinois University

FH60BA
PUBLISHED BY
SOUTH-WESTERN PUBLISHING CO.
CINCINNATI   WEST CHICAGO, IL   CARROLLTON, TX   LIVERMORE, CA

Photo Credits

COVER PHOTO: © Harvey Lloyd/The Stock Market

Page 3: Mimi Forsyth/MONKMEYER PRESS PHOTO SERVICE

Page 201: Dave Schaefer

Page 267: Century 21 Real Estate Corporation

Page 307: Peter Glass/MONKMEYER PRESS PHOTO SERVICE

Page 339: Dave Schaefer

Page 363: David Strickler/MONKMEYER PRESS PHOTO SERVICE

Page 401: Arlene Collins/MONKMEYER PRESS PHOTO SERVICE

Page 433: Photo by Richard Younker

Page 473: © 1988 Karelle Scharff

Page 499: Photo by Richard Younker

Page 561: Arlene Collins/MONKMEYER PRESS PHOTO SERVICE

Page 585: Christie's, New York

Page 621: H. ARMSTRONG ROBERTS

Page 659: H. ARMSTRONG ROBERTS

ISBN: 0-538-80057-7
Library of Congress Catalog Card Number: 87-63016

1 2 3 4 5 6 7 8 D 5 4 3 2 1 0 9 8

Printed in the United States of America

Preface

Managing personal finances has become increasingly complex in the past few years. Financial institutions are subject to fewer regulations and offer consumers many different types of savings and checking plans. Home buyers are faced with a large array of alternative mortgages. Car buyers may often face the choice between a cash rebate or lower finance charges. These are but a few areas that require consumers to evaluate alternative financial choices and to make financial decisions.

Students today are interested in the practical applications of concepts and techniques in managing their personal finances. This book has been written for them. By using a variety of special features, the book will help students to live the type of life styles they want to live.

Special Features

Personal Finance (FH60BA) includes a number of special features designed to draw the students' attention, communicate the factors involved in analyzing financial situations, and help them make better financial decisions.

1. Each chapter opens with a vignette or real-life example, highlighting a major theme covered in the chapter.
2. End-of-section spot quizzes help the student test his or her understanding of the subject materials.
3. Important terms in the text appear in **boldface type**.
4. Highlighted text and cartoons are utilized extensively throughout the book and help illustrate important personal finance concepts.
5. End-of-chapter case problems are designed to let the reader test his or her knowledge by arriving at financial solutions to problems.
6. References provided at the end of each chapter can be used to explore certain topics in greater detail.
7. A glossary is provided at the end of the book and includes in alphabetical order all important terms introduced in the book.
8. An index of important concepts is included for easy reference.

Supplements

Three supplements are available with this book.

Instructor's Manual (FH60BX)

An *Instructor's Manual* is available free to all instructors who adopt the book. Each chapter of the *Instructor's Manual* has the following four sections:

I. Answers to End-of-Chapter Questions

II. Solutions to End-of-Chapter Case Problems

III. Key Concepts

IV. Lotus® 1-2-3® Applications[1]

The *Instructor's Manual* is accompanied by a Lotus 1-2-3 template diskette. The 5¼-inch diskette, for use with the IBM PC[2] and compatible personal computers, contains the following items for many of the chapters:

1. Case problems from the text
2. Solutions to case problems in the text
3. Relevant tables from the text
4. Study-guide case problems
5. Solutions to study-guide case problems

Additional information on the Lotus 1-2-3 template diskette is provided in the preface to the *Instructor's Manual*.

Test Bank (FH60BG)

A separate *Test Bank*, containing over 1,000 true-false and multiple-choice questions, is also available free to adopters. The test questions have been classroom tested and provide the instructor with great flexibility in constructing tests. Additionally, the *Test Bank* is available in conjunction with South-Western's MicroSWAT II (FH60BH81T), which allows for the computerized selection of questions for tests.

---

1. Lotus and 1-2-3 are registered trademarks of Lotus Development Corporation. Any reference to Lotus refers to this footnote.
2. IBM PC is a trademark of International Business Machines. Any reference to the IBM PC refers to this footnote.

Study Guide (FH60BD)

A *Study Guide*, written by Lynette L. Knowles and myself, is available from your local bookstore. Each chapter of the *Study Guide* has the following sections:

- I.   Terms to Know
- II. Key Concepts
- III. Self Tests
    - A. True-False
    - B. Multiple-Choice
    - C. Matching or Fill in the Blanks
- IV. Solved Case Problems
- V. Answers to Self Tests
- VI. Lotus 1-2-3 Applications

The first two sections help the reader in understanding the main ideas in each chapter. Section III helps in testing one's understanding of the materials covered. The fourth section contains one or more case problems with detailed solutions. The fifth section contains answers to self tests.

The *Study Guide* is also accompanied by a Lotus 1-2-3 template diskette that contains the same materials as the diskette in the *Instructor's Manual* with the exception of the solutions to the case problems in the text. The last section of each *Study Guide* chapter is titled "Lotus Application" and generally shows how Lotus 1-2-3 can be applied to a personal finance problem. The Lotus applications are illustrated by utilizing the Lotus 1-2-3 template diskette.

ACKNOWLEDGMENTS

Many have contributed directly or indirectly to the development of this book. My greatest debt is to my students who read the materials included here. Their feedback was very helpful in deciding on the presentation style and on the types of figures and tables to be included in the text.

I am grateful to my colleagues, here at Southern Illinois University at Carbondale and at other universities, who read selected portions of the materials and provided a stimulating environment for developing the book.

I am grateful to Susan Edgren of Southern Illinois University at Carbondale for using my preliminary materials in her personal finance courses

and for providing me with valuable feedback. Laura Sims and Robert Cundiff deserve special thanks for typing portions of the text manuscript. Finally, I am indebted to my family members for their understanding during the writing and revision of this book.

Ike Mathur
Southern Illinois University
Carbondale, Illinois

Contents

Contents

ix

Part 1

Financial Planning

Financial planning is a key requirement for successful personal financial management. Chapter 1, "Careers, Income, and Financial Goals," explains the relationship between life style and personal financial management. Factors that explain differences in incomes are discussed. The chapter also covers choosing a career, preparing a resume, getting a job, and the process of setting personal financial goals.

Chapter 2, "Financial Records: Tools of Financial Management," describes the maintenance of records and the mechanics of preparing income statements and balance sheets. Chapter 3, "Financial Planning and Income Taxes," explains the nature of taxes and how tax returns are prepared. Special topics discussed are capital gains taxes, reducing taxes, and tax assistance.

Chapter 4 is titled "Consumerism: Getting More for Less." Typical consumer frauds are explained, warranties and service contracts are discussed, and consumer protection legislation is outlined. The last part of the chapter outlines a procedure for filing a complaint about a product or service.

Chapter 1

Careers, Income, and Financial Goals

Objectives

After reading this chapter, you will be able to:

- Explain the relationship between life style and personal financial goals.

- Identify factors that explain differences in personal income.

- Discuss factors to consider when choosing a career.

- Prepare a resume.

- Explain how to get a job.

- Explain the procedure for setting financial goals for yourself.

Tom Seifert got a taste of football at the tender age of five when his dad took him to see a game between the Midshipmen of the U.S. Navy and the University of Pittsburgh Panthers. Even though the Midshipmen lost, their impact on Tom was strong. No, Tom didn't go on to become the star quarterback for the team, lead them to the national title, and then become rookie of the year in the National Football League.

What really impressed Tom were the uniforms of the Navy cadets who were sitting in the stands. He wanted to look just like the cadets. So years later, while attending Villanova University, Tom joined the Naval ROTC. Upon graduation, he joined the U.S. Marines. Now, after serving four years in the Marines, Tom is considering resigning and looking for a civilian job.[1]

Why this change of heart after four years in the Marines? Tom has two major reasons for thinking about leaving the Marines: (1) He does not like the periodic separations from his family, and (2) his salary does not allow him to lead the type of life he desires.

Tom is married and has a two-year-old daughter. He and his wife call Jacksonville, North Carolina, home. They own a house worth $29,000, some land worth $12,500, and other assets worth $17,750. They owe $29,300 on the property and the family car. Tom's wife is a part-time schoolteacher. Last year the Seifert family earned about $20,800. Tom's B.A. is in political science, and he is considering enrolling in an M.B.A. program. He believes that he is well qualified to work as a salesperson. What advice do you have for the Seiferts? What financial factors should they keep in mind as Tom begins to think about a new career?

Tom Seifert is not alone in his search for a better life for his family and himself. Most of us share his desire to improve our lives. Our search for a better life, however, is affected by our choice of career and by how well we can plan and manage the financial side of life. This chapter shows how life style and financial plans are tied together, how to choose a career, how to get a job, and how to set financial goals.

LIFE STYLES AND FINANCIAL GOALS

John Bouchard often ends up climbing a wall at work. Many people climb walls at work out of frustration. But not John—he climbs a real, twenty-four-foot granite wall. You see, John and Marie Bouchard are coowners of a company called Wild Things, located in North Conway, New Hampshire. Wild Things is. . . Well, we are getting ahead of ourselves, so let's back up.

John graduated from Dartmouth College in 1978 with an M.B.A. Upon graduation, he accepted a position as an auditor with the accounting firm

---

[1] "Out of Dress Blue, Into Gray Flannel," *Money* (May 1980): 95–100.

of Ernst & Whinney in Boston. After about a year, he decided that he needed more personal space than was provided by the accounting firm, so he quit. The Bouchards relocated to New Hampshire, where John hired out as a mountain-climbing guide. Marie pitched in by sewing clothing items for mountain climbers. These items caught on with the climbers, leading to the formation of Wild Things.

Life Styles

As coowners of Wild Things, neither John nor Marie can rely on a steady paycheck. Instead, their incomes and fortunes are tied to the success of Wild Things. Their desire for independence led them to start their own company. They can decide when to go to work, how many hours to work each day, and, within reason, how much money to earn. Their choice in operating their own business allows them to live the way they want to live. The flip side of the coin is that, as business owners, they also have to plan for their own retirement.[2]

The Bouchard family situation is not unusual. All individuals and families are basically free to follow life styles of their own choosing. Some people choose the security of a 9-to-5 job. The job may provide a steady income, security, and a pension. Others, like the Bouchards, choose the more risky option of running their own businesses. They may choose this career path because it provides more freedom and the opportunity to earn a high income.

The three factors we have mentioned thus far—life style, career choice, and income—are closely related. Figure 1.1 illustrates these relationships. The box at the top of the figure is labeled "Life Style." One family may choose a simple life on a farm, where it raises its own food and is relatively self-sufficient. Another family may choose to live in New York City to enjoy the opera, plays, and night life. These two families have life styles that are quite different from each other. The country family is giving up entertainment for perhaps a less pressured living environment. The city family is giving up closeness to nature in return for the glamour of city life. The career choices for the wage earners in the two families will be different also. The farm family will not be going to work in suits; the city family will not be involved in pitching manure. The incomes of the two families will be different as well.

Basically, the life style that you desire affects your choice of both career and income. Also, your life style is affected by your choice of career and income. As the Seifert family example indicates, the present career of Tom Seifert is affecting both the family's life style and income. He desires to

---

[2] "Rising Off-the-Wall Managers," *Money* (December 1985): 31–32.

Figure 1.1 Personal Financial Management Model

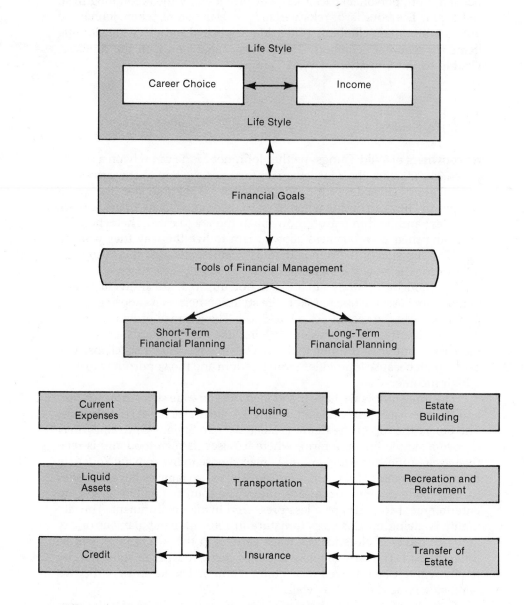

change careers mainly to improve the family's life style and income. Income, too, affects life style and career choice. A person with a high income would be able to lead a life style that is not possible for someone with a lower income. A desire for a particular level of income would point toward certain careers. For example, people who desire a high income

would probably consider favorably professions such as medicine and corporate management.

Financial Goals

The close relationship among life style, career choice, and income is reflected in Figure 1.1. The box at the top encloses smaller boxes labeled "Career Choice" and "Income," indicating that desire for a certain life style may dictate career choice and income. The double arrows between career choice and income indicate that they affect each other directly. The next box in Figure 1.1 is labeled "Financial Goals." The topic of financial goals will be discussed in greater detail later in this chapter. At this point, we can identify three financial goals:

1. Attaining and maintaining a certain life style or quality of living.
2. Accumulating funds for retirement and building an estate.
3. Getting the most for your money.

Financial goals are converted into financial plans by using tools of financial management, such as budgeting and tax planning. Later chapters in this book cover these topics.

The first goal listed deals with current planning—that is, financial planning for the present time. The second goal deals with both long-term and current planning and therefore is not represented by a separate box in Figure 1.1.

Current planning includes the management of liquid assets, such as cash and checking and savings accounts. It also includes the management of credit or loans. Housing and insurance span both current and long-term planning. For example, some portion of the housing payments may be for providing present shelter, whereas the remainder may be for building an estate. Similarly, a portion of insurance expenses may be for life insurance.

Long-term planning, besides housing and insurance, deals with accumulating funds for retirement and for estate building. We plan for retirement so that when we stop producing income, we have sufficient funds to maintain our life style. We are interested in building an estate for a variety of reasons, such as having funds available to educate our children and to leave them or a charity an inheritance.

Notice in Figure 1.1 that a double arrow connects the two boxes labeled "Life Style" and "Financial Goals." The reason is that our life styles dictate what financial goals we should have. Achieving our financial goals helps us to attain or maintain our preferred life style. Consider the example of the Bouchard family. Without planning for retirement, the family would not have funds on hand to maintain its life style after John and Marie retire. Putting into effect a plan for retirement will allow them to retire and live comfortably.

Spot Quiz • Life Styles and Financial Goals

1. Financial goals should be established independently of preferred life style.   T _____   F _____

2. Setting and carrying out financial goals help people achieve a preferred life style.   T _____   F _____

(Answers on page 34)

FACTORS AFFECTING INCOME

As Figure 1.1 emphasizes, choice of career and income are important aspects of life style. From a personal financial management viewpoint, little can be gained by trying to manage an income that does not exist. A variety of factors influence the amount of income a person can generate. To wisely choose a career, it is important to understand the factors that affect income.

Education

Education beyond high school can be of two types. One is attending college full-time for about four years to earn a bachelor's degree. The second type is post-high school vocational training in a specialized area, such as automotive repair or medical technology. In general, people with some education beyond high school earn more money over their lives than people with only high school educations. There is evidence to show that, in general, more education results in a higher income level.

As Figure 1.2 shows, the average (or mean) income (at $12,226) is lowest for persons who complete less than eight years of elementary school education. Income levels rise with the number of years of schooling completed. Mean income is highest (at $30,956) for those who have done some graduate school work. Figure 1.2 shows a direct relationship between years of schooling completed and mean income.

While the data in Figure 1.2 indicate that higher levels of education produce higher income, such is not always the case. Many types of high-paying occupations do not require extensive education beyond high school. For example, people with training in appliance repair, medical technology, or electronics but without college degrees can earn salaries as high as or

Figure 1.2 1984 Mean Income and Education*

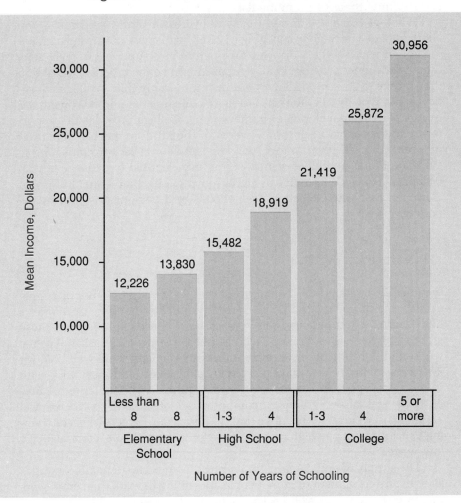

*Mean income is for all year-around, full-time workers 15 years old and over.

Source: Bureau of the Census, U.S. Dept. of Commerce, *Current Population Reports: Consumer Income*, Series P-60, No. 154, 13–14.

higher than those with college degrees. In some areas of study, such as history and sociology, college graduates have a relatively difficult time finding a suitable job. What this means is that it is not necessary for everyone to obtain a college degree to earn a higher income.

While most people would argue that a college education is a worthwhile, enlightening experience, others question the need for a college education. Professor Caroline Bird, a major critic of college education, states that colleges are ghettos for the nation's youth. According to Professor Bird,

the young people of this country go to college or are sent to college because society finds them of no immediate use.[3]

Whether you agree or disagree with Professor Bird's statements, you should not decide to go to college solely for the purpose of earning a higher income. If you feel that you were destined to be a superb auto mechanic, then a vocational program in auto repair might be more beneficial for you than a college education. This is not meant to imply that a college education is not worthwhile. Rather, a college education should be considered from a personal development point of view. College provides the opportunity to expose yourself to new ways of thinking, to meet people from different cultural, ethnic, racial, religious, and social backgrounds, and to gain vocational as well as self-satisfying experiences. If a college education provides you with entry to higher-paying jobs, that's fine. But if that is not the case, the education itself should be a personally satisfying experience.

Nature of the Job

Incomes also depend on the nature of the job and the number of people available to do the job. Some jobs are physically demanding or require a high degree of training and ability. Because of these requirements, these jobs pay higher wages. Workers who helped construct the Alaskan Pipeline worked under difficult environmental conditions and were well paid for it. Professional athletes have very high skill levels and earn very high wages, although their careers are typically quite short. Similarly, because of their specialized training, computer scientists and petrochemical engineers earn high wages. Jobs that do not require special skills or training usually do not pay high wages. Sales clerks, for example, earn relatively low wages.

The supply of and demand for workers in an occupation affects wages also. In any occupation, if more people are willing to work than employers can hire, then wages will be low. Unskilled workers make low wages because of the easy availability of labor. The supply and demand picture, however, is often tempered by the presence of labor unions or professional trade associations. The efforts of such unions as the United Auto Workers and the United Mine Workers have resulted in benefits for workers that cannot be explained by the demand and supply situation alone. Similarly, professional trade associations such as the American Medical Association and the American Bar Association have certain standards that are designed to protect consumers but that also serve to affect wages based strictly on demand and supply.

---

[3] Caroline Bird, *The Case Against College* (New York: David McKay, 1975).

Experience

A look at job listings in newspapers shows that most employers prefer to hire persons with some work experience. Employers are willing to pay experienced workers higher salaries than they are willing to pay workers with no experience. Many jobs involve on-the-job training. During the training period workers are not as productive as they will be after the training. As workers spend more time on their jobs, they become more experienced and productive. Employers recognize the value of experienced workers by paying them higher salaries. Also, as workers spend more time on their jobs, they gain seniority, and wages are often related to seniority on the job.

Experience, seniority, and education come with time, which means that older workers normally earn more than younger workers in a profession. There are exceptions. For example, a person who starts a new career at age 40 is probably going to earn less than someone who is 35 years old but has been in the same profession for 14 years. The relationship among age, education, and income is shown in Figure 1.3. The mean, or average, income for people 30 years of age and with eight years of elementary school education is $7,648. Average income rises to a high of about $15,000 by about age 52 and then starts to decline. A similar pattern is observed for people with four years of high school education. The average income for people 30 years old in this category is $13,496. Income in this education category peaks at about age 52 and then starts to decline. In both of these categories, the decline in income after age 52 is due to lower job mobility for the elderly and lower levels of the types of skills desired in the job market.

Figure 1.3 again shows the benefits of college training. The average income for people 30 years old with four years of college education is shown to be $19,592. Note that, on average, income levels for college-trained people are higher than for non-college-trained people throughout the working life. That is, for any of the age levels shown, a college-trained person can reasonably expect to earn more than a non-college-trained person at the same age. At around age 40, a person with only an elementary school education earns about $13,500 annually, a person with a high school education earns $19,000, and a person with a college education earns $30,000.

Note also in Figure 1.3 that the decline in incomes of college graduates, as related to age, is relatively small. The decline in earnings for people with only an elementary school education is greater. This difference can be explained by the fact that college-trained people have greater job mobility. They can switch jobs more easily than people without college training. Another factor is that as new jobs in new industries emerge, college-trained people can be more readily retrained for a career in a related or different field.

Finally, notice that the average income difference between people with college training and people with eight years of elementary school increases with age. Similar comparisons can be made between those people with

Figure 1.3 1984 Income, Education, and Age Relationships

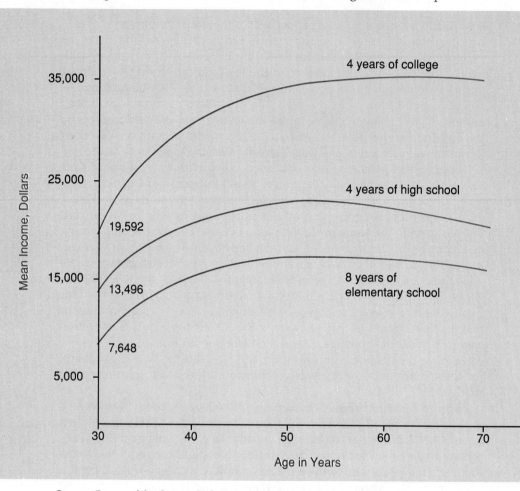

Source: Bureau of the Census, U.S. Dept. of Commerce, *Current Population Reports: Consumer Income*, 1986, Series P-60, No. 151, 126–132.

elementary school educations and those with high school educations. While there are no guarantees, it cannot be overemphasized that more education generally leads to higher income.

Personal Assets

Personal assets, such as abilities, skills, drive, motivation, aptitudes, and value systems, also influence income levels. Some examples of personal

assets are obvious. For example, a person who loves the woods and likes to be outdoors would make a good forest ranger. A person who is five feet tall might excel as a jockey but would have a very difficult time breaking into the lineup of a professional basketball team.

Other examples of ways in which personal assets influence income are not as obvious. The shy, quiet person who does not enjoy meeting people but is majoring in marketing is one example. Marketing majors generally start out in business as sales representatives. But the quiet, shy person does not appear to have the right personal assets to become a successful sales representative. Similarly, a person who does not have any feel for numbers or mathematics probably would not become a good engineer.

These examples emphasize that our personal assets can impact our earnings potential. This impact can be either positive or negative. If we have a good match between our personal assets and our chosen career, then the impact will be positive. A bad match between personal assets and career would affect earnings negatively. In the first example, personal value systems, such as the love of nature, would positively affect income. In the second case, lack of height and ability to compete in basketball would negatively affect income. In the other two cases, personality and skills would have negative effects on incomes. For a further example of how personal assets affect our earnings, see "Law or Computers" below.

Law or Computers

Just before Saigon was overrun by the North Vietnamese, My-Hanh Do and her family fled the city and emigrated to the United States. They eventually arrived at a refugee camp in Arkansas and from there made their way to Chicago. My-Hanh, 15 years old at that time, wanted to be a lawyer when she grew up. Had she stayed in Saigon, she surely would have pursued a career in law. However, when she arrived in the States, she was not very fluent in English, and she felt that even with strong improvement, her communications skills might not be good enough for a successful career in law. Because My-Hanh also had a natural talent for the sciences, she decided to major in electrical engineering at Illinois Institute of Technology. After graduation she started working full-time for AT&T as a programmer. She also earned a master's degree from IIT and now earns in excess of $40,000 a year.

Ms. Do is a good example of a person who was able to match her personal assets to job requirements in the software development field and was able to choose a career well suited to her life style.

Spot Quiz • Factors Affecting Income

1. In general, people with four years of college earn more than people of the same age without a college education.   T _____ F _____

2. Earnings are dependent only on the supply of and demand for workers in any given area.   T _____ F _____

3. In general, more experience means higher earnings.
                                                       T _____ F _____

4. Some personal assets have a great effect on a person's income.
                                                       T _____ F _____

(Answers on page 35)

CHOOSING A CAREER

Education, nature of the job, experience, and personal assets are four major factors that affect income levels. Education and nature of the job are, to a great extent, dictated by the job or occupation. For example, if you want to be a lawyer, completing an education through the necessary professional degree (a J.D. or an L.L.B.) becomes a must. Thus, one step in choosing a career is to obtain more information about various occupations. Second, choosing a career should involve an analysis of personal assets.

Obtaining Information About Occupations

When we seek information about occupations, we need to find out the requirements of the jobs. We also need to understand the future trends in various job areas.

Different jobs have different requirements in terms of education and other training. The *Occupational Outlook Handbook* is issued by the Bureau of Labor Statistics of the U.S. Department of Labor. This *Handbook* lists a lot of valuable information for the job seeker. For example, for any given job, it contains a description of the job, the type of education and training required, the working conditions that exist, and the average salaries paid. Most career placement centers have copies of this *Handbook*. The Bureau of Labor Statistics also issues the *Occupational Outlook for College Graduates*.

This book contains much of the same information as the *Handbook*. In addition, it contains supply and demand statistics for various jobs as well as a forecast for the demand for college graduates in various occupations.

Figure 1.4 provides information on employment growth rates in selected occupations. Three sets of information are listed in this figure. The first set, titled "High Growth," includes those occupations in which

Figure 1.4 Employment Growth Rates in Selected Occupations, 1984–1995

Occupation	Percent Growth Rate	
	Total	Annual
High Growth		
Paralegal personnel	97.5	6.4
Computer programmers	71.7	5.0
Computer and systems analysts	68.7	4.9
Electronics engineers	52.8	3.9
Electronics technicians and technologists	50.7	3.8
Computer operators	46.1	3.5
Securities/financial services sales workers	39.1	3.0
Moderate Growth		
Lawyers	35.5	2.8
Accountants	34.8	2.8
Mechanical engineers	34.0	2.7
Registered nurses	32.8	2.6
Wholesale trade sales workers	29.6	2.4
Physicians and surgeons	23.0	1.9
Teachers	20.3	1.7
Teacher's aides	18.3	1.5
Receptionists and information clerks	18.2	1.5
Licensed practical nurses	17.6	1.5
Low Growth		
Electricians	16.2	1.4
Food service and lodging managers	13.6	1.2
Retail sales workers	12.6	1.1
General office clerks	9.6	0.8
Bookkeeping and accounting clerks	6.0	0.5
Factory supervisors	5.8	0.5

Source: Bureau of Labor Statistics, U.S. Department of Labor, *Occupational Projections and Training Data*, 1986, 12.

both demand and starting salaries are relatively good. The first occupation listed is "paralegal personnel." Between 1984 and 1995 demand for paralegal personnel is expected to grow by 97.5 percent, which is an annual growth rate of about 6.4 percent. Since the U.S. economy is expected to grow by only 2 to 3 percent annually, the growth in this occupation far exceeds the growth rate of the overall U.S. economy. This means that job seekers with paralegal training have excellent prospects for jobs.

Most of the jobs listed in the high growth category are technologically oriented. This factor emphasizes that the United States is becoming an increasingly technologically oriented society. Job seekers in these technical fields can expect to receive above-average salaries.

The second category in Figure 1.4 is titled "Moderate Growth." Occupations in this category are expected to increase at about the same rate as the overall U.S. economy. Some of the occupations in this category, such as lawyers and physicians, allow a person the opportunity to be his or her own boss. Salary expectations in this category are about average.

The last category in Figure 1.4 is titled "Low Growth" and lists occupations where the growth rate in general is smaller than the growth rate of the U.S. economy. Job seekers in these categories will have a more difficult time finding suitable employment and will find that salaries are at the low end.

Choosing the right career can go a long way toward helping you earn a high income. It is possible to identify occupations that do not require a college degree and that do produce high incomes. Skilled technicians, such as electronics technicians, tool and die makers, boilermakers, and plumbers, can and do earn incomes that tend to be higher than those of college graduates. Keep in mind that requirements tend to be different for different occupations. A good fit needs to exist between job requirements and choice of life style and personal assets.

Future Trends in Jobs

When you obtain information about occupations, it is important to find out what the trends in the area will be a few years down the line. You need to know not only whether demand will be high or low but also what is expected to happen to the supply side. For example, it may not be very desirable to go into an area where demand may be high but supply would be even higher. The *Occupational Outlook for College Graduates* provides insights into demand and supply trends in various occupations. Other things being the same, an occupation with high demand levels and low supply levels could be expected to provide excellent prospects as well as high incomes for job seekers. See "Where the Jobs Aren't," page 17, for further information on future job trends.

Where the Jobs Aren't

Some occupations in the United States are showing a decline in the number of workers. A sampling of these occupations "where the jobs aren't" follows:

Occupation	Percent Change in Employment, 1984–1995
Stenographers	−40.3
Shoe sewing operators	−31.5
Telephone repairers	−18.6
Statistical clerks	−12.7
Farm workers	−11.7
University professors	−10.6
Machine operators, plastics	− 9.1
Postal service clerks	− 8.5

The implication of these figures is that under normal circumstances, people would prefer to avoid occupations that are either declining or have very low growth levels.

Determining Personal Assets

A good fit between personal assets and career requirements can help increase income levels. On the other hand, a bad fit between personal assets and career requirements would generally affect earnings negatively. How then does one evaluate personal assets and their impact on earnings potential? For vocational jobs, abilities and skills can be judged through manual dexterity tests. But how can you determine whether you will make a good lawyer or a good accountant? Fortunately, a variety of tests is available for you to take. These tests help determine aptitudes for various careers. The tests can measure intelligence, aptitude, personality, and career interests, among other things. While these tests are not foolproof, they can be extremely helpful in identifying your personal assets and matching them up with the correct career choice.

Most academic institutions have career planning centers where these tests can be taken. Career counselors at these centers can arrange to have these tests administered to you. The counselors can then help explain your best or most suitable career choices based on your test results. An accurate understanding of your personal assets helps to increase your earnings

potential. Most people benefit from taking these tests as a method for choosing careers.

Spot Quiz • Choosing a Career

1. The best way to choose a career is to select the one that has the highest salary levels.   T _____   F _____

2. Based on Figure 1.4, no one should seek to become a teacher.
                                                                 T _____   F _____

3. The results of placement tests should be considered carefully in making a career choice.   T _____   F _____

(Answers on page 35)

GETTING A JOB

After choosing a career and meeting the job requirements for that career, the next step is to obtain a job in the chosen field. Getting a job requires knowing where the jobs are, preparing a resume, doing well on job interviews, and accepting an offer.

Getting Information on Jobs

Two major sources of information on jobs are published materials and contacts and placement services.

Published Sources of Information.   The major source of information on jobs is the *College Placement Annual*. The *Annual* is available at your school's placement center. It lists employers, the types of jobs they have, and the job requirements. The *Annual* also lists job openings by regions. Thus, for example, a civil engineer interested in getting a job in the Southeast will be able to find a list of potential employers in the Southeast.

The classified advertisement section of newspapers and trade journals carry many help-wanted ads. National newpapers such as *The Wall Street Journal* carry nationwide ads. Other papers are local in nature and carry

local ads. If, for example, you are interested in working in Cincinnati, then a subscription to the *Cincinnati Enquirer* may be helpful in identifying potential jobs in that city.

Most academic and public libraries carry *Moody's Handbook* and *Standard & Poor's Register*. These two manuals contain a brief description of most of the publicly held companies, including Procter & Gamble, Ford, Texas Instruments, Kroger, Monsanto, Ralston Purina, General Telephone, and so on. The manuals also provide each company's address and a listing of company officers. If you are interested in a particular company, industry, or technology, then by using these manuals you can prepare a listing of companies that may be interested in talking with you. Additional·information about a company can be obtained by writing a letter to the company's Director of Corporate Relations and requesting a copy of the company's most recent annual report.

Contacts and Placement Services.   You should not hesitate to contact people you know who might be able to help you get a job. If your friend's parent works for a corporation that may be hiring someone with your skills and background, then do not hesitate to give your resume to that person. If you meet someone at a party who might be able to help you, do not hesitate to tell the person that you are in the market for a job and that you would appreciate any help she or he could provide. If you have worked in the summers, ask your bosses on the summer jobs to circulate your resume. Ask your teachers to put you in touch with potential employers. Basically, do not be bashful about seeking help from people you know in trying to get a job. But be sure to express your appreciation for any help that any contact provides you.

Most academic institutions operate a **placement center**. These centers help present and former students to find jobs. You should check with your placement center for the correct procedure to follow. Generally, you will have to register with the center and provide it with a resume and reference letters. Prospective employers may go through your file at the placement center and decide to contact you for an interview. You may also be able to look at the list of employers coming to campus and be able to sign up for interviews.

All states operate **state employment agencies**. You can register with the nearest branch of your state employment agency, which will not charge you any fees for putting you in touch with prospective employers.

You can also register with **private employment agencies**. Private employment agencies typically charge the entry-level employee a fee for job placement services. Upper-level job seekers, such as vice presidents, have their placement fees paid by the companies that hire them. Agency fees can vary from one to six months of salary. If you do not accept a job through the agency, you are under no obligation to pay a placement fee. Read the employment agency contract carefully before signing it.

Preparing a Resume

Most companies require that you provide them with a resume prior to a job interview. A **resume** is a concise listing of your work experience, education, and personal data. Many times a resume is your first contact with a potential employer. If the resume is not well prepared, it may become your *only* contact with a potential employer. Therefore, it is vital to have a well-prepared resume that can sell you and your abilities. A sample resume is shown in Figure 1.5. Notice that the resume is brief and to the point. Personnel officers receive many, many resumes. They generally do not have enough time to thoroughly review lengthy resumes and so appreciate receiving brief, clean, neat, to-the-point resumes.

In general, employers are most interested in finding out what your professional objectives are, what work experience you have, and what your educational background is. This is why the format in Figure 1.5 lists "Professional Objective," "Experience," and "Education" in that order. However, this is only a suggested format. If you feel more comfortable with a different format for the various sections, then you should use that format.

At the top of the resume is the job candidate's name, address, and telephone number. Many employers prefer to contact candidates by phone to expedite the interviews. If you do not have a phone, you might consider listing a number where a message could be left for you.

The first major section, titled "Professional Objective," lists both an immediate objective and a long-term goal. Listing your long-term goal indicates to the prospective employer that you have seriously considered the career path you would like to follow and that you know where you want to go.

The second section is titled "Experience." Work experience is listed with the most recent job first. The names and addresses of employers are listed in case the potential employer wants to contact them. A brief description of each job is also provided. Be careful not to "glorify" your previous job experience. If you worked as a bookkeeper, do not list your job as accountant. If you were shining shoes to put yourself through college, do not call yourself a "footwear maintenance engineer." One personnel manager routinely stamps "BULL" in red ink on resumes containing glorified job descriptions. Don't let this happen to your resume.

Education is also listed in reverse chronological order. You should list your degrees, when they were awarded, the name and address of the degree-granting institution, and major and minor fields of study.

The sections titled "Background" and "Interests and Activities" contain personal information about you. These sections should be kept brief. The section titled "Personal" lists your age, date of birth, marital status, and height. Antibias laws prevent employers from asking for information about your race, color, national origin, religion, sex, age, and physical and mental handicaps. Thus, the information you provide in the "Personal"

Figure 1.5 Sample Resume

```
SUSANNE L. VASQUEZ
300 E. College Street
Chicago, Illinois 60657        Telephone: 312-529-0613


PROFESSIONAL OBJECTIVE         Foreign exchange risk management.
                               Ultimately, manager of international
                               finance division of multinational firm.


EXPERIENCE

July 1988 to present           Harris Rentals, Chicago, Illinois
                               Bookkeeper, inventory clerk.

September 1987 to June 1988    Meridian Hotel, Chicago, Illinois
                               Bar manager with cash register re-
                               sponsibilities.

September 1983 to May 1987     Miscellaneous jobs as sales clerk,
                               waitress, and baby-sitter.

EDUCATION                      M.B.A., expected June 1989
                               Northwestern University, Evanston, Illinois
                               Major: Financial Management

                               B.A., June 1988
                               Loyola University, Chicago, Illinois
                               Major: Psychology; Minor: Mathematics

BACKGROUND                     Native of Chicago. Member of Alpha
                               Kappa Psi and Iota Phi Theta (social
                               sorority). Have traveled extensively
                               in Europe. Fluent in German and Spanish.

INTERESTS AND ACTIVITIES       Active in student chapter of Financial
                               Management Association. Enjoy tennis,
                               racquetball, and swimming.

PERSONAL                       Age: 22; Date of Birth: April 21, 1966
                               Single, 5'6"

REFERENCES                     Available on request.
```

section is optional. If you do not want to provide this information, you are not required to do so.

The last section is titled "References." You can either indicate that references are available on request or you can list the names and addresses of your references. In either case, you should contact potential references and obtain their permission to list them as references.[4]

The Job Interviews

Your first personal contact with a potential employer will be either with a corporate recruiter who is visiting your campus or with the corporate personnel officer. In either case, your first interview will be very short, generally lasting only about 30 minutes. In this short time period the interviewer will have to decide whether to recommend that you be invited for further interviews. Therefore, the first impressions you create fall into three categories:

1. The impression you create as a person.
2. The impression you create about your job-related competence.
3. The impression you create about the fit, or match, between you and the interviewer's company.

The interviewer will develop an impression about you as a person. You can help your image by showing up on time for the interview and by being properly dressed. Interviewers often mention the negative image created by someone who walks into the interview chewing gum, sits down, lights up a cigarette, and starts flicking the cigarette ashes on the floor. Throughout the interview, you should be attentive to what the interviewer has to say and maintain eye contact.

The interviewer will try to gauge your job-related competence by asking you about your education, your work experience, your strengths, and your weaknesses. You should be able to answer the questions in general terms without getting bogged down in the technical aspects of what you would like to do.

In the brief first interview, the interviewer will try to gain an impression of the match between you and the company's requirements. You should be familiar with the company and its operations before you go in for your interview. *Moody's Handbook* and the *Standard & Poor's Register* are useful for learning more about companies. You may also want to ask the interviewer about the company. Questions related to training programs, support for further graduate studies, opportunities for advancement, and

---

[4] There are businesses that can provide you with a professionally prepared resume for a fee, which can vary from a few dollars to hundreds of dollars. However, your college career counseling and placement center can generally provide help with preparing a resume without charge.

so on are perfectly acceptable. At this time you should not ask questions about salaries and fringe benefits, however.

If you have created an overall positive impression on the interviewer, you probably will be invited for a second set of interviews. These interviews are typically held at one of the company's offices. You will meet anywhere from three to fifteen people over a period of one or two days. You will meet your potential supervisor as well as persons with whom you might be working. You probably will be shown around the physical facilities of the company or its plant. If you are interviewing in a new city and if time permits, the company may arrange to show you the community. You should not hesitate to ask questions related to the potential job. At this time, you should become aware of the salary range and the fringe benefits that the company has to offer.

Accepting an Offer

If you made a good impression during your second set of interviews, chances are that you will be offered a job. Most companies will allow you enough time to talk with other companies and to evaluate their offers. Salary and fringe benefits are important, but they should not be the only bases on which you accept a job offer. Geographical location, the work environment, the community, and preferences of other family members are all important factors that should be considered in deciding whether to accept an offer.

Spot Quiz • Getting a Job

1. All job openings are advertised in newspapers.

   T _____   F _____

2. One should not impose on friends by asking them for leads on jobs.

   T _____   F _____

3. A well-written resume is a must in job hunting.

   T _____   F _____

4. In an interview, telling the interviewer what he or she wants to hear is more important than telling your true feelings.

   T _____   F _____

(Answers on page 35)

Setting financial goals

Earlier in the chapter three financial goals were mentioned. The first one, attaining and maintaining a certain life style, is basically short-term in nature. The second, accumulating funds for retirement and building an estate, is a long-term financial goal. The third financial goal dealt with getting the most for your money. Maximizing the quality and quantity that you can buy with limited sums of money is both short-term and long-term in nature. In this section, then, we will take brief looks at the tools of financial planning and at inflation before discussing the setting of short-term and long-term financial goals.

Tools of Financial Planning

Financial goal setting implies using short-term and long-term financial planning to achieve the goals. Financial planning requires preparation of financial statements that show how much income is received, how it is spent, and how the wealth of the person changes over time. The basic financial statements that help in keeping track of money flows are the income statement and the balance sheet. The **income statement** lists income and expenses, while the **balance sheet** lists what the person owns and owes. Financial planning by its very nature requires that estimates be made of future income and expenses. These tools of financial planning are discussed in Chapter 2.

Most individuals are paying or can plan on paying taxes to the federal, state, and local governments. We can make financial plans only for the funds that we actually control. Understanding the tax laws and procedures is helpful in making sure that the individual or family pays no more than its legal, fair share of taxes. Chapter 3 deals with understanding the income tax system and its implications for financial planning.

Consumerism deals with getting the most for your money. The benefits of consumerism are both short- and long-term. By making the best use of available funds, the quality of your life style can be improved. Chapter 4 discusses consumerism.

Inflation

Recognizing the impact of inflation is an important part of financial goal setting and planning. **Inflation** is a steady, sustained increase in the prices of goods and services. Since the mid-sixties we have seen persistent price increases for most goods and services available to consumers. If you have been aware of the rise in new car prices over the past few years, you know what inflation is.

Let's say that you want to buy a new car that costs $9,600. You decide to save $800 per month for twelve months. After one year you have saved

"This inflation is murder! I had to come out of retirement."

Source: *Changing Times*, August 1977, p. 2.

$9,600 (let's ignore the interest income opportunity cost for right now). You go to the dealer showroom to pay cash for your dream car, only to find out that inflation has pushed its price to $10,200. Recognizing inflation in your financial planning would have led to one of two decisions: (1) buy the car now for $9,600 and borrow the money to pay for it or (2) save $850 per month so that $10,200 is accumulated after one year. Financial planning would also have indicated to you the more desirable of these two alternatives. As can be seen from ''Who Benefits From Inflation'' on page 26, inflation hurts some people more than others. But it is always prudent to recognize the impact of inflation in financial planning.

Short-Term Goals

Short-term goals involve a planning horizon of one year or less. As Figure 1.1 indicates, short-term financial planning is needed for managing current living expenses, liquid assets, credit, housing, transportation, and

Who Benefits From Inflation?

The Reagan administration was able to control inflation and keep it around 3 percent annually. However, for much of the 1960s and 1970s, consumers saw high rates of inflation, which in some years were in double digits. You cannot really deduce from this that the U.S. government has finally figured out how to control inflation. However, if we do see high levels of inflation, it doesn't mean that everyone will suffer from the effects. In fact, some people benefit from inflation. For example, those who own real estate benefit from inflation. It has been shown that real estate prices go up at a faster rate when inflation becomes higher. Similarly, people who owe money benefit from inflation. They can pay off their loans with ''inflated'' dollars—that is, dollars that have less buying power. Other beneficiaries include those workers who are represented by unions with strong bargaining power, those who control scarce products or services, and those who own assets such as farms, recreation land, timber, art objects and collectibles, and other real assets.

insurance. In the sections that follow, a discussion of various types of short-term expenses is followed by a comprehensive example of short-term goal setting.

Current Living Expenses. Expenses such as rent or mortgage payments, auto payments, food, recreation, and taxes make up **current living expenses.** Some of these items, such as housing and transportation, are important enough to merit separate discussion. The rest are important enough as a group and require careful financial planning. For example, for food you could either dine out or buy groceries and cook at home. Dining out is more convenient but more expensive than cooking at home. Planning for current expenses would require not only allocating dollars for food but also apportioning the food dollars between dining out and cooking at home. This type of planning requires plans called **budgets** that spell out how much is going to be spent for each expense category. Budgeting for current expenses is a topic taken up in Chapter 5.

Liquid Assets. **Liquid assets** include cash and ''near cash'' assets. We hold cash in currency and in checking accounts. Near cash is money held in savings accounts and in other short-term savings devices, such as certificates of deposit issued by financial institutions. For example, one may have set a goal of taking a vacation around New Year's. One way to accumulate the needed vacation funds would be to use short-term planning to put a certain amount of money in a savings account each pay period. Managing liquid assets is discussed in Chapter 6.

Credit. Careful use of credit allows us to use goods and services prior to paying for them. Credit management involves understanding how credit is granted, how to obtain credit, and how to manage the borrowings. These topics are covered in Chapter 7.

Housing. Housing needs can be met by either renting or buying housing. In both cases different alternatives are available. These alternatives have different costs and benefits. For example, renting an apartment may be cheaper but less private than renting a house with a large yard. Housing requires both short- and long-term financial planning. Managing housing needs is discussed in Chapters 8 and 9.

Insurance. Insurance is another expense category that is both short-term and long-term in nature. Buying insurance calls for periodic payments and therefore requires short-term planning. Costs and benefits of insurance, however, tend to be long-term in nature. Managing insurance needs requires understanding what type of insurance to buy, how much to buy, and from whom to buy. These topics are taken up in Chapters 11–14.

Setting Short-Term Goals. Figure 1.5 showed the resume of Susanne L. Vasquez. Ms. Vasquez plans to graduate in June of 1989 with a master's degree in business administration from Northwestern University. Currently, in January 1989, she is working as a bookkeeper and inventory clerk. She earns $600 per month on a part-time basis. After graduation, she plans to start working in July 1989 for a multinational firm at an estimated salary of $3,600 per month.

Ms. Vasquez's short-term financial goals, which she drew up in December 1988, are listed in Table 1.1. Her first goal is to save $6,000 in 1989 toward buying a condominium. Ms. Vasquez is not in a position to save anything between January and June of 1989. This means that from July to December of 1989, she will have to average $1,000 per month in savings to meet financial goal number 1.

Table 1.1 Short-Term Financial Goals for S. L. Vasquez for 1989*

1. Save $6,000 toward down payment on a condominium.
2. Save $3,000 for a skiing vacation to Switzerland in December 1989.
3. Limit housing costs to $350 per month.
4. Limit new wardrobe expenses to $1,500.
5. Open two or more charge accounts.

*Prepared by Susanne L. Vasquez in December 1988.

Her second goal is to save $3,000 for a vacation. Short-term financial planning for this goal would require her to save an additional $500 per month between July and December of 1989. Financial goal number 3 limits her housing costs to $350 per month. She currently shares an apartment with a fellow student. Meeting this goal would require her to continue the present arrangement through at least the end of 1989.

Her fourth goal is to limit job-related wardrobe expenses to $1,500. She has two options here. She could try to save $1,500/6 = $250 per month from January to June 1989 to buy her wardrobe. However, we already know that she will not be in a position to save any money in the first six months of 1989. The implication here is that she will have to buy her wardrobe on credit. The last goal deals with opening charge accounts. Logically, then, she should have set goal number 5 ahead of goal number 4.

Ms. Vasquez's short-term goals do not include insurance because both medical and life insurance are provided by her employer. Ms. Vasquez has examined these insurance benefits and believes that they are adequate for her needs at the present time.

As the example indicates, short-term goal setting tends to be unique for the individual or family doing the planning. Another person in the same situation as Ms. Vasquez might have chosen to set different short-term goals. The second point to remember is that short-term goals can be met properly only through proper financial planning. It would do Ms. Vasquez little good to set short-term goals without drawing up financial plans to enable her to meet her goals.

Long-Term Goals

Long-term goals involve a planning horizon of over one year. We have already seen some aspects of goal setting and planning that are long-term in nature. Other areas that we cover in this section include estate building, leisure, recreation, retirement, and transfer of estate.

Estate Building. We may wish to build an **estate**, or accumulate wealth, for a variety of reasons. For example, we might build an estate as part of our plan for financing our retirement. Or we might plan to leave an estate for our heirs. Estate building requires saving money as well as carefully investing the money saved. Savings are generated through careful financial planning of expenses. Topics related to managing expenses are discussed in Chapters 2–14. Investing savings is discussed in Chapters 15–19. Tax-related aspects of estates are covered in Chapter 21.

Leisure, Recreation, and Retirement. At some point in the future, most of us will retire, some voluntarily, others involuntarily. Although retirement may be many years in the future, we still need to plan actively for it. Retirement gives us much additional leisure and recreation time.

So retirement planning requires allocating the use of our time. Second, our normal income stops when we retire. So we also need to plan for financing our retirement. These topics are covered in Chapter 20.

Transfer of Estate.   Benjamin Franklin once remarked, ''In this world nothing is certain but death and taxes.'' After death, a person's wealth, or estate, is transferred to her or his heirs. Planning for the transfer of an estate reduces costs and problems for the heirs. Estates can be conveyed to heirs through the use of a legal device called a **will**. Some estate assets can be transferred prior to death. These topics are covered in Chapter 21.

Setting Long-Term Goals.   Besides setting short-term goals, Ms. Vasquez also set her long-term goals in December 1988. These goals are listed in Table 1.2. Her 1990 goals are consistent with her housing plans as well as with her self-perceptions as a professional manager. She plans to buy a condominium in 1991. However, she will run short on funds to furnish the condominium. Therefore, she is planning to sell her car to raise additional funds.

Table 1.2 Long-Term Financial Goals for S. L. Vasquez for 1990–2031*

1990
1. Save $6,000 for condominium down payment.
2. Move to single apartment.

1991
1. Buy condominium.
2. Sell present car.
3. Furnish condominium.

1992
1. Buy new car.
2. Save $6,000 for retirement fund.

*

*

*

2031
1. Buy condominium in Florida.
2. Have fun.

*Prepared by Susanne L. Vasquez in December 1988.

Ms. Vasquez plans to buy a new car in 1992. She is also resuming her savings plan in 1992. This time, though, the goal for savings is to accumulate funds for retirement. In 2031, Ms. Vasquez will be 65 years old. She plans to retire and move to Florida.

As is obvious, some details are missing from Table 1.2. If, for example, Ms. Vasquez marries, her financial goals and plans would most certainly change. If Ms. Vasquez chooses to have or raise children, her financial goals will be affected. Goals will also change as her jobs, responsibilities, and life style change. She obviously cannot anticipate many of these situations now. Her long-term goals reflect the information available to her now. As new information becomes available, she would be in a position to modify her long-term goals.

Spot Quiz • Setting Financial Goals

1. Financial planning should not be affected by inflation.

   T _____ F _____

2. Setting short-term financial goals helps us to control our living expenses.

   T _____ F _____

3. Long-term goals should be changed as new information becomes available.

   T _____ F _____

4. Short- and long-term goals should be related to each other.

   T _____ F _____

(Answers on page 35)

ADVICE FOR THE SEIFERTS

The chapter opened with a discussion of the Seifert family. Tom Seifert is thinking of switching careers and moving back into civilian life. Have you decided what advice you would give the Seifert family? Tom wants to switch to a civilian job to earn more money and provide a better life for his family. Most people would sympathize with Tom in his search for

a better life. However, Tom needs to take certain financial factors into consideration. Although the U.S. Marines may have provided him with valuable job experience, Tom does not have a marketing-related degree. Without a marketing background, he might encounter some problems in obtaining a suitable job in sales.

The Seifert family is accustomed to living on an army salary, which carries with it many fringe benefits. Tom may realize that the same standard of living in civilian life requires an annual income of perhaps $25,000. The Seifert family owns assets worth $59,250, and they owe $29,300. In a financially tight situation, the family could sell its house and land, pay off all the money it owes, and still have enough money left over to live on for eight to twelve months.

Tom might consider taking some tests to determine his aptitudes and the type of job for which he is best suited. Based on the test results, he may want to go back to school full-time while his wife works full-time to support the family. Another alternative for him is to extend his stay in the Marines and work on an M.B.A. on a part-time basis. Right now, though, the alternative of leaving the Marines and then starting a job hunt does not appear to be very desirable from a financial viewpoint.

Summary

Most individuals and families have strong preferences for the life style they want to live. Personal financial management helps people to live their preferred life styles. Life style, career choice, and income are three closely related factors that affect one another.

The income that you earn is greatly affected by your education, the nature of your job, your experience, and your personal assets. In general, income increases with education and experience. Jobs where the supply of workers is low also pay high wages. Finally, a person has a chance of earning higher wages if there is a good match between job requirements and his or her personal skills, aptitudes, drive, and motivation.

In looking for a job it is important to know about the job requirements and future job trends. Personal assets should also be carefully considered. Information on jobs can be obtained from a variety of sources. A well-prepared resume will lead to job interviews.

Before any financial planning can take place, you have to establish both short- and long-term financial goals. Setting financial goals and following up on them ensures that your desired life style will be attained.

Questions

1. Why should life style be important to a person?

2. Briefly explain the three financial goals that you would consider in your own personal financial planning.

3. What is the relationship among life style, career choice, and income? Explain briefly.

4. In general, does education or experience have a greater impact on income? Justify your answer.

5. Cite an example for each of the following situations:
   a. A high-paying job with low education requirements.
   b. A high-paying job that has no experience requirements.
   Do you think that the jobs you have identified here could be easily attained by most people? Explain briefly.

6. What steps would you follow to decide whether you are making the right career choice?

7. What is the importance of a resume in getting a job?

8. What is meant by inflation? Are you being affected by inflation in your current financial situation? Explain briefly.

9. Why should people set short-term financial goals?

10. What is the importance of setting long-term financial goals?

11. Why do certain types of expenses require both short- and long-term financial planning?

Case Problems

1. Write a brief report on the type of life that you want to live. Explain how the right career could help you reach your life style goals.

2. Write a brief report on what you consider to be your important personal assets. How do they relate to your chosen career?

3. What career do you plan to pursue after graduation? Explain how you would find information about your chosen career. Prepare a resume that you could send to potential employers.

4. Prepare a list of short- and long-term financial goals for yourself. Which of your goals are most likely to change after five years?

5. Jamal Ahmed is an engineer working for Westinghouse Corporation in Pittsburgh. He has two sons aged 10 and 12 who are currently living with his ex-wife. Mr. Ahmed's current take-home income is $26,000 annually, out of which he is paying $6,000 a year in child support. He lives in a high-rise apartment overlooking downtown Pittsburgh. Recently, his ex-wife contacted him and asked him to assume custody of the two children, which he has agreed to do. He will stop paying child support when they come to live with him next month.
   a. How might Mr. Ahmed be affected financially by this change in his family situation?
   b. What changes would Mr. Ahmed probably have to make in his short-term financial goals?
   c. What changes should Mr. Ahmed be making in his long-term financial goals?

6. Nancy Kaminski is a 20-year-old junior at a state university. During her high school years she was strongly influenced by the investigative reporting that revealed scandals in various governmental organizations. On entering college, she decided to major in journalism. She has been able to maintain above-average grades in college and has written occasionally for her college newspaper. Recently, she has begun to notice that many journalism graduating seniors with credentials better than hers are not having any luck in finding suitable jobs. Ms. Kaminski has heard that it is easy to obtain jobs in accounting. She feels that she does not have a good aptitude for working with numbers. However, she is considering switching her major to accounting.
   a. What factors should Ms. Kaminski consider before deciding to switch majors?
   b. What career choice advice would you give Ms. Kaminski?

7. Randy Rigsby will be graduating with a bachelor's degree in art history at the end of this spring semester. A few weeks ago, while discussing the job situation with a friend, he found out that a major consumer products company was coming to his campus to interview students for jobs. His friend Eleanor was extremely excited about her upcoming interview with this company. "Actually, Randy, you ought to be interviewing with this company also," Eleanor suggested. "What for?" Randy retorted, "they will have only so many walls that might benefit from art." "True," said Eleanor, "but I have a feeling that you just might make one heck of a sales representative for them."

Randy is a pleasant, outgoing person with a slight aversion to suits and ties. Nonetheless, he is intrigued by Eleanor's suggestion.

a. What suggestions do you have for Randy? Should he sign up for an interview with this company?

b. Assuming that he wants to interview with this company, how should he prepare?

c. Do you have any interviewing tips for Randy?

Bibliography

Bolles, Richard N. *What Color Is Your Parachute?* Berkeley, Calif.: Ten Speed Press, 1988.

College Placement Council. *College Placement Annual*. Bethlehem, Penn.: College Placement Council, annual editions.

"Cram Course in Paying for College." *Changing Times* (October 1986): 49–54.

"Take a Test to Find Your Niche." *Changing Times* (July 1986): 57–60.

U.S. Department of Labor, Bureau of Labor Statistics. *Occupational Outlook for College Graduates*. Washington, DC: U.S. Government Printing Office, biennial editions.

U.S. Department of Labor, Bureau of Labor Statistics. *Occupational Outlook Handbook*. Washington, DC: U.S. Government Printing Office, biennial editions.

"Who Earns the Most—and Why." *Money* (December 1986): 62–66.

Answers to Spot Quizzes

Life Styles and Financial Goals (page 8)

1. F (The life style preferred indicates how financial goals should be established.)

2. T (Realistically set goals help in achieving the preferred life style.)

Factors Affecting Income (page 14)

1. T (Figure 1.3 shows this statement to be true.)

2. F (Activities of labor unions and professional trade associations at times also influence earnings in some areas.)

3. T (Employers are willing to pay an experienced worker a higher salary.)

4. T (Aptitudes, motivation, personality, and other abilities do affect incomes both positively and negatively.)

Choosing a Career (page 18)

1. F (Salary should be only one determinant in choosing a career. Job requirements and their fit with personal assets are also very important.)

2. F (If personal assets and personal interests point in the direction of a teaching career, then you should explore teaching as a career alternative.)

3. T (Placement tests provide valuable information about personal assets and aptitudes for different jobs.)

Getting a Job (page 23)

1. F (Many jobs are not advertised.)

2. F (There is nothing wrong with asking for help in seeking a suitable job.)

3. T (Resumes are your first contact with a potential employer.)

4. F (You may misunderstand what the interviewer wants; the interviewer is well trained to conduct an interview; a job secured through false pretenses may lead to a frustrating work experience.)

Setting Financial Goals (page 30)

1. F (Inflation affects our lives very strongly, and it should be recognized in financial planning.)

2. F (Setting goals by itself does not help control expenses; following through on financial plans does.)

3. T (Goals should reflect all relevant information available.)

4. T (Long-term goals are converted into more detailed short-term goals.)

Chapter 2

Financial Records: Tools of Financial Management

Objectives

After reading this chapter, you will be able to:

- Explain why records are maintained.
- Prepare an income statement.
- Prepare a balance sheet.
- Utilize financial statements.

In 1974 Nelson Rockefeller was nominated to be vice president of the United States. As part of the congressional investigation into his background, Rockefeller was asked to disclose what he owned and owed. It turned out that Mr. Rockefeller had $394,898 in cash. Surely he was worth more than that, you say. Of course, he also owned works of art estimated to be worth more than $33 million, real estate worth $11 million, and other fancy stuff totaling over $64 million. Did he owe anyone anything? Well, he owed about $1.5 million, meaning that at the time, Mr. Rockefeller was worth about $62.5 million. What Mr. Rockefeller owned and owed in 1974 are shown in the article on page 39. If looking at these numbers lets you know more about Mr. Rockefeller's financial situation than you do about your own, then it's time to consider developing a record keeping and financial reporting system for yourself.

Records are very useful for understanding your financial well-being. It is important to know which items to keep and which to discard. The first section of this chapter deals with record keeping. How much you make and how much you spend can be reported on an income statement. A balance sheet, on the other hand, tells what you own and owe. Income statements and balance sheets are also covered in this chapter. The last section deals with using financial statements.

Maintaining records

How many people in the United States would have trouble proving when they were born? Very few? All you have to do is find your birth certificate and the proof is there. Actually, quite a few people would have trouble providing proof of birth. The U.S. Bureau of the Census alone receives requests from about 500,000 persons every year, asking for any records the bureau may have regarding their birth. Quite often, the reason for these requests is that many people do not maintain good records, which includes keeping track of birth records. They may be very good at saving letters from former sweethearts, pieces of string, rubber bands, out-of-style, moth-eaten clothes, and just about anything else except important papers and documents.

Why Maintain Records?

Records should be maintained for five major reasons.

Financial Management.   Maintaining certain financial records helps with personal financial management. Balance sheets, income statements, budgets, and pension and retirement contributions and records fall into

Mr. Rockefeller: What He Owned and Owed in 1974

ASSETS

Cash	$ 394,898
Cash advances	247,891
Notes receivable	1,518,270
Accounts receivable	713,326
New York State Retirement Fund (contributed cost)	21,803
Securities	12,794,376
Partnership interests	157,124
Art (estimated market value)	33,561,325
Real estate	11,252,261
Furnishings	1,191,328
Automobiles, other vehicles, boats, and airplanes	1,767,900
Jewelry	521,136
Coins	12,600
Total	$64,154,238

LIABILITIES

Notes payable	$ 1,567,500
Miscellaneous accounts payable	5,513
Total	$ 1,573,013
Net worth	$62,581,225

Source: *Changing Times*, January 1979, p. 36. Reprinted with permission from *Changing Times* magazine, © Kiplinger Washington Editors, Inc., 1979. This reprint is not to be altered in any way, except with permission from *Changing Times*.

this category. These records are used for short-term as well as long-term management of financial resources.

Legal Evidence. Properly maintained records and documents can serve as legal evidence. Birth certificates, canceled checks, tax returns,

marriage and divorce records, and expired passports can be used as legal evidence.

Property Ownership.   Records such as stock and bond certificates, car titles, and so on are evidence of property ownership.

Legal Rights.   Some documents spell out the consumer's legal rights. Contractual documents such as leases, rental agreements, mortgage papers, insurance policies, and credit notes specify the consumer's rights and obligations.

Verification of Information.   Some documents verify information provided by others. Financial statements from banks, savings and loan associations, and brokerage houses contain information that should be verified. A brokerage house, for example, may be receiving cash dividends on corporate stocks for a client. The client would need to save news of dividend payments to verify the information on the brokerage house statement.

In the following sections, record maintenance requirements for various types of documents are explained. Figure 2.1 provides a listing of records that should be maintained. Notice that the sequence of items listed in this section follows the sequence of topics discussed in this book. Some of the reasons for maintaining certain records for a particular length of time will become more obvious as we discuss the topics later in the book.

Financial Statements

Financial statements include income statements, balance sheets, forecasts of inflows and expenses, budgets, and budget control sheets. Many people prefer to compare current financial figures with last year's figures. Therefore, these statements should be kept at home for the current year and the past year.

Tax Records

Many records are used to justify tax deductions. Payments and records related to interest expenses, property taxes, medical expenses, charitable gifts, educational expenses, and so on should be saved in case the Internal Revenue Service (IRS) asks for documentation. Salary statements can be discarded once they have been verified against the W-2 wage form, which is prepared by the employer at the end of the year.

Checks to doctors and hospitals are acceptable as records of medical expense items. Other checks, such as those to drugstores and maintenance shops, should be accompanied by a receipt or detailed explanation of the expense item. Tax returns and supporting information, canceled checks, W-2 forms, and other records should be saved for seven years at home.

Figure 2.1 Documents and Records to Maintain

Document	Where to Keep	How Long to Keep
Financial statements		
Income statement	Home	1 year
Balance sheet	Home	1 year
Budget	Home	1 year
Tax records	Home	7 years
Warranties and service contracts	Home	Life of appliance
Credit card numbers	Bank	Until card expires
Housing	Bank	Until sale of home
Transportation	Bank	Until sale of car
Insurance policies	Home	Life of insured item
Policy numbers	Bank	
Investments		
Certificates	Bank	Until sale of stock
Statements	Home	7 years
Dividend logs	Home	1 year
Pension benefits	Bank	Until you apply for pension
Vital records	Bank	Indefinitely
Will, original	Attorney's office	Indefinitely
copy	Bank	Indefinitely
Miscellaneous		
Passport	Bank	Indefinitely
Social security stub	Bank	Indefinitely

Warranties and Service Contracts

Many of the items used by a family are covered by warranties. Appliances, tires, batteries, lawn mowers, hair dryers, calculators, even thermometers are all items covered by warranties. In general, it is a good idea to save the warranty for the life of the items. The records should be updated as new warrantied items are purchased and old ones are discarded.

Credit

Credit card numbers and addresses and telephone numbers of the issuing agency should be kept in a safe deposit box at a bank until the cards are

no longer valid. The canceled note from a loan repayment should be kept at home for two years.

Housing

All records related to the purchase or sale of a house should be kept in a safe deposit box. Records of permanent home improvements, such as a new patio, remodeling, air-conditioning, or a new driveway, should be saved also. Records should be updated as needed and kept until the sale of the last house you live in.[1] In many cases this means saving the records until death. A rental lease should be kept until the rental property is vacated and the damage deposit is received.

Transportation

Keep titles of cars in a safe deposit box until the car is sold. If a title is lost, a duplicate can be obtained from the state transportation department in most states.

Insurance

Life insurance policies should be kept at home so that heirs can make claims quickly. Property, car, and health insurance policies should be kept at home so that claims can be filed quickly. A note listing the policy numbers and coverage should be kept in the safe deposit box. Pictures of expensive items should be taken and kept at home. Negatives should be kept at the bank. Certain items, such as jewelry, furs, and diamonds, should be appraised professionally. The appraisals should be kept in the safe deposit box.

Investments

Investors often store their stock and bond certificates with their broker. This is safe and acceptable. Investors who keep their own certificates should do so in a safe deposit box. If certificates are lost, they can be replaced but at a charge of 3 to 5 percent of their value.

Periodic statements from the broker will generally list securities held and current investment transactions. These statements are used to prepare tax returns and should be filed with other tax records.

---

1. Records of permanent improvements must be kept until a family's or individual's last home is sold because the costs involved are used to adjust the holding cost basis for the house. Thus, these capitalized costs reduce the amount of capital gains either rolled over or subject to taxes.

Dividends received should be logged for one year. When the annual dividend statements are received from the firms, then the log can be discarded. Dividend statements should be treated as tax records.

Pension Records

Since pension benefits, profit sharing, and other retirement benefits generally change annually, only the most recent information needs to be maintained. This information becomes very important when a person changes jobs. Often you can receive pension benefits from a previous employer only by applying for them. Saving this information tells you when to apply for benefits.

Vital Records

Birth, death, marriage, and dissolution records are very important. They should be stored in a safe deposit box. Duplicates for lost records can be obtained from an appropriate state agency. The National Center for Health Statistics, Room 8-20, Parklawn Building, 5600 Fishers Lane, Rockville, Maryland 20852, can provide the name and address of the appropriate state agency to contact for a particular vital record.

Wills

A **will** is a legal document that tells how you want your property to be distributed after your death. In order for a will to be useful, however, your survivors must be able to find it. Often the will cannot be readily obtained by heirs and lawyers when it is needed. Many persons, for instance, make the mistake of keeping their wills in safe deposit boxes, which are sealed when a person dies (until they can be opened in the presence of representatives of the estate and the government). A better idea is to leave the original will with an attorney and keep a copy at the bank.

Miscellaneous

An expired or current passport should be kept in a safe deposit box. The stub attached to the social security card should be kept at the bank. See the nearest social security office if either the card or the stub is lost. Keep a list of items in the safe deposit box at home. School records, such as grades and transcripts, should be kept at home, although some people prefer to keep their diplomas in a safe deposit box.

Spot Quiz • Maintaining Records

1. Good record keeping helps in personal financial management.

   T _____   F _____

2. Some records are valid even after the person's death.

   T _____   F _____

3. Records kept at home can be destroyed accidentally.

   T _____   F _____

(Answers on page 58)

INCOME STATEMENT

As the name implies, an **income statement** gives information about a person's or family's income. But an income statement goes far beyond just listing income. It reports money received from sources other than income, such as from the sale of a car. It also lists expenses incurred by the family. More properly, then, an income statement should really be called a "Sources and Uses of Funds Statement." This statement provides a feel for how well a family has done financially over a particular time period.

Sources of Income

The most common source of income is wages or salaries. Many people also receive bonuses and sales commissions. Interest income is received from savings accounts, money market funds, and bonds. Stock purchases lead to capital gains or losses. They also generally provide dividend income for the stockholder.

Other sources of income are listed in Figure 2.2. A person may own rental property that produces rental income. Some people receive tips, pension benefits, or royalties. Selling a piece of property, such as a car, also produces funds. Money can be raised by taking out a loan. Funds received from the various sources are added up to obtain **total income** or **cash inflow.**

Figure 2.2 Sources of Income

Wages, salaries	Disability income
Bonuses, sales commissions	Inheritances
Interest income	Cash gifts
Dividends	Life insurance proceeds
Capital gains (or losses)	Refunds on taxes
Rental income	Sale of property
Tips	Loans received
Pension benefits	Gambling winnings
Royalties	Partnership income

Expense Items

All **expense items** involve spending money. Some major categories of expense items are listed in Figure 2.3. Note that only *major* types of expense items are listed. You know that there are many different ways in which to spend money. The purpose here is to provide an indication of the types of expenses you are apt to encounter.

Figure 2.3 Expense Items

Food	Transportation
Clothing	Payments
Taxes	Gas, oil, maintenance
Federal	Insurance
State, local	Property
Property	Health, life
Loan repayments	Medical
Housing	Doctor
Rents, mortgages	Drugs
Maintenance	Recreation
Utilities	Miscellaneous
Gas, oil	Alimony
Electricity	Gifts
Water, sewer	Education

Income Surplus

The difference between total income and total expenses is called **income surplus**. This is the amount that you would plan to invest. When expenses are in excess of income, the resulting figure is called **income deficit**. An income deficit is not desirable because it means that you are spending more than you are taking in. Income deficits reduce your accumulated savings.

Sample Income Statement

The income statement for 1989 for Norman and Sandy Alstat is shown in Table 2.1. Notice that the income statement covers all incomes and expenses for all of 1989. The first category shown is sources of income. Only the Alstats' take-home income is shown in Table 2.1. Listing the gross income and then showing various deductions, such as taxes and social security withholding, really does not add much to your knowledge of your personal finances. Other sources of income include interest income, dividends, a tax refund, and proceeds from the sale of a car. Total income is shown to be $29,260.

Large expense items for the Alstats include food, housing, transportation, and utilities. Other expenses include clothing, insurance, medical, installment loan, vacation, and entertainment. Small expense items, such as books, donations, and club memberships, have been included in the miscellaneous category. Total expenses for the Alstats for the year are $25,550.

The income surplus is the difference between total income and total expenses, or $29,260 − $25,550 = $3,710. This is the amount of money that the Alstats have left over for investments. Had the Alstats' expenses been greater than their income, they would have needed to make up the income deficit by withdrawing some money from their savings or investments accounts.

Spot Quiz • Income Statement

1. The income statement includes money received from all sources.

   T _____   F _____

2. An income surplus means that take-home wages are greater than total expenses.

   T _____   F _____

(Answers on page 58)

Table 2.1 Income Statement for the Alstats
Year Ending December 31, 1989

Sources of income

Norman's job	$10,230	
Sandy's job	11,110	
Interest	3,190	
Dividends	320	
Tax refund	1,290	
Sale of car	3,120	
Total income		$29,260

Expenses

Food		3,360
Housing		
Mortgage	$4,800	
Taxes	1,200	
Maintenance	300	6,300
Transportation		
Loan payments	1,800	
Gas, oil, etc.	2,150	3,950
Clothing		670
Utilities		
Electricity	3,000	
Water, phone	490	3,490
Insurance, life		2,730
Medical		
Doctor	270	
Drugs	90	360
Installment loan		1,980
Vacation		1,210
Entertainment		600
Miscellaneous		900
Total expenses		25,550
Income surplus		$ 3,710

Balance sheet

The **balance sheet** lists what a family or individual owns and owes at a particular point in time. Whereas an income statement provides a financial picture for the whole time period, the balance sheet shows the financial condition of a family or person for only a certain point in time. The balance sheet has three categories: assets, liabilities, and net worth.

Assets

Everything that a person owns is called an **asset**. Some assets are easy to identify. Cash, whether on hand or in a checking account, is a readily identified asset. So are investments in stocks and bonds. Sometimes whether something should be shown as an asset is questionable. If, for example, a person buys a car and finances it with a loan from a bank, is the car an asset? The answer is yes. All items, whether they are paid for or not, are assets. Thus, financed items, such as cars, homes, and boats, are shown as assets. A listing of major categories of assets is shown in Figure 2.4.

Some assets are not easily recognized as assets. For example, many life insurance policies build up cash values. The cash values of these policies are assets. Similarly, many persons have legal claims for pension benefits. These pension benefits may not be available for use right away, but they are assets nonetheless.

Some families or individuals own all or a portion of a partnership or business. The portion of the partnership or business owned should be listed

Figure 2.4 Assets

Financial	Nonfinancial
Cash	Real estate
Savings	Home
Financial institutions	Rental property
Money market funds	Transportation
Investments	Personal property
Bonds	Household goods
Stocks	Jewelry
Life insurance	Clothing, other
Cash value	Recreational vehicles
Pensions	Partnerships
Loans given	Businesses

as an asset on the balance sheet. Assets that are readily convertible into cash are called **financial assets** and include cash, investments, life insurance, and loans. Assets in the form of physical property are called **nonfinancial assets** and include such items as real estate, cars, boats, and personal property.

Two points should be emphasized about showing assets on the balance sheet:

1. Everything that is owned should be listed, even if it is not paid for fully.
2. Assets should be listed at their current market value.

Liabilities

Money owed by a family or individual is a **liability**. Major categories of liabilities are listed in Figure 2.5. Open-ended credit refers to money owed that is payable in the near future. Examples of open-ended credit are amounts owed on charge accounts, utility bills, and doctor bills. All open-ended credit used needs to be shown on the balance sheet, even if the bill has not been received yet.

Installment loans are borrowed monies that have to be repaid over a period of one to five years. An example is when a car purchase is financed and the loan is repaid in monthly installments over three or more years.

Mortgage loans, which finance real estate purchases, tend to be long-term in nature. Other types of liabilities include education loans and money borrowed from stockbrokers for buying stocks and bonds. Two points need to be emphasized about recording liabilities:

1. All liabilities should be listed on the balance sheet.
2. Only the remaining balance, not the original full amount, of a loan should be listed on the balance sheet.

Figure 2.5 Liabilities

Open-ended credit	Mortgage loans
Charge accounts	Home
Utility bills	Rental property
Doctor bills	Other loans
Installment loans	Educational
Car	Stockbroker
Appliances, other	
household items	Taxes
Cash loans	Miscellaneous

Net Worth

Net worth is what the family or individual would own after paying off all liabilities. Net worth is also called **equity**. The relationship between assets, liabilities, and net worth is

Assets − Liabilities = Net Worth

Nelson Rockefeller, with assets of $64,154,238 and liabilities of $1,573,013, had a net worth of $62,581,225 in 1974 (see page 39).

Sample Balance Sheet

The balance sheet for the Alstats for December 31, 1989, is shown in Table 2.2. Notice that the balance sheet represents the Alstats' financial picture at the end of the day on December 31, 1989. All assets are listed at fair market values. The Alstats have $21,500 in cash and a money market mutual

Table 2.2 Balance Sheet for the Alstats
December 31, 1989

Assets		Liabilities	
Cash		Open-ended credit	
Checking account	$ 500	Charge accounts	$ 320
Money fund	21,000	Utility bills	220
Investments		Other bills	170
Stock	4,000	Installment loans	
Life insurance	970	Car	3,000
Home	80,000	Furniture	1,000
Car	3,900	Other	1,590
Personal property		Mortgage loan	40,000
Furniture	11,000	Stockbroker	1,000
Jewelry	6,000	Total liabilities	$ 47,300
Clothing	3,000	Net worth	86,770
Boat	2,000	Liabilities and net worth	$134,070
Motorcycle	1,700		
Total assets	$134,070		

fund. They have $4,000 worth of stock. The market value of stocks and bonds can be readily determined by looking at financial newspapers such as *The Wall Street Journal*.

The cash value of a life insurance policy can be found by calling your insurance agent or looking at the cash value table included with your life insurance policy. The market value of a house can generally be established by considering the selling prices of similar homes sold recently. Market value for personal property becomes harder to determine. Generally, relatively new furniture can be listed at 50 percent of its cost. Prices of boats, cars, and motorcycles can be established from newspaper advertisements and books that contain used car prices. Total assets for the Alstats are shown to be $134,070.

Liabilities for the Alstats are also shown in Table 2.2. Charge account payments total $320. These include charges billed as well as charges not yet billed. The remaining loan on the car is $3,000. This is not the amount of the original loan. The $3,000 is the amount of money that would be needed to pay off the loan today. The largest loan is for $40,000 for the house. Total liabilities equal $47,300.

The difference between total assets and total liabilities is net worth and equals $134,070 − $47,300 = $86,770 for the Alstats. This means that if the Alstats were to pay off all of their liabilities, they would have $86,770 remaining in assets. The net worth is a true measure of the wealth of a family. The larger the net worth is, the wealthier the family is.

Spot Quiz • Balance Sheet

1. A $4,000 car with a $1,000 loan on it should be listed as an asset worth $3,000.   T _____   F _____

2. If a person's net worth is $9,000 and the person owes $7,000, the person has total assets of $16,000.   T _____   F _____

(Answers on page 59)

USING FINANCIAL STATEMENTS

Financial statements are important documents for managing personal finances. Lending institutions generally require borrowers to prepare finan-

cial statements before evaluating loan applications. By looking at your financial statements, you can determine whether or not you have too much in open-ended credit and installment loans. A look at the income statement can indicate whether too much is being spent on housing, for example. Detailed explanations are provided in later chapters. In this section we will examine changes in the income statement and the balance sheet and the interactions between the two statements.

Income Statement

For most people, total income remains relatively fixed for the year. Some salespeople who work on commission can try to increase total income by increasing their diligence in contacting clients. Also, workers paid on an hourly rate may earn more income by working more hours and receiving overtime pay. Other minor changes could possibly be made by trying to increase interest and dividend income. However, total income generally remains relatively fixed. Thus, the only way to increase income surplus is by trying to reduce expenses. Chapter 5 on budgeting will show how expenses can be controlled so that income surplus is increased.

Balance Sheet

Changes of the same dollar amount within either the assets or liabilities category do not change total assets or total liabilities. For example, if the Alstats withdraw $3,000 from the money market fund and use the money to buy stock, the new entries would be $18,000 in the fund and $7,000 in stocks (see Table 2.2). Total assets would remain the same.

If assets are used to reduce liabilities, net worth remains the same. For example, if $1,000 was taken from the money market fund to pay off the furniture loan, total assets would decline to $133,070, and total liabilities to $46,300, but net worth would remain at $86,770. Similarly, if liabilities are increased to buy assets, net worth would remain the same. For example, assume that the Alstats buy a used car for $2,000. The down payment is $500 and $1,500 is financed. The before and after transactions would affect the balance sheet as shown in Table 2.3. The checking account balance declines from $500 to $0. The car amount is increased by $2,000 to $5,900. Since all other asset entries remain the same, total assets increase by $1,500. Similarly, total liabilities increase by $1,500 as well.

In general, the most important item on the balance sheet is the net worth figure. Net worth is an excellent measure of wealth. A family that has carefully planned its finances should see its net worth rising steadily from year to year.

Table 2.3 Balance Sheet Transactions*

Account	Before		After
Assets			
Checking account	$ 500		$ 0
Car	3,900		5,900
Account totals	$4,400		$5,900
Increase in assets		$1,500	
Liabilities			
Installment loans, car	$3,000		$4,500
Increase in liabilities		$1,500	

*A used car is purchased for $2,000. The down payment is $500, and $1,500 is borrowed.

Increasing Net Worth

As mentioned before, steadily increasing net worth figures reflect increasing wealth. How is net worth increased? First, changes in the values of investment type assets, such as money market funds, stocks, bonds, and rental properties, change net worth. For example, if the stock held by the Alstats increases to $7,000, their total assets will have increased by $3,000. Since their liabilities remain the same, their net worth will have increased by $3,000. On the other hand, if investments decline in value, the Alstats' net worth would also decline. Carefully selected investments are thus important in increasing net worth.

Net worth is also affected by how rapidly the values of some assets decline. For example, in most cases the values of cars decline over time. A car that declines in value less quickly than another car will have a positive effect on net worth. The same also applies to other durable consumption goods.

Finally, and most importantly, net worth is affected by income surpluses and deficits. If asset and liability accounts do not change, then increase in net worth is equal to the income surplus. This cannot be shown for the Alstats because we do not have their beginning of the year balance sheet. However, the example shown in Table 2.4 illustrates this principle. Assume that all transactions are for cash. The person's total income is $20,000, and total expenses are $15,000 for the year. This leaves the person with an income surplus of $5,000 in cash. The January 1, 1989, balance

sheet shows cash of $200, liabilities of $100, and net worth of $100. The
person still has the $100 liability on December 31, 1989. However, cash
now becomes $200 + $5,000 = $5,200. Net worth has increased to $5,100,
an increase of $5,000 that exactly matches the increase in income surplus.

As the example illustrates, larger income surpluses result in relatively
higher net worths. Proper management of expenses can produce higher
income surpluses. The reverse also holds true. Income deficits reduce net
worth. Loosely managed expenses can reduce the amount of growth in
net worth and in some cases might actually reduce its dollar amount. Financial statements demonstrate how well a person or family is achieving stated
financial goals.

Table 2.4   Income Surplus Effect on the Balance Sheet*

Income Statement
for Year Ending December 31, 1989

Total income (all from wages)	$20,000
Total expenses (no loan repayments)	15,000
Income surplus	$ 5,000

Balance Sheet
January 1, 1989

Assets		Liabilities	
Cash	$ 200	Loan	$ 100
Other assets	0	Total liabilities	$ 100
Total assets	$ 200	Net worth	100
		Liabilities and worth	$ 200

Balance Sheet
December 31, 1989

Assets		Liabilities	
Cash	$5,200	Loan	$ 100
Other assets	0	Total liabilities	$ 100
Total assets	$5,200	Net worth	5,100
		Liabilities and worth	$5,200

*Assume that all transactions are for cash.

Spot Quiz • Using Financial Statements

1. Increasing cash by selling stock increases net worth.

　　　　　　　　　　　　　　　　　T _____　F _____

2. Income surpluses in general increase net worth.

　　　　　　　　　　　　　　　　　T _____　F _____

(Answers on page 59)

Summary

A variety of factors, such as the need to manage finances, maintain documents as legal evidence, prove property ownership, and verify information, require the keeping of records. Financial statements, tax records, warranties, credit information, housing records, transportation records, and investment records are some of the documents that should be maintained. Some records can be kept at home, whereas others should be kept in a safe deposit box in a bank.

An income statement lists a family's or individual's income and expenses. The difference between income and expenses is called income surplus if it is positive and income deficit if it is negative. A balance sheet shows what a person owns, which are called assets, and what a person owes, called liabilities. The difference between assets and liabilities is net worth.

Net worth is a measure of a person's wealth. It is financially desirable to manage assets and expenses so that net worth increases. One way to accomplish this goal is to carefully select investments that grow in value over time. Another way of increasing net worth is to generate as large an income surplus as possible.

Questions

1. Briefly explain why you need to maintain records.

2. Explain how some documents can be used to verify information.

3. What types of documents could be used to provide legal evidence? Explain your answer.

4. What types of records are considered to be vital? Why are they vital?

5. Explain briefly the types of tax-related records you should keep.

6. Prepare a list of documents that should be kept in a safe deposit box. Explain briefly why they should be kept there.

7. Would you keep the original of your will in a safe deposit box? Why or why not?

8. What is meant by an income statement? List important major categories on an income statement.

9. What is an income surplus? Why is it important?

10. What is meant by a balance sheet? Briefly explain the three major balance sheet categories.

11. Explain why identical changes in assets and liabilities will not change net worth.

12. Explain how net worth can be increased.

Case Problems

1. Linda Escue expects to have take-home income of $14,300 this year. She received a tax refund of $800 earlier in the year. She will receive about $300 in interest income this year. Her expenses for the year are expected to be as follows: rent, $4,800; food, $1,700; transportation, $1,200; clothing, $600; utilities, $1,400; loans, $1,200; vacation, $900; miscellaneous, $500. Prepare an income statement for Ms. Escue for the current year.

2. Akeem Ahmed has gross income of $27,000 and has taxes and other deductions equaling $9,300 withheld from his paychecks. He received federal and state tax refunds of $327 this year. A savings account will pay him $730 this year. His major expenses include: housing, $4,800; food, $2,400; utilities, $1,800; auto, gas, insurance, $3,600; clothing, $900; vacation, $1,200; other, $1,500. Prepare a current year income statement for Mr. Ahmed.

3. Paula Czarnecki has $200 in a checking account and $910 in a savings account. Her car is worth $5,000. She recently bought furniture for $2,400. Her clothing and jewelry are estimated to be worth $1,300. She owes $170 on a credit card account. Unpaid utility bills total $70. She has a $2,800 loan outstanding on her car. Prepare a balance sheet for Ms. Czarnecki.

4. Whitney Dallas has a savings account with $7,900 in it. She recently checked on the balance in her checking account and found out that she had $1,137. Her furniture and appliances are worth $8,000. She has recently bought clothes worth $1,800 and donated her old clothes to charity. Her credit card has a current balance of $349. She also owes her dentist and her phone company a combined total of $88. Her car, which is worth $9,000, has a remaining loan balance of $4,800. Prepare a balance sheet for Ms. Dallas.

5. The Klimstras had $90,000 in total assets at the beginning of the year. Their total liabilities at that time were $53,000. During the course of the year the Klimstras received $16,900 in take-home wages, $470 in interest income, and $2,200 in dividend income. Their expenses for the year were as follows: food, $3,200; housing, $4,500; transportation, $1,800; clothing, $1,200; utilities, $2,400; miscellaneous, $3,000. What was the Klimstras' net worth at the end of the year? Show all your calculations and explain how you derived the answer.

6. At the beginning of the year, the Adams family had total assets of $100,000. Their total liabilities consisted of a $60,000 mortgage and a $2,000 car loan. During the year the Adamses had gross income of $49,000 and take-home income of $38,000. Their total expenses amounted to $25,000 for the year. These expenses included paying off the car loan and decreasing the mortgage by $900. In addition to their gross income, they also received interest income of $1,200. A signed print by Calder, estimated to be worth $1,500, was donated to charity. What was the Adamses' net worth at the beginning of the year? What was their net worth at the end of the year? Show all your calculations.

7. For the data provided in Table 2.4, assume that the $100 loan was paid off in September 1989. That is, total expenses for the year are $15,100. Redraw the income statement for the year and the balance

sheet on December 31, 1989. What figure do you show for the net worth on December 31, 1989? Explain your answer.

8. At the beginning of the year, the Callahans had total assets of $200,000 and net worth of $110,000. During the year their total assets increased by $10,000, and their total liabilities decreased by $1,500. What is the Callahans' net worth at the end of the year? Show your calculations.

Bibliography

"Which Family Records Should You Hold Onto?" *Changing Times* (December 1974): 37–40.

"Put a Finger on Your Financial Pulse." *Changing Times* (January 1979): 36–38.

"Inflation's Hidden Costs: How to Hit Back." *Changing Times* (December 1979): 7–10.

"Make a Budget for Your Inflation Rate." *Changing Times* (August 1980): 21–25.

"How to Profit From Low Inflation." *Changing Times* (November 1986): 28–34.

Answers to Spot Quizzes

Maintaining Records (page 44)

1. T (For example, good records save time in filing tax returns.)
2. T (For example, a will.)
3. T (Fire can destroy records.)

Income Statement (page 46)

1. T (It lists funds received from all sources.)
2. F (It means that total income is in excess of total expenses.)

Balance Sheet (page 51)

1. F   (The car is an asset worth $4,000.)
2. T   ($16,000 − $7,000 = $9,000.)

Using Financial Statements (page 55)

1. F   (The dollar amount of total assets remains unchanged.)
2. T   (As shown in Table 2.4.)

Chapter 3

Financial Planning and Income Taxes

Objectives

After reading this chapter, you will be able to:

- Describe the basic nature of taxes.
- Decide whether to itemize expenses on your tax return.
- Compute taxes payable.
- Fill out tax forms.
- Describe methods for reducing taxes.
- List sources of tax assistance.

The idea behind the recent major tax overhaul, called the Tax Reform Act of 1986, was to simplify the tax system and make it fairer. The tax reforms were successful in reducing the tax brackets and the maximum tax rate. Also, most of the loopholes in the tax system that allowed people with high incomes to pay little in taxes were eliminated. However, one new group of consumers was affected by the tax reforms—children. Every child who is five years old or older is now required to have a social security number.[1] (See "Tagging the Children" below.)

Taxes are a fact of life, even for children with earnings. The average consumer in the United States will, directly or indirectly, end up paying federal income taxes, state and local income taxes, excise taxes, social security taxes, property taxes, tariffs, unemployment taxes, sales taxes, and personal property taxes. And how about estate taxes, inheritance taxes, and gift taxes? The discussion of taxes in this chapter, including the basics of taxation, filing tax returns, and tax planning, will be limited to federal income taxes.

Tagging the Children

Your college identification number is probably your social security number. You need a social security number to apply for a job or open a bank account. You might even have to list your social security number to apply for a credit card. But why would a five-year-old, who is not going to register for fall classes at a university, apply for a job, apply for a credit card, or open a bank account, need a social security number? Is something sinister afoot? Not really.

The Tax Reform Act of 1986 requires all children who are five years old or older and are claimed as exemptions on tax returns to have social security numbers. Apparently, the IRS wants to identify situations where divorced parents both claim the same child or children as deductions. You can't beat the system in this case. Parents are required to go to their local social security office to fill out an application for a social security number. The child's birth certificate, one other proof of identity, and the parent's ID are needed to apply. Call the social security office to find out the best time to go and to determine what an acceptable "other proof of identity" is.

---

1. "No Kidding: Tax ID Numbers for Children," *Changing Times* (November 1986): 7.

THE BASICS OF TAXES

The original federal income tax laws, dating as far back as 1913, are contained in a tax code that was developed in 1939. Subsequently, the tax laws were changed, amended, and revised a number of times. The Tax Reform Act of 1986 resulted in significant revisions in the tax law and will be explained in this chapter.

Are Taxes Fair?

Ask any taxpayer whether the taxes imposed on him or her are fair. Chances are that the answer will be no. Many people feel that the federal tax laws, as applicable to them, are unfair. The low-income wage earner says that the rich escape paying taxes by utilizing special tax preference provisions. The high-income wage earner complains that he or she supports the young, the elderly, and the unemployed. The middle-income wage earner argues that she or he is too poor to use tax planning and too rich to participate in federal assistance programs.

Very few people would pay taxes voluntarily. Wage earners are required to pay taxes and therefore believe that they have a right to complain about taxes. Taxes are collected for two major reasons: (1) to finance government and (2) to carry out specific social welfare and economic programs. Not all taxpayers agree on how much government support the various social welfare and economic programs should receive. Given each person's unique perspective, it is difficult for anyone to consider taxes "fair." Taxpayers do, however, have the option of influencing government spending through their role in electing government officials. Thus, while taxes could be thought of as not being fair to everyone, a mechanism exists for taxpayers to influence the tax structure.

Complex Nature of Taxes

Federal tax laws are very complex, partly because sources of income are broadly varied. Large differences in the sources of income require differences in methods of taxation, leading to a complex tax law system. Also, the original tax laws have been revised many times. In the process, much more has been added than deleted from the tax laws, contributing to the complexity of the tax system. In addition, taxes not only finance government but also provide a method for carrying out social welfare and economic policies. Translating these policies into tax laws creates additional complexity.

"*Your Majesty is hereby informed that unless your tribute is sent to IRS immediately, we shall lay siege to your castle, sack your vacation home and pillage and plunder your countryside. If payment has already been made, kindly disregard this notice.*"

Source: *Changing Times*, December 1980, p. 38.

Why You Need to Understand Taxes

The tax system is so complex that even experts sometimes differ over the meaning of the law in a certain area. This chapter is not designed to make you a tax expert. Rather, it will provide you with an understanding of how the federal tax system works. Understanding the system better is a must for a variety of reasons. You will not be able to manage your personal finances properly without a reasonable understanding of tax laws. For instance, there is the danger of paying excess taxes because of a lack of understanding of tax laws. Also, a good understanding of taxes can help you avoid computing your taxes incorrectly and having to pay the Internal Revenue Service additional taxes, with both interest and a penalty fee.

Paying a Fair Share

It should be kept in mind that the tax laws are applied to all taxpayers equally. There is nothing especially moral about paying *more* tax than is required. Many people do pay more in taxes than they should because they do not understand tax laws, they do not obtain tax advice from a qualified tax adviser, they neglect to save receipts and documents for tax-deductible expenses, and, quite often, because they are reluctant to take a legitimate

deduction. Paying your fair share of taxes is what the government expects you to do.

Paying your fair share of taxes implies that you need to understand the tax laws well enough to pay only as much in taxes as the law requires. Paying more than the law requires is neither moral nor financially justified. Paying less than the law requires is called **tax evasion** and is illegal. Tax evasion occurs when a person understates earnings or overstates expenses or both. If the IRS detects tax evasion, the taxpayer must pay the taxes evaded with interest and usually with a penalty as well. Tax evasion is not a strategy for managing taxes. Minimizing taxes through financial planning is the strategy to follow.

Tax Rate Schedules.   Table 3.1 shows the tax rate schedules for 1988. For tax purposes, there are four categories of consumer taxpayers. The tax schedules shown apply to **taxable income**, which is equal to gross income less certain deductions. As we explain later, two important deductions are the personal exemption and the standard deduction. For 1988, each person is allowed a **personal exemption** of $1,950 from taxes. Similarly, each category of taxpayer is allowed a certain amount of money, called the **standard deduction**, that can be deducted from gross income. In 1988, the standard deduction for singles was $3,000. The tax tables shown in Table 3.1 as well as the personal exemption and the standard deduction are subject to adjustment for inflation starting in 1990.

Tax Bracket.   The second row for single taxpayers in Table 3.1 shows

$17,850 $43,150 $2,677.50 + 28% $17,850

The first and last figures, $17,850, are the base, or lower taxable income limit. The second number, $43,150, is the upper taxable income limit. These two numbers form a **tax bracket**. The third number contains both a dollar amount and a percent. The amount $2,677.50 is the base tax, and the 28 percent is the percentage applicable to this tax bracket. For example, a person with a taxable income of $26,000 would be classified in this tax bracket.

A Simple Tax Calculation.   Cindy Lapper is a single taxpayer with gross income of $30,000. From this gross income she deducts her personal exemption of $1,950 and standard deduction of $3,000. This gives her taxable income of $30,000 − $1,950 − $3,000 = $25,050, which places her in the $17,850–$43,150 tax bracket. Ms. Lapper's taxes can be calculated as follows:

$$\$2,677.50 + (\$25,050 - \$17,850) \times .28 =$$
$$\$2,677.50 + \$2,016.00 = \$4,693.50.$$

The $2,677.50 is the base tax. It is the 15 percent tax on Ms. Lapper's first $17,850 of taxable income. Her remaining taxable income of $25,050 −

Table 3.1   1988 Tax Rate Schedules[1]

Single Taxpayer[2]

Taxable Income Over	But not over	Tax	Of amount over
$ 0	$ 17,850	$0 + 15%	$ 0
17,850	43,150	$2,677.50 + 28%	17,850
43,150	89,560	$9,761.50 + 33%	43,150
89,560	100,480	$25,076.80 + 33%	89,560
100,480		$28,680.40 + 28%	100,480

Married, Filing Jointly[3]

Taxable Income Over	But not over	Tax	Of amount over
$ 0	$ 29,750	$0 + 15%	$ 0
29,750	71,900	$4,462.50 + 28%	29,750
71,900	149,250	$16,264.50 + 33%	71,900
149,250	171,090	$41,790.00 + 33%	149,250
171,090		$48,997.20 + 28%	171,090

Heads of Household[2]

Taxable Income Over	But not over	Tax	Of amount over
$ 0	$ 23,900	$0 + 15%	$ 0
23,900	61,650	$3,585.00 + 28%	23,900
61,650	123,790	$14,155.00 + 33%	61,650
123,790	134,710	$34,661.20 + 33%	123,790
134,710		$38,264.80 + 28%	134,710

Married, Filing Separately[2]

Taxable Income Over	But not over	Tax	Of amount over
$ 0	$ 14,875	$0 + 15%	$ 0
14,875	35,950	$2,231.25 + 28%	14,875
35,950	113,300	$8,132.25 + 33%	35,950
113,300	124,220	$33,657.75 + 33%	113,300
124,220		$37,261.35 + 28%	124,220

[1]Tax rate schedules are for 1988 taxable income. Starting in 1989, all of the tax brackets will be adjusted for inflation every year. The 33% tax brackets include a 5% surtax.
[2]Assumes one personal exemption.
[3]Assumes two personal exemptions.

$17,850 = $7,200 is taxed at 28 percent. On this $7,200, she pays taxes of $7,200 × .28 = $2,016.00. Her total taxes payable are $2,677.50 + $2,016.00 = $4,693.50.

Marginal and Incremental Tax Rates. The tax rate applicable to the last dollars of taxable income is referred to as the **marginal tax rate**. In Ms. Lapper's case, her marginal tax rate is 28 percent. If Ms. Lapper's taxable income were to increase from $25,050 to $30,000, her marginal tax rate would remain the same. If, however, her taxable income were to increase to $46,000, her marginal tax rate on the increased income would then be 33 percent.

The **incremental tax rate** is the tax rate applicable to a person's increased, or incremental, earnings. Table 3.2 shows the calculation for Ms. Lapper's incremental tax rate, assuming that her income increases from $25,050 to $46,000 during one year.

At a taxable income of $46,000, Ms. Lapper would pay $10,702 in taxes. At $25,050, her taxes are $4,693.50. Her taxable income has increased by $46,000 − $25,050 = $20,950. Her taxes have increased by $10,702.00 − $4,693.50 = $6,008.50. The $6,008.50 tax is the amount paid on the additional, or incremental, income of $20,950. Thus, her incremental tax rate is $6,008.50/$20,950 = 28.67 percent.

People often assume that moving into a higher tax bracket means that their total taxable income will be subject to the higher tax bracket rate. As the above example illustrates, such is not the case. Even though Ms. Lapper moved into the 33 percent tax bracket, only a small portion of her income—the difference between $46,000 and $43,150—was subject to the higher 33 percent rate. As Table 3.1 indicates, the highest marginal tax rate is 33 percent.

Table 3.2 Calculating the Incremental Tax Rate*

Taxable Income	Calculation of Taxes	Taxes
$46,000	$9,761.50 + [($46,000 − $43,150) × .33] =	$10,702.00
$25,050	$2,677.50 + [($25,050 − $17,850) × .28] =	$ 4,693.50
$20,950		$ 6,008.50

Marginal tax rate = $6,008.50 × 100/$20,950 = 28.67%

* Tax rates are from the Single Taxpayers Schedule in Table 3.1.

Average Tax Rate.   The **average tax rate** is the percent tax paid on gross income minus the standard deduction or itemized deductions. The Tax Reform Act of 1986 targeted an average tax rate of 28 percent. Thus, no matter what your income, your average tax rate will never exceed 28 percent on gross income minus the standard deduction. This fact accounts for the 5 percent surtax included in the tax rate schedules in Table 3.1. The 5 percent surtax in the first 33 percent tax bracket makes up for the lower level of taxes in the 15 percent tax bracket. The 5 percent surtax in the second 33 percent tax bracket compensates for the personal exemption. In the first 33 percent tax bracket for the single taxpayer, the surtax is equal to ($89,560 − $43,150) × .05 = $2,320.50. The 15 percent tax bracket is 28 percent − 15 percent = 13 percent less than the 28 percent tax bracket. Thirteen percent of $17,850 equals $17,850 × .13 = $2,320.50. So we note that the surtax in this bracket ''recovers'' the lost taxes associated with the 15 percent tax bracket.

The personal exemption is $1,950. The 28 percent tax on it is $1,950 × .28 = $546. The 5 percent surtax in the 33 percent tax bracket recovers this amount, that is, ($100,480 − $89,560) × .05 = $546.

Finally, let's assume that a single taxpayer has taxable income of $100,480. According to Table 3.1, this person would pay $28,680.40 in taxes. Because gross income − personal exemption − deduction = taxable income, we need to add back personal exemption to taxable income to obtain gross income − deduction, which is equal to $100,480 + $1,950 = $102,430. The average tax rate for this person is $28,640.40/$102,430 = 28 percent. For any taxable income over $100,480, the average tax rate would remain 28 percent because the marginal tax rate is also 28 percent.[2]

Progressive Tax Rates.   Federal income tax rates are progressive. **Progressive tax rates** are rates that increase as a person's income increases. For 1988, a single taxpayer can claim total deductions of at least $1,950 + $3,000 = $4,950. Thus, a single taxpayer with gross income minus deductions equal to or under $1,950 would not have to pay any taxes. For him or her, the tax rate is 0 percent. The maximum tax rate on gross income minus deductions will never be higher than 28 percent. Figure 3.1 shows how the average tax rate for a single taxpayer increases as gross income increases. The figure assumes that the standard deduction and personal exemption are taken. For example, at a gross income minus standard deduction of $40,000, taxable income is $40,000 − $1,950 = $38,050. Taxes on this amount are ($38,050 − $17,850) × .28 + $2,677.50 = $8,333.50. The average tax is $8,333.50/$40,000 = 20.8 percent.

---

2. The ''Married Filing Separately'' category recovers the first 5 percent surtax twice to adjust for uneven incomes for the two spouses filing in this category—($113,300 − $35,950) × .05 = $14,875 × .13 × 2 = $3,867.50.

Figure 3.1 Progressive Tax Rates

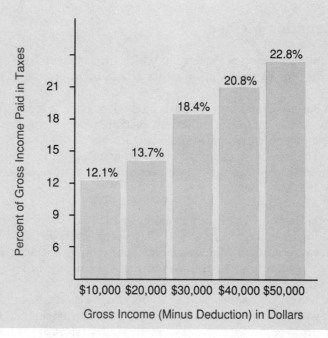

*Tax rates are from the Single Taxpayers Schedule in Table 3.1. A standard deduction is assumed.

Notice in Figure 3.1 that the percent of income paid in taxes increases as income increases. In a **proportional tax rate** structure, the percent of taxable income paid in taxes remains the same irrespective of the level of taxable income. Many states and cities have a proportional income tax. For example, some cities tax their populace 1 percent of income, regardless of the level of income. Some taxes, such as fixed car registration fees, are regressive taxes. With **regressive taxes**, the percent of income paid out in taxes decreases with increases in income.

The Internal Revenue Service

The Internal Revenue Service (IRS) is a division of the U.S. Department of the Treasury. The IRS is the agency in charge of administering and enforcing the Internal Revenue Code and collecting taxes. The IRS implements new tax laws by issuing **regulations**. These regulations provide information to taxpayers on the procedures for complying with tax laws. In special cases where a regulation is not required, the IRS will issue a ruling. A **ruling** is the IRS's interpretation of a law applied to a special situation. The

intent of the regulations and rulings issued by the IRS is to provide information so that taxpayers can know how to comply with the law.

Accounting Method

An accounting method is the way in which the taxpayer keeps financial records. Records can be kept on either a cash or an accrual basis.

Cash Basis.   Under the **cash basis** method, all income actually received and all tax-deductible expenses actually paid are reported for the year. For example, a person works part-time from October 15, 1988, to November 15, 1988. The person does not receive a paycheck until January 7, 1989. Under the cash method, the amount represented by the paycheck is income for 1989, not 1988.

Accrual Basis.   Under the **accrual basis** method, income earned and expenses incurred are recognized as they occur, irrespective of whether any money is received or paid. In the previous example, the taxpayer would recognize the amount of the check as current year income in 1988 because it is earned in 1988.

Once a taxpayer has selected an accounting method, she or he cannot change it without the permission of the IRS. The accrual method involves more record keeping than the cash method. Therefore, most taxpayers prefer to use the cash method.

Spot Quiz • The Basics of Taxes

1. The tax laws are made complex to make it difficult for taxpayers to cheat.   T _____   F _____

2. Paying a fair share of taxes means that a person should try to reduce taxes legitimately.   T _____   F _____

3. In a progressive tax structure, the dollar amount of taxes paid increases at the same rate as gross income.   T _____   F _____

4. The Single Taxpayer Tax Rate Schedule in Table 3.1 indicates that the marginal tax rate on an increase in taxable income from $35,000 to $40,000 will be 28 percent.   T _____   F _____

(Answers on page 97)

DETERMINING TAXES PAYABLE

A step-by-step procedure for determining taxes to be paid is outlined in this section. This procedure is shown in flowchart form in Figure 3.2.

Who Must File a Return?

The first step in determining taxes to be paid is to establish whether a person has to file a tax return. Whether a person has to file a tax return depends on three factors: filing status, exemptions, and gross income. In 1988, each person received an automatic personal exemption of $1,950. Additionally, for each tax return being filed, the taxpayer or taxpayers can claim a **standard deduction**. The standard deduction for 1987 and 1988 for the various filing categories are shown below:

| | Standard Deduction | |
Filing Status	1987	1988
1. Single	$2,540	$3,000
2. Married, filing jointly	$3,760	$5,000
3. Married, filing separately	$1,880	$2,500
4. Head of Household	$2,540	$4,400
5. Qualifying widows, widowers	$3,760	$5,000

Additional deductions are applicable to people who are over 65 years of age or blind or both. A single taxpayer who is over 65 years of age or blind can claim an extra deduction of $750. If both conditions apply, then $1,500 can be claimed. Married taxpayers can claim $600 for each condition. Thus, if both are blind and over 65 years old, they can claim $2,400 in deductions.

For 1988, a single taxpayer with gross income under $1,950 + $3,000 = $4,950 does not have to file a tax return unless he or she expects a refund. Certain combinations of exemptions, filing status, and gross income affect requirements for filing. The process is outlined in Figure 3.3. Note that Figure 3.3 is for 1987 and that the dollar amounts for both the personal exemption and the standard deduction have changed every year since then to keep pace with inflation.

There are some other filing requirements in addition to those shown in Figure 3.3. A person has to file a tax return if she or he:

1. Could be claimed as a dependent by parents and had dividend, interest, and other earned or unearned income of more than $500.
2. Received at least $400 from self-employment.
3. Received tips on which social security taxes were not paid.

Figure 3.2 Flowchart for Determining Taxes to Be Paid

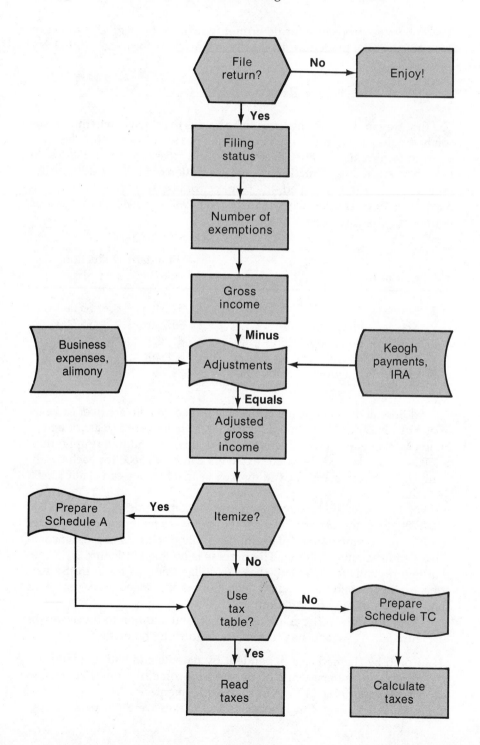

Figure 3.3 Flowchart for Determining Who Must File*

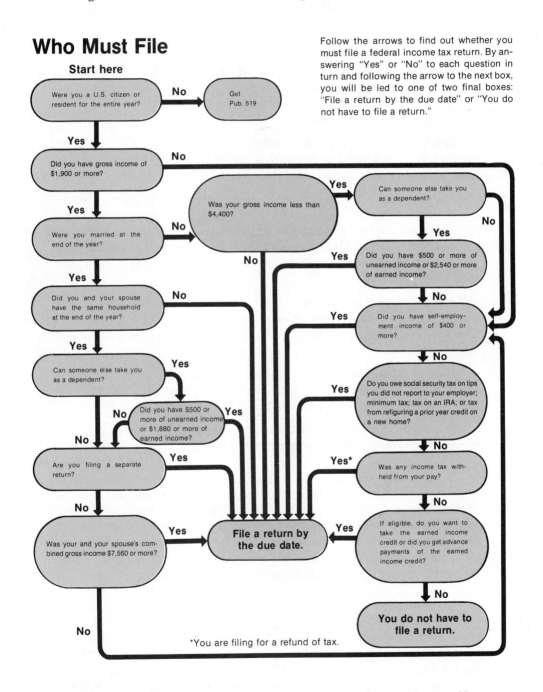

Who Must File

Follow the arrows to find out whether you must file a federal income tax return. By answering "Yes" or "No" to each question in turn and following the arrow to the next box, you will be led to one of two final boxes: "File a return by the due date" or "You do not have to file a return."

Start here

Were you a U.S. citizen or resident for the entire year? — **No** → Get Pub. 519

Did you have gross income of $1,900 or more?

Were you married at the end of the year?

Was your gross income less than $4,400?

Can someone else take you as a dependent?

Did you have $500 or more of unearned income or $2,540 or more of earned income?

Did you and your spouse have the same household at the end of the year?

Did you have self-employment income of $400 or more?

Can someone else take you as a dependent?

Did you have $500 or more of unearned income or $1,880 or more of earned income?

Do you owe social security tax on tips you did not report to your employer; minimum tax; tax on an IRA; or tax from refiguring a prior year credit on a new home?

Are you filing a separate return?

Was any income tax withheld from your pay?

File a return by the due date.

Was your and your spouse's combined gross income $7,560 or more?

If eligible, do you want to take the earned income credit or did you get advance payments of the earned income credit?

You do not have to file a return.

*You are filing for a refund of tax.

*This flowchart for 1987 tax returns has been adapted from an Internal Revenue Service publication and applies only to single and married taxpayers under age 65.

Filing a return does not necessarily mean that a person has to pay additional taxes. For example, if a person expects a tax refund, then he or she would have to file a return to receive the refund.

Filing Status.   Each person falls into one of five tax filing categories. **Tax filing status** affects how much in taxes an individual or family has to pay. Determining filing status is shown in the second box in Figure 3.2, which outlines the procedure for determining taxable income. The five filing categories are listed below.

Single.   A person must file as single if, on the last day of the tax year, the person is unmarried or recognized by the tax law as being separated from his or her spouse and does not qualify to file in another category.

Married, Filing Jointly.   A husband and wife, if they are married on the last day of the tax year, may file a joint return. It does not make any difference whether only one spouse or both spouses had incomes. The incomes and tax-deductible expenses of the two spouses are combined, and taxes are paid on one combined income. In general, this filing status minimizes taxes paid.

Married, Filing Separately.   A husband and wife may file separate returns. Each one must report his or her income and deductions separately. This status may benefit a couple when one spouse had a low income and large number of certain types of deductions.

Head of Household.   An unmarried person may qualify as a head of household if the person has provided at least 50 percent support at home for the whole tax year for another "qualified person."

Qualifying Widows and Widowers.   Under certain circumstances, the surviving spouse qualifies for special tax treatment.

Number of Exemptions.   The third step is to determine the number of exemptions allowed. Claiming the correct number of **exemptions** is important because, for each exemption claimed, the taxpayer can reduce taxable income by $1,950 for 1988. A taxpayer must claim himself or herself as an exemption. Exemptions can also be taken for the taxpayer's children. Other dependents, members of a household, and relatives can also be claimed as exemptions provided they meet certain qualifying tests.

Gross Income.   The fourth step, as shown in Figure 3.2, is to calculate gross income. The basis for paying taxes is **gross income**, which is the total of all income from all sources except those excluded by law. A listing of major categories of income to be included in gross income is shown in Figure 3.4.

Some types of income are excluded from gross income—that is, these incomes are exempt from federal income taxes. Figure 3.5 lists major types of income that are excluded.

Figure 3.4 What Is Included in Gross Income

Alimony	Pensions
Annuities	Prizes
Awards	Rents received
Back pay	Retirement pay
Bonuses	Rewards
Business income	Royalties
Commissions	Salaries
Debts forgiven	Severance pay
Dividends	Strike benefits
Fees	Supplemental unemployment
Free tours	benefits
Gains from sale of property	Tips
Interest received	Travel allowance
Mileage allowance	Wages
Partnership income	

Figure 3.5 What Is Excluded from Gross Income

Accident insurance proceeds	Military allowances
Annuities (limited)	Relocation payments
Child support payments	Scholarships (limited)
Death benefits (limited)	Social security benefits
Disability benefits	Unemployment compensation
Fellowship grants (limited)	Veterans' benefits
Gifts, inheritances	Welfare payments
Life insurance proceeds	Workers' compensation

Adjusted Gross Income.   Certain expense items may be deducted from gross income to arrive at **adjusted gross income**. Business expenses involving travel can also be deducted. Commuting expenses between home and the workplace are not deductible. Subject to certain limits and requirements, payments made to retirement accounts (IRA and Keogh) are also deductible.

Alimony and separate maintenance payments are deductible by the spouse making the payments but only if a written agreement or court decree requires that the payments be made. Disability income up to $5,200 per year may be excluded from gross income. If adjusted gross income (without the disability income exclusion) is more than $20,200, then this deduction cannot be taken.

Itemized Expenses.   The Internal Revenue Code allows expenses in six categories to be itemized and deducted from adjusted gross income.

Who May Itemize?   As mentioned previously, a single taxpayer could claim a standard deduction of $3,000 in 1988. Therefore, a single taxpayer should not itemize unless expenses exceed $3,000. If itemized deductions are greater than the standard deduction, then the taxpayer should itemize. Even if a taxpayer claims the standard deduction, he or she can still deduct the following expenses in addition to the standard deduction.

1. Contributions to individual retirement accounts (if applicable).
2. Contributions to a self-employed retirement plan (Keogh plan).
3. Alimony paid.

Who Must Itemize?   Some taxpayers are required to itemize even if their itemized deductions are less than the standard deduction. For example, a taxpayer must itemize if she or he is married, filing separately, and has a spouse who is itemizing expenses. Certain other situations also call for itemizing.

What Can Be Itemized?   Seven categories of expenses can be itemized. **Medical and dental expenses**, such as fees for doctors, fees for hospital services, health insurance premiums, and expenses for false teeth, eyeglasses, medicines, and drugs, can be deducted subject to certain limitations. Payment for transportation for medical care also qualifies as a medical expense.

Some **taxes**, such as state and local income tax, real estate tax, personal property tax, and certain other taxes, are deductible. Other taxes, such as sales tax, social security tax, gift tax, estate taxes, gasoline tax, and cigarette taxes, are not deductible.

Interest is payment for the use of money. One hundred percent of mortgage interest (on both first and second mortgages) can be itemized

and deducted. Interest on consumer loans and car loans and finance charges and interest on credit card borrowing is called **consumer interest**. Only the following percentages of consumer interest qualify as a tax deduction for the specified year:

Year	Percent of Consumer Interest Deductible
1987	65%
1988	40%
1989	20%
1990	10%
1991 and after	0%

The interest paid on money borrowed to buy investment property, such as stocks and bonds, is called **investment interest**. **Investment income** includes interest received, dividends, rents, royalties, and capital gains. Investment interest up to the amount of investment income can be itemized and deducted.

Contributions to qualified organizations are deductible. Contributions may be in cash or property.

Casualty and theft losses not covered by insurance are deductible. Losses caused by fire, floods, storms, and other sudden, unexpected, or unusual events are deductible.

Moving expenses may be deducted if they are reasonable and if they meet certain requirements.

The last expense category, miscellaneous deductions, can be deducted subject to certain limitations. Union dues, employment agency fees, small tools and supplies, and uniforms are examples of expenses included in this category. Personal legal expenses, bribes, lost property, and penalties are not deductible. All itemized deductions are reported on Schedule A.

Taxes Payable. Itemized deductions, if any, or the standard deduction are subtracted from adjusted gross income. From this balance, the personal exemption amount times the number of exemptions claimed is subtracted to obtain **taxable income**. The last step is to determine taxes payable. The Tax Table must be used to determine taxes payable if taxable income is less than $50,000. A portion of the 1987 Tax Table is shown in Table 3.3. If the $50,000 taxable income limit is exceeded, then the Tax Rate Schedules must be used to determine taxes.

Table 3.3 Sample Tax Table

1987 Tax Table

Based on Taxable Income

For persons with taxable incomes of less than $50,000.

Example: Mr. and Mrs. Brown are filing a joint return. Their taxable income on line 36 of Form 1040 is $25,325. First, they find the $25,300–25,350 income line. Next, they find the column for married filing jointly and read down the column. The amount shown where the income line and filing status column meet is $3,679. This is the tax amount they must write on line 37 of their return.

At least	But less than	Single	Married filing jointly *	Married filing sepa-rately	Head of a house-hold
		Your tax is—			
25,200	25,250	4,807	3,664	5,374	3,973
25,250	25,300	4,821	3,671	5,391	3,987
→ 25,300	25,350	4,835	(3,679)	5,409	4,001
25,350	25,400	4,849	3,686	5,426	4,015

If line 36 (taxable income) is—		And you are—			
At least	But less than	Single	Married filing jointly *	Married filing sepa-rately	Head of a house-hold
		Your tax is—			
$0	$5	$0	$0	$0	$0
5	15	1	1	1	1
15	25	2	2	2	2
25	50	4	4	4	4
50	75	7	7	7	7
75	100	10	10	10	10
100	125	12	12	12	12
125	150	15	15	15	15
150	175	18	18	18	18
175	200	21	21	21	21
200	225	23	23	23	23
225	250	26	26	26	26
250	275	29	29	29	29
275	300	32	32	32	32
300	325	34	34	34	34
325	350	37	37	37	37
350	375	40	40	40	40
375	400	43	43	43	43
400	425	45	45	45	45
425	450	48	48	48	48
450	475	51	51	51	51
475	500	54	54	54	54
500	525	56	56	56	56
525	550	59	59	59	59
550	575	62	62	62	62
575	600	65	65	65	65
600	625	67	67	67	67
625	650	70	70	70	70
650	675	73	73	73	73
675	700	76	76	76	76
700	725	78	78	78	78
725	750	81	81	81	81
750	775	84	84	84	84
775	800	87	87	87	87
800	825	89	89	89	89
825	850	92	92	92	92
850	875	95	95	95	95
875	900	98	98	98	98
900	925	100	100	100	100
925	950	103	103	103	103
950	975	106	106	106	106
975	1,000	109	109	109	109
1,000					
1,000	1,025	111	111	111	111
1,025	1,050	114	114	114	114
1,050	1,075	117	117	117	117
1,075	1,100	120	120	120	120
1,100	1,125	122	122	122	122
1,125	1,150	125	125	125	125
1,150	1,175	128	128	128	128
1,175	1,200	131	131	131	131
1,200	1,225	133	133	133	133
1,225	1,250	136	136	136	136
1,250	1,275	139	139	139	139
1,275	1,300	142	142	142	142
1,300	1,325	144	144	144	144
1,325	1,350	147	147	147	147
1,350	1,375	150	150	150	150
1,375	1,400	153	153	153	153

If line 36 (taxable income) is—		And you are—			
At least	But less than	Single	Married filing jointly *	Married filing sepa-rately	Head of a house-hold
		Your tax is—			
1,400	1,425	155	155	155	155
1,425	1,450	158	158	158	158
1,450	1,475	161	161	161	161
1,475	1,500	164	164	164	164
1,500	1,525	166	166	167	166
1,525	1,550	169	169	171	169
1,550	1,575	172	172	174	172
1,575	1,600	175	175	178	175
1,600	1,625	177	177	182	177
1,625	1,650	180	180	186	180
1,650	1,675	183	183	189	183
1,675	1,700	186	186	193	186
1,700	1,725	188	188	197	188
1,725	1,750	191	191	201	191
1,750	1,775	194	194	204	194
1,775	1,800	197	197	208	197
1,800	1,825	200	199	212	199
1,825	1,850	204	202	216	202
1,850	1,875	207	205	219	205
1,875	1,900	211	208	223	208
1,900	1,925	215	210	227	210
1,925	1,950	219	213	231	213
1,950	1,975	222	216	234	216
1,975	2,000	226	219	238	219
2,000					
2,000	2,025	230	221	242	221
2,025	2,050	234	224	246	224
2,050	2,075	237	227	249	227
2,075	2,100	241	230	253	230
2,100	2,125	245	232	257	232
2,125	2,150	249	235	261	235
2,150	2,175	252	238	264	238
2,175	2,200	256	241	268	241
2,200	2,225	260	243	272	243
2,225	2,250	264	246	276	246
2,250	2,275	267	249	279	249
2,275	2,300	271	252	283	252
2,300	2,325	275	254	287	254
2,325	2,350	279	257	291	257
2,350	2,375	282	260	294	260
2,375	2,400	286	263	298	263
2,400	2,425	290	265	302	265
2,425	2,450	294	268	306	268
2,450	2,475	297	271	309	271
2,475	2,500	301	274	313	274
2,500	2,525	305	276	317	277
2,525	2,550	309	279	321	281
2,550	2,575	312	282	324	284
2,575	2,600	316	285	328	288
2,600	2,625	320	287	332	292
2,625	2,650	324	290	336	296
2,650	2,675	327	293	339	299
2,675	2,700	331	296	343	303

If line 36 (taxable income) is—		And you are—			
At least	But less than	Single	Married filing jointly *	Married filing sepa-rately	Head of a house-hold
		Your tax is—			
2,700	2,725	335	298	347	307
2,725	2,750	339	301	351	311
2,750	2,775	342	304	354	314
2,775	2,800	346	307	358	318
2,800	2,825	350	309	362	322
2,825	2,850	354	312	366	326
2,850	2,875	357	315	369	329
2,875	2,900	361	318	373	333
2,900	2,925	365	320	377	337
2,925	2,950	369	323	381	341
2,950	2,975	372	326	384	344
2,975	3,000	376	329	388	348
3,000					
3,000	3,050	382	334	394	354
3,050	3,100	389	341	401	361
3,100	3,150	397	349	409	369
3,150	3,200	404	356	416	376
3,200	3,250	412	364	424	384
3,250	3,300	419	371	431	391
3,300	3,350	427	379	439	399
3,350	3,400	434	386	446	406
3,400	3,450	442	394	454	414
3,450	3,500	449	401	461	421
3,500	3,550	457	409	469	429
3,550	3,600	464	416	476	436
3,600	3,650	472	424	484	444
3,650	3,700	479	431	491	451
3,700	3,750	487	439	499	459
3,750	3,800	494	446	506	466
3,800	3,850	502	454	514	474
3,850	3,900	509	461	521	481
3,900	3,950	517	469	529	489
3,950	4,000	524	476	536	496
4,000					
4,000	4,050	532	484	544	504
4,050	4,100	539	491	551	511
4,100	4,150	547	499	559	519
4,150	4,200	554	506	566	526
4,200	4,250	562	514	574	534
4,250	4,300	569	521	581	541
4,300	4,350	577	529	589	549
4,350	4,400	584	536	596	556
4,400	4,450	592	544	604	564
4,450	4,500	599	551	611	571
4,500	4,550	607	559	619	579
4,550	4,600	614	566	626	586
4,600	4,650	622	574	634	594
4,650	4,700	629	581	641	601
4,700	4,750	637	589	649	609
4,750	4,800	644	596	656	616
4,800	4,850	652	604	664	624
4,850	4,900	659	611	671	631
4,900	4,950	667	619	679	639
4,950	5,000	674	626	686	646

* This column must also be used by a qualifying widow(er).

Continued on next page

Page 41

Spot Quiz • Determining Taxes Payable

1. A taxpayer who is single and under age 65 must file a return for 1988 if she earns $4,200 working as a sales clerk.   T _____   F _____

2. A family not itemizing expenses would pay taxes on adjusted gross income.   T _____   F _____

3. A head of household with $2,800 in deductible expenses for 1988 should not itemize them.   T _____   F _____

4. A married taxpayer filing jointly and paying $604 in taxes has at least $4,800 in taxable income.   T _____   F _____

(Answers on page 98)

SAMPLE TAX RETURNS

Most taxpayers choose either Form 1040EZ, Form 1040A, or Form 1040 to file their income tax returns. This section shows how to fill out all of these forms.

Which Form to Use

As you might guess, Form 1040EZ is the easiest form to use. For that reason, you should use Form 1040EZ unless you are required to use one of the other forms or would benefit from using one. Because Form 1040EZ is designed to be uncomplicated, it does not provide for more than the simplest circumstances. Form 1040EZ can be used only if you are single, have only one personal exemption, have income only from wages, salaries, or tips totaling less than $50,000, have interest income of $400 or less, have no dividend income, and have no tax credits.

The next simplest form is Form 1040A. You can use this form even if you are married or the head of a household, if you have dependents, or if you have interest or dividend income.

If you earn more than $50,000, itemize deductions, have other forms of income (as from self-employment), or otherwise don't qualify for one of the forms just described, you must use Form 1040.

Sample Form 1040EZ

James W. Linch is single and works as a technician. He has no other dependents. He earned $8,140 in 1987. He has invested in a money market mutual fund that has paid him $350 in interest income. A total of $547 in income taxes was withheld from Jim's paychecks.

"You forgot Form 1040-Q, 'Ill-gotten gains.'"

Source: *Changing Times,* February 1981, p. 42.

Jim does not itemize deductions. His interest income is less than $400. Therefore, he can file Form 1040EZ, shown in Table 3.4. His adjusted gross income is $8,490. He is not claimed as a dependent on another person's return. Therefore, he can take the standard deduction, which for 1987 was $2,540, and the personal exemption, which was $1,900 for 1987. His taxable income is $4,050. The tax table in Table 3.3, under singles, in the $4,000–$4,050 bracket, shows that he has to pay $532 in taxes. Since he paid $547 in taxes, he will receive a refund of $15.

Sample Form 1040A

Craig C. and Patty R. Kowalski are employed as managers of a fast food restaurant. They have a five-year-old daughter, Lisa Jane, who spends half days in kindergarten and half days at a day care center. Together the Kowalskis earned $34,175 in 1987 ($19,240 for Patty and $14,935 for Craig). They had interest income from a certificate of deposit of $435 and own some shares of common stock in the restaurant chain that paid $185 in dividends in 1987. Craig, Patty, and Lisa live in an apartment. Craig and Patty file a joint return and do not itemize deductions.

Craig and Patty are married and they have a dependent, so they cannot file Form 1040EZ. They can, however, file Form 1040A, shown in Tables 3.5a and 3.5b, since they do not itemize deductions. Craig and Patty have

Table 3.4 Sample Form 1040EZ

Department of the Treasury - Internal Revenue Service

Form 1040EZ

Income Tax Return for Single filers with no dependents (0) **1987**

OMB No. 1545-0675

Name & address

Use the IRS mailing label. If you don't have one, please print.

Please print your numbers like this:

0 1 2 3 4 5 6 7 8 9

▶ JAMES W. LINCH
Print your name above (first, initial, last)

3407 McKnight Rd.
Present home address (number and street). (If you have a P.O. box, see instructions.)

Pittsburgh, PA 15237
City, town, or post office, state, and ZIP code

Your social security number

329 44 1302

Please read the instructions for this form on the reverse side.

Presidential Election Campaign Fund
Do you want $1 to go to this fund?

Note: Checking "Yes" will not change your tax or reduce your refund.

Yes No
☒ ☐

	Dollars	Cents

Report your income

1 Total wages, salaries, and tips. This should be shown in Box 10 of your W-2 form(s). (Attach your W-2 form(s).) **1**

08,140.00

2 Taxable interest income of $400 or less. If the total is more than $400, you cannot use Form 1040EZ. **2**

350.00

Attach Copy B of Form(s) W-2 here

3 Add line 1 and line 2. This is your **adjusted gross income.** **3**

08,490.00

4 Can you be claimed as a dependent on another person's return?
☐ Yes. Do worksheet on back; enter amount from line E here.
☒ No. Enter 2,540 as your standard deduction. **4**

2,540.00

5 Subtract line 4 from line 3. **5**

05,950.00

6 If you checked the "Yes" box on line 4, enter 0.
If you checked the "No" box on line 4, enter 1,900.
This is your **personal exemption.** **6**

1,900.00

7 Subtract line 6 from line 5. If line 6 is larger than line 5, enter 0 on line 7. This is your **taxable income.** **7**

04,050.00

Figure your tax

8 Enter your Federal income tax withheld. This should be shown in Box 9 of your W-2 form(s). **8**

00,547.00

9 Use the **single** column in the tax table on pages 32–37 of the Form 1040A instruction booklet to find the **tax** on the amount shown on **line 7** above. Enter the amount of tax. **9**

00,532.00

Refund or amount you owe

10 If line 8 is larger than line 9, subtract line 9 from line 8. Enter the **amount of your refund.** **10**

0,015.00

Attach tax payment here

11 If line 9 is larger than line 8, subtract line 8 from line 9. Enter the **amount you owe.** Attach check or money order for the full amount, payable to "Internal Revenue Service." **11**

,.00

Sign your return

I have read this return. Under penalties of perjury, I declare that to the best of my knowledge and belief, the return is true, correct, and complete.

Your signature _James W. Linch_ Date _2/29/88_

For IRS Use Only—Please do not write in boxes below.

For Privacy Act and Paperwork Reduction Act Notice, see page 31.

Form **1040EZ** (1987)

Table 3.5a Sample Form 1040A (page 1)

Form **1040A**	Department of the Treasury—Internal Revenue Service **U.S. Individual Income Tax Return** 1987	

Step 1
Label

Use IRS label. Otherwise, please print or type.

Your first name and initial (if joint return, also give spouse's name and initial) Last name
CRAIG C. AND PATTY R. KOWALSKI

Your social security no. 914 57 6676

Present home address (number and street). (If you have a P.O. Box, see page 9 of the instructions.)
1229 Hilbrook Place

Spouse's social security no. 219 63 4522

City, town or post office, state, and ZIP code
Jackson TX 76102

OMB No. 1545-0085

For Privacy Act and Paperwork Reduction Act Notice, see page 31.

Presidential Election Campaign Fund

Do you want $1 to go to this fund?.................. ☐ Yes ☒ No
If joint return, does your spouse want $1 to go to this fund?. ☒ Yes ☐ No

Note: *Checking "Yes" will not change your tax or reduce your refund.*

Step 2
Check your filing status
(Check only one)

1 ☐ Single (See if you can use Form 1040EZ.)
2 ☒ Married filing joint return (even if only one had income)
3 ☐ Married filing separate return. Enter spouse's social security number above and spouse's full name here.
4 ☐ Head of household (with qualifying person). If the qualifying person is your child but not your dependent, enter this child's name here.

Step 3
Figure your exemptions
(See page 12 of instructions.)

If more than 7 dependents, attach statement.

Attach Copy B of Form(s) W-2 here.

Caution: If you can be claimed as a dependent on another person's tax return (such as your parents' return), do not check box 5a. But be sure to check the box on line 14b on page 2.

5a ☒ Yourself   5b ☒ Spouse

c Dependents: 1. Name (first, initial, and last name)	2. Check if under age 5	3. If age 5 or over, dependent's social security number	4. Relationship	5. No. of months lived in your home in 1987
Lisa J. Kowalski		— — : — — : — — — —	daughter	12

No. of boxes checked on 5a and 5b 2
No. of children on 5c who lived with you 1
No. of children on 5c who didn't live with you due to divorce or separation —
No. of parents listed on 5c —
No. of other dependents listed on 5c —

d If your child didn't live with you but is claimed as your dependent under a pre-1985 agreement, check here .... ▶ ☐

e Total number of exemptions claimed. (Also complete line 16.)

Add numbers entered on lines above 3

Step 4
Figure your total income

Attach check or money order here.

6 Wages, salaries, tips, etc. This should be shown in Box 10 of your W-2 form(s). (Attach Form(s) W-2.) 6 34175 00

7a **Taxable** interest income (see page 17). (If over $400, also complete and attach Schedule 1, Part II.) 7a 435 00

b **Tax-exempt** interest income (see page 17). (DO NOT include on line 7a.) 7b

8 Dividends. (If over $400, also complete and attach Schedule 1, Part III.) 8 185 00

9 Unemployment compensation (insurance) from Form(s) 1099-G. 9 0 00

10 Add lines 6, 7a, 8, and 9. Enter the total. This is your **total income.** ▶ 10 34795 00

Step 5
Figure your adjusted gross income

11a Your IRA deduction from applicable Worksheet. New rules for IRAs begin on page 18. 11a 0 00

b Spouse's IRA deduction from applicable Worksheet. New rules for IRAs begin on page 18. 11b 0 00

c Add lines 11a and 11b. Enter the total. These are your **total adjustments.** 11c 0 00

12 Subtract line 11c from line 10. Enter the result. This is your **adjusted gross income.** (If this line is less than $15,432 and a child lived with you, see "Earned Income Credit" (line 21b) on page 27 of instructions.) ▶ 12 34795 00

Form **1040A** (1987)

Table 3.5b Sample Form 1040A (page 2)

1987	**Form 1040A**	Page 2

Step 6

Figure your standard deduction,

13 Enter the amount from line 12. **13** 34795 00

0 00

14a Check if: ☐ You were 65 or over ☐ Blind **Enter number of boxes checked ▶ 14a** ☐
☐ Spouse was 65 or over ☐ Blind

b If you can be claimed as a dependent on another person's return (such as your parents' return), check here . . . . ▶14b ☐

c If you are married filing separately and your spouse files Form 1040 and itemizes deductions, check here . . . . ▶14c ☐

d Standard deduction. If you checked a box on line 14a, b, or c, see page 22 for amount to enter on line 14d. If no box is checked, enter amount shown below for your filing status.

Filing status from page 1 { Single or Head of household, enter $2,540
Married filing joint return, enter $3,760
Married filing separate return, enter $1,880 } **14d** 3760 00

Exemption amount, and

15 Subtract line 14d from line 13. Enter the result. **15** 31035 00

16 Multiply $1,900 by the total number of exemptions claimed on line 5e. Or, figure your exemption amount from the chart on page 24 of the instructions. **16** 5700 00

Taxable Income

17 Subtract line 16 from line 15. Enter the result. This is your **taxable income.** ▶ **17** 25335 00

If You Want IRS To Figure Your Tax, See Page 24 of the Instructions.

Step 7

Figure your tax, credits, and payments (including advance EIC payments)

Caution: If you are under age 14 and have more than $1,000 of investment income, see page 24 of the instructions and check here . . . . ▶ ☐

18 Find the tax on the amount on line 17. Check if from: ☒ Tax Table (pages 32–37); or ☐ Form 8615, Computation of Tax for Children Under Age 14 Who Have Investment Income of More Than $1,000. **18** 3679 00

19 Credit for child and dependent care expenses. Complete and attach Schedule 1, Part I. **19** 0 00

20 Subtract line 19 from line 18. Enter the result. (If line 19 is more than line 18, enter -0- on line 20.) This is your **total tax.** ▶ **20** 3679 00

21a Total Federal income tax withheld. This should be shown in Box 9 of your W-2 form(s). (If line 6 is more than $43,800, see page 26.) **21a** 3839 00

b Earned income credit, from the worksheet on page 28 of the instructions. Also see page 27. **21b** 0 00

22 Add lines 21a and 21b. Enter the total. These are your **total payments.** ▶ **22** 3839 00

Step 8

Figure your refund or amount you owe

23 If line 22 is larger than line 20, subtract line 20 from line 22. Enter the result. This is the **amount of your refund.** **23** 160 00

24 If line 20 is larger than line 22, subtract line 22 from line 20. Enter the result. This is the **amount you owe.** Attach check or money order for full amount payable to "Internal Revenue Service." Write your social security number, daytime phone number, and "1987 Form 1040A" on it. **24**

Step 9

Sign your return

Under penalties of perjury, I declare that I have examined this return and accompanying schedules and statements, and to the best of my knowledge and belief, they are true, correct, and complete. Declaration of preparer (other than the taxpayer) is based on all information of which the preparer has any knowledge.

Your signature   Date   Your occupation

X *Patty R. Kowalski*   3/07/88 *Manager*

Spouse's signature (if joint return, both must sign)   Date   Spouse's occupation

X *Craig G. Kowalski*   3/07/88 *Manager*

Paid preparer's use only

Preparer's signature   Date   Preparer's social security no.

X

Firm's name (or yours if self-employed)   Employer identification no.

Check if self-employed ☐

Address and ZIP code

a total income of $34,795. They do not make any individual retirement ac-
count (IRA) payments. Thus, their adjusted gross income is $34,795. They
claim a standard deduction of $3,760 and personal exemptions of $5,700,
giving them taxable income of $25,335. From the tax table in Table 3.3 (see
upper right corner), you can see that they have to pay taxes of $3,679. Since
they have paid $3,839 in taxes, they are entitled to a refund of $160.

Sample Form 1040

Bonita M. and Jerry O. Tinajaro work as managers for firms in Chicago.
Their combined wages were $64,900. They received $800 in interest income
and $600 in dividends from jointly owned stocks. Jerry is paying $300 per
month in alimony to his ex-wife. A total of $6,549 in federal income taxes
was withheld from Bonita's and Jerry's paychecks. They file Form 1040
because they itemize their deductions. Their deductible expenses are
numerous and are summarized on a tax schedule that will be explained
later. Their prepared tax return is explained here.

Table 3.6a shows the front of Form 1040. The Tinajaros are filing a married, joint return. They have two children, Christa and Antonio. Total exemptions are four. Interest income and dividends are declared on Schedule
B (Table 3.8). Income from all sources is listed and totals to $66,300 (line
22 of Form 1040). Adjustments to income equal $3,600. Adjusted gross in-
come is $62,700 (line 30).

The back of form 1040 is shown in Table 3.6b. Adjusted gross income
is shown on line 31. Before further computations can be made on Form
1040, Schedule A (Table 3.7) needs to be completed. Only medical and dental expenses in excess of 7.5 percent of adjusted gross income are deductible. The Tinajaros do not have medical and dental expenses in excess of
this amount, so they enter $0 for this itemized deduction category. Most
people do not have expenses at this level, so this deduction category is
usually not significant. Other deductions are self-explanatory. Total deductions are $19,875 (line 26).

The itemized deductions of $19,875 (from line 26, Schedule A) are
entered on line 33a (Form 1040). Taxable income before exemptions is
$62,700 − $19,875 = $42,825. A total of $7,600 in exemptions is subtracted
to give taxable income of $35,225 (line 36). The Tinajaros use the Tax Table
because their taxable income is less than $50,000. Taxes on $35,225 for "Married Filing Jointly" are $6,103. This tax amount is entered on line 37 of
Form 1040. Line 53 shows total taxes due of $6,103. Because the Tinajaros
had $6,549 withheld in taxes, they are due a refund of $446.

This section has shown how Forms 1040EZ, 1040A, and 1040 should
be filled out. For clarity, the examples have been simplified. In real life
most people probably encounter more complex versions of Linch's, the
Kowalskis', and the Tinajaros' tax returns.

Table 3.6a Sample Form 1040 (page 1)

Form **1040** Department of the Treasury—Internal Revenue Service
U.S. Individual Income Tax Return 1987

For the year Jan.–Dec. 31, 1987, or other tax year beginning _____, 1987, ending _____, 19___ | OMB No. 1545-0074

Label	Your first name and initial (if joint return, also give spouse's name and initial)	Last name	Your social security number
Use IRS label. Otherwise, please print or type.	JERRY R. AND BONITA M.	TINAJARO	332 29 1611

Present home address (number and street or rural route). (If you have a P.O. Box, see page 6 of Instructions.) — 3517 N. Sheridan Dr. — Spouse's social security number 327 97 5551

City, town or post office, state, and ZIP code — Chicago, IL 60640 — For Privacy Act and Paperwork Reduction Act Notice, see Instructions.

Presidential Election Campaign ▶ Do you want $1 to go to this fund? . . . . . [X] Yes [ ] No — Note: Checking "Yes" will not change your tax or reduce your refund.
If joint return, does your spouse want $1 to go to this fund? . [X] Yes [ ] No

Filing Status
Check only one box.

1 [ ] Single
2 [X] Married filing joint return (even if only one had income)
3 [ ] Married filing separate return. Enter spouse's social security no. above and full name here. _____
4 [ ] Head of household (with qualifying person). (See page 7 of Instructions.) If the qualifying person is your child but not your dependent, enter child's name here. _____
5 [ ] Qualifying widow(er) with dependent child (year spouse died ▶ 19___). (See page 7 of Instructions.)

Exemptions
(See Instructions on page 7.)

Caution: If you can be claimed as a dependent on another person's tax return (such as your parents' return), do not check box 6a. But be sure to check the box on line 32b on page 2.

6a [X] Yourself   6b [X] Spouse

| No. of boxes checked on 6a and 6b | 2 |

c Dependents

(1) Name (first, initial, and last name)	(2) Check if under age 5	(3) If age 5 or over, dependent's social security number	(4) Relationship	(5) No. of months lived in your home in 1987
Christa		379 00 2774	Daughter	12
Antonio	✓		Son	12

No. of children on 6c who lived with you ▶	2
No. of children on 6c who didn't live with you due to divorce or separation ▶	0
No. of parents listed on 6c ▶	0
No. of other dependents listed on 6c ▶	0

If more than 7 dependents, see Instructions on page 7.

d If your child didn't live with you but is claimed as your dependent under a pre-1985 agreement, check here . ▶ [ ]
e Total number of exemptions claimed (also complete line 35)

| Add numbers entered in boxes above ▶ | 4 |

Income
Please attach Copy B of your Forms W-2, W-2G, and W-2P here.
If you do not have a W-2, see page 6 of Instructions.

7	Wages, salaries, tips, etc. (attach Form(s) W-2)	7	64900 00
8	Taxable interest income (also attach Schedule B if over $400) . .	8	800 00
9	Tax-exempt interest income (see page 10). DON'T include on line 8	9	
10	Dividend income (also attach Schedule B if over $400)	10	600 00
11	Taxable refunds of state and local income taxes, if any, from worksheet on page 11 of Instructions. .	11	
12	Alimony received	12	
13	Business income or (loss) (attach Schedule C).	13	
14	Capital gain or (loss) (attach Schedule D)	14	
15	Other gains or (losses) (attach Form 4797)	15	
16a	Pensions, IRA distributions, annuities, and rollovers. Total received	16a	
b	Taxable amount (see page 11)	16b	
17	Rents, royalties, partnerships, estates, trusts, etc. (attach Schedule E)	17	
18	Farm income or (loss) (attach Schedule F)	18	
19	Unemployment compensation (insurance) (see page 11)	19	
20a	Social security benefits (see page 12)	20a	
b	Taxable amount, if any, from the worksheet on page 12	20b	
21	Other income (list type and amount—see page 12) _____	21	
22	Add the amounts shown in the far right column for lines 7, 8, and 10–21. This is your total income ▶	22	66300 00

Please attach check or money order here.

Adjustments to Income
(See Instructions on page 12.)

23	Reimbursed employee business expenses from Form 2106 .	23	
24a	Your IRA deduction, from applicable worksheet on page 13 or 14	24a	
b	Spouse's IRA deduction, from applicable worksheet on page 13 or 14 .	24b	
25	Self-employed health insurance deduction, from worksheet on page 14 .	25	
26	Keogh retirement plan and self-employed SEP deduction. .	26	
27	Penalty on early withdrawal of savings	27	
28	Alimony paid (recipient's last name Mishkin and social security no. 369 08 4961).	28	3600 00
29	Add lines 23 through 28. These are your total adjustments . . . . . ▶	29	3600 00

Adjusted Gross Income

| 30 | Subtract line 29 from line 22. This is your adjusted gross income. If this line is less than $15,432 and a child lived with you, see "Earned Income Credit" (line 56) on page 18 of the Instructions. If you want IRS to figure your tax, see page 15 of the Instructions . . . ▶ | 30 | 62700 00 |

Table 3.6b　Sample Form 1040 (page 2)

Form 1040 (1987)			Page **2**

Tax Compu-tation	**31**	Amount from line 30 (adjusted gross income)	**31** 62 700 00
	32a	Check if: ☐ **You** were 65 or over ☐ Blind; ☐ **Spouse** was 65 or over ☐ Blind. Add the number of boxes checked and enter the total here . . . . ▶	**32a**
	b	If you can be claimed as a dependent on another person's return, check here . . ▶ **32b** ☐	
	c	If you are married filing a separate return and your spouse itemizes deductions, or you are a dual-status alien, see page 15 and check here . . . . ▶ **32c** ☐	
	33a	**Itemized deductions.** See page 15 to see if you should itemize. If you don't itemize, enter zero. If you do itemize, attach Schedule A, enter the amount from Schedule A, line 26, **AND** skip line 33b .	**33a** 19875 00
Caution: ◀— If you checked any box on line 32a, b, or c and you don't itemize, see page 16 for the amount to enter on line 33b.	**b**	**Standard deduction.** Read **Caution** to left. If it applies, see page 16 for the amount to enter. If **Caution** doesn't apply and your filing status from page 1 is: { Single or Head of household, enter $2,540 / Married filing jointly or Qualifying widow(er), enter $3,760 / Married filing separately, enter $1,880 }	**33b**
	34	Subtract line 33a or 33b, whichever applies, from line 31. Enter the result here . . .	**34** 42825 00
	35	Multiply $1,900 by the total number of exemptions claimed on line 6e or see chart on page 16 .	**35** 7600 00
	36	**Taxable income.** Subtract line 35 from line 34. Enter the result (but not less than zero) . .	**36** 35225 00
		Caution: If under age 14 and you have more than $1,000 of investment income, check here ▶☐ and see page 16 to see if you have to use Form 8615 to figure your tax.	
	37	Enter tax. Check if from ☒ Tax Table, ☐ Tax Rate Schedules, ☐ Schedule D, or ☐ Form 8615	**37** 6103 00
	38	Additional taxes (see page 16). Check if from ☐ Form 4970 or ☐ Form 4972	**38** 0 00
	39	Add lines 37 and 38. Enter the total . . . . ▶	**39** 6103 00
Credits (See Instructions on page 17.)	**40**	Credit for child and dependent care expenses (attach Form 2441) **40**	
	41	Credit for the elderly or for the permanently and totally disabled (attach Schedule R) **41**	
	42	Add lines 40 and 41. Enter the total	**42** 0 00
	43	Subtract line 42 from line 39. Enter the result (but not less than zero)	**43** 6103 00
	44	Foreign tax credit (attach Form 1116) **44**	
	45	General business credit. Check if from ☐ Form 3800, ☐ Form 3468, ☐ Form 5884, ☐ Form 6478, ☐ Form 6765, or ☐ Form 8586 . . **45**	
	46	Add lines 44 and 45. Enter the total	**46** 0 00
	47	Subtract line 46 from line 43. Enter the result (but not less than zero) . . . . ▶	**47** 6103 00
Other Taxes (Including Advance EIC Payments)	**48**	Self-employment tax (attach Schedule SE)	**48**
	49	Alternative minimum tax (attach Form 6251)	**49**
	50	Tax from recapture of investment credit (attach Form 4255)	**50**
	51	Social security tax on tip income not reported to employer (attach Form 4137) . .	**51**
	52	Tax on an IRA or a qualified retirement plan (attach Form 5329)	**52**
	53	Add lines 47 through 52. This is your **total tax** . . . . ▶	**53** 6103 00
Payments Attach Forms W-2, W-2G, and W-2P to front.	**54**	Federal income tax withheld (including tax shown on Form(s) 1099) **54** 6,549 00	
	55	1987 estimated tax payments and amount applied from 1986 return **55**	
	56	Earned income credit (see page 18) **56**	
	57	Amount paid with Form 4868 (extension request) . . . **57**	
	58	Excess social security tax and RRTA tax withheld (see page 19) **58**	
	59	Credit for Federal tax on gasoline and special fuels (attach Form 4136) **59**	
	60	Regulated investment company credit (attach Form 2439) . . . **60**	
	61	Add lines 54 through 60. These are your **total payments** . . . . ▶	**61** 6549 00
Refund or Amount You Owe	**62**	If line 61 is larger than line 53, enter amount **OVERPAID** . . . . ▶	**62** 446 00
	63	Amount of line 62 to be **REFUNDED TO YOU** . . . . ▶	**63** 446 00
	64	Amount of line 62 to be applied to your 1988 estimated tax . . ▶ **64**	
	65	If line 53 is larger than line 61, enter **AMOUNT YOU OWE.** Attach check or money order for full amount payable to "Internal Revenue Service." Write your social security number, daytime phone number, and "1987 Form 1040" on it . . . . Check ▶ ☐ if Form 2210 (2210F) is attached. See page 20. **Penalty: $**	**65**

Please Sign Here	Under penalties of perjury, I declare that I have examined this return and accompanying schedules and statements, and to the best of my knowledge and belief, they are true, correct, and complete. Declaration of preparer (other than taxpayer) is based on all information of which preparer has any knowledge.		
	Your signature ▶ _Jerry R. Tinajaro_	Date 3/17/88	Your occupation _Manager_
	Spouse's signature (if joint return, BOTH must sign) ▶ _Bonita M. Tinajaro_	Date 3/17/88	Spouse's occupation _Manager_
Paid Preparer's Use Only	Preparer's signature ▶	Date	Check if self-employed ☐ Preparer's social security no.
	Firm's name (or yours if self-employed) and address ▶		E.I. No. ZIP code

Table 3.7 Sample Schedule A — Itemized Deductions

SCHEDULES A&B (Form 1040) Department of the Treasury Internal Revenue Service	**Schedule A—Itemized Deductions** (Schedule B is on back) ▶ Attach to Form 1040. ▶ See Instructions for Schedules A and B (Form 1040).	OMB No. 1545-0074 **1987** Attachment Sequence No 07

Name(s) as shown on Form 1040   JERRY R. AND BONITA M. TINAJARO   Your social security number 332 29 1611

Medical and Dental Expenses (Do not include expenses reimbursed or paid by others.) (See Instructions on page 21.)	**1a** Prescription medicines and drugs, insulin, doctors, dentists, nurses, hospitals, insurance premiums you paid for medical and dental care, etc.	1a		
	b Transportation and lodging	1b		
	c Other (list—include hearing aids, dentures, eyeglasses, etc.) ▶............................	1c		
	2 Add lines 1a through 1c, and enter the total here	2		
	3 Multiply the amount on Form 1040, line 31, by 7.5% (.075) . .	3		
	4 Subtract line 3 from line 2. If zero or less, enter -0-. **Total medical and dental** . . ▶	4		0 00
Taxes You Paid (See Instructions on page 22.)	**Note:** Sales taxes are no longer deductible.			
	5 State and local income taxes	5	1850 00	
	6 Real estate taxes	6	3700 00	
	7 Other taxes (list—include personal property taxes) ▶........	7		
	8 Add the amounts on lines 5 through 7. Enter the total here. **Total taxes** . . ▶	8		5550 00
Interest You Paid (See Instructions on page 22.)	**Note:** If you borrowed any new amounts against your home after 8/16/86 and at any time in 1987 the total of all your mortgage debts was more than what you paid for your home plus improvements, attach Form 8598 and check here . . ▶ ☐			
	9a Deductible home mortgage interest you paid to financial institutions (report deductible points on line 10)	9a	11700 00	
	b Deductible home mortgage interest you paid to individuals (show that person's name and address) ▶..................	9b	0 00	
	10 Deductible points	10		
	11 Deductible investment interest	11	800 00	
	12a Personal interest you paid (see page 22) . .	12a	500	
	b Multiply the amount on line 12a by 65% (.65). Enter the result .	12b	325 00	
	13 Add the amounts on lines 9a through 11, and 12b. Enter the total here. **Total interest** ▶	13		12825 00
Contributions You Made (See Instructions on page 23.)	**14a** Cash contributions. (If you gave $3,000 or more to any one organization, report those contributions on line 14b.)	14a	1500 00	
	b Cash contributions totaling $3,000 or more to any one organization. (Show to whom you gave and how much you gave.) ▶....................	14b		
	15 Other than cash. (You must attach Form 8283 if over $500.). .	15		
	16 Carryover from prior year	16		
	17 Add the amounts on lines 14a through 16. Enter the total here. **Total contributions** ▶	17		1500 00
Casualty and Theft Losses	**18** Casualty or theft loss(es) (attach Form 4684). (See page 23 of the Instructions.) . . . . ▶	18		0 00
Moving Expenses	**19** Moving expenses (attach Form 3903 or 3903F). (See page 24 of the Instructions.) . . . . ▶	19		0 00
Miscellaneous Deductions Subject to 2% AGI Limit (See Instructions on page 24.)	**20** Unreimbursed employee business expenses (attach Form 2106)	20	0 00	
	21 Other expenses (list type and amount) ▶.....................	21	0 00	
	22 Add the amounts on lines 20 and 21. Enter the total.	22	0 00	
	23 Multiply the amount on Form 1040, line 31, by 2% (.02). Enter the result here	23	0 00	
	24 Subtract line 23 from line 22. Enter the result (but not less than zero) . . . . ▶	24		0 00
Other Miscellaneous Deductions	**25** Miscellaneous deductions not subject to 2% AGI limit (see page 24). (List type and amount.) ▶..................................... ▶	25		0 00
Total Itemized Deductions	**26** Add the amounts on lines 4, 8, 13, 17, 18, 19, 24, and 25. Enter the total here and on Form 1040, line 33a. . . . . ▶	26		19875 00

For Paperwork Reduction Act Notice, see Form 1040 Instructions.   Schedule A (Form 1040) 1987

Table 3.8   Sample Schedule B — Interest and Dividend Income

Schedules A&B (Form 1040) 1987

Name(s) as shown on Form 1040. (Do not enter name and social security number if shown on other side.)

OMB No. 1545-0074   Page **2**

Your social security number

Schedule B—Interest and Dividend Income

Attachment
Sequence No. **08**

**Part I
Interest
Income**

(See
Instructions on
pages 9 and 24.)

Also complete
Part III.

Note: If you
received a Form
1099–INT or
Form 1099–OID
from a
brokerage firm,
enter the firm's
name and the
total interest
shown on that
form.

If you received more than $400 in taxable interest income, you must complete Part I and list ALL interest received. If you received, as a nominee, interest that actually belongs to another person, or you received or paid accrued interest on securities transferred between interest payment dates, see page 24.

Interest Income		Amount
1 Interest income from seller-financed mortgages. (See Instructions and list name of payer.) ▶	1	0 00
2 Other interest income (list name of payer) ▶ *Federal Savings & Loan*		800 00
	2	
3 Add the amounts on lines 1 and 2. Enter the total here and on Form 1040, line 8. ▶	3	800 00

**Part II
Dividend
Income**

(See
Instructions on
pages 10 and
25.)

Also complete
Part III.

Note: If you
received a Form
1099-DIV from a
brokerage firm,
enter the firm's
name and the
total dividends
shown on that
form.

If you received more than $400 in gross dividends and/or other distributions on stock, complete Part II. If you received, as a nominee, dividends that actually belong to another person, see page 25.

Dividend Income		Amount
4 Dividend income (list name of payer—include on this line capital gain distributions, nontaxable distributions, etc.) ▶ *Braintech, Inc.*		600 00
	4	
5 Add the amounts on line 4. Enter the total here	5	600 00
6 Capital gain distributions. Enter here and on line 13, Schedule D.*	6	0 00
7 Nontaxable distributions. (See Schedule D Instructions for adjustment to basis.)	7	0 00
8 Add the amounts on lines 6 and 7. Enter the total here	8	0 00
9 Subtract line 8 from line 5. Enter the result here and on Form 1040, line 10 . . . ▶	9	600 00

*If you received capital gain distributions but do not need Schedule D to report any other gains or losses or to figure your tax (see the Tax Tip under Capital gain distributions on page 10), enter your capital gain distributions on Form 1040, line 14. Write "CGD" on the dotted line to the left of line 14.

**Part III
Foreign
Accounts
and
Foreign
Trusts**

(See
Instructions
on page 25.)

If you received more than $400 of interest or dividends, OR if you had a foreign account or were a grantor of, or a transferor to, a foreign trust, you must answer both questions in Part III.

	Yes	No
10 At any time during the tax year, did you have an interest in or a signature or other authority over a financial account in a foreign country (such as a bank account, securities account, or other financial account)? (See page 25 of the Instructions for exceptions and filing requirements for Form TD F 90-22.1.)		X
If "Yes," enter the name of the foreign country ▶		
11 Were you the grantor of, or transferor to, a foreign trust which existed during the current tax year, whether or not you have any beneficial interest in it? If "Yes," you may have to file Forms 3520, 3520-A, or 926 . .		X

For Paperwork Reduction Act Notice, see Form 1040 Instructions.   **Schedule B (Form 1040) 1987**

Spot Quiz • Sample Tax Returns

1. If Jim Linch's earnings had been $40 lower, his take-home income would have decreased by $32.   T _____   F _____

2. The Tinajaros would have been able to deduct some medical expenses if the expenses had been at least $3,000.   T _____   F _____

(Answers on page 98)

SPECIAL TOPICS IN TAXES

What is the tax treatment for gains or losses from sales of property? Does the owner of a business have deductions that are advantageous from a tax viewpoint? Where can you find assistance in filling out a tax return? What do you do if the IRS audits your return? These special questions will be answered in this section.

Capital Gains Taxes

Gains and losses can result from sales of certain types of properties called capital assets, which are assets that are owned for either personal use or investment. Examples of capital assets are cars, houses, real estate, stocks, bonds, coins, antiques, fur, and jewelry. Assets that are owned for the operation of a business are not considered capital assets.

A **capital gain** occurs when a capital asset is sold or exchanged for more than its cost of purchase. Both cost and selling price are adjusted for any fees or commissions paid for the transactions. A **capital loss** occurs when the cost is higher than the sales price. Prior to the Tax Reform Act of 1986, capital gains and losses were classified as either long-term or short-term, depending on whether the assets had been owned for more than one year. However, such is not the case now.

All gains and losses from sales of capital assets are treated as ordinary income or losses. All capital losses are offset against capital gains, and only the net capital gains are reported as ordinary income. If capital losses are greater than capital gains, then up to $3,000 of net capital losses can be offset against other ordinary income. If net capital losses are greater than $3,000, then the balance over $3,000 can be carried forward to offset future income.

Taxpayer A has $10,000 in capital gains and $3,000 in capital losses. A's net capital gain is $10,000 − $3,000 = $7,000, which is reported as ordinary income. Taxpayer B has $5,000 in capital gains and $6,000 in capital losses. B has a net capital loss of $1,000 that can be deducted from ordinary income. Taxpayer C has $1,000 in capital gains and $8,000 in capital losses in 1988, for a net capital loss of $7,000. Only $3,000 of this $7,000 net loss can be deducted from ordinary income in 1988. The remaining $4,000 net loss is carried forward to 1989. If C has capital gains in 1989, this $4,000 is offset against these gains. If C has no capital gains in 1989, then $3,000 of this $4,000 loss is offset against ordinary income in 1989, and the remaining $1,000 is carried forward to 1990.

Tax Treatment on Selling a Home

Tax laws allow people to defer paying taxes on capital gains incurred on the sale of a home under certain circumstances. If the taxpayer buys or starts construction on a new home within two years of selling the existing home, no capital gains taxes are paid unless the purchase price of the new house is less than the selling price for the previous home. The following examples illustrate the tax treatment (assume that the existing home was purchased for $60,000):

Situation	Selling Price Old Home	Purchase Price Old Home	Purchase Price New Home	Gains	Capital Gains Tax On
A	$80,000	$60,000	$90,000	$20,000	$ 0
B	$80,000	$60,000	$80,000	$20,000	$ 0
C	$80,000	$60,000	$72,000	$20,000	$ 8,000
D	$80,000	$60,000	$ 0	$20,000	$20,000

In all situations, the existing home is purchased for $60,000 and sold for $80,000, resulting in a capital gain of $80,000 − $60,000 = $20,000. In situations A and B, the purchase price of the new home is not less than the selling price of the existing home, and capital gains are not subject to taxes. In situation D, no new home is purchased, and the full amount of the gain is subject to taxes.

For tax purposes, the cost of the new home is adjusted by the amount of the gain on which no taxes are paid. Thus, for example, in situation A, the purchase price of the new home is considered to be $90,000 − $20,000 = $70,000. This tax treatment allows homeowners to defer taxes on homes indefinitely. Homeowners who are over age 55 are allowed a one-time-only exclusion of $125,000 of gains from taxes.

Reducing Taxes

A variety of methods can be used to reduce taxes. Two common methods—
bunching deductions and depreciation—are discussed here.

Bunching Deductions. The timing of some tax deductions is
unavoidable. However, some deductions can be planned. For example,
extensive dental work can be scheduled with taxes in mind. Small medical
expenses two years in a row may not produce any deductions at all, but
tax deductions might be realized if all medical deductions are bunched in
one year. Similarly, if itemized deductions are near the standard deduction amount, then by bunching deductions, you can itemize one year, take
the standard deduction the next year, and reduce taxes.

Depreciation as a Tax Shield. Depreciation refers to expensing the
wear and tear of long-lived assets used in business. For example, a salesperson uses a car to conduct his or her business. The car's cost can be ex-
pensed over five years. Say that the car was bought for $10,000 and is used
exclusively for business. A total of $2,000 can be expensed each year for
five years as a business expense. This expensing, or depreciation, is a noncash expense that reduces taxable income. An example of a single person
depreciating $2,000 is provided in Table 3.9. Taxes are from Tax Rate
Schedule for Singles, shown in Table 3.1.

Table 3.9 Depreciation as a Tax Shield*

	Without Depreciation	With Depreciation
Taxable income before expenses	$25,000	$25,000
Minus depreciation	0	2,000
Taxable income after expenses	$25,000	$23,000
Taxes	4,680	4,120
Take-home income	$20,320	$18,880
Add in depreciation	0	2,000
Cash in hand	$20,320	$20,880

* Taxes are calculated from the Tax Rate Schedule for the single taxpayer, shown in Table 3.1.

Table 3.9 shows taxable income of $25,000. After taxes of $4,680, the taxpayer is left with income of $20,320. Assuming that all transactions are for cash, the taxpayer has $20,320 in cash. With depreciation, taxable income is $23,000, and income after taxes is $18,880. However, depreciation is a noncash expense and does not have to be paid. Thus, the taxpayer's cash position is $20,880. Alternatively, the taxpayer paid out $4,120 in taxes from $25,000, leaving him or her with $25,000 − $4,120 = $20,880. Additional cash in hand, using depreciation, is equal to $20,880 − $20,320 = $560. Note that this amount is equal to the depreciation amount times the tax rate: $2,000 × .28 = $560.

Two common methods for reducing taxes were discussed in this section. More complex methods, called **tax shelters**, were available before the Tax Reform Act of 1986. However, under the current law, tax shelters are being phased out and after 1990 will no longer be available as devices for sheltering income from taxes.

Tax Assistance

Tax laws and tax forms tend to be complex. Fortunately, many people have simple income sources, and their deductions are not complex. These people generally prepare and file their own income tax returns. Others seek tax assistance from either the IRS or private sources.

Assistance From the IRS. The IRS offers many publications to the taxpayer free of cost. One handy booklet is IRS Publication No. 17, *Your Federal Income Tax*. This booklet provides detailed information and examples for use in preparing tax returns.

The IRS will also compute a person's taxes if the person is eligible to file Form 1040A. The returns have to be filed no later than April 15 if the IRS is to compute taxes.

The IRS also provides tax assistance by telephone and in person at their local offices. Advice from the IRS is not completely error-free. Like any advisory service, the IRS can provide incorrect information. Advice from the IRS is merely that—advice. It is not binding and not a ruling. Also keep in mind that the role of the IRS is to collect taxes. Its advice will not be designed to give the taxpayer a break.

Private Assistance. Some taxpayers choose to seek help in filling out their tax forms from tax preparation services. If income and expenses are fairly simple, then assistance can be sought from a preparation service such as H & R Block. Local offices of national tax preparation services can generally provide adequate assistance in the preparation of simple returns. However, they may not be equipped to handle complex tax returns.

People with complex situations should seek assistance from a certified public accountant (CPA) or a tax attorney. CPA and attorney fees may seem

"Remember that $3 you sent for income tax advice? Here it is. It says, 'Pay it!' "

Source: *Changing Times,* February 1979. p. 8.

expensive, but these professionals provide valuable assistance. You can ask friends, acquaintances, and colleagues for references to a good CPA or tax attorney.

The IRS administers a nine-hour examination in tax accounting. An accountant who passes this examination is allowed to represent clients before the IRS. The examination is rigorous, and passing it implies a competent understanding of tax laws. The local IRS office should be able to help identify people who have passed this examination.

People who prepare tax returns for a fee are required by law to sign the tax returns. They are expected to be diligent in preparing returns for their clients. Despite their diligence, errors do creep into returns. The taxpayer should go over the return carefully before signing it and mailing it to the IRS.

IRS Tax Audit

Every year the IRS selects a certain number of tax returns to audit, meaning that it examines the returns closely. Tax returns are generally selected

for audit for three reasons. The IRS uses a computer program called Discriminant Function System (DIF), which selects tax returns on the basis of the probability that an error has occurred. The higher the probability of an error is, the higher are the chances of being audited. Second, under the Taxpayer Compliance Measurement Program (TCMP), some returns are randomly selected by the IRS to examine for accuracy. Third, some returns are selected for audit because information listed on the tax return does not match information provided on a matching document. For example, the interest income reported on the return may not match the amount of interest paid reported by a financial institution.

Generally, the audit or examination takes place at the local IRS office, but in some cases it may take place at the taxpayer's home or place of business. The IRS sends the taxpayer a notice of the audit and asks for additional documentation. Upon presentation of the documentation, the IRS agent will explain any proposed changes in the taxpayer's tax liability. If the taxpayer agrees to the changes, she or he signs a form to that effect. Any taxes due can be paid at the time the agreement is signed.

If the taxpayer does not agree with the auditor's findings, he or she can appeal the findings to the Appeals Office of the IRS. Appeals beyond this point may go to the U.S. Tax Court, Claims Court, or the U.S. District Court. Disputes of under $5,000 can be handled under the *Small Tax Case* procedures. It is usually desirable to have a qualified person represent the taxpayer before the Appeals Office or the courts.

Spot Quiz • Special Topics in Taxes

1. All net capital losses can be offset against ordinary income in the same year.   T _____   F _____

2. Capital gains taxes on sales of homes can be deferred by following certain procedures.   T _____   F _____

3. Deductions should be bunched even if they do not exceed the standard deduction.   T _____   F _____

4. Depreciation charges involve paying out cash.   T _____   F _____

(Answers on page 98)

Summary

Taxes provide financing for the government and allow the population as a whole to put into effect various social welfare and economic programs. No one is completely satisfied with the tax structure, yet most people are required to pay taxes. Federal tax laws are complex. However, understanding how the system works helps in financial planning. Managing taxes calls for paying one's fair share of taxes.

U.S. tax rates are progressive, that is, people with higher incomes generally pay proportionally more in taxes. The Internal Revenue Service (IRS) is the federal agency that collects taxes and enforces tax laws. Tax records can be kept on either a cash or an accrual basis.

A certain amount of income, called the standard deduction, is exempt from taxes. The standard deduction, the number of tax exemptions, filing status, and gross income combine to establish whether a person has to file a tax return. Taxable income is based on gross income, which includes all types of income except those excluded by law. Certain expenses are deducted from gross income to derive adjusted gross income. Either the standard deduction or itemized deductions are subtracted from adjusted gross income to arrive at taxable income. Based on taxable income, either the Tax Tables or the Tax Rate Schedules are used to determine taxes payable.

Capital gains and losses result from the sale of capital property and are treated as ordinary income or losses. Capital gains on the sale of a home can be deferred if another home whose cost is more than the selling price of the existing home is bought within two years.

Taxes can be reduced by bunching deductions and using depreciation. Tax assistance on filing returns can be obtained from the IRS or from private sources. Every year the IRS selects some returns for further examination. Maintaining good records helps in answering the questions that the IRS might have.

Questions

1. Do you personally believe that taxes are fair? Explain your answer.

2. Why is it important for the government to collect taxes?

3. Why are tax laws complex?

4. Why is it important to understand how the tax laws work?

5. Explain what is meant by paying one's fair share of taxes.

6. Why are federal income taxes considered to be progressive?

7. Explain what is meant by the marginal tax rate.

8. Briefly explain how the IRS operates.

9. What is the difference, if any, between the cash and accrual methods of record keeping?

10. Explain why a person who does not have to file a return would file one.

11. Describe the five tax filing categories.

12. List some items that are included in gross income.

13. List some items that are excluded from gross income.

14. What types of expenses can be deducted from gross income to determine adjusted gross income?

15. List the seven categories of expenses that can be itemized.

16. What special tax treatment is available to a person over age 55 who sells an existing home?

17. How can bunching deductions reduce taxes?

18. Explain why depreciation reduces taxes.

19. What type of tax assistance does the IRS provide?

20. Why might a taxpayer's return be audited?

Case Problems

1. Liz Capps is single with gross income of $32,000. She claims the standard deduction. Calculate the amount she would have to pay in taxes. What percent of her gross income is paid in taxes? Assume that she has to use the Tax Rate Schedules.

2. Dan Renaro's taxable income increases from $16,000 to $19,000. Use Table 3.1 to calculate the incremental tax rate applicable to the additional $3,000 in his taxable income. Dan is single and qualifies for one exemption.

3. Paula Angeles earned $8,360 from her part-time job as a security guard. She is single and qualified for one exemption. A total of $882 in taxes was withheld from her paychecks. Use the format of Form 1040EZ and Table 3.3 to calculate the amount of taxes to be refunded to her or the balance due her.

4. The Kaufmans received $79,600 in total income. Adjustments to gross income totaled $5,300. Deductible itemized expenses from their Schedule A amounted to $9,715. They have three children and can claim five exemptions. The Kaufmans will be filing a joint return.
   a. Use the format of Form 1040 to calculate their taxable income (line 37, Form 1040).
   b. Calculate their income tax.

Bibliography

"Answers to Your Questions on the New Tax Law." *Money* (December 1986): 105–106.

"And in the Far Corner . . . The IRS!" *Money* (March 1985): 80–86.

"Tax Audits: Improving Your Odds." *Consumer Reports* (March 1986): 155–158.

"Some Disappointing Facts About the New Tax Law." *Money* (November 1986): 195–200.

Answers to Spot Quizzes

The Basics of Taxes (page 70)

1. F (Tax laws are complex because of the diverse nature of income.)

2. T (Minimizing taxes legitimately identifies the fair share tax amount.)

3. F (The dollar amount of taxes paid increases faster than gross income.)

4. T (Both amounts are in the same tax bracket, and the applicable rate is 28 percent.)

Determining Taxes Payable (page 79)

1. F (A return needs to be filed only if income exceeds $4,950.)

2. F (The family would need to subtract the personal exemption times the number of exemptions claimed, and the standard deduction.)

3. T (The standard deduction for head of household is $4,400.)

4. T (Taxable income is between $4,800 and $4,850 [from Table 3.3].)

Sample Tax Returns (page 89)

1. F (His taxes would have remained the same, and his take-home income would have decreased by $40.)

2. F ($3,000 is less than 7.5 percent of their adjusted gross income.)

Special Topics in Taxes (page 94)

1. F (Only $3,000 in net capital losses can be offset against ordinary income in any given year.)

2. T (They can be deferred indefinitely.)

3. F (Deductions should be bunched only if they exceed the standard deduction.)

4. F (Depreciation charges are noncash expenses.)

Chapter 4

Consumerism: Getting More for Less

Objectives

After reading this chapter, you will be able to:

- Recognize consumer frauds.
- Evaluate warranties and service contracts.
- Explain consumer protection legislation.
- Describe and use complaint procedures.

Jordan Goodman is a part-time volunteer worker for the Better Business Bureau of Metropolitan New York. His job is to answer the bureau's complaint telephone lines. Answering the phone lines makes him think that there is perhaps some truth to the statement that there is a sucker born every minute. He tells of callers being promised high-paying jobs for a fee of $3,000, paid in advance. He tells about the elderly woman who paid a $250 fee to a Manhattan marriage broker. The first man referred to her wanted her to take out a large loan so both of them could go on a luxurious vacation. The second person referred to her tried to sell her swampland in Florida.[1]

The situations that Mr. Goodman talks about are not uncommon. There seems to be an almost unending stream of unethical and deceptive practices for consumers to encounter. No amount of legislation can completely eliminate these unethical and deceptive practices. The sure way to combat them is for consumers to be alert to the possibility of being exposed to unfair practices. Without a victim, it becomes difficult to commit a crime. The purpose of this chapter is to show you how to recognize unfair practices and how to get more out of life for less money.

CONSUMER FRAUDS

The motto *caveat emptor,* or "let the buyer beware," has applied ever since the beginning of trade between human beings. In general, when one person tries to sell something to someone else, it is for the purpose of economic gain. The seller, in pursuit of his or her own benefits, does not necessarily look out for the economic interests of the buyer. Therefore, the motto *caveat emptor* takes on great significance. If the buyer does not look after his or her own interests, no one else will either.

Increasing government regulation of business practices may lead a buyer to feel relatively confident when engaging in a business transaction. But the buyer needs to keep in mind that the existence of laws is different from assuming that all sellers operate within the laws. *Caveat emptor* is just as important today as it was two hundred or even two thousand years ago. Knowing about the types of frauds that sellers can commit, knowing about the laws that are designed to provide protection for the consumer, and knowing how to seek corrective action if fraud takes place are the best protection for the consumer. Various types of consumer frauds are covered in this chapter. Keep in mind that the word *fraud* is used here in a very general sense. The term *consumer fraud* implies a deception. It does not necessarily mean a criminal act by the seller or manufacturer.

---

1. "Confessions of a Better Business Bureau Complaint Taker," *Money* (September 1981): 136.

Deceptive Advertising

The main purpose of advertising is to sell the product being advertised. The advertiser really has no interest in emphasizing the product's undesirable points. Therefore, only the desirable aspects of a product are advertised. For example, the manufacturers of some cereals will tell television viewers how good the cereals taste, but they will not mention that some of their cereals are 50 percent sugar. A meat processor will not advertise the fact that its ground beef may be 30 percent fat by weight. Some people may argue that what is *not* said about a product may be considered deceptive advertising.

Sometimes advertising can be considered deceptive because of the way in which a statement is made. When an advertisement says that a product contains the pain reliever most prescribed by doctors, it is really talking about aspirin. So why not simply say, "This product contains aspirin"? Some television advertisements, particularly those for detergents and other household products, show a "hidden camera" interview. The announcer emphasizes that the camera is hidden. Does this mean that the actor shown in the advertisements was unaware that a commercial was being filmed? Does it mean that the actor's comments about the product were spontaneous and unrehearsed? Or does it mean that the actor was aware of the commercial, was coached on the correct response to be given, and was aware that the camera was hidden? By referring to a "hidden camera," the advertisement is trying to create an illusion of spontaneity when such may not be the case. Some people argue that these commercials, while technically truthful, are deceptive because they create an impression that is not correct.

Space limitations prevent the citation of many other forms of deceptive advertising. The best safeguard for a consumer is to critically challenge the assertions made in advertisements. Does a mouthwash really overpower the odor of onions on a person's breath? Will a toothpaste make a person look sexy? Who are the nine out of ten doctors recommending something? Does the celebrity really drive daily the small car he or she is promoting? Careful answers to critical questions raised when viewing advertisements can go a long way toward avoidance of victimization by deception. See "If It Sounds Too Good to Be True, It Isn't True," on page 102, for further examples of deceptive advertising.

Bait and Switch

Despite being illegal, the business practice of bait and switch is alive and well in the United States. Even a major United States retailer was accused by the government of using bait and switch tactics. In **bait and switch**, the retailer advertises an item at a very low price. Generally, the items are

If It Sounds Too Good to Be True, It Isn't True

An Allentown, Pennsylvania, couple seeking to supplement their income saw an advertisement for an earthworm-farming franchise. The couple went to an informational seminar. Based on what they heard—that earthworms were highly profitable—the couple spent over $10,000 acquiring a franchise. Only later did they discover that the earthworm farming business had little, if any, potential.

An advertiser ran ads for very inexpensive digital watches. Ad readers sent in over $1.7 million to buy these watches. The advertiser did not fill a single order for the watches. Fortunately, the advertiser was caught, and about half of the money that had been collected in response to the ad was recovered.

Enticing newspaper advertisements and telephone calls hold out promises of making you rich in a hurry. Many consumers, convinced that they have found the road to riches, discover too late that they have been victimized by scams. By the time the law enforcement agencies start investigating, the crooks and the consumers' money have disappeared. Just remember: If it sounds too good to be true, it isn't true.

durable goods and large-ticket items, such as washers, dryers, air conditioners, and sewing machines. The advertised item is the "bait"—the low price is meant to attract buyers into the store. Once the consumer enters the store, she or he may be told that the advertised item has sold out but that a better-quality item is available at a comparable discount. The alternate item being offered is the "switch." Consumers at times believe that the alternate is a good bargain and buy it, but comparative shopping may reveal that the same product is available at lower prices elsewhere. In this situation, the consumer is baited and switched to a higher-priced product.

A variation on bait and switch is to display the bait in poor lighting. The bait may not look great in the first place. The salesperson then usually points out the disadvantages of the bait and tries to switch the shopper to a higher priced item.

The best protection for consumers is to know in advance what they want to buy and how much they are willing to spend. If the bait, as shown, is acceptable, then it should be purchased regardless of the opinion of the salesperson. If, on the other hand, the bait is really an inferior product, then the consumer should shop elsewhere for a product that meets financial and performance requirements. In no case should the switch be purchased. The alert consumer should report incidences of bait and switch practices to the appropriate authorities.

Labeling and Size of Package

The label on a package should adequately describe the product inside the package. Sometimes the product inside the package barely resembles the picture on the package. If a label says "all necessary installation hardware included," then the package must have sufficient quantities of nuts, bolts, and other hardware needed to complete installation. Did the package say "no tools required for assembly," yet assembly required a screwdriver? If the labeling appears to be deceptive, then the consumer has every right to demand that the retailer replace the merchandise or refund the money.

Often, package sizes appear to serve the sole purpose of trying to confuse the consumer. Why else would there be a $7\frac{5}{8}$-ounce tube of toothpaste? Odd sizes can keep the consumer from comparing the cost per unit of the same product manufactured by different producers. Fortunately, many stores now reveal the price per unit of particular items. Thus, the consumer can directly compare $5\frac{3}{8}$ ounces of toothpaste for $.95 with $7\frac{5}{8}$ ounces selling for $1.49 because for both toothpaste tubes the price will be stated in cents per ounce. In general, consumers are better off shopping at retailers that display **unit pricing**—that is, at retailers that provide information on price per unit for products they sell. In some cases, the physical size of the package is not in keeping with the quantity or size of the product inside. A 24-by-14-by-2-inch package may contain a game board, dice, and some wafer-thin plastic discs, all of which could fit in a ½-inch-deep box. The consumer may well question the need for a box 2 inches deep. Cereal manufacturers argue that cereals settle during shipment, and therefore cereal boxes usually have a note stating that contents are sold by weight, not volume. But what about products that do not "settle" during shipment and are packaged in larger-than-necessary containers? The consumer needs to ask whether the manufacturer's intention is to deceive the buyer.

Inferior Products

American consumers are apt to find a lot of inferior products in the marketplace. Such products can range in price from a few cents to thousands of dollars. Some products are designed to be inferior. Their producers figure they can make fast bucks before consumers become thoroughly disgusted with the product. Some manufacturers try to produce quality products, but in their efforts to lower costs, they use cheaper materials and end up producing inferior products. Other manufacturers produce a quality product that becomes inferior because of inadequate quality control.

An inferior product, irrespective of its price, is not going to provide the consumer with any great amount of satisfaction. Unfortunately, no law can prevent a manufacturer from deliberately selling inferior products to consumers. The best way to avoid inferior products is to carefully examine

the product and try to determine if it can be reasonably expected to do what it is supposed to do. Consumers may discover that it is more desirable to buy a more expensive, quality product than a cheap, inferior item.

Lack of Warranties

Warranties are guarantees issued by a product's manufacturer. A warranty, to a considerable extent, is the consumer's assurance that the product will work as it is supposed to. Some manufacturers choose not to warrant their products. The lack of a warranty in itself is not a deceptive trade practice. However, a consumer should ask this question: If the manufacturer has confidence in its product, then why is the product not warranted? There may be a perfectly good reason. But unless the reason is forthcoming or obvious, it is safe to assume that the seller or manufacturer may not have much confidence in the product. Think about buying a used car from a used car dealer that is sold in ''as is'' condition.

The mere presence of a warranty, however, does not guarantee that a product will perform satisfactorily. The warranty is discussed in more detail later.

Source: Reprinted from *The Saturday Evening Post* © 1978 The Curtis Publishing Company.

Pricing

Pricing deceptions are of two types. A seller cannot sell a product at a "reduced" price if the price, in fact, has not been reduced. Say that an appliance is normally sold for $30. The seller cannot raise the price to $40 and then announce a "25 percent price reduction" to $30.

A second type of price deception is not legally a deception, but its intent clearly is to deceive the consumer. We are talking about the popular practice of pricing products at X dollars and 99 or 95 cents. A product selling for $9.95 could just as easily be sold for $10.00. The idea behind pricing the product at $9.95 is to create the illusion that the product is selling for "nine dollars plus some odd cents." This pricing mechanism does not simplify the consumer's task of getting the most for his or her money. The best way to cope is to round up the price to the nearest dollar. Thus, something selling for $9.95 should be thought of as selling for $10.00. Some consumers find it interesting to note that while a $9.95 product is acceptable to them, they might not buy the same product at $10.00.

Free or Easy Credit

In these days of high interest rates, free credit might look like a gift horse— and who would ever even think of looking a gift horse in the mouth? In this case, though, not only should you look into the mouth of the gift horse but you should check its teeth with pliers as well. There is no such thing as "free" credit. If a merchant advertises "90 days same as cash," rest assured that the merchandise is priced high enough to cover the merchant's extension of "free" credit.

Some firms extend **easy credit**. "Easy" credit means that very few credit applicants are rejected. If a business extends easy credit, it will accept many clients who are not worthy of credit. These clients will generally have more delayed payments, more delinquencies, and more loan defaults than creditworthy clients. As a result, this business will have a high cost of operation. Higher operational costs mean higher prices for goods. There are, of course, exceptions to this rule. You could feel comfortable patronizing an easy credit business if (1) its merchandise quality and price is similar to stores without an easy credit policy and (2) its credit terms, such as interest rates, down payments, and collection policies, are in line with those of other businesses.

Free Goods

Many businesses advertise products at no or low cost. For example, one national chain store frequently advertises a "1-cent" sale on some of its products. For example, "Buy a gallon of paint at the regular price and get the second gallon for 1 cent." This tactic is not legally fraudulent, but keep

in mind that the *true* cost of the second gallon of paint is not 1 cent. If you think it is 1 cent, try buying just the second gallon for that price. "Free" goods that are conditional on the purchase of other goods or services are not free. If you need the "free" good, then go ahead and price the package that includes the free good. But if you don't really need the second gallon of paint, just price the first gallon and shop around.

Winning a Contest

"Congratulations! You have just won a free prize. Please call 555-3794 for instructions on collecting your prize." So says a letter that has your name and address carefully typed on an original letter. Do not feel too flattered. The modern-day miracle of word processors, high-speed printers, and computerized mailing lists ensures that every one of the million "prize" winners will receive an original letter. It turns out that if you call the number, you receive a sales pitch immediately. The whole idea behind the letter is to get you to call the number so a sales pitch can be made. The prize? Oh yes. It's a ballpoint pen. If you just go to an address in Bozeman, Montana, and sign a receipt, the firm would be pleased to award the prize to you in person. (See "The High-Pressure Sales Pitch" below).

Or how about the national "giveaway" promotion that offers a $100,000 prize, no purchase needed. No purchase is needed, so what do you have to lose by mailing in the response? Well, a couple of things. Sometimes the "Yes, I will buy your product" responses are to be returned in an

The High-Pressure Sales Pitch

The postcard arrives in the mail, addressed not to "Occupant" but personally to Mr. and Mrs. Smith. The postcard contains an invitation for the Smiths to claim one of three prizes: a brand new car, a vacation for two, or a relatively inexpensive electrical appliance. All the Smiths have to do to claim their prize is go to a nearby resort community and listen to a one-hour presentation extolling the virtues of buying property in the resort.

The Smiths figure that they can listen through a brief presentation so that they can satisfy their curiosity about whether they won the new car as a prize. Unfortunately, the Smiths and others who respond to similar promotions find out that the presentations are intense sales pitches. Often people end up buying resort properties at inflated prices simply to escape the sales pressure. If you are in doubt about the viability of a prize giveaway, check with your state's attorney general's office, state consumer protection agency, or your local Better Business Bureau.

envelope that is a different color from "No, I don't want what you are selling, but enter me in your contest anyway" responses. Some people in the no group might feel that they could lose out on the $100,000 if they said no; why else would their envelopes be a different color? So they might buy a product they do not need just so they know they will be entered in the contest. But the color of the envelope is not important. If the product is not wanted and the contest looks attractive, go ahead and say no and send in the contest form. The chances for winning the contest are the same irrespective of the color of the envelope.

But should you enter the contest at all? Probably five million other people will enter. Five million people will collectively spend over $1 million in postage to win $100,000. Is it worth it? Probably not. You, the consumer, are the best judge, though.

The average consumer receives many contest offers every year. Each one appears to promise something enticing. The best thing to do is to estimate your odds of winning or receiving a prize worth something. Chances are that the odds for winning something important are one in millions. Gamblers like those odds. Contests should be left to gamblers. A nearby store sells a good ballpoint pen for 39 cents!

Appliance Repairs

Sometimes contracting for repair of an appliance such as a color television or an automobile results in unneeded repairs being made. The consumer might be billed for imaginary or exaggerated repairs. Soldering a loose wire inside a television might become "rewiring a high-voltage circuit." A job that requires replacement of a seal might be explained as a major engine overhaul. Consumer-oriented magazines frequently report on deceptions practiced by repair shops. The best safeguard against fraudulant repair practices is to go to a reputable repair shop. Seek referrals from friends and neighbors. Check with the Better Business Bureau on complaints about a repair shop. You can also seek a second diagnostic opinion from another reputable shop. And you should always get an estimate in writing. Preferably, obtain a guarantee on the maximum repair bill. Taking precautions can save you a lot of money on unneeded appliance and automotive repairs.

Home Repairs

Home repairs generate large numbers of complaints from consumers. The classic frauds continue to exist. For example, someone might claim to have just finished repairing a driveway in the neighborhood. The person has some "pavement sealer" left over, and rather than throw it away, would like to seal your driveway for a very low cost. You pay $50–$200 to have the "sealer" spread on your driveway. But chances are the sealer is nothing

more than used crankcase oil that will wash away with the first heavy rain. In the meantime, it may actually harm the driveway.

Some criminals pose as official furnace "inspectors." They will inspect the furnace, declare it dangerous, and then volunteer to have a "reliable furnace repairer" fix it for only $150. Of course, nothing is wrong with the furnace, but consumers are frightened into having it fixed anyway. Government agencies do not send out furnace, water heater, or any other types of inspectors. If one of these "inspectors" shows up at your door, ask for proper identification, and call the police. The "inspector" is probably a rip-off expert.

Fraudulent home repair schemes of all sorts abound. As with other repair situations, seek references, check with the Better Business Bureau, and seek another opinion. Be wary of cut-rate prices on services that were not obviously needed.

Energy-Related Schemes

The increasingly high cost of conventional energy sources has spawned a new breed of con artist. These people specialize in selling devices that will dramatically lower home energy usage costs. Solar cells, heat collectors, sunroofs, chimney flue dampers, special thermostats, and many other items are touted as energy savers. Some of these products work, but many do not. Often the cost of installing an energy-saving device is not justified by the savings it generates. A $200 device that saves $5 annually in energy costs is no bargain. A $20,000 windmill that generates $1,000 worth of electricity per year is a misuse of hard-earned money. The field of energy conservation is new and has more than its share of bad deals. Seek the advice of an expert, sometimes even from a public utility company, before buying anything that promises to save energy.

The list of fraudulent practices could go on and on—we have merely suggested the types of frauds that can be perpetrated on consumers. Avoidance of greed, careful consideration of costs and benefits, and a genuine need for the products and services in question can go a long way toward preventing victimization by fraudulent schemes.

Spot Quiz • Consumer Frauds

1. A product or service at a bargain price is always a good buy.
                                                         T _____ F _____

2. Consumer rip-off schemes are successful because victims are often motivated by greed.   T _____ F _____

3. The idea behind "bait and switch" is to get the consumer to buy a higher-priced item.   T _____   F _____

(Answers on page 126)

Warranties and Service Contracts

Warranties are guarantees issued by manufacturers or suppliers of goods and services that explain their obligations and, generally, the user's or buyer's responsibilities also. **Service contracts** are agreements applicable to the repair of appliances. Understanding how warranties and service contracts work is important for consumers for a variety of reasons. Some products, if not adequately protected by warranties or service contracts, may cost consumers large sums of money for repairs. However, warranties and service contracts, either directly or indirectly, cost consumers money. Indiscriminate use of these devices can lead to unduly high costs for the purchase or maintenance of appliances.

Warranties

Before 1975, firms issuing warranties could offer "unconditional" warranties, which were not very useful as far as consumers were concerned. In 1975, Congress passed a law called the *Magnuson-Moss Warranty Act*. The act was designed to remove deceptive language from warranties. Additionally, the act required clear disclosure of coverage provided. The act also required that, for any item priced over $15, the buyer be allowed to see and read the warranty before making a purchase.

The purpose of this law was to allow consumers to use the warranty as a shopping tool. Lawmakers believed that if enough consumers read warranties before purchasing goods, manufacturers would have a stronger incentive to offer better warranties and, therefore, better products. (Many people believe that such has not been the result, however.)

Because the cost of making good on warranties is built into the prices of products, it makes sense to evaluate the warranty at the same time as the physical product. The consumer should note whether a warranty is "full" or "limited." (See "Out of Warranty, Out of Luck?" on page 110).

Out of Warranty, Out of Luck?

Suppose an appliance problem you had fixed under warranty crops up again shortly after your warranty protection expires. Is there anything you can do about it if you don't have an appliance service contract? Yes. First call the firm that provided the warranty service. Explain the situation and ask that the product be repaired again without charge. If you're turned down, write to the manufacturer and ask that your case be given special treatment.

If that doesn't work, contact the Major Appliance Consumer Action Panel, a group sponsored by the industry to resolve consumer complaints. MACAP reports that even without its intervention, many firms "will consider handling problems which occur shortly after warranty expiration on an in-warranty basis if proof of an identical in-warranty problem exists." The best proof, of course, is your receipt for a warranty service call. Make sure you obtain and file such receipts even when no charge is involved. If you didn't get a receipt at the time of service, ask the firm that made the repair to check its records and send you confirmation.

Even if there has been no warranty service, you're not necessarily out of luck when a breakdown occurs shortly after the warranty ends. The manufacturer or the dealer who sold you the product might pay all or part of the repair bill. A spokesperson for the Electronic Industries Association notes that manufacturers have an interest in return customers and may be willing to give special consideration to just-out-of-warranty problems.

"If you get one month past the warranty and a major component goes bad, you get into a gray area," she explains. "On a case-by-case basis, the manufacturer is likely to opt in favor of a consumer. If it's a year after the warranty, that's a different matter, but still the manufacturer might split the bill half and half with you." Cases that fall in these gray areas are handled individually. Among the factors considered are how close to the end of the warranty period the problem occurs, how long the component in question could reasonably be expected to last, and whether there is evidence of product abuse.

Most consumer complaints handled by MACAP involve problems that aren't covered by a warranty. And most consumers who take their cases to MACAP go home satisfied. In 1979, MACAP resolved more than 1,000 cases to the consumer's satisfaction; the panel ruled that fewer than 400 cases involved unjustified or unsubstantiated complaints.

If you have an appliance problem that isn't satisfactorily resolved by the dealer or manufacturer, you can request MACAP's help by writing to Major Appliance Consumer Action Panel, 20 N. Wacker Dr., Chicago, IL 60606.

Source: *Changing Times*, November 1980, p. 55. Reprinted with permission from *Changing Times* Magazine, © Kiplinger Washington Editors, Inc., 1980. This reprint is not to be altered in any way, except with permission from *Changing Times*.

Full Versus Limited Warranties.   A **full warranty** provides extended coverage of the product. A fully warranted item is replaced or repaired free of charge during a reasonable time. What is a reasonable time has not been specifically defined, but typically repairs should be performed within 30 days. A full warranty also provides for reasonably easy warranty service. Thus, a central air-conditioning unit would not have to be returned to the factory to obtain service. A full-service warranty is good for the duration of the warranty period. That is, the warranty can be transferred from the original buyer to another buyer.

A full warranty is very desirable for the consumer if it turns out that the product is subject to frequent breakdowns. In this case, the consumer can request a free replacement or the return of the purchase price.

A **limited warranty** is less comprehensive than a full warranty. Some features of a limited warranty are explained in Figure 4.1. Repairs under a limited warranty are more costly than under a full warranty. If the item must be replaced, the manufacturer offers only a *pro rata* refund on the purchase price. For example, a person pays $60 for a car battery that is covered by a 40-month limited warranty. After ten months the battery fails to hold a charge. The manufacturer may credit the consumer with only $30 \times \$60/40 = \$45$ toward the purchase of a replacement battery. Under a full warranty, the consumer would have received a $60 credit.

Warranties may or may not cover **consequential damage**. For example, the compressor on a refrigerator under warranty fails, and food inside the refrigerator is spoiled. A warranty providing for consequential damages would pay for the spoiled food in addition to the repairs on the

Figure 4.1   Full versus Limited Warranties

Full Warranty	Limited Warranty
1. The defective item is fixed or replaced free.	1. Generally, parts are covered but not labor.
2. Warranty service is provided reasonably.	2. Warranty service requires returning the product to a service center.
3. The warranty is good for the duration of the warranty period.	3. The warranty is good only for the original buyer.
	4. The defective item is replaced on a *pro rata* basis.

compressor. This feature can be excluded from both full and limited warranties in most states.

Virtually all products are covered by **implied warranties,** which simply means that a product is capable of doing what it is supposed to do. Thus, for example, an electric shaver should shave hair, and an air-conditioner should blow out cool air. However, a seller can exclude most implied warranties by stating that the product is not covered by a warranty and is sold in "as is" condition.

Evaluating Warranties.   The **coverage** provided by a warranty should be carefully evaluated. Occasionally a manufacturer will provide a limited warranty on the product and a full warranty on certain components in the product. Thus, for example, an air-conditioner may come with a limited warranty, but the motor inside it may have a full warranty. You should check to see whether the coverage provided is comparable with warranties on competing products.

The warranty claims procedure should be explained clearly and should not be unduly bothersome. One warranty, for example, required that the product be returned to the factory in its *original* carton. Most of us are not in the habit of saving packing and shipping cartons. This procedure is clearly designed to discourage warranty claims.

The claims adjustment procedure should be simple. Often manufacturers require that items be returned to a service center for repair. One company used to charge a $5 service and handling fee for repairs to its watches, which sold for $9. Most people would probably choose to discard the watch rather than spend $5 to have it repaired. In this case, the adjustment procedure is such that the warranty does not have much value for the watch buyer.

It is generally advisable to check the warranty, what it covers, who it covers, and the claim and adjustment procedures before purchasing a product. A product backed by a good warranty can save a consumer dollars as well as mental anguish.

Service Contracts

Tony Bessoti bought a color television some time ago. On Sunday he was watching his favorite tenor in his favorite opera when, horror of horrors, the set went on the blink right in the middle of a passionate scene. The warranty on the set had, of course, expired. The repair shop charged Tony $250 to install a new picture tube. Tony's neighbor, Andrea Holt, had a slightly different experience with her set. The Redskins' rookie fullback had just broken through the middle and appeared to be on his way to a 79-yard scamper into the end zone, when, poof—the screen went blank. Andrea, whose set was covered by a service contract, called a repair shop. Her set was repaired in time for her to see the rookie score the touchdown.

Well, not quite. Lucky Andrea, though—she had a service contract. Should everyone have service contracts on their appliances? Probably not.

People like Andrea will be able to take full advantage of their service contracts sometimes. However, chances are that the cost of the service contract will be high. Robert T. Lund of the Massachusetts Institute of Technology studied service contracts covering appliances such as color television sets, washers, ranges, and refrigerators. Mr. Lund compared, for example, the cost of a service contract on a color TV with the set's anticipated repair bills. The study concluded that the service contract cost was about ten times the cost of the expected repair bills. He commented on the cost of service contracts: "They're overpriced. If you are a reasonable person and you look at it from an economic point of view—comparing the cost of the contract with the expected cost of repairs—you wouldn't buy a service contract."[2]

Sellers of Service Contracts. Service contracts are sold by just about anyone involved in the marketing of appliances. These include manufacturers, retailers, repair shops, and independent repair persons. Every time a new appliance is purchased or an old one is serviced, the consumer will probably be offered a service contract. Maytag Corporation, the company that advertises the dependability of its appliances by using the lonely repairman theme, does not sell service contracts. The company states that, based on its experience, its clients are better off without a service contract.

Cost of Service Contracts. Service contracts vary in price, depending on local labor costs and what is offered in the contract. Many companies offer unlimited service calls and unlimited repairs during the contract period. A major chain store typically charges about $40–$70 for a contract on an appliance during the second year of ownership. The first year of ownership is covered by a warranty. A one-year service contract for $40 on a $1,000 refrigerator might sound like a bargain until you realize that very few refrigerators need repairs during their early years.

Before buying a service contract, you should establish that the contract will not cover what is already covered by a warranty. A contract should be purchased from either the manufacturer of the appliance or a reputable dealer or repair shop. In general, though, you are probably better off not buying a service contract. Appliances do need repairs, however, so one way of handling the trauma of a large, unbudgeted repair bill is to include repair expense in the family budget. Repair bills can then be paid from funds already accumulated.

---

2. "Appliance Service Contracts," *Changing Times* (November 1980): 53.

Spot Quiz • Warranties and Service Contracts

1. Since 1975, an "unconditional" warranty covers all repairs on products.

   T _____   F _____

2. Consequential damages are always covered by full warranties.

   T _____   F _____

3. A service contract can save the consumer a large repair bill.

   T _____   F _____

(Answers on page 127)

Consumer Protection

In 1962, President John F. Kennedy, in a special message to the U.S. Congress, set forth the basic consumer rights as follows:

1. Consumers have the right to safety. That is, they should not be exposed to products and services that may be injurious to them.
2. Consumers have the right to be informed. They should be given the facts needed to make informed decisions.
3. Consumers have the right to choose. Competitive products should be available so that consumers have a choice.
4. Consumers have a right to be heard so that appropriate consumer laws can be enacted.

This list of consumer rights is a far cry from the situation that prevailed a few decades ago. But, you might ask, do today's sophisticated consumers really need protection?

Is Consumer Protection Needed?

What is the difference between a personal computer with 640K bytes dynamic RAM and one with 20Kb 200 nsec RAM and a 2K bootstrap PROM? If you do not know the answer, you have lots of company. Products are becoming increasingly complex. A consumer cannot reasonably be expected to know all the technical details about a wide variety of products. Consumer protection legislation can simplify the decision-making process for consumers by providing adequate safeguards.

Frequently, the side effects of using a product may not become apparent for quite some time. And in many cases, the consumer may not even know that the product in question is harmful. Lead-glazed pottery, whose continued use may cause brain damage, is an example. A drug such as Thalidomide, which is now banned because use by pregnant women often resulted in birth defects in babies, is another example. The effects of usage of some products may not become apparent to the consumer for twenty or thirty years. Consumer protection legislation can provide a measure of relief by requiring that products meet safety and performance standards.

Consumer protection legislation can also help prevent some of the consumer frauds mentioned previously in this chapter. But consumer protection legislation has drawbacks. Restrictive legislation will impose extra costs on the manufacturer, who will in turn try to pass these costs on to consumers in the form of higher prices. If consumer laws become too restrictive, some manufacturers may choose to withdraw their products from the markets, thereby limiting choice.

Overall, consumer protection legislation is needed. A balance has to be struck between too little and too much protection. As we shall see in the next two sections, consumers today appear to be amply protected.

Consumer Protection Legislation

Many laws have been enacted at federal, state, and local levels to control various business practices. The purpose of these laws is to protect consumers from unfair, unethical, and dangerous business practices. General categories of laws, rather than the specific laws themselves, are explained in this section.

Antitrust Legislation.　Laws that are designed to maintain or increase competition in the marketplace are called **antitrust laws**. Thus, for example, the manufacturer of Levi's jeans would not be allowed to buy out the manufacturer of Lee's jeans.

The idea behind antitrust laws is to make sure that companies compete with each other. Because of competition, firms are expected to offer consumers the highest-quality products at the lowest prices possible. Competition in the marketplace thus benefits consumers. In some areas, competition is not considered to be desirable. In such situations the government permits one company to provide services to consumers, but these companies are then closely regulated by government agencies. Examples are public utilities, such as telephone and power companies.

Consumer Well-Being.　Some laws are enacted to make life safer for consumers. Such laws apply to a wide variety of products used by consumers, including lawn mowers, ladders, toys, drug packaging, microwave ovens, and automobiles.

Quality of Products.   A variety of laws has been enacted to ensure that products sold to consumers are wholesome. For example, these laws regulate the permissible level of various additive ingredients in food items. Thus, hamburger meat cannot contain more than a certain percentage of fat, and a beef hot dog cannot contain any other meat, such as pork or chicken. Ice cream must have a minimum specified level of fat content.

Drugs are extensively tested and must be approved by the Food and Drug Administration before they can be sold in the United States. This procedure tries to minimize the exposure of U.S. residents to harmful side effects of drugs. Foods processed in the United States are subject to strict governmental regulation. The government also rates various food items. For example, beef can be "prime" or "choice" quality. Laws in this category are frequently revised and upgraded to reflect new information about food substances.

Deceptive Practices.   Deceptive trade practices are prohibited by various laws. Thus, a food package that lists net contents as 16 ounces must contain 16 ounces of food. Violation of these laws can result in fines for manufacturers. Deceptive practices in advertising and pricing are also illegal. These laws also cover door-to-door and mail order selling as well as retail sales.

Disclosure.   Many laws enacted in recent years require manufacturers and sellers to provide more information to consumers. The purpose of these laws is to give consumers sufficient information to make good decisions. Food packages, for example, must list the contents or ingredients in order of decreasing weight. If a jar of mixed nuts lists its ingredients as pecans, cashews, peanuts, salt, and spices, then it must contain more pecans and cashews than peanuts. Disclosure requirements also apply to consumer loan transactions, such as borrowing and credit cards.

The laws in the various categories just discussed are designed to let consumers make the best decisions possible about spending their money. The assortment of goods and services available to consumers is indeed very broad. There will always be situations that may not be desirable for consumers but that are not covered by any laws. Chances are that ultimately these situations will be affected by laws. Until then, the burden is on the consumer to make informed decisions.

Consumer Protection Agencies

Consumer protection agencies exist at all levels of government. Volunteer agencies also are available to resolve consumer-related issues. Federal agencies are generally concerned with prosecuting businesses engaged in illegal practices and enforcing federal laws, rules, and regulations. Federal agencies do not mediate disputes between individual consumers and businesses. State and local agencies can and frequently will mediate

disputes between consumers and businesses. Some offer arbitration as a device for resolving consumer-merchant conflicts. In this section, major federal agencies and other agencies concerned with consumer protection are described.

Federal Agencies. The *Federal Trade Commission (FTC)* is the agency responsible for providing consumers with protection from misleading business practices. The FTC is organized into a number of different operating divisions. The *Division of Product Reliability and Standards* oversees warranty and certification programs. Product performance standards generally are developed in this division. The *Division of Advertising Practices* monitors advertisements and requires that advertisers substantiate claims made in advertisements. The *Division of Credit Practices* oversees credit-related issues and is responsible for enforcing the various credit-related laws. The *Division of Marketing Abuses* is concerned with potential areas of deceptive marketing practices. Trade schools, land and condominium sales, and energy conservation devices are some of the areas where this division exercises its responsibilities.

The *Food and Drug Administration (FDA)* is responsible for making sure that food, drugs, and cosmetics available to consumers are safe. The FDA is required by law to establish that new drugs are safe and effective. When a drug company wants to introduce a new drug in the U.S. market, it must engage in extensive testing of the new drug to satisfy the FDA's requirements. Drug companies argue that it takes the FDA too long to approve a new drug. Consumer groups, on the other hand, frequently blame the FDA for not acting quickly enough to remove potentially harmful food and drug products from the market. Occasionally, a drug that is judged by the FDA to be ineffective is still demanded by the public. For example, Laetrile is considered by the FDA to be ineffective for fighting cancer, yet the public wants to use it. The FDA has thus become a controversial agency that is criticized from many different directions.

The *Consumer Products Safety Commission (CPSC)* was created in 1972. Its role is to prevent potentially harmful products from being sold to the public. It conducts safety tests on products, establishes safety standards, and occasionally bans the sale of hazardous products. It can also require the recall, repair, or replacement of potentially dangerous products.

The *Federal Communications Commission (FCC)* oversees the licensing and operation of radio and television stations. The FCC is empowered to protect the public interest. For example, in 1969 it banned cigaret advertising on television. Some critics argue that the FCC has not done enough. For example, some consumer groups would like the FCC to either ban or limit advertising during children's television programs.

State and Local Agencies. Many states and municipalities have enacted laws designed to protect consumers. State agencies are generally concerned with product quality and safety and with deceptive sales and

trade practices. Many large cities also have legislation designed to protect consumers. The effectiveness of the state and local agencies varies. Some are very rigorous in protecting consumer rights, and others actually discourage consumer complaints. A call to your local government office will help you identify any local consumer protection agencies in your area. Generally, the state and local agencies are better equipped than federal agencies to help resolve individual consumer complaints.

Voluntary Agencies. Many volunteer consumer protection agencies, such as the Consumer Federation of America and the National Consumer Congress, assist consumers with their problems. These agencies can be helpful in resolving problems with businesses. The Office of Consumer Assistance, 330 Independence Avenue, Washington, D.C. 20201, can provide information on forming a local volunteer agency.

Spot Quiz • Consumer Protection

1. Because products are becoming increasingly complex, consumer protection laws can help establish the safety and effectiveness of products.
   T _____   F _____

2. Antitrust legislation leads to reduced competition in the marketplace.
   T _____   F _____

3. The FTC determines whether new drugs are safe and effective.
   T _____   F _____

4. Federal agencies generally do not mediate disputes between consumers and sellers.   T _____   F _____

(Answers on page 127)

COMPLAINT PROCEDURES

Once in a while, as a consumer, you will feel the need to complain about a product or service you have purchased. This section explains the procedures you should follow to satisfactorily resolve a dispute involving a product or service.

The Nature of the Complaint

First, you should fully understand what is unsatisfactory about the product or service. A toaster should toast slices of bread. If it does not, you have a legitimate complaint. If it does not properly toast marshmallows, you may not have a valid complaint. Generally speaking, a consumer will have much better success obtaining satisfaction on products and services that do not perform as they are expected to. Less successful are complaints that are vague and general, indicate a misuse of the product in question, or reflect a change in the buyer's attitude toward the product or service.

Before a complaint is made, you should examine any warranty accompanying the product or service. It may be that the warranty will cover the defective product or service.

Documenting a Complaint

Obtaining satisfaction on a complaint is largely influenced by the timely documentation provided by the buyer. The key word here is *timely*. It does not do any good to wait for weeks or months before making a complaint. A complaint should be registered as soon as the product or service is judged to be defective.

Documenting a complaint requires compiling all necessary papers related to the purchase of the product or service. These papers include sales receipts, shipping documents, warranties, and credit agreements. If repairs to the product or service in question were needed, then related invoices and bills should also be compiled.

Next, prepare a note that lists the following information:

1. Name of the business where the product was purchased.
2. Date of purchase.
3. Cost of the product.
4. Description of the product.
5. Nature of the complaint.
6. Action desired.

The description of the complaint (item 5) should be brief and clear. Item 6 should state whether the product should be repaired, replaced, or returned for credit or cash. One copy should be made of each document.

Step One: The Selling Store

Many consumer complaints are handled at the selling store level. Check first with the customer service department in the store. Bring the complaint to the department's attention. Present the department with the six-step note you have prepared. If it is convenient, you should take in the defective product at the time you make the complaint. In the absence of a

customer service department, explain the complaint to the department manager. If he or she is not helpful, talk with the store manager. Many complaints are resolved at this level. Legitimate businesses try not to irritate customers, and they want customers to return to the store. Therefore, most of them are willing to accommodate complaints. In a complaint adjustment, the buyer should be willing to pay a fair price for the amount of time that the product performed satisfactorily.

Step Two: The Parent Firm

Many stores are branches of a chain. If the local store does not offer satisfaction, the next step is to write to the president of the store's parent firm. To the six-step procedure already listed, add two more steps:

7. Briefly explain what occurred when the local store was asked to resolve the complaint.
8. List a deadline for corrective action.

A reasonable deadline is four weeks from the mailing of the complaint. Send copies of all related documents. Save the original documents for future use. This step, of course, does not apply if you are dealing with a strictly local firm.

Step Three: The Manufacturer

Occasionally, a store may have a policy that it simply will not handle any product complaints. Or it may be more appropriate to go directly to the manufacturer. Write a letter to the manufacturer, listing items 1–6 and 8, and possibly 7. Again, only copies of the documents should be sent.

Step Four: Better Business Bureau

Many cities have a **Better Business Bureau (BBB)**, which is financed by dues paid by member businesses. BBBs are good sources of information about a business *before* a product or service is purchased. BBBs also will quite often help in resolving a consumer complaint. Many BBBs have established arbitration boards. Some BBB arbitration boards charge a small fee to hear consumer complaints; others provide the service free. An arbitration board hears both the consumer complaint and the business's response. Then it makes a settlement. Many consumers believe that BBBs are fair in their dealings with consumers. Call your local BBB for information on filing a complaint. (See "What Consumers Are Telling the BBB" on page 121.)

What Consumers Are Telling the BBB

There was an upsurge in the number of complaints and inquiries about businesses involved in home construction, remodeling, and maintenance. But mail-order companies still held down the top spot as the most-complained about business, and the product category that attracted the most gripes was—you guessed it—automobiles.

Those were some of the findings in a report of the Council of Better Business Bureaus on the activities of its 143 local bureaus in 1978. The survey showed that of 5 million requests for information about businesses, more than 30 percent involved home services companies, such as remodelers, roofers, heating and air-conditioning contractors, and builders. Complaints about remodelers jumped 39 percent in two years. The council attributed the increase to an active housing market, a high incidence of weather-related damages and repairs, and a heightened interest in insulation.

The top five winners/sinners in each of the main survey categories were:

Most complained-about products: automobiles, clothing and accessories, furniture, major appliances (mostly for kitchens), television sets.

Most-complained-about businesses: mail-order companies, franchised auto dealers, home furnishings stores, independent auto repair shops, miscellaneous home maintenance companies.

Businesses most likely to settle complaints: banks, department stores, chain food stores, insurance companies, telephone companies.

Businesses least likely to settle complaints: ''Vacation certificate'' companies (such as those that offer free or cut-rate hotel accommodations as a come-on for a land sales pitch), work-at-home companies, ''business opportunity'' companies (especially those involving sales or franchise operations), paving contractors, dentists.

Source: *Changing Times*, September 1979, p. 36. Reprinted with permission from *Changing Times* Magazine, © Kiplinger Washington Editors, Inc., 1979. This reprint is not to be altered in any way, except with permission from *Changing Times*.

Step Five: Local or State Agency

Local or state consumer protection agencies can be identified in the Yellow Pages listings for local and state governments. A call to the agency will tell the consumer the procedure to be followed in filing a complaint. Most agencies have a complaint form that needs to be filled out before the agency will take any action. The complaint form, if required, should be filled out and submitted with any supporting documents requested.

Step Six: Legal Action

Legal action is the last step in resolving a consumer complaint. Because of the cost and effort involved, legal action is not recommended for situations involving small sums of money. Small claims courts and regular courts can be used for pursuing legal action.

Small Claims Court. Most states have **small claims courts**. The amount of money that can be recovered through small claims court varies from state to state but is usually less than $1,000. It is relatively simple to file a claim, and the filing fee is nominal. The court sets a date for the hearing and issues a notice of appearance to the business being sued. At the court hearing, both sides present their arguments. The judge then makes a decision.

If the consumer wins the case and the defendent pays, there is no problem. However, if the defendent refuses to pay, then the consumer has to take additional legal action to recover the judgment awarded him or her. Because of the time investment involved, the consumer should consider this option carefully before proceeding.

Regular Court. If the dollar amount involved is large enough, the consumer may consider pursuing legal action through regular courts. At the outset, the consumer will need to be represented by a lawyer. The case may take some time before it is heard by the court. Lawyers' fees and other court costs can be high enough to keep most consumers from following this alternative.

Spot Quiz • Complaint Procedures

1. Timely filing of a complaint is important for its resolution.

   T _____   F _____

2. A BBB can help mediate a complaint.   T _____   F _____

3. Low costs for going to small claims court mean that this option should always be pursued.   T _____   F _____

(Answers on page 127)

"*And if you're not 100% satisfied, may God grant you the wisdom to accept the things you cannot change.*"

Source: Reprinted from *The Saturday Evening Post* © 1978 The Curtis Publishing Company.

Summary

As long as there are consumers, there will be frauds in selling goods and services. Consumers are subjected to deceptive advertising, shoddy products, misleading sales pitches, and promises that are not kept. They are charged for repairs not made properly, if at all, for home repairs that are not needed, and for energy-saving devices that do not work. *Caveat emptor* is a motto that applies to all consumers.

Warranties are guarantees explaining the manufacturer's responsibilities. Warranties can be either full or limited. The coverage provided by a warranty should be carefully understood before the product or service is purchased. Service contracts provide for service of covered appliances. In general, service contracts are not justified on the basis of their costs.

The increasing complexity of products calls for consumer protection. Consumer protection laws have been passed at all levels of government. Legislation generally deals with business collusion, consumer well-being, quality and safety of products, deceptive practices, and disclosure.

Consumer protection agencies exist at all levels of government. In addition, private organizations are also involved with consumer protection. The Federal Trade Commission, the Food and Drug Administration, and the Federal Communications Commission are major federal government agencies involved with consumer protection.

A consumer can follow a complaint procedure if she or he is not satisfied with a product or service. The complaint should be timely and properly documented. The various complaint steps include talking with the appropriate local store supervisor, writing to the parent firm, writing to the manufacturer, contacting the Better Business Bureau, contacting the local or state consumer-protection agency, and taking legal action. The last step can be costly and time-consuming and therefore is not suggested unless a large sum of money is involved.

Questions

1. What is meant by *caveat emptor*? How does the concept apply to the modern-day consumer?

2. Give two examples of deceptive advertising. Why are these considered deceptive?

3. What is meant by bait and switch? Cite an example of a bait and switch practice.

4. Discuss this statement: "Requiring that packages be the same size for different brands of the same product reduces consumer choice in the marketplace."

5. Should all products be accompanied by warranties? Explain your answer.

6. Is selling products for $X.99 an example of deceptive pricing? Explain your answer.

7. Explain the circumstances under which "free" or "easy" credit is in fact free or easy.

8. Do contests and lotteries add to general consumer welfare? Why or why not?

9. How can appliance and home repair frauds be prevented?

10. What is a warranty? Explain the difference between a full and a limited warranty.

11. Explain the concept of an "implied warranty."

12. What is a service contract? Is it desirable to have service contracts on appliances? Why or why not?

13. Explain briefly the four basic consumer rights.

14. Is consumer protection needed? Explain your answer.

15. Explain what antitrust legislation is.

16. How do disclosure laws provide consumer protection?

17. Explain what the FTC does to protect consumers.

18. How does the FDA provide protection for consumers?

19. Briefly explain the alternatives you have in pursuing a product- or service-related complaint.

20. How do small claims courts operate? Is it desirable to take complaints there? Explain your answer.

Case Problems

1. The following advertisement appears in a local newspaper:

     16-FOOT FREEZER
     Just what you need to store meat and food at
     wholesale prices. Special price, THIS WEEK ONLY,
     $249

     John Brennan goes to the store in question to buy the freezer. The salesperson points out that the freezer is cheaply built and does not have a built-in light, a thermostat, or a freezer door lock. A better-quality model, also on sale for only $699, has all the desired features. How would you characterize the business practice involved here? What is the common name of the practice? Justify your answer. What advice do you have for John Brennan?

2. Sandra Witt is considering buying a small, color, portable television for $299. The store is offering to sell a one-year service contract on the television for $70. The contract would cover all labor and parts needed to repair the set if it breaks down during its first year of purchase. Furthermore, if service is needed, a service vehicle would be sent to Sandra's residence. Should Sandra buy the service contract? Explain your answer.

3. Jon Gehr purchased a food processor for $100 from a local store. The processor came with a one-year replacement warranty. After 15 months of use, the motor burned out. Jon took the food processor back to the store. The manager agreed that the motor had failed prematurely but was not willing to replace it or refund Jon's money. He has suggested that Jon have the store's repair department replace the motor for $40 ($30 for parts, $10 for labor). Explain briefly the options that Jon has at this time. What are the possible outcomes of those actions that involve either the store or the manufacturer? What should Jon do?

Bibliography

"Know and Use Your Warranty Rights." *Changing Times* (August 1978): 45–47.

"Appliance Service Contracts." *Changing Times* (November 1980): 53–55.

"A Hard Look at Washington's Safety Watchers." *Money* (October 1977): 89–94.

"Confessions of a Better Business Bureau Complaint Taker." *Money* (September 1981): 136, 142, 144, 146.

"Everything Has Its (Lower) Price." *Money* (March 1985): 137–140.

In addition to the above references, most issues of *Changing Times, Consumer Reports,* and *Money* contain articles on consumerism.

Answers to Spot Quizzes

Consumer Frauds (page 108)

1. F (It is not a bargain if the product or service is not needed.)

2. T (Many rip-off schemes prey on the consumer's greed.)

3. T (This is the "switch" part.)

Warranties and Service Contracts (page 114)

1. F (Since 1975, the word *unconditional* does not have any specific meaning as far as a warranty is concerned.)

2. F (They may not be covered.)

3. T (That may very well be the case.)

Consumer Protection (page 118)

1. T (They can simplify the decision-making process for consumers.)

2. F (Antitrust legislation maintains or increases competition.)

3. F (The FDA does.)

4. T (Federal agencies generally do not involve themselves in mediating disputes.)

Complaint Procedures (page 122)

1. T (The details of the complaint are still fresh. The urgency of the complaint is demonstrated.)

2. T (BBBs are helpful in mediating and resolving complaints.)

3. F (The time involved and problems with collecting the judgment should also be considered.)

Part 2

Budgeting, Cash, and Credit

Short-term financial management is very important for the consumer. The first step in short-term management is to develop a system of record keeping that allows you to monitor cash inflows and expenses. Chapter 5, "Budgeting for Current Expenses," explains the budgeting process and provides guidelines for controlling expenses. A system that permits flexible budgeting is explained.

Chapter 6 is entitled "Managing Liquid Assets." Liquid assets include cash on hand, checking account balances, and savings accounts. The chapter describes different types of checking accounts and explains how to open and use a checking account and a savings account. Different methods of payment and special services offered by banks are explained. Finally, a variety of savings instruments is discussed.

"Managing Credit" is the title and topic of Chapter 7. The advantages and disadvantages of using credit and its costs are discussed. Different sources of credit are explained. Open-ended credit and installment loans are analyzed. Consumer credit protection laws are explained, and alternatives for managing excessive credit are considered.

Chapter 5

Budgeting for Current Expenses

Objectives

After reading this chapter, you will be able to:

- State the reasons for budgeting.
- Discuss the role of the budget manager.
- Explain the procedures for setting up a budget.
- Forecast fixed and variable expenses.
- Record and control expenses.
- Maintain a flexible budget.

John Dunmore is a tax accountant who works for the U.S. government. Mr. Dunmore's annual salary is $22,000. His wife, Mary, does not work for a salary, and they have no children. The Dunmores earn about $1,400 annually from their stocks and savings. Despite increases in prices due to inflation, the Dunmores' total annual spending has declined for the past three years. In some years they have cut food expenses from the previous year. For this year, compared to last year, they have reduced department store spending by 52 percent; books, magazines, and dues expenses by 33 percent; and insurance expenses by 5 percent. Last year they spent $1,821 for a leisurely vacation in Florida. This amount was up from $987 the year before last.

How can a family reduce expenses in the face of inflation? How can a family control expenses to free up more funds for leisure and recreation? What is the Dunmores' secret? The answer is simple. The Dunmores use basic principles of money management. They budget all their incomes and expenses. They carefully draw up a spending plan. Additionally, they try very hard to keep their spending in line with the amounts budgeted.[1]

Like the Dunmores, anyone can use budgeting procedures to hold down living expenses and free up funds for savings, retirement, recreation, or other reasons. Budgeting procedures are explained in this chapter.

PLANNING FOR BUDGETING

Budgeting is a system of record keeping. When you budget, you identify all sources of income and plan your expenses so that your income will cover all your expenses. Budgeting also involves keeping tabs on actual expenses. As the Dunmore example illustrates, there are definite benefits from and needs for budgeting.

Why Budget?

Budgeting allows you to plan for expenses. Expenditures can be controlled and channeled in ways that lead to maximum benefit for the family. Certain factors also *require* budgeting.

Advantages of Budgeting.   Most families can easily adjust to spending *more* money. However, once consumption levels are established, very few families can adjust to spending *less*. Budgeting calls on a family to *plan* its expenditures. Because expenditures are planned, they can be more easily reduced if decreases in income call for a reduction in expenses.

---

1. "One Family's Budgeting Plan—It's Easy and It Works," *Changing Times*, (July 1977): 43–47.

Consumers have a tendency to increase spending from one time period to the next. Many of us give in to our desires when we see certain items attractively displayed for sale. That is, many of us spend money on impulse. We spend money when we had not planned to spend it. **Impulse buying**, or buying something when you had not planned to buy the item, can frequently lead to spending more than you can afford. Budgeting provides a realistic look at incomes coming in. You can then plan your spending accordingly. Budgeting makes you conscious of your expenses and therefore gives you more control over them.

Better control of your expenses and reducing the amount of money you spend on impulse buying increases the amount of money that you can save. This increased saving can be systematically invested to build a larger retirement fund or estate. Alternatively, portions of this increased savings can be used to better your current life style. The Dunmores, for example, can afford to spend more on a vacation because they have better control of their expenses. Budgeting allows a family to enjoy life more now by increasing funds for leisure and recreation. Budgeting also allows for a better life later by increasing investment funds for retirement.

"Now I'd like to introduce our new organist and say a few words about our budget. . . ."

Source: Reprinted from *The Saturday Evening Post*
© 1979 The Curtis Publishing Company.

Budgeting Is Needed. Chapter 1 identified three financial goals: (1) attaining and maintaining a certain quality of life, (2) saving funds for retirement, and (3) getting the most for your money. Budgeting can be directly linked to the first two financial goals. Maintaining a certain quality of life implies that the individual prefers certain activities over others. Budgeting allows control over expenses so that more money can be spent on the more desirable activities. In the Dunmores' case, budgeting has allowed them to spend more on leisure and recreation activities.

The second financial goal requires a deliberate strategy of saving. For many of us, it is not pleasant to forego current consumption so that funds can be accumulated for future consumption. Budgeting provides a mechanism so that current expenses can be controlled, and more funds can be made available for retirement planning. Without budgeting, the discipline may not be there to allow systematic saving. (See ''Save That Buck!'' below.)

Since the late 1960s, inflation has been an important economic issue for the consumer. In recent years, the price of consumer goods and services has increased by about 3 to 10 percent every year. For many wage earners, salary increases simply have not kept pace with inflation. Still other consumers are on fixed incomes, such as pensions and retirement benefits. Maintaining the same standard of living under inflation becomes increasingly burdensome. Budgeting allows a family to plan for situations when

Save That Buck!

''Hey man, there's only one way to live: To spend megabucks you gotta make megabucks.'' This was the advice one college senior was overheard giving to another. The advice is questionable, and we know one fact for sure: Spending megabucks is a lot easier than earning megabucks. Even if we aren't interested in spending megabucks, there will be times when our expenditures will exceed our earning capacities—for example, during vacations and during retirement. So how do we meet these needs? By saving, saving, and more saving.

Notice from the discussion in the text that savings are considered to be part of fixed ''expenses.'' That's one way to save. Another is to continue making loan payments after the loan has been paid off. No, not to the lender but into your savings account. Still another way to save is to periodically skip a routine expenditure. If, for example, you buy lunch every day, then brown bagging your lunch once or twice a week will generate savings. Or how about putting every quarter you receive into a savings jar or piggy bank? If you think about it, you will find many different ways to save a quarter here and a buck there, and it all builds up your savings.

increases in income do not keep pace with increases in expenses. Budgeting can show a family where expenses can be selectively reduced.

Without proper budgeting, there may be months when not all of the bills due get paid. When situations like this occur too often, a family's credit rating can be seriously damaged. Budgeting allows a family to maintain its credit rating and enjoy the benefits of credit.

Finally, all members of a family should have reasonable access to the family's income. For example, mismanagement of family income does not mean that teenage members of the family should not receive a weekly or monthly spending allowance. Budgeting provides family members with a better understanding of incomes and expenses. No one family member feels that he or she is being treated unfairly. Budgeting allows a family to reasonably resolve conflicts over expenditures.

Involve the Family

Each member of the family needs to understand the importance of budgeting and the dangers of operating an out-of-balance budget. Some steps can be followed to involve the family in the budgeting process.

The Budget Managers.   Many families are now **dual-career families**, in which both spouses work. For dual-career families, it is important to recognize that there is no such thing as "your money" and "my money." Both incomes should be recognized as "family" income. For a family with a single wage earner, the contributions of the homemaker (whether husband or wife) should be fully recognized. In this setting, both spouses are equal budget managers. If one spouse takes on more budgeting responsibility than the other, it should be on the basis of budgeting expertise only. The role of wage earner or homemaker should not give a person greater consideration as a budget manager.

Noneconomic Spending.   **Noneconomic spending** includes expenses that cannot be related to quality, price, or family consumption needs. Perhaps the biggest category of noneconomic spending is "prestige" goods purchased to gain status. A family with an average income that buys a Cadillac Seville for basic transportation is incurring extra expenses for noneconomic reasons. Another spur to noneconomic spending is peer group pressure. For example, a teenager may want a brand-new wardrobe based on the latest fashions because "that's what everyone else is wearing." Or a wage earner who has been promoted may want to buy a new car because that's what other recently promoted employees have done.

Noneconomic spending tends to reduce the quality of living for most families because it draws resources away from other expense categories.

The average-income family buying the Seville has to crimp on other expense categories to make the car payments. Perhaps a much-needed annual vacation is sacrificed for the car payments. Noneconomic spending may provide temporary psychological satisfaction for one or more family members, but in the long run, it will negatively affect the family's quality of living.

Involving the Family. The whole family should be involved in the budgeting process. Some people may feel that perhaps children should not be involved in such decisions as the type and location of a new home or the make of a new car. Some aspects of these decisions, such as real estate taxes, quality of construction, quality of the car, and commuting needs, understandably would not involve the children. However, all of the family should be included in the deliberation of the budgeting aspects of these decisions. The decision to spend money in one expense category affects the family's ability to spend money in other expense categories. For example, the decision to buy a new car may affect expenditures on food, clothing, recreation, and vacations. All family members are consumers in these expense categories, and they should have a say in how their consumption of these goods and services will be affected by new potential expenses.

Flexible and Simple Budgets. An overly restrictive budget can cause family members to rebel. One way to avoid such a situation is to allow for some flexibility in certain expense categories. Flexibility can also be gained by establishing a ''red bread'' expense category. **Red bread** stands for deficit spending. If not all the funds reserved in this category are spent, then the family has extra money on hand to invest or to spend as it pleases.[2]

In addition to being flexible, the budget should be simple. A budget that is too detailed will make it difficult to keep track of insignificant amounts of money. A simple budget permits a family to keep good records without spending a lot of time on the records.

Spot Quiz • Planning for Budgeting

1. Some families do not need to budget.   T _____   F _____

2. The process of budgeting expenses requires the attention of the family wage earner only.   T _____   F _____

---

2. *Red* refers to deficit, and *bread* to money. The term *red bread* signifies money to cover deficit spending.

3. A simple budget encourages all family members to participate.

T _____   F _____

(Answers on page 153)

THE BUDGETING PROCESS

The budgeting process needs to be simple. Major steps involved in budgeting include:

1. Forecasting cash inflows.
2. Forecasting expenses.
3. Recording transactions.
4. Controlling expenses.

The first two items combined provide the **forecasted budget**. Prior to getting started on budgeting, a suitable budgeting period needs to be established. For most people, budgeting on a monthly basis is best because expenses generally occur on a monthly basis. However, some people may find it easier to budget on a twice-a-month basis. Those who have few expense categories may get by with setting up budgets on a once-every-other-month basis. Keep in mind that the budget needs to be simple and should reflect the income and expense habits of the family.

Forecasting Cash Inflows

Some **cash inflow** sources are obvious. Wages, dividends, and interest income can all be estimated easily. However, other sources of inflows should not be overlooked. Fees, scholarships, grants, gifts, loans, income tax refunds, sickness benefits, strike benefits, and social security benefits are other possible sources of cash inflows.

Table 5.1 shows Statement 1: Forecasting Cash Inflows for the Dardens. The forecast is for the year beginning January 1989. The first row is wages, which are shown to be $1,600 per month for the first six months. Wages are expected to rise to $1,730 per month during the last six months because of an anticipated salary increase. The last column shows the yearly total of $19,980 for wages. Interest income is from a money market mutual fund and is received monthly. Dividends are received quarterly on 100 shares of stock. An income tax refund of $440 is expected in April. The Dardens plan to hold a garage sale in August and expect to sell about $200 worth of items. The last row shows monthly inflow totals. For example, the total

for January is $1,690. All entries in the last row and in the last column sum to $21,380. If the last row and the last column sums are not the same, then one or more errors have been made in adding up the rows and columns.

When you prepare a **cash inflow forecast**, you should err on the conservative side. That is, if you are unsure about an estimate, then use a lower estimate. Cash inflows should be entered only for the months in which they are to be realized. The sources shown in Table 5.1 can be adjusted to suit a family's particular needs.

Forecasting Expenses

Forecasting expenses is more complex than forecasting cash inflows because there are more expense categories. Figure 5 1 shows the major categories and subcategories of expense items. As the figure shows, expenses can be classified as either fixed or variable, and some expenses have both fixed and variable portions.

Table 5.1   Statement 1: Forecasting Cash Inflows

Name _Dardens_   Forecast for (year) _1989_

Source	Jan	Feb	Mar	Apr	May	June	July	Aug	Sept	Oct	Nov	Dec	Yearly Totals
Wages Take-home	1,600	1,600	1,600	1,600	1,600	1,600	1,730	1,730	1,730	1,730	1,730	1,730	19,980
Interest income	50	50	50	50	50	50	50	50	50	50	50	50	600
Dividends	40			40			40			40			160
Income tax refund				440									440
Loans													
Commissions													
Other								200					200
Totals	1,690	1,650	1,650	2,130	1,650	1,650	1,820	1,980	1,780	1,820	1,780	1,780	21,380

Figure 5.1 Major Budget Expense Items

FIXED EXPENSES

Housing
Rent or mortgage

Transportation
Installment payment

Taxes
Property taxes
Other taxes

Loans, Credit
Installment loan payment
Credit card

Insurance
Property insurance
Car insurance and
registration
Life insurance
Health insurance

Savings and Investment
Investment fund
Vacation fund

VARIABLE EXPENSES

Housing
Repairs
Improvements

Transportation
Gas, oil
Repairs, parking
Public transportation

Food
At home
Restaurants

Utilities
Gas or oil
Electricity
Telephone
Water, sewer

Household, Personal
Housekeeping supplies
Toiletries, cosmetics
Barber, hairdresser
Postage, paper, pens

Pocket Money
Father
Mother
Children

Gifts

Clothing
Father
Mother
Children
Repairs, etc.

Medical, Dental
Drugs, medicines
Doctors' bills
Hospital

Recreation, Entertainment
Alcoholic beverages
Pet foods
Tobacco
Sporting goods
Music, albums
Camera, film
Miscellaneous
Books, newspapers,
magazines

Education
Books, supplies
Tuition

Charities

Red Bread

Miscellaneous

Fixed Expenses. All **fixed expenses** tend to be variable over the long run. However, for the one-year budgeting horizon, these expenses can be viewed as fixed. Housing expenses can be either rent or mortgage payments. Installment payments on a car loan are also fixed. Notice that the budget deals only with cash inflows and cash expenses. Therefore, the purchase price of the car is not shown on the budget. In the insurance category, car insurance and registration are shown together. Since insurance is usually paid only once or twice a year and the car is registered only once a year, the two expenses have been lumped together for convenience.

Savings and investments are also shown as fixed expenses. It is important to recognize that most people must force themselves to save. If savings and investments were not viewed as fixed budgeted expenses, a person would tend not to save.

Forecasting Fixed Expenses. Fixed expenses are relatively easy to forecast. Contractual obligations often determine the size of a fixed expense. Table 5.2 shows Statement 2: Forecasting Fixed Expenses.

Table 5.2 Statement 2: Forecasting Fixed Expenses

Name _Dardens_   Forecast for (year) _1989_

Expense	Jan	Feb	Mar	Apr	May	June	July	Aug	Sept	Oct	Nov	Dec	Yearly Totals
Housing Mortgage	350	350	350	350	350	350	350	350	350	350	350	350	4,200
Transportation Installment	160	160	160	160	160	160	160	160	160	160	160	160	1,920
Taxes Property								380	380				760
Other													
Loans Installment	40	40	40	40	40	40	40	40	40	40	40	40	480
Cr. Card	60	60	60	60	60	60	60	60	60	60	60	60	720
Insurance Property		330											330
Car, regis.						40			120	120			280
Life					130						130		260
Health													
Savings Investment	150	150	150	150	150	150	150	150	150	150	150	150	1,800
Vacation	100	100	100	100	100	100	100	100	100	100	100	100	1,200
Totals	860	1,190	860	860	990	900	860	1,240	1,360	980	990	860	11,950

Mortgage payments on principal and interest are $350 per month, for a yearly total of $4,200. Car payments are $160 per month. The other entries are self-evident. The payment patterns for some items, such as property taxes, property insurance, car insurance, and life insurance, are contractually determined. They cannot be shifted forward or backward during the planning period. Thus, for example, the September property tax of $380 cannot be shifted to October to smooth out the expenses. Notice that savings-investment is treated as a fixed expense. The sum of $150 per month is budgeted for investing.

The last column shows annual totals for each expense category. The last row shows monthly totals for all expense categories. Total fixed expenses for January are forecasted to be $860. The sum of the last row entries and that of the last column entries is $11,950.

Variable Expenses.   **Variable expenses** vary from month to month. Unlike fixed expenses, these expenses can be controlled and managed to some extent. Figure 5.1 lists major categories of variable expenses. The variable portions of housing and transportation expenses show up here. The "red bread" expense category, which lends flexibility to the budget, is listed as a variable expense. Gifts, charities, and miscellaneous expenses may or may not be part of a person's budget. Items such as lawyer's fees, union dues, losses due to thefts, and noncategorized expenses can be listed in the miscellaneous section. Depending on a family's needs, the list of variable expenses can be expanded or contracted.

Forecasting Variable Expenses.   Variable expenses can be more difficult to forecast than fixed expenses. At times it is helpful to go back and review your checkbook register to identify most of the variable expense categories and the anticipated expenses. Table 5.3 shows Statement 3: Forecasting Variable Expenses.

The expense categories shown in Table 5.3 are based on the list in Figure 5.1. Transportation is expected to be $60 every month, except for August, when the Dardens plan to go on vacation, and for December, when they plan to commute less. The total annual budgeted amount for gas and oil is $760. Repairs and maintenance do not occur every month. However, the Dardens budget $20 every month. This $20 accumulated for three or four months allows them to have routine maintenance performed. Recreation includes most of the items listed under "Recreation" in Figure 5.1. The Dardens choose not to make separate forecasts for the subcategories of recreation. "Red bread" is the expense category that allows the Dardens flexibility in their budget. Deficit spending in some expense categories will be covered by money from the red bread category.

The January total is $905. The yearly total is $9,440. The fixed expenses from Table 15.2 are $11,950. Total annual expenses are $11,950 + $9,440 = $21,390. This amount equals the cash inflow amount shown in Table 5.1. The inflows and outflows must balance. In reality, what the Dardens

Table 5.3　Statement 3: Forecasting Variable Expenses

Name _Dardens_　　　　　　　　Forecast for (year) _1989_

Expense	Jan	Feb	Mar	Apr	May	June	July	Aug	Sept	Oct	Nov	Dec	Yearly Totals
Housing									100				100
Transportation Gas, oil	60	60	60	60	60	60	60	120	60	60	60	40	760
Repairs	20	20	20	20	20	20	20	20	20	20	20	20	240
Food At home	150	150	150	150	150	150	150	40	150	150	150	150	1,690
Restaurant	30	30	30	30	30	30	30	300	30	30	30	30	630
Utilities Gas	150	150	150	100						200	100	150	1,000
Electricity	30	30	30	30	50	90	120	60	60	30	30	30	590
Phone	30	30	30	30	30	30	30	20	30	30	30	40	360
Water, sewer	20	20	20	20	20	30	30	30	20	20	20	20	270
Household Supplies	15	15	15	15	15	15	15	15	15	15	15	15	180
Toiletries	20	20	20	20	20	20	20	20	20	20	20	20	·240
Misc.	30	30	30	30	30	30	30	30	30	30	30	30	360
Pocket money	30	30	30	30	30	30	30	30	30	30	30	30	360
Clothing	200				200			260					660
Medical Drugs	10	10	10	10	10	10	10	10	10	10	10	10	120
Doctor	20	20	20	20	20	20	20	20	20	20	20	20	240
Recreation	40	40	40	40	40	40	40	40	40	40	40	40	480
Education													
Gifts					100							200	300
Charities												200	200
Red bread	50	50	50	50	50	50	60	60	60	60	60	60	660
Misc.													
Totals	905	705	705	655	875	625	665	1,075	695	765	665	1,105	9,440

have done is determine how much money they have left for meeting variable expenses. This amount of $9,440 is then logically distributed over the various expense categories in Table 5.3. The Dardens did this because Table 5.3 entries represent controllable costs.

Some families prefer to prepare a preliminary Statement 3. If forecasted expenses are greater than the amount left over to meet variable expenses, then Statement 3 figures are carefully adjusted downward. For example, the Dardens' preliminary forecast might have shown variable expenses of $10,500. Selected cuts would then have been made in the budget to reduce the total to $9,440. If forecasted expenses are less than the amount available to meet variable expenses, then the investments in Table 5.2 are increased accordingly. For example, if the Dardens had variable expenses of $8,760, they would increase the amount of investments in Table 5.2 by $9,440 − $8,760 = $680. Finally, for families with few expense categories, all forecasted expenses could be easily listed on one statement.

The forecasts for cash inflows and expenses provide the budget. This section has shown how a budget can be prepared. The next section deals with recording transactions and controlling expenses.

Spot Quiz • The Budgeting Process

1. Statements 2 and 3 can be combined into one if a family does not have many expense categories. T _____ F _____

2. Fixed expenses remain fixed for many years. T _____ F _____

3. Forecasted cash inflows can actually change over time.
T _____ F _____

(Answers on page 153)

CONTROLLING EXPENSES

Once the forecasted budget has been established, the next step is to set up procedures for recording and controlling expenses.

Recording Expenses

An **Expense Record Book** should be used for recording expenses. A looseleaf binder works well as an expense record book. Those fixed and variable expenses that occur only once a month or less frequently should be entered directly onto Statement 4: Budget Control Sheet (discussed later). Expenses that are incurred more than once a month should each have a separate page in the Expense Record Book.

For the expenses listed in Table 5.3, the Dardens believe that Transportation—Gas, oil; Food—At home; Household—Supplies; Household—Toiletries; Household—Misc.; and Recreation expenses will be incurred more than once a month. Thus, they have set up separate pages for these expense categories in the Expense Record Book. Figure 5.2 shows these pages.

Table 5.4 shows the Expense Record Page for the Dardens' Food—At home expense category. The 1/1/89 beginning balance is the budgeted amount of $150. At the end of January, $157 has been spent on groceries, leaving a negative balance of $7. On 2/1/89, $150 is added, giving a cumulative balance of $143. Expenses of $138 in February leave a cumulative balance of $5.

Figure 5.2   Expense Record Book: Sample Pages

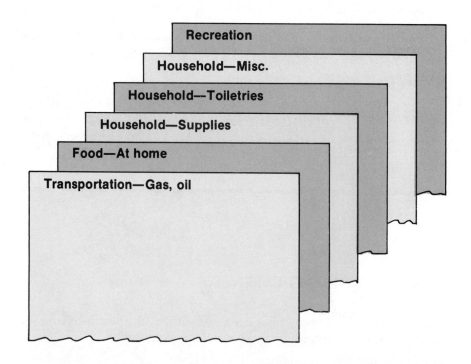

Table 5.4 Expense Record Page—Food at Home

Date	Item	Amount Spent	Monthly Total	Cumulative Balance
1/1/89	Beginning	—		$150
1/5/89	Groceries	42	—	108
1/12/89	"	37	—	71
1/21/89	"	40	—	31
1/28/89	"	38	$157	−7
2/1/89	Beginning	—	—	143
2/5/89	Groceries	32	—	111
2/14/89	"	30	—	81
2/21/89	"	35	—	46
2/28/89	"	41	138	5
3/1/89	Beginning	—	—	155

At the end of each month, the monthly totals and the cumulative balances from the Expense Record Book are posted on Statement 4: Budget Control Sheet (Table 5.5). A few important factors about expense records need to be emphasized. First, expenses should be promptly recorded. If expenses are not recorded quickly, they may be ignored. Thus, although money has been spent, it will not show up as an expense, and there will be problems in reconciling income, expenses, and money left over. Second, generally the person who incurs the expense should record it. Finally, if an item is purchased on credit rather than paid for in cash, then the expense should be entered immediately. Some people wait until the charge is due before recording it, but this procedure can lead to deficit spending in some expense categories.

Controlling Expenses

The final step in the budgeting process is controlling expenses. Statement 4: **Budget Control Sheet**, shown in Table 5.5, is utilized for this purpose. Because fixed expenses, by definition, remain fixed for the year and payments occur once a month or less frequently, there generally is no need to prepare a Budget Control Sheet for them. Table 5.5, therefore, shows only the variable expense items.

Table 5.5 Statement 4: Budget Control Sheet

Name _Dardens_   Year __1989__

Expense	January			February			March			April			Adjustment
	Cum budget	Actual	+ or -	Cum budget	Actual	+ or -	Cum budget	Actual	+ or -	Cum budget	Actual	+ or -	
Housing													
Transportation Gas, oil	60	58	2	62	55	7	67	65	2	62	63	-1	
Repairs	20	0	20	40	0	40	60	0	60	80	86	-6	
Food At home	150	157	-7	143	138	5	155	158	-3	147	141	6	
Restaurant	30	10	20	50	42	8	38	45	-7	23	15	8	
Utilities Gas	150	160	-10	140	170	-30	120	170	-50	150	105	45	100
Electricity	30	35	-5	25	35	-10	20	32	-12	33	29	4	15
Phone	30	18	12	42	23	19	49	45	4	34	31	3	
Water, sewer	20	18	2	22	18	4	24	20	4	24	23	1	
Household Supplies	15	20	-5	10	0	10	25	22	3	18	16	2	
Toiletries	20	30	-10	10	8	2	22	18	4	24	18	6	
Misc.	30	15	15	45	5	40	70	20	50	20	10	10	-60
Pocket money	30	30	0	30	30	0	30	30	0	30	30	0	
Clothing	200	160	40	40	60	-20	-20	0	-20	-20	0	-20	
Medical Drugs	10	7	3	13	6	7	17	21	-4	6	8	-2	
Doctor	20	0	20	40	20	20	40	38	2	22	0	22	
Recreation	40	60	-20	20	20	0	40	40	0	40	45	-5	
Education													
Gifts													
Charities													
Red bread	50	0	50	100	0	100	150	0	150	145	0	145	-55
Misc.													
Totals	905	778	127	832	630	202	907	724	183	838	620	218	0

The expense entries in Table 5.5 are the same as in Table 5.3. Three columns are shown for each. The first is titled "Cumulative Budget." For January, the forecasted variable expenses from Table 5.3 are entered in column 1. The second column is titled "Actual." The actual expenses incurred during the month are recorded in this column. In the Dardens' case, some expenses, such as utilities and medical expenses, occur once a month or less frequently. These expenses are recorded directly on the Budget Control Sheet. Other expenses, such as Food—At home and Household—Supplies are incurred more than once a month and are entered in the Expense Record Book first. Once a month these expenses are transferred from the Expense Record Book to the Budget Control Sheet.

The third column for each month is titled "+ or −." A surplus is indicated by the + symbol, and the − indicates a deficit. The actual expenses are deducted from the budgeted amount to find the surplus or deficit. If the budgeted amount is larger than the actual amount, a surplus results. More spending than the budgeted amount results in a deficit.

The January budgeted amount for the Dardens for Food—At home was $150. Actual expenses were $157, producing a deficit of $7. For February, the budgeted amount is $150. From this $7 is subtracted to give a February cumulative budget of $143. February expenses are $138, leaving a surplus of $143 − $138 = $5. Notice that the cumulative budget, the actual expense, and the surplus or deficit can be readily transferred from the Expense Record Book.

The January budget was $905. Actual expenses were $778, leaving a surplus of $127. This surplus does not necessarily mean that the family did not spend enough. Some expense items are designed to accumulate large surpluses so that periodic large expenses can be paid for. For example, the Transportation—Repairs category accumulated $80 in four months for a repair or maintenance job in April.

Spot Quiz • Controlling Expenses

1. An Expense Record Page should be maintained for all expense items.
   T _____   F _____

2. It is not necessary for budgeted and actual expenses to be equal.
   T _____   F _____

(Answers on page 154)

Maintaining budgeting flexibility

Some families prefer budgets that are not flexible. They prefer not to see any deficits in the "+ or –" column. By forcing actual expenses to be no more than budgeted expenses, they can control costs and achieve financial goals. Unfortunately, such rigid budgeting generally leads to tension and disharmony in the family. Budgeting needs to be flexible for a variety of reasons. A family could underestimate expenses. Thereafter, it would be very difficult to keep actual expenses in line with the budgeted amounts. Family members may feel that they are being asked to make unreasonable sacrifices just for the sake of balancing the budget. Unanticipated inflation can also lead to higher-than-expected expenses. In this section we discuss flexibility in budgeting. (See "The Ballad of the Painless Dentist" below.)

Reevaluating the Original Budget

Periodically, perhaps every three or four months, the original forecasted figures should be reviewed. For the Dardens, for example, Statement 1 should be reviewed in June or July to see whether the actual salary raise is different from the forecasted increase. A logical revision can be made in July.

Sometimes the family situation changes. For example, a son or daughter may decide to live away from home or a nonworking spouse may decide to start working full- or part-time. Both income and expense forecasts

The Ballad of The Painless Dentist

Mom and Dad took their young son to a new dentist because they had heard that she was a painless dentist, meaning that she could treat their child without putting him through much trauma. The child emerged from the dentist's office with a sad face and told his parents, "She wasn't a painless dentist; she screamed just like the rest of them when I bit her finger."

Many consumers tend to view their budgets as painless dentists. They set up budgeting systems to curb their spending habits and to ease the strain on family finances. However, when they bite the dentist's finger—that is, overspend in certain expense categories—then the dentist/budget screams. Don't bite the dentist! Instead, build some flexibility into the budget. Review your budget periodically and revise it as needed.

should be revised when family conditions change unless the change is expected to be temporary. For instance, if income levels are expected to increase temporarily, expenditure patterns should not be changed. Rather, the extra income should be viewed as extraordinary funds for investments.

At times it might be difficult to forecast food, gas, and utilities expenses because of inflation. When inflation makes it difficult to stay within budgeted amounts, that is a good time to reevaluate the budget.

Flexible Budgeting

The budgeting system presented in this chapter is flexible. The last column in Table 5.5, titled "Adjustments," is designed to allow for periodic adjustments in the various expense categories. The "Red bread" expense category is what allows this flexibility. This expense category permits a $50 to $60 monthly variation in the budget.

Table 5.5 shows that in the Utilities—Gas account, the Dardens are exceeding their budget. The cumulative deficit by March is $50. Clearly, the Dardens underestimated gas expenses. The amount budgeted for April, as shown in Table 5.3, was $100. The actual expenses for April were $105. Without flexible budgeting, the April entries would have been

Cumulative Budget	Actual	+ or −
50	105	−55

The first entry would be $100 − $50 = $50. The last entry would be $50 − $105 = $−55. As it turns out, the Dardens shifted $100 from the Red bread account to gas. Thus, the cumulative budget amount becomes $50 + $100 = $150, and the surplus is $150 − $105 = $45. The adjustment column shows this $100 transfer to the Utilities—Gas expense category.

Other adjustments in Table 5.5 are a transfer of $15 to the Utilities—Electricity category and a transfer of $60 out of the Household—Miscellaneous account. All these adjustments are to the Red bread account. The adjustment for the Red bread account is

Transfer to Utilities—Gas	$100
Transfer to Utilities—Electricity	15
Total transfers out	$115
Transfer from Household—Miscellaneous	60
Net transfer out	$ 55

The April cumulative budget amount for Red bread becomes $200 − $55 = $145. Note that no expenditures actually take place in the Red bread account. Funds are only transferred in or out.

The budget planner should include an "Adjustment" column on the Budget Control Sheet every three or four months. Adjustments to the budgets can then be made a few times a year. Under this system the original forecasts do not need to be changed at all. All adjustments can be handled directly on the Budget Control Sheet. The simplicity of the system permits flexible budgeting without the investment of a great deal of time.

Spot Quiz • Maintaining Budgeting Flexibility

1. Budgets are cast in concrete, never to be changed.

                                              T _____   F _____

2. Sometimes differences between budgeted amounts and actual expenses are beyond the control of the family.   T _____   F _____

(Answers on page 154)

Summary

Budgeting is a system of record keeping that allows you to plan for expenses. Budgeting helps us understand the nature of our expenses so that we can control the expenses better. Better control of expenses improves the quality of living. Budgeting is also needed to cope with inflation.

Each member of the family should understand why budgeting is needed. Both spouses should be actively involved in managing the budget. To the extent possible, all family members should have a voice in how the family income is spent.

The first step in budgeting is forecasting cash inflows. Next, fixed expenses are forecasted. Forecasting variable expenses requires more attention to detail. Frequently incurred expenses should be recorded in an Expense Record Book as soon as they are incurred. The budget is controlled by comparing actual expenses with forecasted expenses.

The budgeting system used should be simple and flexible. Flexibility allows the budget managers to adjust to factors such as changing family conditions and inflation.

Questions

1. What is meant by budgeting?

2. What are the advantages of budgeting? Explain briefly.

3. Explain how budgeting can help a family cope with inflation.

4. Critique this statement: "Budgeting is a necessity, not a luxury."

5. Should the wage earner in the family also be the budget manager? Why or why not?

6. What is meant by noneconomic spending? What effect does such spending have on the quality of life?

7. How can the family be involved in the budgeting process?

8. Why should budgets be simple?

9. List the steps involved in the budgeting process.

10. What is meant by fixed expenses? Give three examples of fixed expenses.

11. Are variable expenses easier to forecast than fixed expenses? Explain your answer.

12. What purpose does an Expense Record Book serve in the budgeting process?

13. Briefly explain a procedure that can be used for controlling expenses.

14. Why is it important to maintain budget flexibility?

15. How often and why should a budget be reevaluated? Explain.

16. Explain the "red bread" procedure for maintaining budgeting flexibility.

Case Problems

1. The Prasad family has two wage earners. Both spouses are engineers working in Pittsburgh. Their joint take-home income is $3,100 per month. In June, their take-home income is expected to increase to

$3,400 per month. They also expect to receive $100 per month in interest income. They expect a tax refund of $1,200 in April. They have loaned money to a relative, who is making loan repayments of $110 each month. Prepare a cash inflow forecast for the Prasads for the January–December period.

2. The Prasads pay $750 each month in mortgage and real estate taxes payments. They are paying $270 per month on a car. Their credit card payments average $200 per month. A property insurance payment of $510 is due in October, and a car insurance payment of $600 is due in April. Health insurance is provided free of charge by their employers. They plan to save $300 per month and are putting away $160 per month for a vacation. Forecast their fixed expenses for January through June.

3. From the data provided in Case Problems 1 and 2, show how much money the Prasads would have left over each month for meeting variable expenses. Show your answer for the January–December period.

4. Lisa Argent teaches in a junior college and is paid on a nine-month basis. For January through June her take-home income is $1,900. She is expecting a 5 percent increase in her take-home pay for October through December. She does not receive a salary for July, August, and September. Her husband, Jim Argent, works as a real estate sales agent and averages about $1,200 per month in take-home commissions. The Argents receive about $150 per month in income from a money market mutual fund. They own stock in a company that pays them quarterly dividends of $50 in March, June, September, and December. They expect a tax refund of $400 in May. Prepare a cash inflow forecast for the Argents for the January–December period. What factors should the Argents take into consideration when they analyze their cash inflow statement?

5. The Argents pay $700 per month in mortgage payments. Other house-related expenses (real estate taxes, utilities, and so on) average $300 per month. Other monthly expenses are as follows: automobile, $210; home equity loan, $200; vacation fund, $150; savings, $200; property insurance, $50. Prepare a monthly forecast of fixed expenses for the year for the Argents.

6. Based on Case Problems 4 and 5, what is the maximum amount that the Argents can spend each month on their variable expenses? What advice do you have for the Argents?

Bibliography

"One Family's Budgeting Plan." *Changing Times* (July 1977): 43–47.

"Where Does All the Money Go?" *Consumer Reports* (September 1986): 581–591.

"How to Stop Family Fights Over Money." *Good Housekeeping* (May 1978): 65.

"What Are You Really Fighting About When You Fight About Money?" *Ladies Home Journal* (August 1978): 31.

"How to Set Up a Budget Your Family Can Live With." *McCall's* (September 1978): 64.

"Some Advice From the Friedmans." *Money* (May 1980): 58–60.

"Personal Budgeting for Hard Times." *Money* (May 1982): 157–167.

"Where the Money Goes." *Parents Magazine* (December 1978): 98–101.

Answers to Spot Quizzes

Planning for Budgeting (page 136)

1. F (All families need to budget.)

2. F (All family members should be involved in the budgeting process.)

3. T (A simple budget is highly desirable.)

The Budgeting Process (page 143)

1. T (It is more convenient this way.)

2. F (They can change under certain circumstances.)

3. T (For example, the Dardens' raise may be lower than expected.)

Controlling Expenses (page 147)

1. F (Some expenses are not incurred often enough to justify a separate Expense Record Page.)

2. T (Forcing actual expenses to equal budgeting expenses can lead to budgeting that is too rigid.)

Maintaining Budgeting Flexibility (page 150)

1. F (Budgets can and should be revised.)

2. T (Some expenses are greatly affected by the economy or the government.)

Chapter 6

Managing Liquid Assets

Objectives

After reading this chapter you will be able to:

- Discuss the factors to consider in choosing a bank.
- Explain the various types of checking accounts available.
- Describe how checks are processed between banks.
- Prepare a checking account reconciliation.
- Tell why most people need a savings account as well as a checking account.
- Explain the difference between nominal and effective interest rates.
- Describe various kinds of savings institutions, and explain the differences among them.

Peggy Bateman of Fort Lauderdale, Florida, has not been inside a bank for over a year now. This does not mean that she does not use banking services. Quite the contrary—she uses her bank's services often. But she is willing to use the electronic banking services that her bank offers. For example, she can use her push-button telephone to call her bank and electronically order the bank computer to pay her bills. Similarly, she can go to a convenience store and use a machine called an automatic teller to make deposits, obtain cash, and complete other banking transactions.[1]

Is electronic banking something that might persuade you to open an account at a particular bank? Or would you choose a bank based on the interest rate it pays on your checking account? People who expect high interest rates on their checking accounts would not have their accounts at banks. Rather, they would deposit their money in money market mutual funds, which are designed to allow fund owners to write checks against their deposits. Keeping money in money market mutual funds may be somewhat nontraditional. More traditional is opening and maintaining a checking account at a bank or any other financial institution. Before opening a checking account, you will need to understand the different types of checking accounts and other services offered by different financial institutions.

Cash, checking accounts, money market mutual funds, and savings accounts are called liquid assets. The term **liquid assets** means that these funds are readily converted into cash. This chapter deals with methods of managing liquid assets.

THE NEED FOR LIQUID ASSETS

In their daily lives, consumers shop for food, pay rent, pay utility bills, make payments on charge accounts, buy clothing, and pay for other incidental and planned expenses. Most people will pay cash for some of these expenses. However, for many of these payments, the average person will write a check. Typically, rent, utilities, food, and other planned expenditures are paid for by check. Making payments by check is convenient because large sums of cash need not be carried around. In addition to convenience, the use of checks also provides a method for keeping track of various types of expenses. Checks, when they are cashed by the **payee** (the person to whom the check is made out), constitute proof that payment was made.

The convenience and record-keeping aspects of checks appeal to most consumers. To write checks, you need to have a checking account at a financial institution. A regular checking account at a bank is called a **demand deposit account** because it allows the account owner to withdraw funds on demand. When a valid check is presented to a bank for collection, the

---

1. "The Glories and Glitches of Electronic Banking," *Money* (March 1980): 103.

bank is required to honor the check immediately and to pay the amount of the check—provided, of course, that the account contains sufficient funds.

Banks and savings and loan associations also offer interest-bearing checking accounts called **negotiable orders of withdrawal**, or **NOW accounts**. Typically, NOW accounts pay interest at about the same rate as regular savings accounts. Credit unions offer checking accounts called **share draft** accounts.

Some types of planned expenditures occur infrequently. For example, some homeowners may pay property taxes every six months. These homeowners do not need to have money sitting in checking accounts for six months before paying their property taxes. For them, a more desirable alternative would be to keep the money in a **savings** or **time deposit account**. Savings accounts allow the account owner to receive interest on deposits.

A time deposit account may be maintained at financial institutions such as banks, savings and loan associations, and credit unions. Savings account institutions need not honor a withdrawal request immediately, but in practice most of them do. That is, the law does not require that immediate payment be made on a savings account withdrawal. The institution may, at its option, wait for a specified number of days before honoring the savings account withdrawal. Most times, though, institutions go ahead and pay immediately unless the amount to be withdrawn is very large.

Savings accounts are more desirable than checking accounts when payments are relatively infrequent and large. A family may choose to keep money in a savings account pending the purchase of a car. This way the family earns interest on its money until it is spent. Many people also keep cash in a savings account for emergencies. The possibility of emergency automobile and home repairs, for example, may lead some consumers to maintain a savings account. Alternatives to checking and savings accounts are money market mutual funds, certificates of deposit (CDs), and savings bonds. These topics are discussed in detail in later sections.

Spot Quiz • The Need for Liquid Assets

1. A bank is not required to pay a valid check drawn on a demand deposit account immediately.   T _____   F _____

2. Most consumers find it useful for managing money to maintain a checking account as well as a savings account.   T _____   F _____

(Answers on page 198)

TYPES OF CHECKING ACCOUNTS

Most financial institutions offer a variety of checking accounts with different benefits and service costs. From a legal viewpoint, there is a distinction between a demand deposit account, a NOW account, and a share draft account. From a practical viewpoint, however, the consumer needs to be concerned only with the costs and the benefits of these alternative accounts. The same types of accounts are available at most financial institutions under different names. The most common types of account are activity, minimum checking balance, minimum savings balance, free, and special package. These accounts are described in the following section, and their characteristics are summarized in Table 6.1

Activity Account

For an **activity account**, the institution charges fees based on the use of the account. Typically, an institution will charge around $1 as a monthly account service fee. In addition, the institution will charge 8 to 15 cents each time a check is written and processed on the account, and 10 to 15 cents each time a deposit is made into the account. For example, Ms. Arrigo maintains an activity checking account at a bank that charges a $1 per month service fee, 10 cents per check, and 15 cents per deposit. In a recent month, Ms. Arrigo wrote nine checks and made two deposits. Her service charge for the month would be:

Service fee	$1.00
Nine checks at 10 cents each	0.90
Two deposits at 15 cents each	0.30
Total service charge	$2.20

Activity accounts are more desirable for people who do not write checks very frequently.

Minimum Balance Checking Account

In a **minimum balance checking account**, the institution requires the account owner to keep a specified dollar amount in the account at all times.

Table 6.1 Checking Account Types and Costs

Account	Minimum Balance	Appropriate Service Charges	Special Services
1. Activity	None	Maintenance fee $1.00 per month; 8¢ to 15¢ per check; 10¢ to 15¢ per deposit	None
2. Minimum checking balance	$200 to $600	None	None
3. Minimum savings balance	$300 to $700	None	None
4. Free	None	None	None
5. Special package	None	$1.50 to $5.00 per month	Safe deposit box, lower interest rate, and others

For instance, Mr. Coracy's bank requires him to maintain at least $200 in his checking account at all times. In any given month, if Mr. Coracy does not let his account balance drop below $200, he does not have to pay any service fees.

Some institutions require that the account owner maintain an absolute minimum balance in the checking account. If at any time the balance falls below the minimum, the institution imposes a service fee of $4 to $6. Mr. Coracy, for example, must pay a $5 service fee if his account balance drops below $200 in any given month.

Other institutions, rather than requiring an absolute minimum balance, require that account holders maintain an average minimum balance. Say that an institution requires an *average* minimum balance of $200. An account owner would not be assessed service fees as long as days when the balance is below $200 are offset by days when the balance is higher than $200. Thus, 15 days of $100 balances can be offset by 15 days of $300 balances or 9 days of $500 balances. In each case the calculations are:

$$(15 \times \$100) + (15 \times \$300) = \$6,000$$
$$(15 \times \$100) + (9 \times \$500) = \$6,000$$

In both cases the average balance is $6,000/30 days = $200 per day.

A minimum balance account appears to be free but is not because the account owner loses interest on the minimum balance required. At an interest rate of 5 percent, Mr. Coracy's account costs him $200 × .05 = $10 per year. In general, minimum balance accounts are very desirable for people who write large numbers of checks every month.

Minimum Savings Balance Account

With a **minimum savings balance account**, the institution requires the checking account owner to maintain a minimum balance in a savings account. As long as this minimum savings balance is maintained, the institution does not charge any fees for the checking account. Typical minimum balance requirements range from $300 to $700. The institution will assess a checking account service fee of $4 to $6 if the customer lets the savings account balance fall below the minimum level.

This type of account is advantageous for the customer because the institution pays interest on the minimum savings balance. The disadvantage is that the customer may be giving up a higher-earning alternative to the savings account. However, this type of account is generally more desirable than the minimum checking balance type of account.

Free Checking Account

A **free checking account** is exactly that. The customer does not pay service charges of any kind on the checking account. Free checking is very popular in large cities where institutions must compete for customers. This is by far the best type of checking account for most people. Some savings and loans offer non-interest-paying NOW accounts that have no service charges and no minimum balance requirements.

Special Package

Many institutions offer a checking account as part of a special package of financial services. An institution may offer such services as checking, a charge card, a safe deposit box, free cashier's checks, free traveler's checks, free money orders, and lower rates on loans for a package charge that may be $4 to $6 per month.

A special package may be desirable for people who were planning to use the package services anyway. For example, the Smiths are trying to decide whether a special package offered from a bank is suitable for their needs. The package includes checking, a safe deposit box, free traveler's

checks, and a loan rate that is 1 percent below regular rates. The bank also offers free checking. The Smiths had planned to rent a safe deposit box for an annual fee of $20. They travel once or twice a year and usually pay a fee of about $30 for traveler's checks that they buy. Every three years they buy a new car and finance it through a bank. On the average, they pay $200 annually in interest charges on the car loan. The 1 percent lower rate will save them about $20 per year in interest expense. Is the special package suitable for the Smiths if it costs $5 per month ($60 per year)? By using this package, the Smiths will save $20 + $30 + $20 − $60 = $10 annually. Clearly, the package is better than free checking for them.

Many people do not use all the services that are typically available in special packages. But for others, a package account is desirable.

Selecting an Account

Of the accounts just described, the best for most persons is free checking. It has no restrictive requirements, such as minimum balances, nor does it involve any service charges. If free checking is not available, then the desirability of the other plans depends on the number of checks being written and account requirements. People who require special financial services may find the special package account suitable for their needs. People who rarely write checks but want to maintain a checking account may prefer to go with the activity account.

Most financial institutions offer interest-bearing minimum balance checking accounts in the form of NOW accounts. These accounts are equivalent to minimum savings balance accounts. An interest-bearing NOW account or a minimum savings balance account may be desirable for people who write checks frequently.

Spot Quiz • Types of Checking Accounts

1. The activity account is desirable for people with very active checking accounts.   T _____ F _____

2. From the customer's viewpoint, average minimum balance checking requirements are better than absolute minimum balance checking requirements.   T _____ F _____

3. Free checking is always better than all other types of accounts.
                                                      T _____ F _____

(Answers on page 198)

Opening and Using a Checking Account

Opening a checking account is simple, but the process of selecting a financial institution requires research and comparison. Once you have chosen an institution and opened an account, you need to follow proper check-writing procedures.

Selecting an Institution

In recent years the competition among financial institutions has become intense. As a result, more services and new services are being offered to customers. When you select an institution, convenience in conducting financial transactions is very important. You should also consider the personalities and friendliness of the institution's employees. (See "People Make People Switch Banks" on page 163.) The types of services that the institution offers should be evaluated as well. For example, if you do not have time to go to the bank during weekdays, you might want to choose a bank that is open evenings and weekends. The cost of financial services and lending rates should also be evaluated.

Opening a Checking Account

Once you have selected an institution, you will go to its new account department. There you will be asked to fill out an information sheet. This sheet provides the institution with your name, address, workplace, occupation, and certain other details. Next, you will sign one or two signature cards in exactly the same way as your signature would appear on a check. (The **signature cards** are occasionally used to verify a customer's signature on a check.) Upon depositing some money into the checking account, you will be provided with some temporary checks. After a few days (or weeks), you will receive personalized checks, which will have your name printed on them.

A checking account can be either a single account or a joint account. A **single account** is in the name of one person only. A **joint account** is in the name of two or more persons. One type of joint account requires that all account owners sign a check for the check to be valid. Another type of joint account allows either account owner to sign a check. This type of account is popular with couples because it allows either partner to issue a valid check.

People Make People Switch Banks

An industry survey of customers of banks and thrift institutions in several cities revealed that deficiencies in the institutions' human relations and personal service caused respondents to change institutions more often than did interest rates or loan costs. Of those people who switched institutions, 19 percent did so because of errors in their accounts, 16 percent because of poor service, 13 percent because of rude or unhelpful employees, 11 percent because of cold or impersonal service. Only 12 percent switched to get higher interest rates on savings and 8 percent to get free checking.

Free checking was by far the most desired of six banking services rated. Next, in order of preference, were drive-in banking, evening and Saturday hours, cash machines, automatic loan arrangements, and free credit cards.

According to the report, 82 percent of the respondents recognize that the different kinds of institutions pay different rates on savings accounts (thrifts are permitted to pay slightly higher interest rates on savings than commercial banks). The report also revealed that most people deal with several types of institutions. Commercial banks have more customers than any other type, but their share of patrons dips slightly in areas that also have savings banks. Overall, 86 to 98 percent of those surveyed use commercial banks, 44 to 77 percent use savings banks, 37 percent use savings and loans, and 30 percent use credit unions.

Source: *Changing Times*, October 1978, p. 36. Reprinted with permission from *Changing Times* Magazine, © Kiplinger Washington Editors, Inc. 1978. This reprint is not to be altered in any way, except with permission from *Changing Times*.

Writing Checks

Checks should be written clearly in indelible ink. Five important items should be written in on a check. First, the date should be written on the check. A good practice is to date the check for the day on which the check is written. A check dated ahead of the day the check was written is called a **postdated check**. For example, a check written on May 13 and dated May 20 would be a postdated check. A financial institution will not honor a postdated check if it is presented for collection.

Second, the payee's name should be written. In Figure 6.1 the payee is a company called "International Boutique." The payee's name follows the words *Pay to the order of*. In general, it is not good practice to make out a check to "bearer" or "cash." A check made out to "cash" can be cashed by anyone. For instance, a person may try to pay a bill through the mail by sending a check made out to "cash." If the check is intercepted

and cashed by someone other than the expected payee, the check writer loses money equal to the amount of the check.

Third, the amount of the check is written in numerals. Figure 6.1 shows that the amount of the check is $31.67. In general, it is good practice to write the figure as $31 67/100 rather than $31.67. Both denote the same amount, but someone could alter the check or someone could process the check as $3,167 instead of $31.67.

Fourth, the amount is written out in words. It is generally desirable not to leave any blank space before the word *dollars*. Thus, "thirty one" is shown as "thirtyone" in Figure 6.1. Amounts less than $1 should be written as "67/100," "sixtyseven cents," or "67 cents."

Fifth, the check writer must sign the check. The signature should appear the same as on the bank's signature cards. The signature is authorization for the bank to honor the check. Therefore, you should never sign a blank check.

If any item on the check needs to be changed, the best thing to do is to write a new check. The old one should be torn and "void" entered in the check register to indicate that the check was destroyed. Checks with corrections or alterations may sometimes be processed, but in general, banks will refuse to honor such checks.

The check shown in Figure 6.1 contains two additional items that should be mentioned. First, the upper right corner of the check bears the

Figure 6.1 Writing a Check

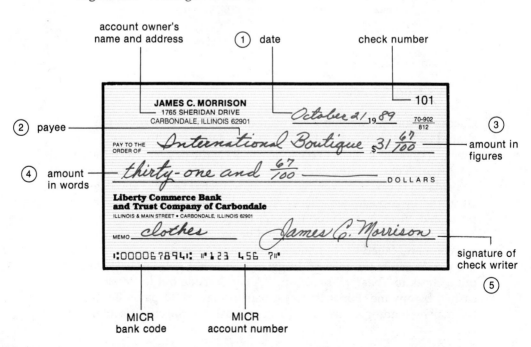

number 101. This is the check number. In the top left, the check carries the account owner's name and address. Most customers prefer to buy checks that have been personalized and numbered. If checks have not been numbered, then it is a good idea to go ahead and number them sequentially. This makes it easier to reconcile checking account statements every month. (Checking account statement reconciliation is discussed later in the chapter.)

How a Check Is Processed

A customer in St. Louis buys merchandise from a firm in Denver and pays with a check. The check is mailed in St. Louis and received in Denver. The Denver firm deposits this check with its bank in Denver. Then what happens?

The U.S. government has divided the country into various **Federal Reserve Bank (FRB) Districts**. Denver is in FRB District 10, whereas St. Louis is in FRB District 8. The Denver bank deposits this check with the Federal Reserve Bank for District 10, which sends the check to the Federal Reserve Bank for District 8. The Federal Reserve Bank in District 8 sends the check to the St. Louis bank, which deducts the check amount from the account of its St. Louis customer.

The St. Louis bank keeps money on deposit with the District 8 FRB. Once the check has been honored, the St. Louis bank authorizes the District 8 FRB to deduct the amount from the money that the bank has on deposit with the FRB. The District 8 FRB pays the District 10 FRB, which credits the money to the Denver bank. The Denver bank credits the amount to the Denver firm. If this process sounds complicated, that's because it *is* complicated.

The check-clearing process is expedited through the use of **Magnetic Ink Character Recognition (MICR)** characters. In the lower left corner of Figure 6.1 are two sets of MICR characters. The first set identifies the bank where the account is maintained. The second set of MICR characters identifies the account number of the check writer. A third set of MICR characters, not shown in Figure 6.1, would appear in the lower right corner and would be the amount of the check coded in MICR characters by the bank that receives the check. The three sets of MICRs expedite the check-clearing process.

Making a Deposit

When customers receive their personalized checks, they also receive personalized deposit tickets. An example of a personalized deposit ticket is shown in Figure 6.2. Most banks require that you list currency, coins, and checks separately on the deposit ticket. As shown in Figure 6.2, the depositor is depositing zero dollars in currency, $4.75 in coins, one check

Figure 6.2 Deposit Ticket

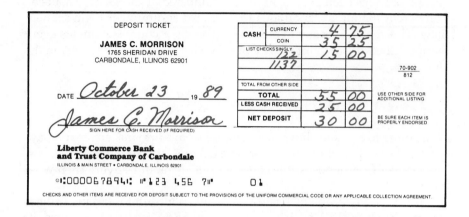

for $35.25, and another check for $15.00. The total of these amounts is $55.00. The customer wants to receive $25.00 in cash. The net deposit is $30.00. Because the customer is receiving cash, he has signed the deposit ticket on the appropriate line. Note that the deposit ticket has MICR characters for both the bank and the account number.

Generally, checks should be deposited or cashed soon after they are received. Checks received from local institutions are honored much more quickly than checks drawn on out-of-town institutions. Typically, institutions make funds available immediately after a check has been deposited. However, they can, if they wish, delay crediting the depositor's account until the check has cleared through the check writer's institution.

Endorsing a Check

A check must be endorsed before it can be either cashed or deposited. **Endorsement** means that the payee has signed his or her name on the back of the check. The check must be endorsed the way the payee's name is spelled on the check. An endorsed check can be cashed or deposited. Thus, the payee should not endorse the check until he or she plans to cash or deposit the check.

There are three methods for endorsing a check. A **blank endorsement** is simply the payee's signature on the back of the check. A blank endorsement is not desirable unless the depositor is cashing the check at a financial institution because a check that has a blank endorsement and is lost can be cashed by the finder.

An alternative to a blank endorsement is a **restrictive endorsement**, which limits the manner in which a check can be negotiated. As the two entries in Figure 6.3 show, the restrictive endorsement specifies that the

Figure 6.3 Types of Endorsements

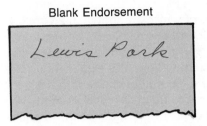

Blank Endorsement

Lewis Park

Restrictive Endorsement

For deposit only
Lewis Park

Restrictive Endorsement

For deposit only
Acct # 42-1316
Lewis Park

Special Endorsement

Pay to the order of
Phil Parsons
Lewis Park

checks be deposited only in the bank account of Lewis Park. A restrictive endorsement is desirable if cash is not needed or if the deposit is to be mailed to the bank.

Another alternative is the **special endorsement**. A check does not have to be cashed by the payee. The payee can pass ownership of the check to another person by endorsing it ''Pay to the order of . . . .'' In Figure 6.3, Lewis Park has given ownership of the check to Phil Parsons by writing ''Pay to the order of Phil Parsons'' on the back of the check and endorsing it. At this point Phil Parsons can cash the check, deposit it, or endorse it over to someone else.

Maintaining the Checking Account Register

All checks written or voided and all deposits made should be entered in the **checking account register**, examples of which are shown in Figure 6.4. In making entries in a check register, either the single entry or the double entry method can be used. As Figure 6.4a shows, in the **single entry method** all checks and deposits are listed without any explanation. The check numbers, date, payee's name, and amount of check or deposit are entered in the appropriate columns. The amount of the check is subtracted from the previous balance. The amount deposited is added to the previous balance to give the current balance.

Figure 6.4b shows an example of the **double entry method** for check registers. The basic entries for a check or a deposit are the same as with the single entry method. In addition, on the line after each entry, a notation is made explaining why the check was written. The double entry

Figure 6.4 Checking Account Register

(a) Single Entry Method

NUMBER	DATE	DESCRIPTION OF TRANSACTION	PAYMENT/DEBIT (-)	√ T	FEE (IF ANY) (-)	DEPOSIT/CREDIT (+)	BALANCE 352 16
99	10/15	Kroger	14 55	√			337 61
100	—	Void	— —				337 61
101	10/21	International Boutique	31 67				305 94
102	10/22	Stan's Auto Repair	62 41				243 53
—	10/23					30 00	273 53

RECORD ALL CHARGES OR CREDITS THAT AFFECT YOUR ACCOUNT

(b) Double Entry Method

NUMBER	DATE	DESCRIPTION OF TRANSACTION	PAYMENT/DEBIT (-)	√ T	FEE (IF ANY) (-)	DEPOSIT/CREDIT (+)	BALANCE 352 16
99	10/15	Kroger groceries	14 55	√			337 61
100	—	Void error in amount	— —				337 61
101	10/21	International Boutique clothes	31 67				305 94
102	10/22	Stan's Auto Repair tuneup	62 41				243 53
—	10/23	4.75 coin + 35.25 + 15.00 - 25.00				30 00	273 53

RECORD ALL CHARGES OR CREDITS THAT AFFECT YOUR ACCOUNT

system provides a good way of keeping track of expenditures for preparing personal budgets.

Overdrafts and Stop Payments

In two fairly common situations, a bank does not pay a check even though it is properly filled out and signed by the account owner. In one of these situations, the overdraft, the bank is protecting its own interests; in the other, a stop payment situation, the bank is protecting the interests of the depositor.

Overdrafts.   An **overdraft** occurs when a check presented to an institution is for an amount that is greater than the checking account balance. The institution has two options when it is presented with an overdraft. First, it can simply stamp the check with the words *insufficient funds* and return the check to the payee or the payee's institution. When overdrafts occur and the check is returned, we say that the check has "bounced." That is why checks that are returned for insufficient funds are often called "rubber checks." Most institutions follow the procedure of bouncing checks when faced with overdrafts. Institutions do not like to deal with overdrafts and therefore typically charge the account holder a fee of $5 to $10 for each check returned due to insufficient funds. When checks are returned due to insufficient funds, the institution notifies the account holder of its action.

Most overdrafts occur because of poor checking account register maintenance. Institutions generally assume that the overdraft occurred because of negligence by the account holder. However, if the institution becomes convinced that the overdraft was intentional, then it may choose to prosecute the account holder for fraud. If the payee for the bounced check is a department store or supermarket, it, too, may assess the check writer a processing fee of $5 to $10.

The second alternative the institution has when faced with an overdraft is to honor the check. Paying the amount of the check when sufficient funds are not available to cover it requires the institution to give the account holder a temporary loan. After honoring the check, the institution will notify the account holder of its action and request that the account holder deposit funds to cover the overdraft amount. The account holder will still pay the $5 to $10 service fee.

Institutions will cover checks when there are insufficient funds only in two situations. If the institution and the account holder have a very good banking relationship, the institution will honor the check as a courtesy to the account holder. The account holder may also have arranged for automatic overdraft protection. In this arrangement, the institution establishes a line of credit for the account holder. When an overdraft situation occurs, the institution transfers enough money from the credit line to the checking account to honor the check. The customer is not assessed

a fee or penalty for the overdraft. However, she or he still has to pay interest on the credit line borrowing.

In general, unless automatic overdraft protection is arranged through the institution, checks should not be written when the account contains insufficient funds. The best way to avoid overdrafts is to enter the check amount in the account register and show the new balance immediately.

Stopping payment.   Occasionally a person may need to **stop payment** on a check. For example, if the check has been lost, stopping payment on it is desirable to prevent the loss of money. Or a check may have been written for merchandise that proved to be defective, and the check writer wishes to return the merchandise rather than pay for it. The procedure for stopping payment is to notify the financial institution.

The institution will require the account holder to fill out a stop payment form. On this form the check issuer will list the check number, the date of issue, amount of check, and name of payee. The stop payment form, which must be signed by the account holder, also contains a statement that relieves the institution of liability in case it cashes the check by error. (Some institutions allow stop payment requests to be phoned in, provided the customer comes in and signs the proper forms.) The stop payment procedure does not guarantee the check issuer that the check will not be cashed, but the institution notifies its tellers to not accept or cash the check. The check and account numbers are also entered into the institution's electronic check-processing equipment to prevent the check from being processed. Institutions usually charge a fee of $5 or more for stopping payment on checks.

Spot Quiz • Opening and Using a Checking Account

1.   Postdating a check means cashing it after the date shown on the check.

T _____   F _____

2.   A blank endorsement is more desirable than a restrictive endorsement.

T _____   F _____

3.   Overdrafts are useful when one is low on funds.

T _____   F _____

4.   A stop payment order on a check guarantees that the check will not be cashed.

T _____   F _____

(Answers on page 199)

Checking account reconciliation

Each checking account involves two different sets of records. One set is maintained by the institution. The second set of records is the checking account register maintained by the account owner. The institution sends periodic statements to its customers. These statements are used to verify that the two sets of records agree, or **reconcile**.

Institution Statements

Institutions mail out periodic statements to their checking account clients. Most of the time these statements are monthly. An example of a monthly bank statement is shown in Figure 6.5. As you can see from the figure, institutions do not prepare statements on a calendar month basis. Rather, statements are staggered, and the statement period starts on different days for different groups of customers. In the statement shown, the period is from September 19, 1989, through October 17, 1989.

The account number is listed in the bottom left corner. The account activity is summarized in the lower portion. No service charges were assessed against the account. The beginning account balance was $293.88. Nine checks were written, for a total of $386.27. Two deposits, for a total of $430.00, were made during the period. The ending balance for the period was $337.61. This statement provides the bank's version of the activity in the account during the specified time period. Along with the statement, the bank also sends to the account holder all canceled checks and, in many cases, all deposit slips processed during the period.

Account Reconciliation

The idea behind account reconciliation is to verify that the institution's records match the records kept by the account owner. The ending balance shown on the institution statement should be compared with the balance shown in the checking account register. If the amounts match, a reconciliation is generally not needed. In Figure 6.4, the register balance is shown as $273.53. Since the bank statement balance is $337.61, a reconciliation is needed.

A reconciliation has two benefits. The accuracy of the institution's records, as well as the account owner's, is verified. The institution may have cashed a check for the wrong amount or the check register may contain incorrect figures. These types of problems are identified in a reconciliation. Second, any service charges or fees that are shown on the institution statement are transferred to the check register to bring its balance up to date.

Differences between the institution's balance and the check register balance can have five explanations:

1. Checks written have not yet been processed by the institution.
2. Deposits made have not yet been processed by the institution.
3. Service fees charged by the institution are not shown in the check register.

Figure 6.5 Bank Statement

Liberty Commerce Bank
and Trust Company of Carbondale

ILLINOIS & MAIN STREET • CARBONDALE, ILLINOIS 62901

MEMBER F D I C

James C. Morrison
1765 Sheridan Drive
Carbondale, Illinois 62901

STATEMENT
OF
ACCOUNT

DATE	CHECKS		DEPOSITS	BALANCE
				293.88
SEP 19	23.40	17.62		252.86
SEP 27	43.29			209.57
OCT 1	200.00		350.00	359.57
OCT 7	7.05			352.52
OCT 12	39.42		80.00	393.10
OCT 15	27.11	13.83		352.16
OCT 17	14.55			337.61

ACCOUNT NUMBER	STATEMENT DATE	CLEARING ITEMS DEPOSITED	OUT OF TOWN ITEMS DEPOSITED	SERVICE CHARGE	AVERAGE BALANCE
123-456-7	OCT 17, 89	1	2	0.00	318.91

BALANCE LAST STATEMENT	NO. OF CHECKS	TOTAL AMOUNT OF CHECKS	NO. OF DEPOSITS	TOTAL AMOUNT OF DEPOSITS	BALANCE THIS STATEMENT
293.88	9	386.27	2	430.00	337.61

4. The institution made an error in recording one or more items.
5. The account owner made an error in recording one or more items.

The statements mailed by institutions generally have forms on the back to help the customer reconcile the checking account. The back portion of a statement is shown in Figure 6.6. As indicated there, the following steps are involved in reconciling the account:

Figure 6.6 Reconciling the Checking Account

THIS FORM IS PROVIDED TO HELP YOU BALANCE
YOUR BANK STATEMENT

CHECKS OUTSTANDING—NOT
CHARGED TO ACCOUNT

| NO. | *101* | $ *31* | *67* |
| | *102* | *62* | *41* |

BANK BALANCE SHOWN
ON THIS STATEMENT $ *337.61*   (1)

ADD +

DEPOSITS NOT CREDITED
IN THIS STATEMENT
(IF ANY) $ *30.00*   (2)

TOTAL $ *367.61*   (3)

SUBTRACT —

CHECKS OUTSTANDING $ *94.08*   (4)

BALANCE $ *273.53*   (5)

SHOULD AGREE WITH YOUR CHECK BOOK BAL-
ANCE AFTER DEDUCTING SERVICE CHARGE (IF
ANY) SHOWN ON THIS STATEMENT

TOTAL $ *94* | *08*

EXPLANATION OF SYMBOLS USED ON FACE OF STATEMENT

DC - DEPOSIT CORRECTION	CC - CERTIFIED CHECK
ER - ERROR CORRECTION	DM - DEBIT MEMO
CB - CHARGE BACK	RT - RETURNED CHECK
MS - MISC. CHARGE	SC - SERVICE CHARGE
CA - CLOSED ACCOUNT DEBIT	CM - CREDIT MEMO
LS - LISTING OF CHECKS	SS - SPECIAL STATEMENT

1. Sort checks numerically or by the date of issue. Compare the checks with the entries in the check register and place a checkmark (✔) on the register after each check that has been paid and canceled by the bank. In Figure 6.4, a checkmark has been placed in the appropriate column for check number 99.

2. Reduce the check register balance by any service fees shown on the statement. In the example given here, no service charges are shown.

3. Enter the statement balance on a balance form of the type shown in Figure 6.6. In Figure 6.6, $337.61 is entered on line 1 of the balance form.

4. Enter on the balance form any deposits made but not shown in the statement. The check register shows a deposit of $30.00 on October 23, which is not shown on the statement. This amount is entered on line 2 of the balance form in Figure 6.6. Total lines 1 and 2, which add up to $367.61, as shown on line 3 in Figure 6.6.

5. List and total all checks not shown in the statement. The full check register is not shown. However, Figure 6.4 shows that check numbers 101 and 102 had not cleared the bank as of October 17, 1989. Assume that these are the only two checks that have not cleared yet. They are listed in Figure 6.6 and total $94.08. This amount is entered on line 4 of the balance form in Figure 6.6.

6. Subtract line 4 from line 3. The balance of $273.53 on line 5 should be and is the same as on the check register in Figure 6.4.

7. After Step 6, if the balance form amount is different from the check register amount, it means one or more errors in the checking account statement and/or the check register. Carefully check the amount of each canceled check on both the check register and the statement. Correct any incorrect figures. Next, check the additions and subtractions on the check register and make corrections. Enter the corrected amounts in the balance form. The statements should now agree. If an error is found in the institution's statement, its accounting department should be contacted for correction of the error.

Canceled checks, institution statements, and check registers should be retained for at least five years. Canceled checks are proof of payment. They also form the basis for basic record keeping. They are useful for justifying tax-deductible expenses in case of an IRS audit as well.

Spot Quiz • Checking Account Reconciliation

1. The idea behind account reconciliation is to determine whether the institution has made an error.　　　　　　　　T _____ F _____

2. Incorrect entries in the check register are a common reason for the account not reconciling with the institution checking account statement.
                                                T _____   F _____

(Answers on page 199)

Special payment methods

Most people usually find it convenient to write checks to pay for goods
and services. However, there are occasions when checks written on regular
checking accounts will not do. For example, a person may need to make
a payment to a stranger who will accept only a check that is guaranteed
payable. In such cases, cashier's checks, certified checks, traveler's checks,
and money orders are acceptable forms of payment.

Cashier's Checks

A **cashier's check** is one that the institution writes on itself. Suppose that
a person wants to send money to a mail order firm in another state. The
person can go to a financial institution and present the payment amount,
and the institution will make out a check drawn on its own account and
payable to the mail order firm. Because cashier's checks are issued by financial institutions, they are readily accepted. Because a cashier's check is made
out to a specific payee, it is considered safe for mail payments.
    The canceled cashier's check is kept by the institution—the customer
does not get it back. However, the institution does provide the customer
with a nonnegotiable duplicate of the cashier's check. Further, the institution can provide verification that the check was cashed by the payee. Most
institutions issue cashier's checks to their customers free of charge. Non-
customers are charged a small service fee.

Certified Checks

To get a check certified, the account holder writes the name of the payee
and the amount on the check. The check is then presented to an institution official, who verifies that the account contains sufficient funds to cover
the check. The amount of the check is immediately deducted from the account, the word *certified* is stamped on the check, and an institution official initials the check. The certification means that the institution has
already deducted the check amount from the account and is guaranteeing
payment on the **certified check**.

Most institutions will certify checks free of charge; some assess a small service fee. When a certified check is presented for payment, it is retained by the institution. The institution sends a note with the account statement indicating that the check has been cashed.

Traveler's Checks

People who are traveling find it convenient to carry traveler's checks rather than cash. **Traveler's checks** have two major advantages over both cash and traditional checks. First, unlike cash, the loss of traveler's checks does not result in any loss for the traveler. When cash is lost or stolen, it cannot be replaced. When traveler's checks are lost or stolen, they can be quickly replaced, provided the traveler has retained the serial numbers. Second, businesses, hotels, gas stations, restaurants, and so on are reluctant to accept out-of-town checks. A vacationer from Idaho may find that not many retail shops in Arkansas are interested in cashing his or her personal check. However, they will readily accept a traveler's check. Traveler's checks are widely accepted in the United States and abroad.

Traveler's checks are issued by such financial institutions as American Express, Bank of America, Thomas Cook's, and Barclays Bank. They are sold by many financial institutions. Traveler's checks come in denominations ranging from $10 to $1,000. The typical service charge for traveler's checks is $1 per $100 of checks. However, some financial institutions issue them free of charge to their customers.

The person buying the traveler's checks must sign them in front of an institution teller or official. Later, to cash a check, the buyer writes in the name of the payee and signs the check a second time. The payee verifies that the two signatures match before cashing the check. The buyer is provided with the serial numbers of the checks bought and keeps a record of the serial numbers as the checks are cashed. If the traveler's checks are lost or stolen, the buyer can provide quickly the serial numbers of the missing checks. It is important to remember that the serial number records should be kept separate from the traveler's checks.

Traveler's checks carry no time limit and can be kept indefinitely. However, there is an opportunity cost of keeping uncashed traveler's checks on hand. For example, a person who has kept $100 in uncashed traveler's checks for one year has given up interest on that $100 for the year. At a 5 percent interest rate, the opportunity cost of keeping the checks for a year is $5. In general, if no travel is anticipated within the next three months, it is wise to go ahead and cash the unused traveler's checks.

Money Orders

A **money order** can be obtained from the U.S. Postal Service and from financial institutions. Money orders are readily accepted and easily negotiable

and so are widely used in making payments through the mail. The issuing institution usually charges a small fee for a money order. The money order is for a specific amount, and the buyer needs to write the name of the payee on it. The buyer is provided with either a nonnegotiable duplicate or a stub as proof of purchase of the money order.

Money Market Mutual Funds

As indicated in the opening paragraph of this chapter, many persons expect, and are getting, up to 10 percent interest on their "checking" accounts. These checking accounts are not with financial institutions; rather, they are with **money market mutual funds**, or **money funds**. A money fund is a mutual fund (explained in detail in Chapter 18) that has invested its assets in extremely safe, short-term government and private securities. Money funds are of two types: taxable money funds and tax-free money funds.

Taxable Money Funds.   Taxable money funds invest their assets in high-grade government and private securities. Returns on these invested assets tend to vary with interest rates. At times, returns have been around 20 percent. The fund managers keep about .75 percent of returns as their management fee and pay out the rest to their investors. Thus, if a fund's investments are earning 10.0 percent, its investors are getting 10.0 percent − .75 percent = 9.25 percent on their investments in the money fund.

A person who wants to use a money fund opens an account with a fund. All transactions, such as deposits and withdrawals, are handled by mail, telephone, or wire. Money funds usually do not charge fees for either monthly statements or checks processed. However, they do have certain minimum balance requirements. Some require a minimum deposit of $1,000 to open an account; others require minimum deposits of up to $10,000. A second limitation is that all funds have minimum requirements for the amount of the check. Most of the time this minimum requirement is $500. Robert Leshner, president of Midwest Income Investment Co., has the following advice for getting around this problem: "A lot of people put all their money in the fund, and as they need it they just write themselves a check for $500 and deposit it in their regular little checking account."[2]

Tax-Free Money Funds.   Tax-free money funds invest their assets in highly secure municipal bonds. The returns from municipal bonds are free from federal taxes, although they may be subject to state and local taxes. The yields on tax-free money funds are lower than the yields on taxable money funds. However, a 6.5 percent tax-free yield to someone in the 35

2. "How to Earn 10% on a Checking Account," *Money* (February 1979): 99.

percent tax bracket is equivalent to a 10 percent before-tax yield. Tax-free money funds appeal to people in high tax brackets. In all other respects, taxable and tax-free money funds are identical for check writing purposes.

Spot Quiz • Special Payment Methods

1. Cashier's checks are made out to "bearer" and are easily negotiated by anyone.   T _____ F _____

2. Certified checks are written on the institution's own account.
   T _____ F _____

3. Traveler's checks are a good alternative to carrying cash since they can be replaced if they are lost or stolen.   T _____ F _____

4. Money funds allow a person to write checks and collect interest on the account balance at the same time.   T _____ F _____

(Answers on page 199)

SPECIAL SERVICES OF FINANCIAL INSTITUTIONS

In addition to the services discussed previously, financial institutions offer a variety of other services. Some of the more popular ones are discussed in this section.

Safe Deposit Boxes

Safe deposit boxes are locked metal boxes in an institution's vault. They vary in size from a shoebox to a filing cabinet. A small safe deposit box can be rented for $15 to $50 per year. A box can be opened only by using two keys. The box renter has one key, and the institution has the other key. Both keys are required to open a box.

A safe deposit box is valuable for storing items that are hard to replace. These include passports, birth and naturalization certificates, bonds, stock certificates, titles, deeds, and other important documents, and jewelry. A renter who wants access to his safe deposit box has to sign in and show proper identification to institution officials. An institution official and the

renter then jointly open the box. If the renter dies, the safe deposit box is sealed and opened only in the presence of legal authorities. Therefore, wills and savings passbooks should not be kept in safe deposit boxes.

Institutions do their best to make sure that safe deposit boxes are not tampered with. Everyone who enters the vault is carefully screened. Institutions do not keep master keys to safe deposit boxes, so it is very difficult for an institution's employee to pilfer the contents of these boxes. Institutions do not guarantee against loss of contents of the boxes, however. In general, institutions do not know what people keep in safe deposit boxes; this, perhaps, explains why institutions are not held liable for the loss of box contents. A renter should carefully prepare an inventory of all items placed in a safe deposit box.

Electronic Terminals

More and more institutions are installing **electronic terminals**, or **automatic teller machines (ATMs)**, to handle routine customer transactions. ATMs allow a customer to deposit to or withdraw funds from checking and savings accounts, move funds from one type of account to another, make mortgage payments, and take out small loans. ATMs are designed to be fairly tamper-proof. Normally, the customer has to insert a magnetically encoded plastic card into the ATM. The machine then asks for a four- to six-digit **personal identification number (PIN)** that only the customer knows. If the customer can provide the correct PIN, he or she can go ahead and make the transaction. If the PIN is wrong, the customer is given one or two more chances for correct identification. If the correct PIN still is not forthcoming, the ATM keeps the plastic ID card. The customer may retrieve the card and find out his or her correct PIN during normal business hours.

The principal advantage of ATMs is that they can operate 24 hours a day. The customer can handle routine financial tasks at his or her convenience rather than during regular banking hours.

Drive-In Windows

Some institutions offer **drive-in** and **walk-up windows**. These are convenient from the customers' viewpoint, because routine business can be transacted without going inside the institution. Drive-in and walk-up services are usually available beyond normal banking hours.

Investment Management Services

Many institutions offer **investment management services** to their customers. These institutions have investment experts who are well versed in various investment strategies. People with funds to invest but with

"Sir—Our drive-up service is outside."

Source: Reprinted from the *Credit Union Magazine*, April
1980, p. 54. Used with permission.

limited time to manage their funds may find it convenient to let an institution handle their portfolio. The investment management service fee also
includes all the necessary record keeping. One problem is that institutions
typically require a minimum of $25,000 in an investment account.

Spot Quiz • Special Services of Financial Institutions

1. Safe deposit boxes are theft-proof and guaranteed against loss.

   T _____   F _____

2. Electronic terminals can completely replace a live teller.

   T _____   F _____

(Answers on page 199)

SAVINGS ACCOUNTS

Consumers need to hold cash for day-to-day transactions, such as utility
bills, groceries, rents, and repairs. Such needs are typically met by maintaining a checking account. Most consumers also encounter unexpected
expenses. These unexpected or emergency needs for cash can be met by
holding extra money in a checking account. However, typical checking ac-

counts do not provide the account owner with adequate returns. For maintaining emergency funds, an alternative to the checking account is a savings account. A savings account, or time deposit account, is very safe, the funds in it are readily available, and monies on deposit in the account earn interest. This is a major reason for maintaining a savings account.

There are other reasons for maintaining a savings account. Typically, a savings account is insured. Most savings institutions provide for insurance up to $100,000 for accounts. If a person has an account at an insured savings institution, there is no danger of loss of principal. Thus, many people view savings as an investment. That is, for these people, savings is part of their overall program for investing excess funds.

Some people also use savings accounts for temporary investments. For example, a person may wish to invest $500 periodically in stocks; however, the person can save only $200 each month in a savings account until the $500 has been accumulated. Another example is a person who wishes to withdraw funds temporarily from stock investing. The person may temporarily invest these funds in a savings account until he or she is ready to go back into the stock market.

A final reason for maintaining a savings account is that it allows you to accumulate money to spend on a particular item. Many people find themselves in a cash bind when the time comes for year-end gift giving. These persons might find it convenient to open a savings account and deposit, for example, $5 in it every week. After 50 weeks they will have accumulated over $250, which can then be used to buy gifts. Similarly, savings accounts can be opened to accumulate funds for specific purposes, such as buying a new car, going on a vacation, or making a down payment on a house.

As these examples indicate, savings accounts are an important part of a consumer's strategies for personal financial management. Savings accounts differ in the way interest is computed and in the type of savings institution offering the account. Also, there are alternatives to savings accounts that consumers should consider. These topics are covered in the remainder of this chapter.

Spot Quiz • Savings Accounts

1. Savings accounts can be opened to achieve specific financial goals.

   T _____   F _____

2. Two separate savings accounts should be maintained for holding precautionary and investment funds.   T _____   F _____

(Answers on page 199)

INTEREST PAID ON SAVINGS

The amount of interest paid on a savings account depends on (1) which method is used to compute interest payments and (2) how the real or effective interest rate is determined.

Nominal and Effective Interest Rates

Different types of financial institutions pay different interest rates on savings accounts. Financial institutions of the same type normally pay the same **nominal interest rate**. The nominal interest rate is the stated or advertised interest rate. For instance, savings and loan (S&L) associations typically pay 5.25 percent interest on regular savings accounts. Even though two S&L associations have the same nominal interest rate, however, their effective interest rate may be different. The **effective interest rate** is the interest rate that is actually received by the account owner.

The difference between nominal and effective interest rates occurs because interest can be paid, or **compounded**, in different ways. Let's assume that the nominal rate is 5.25 percent, and interest is paid annually. The beginning amount, or principal, is $100. After one year, the principal would earn 5.25 percent interest, or $100 × .0525 = $5.25. The total principal after one year becomes $100 + $5.25 = $105.25. The second year this amount earns $105.25 × .0525 = $5.53 in interest, and the new principal becomes $105.25 + $5.53 = $110.78. These calculations are shown in Table 6.2a.

If interest is paid biannually, or every six months, then the 5.25 percent annual rate becomes 2.625 percent every six months. As Table 6.2b indicates, after six months the interest earned is $2.63, and the new amount is $100 + $2.63 = $102.63. For the second six-month period, interest earned is $102.63 × .02625 = $2.69, and the principal after one year is $102.63 + $2.69 = $105.32. At the end of two years the principal is $110.92. This amount is higher than the ending principal when interest is paid annually.

The difference between the ending amounts with biannual and annual compounding is due to the fact that with biannual compounding, interest is received at the end of six months, and this interest also earns interest for the second six-month period. With biannual compounding, interest paid during the first year was $2.63 + $2.69 = $5.32. Annual compounding resulted in an interest payment of $5.25. The difference, $5.32 − $5.25 = $.07, is equal to $2.63 × .02625 = $.07. Thus, the more frequently interest is compounded and paid, the higher will be the effective interest rate.

Table 6.2 How Interest Compounding Works

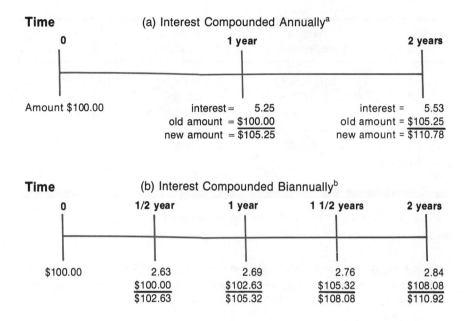

aThe nominal interest rate is 5.25 percent per year.
bThe effective interest rate in this case becomes 5.32 percent.

Table 6.3 shows how the accumulated principal varies with changes in the compounding method. Ten thousand dollars, compounded at a rate of 5.25 percent per year for ten years, becomes $16,680.96. The same amount, with the same nominal interest rate but with monthly compounding, becomes $16,885.24 after ten years. With daily compounding, the amount becomes $16,903.95. As Table 6.3 shows, when the nominal rate is 5.25 percent, the effective rate for annual, monthly, and daily compounding is 5.25 percent, 5.38 percent, and 5.39 percent, respectively. In general, other things being the same, the more often interest is compounded and paid, the more desirable is the savings plan.

How Interest Is Computed

Differences in interest received can be explained by differences in the frequency of compounding. A second explanation is differences in the manner in which interest is computed on the account. Two S&L associations

Table 6.3 Compounding Period and Effective Interest Rates*

Year	Annual Compounding	Monthly Compounding	Daily Compounding
1	$10,525.00	$10,537.82	$10,538.99
2	11,077.56	11,104.56	11,107.02
5	12,915.48	12,994.32	13,001.52
10	16,680.96	16,885.24	16,903.95
Effective interest	5.25%	5.38%	5.39%

*The beginning principal is $10,000. The nominal interest rate is 5.25 percent.

could have the same effective interest rate, and the interest they pay could still differ. Four basic methods for computing interest are widely used: low-balance; first-in, first-out; last-in, first-out; and day-of-deposit-to-day-of-withdrawal.

Low Balance. Under the **low-balance method**, interest is paid on the lowest balance on deposit in the account during the interest period. Let's assume, for example, that the interest period is from January 1 through March 31. A savings account and its related transactions are shown in Table 6.4. The beginning balance was $1,000. One deposit of $2,000 was made on January 20, and another one of $1,000 was made on February 1. On February 15, $1,500 was withdrawn. On March 1 the same amount was deposited, and on March 15, $1,000 was withdrawn. The interest is 5.25 percent, paid on a quarterly basis. The low balance for the quarter is $1,000. Therefore, interest paid is $1,000 × .0525/4 = $13.13. This method penalizes withdrawals from the account.

First-In, First-Out (FIFO). Under the **first-in, first-out (FIFO) method**, withdrawals are deducted from the beginning balance first. If the beginning balance is not enough, then the remaining withdrawal is deducted from later deposits. The use of this method results in the loss of interest on the amount withdrawn from the beginning of the period rather than from the date of withdrawal. In the example cited, for interest computation purposes, the February 15 withdrawal results in the January 1 deposit being treated as $0. The balance on January 20 becomes $1,500 because $500 of the withdrawal could not be charged to the beginning balance and was charged to the January 20 deposit. The March 15 withdrawal further reduces the January 20 deposit to $500. Thus, $500 was on deposit from

Table 6.4 Account Transactions for Savings Account

Date	Withdrawal	Deposit	Interest*	Balance
January 1				$1,000
January 20		$2,000		$3,000
February 1		$1,000		$4,000
February 15	$1,500			$2,500
March 1		$1,500		$4,000
March 15	$1,000			$3,000
March 31			$X	

*Interest posted on account will be as follows for the various account types: Low balance, $13.13; FIFO, $20.42; LIFO, $30.63; DD/DW, $36.42. The interest rate is 5.25 percent paid and compounded quarterly.

January 20 to January 31, $1500 was on deposit from February 1 to February 18, and $3,000 was on deposit from March 1 to March 31. The interest paid under FIFO is $500 × .0525/(12 × 3) + $1,500 × .0525/12 + $3,000 × .0525/12 = $20.42.

Last-In, First-Out (LIFO). Under the **last-in, first-out (LIFO) method**, withdrawals are deducted from the last deposit first and then from the most recent ones. Under LIFO, withdrawals do not penalize the saver as much as under the FIFO method because withdrawals result in loss of interest for the shortest time periods. Under LIFO, $1,000 of the $1,500 withdrawal is charged against the February 1 deposit, and the other $500 is charged to the January 20 deposit. The March 15 withdrawal is charged against the March 1 deposit. Thus, $1,000 is on deposit from January 1 to January 20 (2/3 of a month), $2,500 is on deposit from January 21 to February 28 (4/3 months), and $3,000 is on deposit from March 1 to March 31. Interest paid under LIFO is ($1,000 × .0525/12)(2/3) + ($2,500 × .0525/12)(4/3) + ($3,000 × .0525/12) = $30.63.

Day-of-Deposit-to-Day-of-Withdrawal (DD/DW). Under the **day-of-deposit-to-day-of-withdrawal (DD/DW) method**, interest is paid on the actual balance on deposit. For the account in Table 6.4, interest would be paid on $1,000 for 20 days, on $3,000 for 11 days, on $4,000 for 15 days, on $2,500 for 13 days, on $4,000 for 15 days, and on $3,000 for 16 days. Total interest paid using the DD/DW method would be ($1,000 × .0525)(20/365) + ($3,000 × .0525)(27/365) + ($4,000 × .0525)(30/365) + (2,500 × .0525)(13/265) = $36.47. This method is the preferred one from

the customer's viewpoint because all the money in the savings account is earning interest.

When you select a savings institution, inquire about the effective interest rate and the method used to compute interest. A large number of financial institutions offer **continuous compounding** of interest, which results in an effective interest rate that is practically the same as the rate for daily compounding.

Spot Quiz • Interest Paid on Savings

1. The shorter the period over which compounding occurs, the higher the effective interest rate is.   T _____   F _____

2. The low-balance method of computing interest encourages savings.
                                                                         T _____   F _____

3. Money should be saved at an institution that offers payment of daily interest.   T _____   F _____

(Answers on page 199)

COMPARING FINANCIAL INSTITUTIONS

You can save money at a variety of financial institutions, which vary in the types of services and savings vehicles they offer. The four principal institutions for savings are commercial banks, savings and loan associations, credit unions, and mutual savings banks.

Commercial Banks

Commercial banks typically advertise themselves as "full-service banks" because they offer a full range of services to the consumer. These services include demand deposit accounts, savings accounts, special accounts, NOW accounts, and other services mentioned previously. For savings purposes, commercial banks offer a range of accounts, such as regular savings accounts, special savings accounts, club accounts, and certificates of deposit.

Regular Passbook Savings Accounts.   Under this plan, the bank issues the saver a passbook in which all deposits and withdrawals are recorded. Some banks now issue plastic identification cards instead of passbooks and provide their savings account customers with periodic statements on their accounts. There are no regulations about the maximum allowable rate that banks can pay on regular savings accounts. As Table 6.5 indicates, banks typically pay 5.0 to 5.25 percent on savings accounts. (See "Financial Institutions Love Those Savings Accounts" on page 188.)

A government agency, the **Federal Deposit Insurance Corporation (FDIC)**, provides insurance for accounts held at banks. Currently the maximum amount of insurance per account is $100,000. Most banks carry FDIC insurance. These banks prominently display signs indicating they are a member of the FDIC and that their accounts are insured by the FDIC.

A variety of savings accounts can be opened at a commercial bank. A **single account** is in the name of one individual only. A **joint account** is in the name of more than one individual. A **tenancy in common account** requires that all account owners sign the withdrawal form before the bank

Table 6.5 Interest Rates and Insurance for Financial Institutions

Savings Institution	Average Interest Rates	Insuring Agency	Insurance Limit per Account
Commercial bank	5.0–5.25%	Federal Deposit Insurance Corp.	$100,000
Savings and loan association	5.25–5.5%	Federal Savings and Loan Insurance Corp.	$100,000
Credit union	5.5–6.5%	National Credit Union Administration	$100,000
Mutual savings bank	5.25–5.5%	Federal Deposit Insurance Corp.	$100,000

Financial Institutions Love Those Savings Accounts

Prior to April 1986, banks were restricted to paying a maximum of 5.5 percent interest rate on savings accounts. In April 1986, the U.S. government removed all interest rate ceilings from savings accounts, and banks and other financial institutions were free to pay whatever interest rate they wanted. Most institutions, however, have continued to pay 5.5 percent interest on savings accounts. For sources of funds other than these savings accounts, institutions generally have had to pay higher interest rates. Thus, these savings accounts provide institutions with loans that have bargain basement interest rates. Bank analysts estimate that banks' borrowing costs in the United States are about $7 billion less than they should be because of the low interest rates paid on savings accounts. No wonder financial institutions love these savings accounts.

will allow funds to be withdrawn. A **trust account** is owned by one person on behalf of another. For example, a parent may open a trust account for a child. The trustee, or account owner, retains the right to change the beneficiary at any time. A **minor's account** allows a minor to own an account with the permission of his or her legal guardian.

Special Savings Accounts. Certain restrictions are placed on these accounts. For example, banks may require special accounts to give 30 or 60 days notice prior to withdrawal of funds or banks may require a

"*What should I 'member 'bout F.D.I.C.?*"

Source: *Changing Times*, January 1980, p. 14.

minimum balance of $500 to $1,000. In return, the bank pays an interest rate on these accounts that is .25 to .5 percent higher than on regular passbook savings accounts.

Club Accounts.   Consumers may wish to accumulate a sum of money to be spent for a specific purpose. Banks promote these accounts to encourage regular savings. Typical of these club accounts are Christmas, Hanukkah, and vacation accounts. Many banks even furnish precoded coupon books to encourage regular savings. A coupon book may contain 50 coupons, each imprinted with the weekly due date and the amount of deposit. A consumer wishing to accumulate $500 for Christmas shopping could open a club account and attempt to deposit $10 in the account each week. Because of the bookkeeping and the small deposit sums involved, the interest paid on club accounts is lower than the interest on regular passbook accounts.

Certificates of Deposit.   **Certificates of deposit (CDs)**, are typically issued in amounts that start out at $1,000. CDs are different from regular savings accounts in the sense that the CD buyer is committed to leaving the money on deposit for a fixed time period, which varies from 90 days to a few years. A 90-day CD, for example, requires the saver to leave the money on deposit for at least 90 days. At the saver's option, the 90-day CD may be renewed for another 90-day period. CDs pay an interest rate that can be considerably higher than the interest rate on regular savings accounts. Federal laws require a substantial interest penalty if the saver withdraws his or her money from a CD prior to the maturity date. An early withdrawal may result in the forfeit of interest for up to one quarter, plus the reversion of the interest rate to the rate paid on regular savings.

Savings and Loan Associations

Savings and loan (S&L) associations specialize in offering savings accounts, NOW accounts, and CDs, and in providing mortgage funds. In some states, S&Ls are also known by a variety of other names. Most S&Ls are locally owned and operated. Some of them are owned by the depositors, and others, by the officers of the S&L. S&Ls are chartered, or authorized to do business, by either the state or the federal government. Federally chartered S&Ls must belong to the **Federal Savings and Loan Insurance Corporation (FSLIC)**. The FSLIC insures S&L accounts for up to $100,000.

The interest paid by S&Ls is usually higher than the interest paid by banks. S&Ls in general pay about 5.25 to 5.5 percent in interest. S&Ls offer regular savings accounts, special savings accounts, club accounts, and certificates of deposit. S&Ls are safe places to save because of FSLIC or state insurance of accounts and the secure nature of the loans issued by S&Ls.

Most cities have S&Ls with numerous branches scattered throughout the city, which makes it convenient to maintain an account at an S&L.

Credit Unions

A **credit union** is a financial institution whose depositors are also its owners. A credit union lends money only to its owners. That is, a credit union is a mutual savings institution, which attracts funds from its owners and then lends these funds to other owners. Generally, membership in a credit union is limited to people who have a common interest or association. Thus, for example, all employees of a firm would be eligible to join any credit union operating for their benefit. An eligible person who wishes to join a credit union would start out by making at least the minimum deposit. The minimum deposit is typically around $20. Each deposit amounts to buying shares of the credit union.

As Table 6.5 indicates, in general, credit unions pay an interest rate of 5.5 to 6.5 percent. At the end of its tax year, it will see what is left over after paying expenses. The amount left over, or "profits," are then equitably distributed to its owners. Like banks and S&Ls, credit unions offer a variety of CDs, with interest rates higher than on their savings accounts.

Since many credit unions are job-related, it is easy to start an automatic payroll deduction plan to encourage savings. Interest paid by credit unions is typically higher than at S&Ls. Borrowing costs at credit unions tend to be lower than at other financial institutions. Accounts at credit unions can be insured for up to $100,000 through the **National Credit Union Administration**. Most credit unions offer "share draft" plans, which are similar to NOW accounts and allow credit union members to write checks on their accounts. One problem is that some credit unions are not professionally managed, which may result in lower than expected interest on deposits. If the credit union is not insured, the lack of professional management may put the funds on deposit in danger of loss. Overall, though, credit unions are desirable places to save and to shop for loans. (See "Why Not Deal With a Credit Union?" on page 191.)

Savings Banks

Savings banks are located in some New England and eastern states. Some savings banks are owned by stockholders; others are owned by depositors and are called mutual savings banks. The ceiling on interest paid by savings banks is 6.25 percent. Accounts are insured for up to $100,000 by the FDIC. Savings banks provide services that are similar to those provided by commercial banks. Many savings banks also offer NOW accounts, discussed previously.

Why Not Deal With a Credit Union?

Nancy Lyon, a worker with the Pacific Bell Telephone Company, needed $500 for moving expenses. She joined the company's credit union by phone and received her loan the next day. Commenting on the quick approval of her loan request, Ms. Lyon said, "They knew where to find me. They knew where I'd get the money to pay them back."* Since then Ms. Lyon has taken out other loans from her credit union.

About 53 million Americans have joined credit unions. Interest rates they receive on savings accounts tend to be higher than at other financial institutions. Interest paid on loans tends to be lower than elsewhere. Credit unions now have begun to offer services such as credit cards, individual retirement accounts, stock brokerage services, automated teller services, electronic transfer of funds, and so on. Most of them still retain one of their strong points—the personal touch. That's why credit unions are a good deal.

*The Wall Street Journal, August 30, 1985, p. 11.

Insurance of Accounts

As Table 6.5 indicates, accounts at financial institutions are insured for up to $100,000. Normally an individual cannot increase the limits for himself or herself by opening two separate accounts at the same institution. The $100,000 limit applies to all accounts owned by an individual "in the same capacity and the same right." However, a person can extend the limits by opening accounts in different capacities and rights. A husband and wife can, for example, extend their insurance to $500,000 by opening the following accounts:

Husband, single account	$100,000
Wife, single account	100,000
Husband-wife, joint account	100,000
Husband, in trust for wife	100,000
Wife, in trust for husband	100,000
Total insured savings	$500,000

Further, this same couple can obtain $1,000,000 in coverage by replicating the above accounts at another institution. Fortunately or unfortunately, most of us do not have to worry about insuring savings in these amounts.

Spot Quiz • Comparing Financial Institutions

1. Financial institutions have complete freedom in adjusting their interest rates to market conditions.   T _____ F _____

2. Club accounts are highly desirable for saving money for specific purposes.   T _____ F _____

3. Because of the interest rate, credit unions are a good place to save.
                                                       T _____ F _____

(Answers on page 200)

OTHER TYPES OF SAVINGS INSTRUMENTS

Other types of savings instruments include U.S. savings bonds, annuities such as life insurance, and pension plans. Putting money in these savings instruments is somewhat different from putting money in a savings account at a bank, S&L, or credit union. Consumers typically maintain savings accounts to meet large, infrequent expenses and for emergencies. In these cases, consumers expect to be able to withdraw their funds quickly as the need for funds arises. With the savings instruments discussed in this section, it is generally not possible to withdraw funds quickly. Putting money in these savings instruments is really part of the long-term investment strategy of consumers.

U.S. Savings Bonds

The federal government issues **U.S. savings bonds** as one way of financing its activities. U.S. savings bonds are nonnegotiable, which means that they are registered in the name of a specific person or persons and are not transferable to anyone else. The registration feature is desirable because it prevents loss due to theft, misplacement, or accidental destruction.

Since U.S. savings bonds are fully backed by the U.S. government, they are extremely safe. There is virtually no chance that the U.S. government would fail to redeem the bonds when they mature. Another advantage is that they can be readily purchased from financial institutions without any service charge. Finally, they can be purchased in small denominations. For people interested in saving a small amount periodically, this last feature is very desirable.

In general, U.S. savings bonds are a good deal for the investor with a small amount of money to invest. The bonds pay a market-based interest rate that is guaranteed to be a minimum of 7.5 percent if the bond is held for at least five years. The effective interest rate could be higher than 7.5 percent if market rates are sufficiently high. Two types of bonds are discussed in the following sections: Series EE bonds and Series HH bonds.

Series EE Bonds.   Series E bonds could be purchased prior to January 1980. Series E bonds were purchased at 75 percent of face value. They could be redeemed after 60 days, although their maturity period was five years. Interest was paid on a sliding scale, with interest rising as the bond was held longer.

In January 1980 Series E bonds were replaced by **Series EE bonds**. Series EE bonds are purchased at 50 percent of face value. They mature in no more than ten years and in less than ten years if the market-based interest rate paid on Series EE bonds is higher than 7.5 percent. An individual is allowed to purchase a maximum of $15,000 of Series EE bonds per year. If the bonds are held to maturity, the effective interest rate is at least 7.5 percent.

Series EE bonds do not produce any current income—interest on these bonds is received only upon redemption. Thus, these bonds are not suitable for people who desire current income. A very favorable feature of Series EE bonds is that taxes on interest earned is not paid until the bonds are redeemed.

Series HH Bonds.   Until January 1980, Series H bonds were issued by the federal government. Series H bonds paid interest varying from 4.2 percent if held for six months to 6.09 percent if held for ten years. In January 1980, Series H bonds were replaced by **Series HH bonds**. Series HH bonds have an interest rate that is the same as the interest rate on series EE bonds. However, Series HH bonds cannot be purchased outright. They can be acquired only in exchange for Series E or Series EE bonds. Series HH bonds produce current income for the holder, with interest paid every six months.

Annuities

An **annuity** is a savings or investment plan that provides for monthly income at a later stage in life. Life insurance and pension plans are forms of annuities. With both, a person contributes a fixed sum of money periodically. These monies are invested to accumulate a larger sum. Upon retirement, the person stops contributing money to the annuity. The sum accumulated is then paid out to the person on a monthly basis. These annuity savings plans are treated in greater detail in Chapter 20.

Spot Quiz • Other Types of Savings Instruments

1. U.S. Savings Bonds sacrifice yield for safety.   T _____   F _____

2. Series HH bonds provide for deferment of income taxes until redemption.   T _____   F _____

3. Annuities are savings plans designed to provide retirement income.
                                                      T _____   F _____

(Answers on page 200)

Summary

Consumers need to have money on hand to pay their bills. Many of these payments are planned and can be met by writing checks. Some expenditures are infrequent or of an emergency nature. These can be met by maintaining a savings account.

Five common types of checking accounts are activity, minimum checking balance, minimum savings balance, free, and special package. The suitability of the type of account depends on the account activity.

Checking accounts can be opened as either single or joint accounts. Care should be exercised in writing checks. A check received can be cashed after it has been endorsed. Endorsements can be blank or restricted. Periodically, checking accounts should be reconciled against the records kept by the bank.

In addition to paying by check, payments can be made by using cashier's checks, certified checks, traveler's checks, and money orders. All are acceptable forms of payments. Putting your money into money market mutual funds allows you to earn interest while being able to write checks against the fund balance.

Financial institutions provide a variety of services to their customers, including safe deposit boxes, electronic terminals, drive-in windows, and investment management services.

Savings accounts are held by consumers to pay for infrequent or emergency expenditures, to save temporarily, and to save for specific purposes. The effective interest rate paid on savings accounts is different from the nominal interest rate. The amount of interest received also depends,

in part, on the method used to compute interest. Commercial banks, savings and loan associations, credit unions, and savings banks offer various savings plans. Various government agencies provide insurance on accounts at financial institutions. Other types of savings methods include U.S. savings bonds and annuities.

Questions

1. Why do consumers need to have cash on hand?

2. Briefly explain the various types of checking accounts available. Which one appears to be best? Why?

3. What factors should be considered in selecting a type of account? Explain briefly.

4. What factors should be considered in selecting a financial institution? Explain briefly.

5. Briefly explain some of the mistakes that should be avoided in writing checks.

6. Explain how a check written in New York to a person in San Francisco is processed. (Remember that New York and San Francisco are in different Federal Reserve Bank Districts.)

7. Describe the key steps in reconciling a checking account.

8. List the differences, if any, between:
   a. A cashier's check and a money order.
   b. A cashier's check and a certified check.
   c. A NOW account and a demand deposit account.

9. What is meant by money market mutual funds? What are the advantages and disadvantages of maintaining funds with a money fund?

10. Briefly explain some of the special services of financial institutions.

11. Why do consumers want to maintain savings accounts?

12. Explain the difference between nominal and effective interest rates. Why does this difference occur?

13. Briefly explain the methods used for computing interest on savings accounts.

14. Is it possible for bank A to have a lower effective interest rate than bank B yet pay higher dollar interest on identical accounts? Explain.

15. What is a CD? How does a CD differ from a regular passbook savings account?

16. What are the major differences, if any, between S&Ls and credit unions?

17. Explain the major features of Series EE bonds. Who would want to buy Series EE bonds and for what reasons?

18. How are Series EE bonds different from Series HH bonds?

19. Explain briefly what is meant by an annuity.

Case Problems

1. Judy Zimra estimates that she would be writing, on the average, seven checks each month. An activity account would carry a service fee of 90 cents per month. The bank has a service charge of 8 cents per check and a deposit charge of 10 cents per deposit. Ms. Zimra would be making about two deposits per month. The bank also offers a minimum checking balance. With this account, the bank would not charge any service fees as long as Ms. Zimra maintained a minimum balance of $300. Ms. Zimra could withdraw $300 from her credit union account, which is currently paying 7 percent interest. Should Ms. Zimra open the activity account or the minimum-balance account? Why?

2. Tony Kim writes about ten checks and makes about two cash deposits each month. The local bank has offered him two service packages. The first package would carry a service charge of $1 per month. Each check written and each deposit made would carry a service charge of 15 cents. The second package has a service charge of $4 per month, and no service charges are assessed for either checks or deposits. Which of these checking packages is the better deal for for Mr. Kim? Explain your answer.

3. The Heidens can open a special package account, which would include free checking, free traveler's checks, a safe deposit box, and an 8 percent rebate on interest charges on loans taken out. The cost of the package account is $6 per month. The Heidens can open an activity account that would cost, on the average, $3 per month. A safe deposit box can be rented for $15 per year. The Heidens borrow regularly from the bank and expect that they would pay about $200 in interest every year. The Heidens do not travel regularly, although they are considering taking an annual one-week vacation. Which plan appears to be better for the Heidens? Justify your answer.

4. The checking account register for T. Geisler is shown below:

Number	Date	Description	Payment	Deposit	Balance
201	11/03	Kroger, food	47.35		210.53
202	11/05	Bell, phone	37.60		172.93
203	11/05	CGE, electricity	98.20		74.73
	11/09	Deposit, car parts		80.00	127.73
204	11/17	IGA, food	17.95		109.78
205	11/20	Cash, pocket	60.00		49.78
206	12/01	Sears, clothing	210.25		(160.47)
207	12/01	Ross Realty, rent	350.00		(510.47)
	12/01	Deposit, paycheck		769.22	258.75
208	12/03	IGA, food	32.37		226.38

The bank statement for T. Geisler's account is as follows:

T. Geisler			Beginning balance		$259.88
1009 W. Grand			plus deposits		849.22
St. Louis, MO	63130		less checks		823.35
			less service charge		2.20
			Ending balance		$283.55

Checks	Checks	Checks	Deposits	Date	Balance
47.35				11/05	210.53
37.60	98.20		80.00	11/09	154.73
17.95	60.00		1½0	76.78	
			769.22	12/01	846.00
210.25	350.00	2.20 SC*		12/04	283.55

*SC = Service charge

From the information provided, prepare an account reconciliation for T. Geisler.

5. Erika Schnell wants to buy a $1,000 certificate of deposit for one year. S&L A offers her 6.2 percent interest paid and compounded annually. S&L B offers her a 6.0 percent annual interest paid and compounded quarterly. What are the effective interest rates for these two CDs? Which one should Erika select? Why?

6. J. Lemaster has $300 in traveler's checks left over from a vacation she took recently. She plans to take another vacation in three months. She can either keep the $300 in traveler's checks for her next vacation or cash them and put the money in a savings account that pays 5.25 percent effective interest using the DD/DW method. The bank charges her a service fee of 1 percent for issuing traveler's checks. What should she do? Why?

Bibliography

"Your Bank Wants You to Change Your Ways." *Changing Times* (May 1985): 46–49.

"The Great Banking Bazaar." *Changing Times* (August 1985): 28–33.

"How Safe Is Your Money?" *Changing Times* (August 1985): 34–37.

"Ways to Earn Higher Yields." *Changing Times* (November 1985): 32–38.

"All-in-One Accounts." *Changing Times* (June 1986): 35–37.

"Will the Real Yield Please Stand Up?" *Changing Times* (January 1987): 125–132.

"You and the Banks." *Consumer Reports* (September 1985): 508–516.

"How Safe Are Your Savings?" *Money* (May 1985): 56–59.

"Banks by Other Names." *Money* (September 1985): 80–81.

Answers to Spot Quizzes

The Need for Liquid Assets (page 157)

1. F (The bank has to immediately pay on a valid demand deposit account check.)

2. T (Both provide the consumer with certain advantages.)

Types of Checking Accounts (page 161)

1. F (The activity account is suitable for those who do not write many checks.)

2. T (Average minimum balance allows a customer to let the balance drop below the minimum and then make it up; absolute minimum balance does not.)

3. F (As explained in the text, sometimes special package accounts are preferred to free checking.)

Opening and Using a Checking Account (page 170)

1. F (Postdating means that the date shown on the check is later than the date the check was written.)

2. F (A restrictive endorsement gives the payee more protection.)

3. F (Fraudulent use of overdrafts can result in criminal prosecution.)

4. F (The bank will try to keep the check from being cashed, but it does not guarantee results.)

Checking Account Reconciliation (page 174)

1. F (It is one of the reasons but certainly not the only one.)

2. T (It is quite common to make incorrect entries in the check register.)

Special Payment Methods (page 178)

1. F (Cashier's checks are made out to a specific payee and are not negotiable by anyone else.)

2. F (Certified checks are written on the account holder's account.)

3. T (This is the reason for carrying traveler's checks.)

4. T (Money funds are like interest-paying checking accounts.)

Special Services of Financial Institutions (page 180)

1. F (They are very safe but not theft-proof.)

2. F (Some functions, such as issuing cashier's or certified checks, cannot be handled by an ATM.)

Savings Accounts (page 181)

1. T (Savings accounts can be opened to achieve specific goals, such as accumulating funds to buy a new car.)

2. F (There is no compelling reason to maintain two separate accounts.)

Interest Paid on Savings (page 186)

1. T (Daily compounding, for example, results in higher interest payments than quarterly compounding.)

2. F (The low-balance method actually discourages savings.)

3. F (The choice also depends on the effective interest rate being paid.)

Comparing Financial Institutions (page 192)

1. T (After deregulation, institutions are free to pay whatever they want to.)

2. F (While that is the stated purpose, club accounts pay low interest and are not very desirable.)

3. T (Typically, credit unions have a higher interest rate than S&Ls and banks.)

Other Types of Savings Instruments (page 194)

1. F (Savings bonds provide a good yield, and the bonds are the safest.)

2. F (Series EE bonds provide for tax deferment.)

3. T (That's the idea behind annuity plans.)

Chapter 7

Managing Credit

Objectives

After reading this chapter you will be able to:

- Describe the advantages and disadvantages of credit.
- Judge when and how much credit to use.
- Analyze the cost of credit.
- Explain how to request credit.
- Compute interest charges on open-ended credit.
- Explain the terms of installment contracts.
- Describe consumer protection information.

Mrs. Mary R. Mansour of Akron, Ohio, was very, very fond of two words a few years ago: "Charge it." She and her spouse had a stable family income. Opening charge accounts was no problem at all. In fact, companies welcomed charges by the Mansours. The family felt a strong need for the good things in life. A sparse wardrobe was brightened by running up a $500 charge at one clothing store alone.

Slowly, the family started to spend more on goods charged than it could afford if it had been paying cash. No attention was paid to the total balances outstanding as long as minimum payments could be made. Groceries, haircuts, car repairs—even doctors' services—were charged. Suddenly, the family realized that it was well over $4,000 in debt on charge accounts.

Payments on the balances due started to become bigger than the cash available to pay them. Late charges and service charges were being added to interest charges. Finally, the family realized that its use of credit was out of control. It stopped using its charge accounts. Slowly, it started whittling down the outstanding balances. Mrs. Mansour believes that credit can be like disease in a weakened body. The road back from "Charge it" can be awfully rough.[1]

As the situation of the Mansour family indicates, uncontrolled use of credit can be very damaging to a family. This chapter explains what credit is, how it works, when to use it and when not to use it, and where credit can be obtained.

THE BASICS OF CREDIT

A person buys a used car for $6,000 and finances the purchase with a loan from a bank. Another person buys tires from Sears and charges the purchase on a Sears credit card. A family pays for a flight to Europe by using Visa. What do all these consumers have in common? They are using credit. Credit is involved whenever an institution, whether it is a bank or a store, lends money to someone to finance the purchase of goods and services. In the first case, the bank is providing credit to the car buyer. In the other two cases, credit is provided by Sears and by the bank that issued the Visa card. **Credit** includes all borrowing other than home financing.

Advantages of Credit

Credit can benefit the consumer by providing convenience and economic benefits during periods of high inflation.

---

1. "Hooked on Credit and Out of Control," *Changing Times* (February 1977): 34.

Convenience. Many consumers consider the use of credit a substitute for paying with cash. Thus, instead of carrying cash or checks, many people carry charge cards such as Visa and MasterCard. They charge goods and services throughout the month and pay only once when the charge card statement is received. While this use of credit is justified, it should be undertaken only with a good budgeting system. Otherwise, as the case of the Mansours indicates, it is easy to spend more than you would if you always paid cash.

Buying High-Cost Goods. Credit is useful for the purchase of large-ticket items. Many consumers use credit to finance the purchase of such items as cars and appliances. The funds borrowed can be systematically repaid by including them in the forecast of fixed expenses.

Emergency Use. Credit can come in handy during emergency situations. Say that you are returning from a vacation. Five hundred miles from home, the car's transmission gives up. The repair shop presents a bill of $327. You have only $40 left in cash, and, fortunately, a bank charge card. You use the charge card to pay for the repairs and soon resume the trip. When credit is used in an emergency, appropriate entries should be made immediately on the budget control sheet under actual expenses.

Protection Against Inflation. During periods of high inflation, the prices of some goods and services can increase surprisingly fast. The use of credit allows the purchase of these goods and services before large increases. For example, a family may save for three years to buy a family car. However, over three years the price of their favorite car may go up 25 to 30 percent. The use of credit permits purchase at lower prices as well as earlier use of the product. Keep in mind, though, that the use of credit to hedge against price increases should include an analysis of interest paid on the borrowed funds.

Disadvantages of Credit

The use of credit is not without its disadvantages.

Overextension. The major disadvantage of using credit is that a family can easily overextend itself. **Overextension** means that the family is spending more than it can afford. The Mansours overextended themselves by using a lot of credit. One way to avoid overextension is to record all credit purchases as expenses immediately on the budget control sheet. Good budgeting can prevent overextension and allow a family the benefits of credit.

Contributory to Inflation.   The use of credit by a few families would not make a dent in the inflation rate in the economy. But widespread use of credit by many consumers in society increases the rate of inflation. The reason is that when they use credit, consumers borrow against their purchasing capacity in the future. This increased level of current purchases cannot be adequately met through production. That is, demand exceeds supply. Thus, manufacturers can raise prices, resulting in higher price levels for consumer goods, or inflation.

High Cost.   Often the cost of credit is very high. Consumers may end up paying interest rates of 21 percent or higher on the funds borrowed. High interest rates can reduce the amount of money available for meeting variable expenses, thereby lowering the family's standard of living. If credit is carefully used in conjunction with good budgeting practices, however, a family can enjoy a better standard of living. (See ''Loans and Taxes: Renters Weepers, Homeowners Keepers,'' on page 205.)

Should You Use Credit?

Quite a few people in the United States have never used credit. Some of them, of course, are so wealthy that they do not have to rely on credit at all. Still others worry that the use of credit will force them into bankruptcy. Thus, for them, avoiding credit is a way of avoiding bankruptcy. For some people, credit conjures up images of no jobs, bread lines, and bills to pay. If this sounds vaguely familiar, read up on the Great Depression, which occurred during the 1930s. People who grew up then or who were exposed to that era have a natural dislike of credit. The question still remains, though: Should you use credit?

The advantages of credit were mentioned previously. If you decide to use credit two questions remain: When should you use credit? And how much credit should you use?

When to Use Credit.   As mentioned previously, mortgages or home loans are not considered credit. Credit can be used to finance just about anything. In general, though, a good rule to remember is not to use credit to finance purchases of consumption goods or planned discretionary expenditures. **Consumption goods** include food, groceries, gasoline, eating at restaurants, and clothing. To the extent possible, these items should be paid for in cash or by check. If credit is utilized, it should be only to the extent shown on the budget. Any consumption goods charged should be entered on the budget control sheet immediately. The urge to charge beyond the budgeted amounts should be resisted.

Planned discretionary expenditures include items such as vacations and visits to doctors. Ideally, you should allow for these items in the budget

Loans and Taxes: Renters Weepers, Homeowners Keepers

The 1986 Tax Reform Act put the squeeze on deducting **personal interest expense**, which is interest paid on automobile loans, student loans, credit card balances, charge accounts, credit card advances, and so on. Through 1986, 100 percent of the interest expenses were deductible if the person itemized. However, starting in 1987, only the stated portion of these interest expenses is tax deductible: in 1988, 40 percent; in 1989, 20 percent; in 1990, 10 percent; and after 1990, 0 percent. That is, if you have $1,000 in personal interest expenses in 1988, only $400 is tax deductible.

However, home mortgage interest continues to be fully deductible. Another interesting feature of the Tax Reform Act is that interest expense on home equity loans is fully tax deductible, even if they are used to buy automobiles or to finance a college education. A **home equity loan** is money a person borrows using the net worth in his or her home as collateral. Let's say that two years ago you bought a home for $60,000 and have a $48,000 mortgage balance on it. The house is now worth $70,000. Your equity in it is $70,000 − $48,000 = $22,000. A bank may agree to lend you money against your home equity as long as the loan and the mortgage balance do not exceed 80 percent of the value of the house. Eighty percent of $70,000 is $56,000. The mortgage balance is $48,000, so the banker would be willing to lend you up to $56,000 − $48,000 = $8,000. This loan against your equity in the home is called a home equity loan.

Interest expenses paid on home equity loans are fully deductible. For example, a family wants to buy a new car. A loan from a financial institution, with the car as collateral, would result in only partial deductibility of interest expense through 1990 and no deductibility thereafter. But a home equity loan for the same amount to finance the car purchase would result in total deductibility of interest expenses. Because renters cannot borrow against any home equity, their personal interest expenses do not enjoy the same tax deductibility as the interest of homeowners who use home equity loans to finance various purchases.

and accumulate a surplus. Only when the surplus is large enough should the expenditure occur. Thus, planning for a 1991 vacation should really begin in 1990. Funds for the vacation should be accumulated and then withdrawn to be spent. A common mistake is not to budget for expenses such as vacations. Then July rolls around, and the family hollers loud and clear for a vacation. A trip is taken to the Grand Canyon, and all expenses are charged. The budget gets thrown off track for the next 12 to 15 months. Situations like these should be avoided.

How Much Credit to Use.   Some financial planners say, jokingly of course, that if one never has to repay a loan or interest on it, then the best strategy is to borrow as much as one can. This tongue-in-cheek remark highlights the basic fact in the use of credit—the loans have to be repaid, in keeping with the rules set by the lender. How much credit to use depends on the family's need for goods and services and the family's ability to properly budget loan repayment.

Most families believe that the greater their consumption of goods and services is, the better off they are. This reasoning implies that greater use of credit is desirable. However, greater use of credit increases loan repayment amounts and therefore takes away from some other budget categories. Thus, the need for goods and services should be evaluated with the budget in mind. For example, a family may feel that a new car is a must. Credit can be used to buy a car. The amount of the purchase price that should be financed and how much should be spent on the car become budget expense considerations. If payments for the use of credit for buying the car take away from areas such as food, clothing, and medical expenses, then the family is using more credit than it should.

Another rule of thumb to remember is that no more than 20 percent of a family's take-home earnings should go toward meeting credit payments. For example, for a family with take-home income of $2,000 per month, no more than $400 should go toward making car payments, credit card payments, and other installment loan payments. Table 7.1 shows how this calculation can be performed. The family has $1,780 in monthly take-home income. Its credit payments are $278 per month. The family is spending $278 × 100/$1,780 = 15.6 percent of its take-home income to meet credit payments.

In the example given in Table 7.1, the family is well within its credit limit of 20 percent of take-home income. Assume now that the family would like to trade in the old car on a new one. The remaining loan on the old

Table 7.1 Determining Credit Use

Monthly take-home income		$1,780
Credit payments:		
Car loan	$150	
Credit card	30	
Cash loan	98	
Total credit payments		278
Credit payments as % of income $= \dfrac{278 \times 100}{1{,}780} = 15.6\%$		

car is paid off by combining the sum with a loan for the new car. How much can this family afford in payments on the new car? The calculations are shown in Table 7.2. Twenty percent of the family's take-home income is $356. Its credit payments, other than the car loan, equal $128. Thus, the family has $356 − $128 = $228 in additional credit payment capacity. It can, for example, buy and finance a new car whose monthly payments do not exceed $228. Of course, it is not suggested that a family deliberately try to stay at the 20 percent level.

One way of reducing credit payments is to finance the loan for a longer time period. Thus, financing a car over 42 rather than 36 months would reduce credit payments. However, if a family has to resort to extending loan repayment times to lower monthly loan payments, then chances are the family is using more credit than it should. The correct thing to do is to reduce the use of credit rather than extend the loan repayment time.

Finally, it is acceptable to occasionally have outstanding loan balances on a bank credit card. However, if there is always a loan balance on a bank credit card, the family is using more credit than it should. In this case, further charges on the bank credit card should be avoided, and the loan balance should be paid off as rapidly as possible.

Table 7.2 Determining Credit Limit

Monthly take-home income	$1,780
20% of take-home income (.2 × $1,780)	356
Credit payments less car loan ($30 + $98)	128
Credit payment capacity available	$ 228

Spot Quiz • The Basics of Credit

1. Limited use of credit allows a family to increase its standard of living.

   T _____ F _____

2. Credit should be used by everyone. T _____ F _____

3. The use of credit can help during inflationary periods.

   T _____ F _____

(Answers on page 244)

Cost of Credit

A person borrows $1,000 from a bank. The loan is repaid in 12 equal monthly installments of $91.68 each. The person has paid $100 in interest on the loan. What is the interest rate on the loan? Let's see: $100 interest on a $1,000 one-year loan turns out to be 10 percent interest. Right? Wrong! The interest rate paid on this loan is actually 18 percent. The person has had the use of the $1,000 for one month only. The first loan payment of $91.68 includes $15 in interest and $76.68 in loan repayment. Thus, for the second month, the person has the use of only $1,000 − $76.68 = $923.32. Each month the outstanding loan balance declines. Thus, the borrower has the use of about $555 on the average for the year. The interest rate on the average loan is $100 × 100/$555 = 18 percent.

As the example shows, interest rates are not always what they appear to be. Also, how is the first payment of $91.68 broken down into interest and loan repayment portions? These topics are covered in this section.

Annual Percentage Rate

The **annual percentage rate (APR)** is the effective interest rate applicable to a loan. The Truth-in-Lending Act requires lenders to disclose the APR on loans. The lender is required to include interest charges, carrying costs, and service charges in the calculation of the APR. While typical sources of credit provide the APR to the borrower, some sources, such as leasing arrangements, do not include the APR. Approximate APRs can be calculated by using the formula

$$\text{APR} = \frac{200 \times I \times n}{L \times T}$$

where

I = Total dollar amount of interest
n = Number of payments per year
L = Loan amount
T = Total number of payments plus one

Applying the formula to the example given previously, the APR is

$$\text{APR} = \frac{200 \times 100 \times 12}{1000 \times 13} = 18.46\%$$

The APR thus calculated is approximate. The formula for calculating the exact APR is complicated and so is not given here. The formula for calculating approximate APRs does not work if payments are not regular and constant. If payments are made at varying intervals or if the amount of the payment varies, this formula will not work.

The Truth-in-Lending Act

The **Consumer Credit Protection Act of 1968**, popularly known as the **Truth-in-Lending Act**, became effective July 1, 1969, and was amended in October 1975. The law applies to all credit for amounts up to $25,000 and to all real estate mortgages for any amount. Credit extended to businesses is not covered by the law. Anyone, whether an individual or a business, who regularly offers credit (including mortgage loans or loans to individuals, families, and farmers) is covered by the law. Typically, banks, credit unions, savings and loan associations, retail stores, contractors, and credit card companies extend credit to consumers. All these institutions are subject to the Truth-in-Lending Act.

The law requires that lenders disclose specific information about the loan they are making. The disclosures fall into three major categories. First, credit cost—the APR, the total dollar amount of the finance charge, and the method used for computing interest—must be explicitly disclosed.

Second, information about payments must be disclosed. The number of payments to be made, the amount of each payment, and due dates for payments are written out. For credit cards, the minimum payment must also be specified. Finally, any fees for late payment or fees for paying off the loan before it comes due have to be explained.

A borrower, by signing the loan papers, is not only agreeing to the terms of the loan but also acknowledging that the law's disclosure requirements have been met. It is therefore important not to sign the loan papers without reading them carefully.

Loan Repayments

When credit is used, typically the amount of the loan remains the same. Similarly, the frequency of payment remains the same from one loan source to the next. Say that a person is buying a new car for $8,000. The person has a down payment of $2,000 and wants to finance $6,000. Virtually all financial institutions offering car loans will want the borrower to make monthly payments. Both the loan amount ($6,000) and frequency of payments (monthly) are fixed. Two factors determine the amount of the periodic payments and the total interest paid—the APR and the loan maturity.

APR and Loan Repayment. Both the monthly payments and the total interest paid increase as the APR increases. This is shown in Figure 7.1. For the $6,000 car loan, it is assumed that APRs vary from 12 percent to 20 percent. At the 12 percent APR, monthly payments are $199.29, and total interest paid is $1,174.44. At an APR of 20 percent, monthly payments go up to $222.99. However, total interest paid increases more sharply to $2,027.64. Clearly, the lower the APR is, the lower the monthly payment

Figure 7.1 Effect of APR on Loan Repayment*

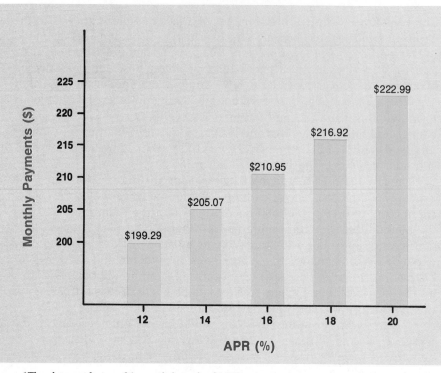

*The data apply to a 36-month loan for $6,000.

will be. In shopping for an installment loan, you are better off borrowing from the lender with the lower APR.

Maturity and Loan Repayment. **Maturity** refers to the length of time over which the loan is repaid. As loan maturity increases, monthly payments decline. As Figure 7.2 shows, the monthly payments for a $6,000, 24-month, 20 percent APR loan are $305.38. The payments go down to $199.79 when loan maturity increases to 42 months. As Figure 7.2 illustrates, the same holds true for the other APRs.

Total interest paid increases as loan maturity increases. Total interest paid can be calculated by using the formula

$$I = P \times N - L$$

where

I = Total interest paid
P = Periodic payments
N = Total number of periodic payments
L = Loan amount

Figure 7.2   Effect of Maturity on Loan Repayment*

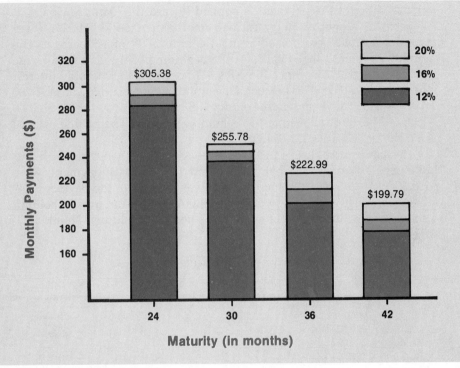

*The data apply to a $6,000 loan.

For the $6,000, 24-month, 20 percent APR loan, total interest paid is

$$I = \$305.38 \times 24 - \$6,000 = \$1,329.12$$

For 42-month maturity, total interest paid is $I = \$199.79 \times 42 - \$6,000$ = $2,391.18. The principle that total interest paid increases with increases in maturity holds true for all other maturities and APRs also.

When you shop for a loan, if your budget permits, a loan with a shorter maturity is more desirable than one with a longer maturity. In this way you will pay less in total interest even though your monthly payments will be higher.

Loan Amortization

In previous sections we discussed the repayment of loans. The systematic repayment of the loan principal and interest is called **loan amortization**. Traditional mortgages, car loans, installment loans, and many other types of loans are generally amortized. For an amortized loan, the amount of

the periodic payment remains fixed. In early months of the loan, smaller portions of the repayment apply to reducing the loan balance. In later months, more of the payment is applied toward the loan principal.

Table 7.3 shows how a typical loan amortization works. The borrower takes out a $1,200 loan for eight months at an APR of 1.5 percent. The monthly payments are $160.30. At the beginning of the first month, the loan balance is $1,200. Since the APR is 18 percent, the monthly interest rate is 18 percent/12 = 1.5 percent. One month's interest on $1,200 is $1,200 × .015 = $18. This is shown in column 4. Since $160.30 was paid, $160.30 − $18 = $142.30 is applied to the beginning balance. The ending balance is $1,200 − $142.30 = $1,057.70.

The same procedure is followed every month. When the eighth and last payment is made, the loan is fully paid off. Total loan payments were $160.30 × 8 = $1,282.40. Since the loan was for $1,200, the payments included $1,282.40 − $1,200 = $82.40 in interest. The amounts in column 4 should add up to $82.40. Similarly, the amounts in column 5 should total $1,200.

Table 7.3 Loan Amortization Schedule*

1	2	3	4	5 = 3 − 4	6 = 2 − 5
Month	Beginning Balance	Monthly Payment	Interest at 18%	Loan Repayment	Ending Balance
0	$1,200.00	$ —	$ —	$ —	$1,200.00
1	1,200.00	160.30	18.00	142.30	1,057.70
2	1,057.70	160.30	15.87	144.44	913.26
3	913.26	160.30	13.70	146.60	766.66
4	766.66	160.30	11.50	148.80	617.86
5	617.86	160.30	9.27	151.03	466.83
6	466.83	160.30	7.00	153.30	313.53
7	313.53	160.30	4.70	155.60	157.93
8	157.93	160.30	2.37	157.94	—

*The loan is for $1,200, with APR of 18 percent and eight equal monthly payments.

Spot Quiz • Cost of Credit

1. A loan at 12 percent annual interest that has service fees will have an APR of 12 percent.   T _____ F _____

2. The Truth-in-Lending Act protects consumers from paying high interest rates. T _____ F _____

3. A $1,000, 14 percent APR loan will always have monthly payments that are lower than those for a $1,000, 19 percent APR loan. T _____ F _____

(Answers on page 244)

GETTING READY FOR CREDIT

When you seek credit, you should know what documentation you will need and what questions you should ask the lender.

Documentation Needed

A lender will want to know a number of facts before approving your loan application. First, the lender will want to know how much money you need. This may sound trivial, but many would-be borrowers have no idea of the amount of money they need. In something like car financing, the amount to be borrowed is easily determined. But in home remodeling, for example, it may be more difficult to estimate the amount needed. The lender will be impressed by the credit applicant who has a good estimate of the amount of the loan.

The lender will also want to know why the applicant wants to borrow. The borrower should draw up a balance sheet to answer any questions the lender may have. Generally, the answer is the lack of ready cash to pay for goods or services to be bought.

The lender will try to gauge the applicant's financial strength by examining the applicant's balance sheet and net worth statement. These should be prepared ahead of time. The lender will judge the applicant's ability to repay the loan by examining the applicant's income statements, some version of a budget, and utilization of existing credit. The applicant should prepare a budget that clearly reflects the ability to repay the loan requested.

The lender will also try to gauge the applicant's willingness to repay debt obligations on time. The lender may check with others who have provided credit to the applicant. The lender will also look at the applicant's employment and income history. The applicant should prepare a record of past debt payments and explanations for tardy or missed payments. A record of employment and salary history should also be prepared. Documentation of credit should be provided to the lender by listing various sources of credit used in the past.

These are the basic items the lender will need to know. Sometimes lenders may have additional credit-related questions. Applicants should make sure that the information provided is as accurate as possible.

What to Ask the Lender

The credit applicant should not hesitate to ask the lender questions. In fact, it is best to ask the same questions of several lenders before formally applying for a loan. First and foremost, find out if the lender is capable of providing the amount of loan requested. It does no good to ask questions only to find out that the lender cannot or will not provide a loan of the size requested.

As mentioned in previous sections, the APR and the loan maturity have direct effects on the size of the loan repayment amounts. Ask the lender for the APR and for the maturities. It is not always desirable to extend the loan maturity, but extension is a useful tool for managing monthly payments. For example, some lenders may be willing to finance a new car only over 36 months, whereas others may finance it over 42 or 48 months. Loan maturity provides budgeting flexibility, and the applicant needs to be aware of the alternatives.

The applicant should also ask about the repayment schedule. Typically, installment loans call for monthly payments, but occasionally a lender may be willing to defer the first payment for a couple of months. A feature like this may be handy around holiday time. The applicant should inquire about penalties for late payments and prepayments. Penalties for late payments are fairly common and are to be expected. Some lenders do not impose prepayment penalties. Borrowing from these lenders provides the credit applicant the opportunity to repay a loan before it matures without a penalty.

Some lenders have less restrictive requirements than others when it comes to collateral for securing loans. The applicant should ask the lender how much and what kind of **collateral** is needed to borrow the amount requested.

Sources of Credit

A person can obtain credit in two ways. First, the lender can provide the borrower with cash. The borrower can then use this cash to buy whatever

goods or services the person had in mind. Alternatively, the lender may provide a credit line for the borrower, who can then purchase goods and services against the credit line provided. In either case, an institution acts as a supplier of credit. Also, loan repayments may involve one payment only, many fixed payments, or many flexible payments. The same institution may be involved with cash and credit loans and various payment plans. Therefore, in the subsections that follow, we discuss various sources of loans, irrespective of whether the loan is cash or credit and whether it requires single or multiple payments. This information is summarized in Table 7.4.

Kith and Kin.   Relatives and friends can be approached for loans. For a family just starting out and without an established credit history, relatives and friends may be the only source of credit available. The major advantage is the informality involved in the borrowing. Generally, there are no service fees or transaction costs. Furthermore, the maturity of the loan and the repayment schedule can be arranged to suit both parties. Because the intermediary—a financial institution—is bypassed, both lender and borrower can benefit. The lender can usually receive an interest rate that is higher than what could be obtained by investing in an intermediate term security, such as a certificate of deposit. The borrower can pay an interest rate that is lower than at a financial institution.

A disadvantage of borrowing from friends and relatives is the tendency to be lax in repayment. Such a temptation should be avoided by all means. The quickest way to lose a friend or estrange a relationship is to not repay a loan or not stay with the repayment schedule. (See ''Borrowing From Your Relatives'' on page 217.)

Loan Sharks.   Lenders who operate outside the legal limits imposed by state and federal laws are called loan sharks. Most states have usury laws that specify the maximum interest a lender can charge. Rates charged by loan sharks are far in excess of state interest rate ceilings. Typical loan shark practices include extremely high interest rates, having the borrower sign a promissory note for an amount greater than the loan, and dating the loan before the money is actually lent. Loans from nonlicensed sources offer no advantages. We recommend that you never negotiate a loan with a disreputable source of credit.

Pawnbrokers.   **Pawnbrokers** lend money secured by the borrower's goods. A person borrowing at a pawnshop will present an article to the pawnbroker. The broker will judge the resale value of the item and will offer a loan equal to about 50 percent of the article's resale value. The borrower is given the loan as well as a pawn ticket listing the item pawned, the amount of the loan, the APR, the amount to be repaid, and the due date for the loan. If the loan is not repaid by the due date, the pawnbroker can legally sell the article pawned to recover his or her loan.

Table 7.4 Summary on Sources of Credit*

Source	APR	Loan Amount	Maximum Maturity	Collateral Required	Eligibility
Relatives, friends	Varies	No limit	No limit	Generally no	Relatives, friends
Loan sharks	50–900%	No limit	No limit	Usually none	Anyone
Pawnbrokers	30–120%	50% of resale value	6–12 months	Property of borrower	Anyone
Credit unions	12–18%	$100–$25,000	1–5 years	Only on secured loans	Members with good credit rating
Life insurance companies	5–13%	Cash value of insurance policy	No limit	Life insurance policy	Policyholder
Commercial banks	12–22%	$800–$30,000	1–10 years	Generally yes	Anyone with good credit rating
Savings and loan associations	Passbook interest rate + 1 to 2%	90–100% of savings account balance	1–3 years	Savings account	Savings account holders
Consumer finance companies	18–50%	$500–$30,000	1–10 years	Generally yes, or cosigner	Anyone with acceptable rating

*APRs, loan amounts, and the maximum loan maturities are often subject to state laws. General trends are identified in this table; the actual figures will vary from state to state.

Borrowing from Your Relatives?

Your old set of wheels, after a long period of wheezing, coughing, and quitting on you periodically, has finally given out. But with tuition, rent, food, books, and entertainment, you don't have any money left to replace your old car with a new one. What to do? Why not use the emergency hotline and say, "Hey, Pops, how 'bout lending me a few grand for a new car? I'll pay you and mom back after I graduate." So, Ma and Pa spring for the $11,000 super-duper apartment-to-campus transporter. No interest charges on the loan, and you don't have to start repaying till you graduate next summer or maybe the summer after.

Sound like a good deal? Not for Ma and Pa if they understand the tax laws. The U.S. government was worried that wealthy parents would lend money at low or no cost to their children, who would invest the money and pay taxes at their lower tax brackets, thus generating tax savings for the parents. So, the tax law requires that on loans in the family, the lender has to pay taxes on the interest that normally would have been received on the loan. The IRS determines the interest rate that would apply on family loans. The major exception to this rule is that the IRS does not worry about loans of less than $10,000. So when talking to Pops, just ask for enough money to buy the semi-super-duper model selling for $9,999.99.

Pawnbrokers are willing to accept a wide variety of articles for security. They can loan funds on such items as watches, guitars, cameras, and jewelry. The transaction is very quick and easy. Pawnbrokers do not investigate the creditworthiness of the borrower because the loan is secured with goods. No financial statements are needed to obtain the loan. The major disadvantage is that pawnbroker loans carry high APRs. If the item is not reclaimed by the due date, it is for all practical purposes sold at a price much below its resale value. In general, a pawnbroker is not a desirable source of credit.

Credit Unions. A **credit union** is a not-for-profit institution. It accepts deposits from its members and lends these funds only to its members. Credit union members are part of a common group. A hospital's employees, for example, constitute a common group and could start their own credit union.

Credit unions, in general, offer loans at low APRs. This is possible because typical credit unions are housed in space provided by the members' employer, who is known as the sponsor. Officers for the credit union are elected and often are not paid for their services. Low operating costs thus allow a credit union to offer loans at low APRs. Additionally, credit unions allow prepayment of loans without penalty.

However, borrowing from credit unions has certain disadvantages. The loan evaluation committees at credit unions are made up of fellow members. Some borrowers may hesitate to reveal personal financial data to fellow employees. Second, not everyone can join a credit union. Only eligible members can join. However, sometimes a family can make itself eligible by joining a social organization or club that sponsors a credit union. In general, if it is at all possible, a person in need of credit should consider joining a credit union. Additional information on credit unions is summarized in Table 7.4.

Life Insurance Policies.   Life insurance policies, other than term insurance, build up cash values over time. At any point in time the policyholder can surrender her or his policy and receive the cash value of the policy. The policyholder can also take out a loan for up to the policy's cash value. The APR for the loan is specified in the policy itself.

The principal advantage of a loan against a life insurance policy is the low APR. Policies taken out in the 1960s, for example, carry an APR of 5 percent. Recent policies carry higher APRs to discourage policyholders from borrowing on their policies. The loan amount does not have to be repaid by a certain time. In theory, a policyholder could take out a loan for an indefinite time period. Interest on the loan is payable annually. Since the loan is secured by the insurance policy, the insurance company does not need a credit check, credit history, or financial statements to issue the loan.

One disadvantage of borrowing on a policy is that the face value or death benefit of the policy is decreased by the amount of the loan. For example, a $50,000 policy may have a $10,000 cash value. If the policyholder takes out an $8,000 loan on the policy, the death benefit of the policy is reduced to $50,000 − $8,000 = $42,000 during the time that the loan is outstanding. If the family needs $50,000 in protection, then one way of overcoming this disadvantage is for the policyholder to take out an $8,000 term life insurance policy. A second disadvantage is that the discipline of regular repayments is not built into an insurance policy loan. Some borrowers find out that a short-term loan on an insurance policy has become a permanent loan.

In general, life insurance policies are good sources of relatively cheap credit. Unfortunately, it takes quite a few years for policies to build up decent cash values. Thus, this alternative is available only to those who have had life insurance for at least five or six years.

Commercial Banks.   Banks provide a variety of loans to their clients, including secured installment loans, unsecured installment loans, bank credit cards, and overdraft privileges. **Secured installment loans** include loans for cars, home improvements, boats, furniture, appliances, and other durable goods. Banks screen their clients carefully, so their bad debt losses

tend to be low. As a result, banks can offer relatively low APRs on secured loans.

Banks are willing to make **unsecured installment loans** to people with very good credit ratings. APRs on unsecured loans tend to be higher than APRs on secured loans. Banks also issue credit cards, which represent unsecured credit. MasterCard and Visa are the most popular bank credit cards. APRs on credit card charges are generally higher than APRs on unsecured cash loans.

Many banks provide creditworthy clients with overdraft privileges. An **overdraft** results when a person writes a check for an amount greater than the funds available in the person's checking account. Under this system, the checking account is coupled with a line of credit. For example, a person may have $120 in the checking account and a $500 overdraft privilege. The person can write checks for up to $620 without bouncing them. Overdraft borrowing is systematically repaid through automatic withholdings by the bank.

To summarize, because commercial banks have strict credit requirements, they can offer relatively low APRs on their loans. They also offer a variety of alternatives to the borrower. For the person with established credit, there are no disadvantages to bank borrowing. People with a spotty credit record will have difficulty borrowing from a bank.

"That's not our interest rate. It's our how-many-times-we-say-yes rate."

Source: *Changing Times*, February 1975, p. 34. Reprinted with permission from *Changing Times* magazine, © Kiplinger Washington Editors, Inc., 1975. This reprint is not to be altered in any way, except with permission from *Changing Times*.

Savings and Loan Associations. Savings and loan associations (S&Ls) can make passbook savings loans as well as loans for home improvements. Depending on the charter conditions, an S&L can loan from 90 to 100 percent of the borrower's savings account balance. Since the S&L holds the savings book for collateral, no credit investigation or financial statements are needed from the borrower.

S&L passbook savings loans are quick and convenient. The APR, while low, is not the lowest. Most S&Ls pay 5.25 percent interest on passbook savings. The borrower can withdraw money from the account to buy goods and services. Then, rather than making installment payments on the loan, the person could put the same amount each month into the savings account. Following this procedure gives an APR of 5.25 percent.

Savings are considered to be emergency funds. Borrowing against savings thus defeats the purpose of such a fund and in general is not very desirable.

Consumer Finance Companies. **Consumer finance companies** are also called **small loan** or **finance companies**. They range in size from the industry giants, such as Household Finance and Beneficial Loan, to one-location, neighborhood operations. Finance companies have less strict lending requirements than commercial banks. As a result, people who were turned down for a loan at a bank might be able to secure one at a finance company. Reflecting the risky nature of their loans, finance companies have relatively high APRs. Finance companies are, however, subject to state usury regulations as well as to the federal Truth-in-Lending Act.

The advantages of finance companies are (1) they are willing to lend to people who may have difficulty obtaining a loan from a bank, (2) they are more flexible than banks in terms of loan amounts and maturities, and (3) they will accept as collateral items that a bank will not accept.

The major disadvantage of a finance company loan is the high APR. APRs vary from state to state but can be as high as 50 percent. The high APRs are justified by the nature of loans made and the collateral accepted by finance companies. In general, a borrower should approach a commercial bank before seeking a loan from a finance company.

Other Sources. A variety of federal and state loan programs are available to students. Generally, interest rates on these loans are lower than existing interest rates on commercial bank loans. Repayment is generally deferred until a few months after graduation. Additionally, some colleges and organizations have loan programs. The financial aid office at any university or college can provide up-to-date information on loan programs for students.

Spot Quiz • Getting Ready for Credit

1. The borrower should prepare financial statements prior to applying for a loan. T _____ F _____

2. The lender will grant a loan based on the borrower's ability to repay the loan. T _____ F _____

3. The APR is the most important factor from the borrower's viewpoint. T _____ F _____

4. In general, credit unions are very desirable sources of credit. T _____ F _____

5. Borrowing from a finance company is desirable since such companies specialize in consumer loans. T _____ F _____

(Answers on page 244)

OPEN-ENDED CREDIT

Open-ended credit refers to charge accounts and credit cards issued by stores, oil companies, banks, and other companies. Some stores open charge accounts without issuing a credit card. Other stores, such as Sears and J.C. Penney, issue charge cards. Oil companies issue credit cards so customers can charge gasoline and other products and services at their gas stations. Cards such as Visa, American Express, MasterCard, and Diners Club can be used at a wide variety of retail businesses. In this section, charge accounts and credit cards and some general features of open-ended credit are discussed.

Charge Accounts

There are three major types of charge accounts: regular (30-day) charge accounts, budget charge accounts, and revolving charge accounts.

Regular (30-Day) Charge Accounts. Regular (30-day) charge accounts are offered by many businesses for the convenience of their customers.

Customers charge purchases and then have 30 days in which to pay their accounts. Doctors, repair shops, telephone companies, and other suppliers of services frequently offer these accounts.

Budget Charge Accounts. With a **budget charge account**, rather than having to pay all of the bill at once, the customer may pay only a portion of the bill. The issuer usually specifies the minimum amount that has to be paid on the bill. The customer therefore has the option of paying any amount equal to or more than the minimum payment, up to the full amount of the bill. The minimum payments are established at a level that allows the customer to pay off the bill in 12 to 24 months. An interest charge is imposed on unpaid balances.

Revolving Charge Accounts. A **revolving charge account** is similar to a budget charge account in that the customer needs to make only partial payments on the bill, and interest is charged on the unpaid balance. In addition, the customer has the option of adding purchases to the charge account as long as a specific credit limit is not exceeded. This type of account is frequently offered by department and retail stores.

Credit cards are usually associated with budget and revolving charge accounts. Many large department and retail stores that offer credit issue their own credit cards. Sears, J.C. Penney, Saks Fifth Avenue, Macy's, and Bloomingdale's are some of the better-known stores that have their own credit cards. Small retail stores may offer charge accounts but not charge cards.

Bank Credit Cards

Close to half of all American families have one or more bank credit cards. The most widely used of these are MasterCard and Visa. They are widely accepted at stores, restaurants, hotels, and other places frequented by consumers. In some cases, the consumer does not have to pay for the use of the card. Generally, however, banks charge an annual fee ranging from $20 to $30. Merchants accepting these cards pay a fee of 3 to 6 percent of the dollar amount of goods or services charged. The merchants pay the fees because they believe that accepting bank credit cards increases their sales volume. Some popular features of bank credit cards are discussed in this section.

Monthly Statement. The bank issuing the credit card mails a monthly statement to the cardholder. The statement shows all of the transactions and the related amounts. Also shown are the previous balance, payments and credits, any adjustments, the finance charge, new transactions, and the new balance. The statement also lists the balance subject to the finance charge, the periodic (daily or monthly) interest rate, and the APR.

Closing Date and Due Date. The statement also shows the closing date. All transaction notifications and payments received by the closing date are shown on the statement. The due date is the date by which the cardholder must remit either full or partial payment on the outstanding balance.

Minimum Payment Due. Bank credit cards are very similar to revolving charge accounts. The cardholder need not pay the total balance outstanding. The statement will list a minimum payment due, which the cardholder can pay by the due date and still maintain his or her credit rating.

Maximum Credit Limit. Bank credit cards have an upper credit limit, usually about $800 to $2,000. The cardholder cannot exceed this limit. That is, at any time, the total of the balance outstanding plus new charges cannot exceed the maximum limit. The monthly statement will show the maximum limit as well as the amount of credit not utilized on the closing date.

Cash Advances. Bank credit cardholders can obtain cash advances on their cards for amounts up to the credit available limit. A cardholder without any charges outstanding would be able to obtain a cash advance of up to the maximum credit limit. A Visa holder, for example, can go to any bank providing Visa services and obtain a cash advance on the card. Interest on the cash advances begins to accumulate from the day the advance is received by the cardholder. In some states, the APR on cash advances is lower than the APR on purchases.

National Credit Cards

American Express, Diners Club, and Carte Blanche are examples of national credit cards. They are very similar to bank credit cards in use. Like bank credit cards, they can be used to charge goods and services at many hotels, motels, restaurants, airlines, travel agencies, car rental companies, and stores. Because of their greater use for charging meals, lodging, and travel, they are often called **travel and entertainment**, or **T & E, cards**.

There are some important differences between bank cards and national credit cards. Athough some bank cards are free, all national cards charge an annual fee of about $30 to $60. Bank cards offer revolving credit, whereas national cards do not. Bank cards are accepted by substantially more businesses than are national cards. For example, your local hardware store will accept a bank credit card but not a national credit card. In contrast, some restaurants will accept national cards but not bank cards. In general, though, unless you entertain at certain restaurants, a bank credit card will do just about everything—and maybe even more than—a national card would do. (See ''Credit Card Deals'' on page 224.)

Credit Card Deals

After American Express, Diners Club, and Carte Blanche came Visa and MasterCard. Then came Sears, Roebuck with its Discover card. Now, Shell Oil has hit the market with its Signature card, and Amoco Corporation, with Multicard. The market for credit cards is saturated. So the new cards and some of the existing ones have had to resort to special programs to induce consumers to apply for and use their cards. Sears is trying to push Discover for financial services as well as general purposes. With Discover, a person has access to individual retirement accounts, money market mutual funds, and merchandise and services at Sears and other establishments. All in all, the competition in the credit card industry may provide some good deals for consumers.

Computing Interest Charges

The Truth-in-Lending Act requires issuers of open-ended credit to disclose the APR charged and the way the outstanding balance (on which interest is charged) is computed. Keep in mind that if the full amount billed, or the new balance, is paid by the due date, then generally no interest charges are paid by the cardholder.

Interest charges billed are calculated by multiplying the outstanding balance by the periodic interest rate. If the APR is 18 percent, then the monthly, periodic interest rate is 1.5 percent. If the outstanding balance subject to finance charges is $300, the cardholder would be billed for $300 × .015 = $4.50 in interest charges. The applicable APR is easy to determine, because it is stated. However, credit issuers can use any of three methods for computing the outstanding balance. How the outstanding balance is computed affects the dollar amount of interest charged. The three methods—previous balance, adjusted balance, and average daily balance— are discussed below.

Previous Balance Method. When this method is used, interest is charged on the total balance outstanding at the end of the previous month. No credit is given for payments made during the current billing month. This method results in the highest interest charges for the cardholder. This method is used quite often by credit card companies, although its use is being curtailed through state laws.

Adjusted Balance Method. With this method, the interest is charged on the outstanding balance after it has been adjusted for payments and credits. Use of this method typically results in the lowest finance charges for the cardholder. Unfortunately, this method is not widely used by issuers of open-ended credit.

Average Daily Balance Method.   With this method, interest is charged on the average daily balance outstanding. The average balance is calculated by adding the balances outstanding each day and dividing the total by the number of days in the billing month. Payments made during the billing month reduce the average balance outstanding. Therefore, earlier payments are desirable because they reduce the average balance more than later payments. Many credit issuers also include new purchases as well as credits on returned merchandise in the daily balances from the day notification of the purchase or credit is received. This method is also widely used by credit issuers.

Interest charges are lowest for the adjusted balance method and highest for the previous balance method. If you have a choice and the APRs are the same, the most desirable lender is the one using the adjusted balance method.

Securing Credit

Many consumers possess one or more credit cards. Those who have not established credit will probably apply for credit eventually. This section outlines the process of securing credit.

Applying for Credit.   The first step in securing credit is applying. Credit issuers require that a person fill out an application, which requires information related to an applicant's ability and willingness to repay a loan. Ability to repay is ascertained by asking questions about the applicant's income, assets, and liabilities. Willingness to repay is judged by the applicant's past credit history and payment experience.

Credit Investigation.   Upon receiving an application, the lender investigates the creditworthiness of the applicant. This process involves verifying the information provided on the credit application. At this time the lender will probably check on the applicant's information by calling the local credit bureau. The credit bureau has a history of the applicant's past credit experiences, with information provided by lenders with whom the applicant has dealt in the past. The credit bureau thus acts as a clearinghouse for credit-related information. If the applicant has not lived in town long enough, the local credit bureau will contact the credit bureau in the city where the applicant resided previously. Most of the time, the credit bureau will be able to provide the applicant's credit history in a few minutes over the phone. The credit bureau does not make the credit decision for the lender. It merely supplies data on the applicant's past credit history and experiences.

Credit Decision.   Once the lender has verified the accuracy of the information provided by the applicant, it decides whether or not to extend

credit. Most lenders use a procedure called credit scoring to make the credit decision. In credit scoring, various factors, such as the applicant's income, amount of debt outstanding, pay habits, and nature of job, are assigned points. If the total points exceed the credit cutoff point, credit is granted. Credit is not granted if the applicant does not accumulate sufficient points. In either case, the applicant is notified of the lender's decision. If credit is approved, the applicant is mailed a charge card and materials explaining the terms of credit.

Securing Credit for the First Time.   All consumers must apply for credit for the first time. They may be able to document their ability to pay, but they have difficulty showing their willingness to pay because they have no past credit experiences. Cautious lenders may refuse credit to the first-time credit applicant because of this lack of information.

When you apply for credit the first time, you should recognize the potential difficulty and prepare accordingly. You may have public utilities services, such as telephone, electricity, water, and gas, billed to you. Regular payments by the due date establish your willingness to pay. Some department stores are willing to open small charge accounts for first-time customers. You might open such an account and regularly charge and pay for goods at the scheduled times as a way of establishing a record of pay

"We've simplified our loans. Take out one enormous loan; repay it with one enormous payment."

Source: *Credit Union Magazine,* October 1980, p. 54. Reprinted with permission.

habits. Finally, it may be useful to borrow from a savings and loan association against a passbook savings account. Timely repayment of the loan would be taken into consideration when you make your first major credit application.

Managing Open-Ended Credit

At times open-ended credit is easy to obtain—almost too easy. Achieving personal financial goals requires active management of credit. This section provides some ideas for managing credit.

Interest-Free Loans.   The best use of open-ended credit is to view it as interest-free loans. Open-ended credit provides interest-free loans *if* all new balances are paid in full by the due date. For example, a person charges $200 worth of goods on Visa. If this Visa bill for $200 is paid in full by the due date, no interest charges are incurred. Basically, the cardholder had the use of $200 from the time the goods were charged to the time the bill was paid. Managing credit this way actually increases family income because the $200 can be invested to earn a return. The major thing to remember is to have the discipline to pay the full amounts of the new balances by the due dates.

Limit Debt.   There are times when budgeting and planning calls for not paying the new balance in full. Debt is created and has to be repaid in installments. When this happens, try to pay more than the minimum payment required. Also, if consumption goods such as food, clothing, and entertainment are charged, they should be paid for in full. If debt includes charges for consumption goods, chances are that the individual or family is in or is headed for financial problems.

Watch the APR.   Check on the APRs and the methods for computing outstanding balances. Patronizing a lender whose has a lower APR or uses the adjusted balance method can lead to large savings in interest expense in the long run.

Pay on Time.   Paying late can damage your credit rating. You should protect your credit rating by paying your bills on time. If for some reason it becomes difficult to pay on time, contact the lender at once. Most lenders are willing to grant additional time for the rare payment that is going to be late. However, if payments become habitually late, lenders will not be agreeable to extending the due dates. Habitual lateness in paying is considered a sign of financial problems. It may indicate that debt limits have been exceeded and corrective actions need to be taken.

Spot Quiz • Open-Ended Credit

1. A bank credit card is similar to a regular charge account.

   T _____   F _____

2. The law requires that the APR and method for computing the outstanding balance for open-ended credit be disclosed.

   T _____   F _____

3. Open-ended credit is called open-ended because there is no credit limit.

   T _____   F _____

4. The previous balance method results in the highest interest charges.

   T _____   F _____

(Answers on page 244)

INSTALLMENT LOANS

Installment loans, as the name implies, require that the loans be repaid by making a series of payments. Open-ended credit can be used to buy just about anything. The amount of credit used and the payments made are flexible. Installment loans, on the other hand, are associated with purchases of durable goods and services, such as cars, appliances, and home remodeling. The loan amount as well as the payments are fixed. Important aspects of installment loans are discussed in this section.

Installment Sales Contract

The installment loan is created by an **installment sales contract**, illustrated in Figure 7.3. That contract spells out the agreement of the parties to the installment sale and contains provisions for creating the security interest. The contract also specifies the purchase price, down payment, amount to be financed, finance charges, APR, total payments, and deferred payment price. Important clauses and features of an installment sales contract are discussed below.

Figure 7.3 Sample Installment Sales Contract

(ASSIGNEE-CREDITOR)		**RETAIL INSTALLMENT CONTRACT** [Goods and Services]	DATE	ACCOUNT NUMBER $

Buyer _____
NAME   RESIDENCE ADDRESS   CITY   STATE   ZIP CODE

Buyer _____
NAME   RESIDENCE   CITY   STATE   ZIP CODE

Seller &
Credit
Arranger _____
CORPORATE, FIRM OR TRADE NAME   BUSINESS ADDRESS   CITY   STATE   ZIP CODE

Seller hereby sells and Buyer or Buyers, jointly and severaly, hereby purchase the following goods for the deferred payment price and on the terms set forth in this contract, Buyer acknowledges delivery and acceptance of the goods in good condition.

Make	Model	Serial No.	Description

DISCLOSURE STATEMENT

1. Cash Price .... $_____
2. Less: Cash Down Payment .... $_____
       Trade-In .... $_____
3. Total Down Payment .... $_____
4. Unpaid Balance of Cash Price .... $_____
5. Other Charges:
       Official Fees .... $_____
       Property Insurance .... $_____
       Credit Life Insurance .... $_____
       Credit Disability Insurance...................... $_____
6. Amount Financed—Unpaid Balance .... $_____
7. **FINANCE CHARGE** .... $_____
8. Total of Payments .... $_____
9. Deferred Payment Price
       (1, 5 & 7) .... $_____
10. **ANNUAL PERCENTAGE RATE** .... _____ %

Buyer promises to pay the **"TOTAL OF PAYMENTS"** shown herein to the holder of this contract at its office designated on the reverse side hereof in_____ installments of $ _____ each and a final installment of $ _____ , beginning on _____ , and continuing on the same day of each successive month thereafter until paid in full. Guarantor, if any, guarantees the collection of the above described **"Total of Payments"** and any other indebtedness due hereon upon the failure of the Seller to collect the above amount from the Buyer named herein. Finance charge begins to accrue _____ 19____
(If different from date of transaction)

Buyer agrees that (1) if Buyer shall default in the payment of any installment of the Total of Payments or any other indebtedness due hereon: or (2) Buyer shall fail to perform any agreement or warranty made by Buyer herein; or (3) any loss, theft, substantial damage to, destruction, sale, encumbrance, concealment, removal, attachment, seizure, forfeiture of or levy upon the goods; or (4) a proceeding under any bankruptcy or insolvency statute shall be instituted by or against Buyer or Buyer's business or property, or Buyer shall make an assignment for benefit of creditors, or (5) if Buyer shall die or be adjudged incompetent; or (6) if holder shall, for reasonable cause, deem itself insecure, the holder may declare all installments of the Total of Payments and all other indebtedness secured hereby immediately due and payable without notice or demand. In the event of acceleration, Buyer shall be credited with the same rebate of unearned **Finance Charge** as for voluntary prepayment.

RETAIL INSTALLMENT CONTRACT

Dated: _____ , 19____   BUYER _____

    _____
          SELLER   BUYER _____

By: _____
       TITLE   Instructions: If parent or spouse is a Co-Buyer sign above. Co-Signer's other than parent or spouse Co-Buyer, sign on Guarantor line below.

Security Agreement.   Historically, the security interest in a credit sale was created by one of a number of different types of agreements: assignment, chattel mortgage, trust deed, factor's lien, and conditional sale. Now all states have, by statute, consolidated all of these legal devices into one form of transaction called a **secured transaction**, which is created by a **security agreement**, as shown in Figure 7.4. The rights and obligations of the parties to such a transaction are outlined by state statutes.

Figure 7.4 Sample Security Agreement

SECURITY INTEREST: Seller retains and shall have a purchase money security interest in the property described above and all accessions under the Illinois Uniform Commercial Code until the Total of Payments and all other amounts hereafter to become due from Buyers hereunder are paid in full. Holder has a security interest in the proceeds and the unearned premiums in any insurance required or purchased. Holder has the right of set-off or lien on any deposit or sums hereunder owed by holder to Buyer.

Credit Life and Disability Insurance.   Figure 7.5 shows that the borrower can buy credit life and disability insurance. The middle and right side of Figure 7.5 shows that these items are optional and not required by the lender. **Credit life insurance** is term insurance and is designed to pay off the remaining balance on the loan in case of the borrower's death. **Disability insurance** allows loan payments to be made if the borrower becomes disabled and is unable to work.

The motives behind credit life and disability insurance are fine. However, the decision to buy life and disability insurance should be part of the planning process for insurance coverage. If the borrower has adequate existing life and disability insurance, then more need not be purchased. If the borrower feels that more insurance is needed, then the procedures recommended in Part IV of this book should be followed. In general, if additional insurance is needed, it should not be purchased through the lender because costs will be high. If the lender requires credit life and disability insurance, check premium costs with other insurers before buying through the lender.

Delinquency Charges.   Installment lenders will impose a late payment charge if the payment is not paid within a specified time period. In Figure 7.6, this charge is shown to be 5 percent of the payment. Every effort should be made to avoid late payments. Besides hurting your credit rating, late payment may involve costly penalties.

Figure 7.5   Sample Insurance Agreement

INSURANCE AGREEMENT

Property Insurance may be required by Seller. Buyer may choose the person through whom the insurance is to be obtained. If such insurance is to be obtained through Seller, the cost for the term of the credit will be $_____ .
Credit Insurance is not required by Seller nor is it a factor in approval of the extension of credit. No Credit Insurance is to be provided unless the Buyer signs the appropriate authorization below. Group Credit Insurance is available for the term of the credit at the following costs:
Credit Life Insurance $ _____ Credit Disability Insurance $_____

I Desire Credit Life and Disability Insurance	I Desire Credit Life Insurance Only	I DO NOT want Credit Life or Disability Insurance
_____	_____	_____
(Date) (Buyer's Signature)	(Date) (Buyer's Signature)	(Date) (Buyer's Signature)

NOTICE OF PROPOSED GROUP CREDIT LIFE INSURANCE

If a charge is made in Item (5) above for credit life insurance and if such insurance is to be procured by assignee, the undersigned takes notice that decreasing term insurance written under a Group Credit Life Insurance Policy is to be purchased on the life of the Buyer, whose signature first appears below (unless Joint Credit Life Insurance has been requested), subject to acceptance by the insurer and issuance of a certificate by

_____

(Insurer)   (Home Office Address)
The amount of the premium shown in item (5) above. The term of insurance will commence on the date of this contract and expire on the originally scheduled maturity date of the indebtedness. The initial amount of insurance will be equal to the initial indebtedness, and will decrease as any payment is made on the indebtedness in an amount computed by multiplying the amount of the payment by the ratio of the initial indebtedness. The proceeds of any insurance paid will be applied to reduce or extinguish the indebtedness. If insurance is terminated prior to the scheduled maturity date of the indebtedness, any premium refund will be paid or credited promptly to the person entitled thereto. Refund formula is on file with the Director of Insurance and with creditor. All of the foregoing is subject to the provisions of the certificate of insurance to be issued. SIGNATURE BELOW.

Prepayments.   Figure 7.6 shows that the loan can be repaid before it matures. Most installment loans allow for prepayment of loans. The method most often used for rebating finance charges is called the **Rule of 78**. Assume that a $5,000 loan is taken out for one year. Finance charges on the loan are $1,000. The total payment amount of $6,000 is to be repaid in 12 monthly installments of $500 each. The borrower makes 4 payments of $500, then wants to repay the loan. The total payment amount was $6,000, and $2,000 has been paid already. Does this mean that the borrower will have to repay $4,000?

The $4,000 includes both principal and finance charges. The finance charges portion of $4,000 will be rebated to the borrower by using the Rule of 78:

1. The loan was for 12 months: $1 + 2 + \ldots + 12 = 78$.
2. To reflect the declining principal on an installment loan, the lender will charge 12/78 of the total interest in the first month, 11/78 in the second, and so on until 1/78 is charged for the last month.
3. Four months of finance charges are $(12 + 11 + 10 + 9)/78 = 42/78$ of total finance charges. The rebate fraction is $1 - 42/78 = 36/78$ of total charges. This amount represents the unused portion of the finance charges. It can also be calculated by summing up the charges for the last 8 months: $(8 + 7 + 6 + 5 + 4 + 3 + 2 + 1)/78 = 36/78$.
4. The rebate amount is the finance charge times the rebate fraction, or $\$1{,}000 \times 36/78 = \$462$. The borrower can repay the loan by paying the lender $\$4{,}000 - \$462 = \$3{,}538$. The Rule of 78 is used also in rebating loans with maturities other than 12 months. The 78 is replaced by the sum of the number of total monthly payments. For a loan with 6 monthly payments, the 78 is replaced by $1 + \ldots + 6 = 21$. A loan with 24 monthly payments will have a denominator of $1 + 2 + \ldots + 23 + 24 = 300$.

Prepayment Penalties. Many installment loans carry a prepayment penalty. Figure 7.6 shows that the prepayment penalty is $12. In general, do not prepay a loan if the prepayment penalty is larger than the finance charge rebate.

Figure 7.6 Sample Prepayment and Delinquency Charge Clauses

REBATE FOR PREPAYMENT: Buyer has the right to prepay this contract in full at any time before maturity of the final instalment hereunder, and if he does so, Buyer shall receive a statutory rebate of unearned **Finance Charge** equal to that proportion of the original **Finance Charge**, less an acquisition cost of **$12**, as the sum of the periodical time balances beginning with the next payment period bears to the sum of the periodical time balances under the schedule of instalment payments in this contract. This statutory computation employs the "sum of the digits" method, also known as the "Rule of 78ths". No rebate of less than **$1** will be made. Use of the statutory method for computation will result in a rebate that is less than a proration of the **Finance Charge** for the period after date of prepayment. The difference may be construed as a penalty for prepayment.

DELINQUENCY CHARGES: Buyer agrees to pay a delinquency charge on each instalment in default for a period of not less than **10** days in an amount of **5%** of the instalment or **$5**, whichever is less. In addition, Buyer agrees to pay court costs and reasonable attorneys' fees incurred by Seller in the collection or enforcement of the debt. In the event of any default hereunder, the entire balance may be declared due and payable.

Notes.   The note is a legal document in which the borrower promises to repay the loan under agreed upon terms. In some cases, the lender requires the borrower to sign a note that is separate from the sales contract. In most cases, though, the note is incorporated into the sales contract, and the total document becomes the note.

Undesirable Clauses in Installment Loans

Some lenders still use clauses in lending agreements that are not very desirable from the borrower's viewpoint. In general, borrowing with undesirable clauses in contracts should be avoided.

Wage Assignment or Garnishment.   With this clause, a lender can collect a portion of the borrower's wages if the borrower has defaulted on the loan. A court order is not needed to garnish wages with this clause. If this clause does not exist, the lender would have to obtain a court order to garnish wages.

Confession of Judgment.   The borrower gives up rights to be present at legal proceedings if default on the loan occurs and this clause is in the sales contract. This clause will not be given legal effect in many states.

Balloon Payment.   Sometimes the full amount of the loan is not fully amortized over the loan's life. In other words, the installment payments are too small to fully pay off the loan at maturity. Because only a portion of the loan is repaid, the borrower faces making a relatively large payment when the loan matures. Balloon payment loans generally create hardships when the loans mature. In general, balloon loans should be avoided unless you are certain of large cash inflows before the loan matures. The Truth-in-Lending Act requires disclosure of balloon payments, and some states have outlawed balloon payment loans.

Add-On Clause.   An add-on clause allows the lender to maintain a security interest in all items financed by the lender until all items are repaid. Lenders can legally repossess items already paid for by the borrower if the borrower defaults on an item not yet paid off. To avoid such problems, it is best to have a separate sales contract for each item.

Acceleration Clause.   An **acceleration clause** causes the total loan to become due immediately if the borrower misses a payment. This clause allows the lender to repossess the security if the borrower defaults on a payment.

In general, installment sales contracts with the types of clauses mentioned in this section should be avoided because these clauses give the lender undue power over the borrower. Borrowing from a lender who does

not insist on these clauses leads to a better relationship between borrower and lender.

Repossession

The lender may try to repossess goods purchased on installment contracts if the buyer defaults on the loan payments. The lender usually has the legal right to physically repossess the goods if they have been used as collateral for a loan. Once the item has been repossessed, the lender will probably sell it to satisfy the unpaid loan. The borrower is still liable if the proceeds from the sale are not sufficient to pay off the loan. Sales proceeds in excess of the unpaid loan are returned to the borrower. Repossessions lead to the loss of goods and harm to a person's credit rating. A frank discussion with the lender might lead to a loan repayment schedule that is easier to handle.

Spot Quiz • Installment Loans

1. Credit life insurance is not a good way of handling the liability of paying off a loan.   T _____   F _____

2. The Rule of 78 is used to determine prepayment penalties.
                                                        T _____   F _____

3. An add-on clause allows the lender to possibly repossess a purchase that was already paid for.   T _____   F _____

(Answers on page 244)

Consumer Credit Protection

The Truth-in-Lending Act, discussed earlier in the chapter, requires disclosure of APRs and certain other credit-related items. In addition to this law, a variety of other laws provide consumers with additional credit protection. Some of these protective measures are discussed in this section.

Lost or Stolen Credit Cards

The Truth-in-Lending Act limits a cardholder's liability to a maximum of $50 if a lost or stolen card is used by someone else to charge goods or services. Cardholders are not liable for unauthorized charges that occur after the card issuer has been notified of the card's loss or theft. The best way to notify the card issuer of a credit card loss or theft is by a collect call to the issuer followed by a telegram. Because the maximum liability is a small amount, there is generally no need to buy credit card insurance.

Credit Reporting

An earlier section in this chapter explained that a lender will seek to verify a credit applicant's information by contacting a credit bureau. A good credit reporting system helps those consumers who are good credit risks by screening out poor credit risks. Credit reporting and investigation permit lower credit costs for those who are willing and able to handle credit.

Credit bureaus obtain their information from three sources. First, firms who use the services of credit bureaus provide the bureaus with credit experiences of their clients. Second, credit bureau investigators utilize court records and other public sources to gather information about borrowers. Third, from time to time, these investigators interview friends, neighbors, and coworkers to obtain information about borrowers. There is always a chance that in this information-gathering process an error will be made.

The **Fair Credit Reporting Act**, passed in 1971, is designed to force credit bureaus to keep only correct information about borrowers on file. A rejected credit applicant can request the credit bureau involved to provide information contained in his or her credit file. If the information is incorrect, the credit bureau must correct the information and notify lenders about the correction. If the applicant and the credit bureau do not reach an agreement on the validity of the information, the applicant can place a 100-word explanation in his or her credit file. This explanation must be forwarded to lenders. If a consumer has not been rejected for credit, he or she can still see his or her credit file at the credit bureau by paying a nominal service fee of $5 to $25.

Equal Credit Opportunity

The **Equal Credit Opportunity Act**, passed in 1975, prohibits credit discrimination on the basis of sex or marital status. In other words, a lender must apply the same credit standards irrespective of the sex or marital status of the applicant. Regular alimony and child support payments must be

considered to be part of income. The credit history of the family must be considered when only one spouse is applying for credit.

Disputes on Merchandise Defects

One of the sections of the Truth-in-Lending Law deals with disputes about defective merchandise. This law applies to credit purchases in excess of $50 made in the borrower's home state or within 100 miles of his or her mailing address. The borrower need not pay for the goods or services until the merchant has tried to correct the situation or has taken back the merchandise. This law does not apply if the borrower arranged for the loan independently of the purchase of goods and services.

Billing Procedures and Problems

The Truth-in-Lending Act also covers billing procedures and billing errors. Bills must be mailed at least 14 days prior to the due date. All payments and credits received during the current billing month must be posted to the account.

Notices of billing errors must be acknowledged by the lender within 30 days unless the lender was able to resolve the error within the 30-day period. The lender has 90 days to correct the error or explain why the bill was correct. The lender cannot legally collect the payment in dispute during the time it takes to respond to the borrower. Once the lender has explained the bill, it can proceed with trying to collect the bill.

Important consumer credit protection legislation was discussed in this section. These laws provide consumers with a fair amount of protection. Chances are that in the future even more laws will be enacted to provide consumers with additional credit protection.

Spot Quiz • Consumer Credit Protection

1. Consumer credit protection laws keep lenders from collecting from a delinquent borrower.   T _____ F _____

2. The Fair Credit Reporting Act prohibits discrimination on the basis of sex.   T _____ F _____

(Answers on page 245)

Managing excessive credit

This chapter so far has provided information on credit and credit sources. A family that is actively involved in budgeting can easily identify its capacity to take on more debt. Unfortunately, from time to time some families and individuals find themselves overextended—trying to cope with more debt than they can possibly handle. This section describes a series of steps for managing excessive debt.

Confirmation of Excessive Debt

Certain basic symptoms suggest excessive debt. If you are having trouble meeting loan payments, if you pay only the minimum amount, if lenders are calling to ask for payment—chances are you are overextended. If you are not making savings account deposits or if your savings account balance is dropping, it is probably because of excessive borrowing. For starters, you can go to a bank, credit union, or other financial institution and ask for information about credit counseling. The lending officers at these institutions will probably provide a free analysis of your credit picture. Believe these professionals if they state that you have excessive debt. (See "Too Much Debt?" below.)

Too Much Debt?

Are you too deep in debt? To find out, try out the following quiz:

I am in too much debt if:
   a. My take-home pay is less than five times my total personal debt (all debt except mortgage).

   b. I am spending more than a fifth of my monthly take-home income on servicing personal debt.

   c. It would take me more than 12 months to pay off my personal debts.

   d. After paying for food, utilities, and mortgage, I am using more than a third of what's left to make payments on personal debts.

   e. Any of the above apply.

The answer is e. If any of the four situations apply, you are in too much debt.

Reduce Expenditures

At the first signs of excessive debt, stop all use of credit. Borrowing to repay loans does not help at all. Examine your budget for expenses that can be reduced. A budget should be prepared if you do not have one. Discretionary expenditures should be reduced. Entertainment expenses can be eliminated for a while. You can save on food by eating out less often. Expenditures for clothing and shoes should be postponed. Any funds freed up should be applied to reducing those loans that have the highest APRs. If sufficient funds are not freed up to avoid loan payment delinquencies, contact the lenders at once. Explain the situation to them. Show them how expenses have been reduced and how much is available for loan payments. They may be willing to renegotiate loans, resulting in lower payments.

Some lenders may suggest a **debt consolidation loan**. With debt consolidation, a new loan is taken out to repay the outstanding loans. One debt payment is substituted for many debt payments. This sounds acceptable until you realize that the APRs on debt consolidation loans can vary from 30 to 50 percent. Why give up 18 to 20 percent APR loans for a 30 to 50 percent APR loan? A debt consolidation loan is acceptable only if its APR is about the same as that of the loans it seeks to consolidate.

Seek Credit Counseling

As mentioned before, many financial institutions are willing to provide credit counseling services. If you cannot find counseling, contact the National Foundation for Consumer Credit, 1819 H Street, NW, Washington, DC 20006. This foundation will help you locate a nearby credit counseling service. The service can help you develop an essential expense budget and arrange new payment schedules with lenders. Their services are either free or available for a low cost.

Family counseling services also provide credit counseling as well as information about legal aid. The location of a nearby family counseling service can be obtained by contacting the Family Service Association of America, 44 East 23rd Street, New York, NY 10010.

Bankruptcy

Sometimes even with reduced expenditures and credit counseling, the debt burden remains unmanageable. At this point, one alternative is to declare bankruptcy. **Bankruptcy** is a legal procedure that allows a person to give up certain assets in return for release from certain financial obligations.

A new federal bankruptcy law went into effect in October 1979 and was revised in 1984. It defines two kinds of personal bankruptcies—Chapter 7 and Chapter 13. Some debts, such as alimony, child support, damage awards from drunk driving, and income taxes, cannot be discharged through bankruptcy.

In **Chapter 7 bankruptcy**, or **straight bankruptcy**, certain assets remain exempt; the rest are made available to lenders to satisfy their loan claims. Exempt assets include: $7,500 equity in home; $1,200 equity in car; $200 per item for household goods, clothing, appliances, and so on; $500 in jewelry; $400 in other property; $750 in tools; all health aids. These amounts are doubled for a husband and wife who file joint bankruptcy. Also exempt are social security benefits, pension benefits, alimony, child support, and disability benefits. A petition for bankruptcy is filed with the area U.S. District Court. Assets, liabilities, and earnings have to be listed in the petition. Eventually, the lenders receive notice of discharge of debt, and the borrower is free of his or her debt obligations. A Chapter 7 bankruptcy cannot be filed more often than once every six years.

In **Chapter 13 bankruptcy**, also known as the **wage earner plan**, a new repayment schedule is worked out under court protection. Only partial payment is generally made on the outstanding debt. A Chapter 13 bankruptcy is somewhat similar to a debt consolidation loan under court protection. Under Chapter 13, the borrower is allowed to keep all assets as long as he or she is keeping up with the court-approved repayment schedule. If the borrower is paying at least 70 cents on each borrowed dollar under Chapter 13, then the limitation of a bankruptcy petition no more than once every six years does not apply.

Bankruptcy is a drastic measure that should be resorted to only after other remedies have been exhausted. The overextended borrower should first try to work out an equitable settlement with lenders and should obtain advice from credit counselors.

Spot Quiz • Managing Excessive Credit

1. Often excessive debt can be managed through reducing expenditures.

    T _____   F _____

2. Bankruptcy is an easy way out of paying debts.

    T _____   F _____

(Answers on page 245)

Summary

A person is using credit whenever he or she buys goods or services by borrowing money from someone else. Credit makes shopping convenient, allows the purchase of high-priced items, is handy in emergencies, and can provide some protection from inflation. However, credit carries a high cost, and its abuse can lead to debt overextension.

The cost of credit is measured by the annual percentage rate, or APR. The Truth-in-Lending Act requires lenders to disclose the APR, the total dollar amount of finance charges, and other information about loans. Higher APR loans are more expensive than lower APR loans.

Before applying for credit, a person will need to prepare personal financial statements. The lender will try to gauge the loan applicant's ability and willingness to repay a loan before granting the loan. A person can seek credit from friends, relatives, pawnbrokers, credit unions, life insurance policies, commercial banks, savings and loan associations, and consumer finance companies.

Credit can be open-ended or installment loan. Examples of open-ended credit are charge accounts and bank and other credit cards. Interest charges on balances are affected by the method used to compute outstanding balances. Credit issuers will check on an applicant's prior credit history and experiences before granting credit.

Installment loans carry delinquency charges and prepayment penalties that should be understood. Some installment loan contracts have undesirable clauses affecting the borrower's bargaining power. These contracts should be avoided.

Consumer credit protection laws cover lost and stolen credit cards, credit reporting, discrimination on the basis of sex or marital status, disputes over defective merchandise, and billing problems. Excessive use of debt can sometimes be managed with the help of credit counselors. Other times, a drastic measure such as bankruptcy is the only way out.

Questions

1. What is meant by credit? Give some examples of credit.

2. What was the basic financial problem of the Mansour family, mentioned at the beginning of the chapter? What advice do you have for the Mansours?

3.   What are the major advantages of credit? Explain briefly.

4.   Briefly discuss the major disadvantages of credit.

5.   Explain when credit should be used.

6.   How can a family determine whether it is using too much credit?

7.   What is meant by APR? Explain whether it is a useful tool in making consumer credit decisions.

8.   Briefly explain the disclosure requirements of the Truth-in-Lending Act.

9.   Explain the relationship, if any, between loan maturity and loan repayment.

10.   What is meant by amortizing a loan?

11.   What type of documentation does a person need before applying for credit?

12.   What questions would you ask a lender before applying for a loan?

13.   Briefly explain four popular sources of consumer credit.

14.   Are there any sources of consumer credit that you would not want to use? Explain your answer.

15.   What is meant by open-ended credit? List three sources of open-ended credit.

16.   Explain any similarities and differences between bank credit cards and national credit cards.

17.   Briefly explain the following methods of computing outstanding balances:
      a.   Previous balance.
      b.   Adjusted balance.
      c.   Average daily balance.

18.   Explain the two major criteria used by lenders in deciding whether to grant credit.

19.   Explain the procedure used to verify information supplied by a credit applicant.

20.   What can a person do to prepare for applying for credit for the first time?

21.   Why is it important to make loan payments on time?

22.   What is the difference, if any, between a conditional sales contract and a chattel mortgage?

23.   Should you buy credit life and disability insurance through a lender? Why or why not?

24. Explain briefly how the Rule of 78 works.

25. Briefly explain three clauses that you would prefer *not* to see in an installment loan contract.

26. Why is repossession not desirable from the borrower's viewpoint?

27. What protection does a person have after losing a credit card?

28. What would you do if you felt that the credit bureau had incorrect information about you?

29. What are the borrower's rights if defective merchandise is purchased on credit?

30. How would you have a billing error corrected?

31. How can you determine if you are using excessive credit?

32. What is the role of a credit counselor in a situation involving excessive debt?

33. What are the major differences between Chapter 7 and Chapter 13 bankruptcies?

34. If you had to file for bankruptcy, would you file for Chapter 7 or Chapter 13? Explain your answer.

Case Problems

1. The Adamses have take-home income of $2,200 per month. They are paying $250 per month on a car loan. Other monthly credit payments include $100 for charge accounts and $150 for a cash loan. Analyze the Adamses' credit use to determine whether they are overextended.

2. The Venezias have a monthly take-home income of $2,300. Their monthly credit payments equal $240 per month. They are planning to buy a new car that would require monthly payments of $260 per month. What advice do you have for the Venezias? Provide numerical justification for your advice.

3. Sandy Galetti has a job paying $1,500 per month after all deductions. Recently purchased appliances call for monthly payments of $160 per month for the next two years. She is thinking of buying a new car that would involve monthly payments of $155 per month for 36 months. She is also considering a good used car that would call for payments of $130 for the next 30 months. What advice do you have for Ms. Galetti? Explain your answer fully.

4. The Rahmans need a $3,000 loan for three years. Bank A has offered a $3,000, 36-month loan that is to be repaid with monthly payments of $108. Bank B offers a $3,000, 42-month loan that calls for monthly payments of $94.
   a. Calculate the total interest that would have to be paid with each of the two loans.
   b. Calculate the APRs associated with the two loans.
   c. From which bank should the Rahmans borrow? Why?

5. Henry Chadwick takes out a three-month loan for $500. The monthly interest rate on the loan is 1.5 percent. Mr. Chadwick repays the loan by making three monthly payments of $171.69 each. Prepare a loan amortization schedule for Mr. Chadwick's loan. How much of the $171.69 payment was for interest in each of the three months? (*Hint*: Interest for all three months totals $15.07.)

6. For Case Problem 5, Mr. Chadwick wants to repay the loan after making the first payment. His two remaining payments equal $171.69 × 2 = $343.38. Part of this amount represents interest, which will be rebated by using the Rule of 78. How much of a rebate will Mr. Chadwick receive? Show your calculations.

7. Diane Stutzmann has a $2,500, 15-month loan from a consumer finance company. She is making monthly payments of $200 to pay off the loan. After making nine payments, she decides to pay off the loan. The finance company uses the Rule of 78 to rebate finance charges. It also charges $15 as a prepayment penalty. Calculate the amount of money needed to pay off the loan.

Bibliography

"Five Ways to Lose When You Borrow." *Changing Times* (April 1985): 72–74.

"Should You Hock Your Home?" *Consumer Reports* (November 1986): 739–743.

"The Hidden Power of Plastic." *Consumer Reports* (February 1987): 119–121.

"When It Pays to Use an Out-of State Bank." *Money* (April 1985): 81–86.

"Extracting Cash from Your House." *Money* (April 1986): 97–100.

"If You're So Smart, Why Aren't You Rich?" *Money* (November 1986): 203–208.

Answers to Spot Quizzes

The Basics of Credit (page 207)

1. T (Careful use of credit allows the purchase of goods that can improve the quality of life.)

2. F (Some people should not use credit.)

3. T (Using credit helps especially when goods whose prices are increasing sharply are purchased.)

Cost of Credit (page 212)

1. F (The service fees will make the APR higher than 12 percent.)

2. F (It only requires credit disclosures.)

3. F (Monthly payments also depend on loan maturity.)

Getting Ready for Credit (page 221)

1. T (Information should be organized before seeing a lender.)

2. F (Both ability and willingness are considered.)

3. T (The APR affects the loan repayment amount.)

4. T (Credit unions generally have lower APRs.)

5. F (In general, finance companies have higher APRs.)

Open-Ended Credit (page 228)

1. F (It is similar to a revolving charge account.)

2. T (Both have to be disclosed.)

3. F (Generally, there is a specified maximum credit limit.)

4. T (Charges are highest with this method.)

Installment Loans (page 234)

1. T (Buying insurance requires planning that is separate from incurring debt.)

2. F (It is used to determine finance charge rebates.)

3. T (With the add-on clause, the security agreement is extended to items that may have been paid for already.)

Consumer Credit Protection (page 236)

1. F   (Laws establish consumer rights but do not shelter delinquents.)

2. F   (The act relates to credit files.)

Managing Excessive Debt (page 239)

1. T   (Certain discretionary expenses can be reduced.)

2. F   (Bankruptcy can leave scars.)

Part 3

Housing and Transportation

Part 3 deals with housing, transportation, and appliances. Together, these items account for a very large portion of the expenditures in a family's budget. Chapter 8, "Renting Housing," discusses the advantages and disadvantages of renting versus buying housing. The chapter also discusses the rental agreement.

Chapter 9 is entitled "Buying a Home." Factors to be considered in buying a home as well as sources of financing are explained here. One section is devoted to a discussion of home remodeling.

Chapter 10, "Transportation and Major Appliances," describes the purchase decisions for cars and appliances. Discussion focuses on buying new and used cars. Leasing a car is also explained. The various factors to be considered in buying major appliances are discussed as well.

Chapter 8

Renting Housing

Objectives

After reading this chapter, you will be able to:

- Discuss the advantages and disadvantages of renting housing.
- Discuss the advantages and disadvantages of buying housing.
- Explain how to compare renting with buying housing.
- Tell who may be particularly interested in renting housing.
- Name three factors that are of great importance in renting housing.
- Describe the clauses usually found in a lease.

Meet Melissa Litton, Denver area marketing representative for System Development Corporation. Single, in her late twenties, earning about $18,500 annually, and enjoying the laid-back Denver life style, she has one concern about her status as a renter: "I know I'll have regrets if I don't buy a house before I'm priced out of the market."[1] Ms. Litton, currently living in a rented bungalow, plans to buy a house priced around $55,000. She has decided not to buy a condominium because she feels they will not go up in value as fast as houses.

Basic among human needs is the need for a place to live. Apartments, houses, condominiums, and mobile homes are alternate forms of shelter. For that matter, so are caves, houseboats, and, in a remote Bavarian village, a very large wooden wine barrel.

How does Ms. Litton—or anyone else—decide between buying and renting shelter? What do you have to keep in mind when you rent? Answers to these questions form the subject of this chapter.

RENTING VERSUS BUYING HOUSING

Typically, for any housing that can be rented, a similar type of housing can be bought. For example, houses can either be rented or bought; units in apartment buildings are typically rented, but in some cases they, too, can be bought.[2] This means that when you are looking for shelter, usually your needs can be met by either renting or buying. The decision to either rent or buy depends on the advantages and disadvantages of the two alternatives.

Advantages of Renting

The principal advantage of renting is that it does not involve a substantial financial expenditure. Usually the **tenant** (the person renting the unit) pays one month's rent in advance and a damage deposit before occupying the rental unit. Also, renting does not involve a long-term financial commitment. Rental agreements specify the duration of the agreement, usually one year. The tenant is under no obligation to occupy the rental unit beyond the terminal date specified in the rental agreement. The short-term nature

---

1. "A Solo Plunge into Real Estate," *Money* (March 1979): 57.
2. Apartment-type shelters for sale are called condominiums or cooperative units. These forms of housing are discussed in Chapter 9.

of the rental agreement allows considerable freedom to accommodate personal plans. Students generally find it convenient to rent shelter. A businessperson temporarily assigned to a different city for, say, one year may find it convenient to rent.

More and more rental units belong to large complexes. These complexes often provide swimming pools, tennis courts, saunas, recreation clubs, and other recreational facilities. In addition, owners of rental units usually provide maintenance and repair services. The tenant normally does not have to maintain landscaping, fix plumbing, or repair a leaking roof. Also, because rental units tend to be small, tenants find that housekeeping chores are simplified. Another advantage of renting is that access to public transportation, shopping, and recreational facilities outside the complex may be excellent.

Disadvantages of Renting

The major disadvantage of renting is that the tenant does not build up any **equity** (the owner's interest in a property over and above the amount of the mortgage) in the rental housing over time. That is, all of the rent is an expense for the tenant. A tenant who pays $300 a month in rent pays out $3,600 in rent over one year and has nothing tangible to show for this expense.

Another disadvantage is that renting does not result in tax deductions for the tenant. Thus, the actual cost of obtaining housing is the same as the rent payment. The person paying $300 a month in rent incurs an actual housing expense of $3,600 over one year.

Also, because rental agreements are for short time periods, the **landlord** (the person owning the rental unit) can raise the rent or make other changes in the rental unit. Renting therefore typically does not provide the tenant with protection from increases in shelter costs.

Finally, at times renting does not allow much personal privacy. Poorly constructed or poorly maintained rental units may allow noise and dust to interfere with a person's preferred life style.

Advantages of Buying

How many times have you met a person who proudly states, "I am a homeowner." Home ownership is a source of great personal pride, adding to a person's sense of self-worth. Handling the obligation of owning housing in a responsible manner also increases self-esteem.

Owning housing generally involves borrowing money for a long time period to pay for the housing unit. This loan is generally paid off by making

fixed, periodic payments over a specified time. Owning a home therefore, to a great extent, keeps the cost of housing fairly constant.

The loan payments consist of two parts—principal and interest. The portion of the payment that is applied to reducing the amount of the loan is called **payment on the principal**. The rest of the payment is interest on the amount borrowed. Let's assume that someone has bought a house for $60,000. This person borrows $48,000 from a bank and combines it with $12,000 of her own money to pay for the house. She repays the $48,000 loan by making monthly payments of $600 for a specified number of months. For one year, total loan payments are $7,200. Of this amount, $2,000 is payment on the $48,000 principal, and $5,200 is interest on the principal. After one year, the owner's investment in the house is $12,000 + $2,000 = $14,000. That is, the amount of the loan has been reduced by $2,000 to $46,000. Housing ownership generally provides for periodic saving and an increase in the amount of funds invested.

In the example just cited, the homeowner can take a tax deduction for the $5,200 paid in interest, reducing the actual housing expense. Similarly, property taxes paid on the housing unit are also tax-deductible.

The cost of shelter has been going up steadily. For example, the price of the average new residential house in the United States in November 1982 was $93,000. By June 1987, the price of the average new home had risen to $129,000, an increase of 39 percent. This increase in the price of new houses is fairly typical of increases in other forms of shelter also. Older houses, condominiums, and cooperatives are steadily appreciating in value. Housing ownership provides the owner with a good return on the investment. Let us continue the example of the home bought for $60,000. The owner bought this house by putting up $12,000 of her own money and borrowing $48,000 from a bank. One year later, she sells this house for $66,000. After paying off the remaining bank loan of $46,000, she has $20,000. She had invested $14,000 of her own money, so she is left with a profit of $20,000 − $14,000 = $6,000. This profit is a ($6,000/$14,000) × 100 = 42.8 percent return on her investment of $14,000.[3]

Disadvantages of Buying

Buying shelter has certain disadvantages. Lending institutions will not lend 100 percent of the purchase price. Usually they will lend only up to 80 percent of the purchase price. This means that the buyer has to put up at least 20 percent of the purchase price in cash. The amount of money that the buyer puts up toward the purchase of a house is called the **down payment**.

---

3. The example cited here is simplified in that brokerage and other fees are ignored. These points are clarified in Chapter 9.

Many individuals and families are not able to save enough money for the down payment.

Buying housing also limits the buyer's mobility in the short run. Selling a home may involve brokerage fees and other fees associated with transfer of ownership of the home from the seller to the buyer. Many of these costs are relatively large. A home that is sold within a period of one or two years may not allow the seller even to recover the down payment. Buying typically implies that the person will keep the house for two years or more. If changes in the family situation or jobs are expected to occur over short time periods, then buying housing is not a highly desirable alternative.

Buying housing also requires spending time and/or money for the upkeep of landscaping, plumbing, appliances, and so on. In addition, housing available for purchase may not be situated to allow for convenient use of public transportation.

Comparing Costs of Renting Versus Buying

As the previous sections indicate, advantages and disadvantages are associated with both renting and buying housing. The advantages and disadvantages are monetary as well as nonmonetary. Nonmonetary items cannot be directly compared. However, costs of renting versus buying housing can be compared by looking at the monetary items.

If a housing unit is rented, the tenant has to pay rent, typically utilities, and sometimes insurance. A home buyer has to make loan payments as well as pay utilities, taxes, insurance, and maintenance expenses. The tenant does not receive any tax benefits from paying rent. The homeowner can deduct interest expenses on the loan and taxes. In addition, the buyer's home may go up in value. All of these factors are monetary and are used in comparing renting and buying.

The example that follows is based on a real situation facing a young couple in a university town. The Kims can rent a house for $425 per month. Their expenses for electricity, water, gas, and garbage collection are expected to average $90 a month. They also plan to buy insurance for household belongings, which will cost $8 a month. These costs of renting are summarized in the left column in Table 8.1.

The Kims also have the option of buying this house for $40,000. The bank will provide a 25-year, 80 percent loan, or $40,000 × .8 = $32,000, at 10 percent annual interest if the Kims make a down payment of $8,000. Monthly payments on the loan would be $291. For the first month, $267 of the $291 payment would be interest expense ($32,000 × .10 × 1/12 = $267), and $291 − $267 = $24 would be payment on the principal.

The Kims would still incur utilities expenses of $90. Their homeowner's insurance would be $360 annually, or $30 per month. Property taxes are $1,200 annually, or $100 per month. Routine maintenance expenses are expected to be $60 a month. These expenditures are summarized in the right column in Table 8.1.

Table 8.1 Comparison of Cost of Renting Versus Buying

Item	Rent	Buy
Shelter Expenditures		
Rent	$425	—
Loan repayment	—	$291
Utilities	90	90
Insurance	8	30
Property taxes	—	100
Maintenance	—	60
Total monthly expenditures	$523	$571
Shelter Benefits		
Interest on down payment	40	—
Tax savings, interest	—	67
Tax savings, taxes	—	25
Payment on principal	—	24
Increase in shelter value	—	167
Total benefits	$ 40	$283
Net Cost of Renting, Buying	$483	$288

If the Kims did not buy the house, they could keep the $8,000 down payment in a savings account, which would pay them 8 percent per year in interest. The Kims are in the 25 percent tax bracket. Their benefit from renting would be $8,000 $\times$ .08 $\times$ (1 − .25) $\times$ 1/12 = $40. The Kims receive no other benefit from renting. Their net cost of renting is $523 − $40 = $483.

The interest payment is tax-deductible and produces a benefit of 25 percent, or $267 $\times$ .25 = $67. Similarly, the property taxes also produce a tax savings of 25 percent, or $100 $\times$ .25 = $25. The payment on the loan principal itself was $24. Further, it is expected that after taxes, the price of the Kims' house will increase by 5 percent over one year. The monthly increase is $40,000 $\times$ .05 $\times$ 1/12 = $167. Total benefits of owning are $283. The net cost of owning is $288.

Because the net cost of owning is less than the net cost of renting, the Kims would be better off financially buying rather than renting the house. Keep in mind, though, that this analysis has focused only on monetary items. If, for example, the Kims were planning to move after one year, they might be better off renting.

Spot Quiz • Renting Versus Buying Housing

1. Compared to buying, renting provides more financial flexibility.

    T _____   F _____

2. If the value of apartments increases, tenants benefit through increases in their equity in the apartments.   T _____   F _____

3. The tax benefits of renting are similar to the tax benefits of owning a home.   T _____   F _____

4. In Table 8.1, if the increase in home value were $0, then it would be advantageous to rent rather than buy.   T _____   F _____

(Answers on page 265)

RENTAL CONSIDERATIONS

For reasons mentioned previously, renting housing appeals particularly to students, young families just starting out, and elderly people who no longer have children living at home. Once the decision to rent has been made, a variety of factors should be considered.

Determining Rental Needs

Three factors should be thoroughly evaluated prior to renting housing: location, rent, and offerings.

Location. Location is of prime importance in selecting a desirable rental unit. A bicyclist or pedestrian may prefer a location close to work or school. Elderly people without personal transportation should investigate the access to public transportation, public recreation facilities, and stores. Families with young children should consider the proximity of play areas, parks, and elementary schools.

Rent. How much rent to pay depends on earnings or financial support received. A general rule of thumb is that rent should not exceed one-fourth of take-home income. In the previous example, the Kim family's

take-home income was $1,200 per month. They should not spend more than $300 per month on rent.

A second point to consider in renting is whether the apparently cheaper rental unit is, in fact, cheaper. For example, the Kims may rent one house for $425 or a similar house five miles farther from work for $400. The issue is whether the extra $25 per month savings in rent is more than the extra cost of commuting the additional ten miles each work day. In the Kims' case, renting the house with the higher monthly rent is cheaper because of the savings in gas and commuting time.

Offerings. The third factor in renting is to evaluate what each rental unit has to offer. A checklist for renting apartments is shown in Figure 8.1. Buildings and grounds should be inspected for cleanliness and attractiveness. The services should be carefully checked. At the minimum, the apartments should provide locked mailboxes, parking, trash disposal, and laundry equipment. The living space in the apartment should be examined. Preferably, the unit should be soundproof, clean, attractive, well lit, well ventilated, and easy to maintain, and it should have an effective climate-control system.

In addition, the prospective renter should ask about the availability of recreation facilities such as tennis courts, swimming pools, and recreation centers; day care services; emergency services; and the makeup of tenants in other rental units in the complex.

The Rental Agreement

The usual methods of finding rental units are through classified ads in local newspapers, referrals from acquaintances, rental property managers, and the Yellow Pages. In the preliminary search, the person identifies appropriate rental units in the right location and rent range. The next step is to contact the owner or manager and ask about rental units available. In some cases, vacant units are available for inspection. In other cases, a model rental unit is shown. In either case, the physical condition of the unit to be rented should be verified. Failure to do so could cause tenant-owner problems later.

If the inspected unit is satisfactory, the manager will ask the tenant to sign a lease or rental agreement prior to occupancy. The **rental agreement** is a legal contract that details the rights and obligations of both tenant and owner. Because the rental agreement is prepared by or acceptable to the owner's lawyer, it contains terms or clauses that are generally advantageous to the owner. The tenant should carefully read the agreement before signing it. If some clauses are unclear or unacceptable, the owner should be asked to alter or delete those clauses. Altered or deleted clauses should have the initials of both tenant and landlord on all copies of the lease. If this is not done, the potential tenant should not sign the lease

Figure 8.1   A Checklist for Renters

You can use the list of questions below to check an apartment before you move in. With some exceptions, you can also use it to log complaints about apartment conditions stemming from a landlord's failure to perform proper service or maintenance. Some questions cannot be answered by simple observation and may require interviewing tenants of other apartments in the building or asking the opinion of an expert knowledgeable in building problems (an architect or engineer).

1. What is the rent per month?
2. Is a security deposit required? If so, how much is it and under what conditions is it held?
3. Does the lease say rent can be increased if real estate taxes are raised, sewer or water assessments are hiked, or for any other reason?
4. Do you pay extra (and how much) for such things as utilities, storage space, air-conditioning, parking space, master TV antenna connection, use of recreation areas (such as pool or tennis courts), installation of special appliances, late payment of rent, etc.?
5. Read the lease carefully. Mark any provisions that seem especially objectionable to you and try to have them removed from your lease. List also the provisions (not included) that you would like, such as a sublet clause. Try to have these added.
6. Assess the maintenance services: Is there a resident superintendent? Are maintenance hours (for usual services) restricted? How is emergency service handled?
7. How is refuse disposal handled? Are facilities easily accessible? Are they well kept and clean?
8. Laundry facilities: How many washers and dryers are available? Are they in good working order? (A washer and dryer for every ten apartments is a good ratio.)
9. Building lobby: Is it clean and well lighted? Does it have a lock or other security provisions? Is there a doorman? If so, for how many hours a day? How are deliveries handled?
10. Entrance and exit: Is an elevator provided? If so, is it in good working condition? Are the stairs well lit and in sound condition? Are fire exits provided? Is there a fire alarm or other warning system?
11. Hallways: Are they clean and adequately lit? Are they otherwise in good condition?
12. Are signs of insects present? Of mice or rats?
13. Bathroom(s): Are the plumbing fixtures in good working order and reasonably clean? Does the hot water supply seem adequate? Are the tiles (if room is tiled) sound?
14. Kitchen: Is the sink in good working order, reasonably clean, and provided with drain stoppers? Does the stove seem to be in good working order and reasonably clean? Is the refrigerator in good working order? Does it have a separate-door freezing compartment? If there is a dishwasher, is it in good working order?
15. Air conditioning: Is the entire building air-conditioned? If not, are there separate units and are they functioning properly (if it's summer)?

(Continued on p. 258)

Figure 8.1 *(Continued)*

16. Wiring: Are there enough electrical outlets? (Two or three to a room is the minimum.) Do all the switches and outlets work? Are there enough circuits in the fuse box (or circuit-breaker panel) to handle the electrical equipment you expect to install? (If there is a serious question, get an expert opinion.)

17. Does the heating system seem to be in good working order? Is it providing adequate heat (if it's winter)?

18. Is there a fireplace? If so, are there any signs (such as smoke stains) that it has not worked properly?

19. Windows: Are any broken? Can they be opened and closed easily? Are screens provided? Are there drafts around the window frame? Does the landlord arrange for the outside of the windows (in high-rise buildings) to be cleaned? And if so, how often?

20. Floors: Are they clean? Are they marred or gouged? Do they have any water stains indicating previous leaks?

21. Ceilings: Are they clean? Is the plaster cracked? Is the paint peeling? Do they have any water stains indicating previous leaks?

22. Walls: Are they clean? It the plaster cracked? Is the paint peeling? Does the paint run or smear when rubbed with a damp cloth?

23. Telephone: Are phone jacks already installed? Are they in convenient locations?

24. Television: Is TV (or hi-fi) playing forbidden at certain hours? Is an outside antenna connection provided? Is there a cable TV connection?

25. Is ventilation adequate? is there an exhaust fan in the kitchen?

26. Lighting: Are there enough fixtures for adequate light? Are the fixtures in good working order? Does the apartment get reasonably adequate natural light from the windows?

27. Storage space: Is there adequate closet space? Are there enough kitchen and bathroom cabinets? Is there long-term storage space available in the building for your use?

28. Security: Does the entry door have a dead-bolt lock? A security chain? A through-the-door viewer?

29. Soundproofing: Do the walls seem hollow (when thumped) or solid? Can you hear neighbors upstairs, downstairs, or on either side of you?

30. Outdoor play space: Is it provided? If so, are facilities well maintained?

and should look for housing elsewhere. The following clauses should be fully understood.

Length.   Leases are usually for one year, but leases for shorter periods can often be negotiated. Also, when the lease expires, does it carry the option of renting by the month or is the lease renewed automatically?

Source: *Changing Times*, April 1971, p. 16. Reprinted with permission from *Changing Times* magazine, © Kiplinger Washington Editors, Inc., 1971. This reprint is not to be altered in any way, except with permission from *Changing Times*.

Rent. Is there a penalty for late payment of rent? Is the tenant asked to waive the right to be notified if the rent is going to be raised?

Utilities and Maintenance. The lease should specify the party responsible for utility bills. The lease should also specify the party responsible for maintenance of appliances and repairs to plumbing, wiring, and so on. Is the tenant expected to shovel snow and mow the lawn?

Deposit. Most landlords require a damage deposit. The owner can charge for damages and excessive wear and tear against the damage deposit. The tenant should inquire whether interest is paid on the deposit and whether the deposits are kept in an account separate from the owner's other accounts.

Liability. The lease should identify the party responsible for accidents and mishaps in the rental unit complex.

Decoration and Remodeling. Can the tenant remodel, repaint, or redecorate after moving in? Will the owner share in the expenses? Who owns the improvements made in the rental unit?

Subleasing. The tenant usually cannot sublet the rental unit without the owner's approval. Subleasing details should be specified in the lease.

Miscellaneous Terms. The lease should indicate whether overnight guests are permitted, whether there are any restrictions on heavy furniture, such as a grand piano or a waterbed, and whether loud noises are acceptable after certain hours.[4]

Verifying that the types of items just mentioned are covered in the lease will go a long way toward minimizing tenant-landlord disagreements later.

Tenant-Landlord Relationship

Both tenants and landlords should to try their best to conform to the terms of the lease. Problems typically arise when the tenant becomes tardy in paying rent and when the owner takes excessive time to respond to complaints from the tenant. Landlords can and do attempt to evict tenants who fail to pay their rent. In extreme cases, they can seize and sell the personal belongings of the tenant and apply the proceeds to the rents due. Obligations of both tenants and landlords are summarized in Figure 8.2. (See also "Dealing With the Problem Landlord" below.)

Dealing With the Problem Landlord

The **doctrine of implied warranty of habitability** holds that the landlord is legally bound to provide the tenant with a livable dwelling. Many states have formalized this doctrine by passing specific laws. Despite this doctrine and the presence of laws safeguarding tenants' rights, many landlords persist in trying to shun their responsibilities by not providing livable housing for their tenants. Tenants who believe that they have been wronged

---

4. An excellent explanation of clauses in leases is contained in "How to Read a Lease," *Consumer Reports* (October 1974): 708–711.

have a number of strategies to utilize, including registering complaints with the appropriate housing authority, having the appropriate repairs done and deducting the cost from the rent, withholding rent, organizing rent strikes, starting or joining a renters' organization, and taking their complaints to the public.

If you have not been able to resolve problems satisfactorily with your landlord, then you might consider filing a complaint with the city's housing authority. Most housing codes specify that buildings be heated during the winter, that plumbing and sewage systems be in good working order, that dwellings be free of rodents and pests, and so on. Prepare a list of specific complaints and send a copy to the appropriate housing authority, keeping a copy for the housing inspector and one for yourself. The complaint should ask the housing authority to send an inspector to verify the complaints and the violations of the codes. If the complaints are verified, the housing authority may pursue legal action against the landlord. The threat of legal action, legal action, or the related publicity (or a combination of factors) may force the landlord to make necessary improvements and repairs.

Many states allow renters to withhold rent pending resolution of complaints against the landlord. Of course, a number of tenants who join together in a rent strike have more power than just one individual withholding rent. Another, related option is to have repairs done yourself and deduct the cost from the rent paid. Again, in different states the extent to which repair costs can be deducted from rents varies from no deductions to no maximum limit. Withholding rents and rent strikes ultimately result in the landlord either making the repairs and improvements or seeking to evict the tenants. In the latter case, verification by the housing inspector of code violations is useful in proving that the dwelling is not habitable. If rent is being withheld, it is generally desirable to pay it into an "escrow account" set up for the purpose.

Another alternative is for the tenants to hold an informal get-acquainted meeting to discuss their common problems and form a tenants' organization. An organization of this type has much more bargaining power than an individual renter trying to deal with the landlord one on one. Still another alternative is to seek media publicity. Many college newspapers are interested in printing stories related to renter-landlord conflicts, especially if the landlord has a history of conflicts. Finally, seek the advice of the Student Legal Counsel at your college, if it is available. The counsel is generally funded by assessed student fees and serves as an advocate of students' rights.

Figure 8.2 Obligations of Tenants and Landlords

A *landlord must:*
- Provide an apartment, home, trailer, room, or other dwelling that complies with all applicable housing codes.
- Maintain the dwelling unit so that it is habitable.
- Provide for proper maintenance of common areas for the dwelling, such as hallways, stairs, and elevators.
- Maintain plumbing, electrical fixtures, heaters, and furnaces, and keep other furnished appliances in working order.
- Keep the dwelling free of rodents, insects, and pests.
- Maintain the structural safety of the dwelling.
- Pay taxes and other costs as due.
- Keep the sidewalks free of litter and snow.

A *tenant must:*
- Pay rent as due.
- Vacate the dwelling at the end of the lease unless other terms have been mutually agreed on.
- Use the dwelling in a responsible manner.
- Keep the landlord informed about problems and repairs.
- Keep the dwelling clean.
- Comply with housing codes as they apply to him or her.
- Use plumbing and electrical fixtures and furnished appliances properly.
- Not disturb neighbors.

Spot Quiz • Rental Considerations

1. Location is of prime importance in determining which unit to rent.

   T _____   F _____

2. The rental lease need not specify the expiration date or length of the lease.   T _____   F _____

3. The doctrine of implied warranty of habitability obligates the tenant to pay rent even if the owner refuses to make needed repairs.

   T _____   F _____

(Answers on page 266)

Summary

The need for shelter is a basic human need. Housing can be either rented or bought. Both renting and buying housing have advantages and disadvantages. Renting does not involve large initial cash outlays or a long-term financial commitment. The major disadvantage of renting is that the tenant does not build up any equity in the rental unit. Also, renting does not produce any tax benefits for the tenant.

The principal advantages of buying housing are the buildup of equity in the housing unit and the tax deductibility of certain housing expenses. However, buying housing typically requires substantial cash for the down payment and a long-term financial commitment. A monetary analysis of costs of renting versus buying can be done before buying housing.

Three factors—location, rent, and offerings—are of great importance in selecting rented housing. These factors should be carefully evaluated before a rental agreement is signed. The rental agreement itself should be carefully read and fully understood before it is signed. The lease clauses can be modified or deleted if both tenant and landlord initial all copies of the lease. Tenant-landlord conflicts can be reduced if both parties make an effort to perform their duties.

Questions

1. What is meant by housing? Can it be rented only? Explain your answer.

2. What are the primary advantages and disadvantages of renting housing?

3. What are the advantages and disadvantages of buying housing?

4. Describe how you would go about comparing renting with buying housing. Your answer should be descriptive, not numerical.

5. Is location more important when buying or renting? Briefly explain your answer.

6. Describe two clauses in a rental agreement that need to be carefully evaluated.

7. What is meant by the doctrine of implied warranty of habitability? What advantages does it hold for the renter?

8. Obtain a copy of a lease from a rental agency in your town. Show how you would modify or delete certain lease clauses if you were going to rent from the agency.

Case Problems

1. The Grazianos can rent a home for $310 per month or buy it for $37,000. Assume that whether they buy or rent, maintenance, insurance, and utilities costs will remain the same. Monthly real estate taxes are $50. The house can be bought with a $7,000 down payment. Monthly mortgage payments are $316; $300 is interest, and $16 is payment on the principal. The house is expected to go up in value at a rate of $80 per month on an after-tax basis. If the Grazianos do not buy the house, they will put the $7,000 in a savings account paying 8 percent per year. Their tax rate is 30 percent. Is it cheaper for them to buy or rent? Show your calculations.

2. Solve Case Problem 1 but assume that the Grazianos' tax rate is 0 percent and that the house increases in value at a rate of $125 per month. Show your calculations to indicate whether it is cheaper for them to buy or rent.

3. Carol and Don Anderson are looking for a house. They have located a house that can be either rented or bought. The rent is $350 per month on a 12-month lease. Renters' insurance on the house would be $9 per month. Their utility bills are expected to average $80 per month. The house can be bought for $42,000. A bank is willing to provide an 80 percent loan at 12 percent interest. Monthly payments to repay the loan are $354, of which $336 is for interest, and the rest is payment on the principal. Real estate taxes on the house are $720 per year. Homeowners' insurance is $300 per year. Maintenance expenses are $50 per month. The Andersons' tax rate is 25 percent. The house is expected to increase in value by $140 per month on an after-tax basis. If the Andersons do not buy the house, they will put the down payment amount in a savings account paying 8 percent before taxes. Calculate the net cost of renting and buying. Which is better financially?

4. Chuck Khan is finishing his bachelor's degree at State University and has been accepted to the school's graduate program in agricultural

economics. He will be living in University City for at least two more years. A recent legacy has provided him with $6,000. He has been renting a two-bedroom house for $300 per month. He and his roommate have been splitting the rent as well as utility expenses of $100 per month. Insurance on his personal belongings has been $5 per month. Chuck's landlord has recently asked him if he would be interested in buying the house for $30,000. Chuck would use the $6,000 as the down payment, and the landlord would finance the $24,000 balance at 9 percent interest. Monthly mortgage payments would be $201, composed of $180 in interest and $21 in principal. Real estate taxes would be $900 per year, and homeowner's insurance would be $300 per year. Maintenance expenses would probably average $30 per month.

Chuck's taxes would be very low, probably about 10 percent of his income. If he bought the house, he would continue to share the place with his roommate, charging him rent of $150 per month. They would continue to split the utilities. If he does not buy the house, he can invest the $6,000 in a certificate of deposit paying 6 percent annually. If Chuck sells the house after two years, he should get his $30,000 out of it after selling expenses. Should Chuck buy the house? In solving this problem, you should recognize that rent received is taxable income, but assume that Chuck does not depreciate the house and does not take a tax deduction for maintenance and insurance.

Bibliography

Blumberg, Richard E., and J. R. Grow. *The Rights of Tenants*. New York: Avon Books, 1978.

"Learn to Spot the Traps in a Lease." *Changing Times* (January 1980): 17–18.

Answers to Spot Quizzes

Renting Versus Buying Housing (page 255)

1. T (Renting does not require a large cash outlay for a down payment.)

2. F (Tenants do not possess equity in shelter they rent.)

3. F (The benefits are quite different. Owners can deduct taxes and interest expense; tenants do not have similar deductions.)

4. F (The benefits of buying would be $67 + $25 + $24 = $116. The net cost of owning, $571 − $116 = $455, is still less than the net cost of renting.)

Rental Considerations (page 262)

1. T (A nondesirable location may add to the expense of shelter.)

2. F (Without an expiration date or length of lease, the tenant could vacate the rental unit anytime or the owner could evict the tenant at will.)

3. F (In some states the tenant may be allowed to withhold rent if needed repairs are not made.)

Chapter 9

Buying a Home

Objectives

After reading this chapter, you will be able to:

- Name the important factors to consider when buying a home.
- State the three sources of mortgage funds.
- Describe the types of mortgages available.
- Discuss the most common terms or clauses for a typical mortgage.
- Tell the difference between a title and a deed to property.
- Describe the three types of deeds.
- Explain the tax advantages of owning a home.
- Name three alternatives to buying a house, and discuss the advantages and disadvantages of each.

Tom and Maryann Byrne are both schoolteachers in Boston, Massachusetts. In their search for a suitable place to live, they found for sale a farmhouse in Pembroke, Massachusetts, that had been built in 1840. The seller's asking price for the farmhouse was $79,900. The Byrnes ended up paying $73,000 for the house. In addition, the Byrnes convinced the seller to accept a $15,000 second mortgage at a very reasonable interest rate. Tom Byrne flatly states, "We got a bargain."[1]

The need for housing is met by either renting or buying. Renting was discussed in Chapter 8, and buying housing is discussed in this chapter. What steps and considerations are involved in the decision to buy housing? How do you finance the purchase of shelter? What are the tax implications of home ownership? How about buying a condominium, a cooperative unit, or a mobile home? Should you have a new home built rather than buying an older home? Should existing shelter be remodeled? You will find the answers to these questions in this chapter.

Buying housing

Who is buying houses? Just about anyone who can afford one, plus quite a few people who really cannot afford one. John Wetmore, chief economist of the Mortgage Bankers Association, says, "A lot of people are willing to be house poor for a few years. They put a big percentage of their income into housing because it is such a good investment."[2] Being **house poor** simply means buying more house than you can afford. How much shelter can you afford? What should you look for when you buy housing? How do you go about buying shelter? Answers to these and other questions are found in this section.

How Much Shelter Can You Afford?

How much housing a person or family can afford to buy without becoming overextended can be determined by using some guidelines. Bankers and other lenders use a variety of guidelines. The first guideline is that the cost of the housing should be less than twice the person's or family's gross annual income. Thus, a family whose gross income is $50,000 would be able to buy a house for up to $50,000 × 2.0 = $100,000.

The second guideline is that total housing costs (mortgage payment + taxes + utilities + insurance + maintenance) should be less than one-fourth of monthly gross income. If monthly gross income is $3,000, the

---

1. "Bottom Dollar for a Tip-Top House," *Money* (March 1980): 48.
2. "Who's Buying the 'Median' House," *Money* (July 1978): 54.

person can qualify to buy a house if total housing costs do not exceed $3,000 × .25 = $750 per month.

Total housing costs are affected by the size of the down payment, the interest rate on the mortgage loan, taxes, utilities, insurance, and maintenance. Other things being the same, large down payments reduce housing costs, and higher interest rates increase housing costs. An example is given in Table 9.1. Based on the first guideline, all three families qualify to buy their chosen houses if their annual gross income exceeds $37,500. To qualify based on the second guideline, the Ahmed family needs a gross annual income of $775.22 × 4 × 12 = $37,210.56. With an annual income of $37,210.56, the Ahmed family's monthly income would have to be $37,210.56/12 = $3,100.88; 25 percent of this amount is $3,100.88 × .25 = $775.22.

Similarly, the Baxter family would need an annual income of $861.94 × 4 × 12 = $41,373.12, and the Chens would need $707.07 × 4 × 12 = $33,939.36 to satisfy the second guideline. The amount of housing a person or family can afford to buy depends on gross income, the size of the down payment, the interest rate on the mortgage, and such housing-related costs as taxes, utilities, insurance, and maintenance.

Table 9.1 Comparison of Housing Costs when Down Payments and Interest Rates Vary

Item	Ahmeds	Baxters	Chens
1. Cost	$75,000	$75,000	$75,000
2. Down payment (%)	20%	20%	30%
3. Down payment ($)	15,000	15,000	22,500
4. Mortgage (1 − 3)[a]	60,000	60,000	52,500
5. Interest rate	10%	12%	10%
6. Mortgage payment[b]	545.22	631.94	477.07
7. Taxes, utilities, insurance, maintenance[b]	230.00	230.00	230.00
8. Housing costs[b]	$775.22	$861.94	$707.07

[a]The mortgage is for 25 years at the stated interest rate.
[b]On a monthly basis.

What to Look for When You Buy a House

A variety of important factors should be considered when you buy a home, such as location, zoning, taxes, construction, and living space.

Location.   The most important factor in buying a house is location. Many real estate experts say that when you buy a house, what you are really buying is the neighborhood. Families with young children should be particularly aware of the quality of education in the school district for the house. In addition, it is desirable for these people to locate near an elementary school. People with allergies should obviously avoid areas with high pollen counts or pollution. In general, areas with excessive traffic or smoke should be avoided, as should areas subject to periodic unpleasant odors from nearby factories and sewage treatment plants.

Zoning.   Cities have laws that regulate what type of structure (commercial, factory, apartment complex, single-family residence, and so on) can be built in each area of the city. These are called **zoning laws**. Before buying a house, you should carefully check the applicable zoning laws. From the viewpoint of living environment, it is not advisable to buy a house in an area where zoning laws allow construction or establishment of commercial and industrial buildings.

Taxes.   Within the same geographical area, tax rates may differ in different neighborhoods. For example, a person wishing to buy a house in Pittsburgh will find dozens of different tax districts with varying taxes. Keep in mind that services provided by the different tax districts tend to vary with the taxes. A district with low taxes may not be operating a very good school system, for instance. Thus, a family with school-age children may prefer a district with higher taxes for the educational benefits.

Yard.   The buyer should be sure that the lot is adequate for family needs. Healthy shade trees are always desirable. Additional factors to consider are listed in Figure 9.1.

Exterior Construction.   A variety of materials—stone, brick, wood, and metal—can be used to construct the exterior of the house. The construction should show quality workmanship. Houses in cold climates should be well insulated, with weather stripping and storm windows and doors.

Interior Construction.   The interior walls should not have large cracks. Moldings should be well fitted. It is also desirable to have a house that can be remodeled easily without changing the house's character.

Living Space.   Living space should be adequate. The floor plan should allow traffic to flow easily from one room to the next. The house should

Figure 9.1   Checklist for Buying a House

Outside house and yard

- ☐ Attractive, well-designed house
- ☐ Suited to natural surroundings
- ☐ Lot of the right size and shape for house and garage
- ☐ Suitable use of building materials
- ☐ Compatible with houses in the area
- ☐ Attractive landscaping and yard

- ☐ Good drainage of rain and moisture
- ☐ Dry, firm soil around the house
- ☐ Mature, healthy trees—placed to give shade in summer
- ☐ Convenient, well-kept driveway, walks, patio, porch
- ☐ Yard for children
- ☐ Parking

- convenience—garage, carport, or street
- ☐ Distance between houses for privacy
- ☐ Sheltered entry—well-lighted and large enough for several to enter the house together
- ☐ Convenient service entrance

Outside construction

- ☐ Durable siding materials—in good condition
- ☐ Solid brick and masonry—free of cracks
- ☐ Solid foundation walls—6 inches above ground level—8 inches thick

- ☐ Weather-stripped windows and doors
- ☐ Noncorrosive gutters and downspouts, connected to storm sewer or splash block to carry water away from house

- ☐ Copper or aluminum flashing used over doors, windows, and joints on the roof
- ☐ Screens and storm windows or Thermopane glass
- ☐ Storm doors

Inside construction

- ☐ Sound, smooth walls with invisible nails and taping on dry walls; without hollows or large cracks in plaster walls
- ☐ Well-done carpentry work with properly fitted joints and moldings

- ☐ Properly fitted, easy-to-operate windows
- ☐ Level wood floors with smooth finish and no high edges, wide gaps, or squeaks
- ☐ Well-fitted tile floor—no cracked or damaged tiles—no visible adhesive

- ☐ Good possibilities for improvements, remodeling, expanding
- ☐ Properly fitted and easy-to-work doors and drawers in built-in cabinets
- ☐ Dry basement floor with hard smooth surface
- ☐ Adequate

(Continued on p. 272)

Figure 9.1 *(Continued)*

basement drain
□ Sturdy stairways
with railings,
adequate head

room—not too
steep
□ Leakproof roof—in
good condition

□ Adequate
insulation for
warmth, coolness,
and soundproofing

Living space

□ Convenient floor
plan and paths
from room to room
□ Convenient entry
with foyer and
closet
□ Convenient work
areas (kitchen,
laundry,
workshop) with
adequate drawers,
cabinets, lighting,
work space,
electrical power
□ Private areas
(bedrooms and
bathrooms) located
far enough from
other parts of the
house for privacy
and quiet
□ Social areas (living
and dining rooms,
play space, yard,

porch or patio)
convenient,
comfortable, large
enough for family
and guests
□ Rooms
conveniently
related to each
other—entry to
living room, dining
room to kitchen,
bedrooms to baths
□ Adequate
storage—closets,
cabinets, shelves,
attic, basement,
garage
□ Suitable wall space
and room size for
your furnishings
□ Outdoor space
convenient to
indoor space

□ Windows located
to provide enough
air, light, and
ventilation
□ Agreeable type,
size, and
placement of
windows
□ Usable attic and/or
basement space
□ Possibilities for
expansion
□ Attractive
decorating and
fixtures
□ Extras—fireplace,
air conditioning,
porches, new
kitchen and baths,
built-in equipment,
decorating you like

Source: *Your Housing Dollar* (Chicago: Money Management Institute of Household Finance
Corporation). Reprinted with permission.

be wired to accommodate modern appliances. Enough storage space should
be available to accommodate all the family's belongings. Some additional
items are listed in Figure 9.1.

Avoiding Problems of Buying Defective Houses

Some houses that are for sale are "lemons" and generally should be
avoided. States provide little, if any, protection for the buyer of a poorly

constructed house. Consider the case of the Burnettes. The back yard of their $90,000 Alexandria, Virginia, house began to slide, causing damage to the patio. They sued the constructor for negligence. It appeared that the house had been built on unstable soil, and therefore a jury awarded the Burnettes $73,063. Shortly after the award, the Virginia Supreme Court ruled that state law did not provide legal protection to new home buyers. The trial judge on the Burnette case then threw out their case.[3]

The Burnette case is not an isolated incident. The National Real Estate Inspectors Service of New York City estimates that 35 to 40 percent of houses for resale have major defects. A variety of factors account for badly built houses. Skilled workers, such as plumbers, carpenters, and electricians, tend to be in short supply during peak home construction periods. Homes built during these periods may have defects because less-skilled workers were used. Also, with rising labor and material costs, some contractors reduce costs by using cheaper materials and shoddy construction methods.

Typical problems in poorly built homes are leaky roofs, wet basements, poor drainage, and bad grading. The condition of the roof should be carefully evaluated. A leaking roof can cause structural damage to the house and may result in costly repairs. Basements should be examined for wetness and dampness. Drying up a damp basement permanently may cost thousands of dollars. Wiring, plumbing, furnaces, air-conditioning units, water heaters, and other appliances should be checked for operating condition. The home buyer should not rely on luck to find a well-built home. Two alternative ways to avoid home-buying hassles are warranties and professional inspections. (See "Watch Out for the Problem Home" on page 274.)

Warranties. About 12,000 home builders participate in the **Home Owners Warranty (HOW) program**. Builders in this program guarantee that their workmanship, materials, and construction are up to established standards. The warranty is good for ten years.

The National Association of Realtors sponsors warranty programs on homes for resale. These warranties vary in what they cover and how much they cost. A typical warranty covering the heating, cooling, electrical, and plumbing systems, and the roof, foundation, floors, ceilings, and basement may cost $300–$400. Real estate agents participating in or offering warranty programs usually promote the availability of these programs in their advertisements.

Professional Inspection. A potential home buyer has the option of hiring a professional home inspector to inspect the house under consideration. Preferably, the house should be inspected prior to purchase. The buyer should accompany the inspector on the inspection tour. The inspector may

---

3. "Beware the Badly Built Home," *Changing Times* (June 1979): 31.

Watch Out for the Problem Home

The wonders of modern electronics saved Lori and Richard Masterson a big headache and about $1,500. They were in the process of buying a house in Detroit and had not noticed anything unusual about the plumbing in the house. However, an inspector equipped with an electronic device detected excess moisture in a wall and traced it to corroded and leaking plumbing in a bathroom. As a result, the Mastersons were able to obtain a lower price from the seller (*The Wall Street Journal*, October 22, 1985, 33).

Besides plumbing, a lot of other things can go wrong with a house. The most frequent problems reported are those that can be readily identified—doors and windows that don't close properly, the paint job, the trim, and damage to walls and driveways. However, problems such as leaking roofs, sagging floors, rotted wood, termite damage, cracked or sinking foundations, cracked walls, damaged or improperly lined chimneys, old furnaces and water heaters, and not enough insulation are not readily detected and can cost thousands of dollars to correct. The Real Estate Commission in Texas has prepared forms that advise buyers to have houses inspected before purchase. California and other states require sellers to disclose information on factors such as drainage and remodeling. While these regulations provide some measure of safety, it is still the buyer's responsibility to watch out for the problem home.

provide both an oral and a written report. If the home is to be inspected after the purchase offer has been made, the buyer should include in the purchase offer appropriate safeguards against defects. For example, the purchase offer may state that if any major defects are found in the house, then either the offer can be withdrawn or the owner has to pay for correcting the defects. Buyers should be aware that defects not uncovered during inspection generally become their liabilities.

Identifying a Suitable House

Some houses are for sale by the owner. These houses are advertised in the classified section of the local newspaper, by placing a sign in the front yard of the house, and by word of mouth. A buyer who wants to inspect a house that is ''for sale by owner'' should contact the owner and arrange to tour the house. Typically, the seller will escort the buyer around the house.

Most houses for sale are listed by the owner with a realty company. A **realty company** specializes in the sale of real estate properties. The sales personnel at a realty company are called **real estate brokers** or **agents**. These

agents or brokers are licensed by the state in which they work. Licensing merely ensures a minimum level of expertise in handling real estate transactions. Buyers should check with friends and acquaintances to obtain recommendations on brokers who have a reputation for providing good service.

Brokers who know what they are doing will try to understand the housing needs of the buyers. In addition, they will try to gauge the financial capabilities of the buyers. A competent broker, after figuring out the buyer's needs, will take the buyer on a tour of four to six houses.

Most brokers have two types of listed houses to show buyers. Some houses are **exclusive** listings, shown only by brokers at the realty company where the house is listed. Other houses are **multilisted**, which means that any broker can show the house. Exclusively listed houses are generally automatically multilisted if the listing realty company has not sold it within a certain time period. Once the buyer has identified a suitable house, the price negotiation process begins.

Negotiating a Price

The owner expects the buyer to negotiate on the price. Typically, the asking price is 5 to 10 percent higher than what the seller really expects to obtain for the house. Before deciding on an offering price, the buyer should try to gauge the owner's reasons for selling. An owner who has been transferred is probably more willing to bargain than one who plans to build a new house if the present one is sold.

The buyer should also make a very unemotional assessment of what the house is worth. On occasion, a buyer will fall in love with a particular house and lose the will to pay a realistic price. An inflated or unduly high offer will raise monthly housing expenses and take away funds that could have been enjoyed elsewhere. During the negotiation process, it does not pay to ask the broker for his or her advice. The broker is paid by the seller and represents the seller's interests.

After the buyer's offer has been transmitted to the seller, the seller has three alternatives—to reject the offer, to accept the offer, or to make a counteroffer. If the buyer's offer is rejected, the buyer can either offer a higher price or look for another house. If the offer is accepted, the buyer proceeds with arranging financing for the house. If a counteroffer is made, the buyer can accept the counteroffer, reject it, or make another offer. Negotiations proceed through offers and counteroffers until the final offer is either accepted or rejected.

The Purchase Contract

The buyer makes the offer to buy by signing a purchase contract. The seller accepts the offer by signing the purchase contract also. The **purchase**

contract then becomes a legal contract between buyer and seller. The contract spells out the full details of the purchase transaction and specifies the purchase price. The financing details are also contained in the purchase contract. For example, the contract may specify that the sale is subject to the buyer obtaining suitable financing within a period of six weeks. The date when possession of the house changes hands is also specified. Any other special understandings between buyer and seller are listed in the purchase contract as well.

The purchase contract also specifies the **deposit** or **earnest money** that the buyer has to pay to indicate his or her willingness to follow through on the purchase agreement. The deposit can be either cash or a promissory note.

Spot Quiz • Buying Housing

1. Total monthly housing costs can be reduced by making a larger down payment.   T _____   F _____

2. Generally speaking, the price of a house should be more important than location.   T _____   F _____

3. A professional inspection of a house before purchase will prevent the purchase of a defective home.   T _____   F _____

4. The purchase offer is made by the buyer signing a purchase contract.
                                                                     T _____   F _____

(Answers on page 304)

Financing the House

Very few people are in a position to pay cash for their house purchases. The more usual situation is that the home buyer will put up some cash toward the purchase price and borrow the rest of the money to pay for the purchase. The borrowing for financing a house purchase is called a **mortgage**. Mortgage money can be obtained from different places, and different types of mortgages are available.

Sources of Mortgage Funds

Mortgage funds are available from financial institutions, mortgage assumptions, and land contracts.

Financial Institutions. Savings and loan associations, commercial banks, insurance companies, and credit unions are engaged in home financing. Savings and loan associations have a very high percentage of their total assets invested in home mortgages. This is the first place many home buyers go to find mortgage funds. Commercial banks also finance home purchases, but home mortgages are not a very large portion of their assets. Life insurance companies, while generally involved in providing mortgage money for large commercial and industrial property, on occasion will also finance home purchases. The best source for information on funds from insurance companies may be the home buyer's life insurance agent. Mutual savings banks in the East and homestead associations in the South are also sources of mortgage funds.

Mortgage Assumption. In some home purchase situations, it is possible for the buyer to **assume**, or take over, the mortgage from the owner. For example, the Aakers buy an $80,000 house from the Aguirres. The Aguirres have a $50,000 mortgage on the house they are selling. The Aakers pay the Aguirres $80,000 − $50,000 = $30,000 and also assume the Aguirres' mortgage. The advantage of mortgage assumption is that the interest rate on it will be lower than the going interest rate for mortgages.[4] The disadvantage of assuming a mortgage is that the cash payment the buyer is required to provide is typically larger than the down payment for a new mortgage. For example, on a new mortgage with 20 percent down, the Aakers would have needed only $16,000 in cash.

Land Contract. In a **land contract** (also called a **contract for deed**), the seller provides the financing for the buyer. The deed for the house is held in escrow while the buyer makes the mortgage payments to the seller. The deed is released to the buyer when the mortgage has been paid off. Because the financing arrangements are made by the buyer and seller directly, the terms can be negotiated to accommodate both buyer and seller. If money is tight and financing is difficult to obtain, a land contract may be advantageous to both buyer and seller. The seller has sold the house, and the buyer is able to buy the house. The buyer needs to be aware that if mortgage payments are in default, the seller may have the right to keep the house as well as all mortgage and down payments already made.

---

4. Had the Aakers been able to obtain a mortgage from a financial institution at a rate lower than the rate on the assumption, they would not have assumed the mortgage.

Types of Mortgages

James and Dana Traitz of Florida bought a $200,000 home with a swimming pool. Rather than finance the purchase with a fixed-rate mortgage at 12.5 percent, they selected an adjustable-rate mortgage with an interest rate of 9.5 percent. Their monthly payments with the fixed-rate mortgage would have been $1,654. However, with the adjustable-rate mortgage, their payments are only $1,303 per month. The home buyer can select from one of a variety of mortgages.[5] (See "Shopping for a Mortgage" below.)

Fixed-Rate Mortgage.   The **fixed-rate mortgage** used to be the most prevalent type of mortgage in home financing. However, in recent years interest rates have fluctuated a lot, making fixed-rate mortgages less desirable for lenders. Therefore, their use in home financing has declined quite a bit. With a fixed mortgage, the buyer borrows from a lender the difference between the purchase price and the down payment. The loan

Shopping for a Mortgage

Just because mortgage money has been in relatively tight supply doesn't mean that a potential home buyer can't shop around for a cheaper mortgage. Shopping around can help save large chunks of money. For example, the monthly payments for a $70,000, 25-year, fixed-rate mortgage at 11 percent annual interest are $686.08. However, for the same mortgage at an interest rate of 10 percent, monthly payments are $636.09. The 10 percent mortgage results in monthly payments that are $49.99 lower than for the 11 percent mortgage and saves $14,997 in interest expenses over the mortgage life.

Before going to a mortgage lending institution, check with people connected with real estate, especially lawyers and brokers. They might be able to provide information on special deals available at certain lending institutions. It is also worthwhile contacting lending institutions in neighboring communities. Occasionally, one of them may be able to offer lower rates. Mortgage closing costs are not cast in stone. The lender may be willing to reduce some closing costs, such as mortgage service fees, points, and escrow fee, especially if the borrower is interested in opening checking and savings accounts at the lending institutions. Finally, even on a nonassumable mortgage, ask the lender to allow assumption. Some lenders permit this at an interest rate lower than the current rate.

---

5. "A Call to ARMs," *Money* (July 1985): 123.

is at a set, specified interest rate for a fixed time period. The monthly mortgage payments remain the same over the mortgage life. Mortgage payments include both interest and payment on the loan principal. The payments are at a level so that the mortgage is completely repaid when the last payment is made.

The fixed-rate mortgage is generally uninsured against default. The lender's protection on the loan comes from the amount of the down payment the buyer has made. A larger down payment means a smaller mortgage and a larger margin of safety for the lender. Mortgages with larger down payments generally carry lower interest rates than those with smaller down payments.

The down payments on mortgages are specified by the lending institution. When money is easily available, the lending institution may provide financing with a 10 to 20 percent down payment. During periods of tight money, the same institution may require a down payment of 20 to 40 percent.

Mortgage payments are affected by interest rates and the length of the payment period. Typical payment periods are from 15 to 30 years. Table 9.2 shows the effects of interest rates and payment periods on the mortgage payments. The mortgage amount is $40,000. For a 9 percent, 20-year mortgage, monthly payments are $359.90, with payments going up to $440.43 for a 12 percent, 20-year mortgage. If interest rates remain the same and the payment period is increased, the monthly payment declines, but total interest paid goes up.

As long as economic and financial conditions remain stable, the fixed-rate mortgage is able to put the average home in the hands of average families. However, as inflation causes housing prices to go up, new types

Table 9.2 Effect of Interest Rate and Payment Period on Monthly Payment[a]

Interest Rate	Payment Period	Monthly Payment	Total Interest
9%	20 years	$359.90	$ 46,376.00
9%	25 years	$335.68	60,704.00
12%	20 years	$440.43	65,703.20
12%	25 years	$421.29	86,386.90
15%	20 years	$526.72	86,411.80
15%	25 years	$512.33	$113,699.67

[a]The mortgage amount is $40,000.

of mortgages are needed. The graduated-payment mortgage and the adjustable-rate mortgage are two examples of flexible home financing.

Graduated-Payment Mortgage. A **graduated-payment mortgage (GPM)** is designed to provide lower payments in the beginning years and higher payments in the later years of the mortgage. GPMs are particularly useful for young couples buying their first homes. A GPM is compared with a fixed-rate mortgage in Figure 9.2. For the first four years, GPM payments are lower than payments for a fixed-rate mortgage. Starting in year 5, GPM payments are higher than fixed-rate mortgage payments.

Adjustable-Rate Mortgage. As the name implies, interest rates for **adjustable-rate mortgages (ARMs)** are not fixed. Rather, the rate applicable to the mortgage goes up or down as interest rates in general go up or down. ARMs have become very popular since the early 1980s. In general, lenders can increase the interest rate on mortgages only once every six months. In California, the lenders may not raise the interest rate by more than 2.5 percent over the life of the mortgage. The interest rate charged on ARMs is tied to some financial index. In California, for example, the rates on ARMs are changed based on changes in the "cost of money" index of the Federal Home Loan Bank of San Francisco.

Figure 9.2 Fixed-Rate and Graduated-Payment Mortgages

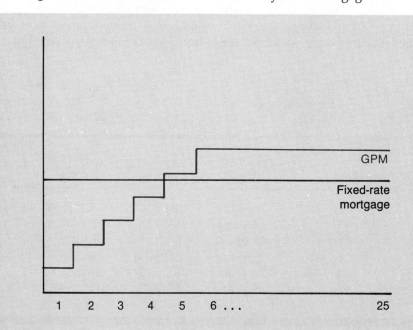

Adjustable-rate mortgages are most desirable for home buyers when interest rates are high. Even when interest rates are low, home buyers may prefer an ARM if they can obtain an interest rate lower than on a conventional mortgage. Lenders typically allow proportionally more ARMs to be assumed than conventional mortgages. Some financial institutions also permit an ARM to be transferred to another house purchased by the ARM borrower. These factors make ARMs attractive for many home buyers.

Other Types of Mortgages. A **rollover mortgage** allows for the interest rate and other loan terms to be renegotiated after a fixed time period. With a **shared-appreciation mortgage**, the lender charges a lower interest rate on the mortgage in return for a share of the profits when the borrower eventually sells the house. In addition to these two, about 30 other types of mortgage plans are available. (See ''Other Types of Mortgages'' below.)

Other Types of Mortgages

Type of Mortgage	Advantages and Disadvantages	Uses
Rollover Mortgage. Due to changes in the interest rates, mortgage terms, including the interest rate, are periodically renegotiated.	Borrowers will pay higher interest rates if they move up; however, the mortgage term and principal can be renegotiated to keep payments fairly constant.	Especially useful for those borrowers whose financial situation might change over time, since renegotiation allows adjustment to the new situation.
Shared-Appreciation Mortgage. The lender shares in the price appreciation of the property in return for giving a lower interest rate loan.	Borrowers' monthly payments are lower due to lower interest rate; borrowers give up part of the gain on the property.	Suitable for those who may not qualify for a loan at normal interest rates because the payments would be too large for their budgets.
Price-Level-Adjusted Mortgage. The interest rate remains fixed, but the mortgage balance and monthly payments are adjusted for inflation periodically.	Borrowers' monthly payments are lower in the early years; mortgage may become a burden for the borrower if income does not keep up with inflation.	Lower payment in the earlier years makes this mortgage desirable for first-time home buyers.

Insured and Guaranteed Loan Programs

Financial institutions are normally reluctant to lend more than 80 percent of the purchase price of the house. To get a loan with a 20 percent down payment, a young family buying a $60,000 house would have to come up with $12,000. For some families, it may be very difficult to save for a large down payment. Two programs designed to assist families in these situations are the FHA and VA programs.

FHA-Insured Loans. The **Federal Housing Authority (FHA)** provides loan insurance to financial institutions. Within certain guidelines, the FHA insurance guarantees the lender that it will not lose any money on an FHA-insured loan. The FHA also specifies the maximum interest rate that can be charged on an FHA-insured loan. When rates on mortgages exceed interest rates on FHA-insured loans, financial institutions become very reluctant to participate in the FHA program. The insurance for the FHA-insured loans costs 0.5 percent of the outstanding balance annually.

VA-Guaranteed Loans. The **Veterans Administration (VA)** offers a loan-guarantee program to enable veterans to buy homes with smaller down payments. The VA Program guarantees the lender against loss for up to 60 percent of the appraised value of the house. The current maximum amount for a VA guarantee is $27,500. The maximum amount of loan guaranteed for a $50,000 house would be $27,500, because 60 percent of $50,000 is $30,000 and is in excess of the maximum amount. A $40,000 house would allow guaranteeing a loan for up to $40,000 $\times$ .6 = $24,000.

VA-guaranteed loans are available to veterans who were on active duty for at least 90 days during World War II, the Korean War, or the Vietnam War or for at least 181 days during nonwar times. The veterans' discharge from the service must have been honorable. The minimum active duty requirement is waived for those veterans who were discharged because of service-related injuries. The guarantee program applies to mobile homes as well as to houses. The guarantee program can be utilized more than once if the veteran has paid off a previous VA-guaranteed loan.

Down Payment

The **down payment** is the cash amount put up by the buyer toward the purchase of a house. Larger down payments result in lower monthly housing costs. However, it is not advisable for a home buyer to apply all of the family savings toward the down payment. For example, a family may have $23,000 in a savings account. It purchases a house for $60,000, and the lender requires a minimum down payment of 20 percent or $12,000. The family should use $12,000 of its savings for the down payment and keep the rest of its money in the savings account for emergencies.

Points

Frequently, the lender will charge the borrower a **loan service fee** for the loan. The service fee is also called **points**. Each point equals 1 percent of the amount of the loan. A lender who charges two points on a $50,000 loan will be paid $1,000 by the borrower in loan service fees. The actual effect of points is to raise the effective interest charged on the loan. Each point increases the effective interest rate on the loan by approximately 0.125 percent. In the example just cited, the borrower is really getting a loan for $50,000 − $1,000 = $49,000. If the borrower is paying 10 percent on the $50,000 loan, his or her effective interest rate will be about 10.25 percent.

When mortgage money is scarce, lenders like to charge points to raise the effective interest rate on the mortgages. The FHA and VA programs prevent the lender from charging points from the buyer. Here, of course, the seller tacks on the required points to the selling price, and the buyer ends up paying them anyway. **Truth-in-lending laws (Federal Reserve Regulation Z)** require that lenders disclose the effective interest rate to the buyer. Any points or service charges are taken into consideration in calculating the effective interest rate.

Mortgage Terms

The typical mortgage calls for the borrower to make monthly payments to the lender for a specified time period. The payments include both interest and principal and are designed to fully repay the loan at the end of the specified period. Mortgages have a variety of terms or clauses. Some of the more critical clauses are explained below.

Escrow Accounts.   Homeowners can lose their homes for nonpayment of real estate taxes. Therefore, most lenders require that borrowers make monthly payments equal to one-twelfth of the anticipated annual real estate taxes and insurance into an account called the **escrow account**. When tax payments or insurance premiums are due, the lender uses the funds in the escrow account to pay them. This procedure assures the lender that taxes and insurance premiums will be paid.

Hazard Insurance.   The borrower pledges the house as security to obtain the mortgage. However, an uninsured, mortgaged house that has been destroyed by fire has provided the lender with little protection. To protect their financial stake in the house, lenders require borrowers to carry **hazard insurance** on the house.

Assumption.   An **assumption clause** allows the owner of the house to transfer the mortgage to a later buyer. In recent years, with interest rates moving sharply up and down frequently, lenders are reluctant to include

an assumption clause in the mortgage contract. However, the buyer who is able to negotiate an assumption clause may have an easier time reselling the house.

Acceleration. The **acceleration clause** allows the lender to take legal action if the borrower becomes delinquent in making mortgage payments. The borrower has the right to stop the legal action undertaken by the lender by curing or correcting all breaches of the loan contract.

Prepayment of Loan. Let's assume that a home buyer has taken out a mortgage at an interest rate of 13 percent. Two years later interest rates drop to 10 percent. It may be advantageous for the home buyer to take out a new loan at 10 percent and repay the 13 percent loan. Lenders frequently try to discourage this type of refinancing by including a clause that allows them to charge the borrower a penalty for repaying a loan before its due date, or prepaying. A home buyer should try to negotiate a loan that does not include a penalty for prepayment.

Future Advances. Some mortgages allow the borrower to borrow additional money at prevailing rates without having to repay the amount borrowed previously. This clause is desirable from the borrower's viewpoint. Its inclusion allows the borrower to undertake, for example, major house remodeling without going through a complete house refinancing.

Spot Quiz • Financing the House

1. It is possible for the seller to finance the house for the buyer through personal resources.   T _____ F _____

2. A fixed-rate mortgage with prepayment penalties is highly desirable during periods when interest rates are high.   T _____ F _____

3. An adjustable-rate mortgage issued during periods of low interest rates is more beneficial for the lender.   T _____ F _____

4. FHA-insured programs guarantee that the borrower will make the monthly mortgage payments.   T _____ F _____

5. Points are charged by lenders to increase the effective interest rate on the mortgage.   T _____ F _____

(Answers on page 304)

Taking title to the house

Once the house has been selected and financing has been arranged, the next step is for the buyer to take possession of the house. The important considerations are deeds and title, and closing costs.

Title and Deeds

A **title** simply means the right to ownership of a property. A **deed** is the legal document that transfers title of the property from the owner to the buyer. A buyer needs to be certain that the title to the property purchased is free of legal claims by any other party. Most of us are familiar with situations where a person finds a good bargain on a used car only to find out after buying the car that it was stolen. The car is returned to the original owner, and the buyer loses the money paid for the car. This is an example of loss suffered because of a defective title. Similar problems can arise if a person buys a house with a defective title.

Title. Typical home buying transactions involve a number of procedures that can limit the buyer's chances of getting a defective title. A **title abstract**, usually performed by a lawyer, is a history of the property, which helps identify any claims outstanding against the property. A **certificate of title** is a lawyer's certification that no claims appear to be outstanding against the property. Neither the abstract nor the certificate guarantees that the title is without prior claims. They indicate, though, that after searching the property's history with due care, no claims have been found.

Title insurance provides the home buyer with insurance against any claims arising from a defective title. Most lenders require that the borrower pay for and buy title insurance. The principal advantage of title insurance is that if any claims against the property are discovered after the purchase, the buyer is not responsible for discharging those claims. Title insurance also involves a **survey** of the property. A survey is an exact geographic description of the location and boundaries of the property. Title insurance is reasonably inexpensive, around $250 to $350, and provides the home buyer with great peace of mind. It can be purchased through a title insurance company.

Deeds. Deeds transfer title from seller to buyer. Deeds are typically recorded with the clerk of the county in which the property is located. A valid deed has to be in writing and has to meet certain legal requirements. The **warranty deed** is the safest one for the buyer because it guarantees that the title is free of any legal claims. A **special warranty deed** only guarantees that the seller has not attached any claims or restrictions on

the property. A **quit claim deed** allows the title grantor to relinquish his or her interest in the property.

Closing Costs

Closing or **settlement** date refers to the day on which title is formally passed to the buyer. On closing day the buyer will pay a variety of costs associated with closing the title transfer transaction. Some common closing costs are listed in Figure 9.3.

The lender will require a report on the creditworthiness of the borrower. The lender will also want the property to be surveyed and inspected for any termite damage. Points are also paid at the closing. Other fees at closing are associated with preparing the documents, insuring the title, and recording the title. All of these items tend to be very technical. It is always advisable for the buyer to be represented by legal counsel during

Figure 9.3 Typical Closing Costs

Item	Amount
Credit report on buyer	$50–$80
Appraisal fee	$80–$350
Termite inspection	$35–$60
Mortgage service fee[a]	Varies
Document preparation	$50–$80
Notary fees	$5–$20
Survey	$150–$300
Title search	$80–$200
Title insurance	$250–$500
Mortgage insurance[b]	Varies
Attorney's fees	$300–$600
Escrow fees	$30–$60
Escrow payments[c]	Varies
Transfer taxes[d]	Varies
Recording fee	$10–$30

[a]Depends on the points being charged by the lender.
[b]Varies with amount of mortgage insured.
[c]Depends on real estate taxes, hazard insurance, and other items on which some prepayment is required.
[d]Some states or counties may impose on the buyer a title transfer tax of about 1 percent of the purchase price.

the closing process. Some of the item charges can be negotiated and reduced. Overall, closing costs can come to almost 5 percent of the purchase price of the house.

Spot Quiz • Taking Title to the House

1. A certificate of title guarantees the buyer that the title is defect-free.
   T _____   F _____

2. A quit claim deed signed by the seller is the same as a warranty deed.
   T _____   F _____

3. It is desirable for the buyer to lower closing costs by not retaining an attorney.   T _____   F _____

(Answers on page 304)

Tax ASPECTS OF HOUSING OWNERSHIP

Owning a house creates certain tax advantages not available to renters. If a homeowner itemizes expenses on the federal income tax return, then real estate taxes and interest on the mortgage loan are completely tax-deductible. Points paid for obtaining the mortgage are also tax-deductible in the year the house was purchased.

Expenses related to the final settlement, such as credit report fees, appraisal fee, notary fees, survey, title search, title insurance premium, attorney's fees, and so on, are not tax-deductible in the year in which the house was purchased. However, these expenses can be added to the cost of the house. For example, the Aguirres bought an $80,000 home. Expenses of the type mentioned above equal $1,500, so the holding cost of their house is $81,500. The holding cost of the house is also known as the **adjusted basis**. Any expenses related to permanent house or property improvements are also added to the adjusted basis.

Profits made from selling a house for more than its adjusted basis are subject to taxes. However, if the owner replaces the house sold with another one within 24 months of the sale of the old home, then it is possible to defer up to all of the taxes due on profits made from the sale of the old home. Let's assume that the Aguirres sell their house for $109,000. Commissions and other expenses related to sale are $7,200. The amount they

realize from the sale is $109,000 − $7,200 = $101,800. Their gain on this sale is computed as follows:

Selling price	$109,000
Less selling expenses	7,200
Net amount realized	$101,800
Adjusted basis	81,500
Gain on sale	$ 20,300

Normally, this $20,300 is subject to taxes. However, the Aguirres buy another house for $110,000. They can defer taxes on the $20,300 by adjusting the basis for the new house as follows:

Purchase price	$110,000
Less gain on sale	20,300
Adjusted basis, new home	$ 89,700

By adjusting the basis for the new home, the Aguirres have been able to defer taxes on the gain from the sale of the old home.

Persons who are 55 or older qualify for a special tax treatment on profits from the sale of a residence. Up to $125,000 of profit from the sale of a house is excluded from the amount subject to taxes. This exclusion can be taken only once in a lifetime. If a person who qualifies sells a house for a $140,000 gain, he or she would pay taxes on only $15,000. The exclusion is not cumulative. That is, if an eligible person sells a house for a profit of $85,000 and excludes this amount from taxes, the other $40,000 exclusion is forfeited. This tax law is very beneficial for people who are ready to retire and move into a smaller home or an apartment.

Spot Quiz • Tax Aspects of Housing Ownership

1. Real estate taxes and interest expenses can always be deducted by the homeowner.   T _____   F _____

2. Gains from the sale of a house can be deferred indefinitely as long as the owner keeps buying more expensive homes.
                                                            T _____   F _____

3. The $125,000 gain exclusion is available to all homeowners.
                                                            T _____   F _____

(Answers on page 304)

HOUSING ALTERNATIVES

The previous section basically discusses the ownership of houses. However, there are a variety of alternatives to owning houses, including condominiums, cooperatives, and mobile homes.

Condominiums

Condominiums, or condos, as they are popularly called, are individually owned units in apartment complexes. A person or family owning a condo owns the individual apartment as well as a proportional share of common areas, such as the lobby, yard, and hallways. Condos are growing rapidly in popularity and now account for almost one-third of this country's new housing units. The demand for condos is so strong in some areas, such as San Diego and Washington, that buyers often put down a deposit on a condo unit before construction even begins.

Condos can be newly constructed or converted from rental units. Newly constructed condos are specifically designed to be condos. It is estimated that over 100,000 new condo units are being built every year. The second type of condos are rental apartment units that have been converted to condos. It has been estimated that the number of apartment units being converted into condos each year equals the number of new condos being constructed each year.

Who Should Buy a Condo? A condo is not for everyone interested in buying shelter. Condos are generally cheaper than detached houses because they utilize less land per unit and share roofs, walls, plumbing, and so on. In a major metropolitan area, a two-bedroom condo might sell for about $80,000, whereas a three- to five-bedroom detached house in the same area might sell for $200,000 to $300,000. Condos therefore allow buyers to live in more expensive neighborhoods for less money than if they were living in a detached house.

Condos are particularly appealing to singles; young, childless couples; and the elderly. In some condo developments, young singles are buying up to 60 percent of the units available.

Persons who work in the downtown area in large cities and live in the suburbs may find the inconvenience and cost of commuting sufficient incentive to move into a condo closer to work. Don and Beth Rowley of Northbrook, a Chicago suburb, rented out their suburban home and moved to a one-bedroom condo in downtown Chicago. Both have more leisure time now and have a short walk to work.[6]

Certain advantages and disadvantages of condo ownership should be kept in mind. Many condos offer "amenity packages," which may include

---

6. "Moving in on the Condominium Boom," *Money* (June 1979): 76.

swimming pools, tennis courts, saunas, game rooms, and other recreational facilities. Most condos provide maintenance services, for which the owner pays a monthly fee. As with other forms of shelter ownership, condos provide deductibility of real estate taxes and interest paid on the mortgage. Finally, condos appreciate in value at about the same rate as detached houses.

In general, condos are harder to sell than detached houses. A condo owner cannot enlarge the condo. Certain activities, as well as ownership of pets, may be prohibited in some condo developments. There is no guarantee that owners of neighboring condos will not be noisy. Finally, decisions and rules about condo development are made by a majority of the condo owners; some condo owners may find it very difficult to live by the rules of the majority.

Tips on Buying a Condo. A real estate agent who is very familiar with condos and a good lawyer are two musts for the first-time condo buyer. The real estate agent will be able to provide vital information on the various condo developments in the area. The lawyer will be able to carefully screen the documents on the condo.

The estimated monthly maintenance charges stated by the condo seller should be carefully verified. Some sellers deliberately underestimate maintenance charges (called **lowballing**) to attract potential condo buyers. The real estate agent should be helpful in obtaining actual maintenance charge information from comparable condo developments.

Some condo developers retain ownership of the amenities and lease them to the owners. The lawyer should be able to tell whether the lease payment on the amenities will increase sharply after all condo units have been sold. The state of Florida prohibits increases in amenities leases. Other states may follow suit to protect the condo buyers' interests.

If the condo development is new, the developer's reputation should be checked with the state's attorney general. If there are any complaints against the developer for poor construction, it's best to shop for a condo elsewhere. If the condo unit has yet to be constructed, site drawings, construction plans, and condo floor plans should be carefully evaluated. If the condo development is a conversion, the age of the building should be ascertained. Heating, plumbing, and wiring should be in good condition. The overall physical condition of the structure should be carefully evaluated. An engineer's report may detect problems with wiring, heating, plumbing and the structure, and should be requested from the seller.

Parking facilities and any related costs should be understood. The buyer should check to see that good maintenance and refuse pickup services are provided. The condo buyer should ascertain that potential neighbors are reasonable and congenial. The condo development's bylaws and rules should be evaluated by the lawyer and thoroughly explained to the condo buyer.

The lawyer and the real estate agent should be helpful in explaining the condo sale papers. The development operating budget and any assessments should be carefully checked. Basically, condo buying calls for the buyer to be patient and very unemotional while looking for the right condo. (See "A Condo on Campus?" below.)

Cooperatives

Cooperative apartments are units in an apartment complex where the owners buy a proportional share of a corporation owning the total complex rather than individual, identifiable units. Let's assume that a cooperative apartment complex (co-op for short) has 30 identical, equally valued apartment units. The total market value of the complex is $1,650,000. A person wants to buy an available co-op apartment in this complex. The person can buy this apartment for $1,650,000/30 = $55,000. For $55,000 the buyer receives 1/30 ownership of the corporation owning the total co-op. This 1/30 ownership share would, of course, include the apartment as well as a proportional share of all common property areas. If the apartments in the co-op are of different values, then each co-op member would own

A Condo on Campus?

You may not find a condo in the middle of campus, right next door to your 8 A.M. class, but it is becoming increasingly easy to buy a condo close to campus. With college enrollments stabilizing, and with families becoming more affluent, real estate developers have been quick to fill the demand for quality housing close to campuses across America. The deal goes down something like this: parents buy the condos and rent them to their college-going sons and daughters. When the students graduate, the parents sell the condos for good profits.

Renting these campus condos owned by their parents is a good deal for the students because it provides them with high-quality living space at reasonable prices. It is a good deal for the parents as well because they receive the benefits of owning investment property.

Campus condo deals may sour, however, if the parents become too emotionally involved with providing housing for their offspring and forget about the investment aspects of the deals. Campus condos should generally be evaluated the same way as other investment deals. In addition, parents should determine the rental appeal of the condos in case they cannot be sold readily. Maintenance and management costs should also be checked carefully. If everything checks out satisfactorily, campus condos can be sweet deals for everyone involved.

a portion of the co-op corporation equal to the ratio of the value of his or her apartment to the value of the whole co-op.

Co-op members are responsible for their proportional share of total common co-op expenses, such as maintenance, repairs, taxes, insurance, and management fees. The advantages and disadvantages of owning co-ops are somewhat the same as those for owning condos. Before a person buys into a co-op, the person should utilize the tips and precautions that apply to condo buying. Additionally, the person should be aware that co-op financing is more complex than condo financing.

Mobile Homes

Mobile homes are prefabricated shelter units that are built in a factory and then moved to their permanent location. Most communities have zoning ordinances that prevent mobile homes from being installed in neighborhoods made up of single-family detached homes. Typically, mobile homes are located in trailer or mobile home parks outside city limits in unzoned areas. Because mobile homes are transported by roads, most of them are relatively narrow, although the recent trend has been to buy two units that can be bolted together to make a wider mobile home.

Because they are relatively inexpensive, mobile homes appeal to the young and the elderly. Typical new mobile homes range in price from $8,000 to $30,000. The lower price of a mobile home means a smaller down payment and smaller monthly mortgage payments. The major disadvantage is that mobile homes do not appreciate in value like the other shelter alternatives discussed previously. Mobile homes, like automobiles, lose their value slowly over time. Thus, the purchase of a mobile home does not result in the buildup of equity.

As with buying houses, location is of prime importance in buying mobile homes. That is, the potential mobile home buyer should find the right mobile home park in the right location and arrange for a suitable site in the park before making the purchase.

Once a suitable site has been located, a reputable dealer handling reputable mobile homes should be identified. At times, mobile homes suffer from faulty construction, not enough insulation, leaking roofs, and squeaky doors. Dealing with a reputable dealer will help the buyer avoid many of these problems.

More and more mobile homes are being financed by financial institutions. Unlike mortgages on houses, loans for mobile homes mature in 7 to 15 years. The faster loan repayment for mobile homes is because mobile homes tend to lose value over time. Lenders want their loans repaid over the 7- to 15-year period to prevent losses due to defaults. FHA-insured and VA-guaranteed loans also are available for mobile home purchases. The interest rate on mobile home loans is typically higher than the rate on other types of housing loans.

Time-Share Homes

As the name implies, a **time-share home** is one in which the buyer purchases the use of the house for a short time period. The principal use of time-share homes is for vacations. Dick and Muriel Deardorff of Arlington, Virginia, liked the Virginia Beach area and wanted to go there year after year for vacations. So in 1975 they bought a two-week time-share in a beachfront, fully furnished, two-bedroom luxury apartment for $8,300. By 1979, similar two-week time-share homes in the area were selling for $18,000.[7]

Time-shares vary from one week to six months. Prices of time-shares also vary, depending on the size and location of the unit and the season. Time-share homes are available in all popular vacation areas, from Hawaii to Cape Cod. The principal advantage of a time-share home is that it guarantees the buyer a place to stay in a desirable vacation spot. Typical time-share arrangements call for a deed for the owner, who can transfer it later in much the same way as a conventional house deed. Time-share homes are a relatively new concept, and potential buyers should not complete a purchase of one without good legal counsel.

Spot Quiz • Housing Alternatives

1. For all practical purposes, condos and co-ops are very similar.

   T _____   F _____

2. Condo and co-op buying requires more legal counseling than does buying a house.

   T _____   F _____

3. All shelter alternatives increase in value over time.

   T _____   F _____

(Answers on page 305)

Home Remodeling

Rather than moving to a new house to accommodate changing shelter needs, many families simply opt for remodeling their existing houses. Additions to the family may call for converting the attic space into a bedroom or adding a new bathroom. The house may be without a garage,

---

7. "Buying a Vacation Home a Week at a Time," *Money* (October 1978): 57.

and the owner may decide to build one. The kitchen may be obsolete, and the owner may decide to modernize it. A second type of remodeling is done for safety or cost reasons. Many homeowners are having burglar alarms installed. Still others are making their houses more energy-efficient. Remodeling and home improvement should be considered from both investment and cost-saving viewpoints.

Investment Aspects of Remodeling

Typical types of home remodeling include adding a bedroom, bathroom, family room, fireplace, or garage, and modernizing the kitchen, bathroom, or living room. The costs of these remodeling jobs is not trivial. Adding a garage may cost $12,000, a new bathroom may cost $7,000, and a kitchen modernization may cost $15,000. Can the homeowner recover the costs of remodeling? That is, if $8,000 is spent on remodeling, will the value of the house increase by $8,000? Surprisingly, the answer is that only in very rare cases will the homeowner be able to recover 100 percent of remodeling costs. As Figure 9.4 shows, adding a new swimming pool to a house will result in the recovery of only 32 percent of the expenses. On the other hand, adding a new fireplace to a house will increase the value of the house by an amount that is more than the construction cost.

The principal reason behind home remodeling is that the present neighborhood or location is very desirable for the owners. Many homeowners choose to remodel rather than move to a new house because of schools, friends, social groups, and the general neighborhood environment. A second reason is that moves tend to be costly and are not always tax-deductible. Moving to a new location may also mean taking out a new mortgage at a much higher interest rate than that on the old mortgage.

Some general pointers should be kept in mind when you consider remodeling. You should not go overboard on improvements. Modest sums should be spent to remodel and renovate. A rule of thumb is that total remodeling costs should not exceed 30 percent of the value of the home. Second, it is not advisable to improve the house to the extent that it no longer fits into the neighborhood. For instance, adding two bedrooms to a three-bedroom house in a neighborhood where typical homes have three bedrooms is not recommended.

Putting money into renovating a house in a deteriorating neighborhood probably is not going to be profitable. On the other hand, if a deteriorating neighborhood is undergoing a change for the better, with many homes being renovated, then remodeling is very desirable. Remodeling that narrows the appeal of the house should be avoided unless the owner plans to live in the house for a long time. Tennis courts, swimming pools, hot tubs, exotic landscaping, and greenhouses fall into this category.

Figure 9.4 Percent of Remodeling Expenses Recovered at House Resale Time*

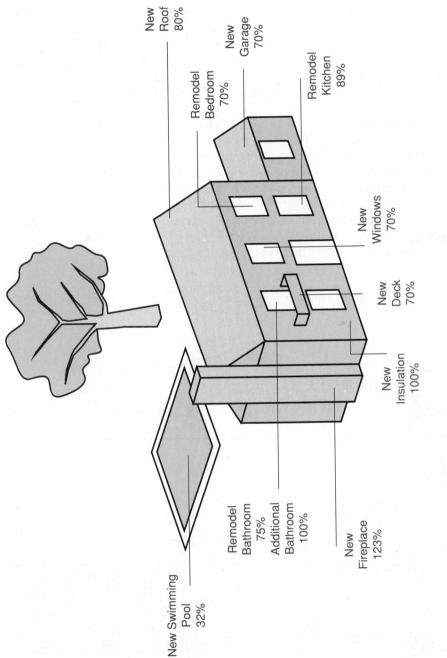

New
Roof
80%

New
Garage
70%

Remodel
Bedroom
70%

Remodel
Kitchen
89%

New
Windows
70%

New
Deck
70%

New
Insulation
100%

New
Fireplace
123%

Additional
Bathroom
100%

Remodel
Bathroom
75%

New Swimming
Pool
32%

*The percents represent the amount of remodeling expenses recovered when the house is sold. The figures apply to an average 17-year-old home with 1,700 square feet, located in the Midwest. The percentages listed here will vary depending on the region, the size of the house, and the quality of materials utilized.

Cost-Saving Remodeling

Cost-saving remodeling results in lower monthly housing costs. The primary purpose of cost-saving remodeling is to reduce utility and insurance costs. Making a house energy-efficient may result in substantial savings for the homeowner. In fact, the cost savings may pay for the remodeling in three to six years. Burglar alarms may reduce insurance premiums as well as the potential of loss from theft.

House Insulation. With fuel and energy prices increasing, more and more homeowners are becoming aware of the need to better insulate their homes. Insulation can reduce heating and cooling bills dramatically. The Princeton Center for Energy and Environmental Studies showed that by adding insulation, caulking, and weather stripping and making other improvements, home heating bills could be reduced by 67 percent. Fifteen hundred dollars spent on insulating may reduce heating and cooling bills by $500 per year. Figure 9.5 shows how fuel bills can be reduced through better insulation and other cost-reduction methods.

Figure 9.5   Savings in Fuel Costs

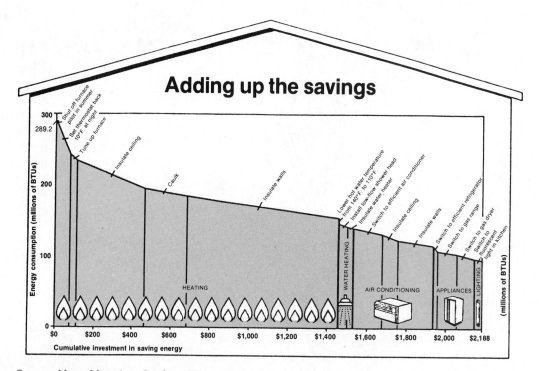

Source: *Money* Magazine, October 1979, p. 60. Reprinted with permission.

The protection against temperature loss provided by an insulating material is measured in R-values. The **R-value** is a standard measure to show how well the material insulates. Twelve inches of loose glass fiber has the same R-value as seven inches of loose cellulose fiber. The United States can be divided into five heat zones. Los Angeles, Phoenix, Dallas, and Atlanta are in heat zone 1. Sioux Falls, Minneapolis, and Burlington, Vermont, are in heat zone 4. The U.S. Department of Energy has certain guidelines for home insulation. For example, its recommended R-values for attic floors are R-26 in heat zone 1 and R-33 in heat zone 4. Twelve inches of loose glass fiber have an R-value of 33. Any insulation dealer will have a chart showing how R-values can be translated into inches of insulation materials.

There are four basic types of insulation materials. Batting and blankets can be easily used between joints and studs. Loose fill can be blown or filled into areas. Foam insulation is injected into walls. Rigid sheets can be used for basement walls. All types of insulation materials are acceptable based on the specific insulation needs.

You should obtain three or four estimates before you hire a contractor to install the insulation. The reputation of the contractors should be carefully checked. The contractors should be asked to provide the estimate on a "cents per unit of R-value" basis as well as the total amount. For example, if the cost for R-33 insulation is 42 cents per square foot, the cost per unit of R-value is 42 cents/33 = 1.27 cents per R per square foot. Remember that your electric or gas utility can provide additional information on insulating needs in the home.

"I figure it's a good time to insulate."

Source: *Changing Times*, October 1979, p. 2.

Wood Stoves. As fuel prices keep going up, more and more homeowners are using wood stoves to heat their homes. Every year approximately 1,500,000 new wood-burning stoves are installed by homeowners. Wood is generally sold by the cord. A **cord** of wood is a 4-by-4-by-8-foot stack of wood. Whether wood stoves result in cost savings depends on the price of wood. For example, if electricity is 5 cents per kilowatt hour, burning wood at up to $184 per cord will produce cost savings. Heating oil at 75 cents per gallon is equivalent to wood at $117 per cord.[8]

Wood stoves vary in price, quality, and features. A good stove will be airtight and have a thermostat to regulate the flow of air into the stove. Some stoves are connected to traditional furnaces; when the wood fire burns out, the regular furnace takes over.

The principal disadvantage of a wood stove is that ashes must be cleaned out regularly. Also, wood stoves do not fuel themselves. Someone has to feed in the wood every few hours. A final disadvantage is that wood stoves can be fire hazards. Some insurance companies charge a 10 to 20 percent insurance premium if the house is heated by a wood stove. The homeowner should check with his or her insurance agent before having a wood-burning stove installed.

Solar Heating. Many new houses are being designed with solar heating systems. These systems are of two types. Passive solar heating systems use certain features of the house to gather or store solar heat. South-facing windows gather solar heat, which may be stored in special floor tiles. Active systems utilize special devices to gather and store solar heat. For example, an active system may use special panels to gather heat. Water may be circulated through the panels to store heat. The heated water may then be transferred to a special holding tank until it is needed.

Very rarely will a solar heating system by itself suffice to heat a home. Normally, a standard furnace is used as a backup to a solar heating system. A solar heating system that can contribute from 30 to 60 percent of the total heating needs of a house may be economical. A solar heating system for a 2,000-square-foot home may cost between $10,000 and $25,000. A system providing 40 to 50 percent of heating needs should pay for itself in 10 to 15 years.

Because no standards have been developed for solar heating systems, care should be exercised before installing one. Estimates should be obtained on initial as well as operating costs. Maintenance and warranties should be thoroughly checked. The contractor should be able to tell whether the roof of the house can support the weight of the solar heating system.

---

8. These comparisons are based on heat output and assume that hardwoods such as ash, oak, and cherry are burnt in a stove with 50 percent efficiency.

Finally, a heating engineer should be consulted to estimate the potential cost savings that would result from the solar heating system.

Burglar Alarms.   Burglar alarms vary from simple to complex. Alarms that can be hung from doorknobs sell for $10 to $30. If the doorknob is turned, the alarm emits a very loud noise. More complex systems can cost up to $500. Some systems are hooked up to doors and windows and are triggered when disturbed. Ultrasonic systems send out sound waves and are triggered when movement is detected. More expensive units use microwaves rather than sound waves. Microwaves can penetrate walls, allowing one system to protect large areas of the house. Many department stores and electronic equipment stores sell burglar alarm systems. The cost of the systems is well worth the protection and peace of mind they provide.

Financing Home Remodeling

The FHA insures loans for permanent, structural home improvements. Additions like bathrooms, bedrooms, and patios are eligible for FHA insurance. The FHA has two different insurance programs. Title I loans have a maximum insurability limit of $15,000. These loans carry a maximum interest rate of 12 percent and maximum maturity of 15 years. Title II loans are for improvements to homes at least 10 years old. The maximum amount insured is $12,000, with a maximum maturity of 20 years. On both types of loans, the FHA charges an insurance premium of 0.5 percent of the loan balance.

A second alternative is to take out a **second mortgage** on the house. For example, the house may be valued at $80,000. The first mortgage is for $50,000. The lender is willing to let the owner carry an 80 percent loan. That is, the owner's borrowing capacity is $80,000 × .8 = $64,000. The first mortgage is for $50,000, so the lender is willing to lend $64,000 − $50,000 = $14,000 on a second mortgage. Second mortgages provide less protection for the lender than first mortgages. Therefore, the interest rate on the second mortgage will be 5 to 8 percentage points higher than the prevailing rate on first mortgages.

The Tax Reform Act of 1986 encourages another type of second mortgage borrowing. Called the **home equity loan**, it allows homeowners to borrow against the equity they have built up in their homes. Home equity loans have become desirable because, under the new law, interest on personal and consumer loans is being phased out gradually, whereas interest on home equity loans will generally remain fully tax-deductible. Interest on home equity loans for all other purposes remain fully tax-deductible as long as the sum of the loan and the mortgage balance does not exceed the original purchase price of the home plus the cost of any home improvements. Most home equity loans carry variable interest rates, and homeowners are generally required to pay for an appraisal of their home

and a loan origination fee of $200 to $1,000. Despite the tax deductibility of interest on home equity loans, the homeowner must guard against excessive borrowing on these loans because inability to repay the loans may result in the loss of the home.

A fourth alternative is to **refinance** the house. In the example of the second mortgage, the owner has the alternative of repaying the first mortgage and taking out another mortgage for $64,000. The advantage is that the owner does not incur the high interest expense of the second mortgage. The disadvantages are that the owner may be giving up a low-interest mortgage. Also, refinancing will involve such costs as points and appraisal fees. A loan officer from the financial institution where the first mortgage originated should be of help in determining whether a second mortgage or refinancing is more desirable for the homeowner.

Spot Quiz • Home Remodeling

1. The ideal remodeling is one in which the increase in the value of the house is more than the cost of remodeling.   T _____   F _____

2. In general, increasing the energy efficiency of the house is economically desirable.   T _____   F _____

3. Solar heating systems are desirable for all homes.
                                                  T _____   F _____

4. The FHA issues home improvement loans.   T _____   F _____

(Answers on page 305)

Summary

Housing can be either rented or bought. Before buying housing, the potential homeowner should determine how much housing he or she can afford. Location, zoning, taxes, yard, exterior and interior construction, and living space are important factors in buying housing. The owner should seek protection against purchasing a poorly constructed home by buying

a warranty or having the house professionally inspected. The buyer makes an offer to buy by signing a purchase contract.

Mortgage funds for financing home purchases are available through financial institutions, mortgage assumption, and land contract. Mortgages can be of the conventional, graduated-payment, or variable-rate type. The FHA and VA have loan insurance and guarantee programs. Many terms or clauses are associated with mortgages.

The title to the house is transferred from buyer to seller by using a deed. Before title can be transferred, the property is surveyed, and the buyer pays a variety of closing costs. Home ownership produces tax-deductible expenses as well as tax deferral of profits under certain circumstances. Besides detached houses, other types of shelters are condos, co-ops, mobile homes, and time-share homes. Each form of housing has special appeal for certain groups of people.

Owners who remodel homes should consider both investment and cost-saving aspects of remodeling. Adding home insulation and installing wood-burning stoves and solar heating systems are examples of cost-saving remodeling. Remodeling can be financed through FHA-insured loans, second mortgages, and refinancing.

Questions

1. What is meant by housing, or shelter? List five different forms of housing.

2. Explain the guidelines that can be used to determine how much housing a person can afford.

3. What procedures can be followed to avoid the purchase of a defective home?

4. What sources are available for financing the purchase of a house?

5. How does a graduated-payment mortgage differ from an adjustable-rate mortgage? What are their advantages for the home buyer?

6. What is meant by points? What is the impact of points on the mortgage interest rate?

7. Explain some key clauses in a mortgage contract.

8. What is the difference between a title and an abstract? How is the homeowner protected from buying a house with a defective title?

9. What tax advantages are gained by buying housing?

10. Briefly explain what condos are. Who would be especially interested in buying a condo?

11. How are co-ops different from condos?

12. What factors should be kept in mind when a person is considering remodeling?

13. What is meant by cost-saving remodeling? Explain by giving an example.

14. Briefly explain the different methods of financing home remodeling.

Case Problems

1. The Frymans want to buy a house for $79,000. Their monthly housing costs (mortgage payment, taxes, utilities, and so on) will amount to $890. The Frymans' gross annual income is $39,000. If the lender uses the gross monthly income rule, do the Frymans qualify for a loan? If not, by how much would they have to reduce their monthly housing costs to qualify?

2. The Loys have annual gross income of $60,000. Using the annual gross income rule, what is the maximum purchase price that they should consider paying for a house? Based on the monthly gross income rule, what is the maximum amount per month that they should plan on spending for housing costs?

3. Karen Crisp is considering making an offer of $100,000 on a ranch house that she likes. Her housing costs other than mortgage payments (that is, taxes, utilities, insurance, and maintenance) would be $500 per month. A lender has indicated to her that with a 20 percent down payment and a 12 percent, 25-year, fixed-rate mortgage, she would just meet the monthly gross income requirement. What is Karen Crisp's annual gross income? (*Hint*: Use the information in Table 9.2.)

4. A. Pham and R. Sulski are thinking of buying houses costing $80,000. Mr. Pham would make a 20 percent down payment, and Ms. Sulski, 30 percent. Both mortgages are for 25 years, with Mr. Pham paying 12 percent interest, and Ms. Sulski, 10 percent. Mr. Pham's and Ms. Sulski's monthly payments are $674 and $509, respectively. Taxes, utilities, maintenance, and insurance are $250 a month for both.

    a. Mr. Pham's annual gross income is $34,000, and Ms. Sulski's is $38,000. If the lender uses the annual gross income rule, do both qualify for a mortgage? Explain your answer.

    b. Using the monthly gross income rule, do both qualify for a mortgage? Explain your answer.

5. Kent and Frieda Chacun bought a house for $40,000, spent $7,000 on home improvements, and then sold the house for $80,000. Sales commissions and other closing costs were $6,000. Three months later they bought a new house for $90,000. What is the adjusted cost basis for the new house purchased?

6. Donna Foy recently bought a new house for $68,000. She sold her old home for $63,000. Commissions and other expenses related to the sale of her old home amounted to $4,300. She had originally purchased the old home for $49,700. Nondeductible purchase expenses associated with her old home are $1,400.

    a. Calculate the taxable gain Donna Foy has on the sale of her old home.

    b. Rather than paying taxes, Ms. Foy adjusts the cost basis for her new home. Calculate the adjusted cost basis for the new home.

Bibliography

"Let a Computer Shop for Your Mortgage." *Changing Times* (June 1985): 43–45.

"Don't Let Your Lender Twist Your 'ARM'." *Changing Times* (July 1985): 39–41.

"When It Pays to Refinance." *Changing Times* (October 1985): 65–66.

"Making Home Improvement Pay Off." *Changing Times* (May 1987): 71–78.

"Bargain for That House Like a Pro." *Changing Times* (May 1987): 45–48.

"Two Ways to Save on a Mortgage." *Consumer Reports* (June 1985): 336–337.

"Time to Refinance Your Mortgage." *Consumer Reports* (October 1986): 646–649.

"Out the Old House and into the New." *Money* (May 1985): 77–80.

"A Call to ARMs." *Money* (July 1985): 123–131.

"How to Keep Your Property Taxes From Going Through the Roof." *Money* (December 1986): 51.

Answers To Spot Quizzes

Buying Housing (page 276)

1. T (A larger down payment reduces the monthly mortgage payment.)

2. F (What good is the price if the location is not very desirable?)

3. F (This statement is generally—but not always—true.)

4. T (The purchase contract, signed by the buyer, is an offer to purchase the house for sale.)

Financing the House (page 284)

1. T (The house is sold on a land contract.)

2. F (If the borrower wants to refinance the house when interest rates decline, he or she would have to pay a penalty.)

3. T (The lender's risk of lowering the interest rate is very small; the lender has more of a chance to raise the interest rate on the mortgage.)

4. F (The program guarantees that the lender will not lose any money on the insured part of the mortgage.)

5. T (Each point increases the effective interest rate on a mortgage by about .125 percent.)

Taking Title to the House (page 287)

1. F (It merely indicates that a diligent search has not revealed any claims against the property.)

2. F (A quit claim deed does not transfer title.)

3. F (Unless the buyer is legally competent in real estate transactions, an attorney should be retained.)

Tax Aspects of Housing Ownership (page 288)

1. F (These expenses can be deducted only if the homeowner itemizes expenses.)

2. T (Current tax laws allow for this situation.)

3. F (The exclusion is available only to persons 55 or older.)

Housing Alternatives (page 293)

1. T (The difference is more legal than practical.)

2. T (Condo and co-op buying involves more complex issues than does buying a house.)

3. F (Mobile homes typically lose value over time.)

Home Remodeling (page 300)

1. T (It is desirable to recover as much as or more than the cost of remodeling.)

2. T (In general, yes. For instance, costs of insulation are usually recovered in three to five years.)

3. F (Many older homes and homes in low-sunshine areas do not benefit from solar heating systems.)

4. F (The FHA only insures loans.)

Chapter 10

Transportation and Major Appliances

Objectives

After reading this chapter, you will be able to:

- Identify transportation needs.
- Determine transportation costs.
- Explain how much to spend on transportation.
- Discuss the selection of a new car.
- Estimate a reasonable price for a new car.
- Negotiate with a car dealer.
- Select and price a used car.
- Describe car purchases from a car rental company.
- Explain how to keep a car running.
- Describe car financing.
- Discuss car leasing.
- Evaluate and buy an appliance.

Ray Magnus was looking around for a nice, clean used car to buy. He spotted an advertisement in a newspaper for a 1982 Ford. He arranged to meet the seller in the parking lot of a shopping center. He arrived at the appointed time and saw the seller with a sharp-looking car. The Ford looked extremely clean inside and out. No rust spots or scratches marred the body. The seller showed him the four new radials on the car. Then he opened the trunk to show the unused spare. Ray was impressed. He was ready to bargain on the price when the seller insisted on showing him the engine. It was absolutely clean. "Oh, by the way," said the seller, "notice the new front shock absorbers." On the seller's insistence, Ray drove the car around the parking lot. It ran just fine.

Used cars have two prices associated with them. The **retail price** is the price at which used car dealers will sell a used car to a consumer. The **wholesale price** is the price at which the used car dealer will sell the car to another used car dealer. For the '82 Ford, the seller was asking a price just below the average retail price. Ray countered with the wholesale price. After some haggling, they agreed on a price somewhat higher than the wholesale price. "What a bargain," thought Ray as he drove the seller to his bank so he could cash the check that Ray had written.

Ray dropped the seller off at a street corner and headed home. About a mile from his house he heard a scraping sound under the car. He stopped and saw that the car muffler was dragging on the street. Muttering under his breath, he pulled into a muffler shop. The complete exhaust system had to be replaced at a cost of $145. One week later, Ray was having the oil and filter changed when a routine checkup resulted in a brake overhaul. Cost: $100 plus. Two months later, Ray noticed blue smoke coming out of the exhaust pipe. . . .

Ray had purchased a lemon—a car that was destined to give him problems constantly. He had made a number of errors in buying the Ford. He had let the car's exterior influence him unduly. He had not checked out the car properly, and had not asked a qualified mechanic to check the car. Ray was asking for trouble. The purpose of this chapter is to provide information for making good decisions about buying new and used cars and new appliances.

TRANSPORTATION NEEDS AND COSTS

Transportation ranges from walking to work to flying on the Concorde to Paris for a business meeting. Of primary concern to the vast majority of consumers is the basic need to get back and forth to work. Public transportation, car or van pooling, bicycling, and motorcycling are some options used by commuters. However, by far the most popular method of transportation is driving a car to work. Therefore, the sections on transportation

will focus on the car. This section also discusses how to identify transportation needs and how to determine—before you purchase the car—how much it is going to cost.

Identifying Transportation Needs

People's needs for owning cars vary. For some, the primary reason for owning a car is to meet transportation needs. For others, a car not only meets the transportation need but also provides status for the owner. Some people will buy expensive cars as a symbol of their wealth. And some will drive a beat-up old clunker as a symbol of their wealth. There is really nothing wrong with buying a car as a status symbol. Buying a car for status is a value judgment that each person is free to make. However, you should recognize that when a car is purchased as a status symbol, it then becomes meaningless to discuss the purchase of cars from a financial viewpoint. Our discussion, then, focuses on car purchases strictly from a transportation viewpoint.

Cars can be classified into five categories: subcompacts, compacts, intermediates, full-size, and specialty. The specialty category includes all cars that do not fit into one of the other four categories. For example, sports cars, such as Corvettes and Triumphs, fall into this category. When you define your transportation needs, you should take into consideration roominess, operating costs, comfort, and reliability. Different categories of cars have different levels of the four features listed.

Roominess. Roominess refers to the internal dimensions of the car's passenger space and the trunk. Subcompacts are less roomy than compacts, intermediates, or full-size cars. Specialty cars tend not to be roomy. If the majority of your driving involves one or two persons, a subcompact or compact is desirable.

Operating Costs. Operating costs include gas, routine maintenance, depreciation, insurance, and repair costs. Operating costs per mile are lowest for subcompacts and highest for full-size cars. Subcompacts, of course, get higher gas mileage than full-size cars. In general, they also have lower insurance costs, lower depreciation rates, and lower maintenance costs per mile than full-size cars. Compacts and intermediates fall between subcompact and full-size cars.

Comfort. Full-size cars have a much more comfortable ride than do subcompacts. Full-size cars, in general, also tend to be more luxurious than compacts or subcompacts. Amenities such as automatic transmission, power steering, and power brakes are readily available as standard or optional equipment on full-size cars. Many subcompacts do not offer these features even on an optional basis.

". . . and you won't have any worries about gas. This baby's got a 400-gallon tank."

Source: *Changing Times*, August 1979, p. 2. Reprinted with permission.

If you drive long distances or over rough roads, full-size cars are much more desirable. Subcompacts are more suited to short commutes.

Reliability. Reliability tends to be a function of the company that manufactured the car. Specialty cars tend to be more exotic and somewhat less reliable than other cars.

In summary, subcompacts and compacts are generally cheaper to operate than intermediate, full-size, or specialty cars. Intermediates and full-size cars, on the other hand, are roomier and provide more comfort than compacts or subcompacts. When you identify your transportation needs, you should compare operating costs with requirements for roominess and comfort.

Determining Transportation Costs

Ten or fifteen years ago, it was fairly common for a car buyer to base his or her decision on comfort, roominess, and the status of the car. Operating and maintenance costs were not high enough to justify serious consideration. Such is not the case these days. Car prices, gasoline and maintenance costs, as well as financing and insurance costs have skyrocketed in the past few years. If anything, it appears that operating costs are now becoming a prime consideration in any car purchase decision. Determining these transportation costs is the topic of this section.

Transportation costs can be divided into two categories: fixed and variable. **Fixed costs** remain the same irrespective of how much the car is driven. Fixed costs include depreciation, insurance, license, fees, sales taxes, parking costs, and loan payments. **Variable costs**, which change with the number of miles driven, include maintenance, repairs, and gasoline.

Table 10.1 shows how transportation costs can be estimated. The table assumes that the new car has been purchased for $8,500. The following depreciation charges are used for new cars: 25.0 percent in year 1, 15.0 percent in year 2, 10.0 percent in year 3, and 7 percent in year 4. Actually,

Table 10.1 Calculating Transportation Costs

Cost	Annual Amount			
	Year 1	Year 2	Year 3	Year 4
Fixed Costs				
Depreciation[a]	$2,125	$1,275	$ 850	$ 595
Insurance[b]	500	550	605	666
Interest on loan[c]	540	540	540	540
Parking, license, etc.[b]	300	330	363	399
Total fixed costs	$3,465	$2,695	$2,358	$2,200
Variable Costs				
Gasoline[b]	750	825	907	998
Maintenance, repairs[b]	250	275	303	333
Total variable costs	$1,000	$1,100	$1,210	$1,331
Total transportation costs	$4,465	$3,795	$3,568	$3,531

[a]The purchase price of the car is $8,500.
[b]These costs are increased by 10 percent every year.
[c]The loan of $6,000 is for four years at an APR of 16 percent. The total loan payment is $8,160. Interest is $2,160 for four years.

there is little consensus on the actual depreciation rate for a new car. Inflation muddles the picture. For example, a car was bought one year ago for $8,000 and can now be sold for $6,000. It appears that depreciation is $8,000 − $6,000 = $2,000. However, if it costs $9,000 to replace the car today, then inflation-adjusted depreciation is $3,000. Table 10.1 shows the depreciation costs for the first four years based on the above percentage charges.

Insurance costs vary from city to city. The insurance cost for the first year is $500. It is shown to increase by 10 percent every year. The car buyer makes a down payment of $2,500 and finances the balance of $6,000 for four years at an APR of 16 percent. APRs were discussed in Chapter 7. The monthly loan repayment amount is $170. Total loan repayment is $170 × 48 = $8,160. Interest on the loan is $8,160 − $6,000 = $2,160, or $540 per year.[1]

---

1. The loan payment amounts on the principal do not show up as transportation expenses because they build up the owner's equity in the car. Including both depreciation and the payments on the principal would result in double-counting costs of ownership.

Parking, license, and so on also vary from city to city. They are estimated to be $300 for year 1 and to increase by 10 percent each year. Total fixed costs for year 1 are $3,465.

Total variable costs for year 1 are $1,000. It is assumed that the car is driven 10,000 miles each year and averages 18 miles per gallon. Total transportation costs for year 1 are $4,465. Because the car is driven 10,000 miles, transportation costs are 44.65 cents per mile for year 1. By year 4, these costs decline to $35.31 cents per mile. These costs are for an intermediate-size car. The cost for a subcompact will be about 3 to 5 cents per mile lower. Full-size car costs will be 3 to 5 cents per mile higher.

As Table 10.1 shows, the largest portion of costs is associated with depreciation. A full-size new car will cost about $800 to $1,000 more to operate than a subcompact. After four years of operation, a full-size car will cost about $500 per year more to operate than a subcompact. These costs should be compared with the requirements for comfort and roominess before deciding on the size of the car.

How Much to Spend on Transportation

After housing and food, transportation is the next largest item in the family budget. In general, transportation expenditures should not be more than 15 percent of a family's take-home income. The information from Table 10.1 can be used to estimate the out-of-pocket expenses of transportation. Note, however, that Table 10.1 includes an entry for depreciation. **Depreciation** is a noncash charge. That is, it reflects wear and tear on the car but does not involve any physical outlay of cash. So in figuring out-of-pocket expenses for transportation, we can remove depreciation as an expense.

Table 10.2 shows total transportation costs of $4,465 for year 1. From this amount we remove $2,125 for depreciation as a noncash charge. The

Table 10.2 Calculating Cash Outflows for Transportation

Cost	Amount			
	Year 1	Year 2	Year 3	Year 4
Total transportation costs[a]	$4,465	$3,795	$3,567	$3,531
Less: depreciation[b]	2,125	1,275	850	595
Plus: loan repayment[c]	1,500	1,500	1,500	1,500
Total cash outflows, annual	$3,840	$4,020	$4,211	$4,436
Total cash outflows, monthly	$ 320	$ 335	$ 351	$ 370

[a]From Figure 10.1.
[b]Depreciation is a noncash charge and is excluded here.
[c]The total loan is $6,000. Annual repayment is $1,500.

car buyer is also repaying the $6,000 loan at a rate of $1,500 per year. This loan amount is added to the transportation expenses shown in Table 10.2. For year 1, total out-of-pocket transportation expenses are $3,840. On a monthly basis, these expenses are $320 for year 1. In later years, these expenses increase somewhat.

Let's assume that the family thinking about buying the $8,500 car has a take-home income of $2,000 per month. This family should not spend more than $2,000 x .15 = $300 per month on transportation. Table 10.2 shows monthly expenses of $320. The family has three options at this time. It can choose to buy a cheaper car, which would lower interest and loan repayment expenses. Second, the family could increase the size of the down payment on the $8,500 car. A larger down payment would reduce the amount to be financed and therefore lower transportation expenses. A third option is to buy the $8,500 car with a $3,500 down payment and reduce some other expenses, such as those on clothing or recreation. In general, though, it is better to stay within budget guidelines rather than increase one expenditure category by trying to decrease another category.

Spot Quiz • Transportation Needs and Costs

1. Transportation costs include only depreciation, gasoline, and maintenance.   T _____   F _____

2. Transportation costs can be different from actual out-of-pocket transportation expenses.   T _____   F _____

(Answers on page 335)

Buying a new car

The last two sections provided information on how much car a family can afford. This section deals with buying a new car. The steps involved are selecting a particular make of car, determining a reasonable price, and negotiating a deal with the car dealer.

Selecting the Make of Car

Within a size category, numerous cars can be considered for purchase. The reliability record, warranty offered, standard and optional equipment available, and resale value should be carefully evaluated.

Reliability. An otherwise attractive car that is constantly breaking down and being towed to a garage is no joy to drive. Owning a reliable car not only saves money but also cuts down on the inconvenience of temporarily being without transportation. To determine which cars are reliable and which are not, start by checking with friends and acquaintances about the reliability of their cars. Remember, though, that this method of judging reliability may not be very accurate because people can hold biased opinions.

Magazines such as *Consumer Reports, Popular Science,* and *Road and Track* publish survey results on a variety of cars and their major features. *Consumer Reports* also publishes an *Annual Buying Guide* in which all major brands of cars are surveyed. In addition, periodically *Consumer Reports* contains detailed write-ups on the same type of car made by different manufacturers. Information from these published sources as well as from friends and acquaintances are useful sources for judging the reliability of various makes of cars.

Warranty. All new cars are covered by a warranty. Many warranties are for 60,000 miles or 60 months, whichever comes earlier. Many manufacturers also offer **extended warranties**, which become effective when the basic warranties expire, at extra cost. The extended warranty excludes routine maintenance and focuses on major repairs to the engine and the drive train. Extended warranties at nominal cost may be a desirable option to consider.

Standard and Optional Equipment. Car manufacturers offer very different standard equipment. Some cars have automatic transmission as standard equipment; others make it available as an option. When you compare cars, note what is available as standard equipment and optional equipment. A person who does not want to drive a car with a manual transmission, for example, would have to exclude from consideration those cars that do not offer automatic transmissions even as an option.

Resale Value. Some cars lose their value much faster than other cars. As a result, the resale values for different makes of cars made in the same year vary. Consumer magazines often report the results of studies to show how resale values vary with the size and make of car. The studies generally compare the average price for a new car with the average wholesale value of the same car three to five years later. For example, in 1987 the average price for a 1983 full-size car was about 40 percent of its 1983 price. That is, the average 1983 full-size car retained about 40 percent of its value in 1987. If the average new full-size car sold for $10,000 in 1983, then its value in 1987 as a used car was $10,000 x .40 = $4,000. For intermediate-size cars, the value retained after four years is about 48 percent, whereas for compacts and subcompacts, it is about 50 percent. On the average, foreign cars hold their value best, at about the 55 percent level after four

years. That is, after four years, the average foreign car can generally be sold for well over half of its original price.

Within the size categories, retained values vary also. In the compact/subcompact category, for example, the Pontiac Firebird Transam retains about 67 percent of its value after four years, whereas its close relatives from other General Motors divisions retain only about 36 to 38 percent of their value after four years. In the foreign car category, Hondas and Toyotas retain about 63 percent of their value after four years; the comparative figures for Mazdas and Subarus are somewhat lower.

Before buying a new car, you should evaluate the resale value of the car. The higher the resale value is, the lower the depreciation costs for the car will be. Lower depreciation costs mean lower transportation costs.

Test Drive. Before buying a new car, you should insist on test driving the car. Different makes of cars have differences in suspension systems, tires, steering mechanisms, engine weights and placements, window sizes and shapes, and many other factors. All of these factors have an effect on how the car rides and drives. Avoid buying a car that does not feel comfortable to drive.

Determining a Reasonable Price

All cars are required by law to carry a "window sticker" price. The **window sticker** shows the manufacturer's suggested list price for the car. The prices of the options on the car are itemized. In addition, the sticker may carry prices of a few options added by the dealer. Very rarely does a car buyer pay the window sticker price. Most of the time, the car is sold at a discount from the listed price.

Profit margins on new cars vary from 10 to 20 percent of list price. If, for example, a new car has a list, or retail, price of $8,000 and its profit margin is 15 percent, then the dealer's cost, or the wholesale price, for this car would be $8,000 × (1 − .15) = $6,800. A number of publications list the wholesale prices of both domestic and foreign cars. *Edmund's New Car Price* lists the retail and the wholesale prices for both the basic car and its available options. *Charlton's New Car Prices* also contains a listing of wholesale prices. **Wholesale price** in this case is the price the dealer pays the car manufacturer for the car and options.

Most dealers are willing to sell a car if they make a profit of about $400 or $500. The price to be paid depends on whether or not there is a trade-in. Wholesale prices for used cars can be estimated from *Edmund's Used Car Prices* or the *Official Used Car Guide* issued by the National Automobile Dealers Association (NADA).

Table 10.3 shows how a reasonable price can be determined for a new car. The left column contains the numbers used when a car is not being traded in. First, the wholesale price for the basic car and options are totaled.

They come to $10,500. Second, destination charges are added in. Destination charges, listed on the window sticker, cannot be reduced because they represent the actual amount billed to the dealer. Next, local dealer preparation charges are added in. These charges should be reasonable. Watch out for dealers who add on $300–$500 in local preparation charges. One dealer listed a charge of $90 for washing the car. Such dealers should be avoided.

The costs add up to $10,940. The dealer is being allowed a profit of $450. The purchase price is $11,390. Sales tax on $11,390 is $570. Title and registration are shown to be $60. These costs add up to $12,020, the reasonable price that buyer is willing to pay.

If a trade-in is involved, the wholesale value of the car being traded in is reduced from the dealer's cost, as shown in the right column of Table 10.3. The dealer's profit remains the same in either case. The sales tax is lower because it is charged on only $9,390. With the trade-in, the buyer should be willing to pay $9,920.

The procedure just described is a general one for determining a reasonable price. Some new cars are in great demand and sell for the window sticker price. For example, high-mileage, economy imported cars generally sell at or close to sticker prices. Occasionally, cars are in such demand that they sell for more than the sticker price. At one time, the diesel-engine VW Rabbit sold for $1,500 to $2,000 over the sticker price in some parts of the country.

Table 10.3 Determining Reasonable Price for a New Car

Item	Without Trade-In	With Trade-In
Wholesale price of car, options	$10,500	$10,500
Destination charge	400	400
Local dealer preparation	40	40
Dealer's cost	$10,940	$10,940
Less: trade-in	0	2,000
Plus: dealer's profit	450	450
Purchase price	$11,390	$9,390
Sales tax (5%)	570	470
Title, etc.	60	60
Buyer pays	$12,020	$9,920

Negotiating With the Dealer

New cars can either be ordered from a dealer or purchased off the dealer's lot. When a new car is ordered, delivery takes five to eight weeks, but the consumer is assured of all the desired options. Buying from the dealer's inventory has the advantage of immediate delivery. And even if the car with the desired color or options is not available, a person with some flexibility can generally find something on the lot that is pretty close to what he or she had in mind in the first place.

The procedure shown in Table 10.3 can be used to negotiate with the dealer. In the example with the trade-in, the dealer may initially offer the car for $9,900 with the trade-in. It does not matter what the dealer offers for the car being traded in. The important figure is the dollar amount that goes with the trade-in. The buyer may counter with an offer of $8,800 and the trade-in. Bargaining back and forth should produce a purchase price of $9,390 with the trade-in. If the dealer is not near the figure, then it is time for the buyer to go to a different dealer.

The buyer should not be swayed by the dealer's offers of "top price" for the trade-in. A buyer should not sign a contract if the price is not right. A buyer should not give the dealer any "earnest money" or a "good faith" check when making an offer. If the dealer's conduct is not satisfactory, negotiations should be terminated. Keep in mind that there is no such thing as a unique car. The same car, or one very similar to it, is available down the street, across town, or in a neighboring city. The car dealers *need* customers. The dealer *needs* a reasonable profit. The car buyer *needs* to pay a reasonable price. A reasonable offer keeps all parties happy. (See "Snowball in Hell?" on page 318.)

Spot Quiz • Buying a New Car

1. The asking price for a car should determine which car should be purchased.   T _____ F _____

2. Higher resale values for new cars mean higher operating costs.
                                                     T _____ F _____

3. A higher trade-in allowance does not necessarily mean a lower purchase price.   T _____ F _____

(Answers on page 336)

Snowball in Hell?

Many savvy observers argue that the unprepared person has about as much chance of getting a good deal from a new car salesperson as a snowball has of surviving in hell. Consumer magazines often report that salespeople aren't above lying to make a sale. For example, one salesperson told a *Consumer Reports* employee that a Mercury Sable costing $14,206 came with air conditioning, power windows, and other items as standard equipment. Only when confronted with contrary evidence did he admit his mistake—the base sticker price for the Sable was $11,126, and most of the equipment mentioned was optional. Apparently, it is quite common for auto dealers to try to sell a lot of optional equipment to increase profits.

How do you increase your chances of getting better odds than the proverbial snowball? Remember four important rules: (1) define for yourself in some detail what you want in a car; (2) don't fall in love with any particular car in a dealer's lot—your love affair will cost you hundreds of dollars; (3) know the dealer's price—otherwise, you will pay too much; (4) keep the cost of buying the new car a separate issue from financing it or from what you might get for a trade-in. Paying attention to these four simple rules will increase your chances of getting a good deal on wheels.

BUYING A USED CAR

Sharp increases in the prices of new cars are forcing many car buyers to give serious consideration to buying a used car. Many people also prefer to buy a used car because they believe they can obtain transportation at a lower cost than if they bought a new car.

Buying used cars also has some distinct disadvantages. For example, the choices of options are limited. Choices of color or style may be limited as well. The biggest disadvantage, however, is the possibility that the buyer is acquiring a "lemon." Some used cars look very clean inside and out. The paint shines, the seats are not torn, the tires are new, the battery cranks well, and the engine looks clean. But two days after buying it, the car needs a new alternator. One week later, the brakes have to be replaced. Then the air conditioner compressor breathes its last. And the list of repairs goes on. Ready to swear off used cars? Don't. This section tells how to buy a good used car, one that is not only dependable to drive but also cheaper to operate than a new car.

Selecting a Used Car

Selecting a used car involves identifying sources for used cars, examining the car, test driving the car, and having it inspected professionally.

Sources for Used Cars.   There are four major sources of used cars. When new car dealers take trade-ins on new cars, the dealers keep the best of the trade-ins for resale and wholesale the rest. Generally, used cars at a new car dealer's lot will be mechanically and physically sound cars. Unfortunately, the new car dealer's used car prices will be high because the dealer knows the cars are good. Also, the dealer will replace decorative trim and chrome and really shine up the car, and someone must pay for the labor involved. The new car dealer's lot should be visited only as a last resort.

Used car dealers generally obtain their cars at auctions and from new car dealers. The cars for sale generally are not in excellent mechanical condition. Thus, you should avoid used car lots if possible. You should also avoid car auctions unless you are mechanically inclined and know how to bid.

Newspaper advertisements carry listings of cars for sale by owners. Bulletin boards at work, in the cafeteria, in shopping malls, and at supermarkets are also good sources for identifying potentially good used cars. Driving around also helps. Some owners park their cars in their front yards with a "For Sale" sign on them. In general, you should begin your search for a used car by looking at what is available directly from owners.

The fourth source for used cars, the car rental agencies, is discussed in the next section.

Examining the Car. Before examining a car, you should already have determined the approximate type and age of car you want to purchase. You should also have estimated the price you are willing to pay for the car.

The first step in selecting a good used car is to examine it thoroughly. Is the physical appearance of the car satisfactory? Does it have rust spots or holes? Is the paint job uniform or are there areas where the paint colors do not match? Are the tires worn? Are there broken lights or glass? Does the car appear to have been involved in a major accident? If the answers to these questions are troublesome, tell the owner that the car is not suitable.

If the appearance of the car is satisfactory, then start the engine. After warming up the engine for a few minutes, listen to it. Does it make loud noises? How much dirt and grime is there on the engine? Does smoke come out of the exhaust pipe? Turn off the engine. Is the oil level okay and is the oil clean? If by this time the car is giving off bad vibes, forget about it. If examining the car gives you a comfortable feeling, then proceed with the next step. (See "Lemon Meringue and Peach Cobbler" on page 320.)

Test Driving the Car.   Take the car out for a test. If the owner or dealer will not allow the car to be test driven, don't bother with it any more. Warm up the engine. Put the car in gear and step on the gas. Does it start to move smoothly? Does the car feel safe to drive? How do the brakes work? (Disc brakes are habitually squeaky; don't worry about them now.) Find a long hill or a smooth stretch of open road. Slow the car down to 25 miles

Lemon Meringue and Peach Cobbler

At the dinner table, anything goes. Nothing is wrong with either lemon meringue or peach cobbler. But when it comes to buying used cars, avoid anything with even a hint of lemon, even if it has a topping of whipped egg whites and sugar.

Inspect the car carefully before test driving it. Look—really look—under the car. If you see any crankcase oil, transmission oil, or radiator leakage, however slow, forget about the car. (But don't mistake the melting condensation from the air conditioner for a radiator leak.)

Start the car, preferably when the engine is cold. Does it keep stalling in the process? It could mean a needed tune-up—or worse. Check for smoke in the exhaust. If you see smoke coming out the exhaust pipe, the car is burning oil. A car with a diesel engine will burn some oil, especially when the car is first started up. However, an oil-burning gasoline engine spells trouble and expensive repairs.

Listen to the engine. The disco car—the one with the shakes, shimmies, knocks, rattles, vibrations, and raps—does not produce music for the ears.

Place the car in gear but keep the hand brake on. Does the brake hold well? If not, the car might need brake work. Test drive the car. Does it handle smoothly? Is the acceleration smooth? Do the gears shift easily? If the ride doesn't feel okay, don't buy the car.

Finally, if the car checks out on all these details, take it to a trusted mechanic for a thorough inspection. If the mechanic says okay, go ahead and negotiate to buy the car. The money you saved buying this peach will pay for a lot of lemon meringues.

per hour and then step on the gas. Does the car start to accelerate smoothly? If not, it may be loosing compression. Get the car up to highway driving speeds. How does it handle? Is the acceleration good? Does the steering shimmy and shake at high speeds? Negative answers could mean high repair costs later on.

How did the test drive feel? If the car didn't feel good to drive, don't bother with it anymore. If the car still looks and feels acceptable, then the final step is to have a mechanic check it out.

Professional Inspection.   The last step is to have a good mechanic or diagnostic center check out the car. The mechanic or center may charge $20-$30 to thoroughly check the car. The expense is minor compared to the expenses involved in fixing up a lemon. The mechanic or center will check out the engine, transmission, power drive, brakes, exhaust, and the electrical system. The mechanic should be able to tell you about the

mechanical condition of the car. Some minor items, such as battery replacement, belt tightening, or a brake job, should not keep you from buying a car. If the mechanic points out major problems, listen to the advice, and look for another used car. If the mechanic gives the car a clean bill of health, then proceed to negotiate with the seller. Minor problems that need to be corrected should be discussed with the seller and factored into the price of the car.

Determining a Reasonable Price

Negotiating a purchase price for a used car is as much an art as negotiating for new cars. A number of publications provide a listing of prices for used cars and popular options. *Edmund's Used Car Prices* provides reasonably current prices for used cars. The *Official Used Car Guide* issued by NADA also provides used car prices.

The condition of the car is a major determinant of used-car prices. All new cars are basically in the same mechanical and physical condition. Different owners, however, place different demands on their cars. As a result, some used cars are in "cream puff" condition, meaning that their physical appearance and their mechanical condition are excellent. Other cars are average, showing some wear and tear and minor rust and are reasonably good mechanically. Still others are "clunkers"—beat up and junky looking.

Some used car guides provide average wholesale and retail prices. Others provide prices for a variety of categories. The buyer, with the help of a mechanic, can gauge the quality of a car. For example, if the car is "average," the buyer can expect to pay a dealer pretty close to the car's listed retail price.

Many times you can buy a used car directly from the owner. Buying directly from the owner requires more caution than buying from a dealer because a private owner will sell a car in "as is" condition, without any warranty. The procedure explained in the previous section should be followed. The owner will typically try to obtain a price that is between the retail and the wholesale values. However, often the actual selling price turns out to be closer to the wholesale value.

Buying From A Rental Company

Car rental companies, such as Hertz, Avis, and Budget, offer their rental cars for sale after they are one to two years old. Jack Heffinger, publisher of a used car price guidebook, says, "The rental companies are one heck of a source for the public to get darned good autos at darned good prices."[2]

---

2. "Warranted Deals on Used Wheels," *Money* (May 1980): 126.

Until the early 1970s, rental companies wholesaled their used cars to volume dealers. In recent years, however, rental companies have been selling their used cars directly to the public.

Cars sold by rental companies have typically been driven about 500 miles each week. The cars are serviced about every other month. The cars are thoroughly checked before they are sold, and "lemons" are wholesaled. All rental companies make available to the used car buyer the use and repair records on the cars.

Prices charged by rental companies are lower than prices charged by used car dealers. Rental companies can sell cars at lower than average prices because they have already realized certain tax benefits from owning the cars. Unlike used car dealers, rental companies do not negotiate on the prices they are asking for a used car. The buyer will have to pay the posted price. Also, rental companies do not accept trade-ins or finance cars.

Major rental companies will offer a one-year or 12,000-mile warranty on their used cars. Used car dealers rarely give a warranty for more than 90 days. Overall, a person considering buying a used car would do well to check out a used car offered for sale by a major rental company.

Spot Quiz • Buying a Used Car

1. A sharp-looking, clean used car is a good investment.

   T _____ F _____

2. Having a mechanic examine a car is a very important step in buying a used car.

   T _____ F _____

3. Used cars from rental companies are mechanically abused and should not be considered.

   T _____ F _____

(Answers on page 336)

KEEPING THE CAR RUNNING

Most people who know about cars will state that any car, with proper care and maintenance, will easily last up to 100,000 miles without major repairs or overhauls. The car owner does not necessarily need to know how to fix or repair a car. Rather, the important factor to know is when to have the car serviced. The maintenance schedule for a car will be specified in the owner's manual. The owner should strictly follow the maintenance

schedule, avoiding the tendency to postpone routine maintenance for a week or two or a few hundred miles. Some additional hints for keeping the car running are provided in this section.

Keep the Car Clean

A clean car not only looks good but also last longer. Only a soap specially suitable for washing cars should be used. Laundry or kitchen detergents are generally too harsh for the car's finish. A gentle stream of water should be used because a harder stream can cause the dirt to scratch the car surface. The underside should be cleaned thoroughly. Rust spots should be sanded, primed, and painted.

Monitor Tire Pressure

Check the tire pressure fairly often, every time the car is filled up. The owner's manual may indicate that, for example, tires should inflated to 28–31 pounds per square inch. Pressures toward the higher end are more desirable.

Check Belts, Hoses, and Battery

Tension on the belts should be checked about once a month. Loose belts can lead to a run-down battery or loss of power steering. Belts should be replaced if they are cracked or worn or if the undersides are too smooth.

Some mechanics suggest that hoses should be changed every three or four years. Hoses should be pliable and should be replaced if they are stiff or cracked. Keep spark plug wires and electrical connections clean.

Battery posts should be corrosion-free. If they are not, remove the cables and clean both the cables and the battery posts. Coat the posts and connections with nonmetallic grease.

Check Fluid Levels

For nonsealed batteries, fluid levels should be checked twice a month. If the fluid is low, distilled water should be added up to the suggested level. Radiator fluid should be checked when the engine is cold. Add antifreeze to fill the radiator to the specified level. Once a year, the radiator should be drained and flushed and new antifreeze installed.

Check the engine oil level twice a month. Make sure that the dipstick is properly seated before reading the oil level. Add oil if it is a quart or more low. Automatic transmission and power steering fluids should be checked once a month.

The above suggestions do not consume much time, but faithfully following them should lead to trouble-free use of a car for years. (See "Gas Savers—and Rip-Offs" on page 325.)

Spot Quiz • Keeping the Car Running

1. Sometimes maintenance should be performed more frequently than suggested by the manufacturer.   T _____   F _____

2. Low levels of various car fluids can lead to costly engine repairs.
                                                         T _____   F _____

(Answers on page 336)

Financing and leasing cars

Once a suitable car has been found and arrangements have been made for its purchase, the next step is to finance the purchase, the topic of this section. Because some people choose to lease rather than buy a car, leasing is also discussed in this section.

Financing a Car

Some people can afford to pay cash for a car, but most of us must seek financing. The idea is to finance a car at the best annual percentage rate, or APR, available. (APRs were discussed in Chapter 7.) Major sources of car loans are credit unions, banks, and dealer financing.

Credit Unions. Credit unions often provide the cheapest financing for buying cars. Thus, the first place to check for a car loan is a credit union. Because credit unions give credit only to members, you must join to obtain a loan. Often you can join a credit union where you work, which may permit payroll deduction of car payments.

Banks. Not every bank will be willing to give a car loan to a noncustomer--some banks restrict their lending to their checking account customers. Thus, you should check with your own bank first. However, keep in mind that some banks promote car loans with APRs that are lower than those offered by other banks in the community. (These banks may

Gas Savers—and Rip-Offs

Now that prices at the pump have topped $1, people are going to great lengths to go greater lengths on a gallon of gas. Some motorists are investing in gas-line heaters, superchargers, spark intensifiers, air injectors, and other contraptions that purport to stretch a gallon of gas as much as 50 percent. Once the focus of country fair sideshows, these devices might have been somewhat effectual in the muscle cars of yesteryear, but they are all but worthless in today's more fuel-efficient vehicles.

One of the most widely touted gadgets is a small canisterlike aerator sold under such names as Ball-Matic Air Injector, Turbo-Dyne Energy Chamber and G-R Gas Saver Valve. It is supposed to stretch your mileage by increasing the air in the fuel mixture. But according to Tom Coultas, an invention evaluator for the National Bureau of Standards, "Present-day carburetors atomize fuel very well. So none of these devices deliver on their promise to improve mileage."

Other devices have proved to be outright rip-offs. According to an Environmental Protection Agency official, one $20 fuel "maximizer" was nothing more than an extra battery cable. Gasoline additives are supposed to produce dozens of miles more. "Many are just mouse milk with a placebo effect," says Coultas.

Government agencies have begun to crack down. The makers of the G-R Valve recently signed a Federal Trade Commission consent order not to make any more mileage claims unless they can be backed up by reliable tests.

You don't have to spend money on gimmicks to save gasoline. A motorist can tot up significant fuel savings just by driving more carefully. It's possible, for example, to reduce the mileage you get on a car rated at 16 mpg by the EPA to 12 mpg through bad driving habits. It's also possible to get as much as 20 mpg in the same car by following all the suggestions below—advice culled from auto and oil companies, government agencies, and automotive engineering firms.

Reduce highway speeds. You could increase your mileage nearly 3 mpg by driving at 55 mph instead of 70.

Drive moderately. By accelerating slowly and maintaining steady speed, you could save 1 mpg in city driving.

Keep your car tuned. A fouled spark plug, for example, could cost you over 1 mpg. By maintaining a record of your gas mileage, you should be able to tell when your car needs a tune-up.

Turn off the air conditioner. This would give you nearly another 1 mpg, especially in city driving.

Roll up the windows. Once you've turned off your air conditioner, if the temperature permits, open the interior vents and keep the windows closed. The reduced wind drag would add just under .5 mpg. Indeed, some

controversial recent tests suggest that at highway speeds certain cars get slightly better mileage even with the air conditioner *on* if turning it off means opening the windows.

Ride on radials. Switching from bias-ply tires to steel-belted radials could give you more than .5 mpg. For several years, though, the savings would be offset by the cost of the new tires.

Increase the tire pressure. Pumping up your tires from, say, 26 pounds to the maximum 32 pounds per square inch would save an additional .5 mpg.

Try one of the new slipperier oils. It could add nearly .3 mpg. Sunoco's version, which goes on sale this fall, will cost 25 cents a quart more than the company's current high-grade oil.

Maintain wheel alignment. Bad alignment can reduce mileage by .2 mpg. You know your wheels need aligning when the car pulls to the right or left; alignment typically costs $16 to $22.

Don't carry excess weight. By lugging around tools and a second spare tire, you could cheat yourself of .2 mpg. A gallon of gas weighs about six pounds, so even driving on a full tank costs you—though not much. If you average half a tankful, you would save about $12 a year.

Source: *Money Magazine*, October 1979, p. 53. Reprinted with permission.

require the opening of a checking or savings account prior to giving the loan.) Also, some banks will give a small discount on the APR if they can automatically deduct monthly car payments from the borrower's checking account.

Dealer Financing. If the car is purchased from a dealer, chances are that the dealer will be able to arrange financing for the car. Some dealers have financing arrangements with banks. Others are tied in with the financing arms of major U.S. automobile manufacturers. In general, rates offered by car dealers are higher than rates you can find on your own. Even if the car is being bought from a dealer, it is a good strategy to check APRs with local banks and credit unions.

In recent years, car manufacturers and dealers have periodically tried to combine the car purchase decision with the financing decision as a method of selling. Dealers and manufacturers, for example, often offer low-cost financing on overstocked cars. If you are seriously interested in buying one of these cars, then the low-cost financing *might* provide some savings. Dealers and manufacturers will also occasionally offer a choice between low-cost financing and a cash rebate. In this situation, the alternatives need to be carefully considered before opting for the low-cost financing. That is, the combination of a cash rebate and financing through

a bank or credit union at regular rates might be cheaper than the low-cost financing.

Leasing a Car

Many people consider leasing as an alternative to buying a car. Leasing offers some advantages over buying. In leasing, for example, generally no down payment is required. Leasing may also result in lower monthly payments. The major disadvantage of leasing is that no equity is built up. After the lease period is over, the car belongs to the lessor, the leasing company. Leases can be either net (closed-end) or open-end.

Net, or Closed-End, Lease.   The lessee—the person who will be using the car—and the lessor agree on the type and make of car to be leased. Then the lease period (generally 36 or 48 months) and the lease payments are established. In a **net lease**, the lessee's financial responsibilities end with the last lease payment. If the car has less than the number of miles specified in the lease and if the car shows only normal wear and tear, the lessee has no remaining financial obligations.

Open-End Lease.   In an **open-end lease**, the make and type of car and length of lease are established. The lessor specifies a wholesale value for the car at the end of the lease period. Lease payments are based on the difference between the new car price and the end-of-lease wholesale value. When the lease is over, the lessee is responsible for any difference between the actual and the agreed-upon wholesale price. For example, an open-end lease is written with a wholesale value of $4,000. At the end of the lease, the car is wholesaled for $3,400. The lessee has to pay the lessor an additional $600. Of course, if the actual value had been $4,300, the lessor would have paid the lessee $300. (See "Tax Reforms and Leasing" on page 328.)

Evaluating a Lease.   A simplified lease-or-buy analysis is shown in Table 10.4. The lease is for 48 months. Total lease payments over 48 months are $199.50 × 48 = $9,576.00.

The same car can be purchased for $8,500. After a $2,500 down payment, $6,000 is financed at 16 percent APR. Monthly payments of $170 lead to total payments of $170 × 48 = $8,160. To this amount we add the down payment of $2,500, sales tax of $425, and license and fees for four years of $160. Total outflow with buying is $11,245. After 48 months the car has a wholesale value of $3,655. The net cost of buying is $7,590. Table 10.4 shows that buying is better than leasing. A simple analysis of this type can show whether leasing or buying is better in any situation.

Tax Reforms and Leasing

The Tax Reform Act of 1986 is gradually eliminating deductions for consumer interest payments. By 1991, the deductions will be totally eliminated, making car buying more expensive because interest paid on the car financing will not be deductible. Because of this loss of interest deductibility, car manufacturers and finance companies are touting the advantages of leasing as compared with buying. Such is not the general case, however. The Tax Reform Act also eliminated a tax benefit called the investment tax credit, which lessors had been able to use to reduce the cost of leasing. Additionally, lessors will have to depreciate the leased cars over a longer time period, resulting in a slower recovery of their car purchase prices and thus higher leasing costs. The net result is that tax reforms have made both car leasing and buying more expensive but have not changed their comparative merits.

Table 10.4　Lease or Buy Evaluation[a]

Cost of Leasing	
Monthly lease payment	$ 190.00
Sales tax (5%)	9.50
Monthly cost	$ 199.50
Total cost for 48 months	$ 9,576.00
Cost of Buying	
Purchase price	$ 8,500.00
Amount financed at 16% APR	6,000.00
Monthly payment	170.00
Total for 48 monthly payments (1)	8,160.00
Down payment (2)	2,500.00
Sales tax at 5% on $8,500 (3)	425.00
License for 4 years (4)	160.00
Cost of buying (1 + 2 + 3 + 4)	$11,245.00
Less wholesale value	3,655.00
Total cost of buying	$ 7,590.00

Advantage to buying $9,576 − $7,590 = $1,986

[a]Interest lost on the down payment as well as certain other tax benefits are omitted here.

Spot Quiz • Financing and Leasing Cars

1. The APR is an important factor in deciding where to obtain a car loan.
   T _____   F _____

2. For some people, the type of lease evaluated in Table 10.4 may be better than buying the car.   T _____   F _____

(Answers on page 336)

Buying appliances

Televisions, refrigerators, freezers, washers, dryers, and air conditioners are important in the lives of consumers. Appliances call for considerable investments, not only in the purchase price but also for maintenance and operations. Appliances are also called **durable goods** because they have long lives, from 8 to 20 years. The importance of appliances in our daily lives, their costs, and their durable nature call for carefully considered purchase decisions. Evaluating and buying appliances are covered in this section.

Evaluating Appliances

Four factors are important in evaluating appliances: service frequency, operating costs, price, and features. Each of these factors has different levels of importance for different types of appliances. For example, a television does not consume much power but is subject to breakdown. Therefore, servicing is important. A refrigerator, on the other hand, may not break down as often, but it does consume a fair amount of energy. Therefore, operating costs are more important for refrigerators.

Service Frequency.   Some appliances require more service than other appliances. For example, televisions in general require more service than refrigerators. Within any category of appliances, some makes and models are less durable than others. Some color television sets will give three or four years of trouble-free performance, whereas others will be in the repair shops every 12 months. *Consumer Reports* magazine, friends, and acquaintances can provide some idea of the durability of various makes of appliances.

Besides service frequency, ease of servicing is important. Some appliances may not break down very often, but when they do, servicing them may be a real problem. The buyer should check on the availability of key repair parts prior to purchase of the appliance. In addition, the buyer should check to see how many dealer and/or independent service organizations are available to work on the appliance.

Many appliance dealers offer to sell a service contract on appliances. The service contract allows the appliance buyer to have the appliance repaired at any time during the contract period free of charge. All indications are that consumers really do not benefit from buying service contracts. Thus, in general, it is advisable not to buy service contracts on appliances. (See "Guidelines for Maintaining Major Appliances" below.)

Operating Costs.   The cost of operating appliances can vary sharply from one make to the next. A 16-cubic-foot brand X refrigerator may use $60 worth of electricity each year, whereas the same size brand Y refrigerator may use $130 of electricity each year. Using $70 more in electricity per year, brand Y is going to cost $700 more to operate over ten years than brand X. Even if it costs more than brand Y, brand X may be the better buy.

Guidelines for Maintaining Major Appliances

Refrigerator.   Vacuum clean the condenser unit about every two months. About every six months, close the refrigerator door on a dollar bill that is partially outside the refrigerator. If the bill pulls out easily, check the refrigerator to make sure that it is level. If it is, replace the door seal. Do not line the shelves with paper or foil. Defrost a manual defrost refrigerator whenever the frost builds up to one-quarter inch.

Oven.   All ovens should be cleaned regularly. Do not use chemical cleaners in a continuous-cleaning oven. Rather, use warm water and a nylon brush to gently clean heavy splatters. Do not block the oven airflow by using foil liners.

Room Air Conditioner.   Clean the air filter once a month. Make sure that curtains and furniture do not block airflow from the air conditioner. Any branches, leaves, plants, and so on that may block free airflow to the air conditioner should be removed.

Central Air Conditioner.   Change air filters every other month during use. Have the compressor unit checked by an expert at the beginning of each season. Make sure that all motors are properly lubricated. Remove debris, leaves, shrubs, and so forth from and around the compressor unit.

Using the maintenance techniques mentioned here will increase operating efficiency and reduce costs.

Some consumer-oriented magazines provide figures on operating costs of appliances. *Consumers' Research Magazine* publishes information on refrigerators and dishwashers. *Consumer Reports* also provides a variety of ratings on appliances, including ratings on operating costs. This information is useful in estimating the cost of operating various makes of appliances. Currently, air conditioners are required by law to carry a rating called **energy efficiency ratio (EER)**. Higher EER ratings mean lower energy costs.

Many manufacturers that produce high-energy-consuming appliances, such as refrigerators, freezers, and air conditioners, are now selling energy-efficient models. Whether to buy one depends on the cost savings generated. Let's assume that an energy-efficient air conditioner sells for $200 more than a comparable but less efficient one. The energy-efficient air conditioner is the better buy if it can provide total cost savings of $200 or more in five years or less. (We limit the savings analysis to five years because beyond this time the value of a dollar becomes significantly less.)

Price. A high-quality appliance can be expected to be relatively more expensive. But a high price does not guarantee high quality. Some poorly made appliances are sold at relatively high manufacturer's suggested list prices. Therefore, the price of an appliance should be carefully judged relative to its quality ratings, operating costs, and features. An appliance should not be bought strictly on the basis of price.

Features. Appliances vary sharply in price. A manufacturer may sell six different models of the same size television. The models may be mechanically similar, with cosmetic differences only. For instance, the basic 19-inch model may sell for $350, whereas the deluxe model with fake walnut trim may sell for $380. Remember that cosmetic features add nothing to the operation of appliances and that chrome on plastic rubs off, fake trims peel off eventually, and fancy knobs break. In general, appliances with fewer cosmetic features are more desirable.

Technical features should be carefully evaluated. Some people prefer to pay a few extra dollars for a television with automatic fine tuning. However, they may decide to do without remote control. Some features are very important. A lock on a freezer may prevent accidental thawing of food. *Consumer Reports* and *Consumers' Research Magazine* evaluate features on appliances. They also point out advantages and disadvantages of various features. The relevant articles in these magazines should be evaluated in light of your own needs.

Shopping for Appliances

The first rule to remember in appliance buying is to never pay the list price. Just about every make of appliance is placed on sale sometime during the

year. Appliances generally go on sale at the end of their peak buying period. For instance, you can obtain tremendous buys on air conditioners in August and September. Most appliances are sale priced in January and February.

Some stores are constantly advertising "Closeouts," "Christmas in July" sales, "Inventory Reduction" sales, "Clearance" sales, and so on. These advertisements should be lightly regarded—a few rarely sought items are deeply discounted and are expected to attract crowds to the stores. Retailers from time to time hold "Scratch and Dent" sales at which they sell floor models. Sometimes excellent bargains can be obtained on appliances that are functionally okay but have a scratch or a dent.

Comparative shopping at different retail stores helps. The large retail chains post a price that the customer is expected to pay. But stores of a well-known discount chain have been known to reduce the posted prices if a customer can bring in an advertisement showing a lower price for the same appliance. Most independent retail stores are willing to negotiate on the asking price. It does not hurt to make a bid on an appliance. If the offer is reasonable, the store might accept the offer. Before you accept a price, make sure what is included in the price. In general, comparative shopping for prices should be for the appliance and for its delivery and installation.

Spot Quiz • Buying Appliances

1. Quality and price are directly related.   T _____   F _____

2. Appliance prices are fixed and nonnegotiable.   T _____   F _____

(Answers on page 336)

Summary

Transportation expenses are important in consumers' budgets. Therefore, they require careful consideration. An evaluation of transportation needs should include analysis of roominess, operating costs, comfort, and reliability. Transportation costs should be estimated prior to purchasing a car and should not exceed 15 percent of a family's take-home income.

When you select a new car, you should evaluate its reliability, warranty, equipment, and resale value. The car should be test driven. A

reasonable offer for most new cars is its wholesale cost plus $400–$500 in dealer profits plus its transportation cost.

Buying a used car requires more caution than buying a new car. The car should be carefully examined and test driven. A mechanic should thoroughly check it out prior to purchase. A good offer is a price slightly higher than its wholesale price. Major rental companies are considered to be good sources of used cars.

Car financing can be arranged at credit unions or banks or through the dealer. Credit unions usually have lowest APRs. Leasing a car is suggested when a person does not have the down payment. Otherwise, leasing is generally more expensive than buying a car.

Before buying a new appliance, its service frequency, operating costs, price, and features should be evaluated. Most appliance dealers are willing to negotiate on prices.

Questions

1. What factors need to be considered when you evaluate transportation needs? Explain briefly.

2. Briefly outline the procedure that you would follow to determine transportation costs.

3. What are the differences, if any, between fixed and variable transportation costs?

4. Briefly explain the procedure for calculating transportation expenses.

5. What factors need to be considered when a person buys a new car? Is one factor more important than the others? Explain.

6. Discuss this statement: "An expensive car with a high resale value is a better buy than a cheap car with a low resale value."

7. Explain the sources for finding out new car prices.

8. Explain the differences, if any, between the processes of buying new and used cars.

9. How would you go about selecting a used car for purchase?

10. Why is a professional inspection important when a person buys a used car?

11. Would you buy a used car from a rental company? Why or why not?

12. Explain the various sources for financing cars. Which is the best place to finance a new car in your town? What APR does this institution offer for an 80 percent, 36-month loan?

13. What is the difference between a closed-end and an open-end lease?

14. What factors should be considered in evaluating appliances? Explain briefly.

15. Would you negotiate with a dealer on the price of a new appliance? Explain your answer.

Case Problems

1. A new car can be purchased for $9,000. Annual depreciation rates for the first three years are 25, 15, and 10 percent of the purchase price. Insurance is $400 for the first year, $440 for the second, and $500 for the third year. The down payment for the purchase would be $3,000, and the car would be financed over four years. Annual interest is $579. Parking, license, and so on are as shown in Table 10.1. Gasoline costs are $800 in year 1. They will increase by 10 percent a year in years 2 and 3. Maintenance and repair costs are as shown in Table 10.1. Calculate the total transportation costs for years 1, 2, and 3.

2. For Case Problem 1, calculate the cash outflows for years 1, 2, and 3.

3. Carol Allen is thinking about buying a new car. The car lists for $9,000. The wholesale price of the car is 18 percent less than its list price. Destination charges are $385. Dealer preparation charges are $60. Estimate a reasonable purchase price for the car. Carol does not plan to trade in her old car on the new one.

4. For Case Problem 3, Carol is thinking of trading in her old car. The car is in good shape, and its wholesale value is $2,700. Estimate the purchase price of the new car with the trade-in.

5. Mac Donald is interested in buying a compact imported car with a manufacturer's list price of $9,600. He notices, however, that the dealer has its own price sticker on the car listing the following dealer-installed accessories: paint sealer, $250; undercoating, $250; rust proofing, $300; fabric protection, $150; additional dealer margin, $700—list price, $11,250. The salesperson tells Mr. Donald that the sales manager would allow a trade-in of $3,000 on his car, which has a wholesale value of about $2,200. What advice do you have for Mr. Donald?

6. Al Starr can lease a new car for $210 per month. Sales tax on the lease is 5 percent. The closed-end lease is for 36 months. Mr. Starr can buy the same car for $9,000. He can finance $7,000 of the purchase at 16 percent for 36 months. Monthly payments would be $246. Sales tax on the car would be 5 percent of $9,000. License costs are included in the lease, but Mr. Starr would pay $40 per year for licensing if the car is purchased. The wholesale value of the car after 36 months would be $4,800. Is it more advantageous to lease or to buy? Show your calculations.

Bibliography

"Your Car Can Last 1,000,000 Miles and More." *Changing Times* (April 1980): 49–52.

"Look Before You Lease a Car." *Changing Times* (July 1980): 28–30.

"The Real Cost of Driving Your Car." *Changing Times* (September 1980); 21–24.

"A Twist of Lemon." *Consumer Reports* (April 1985): 192–194.

"Used Cars: Good Bets and Bad." *Consumer Reports* (April 1985): 248–249.

"How to Get the Best Deal." *Consumer Reports* (April 1986): 211–214.

"Options: Which to Take, Which to Leave." *Consumer Reports* (April 1986): 224–225.

"Auto Service Contracts." *Consumer Reports* (October 1986): 663–667.

"Warranted Deals on Used Cars." *Money* (May 1980): 126, 128, 130.

Answers to Spot Quizzes

Transportation Needs and Costs (page 313)

1. F (Costs also include insurance, license fees, and so forth.)

2. T (The difference is due to depreciation, which is a noncash cost, and principal loan payments.)

Buying a New Car (page 317)

1. F (Reliability, warranty, and so on should also be taken into consideration.)

2. F (Higher resale values lower depreciation costs and thus result in lower operating costs.)

3. T (The purchase price also depends on the new car price asked by the dealer.)

Buying a Used Car (page 322)

1. F (Physical condition does not tell much about the mechanical condition.)

2. T (The mechanic can pick out problem areas.)

3. F (These cars are generally well maintained and in good condition.)

Keeping the Car Running (page 324)

1. T (It depends on the usage.)

2. T (Maintaining proper fluid levels is very important.)

Financing and Leasing Cars (page 329)

1. T (The APR influences how much is paid in interest.)

2. T (For example, leasing may be better for the person who does not have funds for the down payment.)

Buying Appliances (page 332)

1. F (Prices may not reflect quality.)

2. F (Prices are generally negotiable.)

Part 4

Insurance

The basics of insurance are covered in Part 4. Chapter 11, "Risk Management and Insurance," identifies the different types of risks and ways of dealing with these risks. The risk management process is explained. The chapter also contains a general discussion of how insurance works and what is insurable. The procedure for buying insurance is described.

Chapter 12, "Property and Liability Insurance," describes different types of homeowners' insurance policies as well as strategies for managing homeowners' insurance. The discussion of liability risks includes coverage of comprehensive liability insurance. A separate section is devoted to automobile insurance.

Chapter 13, "Health Insurance," looks at different types of health insurance programs and discusses management of health insurance costs. Disability insurance is dealt with in a separate section.

The last chapter in Part 4 is entitled "Life Insurance." Term, whole life, and endowment insurance are explained in this section. Major provisions of life insurance policies are discussed in detail. The last section explains how to make cost comparisons when you shop for life insurance.

Chapter 11

Risk Management and Insurance

Objectives

After reading this chapter, you will be able to:

- Define different types of risk.
- Explain alternative methods of dealing with risk.
- Describe the risk management process.
- Define insurance.
- Explain how insurance works.
- State the types of risks that are insurable.
- Discuss the basic factors to consider when buying insurance.
- Select the insurance coverage needed.
- Explain the major features of an insurance policy.

Kathy Samed bought a new car and went to a local bank to arrange financing for the car. As she was filling out the loan papers, the lending officer casually stated, "Oh, by the way, we make available credit life insurance for only $5.47 per month. The insurance will pay off your auto loan in case of your death prior to full repayment of the loan." Ms. Samed did some quick thinking: $5.47 was about $66 per year. "That's not a bad deal," she thought. "In case I die, the insurance policy would pay off on the remaining balance on an $8,000 loan." Kathy purchased the credit life policy.

Ms. Samed is 28 years old and single with no dependents. She lives in her own condo in Houston and works as a graphic artist for an advertising agency. Did she make the right decision in buying the insurance offered by the bank? The answer is no. Because she has no dependents, her death would not create an economic hardship for anyone. Thus, whether the car is paid off or not if she dies is not important. Even if she had a dependent, credit insurance still might not have been justified if: (1) her dependent did not inherit the car; (2) her dependent inherited the car but did not have any use for the car (in this case, the car would be sold); (3) her dependent was financially capable of making the car payments.

A second point against credit insurance is that even if Kathy needed insurance, something called term life insurance would have provided her with the same protection at a lower cost.

The situation just described is an example of managing personal risks. Different situations create different types of risks, and there are different ways of handling risk. Insurance is one way. But before you buy insurance, you first need to evaluate the risks and then plan a comprehensive risk management and insurance program.

Risk

What is risk? Are there different types of risk? The answers to these questions are provided in this section.

What Is Risk?

Risk can be thought of as the possibility of incurring a loss. Often losses can be measured in economic, or dollar, terms. For example, your home could burn down. A dollar loss would be involved if the house burned down. Thus, owning a home carries with it the possibility of a loss, or risk.

Generally speaking, we do not expect to find our homes burned to the ground when we return to them in the evening. We do not expect to be run over by a truck while we walk to school. Our normal expectations are that our homes will still be in sound condition in the evening and that we will be able to walk to school safely. Although houses are not constantly burning down and we are not often run over by trucks, there is always the possibility that these events could happen. Furthermore, a home burning down and a person getting run over by a truck are both unfavorable events. Thus, risk is also the possibility that an unfavorable event will occur unexpectedly.

Types of Risk

Risk is either speculative or pure. **Speculative risk** involves the possibility of incurring gains as well as losses. An example of a speculative risk is buying a lottery ticket on a new car for $1. A win would produce a gain. People who do not win lose their dollars. Drilling for oil is also an example of incurring speculative risk. Both gains and losses are possible outcomes in oil drilling.

Pure risk involves only the possibility of a loss. Gains are not a possibility with pure risk. Thus, if a home burns down, only a loss is involved. Similarly, becoming disabled involves loss only. Pure risk can be related to property, liability, and a person's well-being.

Property Risk.   **Property risk** is the possibility of the loss of your property. If your home burns down, property is lost. Thus, home ownership involves property risk. Property risk involves both direct and indirect losses. The home burning down is the direct loss. The indirect loss is the cost of temporary shelter, getting estimates on rebuilding the home, and perhaps supervising reconstruction of your home.

Liability Risk.   **Liability risk** is the possibility of economic loss as a result of causing and paying for damages to someone else. Owning a car creates liability risk. The car owner, for example, could damage someone else's car in an accident and would be liable for paying for repairs to the other car.

Personal Risk.   **Personal risks** are associated with personal losses. For example, the possibility of income losses because of disability or premature death creates personal risk. Sickness involves personal risk also because a possibility of loss of income is associated with sickness.

Spot Quiz • Risk

1. Investing in the stock market involves pure risk.

    T _____   F _____

2. An event that is going to occur does not involve risk.

    T _____   F _____

(Answers on page 360)

DEALING WITH RISK

There are four ways of dealing with risk: avoiding it, controlling it, retaining it, and transferring it. These four methods are explained in this section.

Avoiding Risk

Avoiding risk means reducing the possibility of loss from risk to zero. In practical terms, risk avoidance means not engaging in activities that create risk. Thus, the risks of home ownership can be avoided by not owning a home. For example, some people avoid home ownership risks by renting shelter. The risk of death due to mountain climbing can be avoided by not engaging in the activity.

Although some risks, such as those associated with property ownership, can be avoided, other types of risk cannot be avoided. For example, the risk of premature death cannot be avoided. Also, it is not always desirable to avoid risk. Many people believe that the convenience of car ownership far outweighs the risks associated with car ownership.

Controlling Risk

Controlling risk means reducing the possibility of suffering a loss. For example, home ownership risks can be controlled and minimized by following certain safety practices. Fire alarms and smoke detectors may not reduce the chances of fire, but they certainly can help minimize human and property losses due to fire. Keeping a fire extinguisher on hand can reduce losses even further. Nailing down and securing loose carpeting on stairs will reduce the risk of home accidents.

Controlling risk does not mean eliminating risk—a car owner will always incur some risk in owning and driving a car. Controlling risk implies that the car owner can take steps to reduce the potential for loss. Locking a car when it is parked reduces the risk of theft, for example. Snow tires increase the safety of driving in snow.

Because controlling risk carries certain costs, people have different levels of preference for controlling risk. Also, as the costs of controlling risk change, people's preferences for controlling risk change. For example, as the prices of smoke detectors have declined, more homeowners have started installing the devices.

Retaining Risk

The third way of dealing with risk is to retain it. Risk is **retained** when it is neither avoided nor transferred. In other words, the person bears all responsibility in the event that a loss occurs. A homeowner may retain the risk of ownership by not buying homeowners' insurance. If the house burns down, the homeowner suffers the loss. A car owner may prefer not to buy collision coverage on an old car. If the car suffers collision damage, the owner would be financially responsible for any repair costs.

It may sometimes be worthwhile to retain risks. In the car owner's case, the value of the car may be so little that collision insurance costs are more than the car's cost. In this situation, collision insurance is not justified. In other situations, risk retention may not be desirable. The homeowner who elects not to insure his or her home is retaining a very large risk that could cost thousands of dollars just to save a few hundred dollars on insurance premiums. Here, risk retention is not justified.

Risk should be retained when the cost of insurance to cover the risk is not justified by the possible amount of loss. Risk should also be retained if the possible amount of loss is relatively small. In addition, it is advisable to retain risk where the chances of the loss occurring are very small.

Often people retain risk because they are not aware that risk is involved. For example, some occupations may pose extra health hazards for workers, but the risks are not known now. Not much can be done about this type of risk retention. Once in a while, though, people retain excess risk because of their attitudes. A car owner may retain the risks of car ownership by saying, ''I am a safe driver; I won't cause an accident.'' Regrettably, the person may cause an accident and become liable for losses caused to others. If a person is not financially capable of absorbing a loss associated with retained risk, then risk should not be retained. Further financial considerations are discussed in the next three chapters.

Transferring Risk

The fourth method of dealing with risk is to transfer it. Risk can be transferred to another party in a variety of ways. The most popular method

of **transferring risk** is through insurance. For example, the risk of losses due to ownership of a home can be transferred to an insurance company by buying homeowners' insurance. Many types of exposure to risks that consumers face every day can be transferred to insurance companies. These risks include property, liability, and personal risks. Risk can also be transferred by storing property. Thus, risk of loss due to theft of valuables can be transferred to another party by storing receipted valuables with them.

Transfer of risk carries certain costs. Insurance agencies, for example, charge an appropriate premium to insure risks. The insurance premium includes sufficient compensation for the insurance company to assume risks on behalf of the insured person (the person who is to receive the benefits provided by the insurance policy).

Which Method Works Best?

No one method of dealing with risk can be considered better than any other method. In some cases, risk avoidance works best. Controlling risk is useful where the results of commonsense precautions are readily understood. For example, personal risks can be controlled by not driving through red lights. Risk retention may work very well where only small financial losses are involved. Risk transfer may work best where fairly large losses would be involved.

In general, though, most people use a combination of all four methods to deal with risk. For example, the property risks of car ownership can be dealt with by careful driving and buying collision insurance with a dollar deductible clause in the contract. Say that the deductible, which is the amount of loss the insured person agrees to retain, is $250. This means that in case of a collision, the insured pays $250, and the insurance company pays for any damage in excess of $250. Here, careful driving is controlling risk. The $250 deductible is a retained risk—in case of a collision, the insured suffers a maximum loss of $250. The collision insurance represents risk transfer. Identifying a desirable combination of avoidance, control, retention, and transfer of risk is **risk management**, discussed in the next section.

Spot Quiz • Dealing With Risk

1. All risks can be avoided.   T _____ F _____

2. Risk retention is not desirable because it leads to losses.
                                                                  T _____ F _____

3. Risk should be transferred if the financial losses involved are very large.

T _____ F _____

(Answers on page 360)

THE RISK MANAGEMENT PROCESS

The general process of management includes planning a program of action, implementing the program, and controlling the program. The risk management process is no different. An individual needs to understand all the risks confronting him or her or the family. Understanding these risks is an important prelude to managing them. The planning part of the risk management process includes three steps: identifying risks, evaluating them, and choosing an appropriate strategy for dealing with them.

Identifying Risks

The first step in the risk management process is **identifying risk**. As explained previously, people face property, liability, and personal risks. Property risks are usually easy to identify. Homes, cars, recreational vehicles, jewelry, certain investments, clothes, and other personal property can be destroyed, damaged, or stolen. Figure 11.1 lists some common types of property that are subject to risk of loss.

Liability risks are generally associated with owning property. For example, the homeowner is liable if someone trips, falls, and suffers injuries on the home's uneven driveway. Car ownership also involves liabilities. Some liability risks are not associated with property ownership. A surgeon, for example, is liable if he or she is proven to be negligent in performing an operation.

Personal risks for employed persons include premature death, disability, and illness. But a person does not have to earn wages to be considered employed. Homemakers do not earn wages for their services, yet hiring someone to perform the services of a homemaker would cost thousands of dollars every year. Unemployed persons, such as minor children, do not earn wages. However, they are subject to disability and illness risks.

Risks vary from person to person and family to family. Each individual or family needs to carefully identify the types of risks to which they are exposed.

Figure 11.1 Risk Situations, Risks, and Losses

Risk Situation	Risks	Nature of Financial Losses	Severity of Loss
Property			
Home	Damage, destruction	Assets, extra expenses	High
Car	Damage, theft	Assets, extra expenses	Medium
Art, stamps	Damage, theft	Assets	Varies
Other	Damage, theft	Assets, extra expenses	Varies
Liability			
Home	Liability	Extra expenses	High
Car	Liability	Extra expenses	High
Other	Liability	Extra expenses	Varies
Personal			
Employed person	Death, disability, illness	Income, extra expenses, services	High
Unemployed person	Disability, illness	Extra expenses	Varies

Risk Evaluation

After identifying the risks, the next step in the risk management process
is to **evaluate the risks**. The evaluation process includes judging the nature
of financial losses and the severity of losses associated with the risks. As
listed in Figure 11.1, for example, the risk of home ownership can involve
damage to or destruction of the home. Assets are lost in home destruction. In the case of a major fire that burns down the home, not only is
the home lost but also furniture, appliances, clothes, and other assets are
destroyed. In addition, extra expenses are incurred for temporary living
quarters.

The **severity of loss** varies from one risk situation to another and can
range from high to low. In some cases, the losses will be small, and the
severity will be low. In other cases, losses will be large and very severe.
For example, replacing the average home in the United States can cost between $80,000 and $100,000. For most people, a loss of this magnitude
would be very severe. Also, the risk of becoming permanently disabled
can involve large losses. A person who is disabled and whose income would

have averaged $25,000 per year for the next 40 years is faced with a financial loss of $1 million.

Figure 11.1 also shows the severity of typical financial losses. These estimates will vary, of course. A person who owns an eight-year-old full-size car is probably exposed to a small financial loss. Thus, the severity of this loss would be very low rather than medium. Individuals and families should assess risks and associated losses and severities for their own personal situations.

Choosing an Appropriate Strategy

The third step in risk management is to choose an **appropriate strategy** to deal with risk. The four methods of dealing with risk, explained previously, are avoidance, control, retention, and transfer. It is always desirable to avoid and control risks to the extent possible. In general, then, the choice becomes one of retaining or transferring risk or combining the two methods. All strategies involve direct or indirect costs. In retention, the indirect cost is the potential of loss. In transfer, the direct cost is the insurance premium.

In some cases, the answer is simple. For example, insuring an old car against damage may cost $300 per year, whereas the car is worth only $400. In this case, risk retention is more desirable than risk transfer. In most cases, though, the choice of an appropriate strategy is influenced by both subjective and objective factors. In general, the combination of retention and transfer works better than either retention or transfer alone. Full insurance against damage to a new car may cost $500 per year. But by agreeing to pay the first $200 in damages and insuring the rest, the owner may lower the cost to $270 per year. A careful driver will benefit by retaining a small portion of the possible loss. The amount of loss retained is called the **deductible** in an insurance policy.

Implementing the Program

Implementing the program simply means that the strategies selected to manage different risks are executed. Implementation involves reviewing existing insurance policies and updating coverages as needed. Also, new policies may have to be purchased to fully implement the program. If, as suggested previously, some portions of the risk are retained, then the amount of cash necessary to cover that potential loss has to be set aside or accumulated to fully implement the program. If, for example, health insurance to cover illness has a retention feature that requires the insured person to pay approximately $800 for hospitalization, then this amount of money has to be set aside to implement the program. If the program calls for avoiding certain risks, then those risks must be avoided.

Controlling the Program

The final step in the risk management process is **controlling the program**. This step involves periodic review of the risk situations. Often risk situations change, and therefore changes need to be made. For example, old property might be sold or new property acquired. Even if property is retained, the age of the property may require changes in a risk management program. Thus, for example, each car owner faces a decision about dropping damage or collision coverage on a car and retaining the risk of damage as the car becomes older. Similarly, changes in income or health may require a review of the risk management program.

Another suggested time for reviewing the program is when insurance premiums are due. Even if no changes have taken place, it is still worthwhile to review the insurance coverage and its related costs to see if any changes appear desirable.

Spot Quiz • The Risk Management Process

1. Risk is evaluated when the nature of financial losses is established.
   T _____   F _____

2. Risk retention is implemented when sufficient funds are accumulated to pay the retained losses.   T _____   F _____

(Answers on page 360)

Risk Transfer by Insurance

The most common method of risk transfer is buying insurance. This section explains insurance, how it works, and what is insurable.

What Insurance Is

Insurance is a legal contract that transfers the risk of incurring the insured loss to the insurance company. Homeowners, for example, can transfer the risk of loss from fire to an insurance company by buying a homeowners' insurance policy. The payment for the insurance is called a **premium**.

Insurance removes the uncertainty surrounding a possible loss. An uninsured homeowner faces an uncertain situation. The house may burn

down and create a large loss or the house may not burn and may not create any loss at all. Buying insurance removes this uncertainty. Whether the house burns down or not, the homeowner knows what it will cost him or her. Keep in mind that buying insurance does not change the possibility of the risk occurring. Rather, it changes the uncertainty of incurring some financial loss. With insurance, the uncertainty of a loss is replaced by the certainty of a fixed insurance premium.

How Insurance Works

A homeowner may be able to insure a home for $100,000 with a $400 annual premium. How is it possible to cover such a large potential loss with such a small premium? Probability, the law of large numbers, and risk proneness are involved in explaining how insurance works.

Probability. Throughout this chapter, we have been talking about chance and uncertainty. Frequently we say, ''It will probably rain today,'' whereas the weather reporter says, ''There is a 60 percent change of rain today.'' **Probability** is simply the numerical measurement of the chance that an uncertain event will occur. Insurance premiums are generally much lower than the maximum possible losses because the probability that the loss will occur tends to be small. In the home insurance example, the uncertain event is that the home will burn down. There may be only 1 chance in 300 that this event will occur during any year.

Law of Large Numbers. On one flip of a perfectly balanced coin, we would either observe a head or not. On a large number of flips, though, we will observe that close to half of the flips show heads. That is, on many, many flips, the actual number of heads observed would be reasonably close to what is expected. This is called the **law of large numbers**. In other words, when the same event is repeated many times, actual outcomes are numerically close to expected outcomes.

For one homeowner, his or her home may or may not burn down. Let's assume that, during one year, the chances of a home burning down in a certain city are 1 in 300. Then, if there are 3,000 homes in the city, we would normally expect that $3,000 \times 1/300 = 10$ homes would burn down during the year. An example later in this section will show how this law works in insurance.

Risk Proneness. **Risk proneness** means that some people or properties are more likely to incur losses due to risk than others. Thus, male drivers under the age of 25 years are considered to be more accident-prone than the average driver. A person who smokes may be more prone to premature death than a nonsmoker. Insurance companies use screening

devices to identify risk-prone situations. For example, medical examinations are used to identify risk-prone persons. Usually risky situations are either screened out or placed in separate risk categories.

An Example.   In the city of Brightlite, there are 3,000 homes. For the sake of simplicity, let's assume that all homes are worth $100,000 each. The chances of a home burning down in any year in Brightlite are 1 in 300. Thus, on the average, in any year 10 of these 3,000 homes burn down. For any homeowner in any given year without any insurance, the loss would be either $0 or $100,000. Without insurance, the same situation would prevail each year. Presumably, each homeowner would have established a $100,000 cash reserve to replace his or her home in case it burned down.

Now let's assume that everyone buys homeowners' insurance from the same insurance company. The annual premium is $400. The insurance company receives $400 × 3,000 = $1,200,000 in premium income. During the year, 10 homes burn down. The insurance company pays out $100,000 × 10 = $1,000,000 in insurance coverage benefits. The insurance company is left with $1,200,000 − $1,000,000 = $200,000 to cover sales expenses, administrative costs, and profit.

As this simple example illustrates, the homeowner has a choice of risk retention or risk transfer. Risk retention involves a loss of either $0 or $100,000 in any given year. Risk transfer costs $400 every year and does not involve any uncertainty at all. In this situation, most consumers would prefer to transfer rather than retain risk.

What Is Insurable?

Insurance is a nice way of transferring risk, but not all risks are insurable. An **insurable risk** has to satisfy four criteria, described in this section.

Fortuitous Loss.   **Fortuitous losses** are those associated with chance events. Only fortuitous losses can be covered by insurance. A house catching fire is a chance event and is covered by insurance. However, if a homeowner deliberately sets fire to his or her home, then the burning is not a chance event and is not covered by insurance.

Financial Loss.   A **financial loss** must be involved before an event can be covered by insurance. A definite financial loss is involved with a home burning down, and thus a home is insurable. On the other hand, a person who oversleeps and misses a football game on television does not incur financial losses and therefore cannot obtain insurance against oversleeping.

Personal Loss.   An insurable risk must be **personal in nature**. That is, an insurable risk cannot affect all insured persons at the same time. The

actual incidence of the loss has to vary from insured person to insured person. Thus, home ownership creates a risk that is personal in nature. Generally speaking, not all insured homes in a city are going to burn down simultaneously. Similarly, not all car owners are going to have accidents at once. Generally, the occurrence of a car accident is independent of the occurrence of any other car accident. On the other hand, all homes located in an earthquake-prone region are subject to the possibility of loss simultaneously. Thus, under normal circumstances, insurance will not cover earthquake damage, because the risk of loss is not personal in nature.

Insurable Interest.   An insurable risk involves a fortuitous, financial loss that is personal in nature. However, not everyone can take out insurance on any insurable risk. The person buying the insurance has to have an **insurable interest** in the object being insured. If the person seeking to buy insurance would not suffer any personal or economic loss if the insured object suffered a loss, then the person would not be able to buy insurance. For example, you cannot go to an airport and buy insurance on passengers at random with the expectation that if their flights crash, you can collect insurance money. Because you would not have an insurable interest in a stranger, the insurance company would not pay if a crash occurred.

What to Insure

Two factors affect the decision about what should be insured: **probability of occurrence** and **severity of loss**, as explained earlier. In general, when the severity of loss is high, the risk should be transferred, or insured. Thus, for example, homeowners should carry insurance on their homes. Even though the probability of occurrence is very low, the severity of the loss is high and thus justifies carrying insurance.

When the probability of occurrence is low and the severity of loss is low, risks should be retained. For example, an old, cheap car should not be insured for collision damage. When the probability of occurrence is high and the severity of loss is low, then it is probably best to avoid the risk. Insuring such risks may require very high insurance premiums. For example, remote-controlled model airplanes may cost $100 each. A model airplane enthusiast may not be able to fly one very well, leading to frequent crashes and destruction. Insurance to cover this person's hobby may be too expensive. Retention may be expensive also. In this case, the person might consider avoiding the risk by developing a new hobby.

Figure 11.2 shows risk situations and types of insurance policies that are available to cover these risks. For the typical consumer, a homeowners' policy will cover most properties except for a car. Works of art, stamp collections, antiques, collectible items, jewels, fur coats, and other nontypical and expensive items require a special type of insurance policy. Other types

of risks and related insurance policies are also listed in Figure 11.2. These types of insurance will be discussed in greater detail in later chapters.

Figure 11.2   Risk Situations and Insurance Policies

Risk Situation	Type of Insurance Policy
Property	
Home	Homeowners' or renters'
Car	Collision, comprehensive
Art, stamps	Scheduled
Other	Homeowners', scheduled, floater
Liability	
Home	Homeowners' or renters'
Car	Liability
Other	Comprehensive
Personal	
Person or family	Life, disability, health, accident

Spot Quiz • Risk Transfer by Insurance

1. All insured people pay the same insurance premium for the same risk.

    T _____   F _____

2. A loss that is definitely going to occur cannot be insured against.

    T _____   F _____

3. A health-related physical disability is insurable because disabilities occur independently from one person to the next.

    T _____   F _____

4. Risks that have a low probability of occurrence should be insured.

    T _____   F _____

(Answers on page 360)

Buying insurance

This section covers the basics of buying insurance: selecting an insurance agent, an insurance company, and the right coverage, reading and understanding an insurance policy, and the procedure for filing claims.

Basics of Buying Insurance

The premiums for health, life, disability, homeowners', and auto liability and collision insurance can cost more than $300 every month. For many consumers, this expense is more than the money spent on food. Thus, you should keep two principles in mind when you buy insurance: insuring large losses and retaining small losses.

Insuring Large Losses.   Most consumers cannot afford to suffer a large loss. Money saved for travel, retirement, or estate building can easily be consumed in rebuilding a destroyed home or paying off a liability claim from a car accident. Therefore, all possible large losses should be adequately covered by insurance. For most people, premature death, a long disability, destruction of a home, and a severe car accident could create large losses and financial hardships. Thus, life, disability, homeowners', and car liability insurances can provide needed protection.

Retaining Small Losses.   Consumers need to control insurance costs, however. The way insurance works has been explained previously. A higher probability of losses would result in higher insurance premiums because the insurance company would be paying on more insurance claims. Premiums are also affected by the amount of paperwork that the insurance company handles in settling claims. Paperwork costs associated with receiving a claim, verifying it, and paying on it remain fairly constant, irrespective of the size of the claim. The insurance company will charge a premium that will allow it to ultimately recover money paid on claims as well as paperwork costs. Small losses therefore cost proportionally more than large losses to process. Thus, insurance covering small losses is relatively more expensive than insurance covering large losses.

One way to retain small losses is by buying insurance with a **deductible** clause. The deductible clause allows the insured person to retain the loss equal to the deductible amount. Comprehensive car insurance covers losses such as vandalism and glass breakage. A $0 deductible comprehensive car policy will pay for all covered losses and might cost a certain car owner, say, $70 per year. The same coverage, with, for example, $50 deductible, will pay for all covered losses over $50 and might cost the car owner only $40 per year. By retaining the first $50 of a covered loss, this car owner can reduce the premium by $30.

Selecting an Agent

Generally speaking, it does not require much formal education or training to become an insurance agent. Some insurance companies are not too particular about whom they hire as agents as long as the people can sell insurance. As a result, you will find highly competent and knowledgeable agents as well as incompetent agents. A competent agent is interested in helping the client identify his or her risks and in proposing a suitable program for properly managing the insurable risks confronted by the client. An incompetent agent is more interested in selling insurance and will not place sufficient emphasis on proper risk management.

Besides recommending a suitable insurance program, competent agents will also help you select the right deductible to manage insurance costs. They will review the coverage provided by the insurance policy and actively monitor your coverage over time. Insurance agents work for a commission paid by the insurance company. An incompetent agent is no cheaper than a competent one. Therefore, it is most desirable to work with a competent agent.

Most agents specialize in either personal (life, disability, and health) or property and liability insurance. Thus, most people end up selecting two agents to handle their risk management program. Many insurance agents hold professional certifications, such as **Chartered Life Underwriter (CLU)** or **Chartered Property Casualty Underwriter (CPCU)**. These designations are not easy to obtain. Therefore, an agent with a professional certification can be expected to have high technical competence in his or her area of insurance.

The Yellow Pages are useful for obtaining a listing of agents. A phone call or a personal visit with a potential agent can provide some indication of the agent's competence and his or her willingness to help set up a suitable insurance program. Checking with friends and acquaintances can provide good leads also. It is acceptable to ask the agent to provide local references. Most important, avoid an agent who tries to sell insurance without fully understanding your insurance situation.

Selecting a Company

Selecting an insurance company is just as important as selecting an insurance agent. Because many agents work for only one company, selecting an agent and selecting a company has to be done simultaneously. The typical insurance company will be organized as either a stock or a mutual company. A **stock insurance company** is similar to any other corporation. It sells its services to its customers, or policyholders. It raises capital from its stockholders, and all profits (and losses) go to them. A **mutual insurance company** is owned by its policyholders. Theoretically, insurance premiums are set so that a mutual company breaks even every year. That is, a mutual

company can be expected to neither earn profits nor lose money. Thus, mutual companies can be expected to provide insurance policies at a lower rate than stock companies. When you select an insurance company, you should take into consideration prices, financial strength, and settlement practices.

Prices. Prices vary substantially from company to company. Other factors being the same, it is better to buy insurance from a company with lower premiums. Price information on coverage should be readily available from insurance agents.

Financial Strength. Insurance should be purchased only from a financially strong company. *Best's Life Reports* and *Best's Insurance Reports* contain information on the financial strengths of insurance companies. These publications are readily available in public libraries. *Best's* gives financial ratings to firms ranging from A+ to C. Ratings of A+ and A mean excellent financial strength. You should consider buying insurance from a firm that has had an A or A+ rating for the past six years.

Settlement Practices. Claim settlement practices also vary from company to company. Some companies have a reputation for prompt and fair settlement, whereas other companies tend to delay payments on claims for agonizingly long times. Unfortunately, no standard, readily available published sources provide information on the settlement practices of firms. Local newspapers occasionally carry articles on settlement practices. Also, dissatisfied clients can file complaints with their state's insurance department. Thus, a check with this department can provide an indication of settlement practices. Proportionally large numbers of complaints may indicate unfair settlement practices.

Selecting the Coverage

A competent agent should have good advice on selecting the right coverage. Coverage should be high enough to cover potential large losses but not so high that it involves excess, unnecessary insurance premiums. Finally, deductibles should be at a level where the insured person can readily absorb the small losses but still realize savings on the insurance premiums.

Applying for Insurance

Once you have selected an agent and a company, you are ready to apply for insurance. The application requires information about you as well as on what is being insured. A medical examination and a personal medical history are generally required for life and disability insurance. Driving history and driving record are required for auto insurance. A property

description is required when insurance is desired on property. Providing false information on the insurance application may lead to the denial of claims later. Therefore, only correct information should be provided on the insurance application.

Often when insurance covers property or liabilities, insurance agents are authorized to provide coverage starting from the time the application is received by the agent. The **binder** is a temporary contract that allows the agent to provide coverage from the time the application is received by him or her. The binder can be either oral or written, although a written binder leads to fewer disputes if a claim arises before permanent coverage is issued. The insurance applicant can ask the agent to provide a written binder stating who is covered, what is covered and for what amount, and the name of the insuring company.

The Insurance Policy

Keep in mind that the insurance policy is a legal contract. It is usually written in a complex, legal style. Reading a policy may not be quite as enjoyable as reading your favorite magazine; nevertheless, it is something you should do. An insurance policy has five sections: declarations, insuring clauses, exclusions, conditions, and endorsements.

Declarations.   The **declarations section** contains the basic identifying details of the policy. The name of the policy owner, what is insured, the amount of insurance, the cost of the policy, and the time period covered by the insurance are contained in this section.

Insuring Clauses.   The **insuring clauses** section contains the obligations of the insuring company. The perils or risks covered are listed in this section. Definitions of terms are contained here as well.

Exclusions.   The **exclusions section** lists perils and properties that are not covered by insurance. Most policies contain some type of exclusion. Losses due to war are not covered by homeowners' policies, for example. Similarly, health and disability policies exclude preexisting medical problems. Life insurance policies exclude suicides from coverage for the first one or two years that the policy is in force.

Conditions.   The **conditions section** lists the obligations of the policy owner. For example, the insured person may be required to file a claim within a specified time to collect on a claim.

Endorsements.   Endorsements or riders are associated with property and liability coverage. A **rider** or an **endorsement** is a statement attached to an insurance policy that changes the terms of the policy. Typically,

changes in beneficiaries, coverages, premiums, and items insured are handled through the issuance of a rider or endorsement.

Filing Claims

When you incur a loss, the first thing to do is to notify the insurance agent. Some claims are small, and no further action is necessary. For example, on a claim for car towing services, it is generally sufficient to call the agent and mail her or him a receipt for the service. A settlement check should be forthcoming in a few days.

Larger claims may require filing a formal claim. Insurance companies use the services of either their own claims adjusters or independent adjusters to evaluate the insured person's claim. The adjuster determines whether the claim is covered by insurance and whether the claim is justified. In most cases, the claims adjustment and settlement process is easy and fair. Occasionally, the insured person does not obtain satisfaction from the settlement being offered by the adjuster. In such cases, the insured person should refuse any claims settlement check offered and discuss the situation with a lawyer.

Spot Quiz • Buying Insurance

1. Insuring losses of all sizes is a good policy.   T _____   F _____

2. Price is important but is not the only criterion when you select an insurance company.   T _____   F _____

3. The endorsements indicate what is covered in an insurance policy.
                                                        T _____   F _____

(Answers on page 361)

Summary

Risk is the possibility of suffering a loss. Risk can be either speculative or pure. Pure risks involve only the possibility of a loss and are insurable. Property, liability, and personal risks are examples of pure risks.

Four ways of dealing with risk are avoiding, controlling, retaining, and transferring risk. Some risks cannot be avoided, but most risks are controllable to some extent. Risk can be transferred by buying insurance.

In risk management, the first step is to identify the risk. After identification, risks should be evaluated. Next, appropriate strategies should be chosen to deal with risks. Once the strategies have been selected, they should put it into effect. The final step in risk management is periodic review of the program.

Insurance is a legal contract, transferring risk from the insured person to the insuring company. The law of large numbers helps explain how insurance works. Losses that are fortuitous, financial, and personal are insurable. The insured person needs to have an insurable interest in whatever is being insured. Risks that can result in severe losses should be insured.

When you buy insurance, large losses should be transferred, and small losses should be retained. Selection of an insurance company should take into consideration the company's prices, financial strength, and claims settlement practices. The terms of insurance should be understood before you buy any policy.

Questions

1. What is meant by risk? Explain briefly.

2. What is the difference between pure and speculative risks? Why is only one of them insurable?

3. Briefly explain the different types of pure risks.

4. Explain two situations in which it is best to avoid risk.

5. Explain briefly how risk can be controlled.

6. What is meant by retained risk? Under what conditions should risk be retained?

7. Do you agree that risk transfer works better than risk retention? Explain your answer.

8. Very briefly, explain the steps in the risk management program.

9. What is probability? What does it have to do with insurance?

10. How does the law of large numbers help explain the way insurance works?

11. Explain the four criteria that make a risk insurable.

12. Why does the insurance owner need an insurable interest in an item being insured?

13. Briefly give your reason for insuring or not insuring an item where the probability of occurrence and the severity of loss are both low.

14. Explain the two principles for buying insurance.

15. What factors need to be considered when you select an insurance company?

16. What is a binder? Is an oral or a written binder more desirable? Why?

17. What does an insurance claims adjuster do?

Case Problems

1. Richard and Janet Strauss live in Houston. They are renting an apartment and saving money regularly for a down payment on a house. Both Richard and Janet are self-employed, working as partners in a small bookkeeping firm. Both run at least two miles daily and consider themselves to be extremely healthy. An old car provides their transportation. They have health insurance and collision and liability insurance for their car.

    a. Keeping in mind Figure 11.1, explain the risks that Richard and Janet face. How can they best handle these risks?
    b. How might their risk situation change over the next five years? How can they prepare to handle any new risks that might emerge later?

2. Dr. Adam Fulbright, considered by students to be a typical college professor, jumps out of bed at precisely 6:00 A.M. every day. He pulls on his jogging clothes, starts the automatic coffee pot, and by 6:07 A.M., he is on the road, jogging the ten blocks to a newsstand and back again. After a shower and breakfast, he pulls the front door to his house shut behind him and pins a note on the door for the postal worker. He opens the garage door and drives off in his car. On the way to school, he gives a ride to a hitchhiker who is probably a student. What advice about controlling risk would you give Dr. Fulbright?

Bibliography

Greene, Mark R., and J. R. Trieschmann. *Risk and Insurance.* 6th ed. Cincinnati: South-Western Publishing Co., 1984.

"Insurance and an Investment Too." *Changing Times* (May 1986): 73–79.

"You May Already Be Insured for That." *Money* (November 1978): 110–112.

"Weave Your Own Safety Net." *Money* (November 1986): 95–98.

Answers to Spot Quizzes

Risk (page 342)

1. F (It involves speculative risk because profits as well as losses can be expected.)

2. T (It is no longer accidental or speculative.)

Dealing With Risk (page 344)

1. F (Some risk, such as premature death, may not be avoidable.)

2. F (Retaining small losses may be the least expensive way of dealing with the risks involved.)

3. F (Not if the chances of occurrence are very, very small.)

The Risk Management Process (page 348)

1. F (The severity of losses also needs to be considered.)

2. T (Sufficient funds must be on hand to cover retained losses.)

Risk Transfer by Insurance (page 352)

1. F (More risk-prone people pay higher premiums.)

2. T (It is no longer fortuitous.)

3. T (The losses from physical disability are fortuitous, financial, and personal, and the disabled person has an insurable interest.)

4. F (Whether you should insure also depends on the severity of loss.)

Buying Insurance (page 357)

1. F (Small losses should not be covered by insurance.)

2. T (The company's financial strength and its settlement practices are also important.)

3. F (An endorsement only indicates a change.)

Chapter 12

Property and Liability Insurance

Objectives

After reading this chapter, you will be able to:

- Identify real and personal property risks.
- Evaluate home ownership risks.
- Explain the different types of homeowners' policies.
- Discuss the important factors in managing homeowners' insurance.
- Differentiate among types of liabilities.
- List the major features of automobile insurance.
- Discuss the management of automobile insurance.

Nancy Chasen and her husband owned a rental property in Bethesda, Maryland. Careless cigarette smoking led to a fire in the property's kitchen and bathroom. The rest of the home suffered smoke damage. The home was insured by one of the largest insurance companies in the United States. Ms. Chasen believed that the claim would be evaluated fairly by the insurance company and that a settlement check would be forthcoming soon. Such, however, was not the case.

Ms. Chasen was told that the policy she owned provided "actual cash value" rather than "full replacement cost." An "actual cash value" policy pays for the replacement cost *less depreciation* for a damaged item. A "full replacement cost" policy pays for replacing the damaged item. Ms. Chasen's insurance agent did not explain this difference in policies to her when she purchased the actual cash value policy.

The insurance company offered $29,745 in settlement. Ms. Chasen's independent contractors estimated that it would cost about $37,000 to restore the house. Finally, Ms. Chasen wrote to the president of the insurance company, to the Maryland insurance commissioner, and to New York Congressman Benjamin Rosenthal, who has a strong consumer orientation. Within a few weeks after writing these letters, the insurance company offered a settlement that Ms. Chasen considered to be fair.[1]

What would you have done if you had been in Ms. Chasen's place? What properties should a person insure? For how much? These and other liability insurance issues are discussed in this chapter. The chapter covers homeowners' insurance first and then auto insurance.

Managing home ownership risks

There are two types of property: real and personal. **Real property** includes physical structures, such as a house, garage, fences, and any other type of building or structure attached to the land. **Personal property** includes furniture, appliances, clothing, and other personal belongings. Generally speaking, both real and personal property can be insured. Land is real property also. However, because land is not subject to typical risk situations, it cannot be insured. Both real and personal property risks arise with home ownership.

Chapter 11 explained the steps in risk management. These steps are considered here as we discuss managing the risks involved with home ownership.

---

1. "How Not to Get Hosed by Your Fire Insurer," *Money* (December 1979): 85–90.

Risk Identification

Most people probably would be hard pressed to prepare from memory a list of all of their properties. For this reason, it is desirable to prepare a written list of all properties you own. This list, or inventory of properties, can be divided into the two categories of real property and personal property.

Real Property.   Real properties are limited in number and are easily identified. A suggested inventory of real properties is shown in Table 12.1. In the risk identification stage, all real properties are listed in the first column. The other columns relate to risk evaluation and will be discussed in the next section. The types of real properties owned will vary from family to family.

Personal Property.   Personal property is also known as household property. Some people prefer to catalog personal property by type of item. That is, they might identify the number of chairs, the number of beds, and so on. However, this approach creates problems if damage occurs to only a portion of the home. For example, fire damage might be limited to two rooms. In this case, the insurance company is interested in knowing what was located in those two rooms in particular.

An alternative—and preferred—approach is to inventory personal property by location. The contents of each room or area of the house are listed on a separate sheet of paper. An example for a kitchen is shown in Table 12.2. The personal property items are listed in the first column in the table. The remaining columns will be discussed in the next section. Anything of value, no matter how insignificant, should be identified at this stage.

Table 12.1   Identification and Evaluation of Physical Property

Property	Original Cost	Replacement Cost	Accumulated Depreciation	Actual Cash Value
House	$60,000	$100,000	$ 6,000	$ 94,000
Garage	10,000	15,000	2,000	13,000
Swimming pool	8,000	8,000	4,000	4,000
Fences	1,000	2,000	1,000	1,000
Barn	3,000	4,000	1,000	3,000
Storage room	2,000	3,000	1,000	2,000
Other	2,000	3,000	1,000	2,000
Total	$86,000	$135,000	$16,000	$119,000

Table 12.2 Identification and Evaluation of Personal Property: Kitchen

(1) Property	(2) Original Cost	(3) Age	(4) Percent Annual Depreciation	(5) Percent Accumulated Depreciation	(6) Replacement Cost	(7) Value of Accumulated Depreciation	(8) Actual Cash Value
Refrigerator	$ 800	4	7	28	$1,200	$ 336	$ 864
Stove	300	4	7	28	500	140	360
Dining table, chairs	300	4	10	40	600	240	360
Microwave oven	400	1	7	7	500	35	465
Cooking utensils	300	4	7	28	500	140	360
Dishes, silverware	800	4	—	10	1,200	120	1,080
Other	800	3	10	30	1,200	360	840
Total	$3,700				$5,700	$1,371	$4,329

Risk Evaluation

Before you can evaluate risk, you need to understand some basic concepts and terms in the pricing of property. Let's assume, for example, that you buy a sofa for $500. The sofa has a useful life of ten years. After five years, the sofa is destroyed in a fire. Replacing the sofa would cost $800. Because only half of the useful life of the sofa remained, its market value at the time of the fire would have been $1/2 \times \$800 = \$400$. In this example, $500 is the original cost, $800 is the replacement cost, and $400 is the actual cash value. Based on the type of insurance policy coverage, the person would receive either $800 or $400 in settlement for the sofa.

Table 12.2 shows that the original cost of the dining table and chairs was $300. The third column shows that the set is four years old. Insurance companies try to estimate the useful lives of various properties. The annual depreciation charge equals 1 divided by the useful life:

$$\text{Annual Depreciation Charge} = \frac{1}{\text{Useful Life}}$$

The **annual depreciation charge** is simply the decline in the value of a property due to normal wear and tear. For the table and chairs, which have a useful life of ten years, the annual depreciation charge is $1/10 = .1$, or 10 percent.

Age multiplied by the annual depreciation charge gives **accumulated depreciation**:

$$\text{Accumulated Depreciation} = \text{Age} \times \text{Annual Depreciation Charge}$$

The accumulated depreciation for the dining set is $4 \times .1 = .4$. Column 6 in Table 12.2 shows the replacement cost of the property. This is what it would cost to replace the property today. Obviously, not all items can be replaced. If an exact replacement is not available, then you could identify the price of a similar product. The replacement cost for the table and chairs is $600.

The **accumulated depreciation in dollars** is equal to accumulated depreciation times the replacement cost:

$$\text{Accumulated Depreciation in Dollars} = \text{Accumulated Depreciation} \times \text{Replacement Cost}$$

For the table and chairs, it is $.4 \times \$600 = \$240$. The last column in Table 12.2 shows the actual cash value to be $360. **Actual cash value** equals replacement cost minus accumulated depreciation in dollars:

$$\text{Actual Cash Value} = \text{Replacement Cost} - \text{Accumulated Depreciation in Dollars}$$

Annual depreciation charges for personal property can be obtained from depreciation schedules prepared by insurance companies. An example is shown in Table 12.3.

Table 12.3 Depreciation Schedule for Personal Property*

Article	Percent Annual Depreciation	Article	Percent Annual Depreciation
Blankets	7	Furniture, redwood	10
Carpets	10	Furniture, upholstered	10
Clothes	20	Mower	10
Curtains	20	Refrigerator	7
Dishes	Use 90% of replacement cost	Silverware	Use 90% of replacement cost
Dryer	12	Stereo	7
Furniture, desk	5	Television	10

*Source: State Farm Insurance.

Depreciation charges for physical property are much more difficult to calculate. For this reason, estimations of the type shown in Table 12.3 should be done with the help of a qualified insurance agent. Most are willing to help you estimate replacement costs and actual cash values of physical properties.

Table 12.1 shows that the total replacement cost of physical property is $135,000. The replacement cost of the house is $100,000. Table 12.2 in column 6 shows that the total replacement cost of all the personal property in the kitchen is $5,700. If the house and its belongings were totally destroyed in a fire, the cost of replacing them would be at least $100,000 + $5,700 = $105,700. The cost would be much higher if we took into consideration the personal property in other rooms as well.

Choosing a Strategy

As we discussed in Chapter 11, there are four ways to deal with risk: avoid it, control it, retain it, or transfer it. Only by not owning property can you avoid property risks, and this is not a viable alternative for most people.

Risk can be controlled by exercising caution. Homes should be equipped with smoke and fire detectors and fire extinguishers. Combustible materials should not be stored in the house. Exhaust fan filters over

ovens should be cleaned often to remove trapped grease and reduce the possibility of fire. Electrical outlets should not be overburdened with extension cords. Water heaters and furnaces should be cleaned and checked periodically. There are many things that you can do to control the risks of home ownership. One useful thing is to call the local police and fire departments and obtain their brochures on controlling home ownership risks. Putting some of this advice into practice can lower the risk environment of the home.

As mentioned previously, it is generally better to retain only small loss risks. After deciding on a reasonable retention through a deductible clause, the remaining home ownership risks should be transferred by buying a homeowners' insurance policy. This type of insurance coverage will be discussed in detail in the next section.

Once an appropriate strategy has been selected, it needs to be implemented. Part of Chapter 11 dealt with choosing an insurance agent and an insurance company. Those factors should be kept in mind when you buy insurance. You should also remember to reevaluate insurance coverage needs when the insurance policy comes up for renewal. (See "Who Loves Ya, Baby?" on page 370.)

Spot Quiz • Managing Home Ownership Risks

1. For any person, physical property is always more expensive than personal property. T _____ F _____

2. Higher annual depreciation charges mean shorter useful lives for property. T _____ F _____

3. Some personal property depreciates very little over time. T _____ F _____

(Answers on page 398)

HOMEOWNERS' INSURANCE

Six types of homeowners' insurance policies are available to consumers. All six types of policies have four major sections:

1. Declarations page
2. Section I coverage

Who Loves Ya, Baby?

Your house is burning down to the ground. Based on fire drills practiced in the past, the family reaches the front yard safely. Fortunately, your trusted dog Sheba runs back into the house, rummages through your filing cabinet, finds the homeowners' insurance policy, wraps it in a moist towel, brings it out, and deposits it at your feet. You are congratulating yourself on your good fortune for owning Sheba when your insurance agent drives up, assesses the fire damage, and offers to write you a settlement check right then and there. Good fortune times two! You sign some papers and take the check. In the morning, you get bids for rebuilding the house and find out that the minimum bid is quite a bit higher than the settlement check. What to do now?

Some people argue that many consumers would benefit by using the services of public insurance adjusters. For a fee that is about 10 to 15 percent of the settlement, the adjuster will represent the homeowner in negotiating a reasonable settlement with the insurance company. Adjusters can help with preparing a detailed inventory of damaged items, obtaining repair bids, and explaining what is covered by the insurance policy. Consumers who have used adjusters generally state that their services are worth their charges.

In recent years, many insurance companies have improved their claims adjustment procedures to allow for independent third-party resolution of claims that cannot be directly resolved with the homeowners. Thus, the insurance companies argue that homeowners are generally treated fairly and the services of public adjusters are not needed. Who loves ya? It depends on how you are treated.

3. Section II coverage
4. General conditions

Section II deals with liability coverage and will be discussed later in the chapter. The important features of the other sections are discussed here.

Declarations Page

The **declarations page** lists the name and address of the insured person or persons and the location of the insured home. The beginning and ending dates for the policy are listed here. The policy limits on the various types of coverages are stated here also. Any special endorsements to the basic policy are identified on the declarations page. This page also shows a number, such as HO-1 or HO-3, to indicate the type of policy.

Section I Coverage

Section I generally has eight subsections. **Coverage A—House** applies to the house itself and to any other structure, such as a garage, attached to it. **Coverage B—Detached structure** applies to structures that are on the insured property but not attached to the house. For example, many homes have detached garages. **Coverage C—Unscheduled personal property** covers the insured person's property as well as items borrowed by the insured person for use on his or her property. **Coverage D—Additional living expenses** applies when the insured person cannot live in the insured home. For example, fire damage to the home may make it uninhabitable.

The fifth subsection, **Supplementary Coverages**, describes a variety of coverages. Removal of debris is covered in this subsection. This coverage also pays for a fire department's service charge of up to $250. Trees, shrubs, and plants are covered. Losses related to credit cards, forgeries, and counterfeit money are also covered.

The sixth subsection, **Perils Covered Against**, lists the perils or risks against which the person is insured. Certain exclusions are listed here as well. For example, losses due to theft are covered in all policies. However, theft by the insured person is not covered.

The seventh subsection lists **Exclusions**. Losses due to enforcement of local or state laws are excluded from coverage. Also excluded are birds, animals, fish, tape players, CB radios, business property, property in a rented unit, and property of renters.

The last subsection, titled **Conditions**, contains certain conditions, such as the "Coinsurance" clause and the "Apportionment" clauses. Some important conditions are discussed separately later in the chapter. (See "You May Already Be Insured for That" on page 372.)

General Conditions

The **General Conditions** section contains conditions that are common to both Section I and Section II. This section contains the insurance agreement and other conditions of insurance. It contains a statement to the effect that the policy is void if the insured person has deliberately concealed facts about the insurance. It indicates what is uninsurable. The procedure for canceling the policy is also mentioned here. Other conditions cover situations such as the death of the insured, modification of the terms of insurance, and nonrenewal provisions. Finally, there is a statement about what the insured person must do if a loss occurs.

Types of Perils and Policies

There are six types of homeowners' insurance policies. They differ in terms of perils covered and minimum and maximum coverages.

You May Already be Insured for That

Stolen billfolds. After spending all day on the beach, you discover that thieves have broken into your car and stolen your checkbook and wallet. Most policies pay for $100 in stolen cash and $1,000 in forged checks or unauthorized credit card charges. By law, banks absorb losses from forged checks they cash themselves, and credit card companies pay for all but $50 of purchases made with lost or stolen cards (they must take the full loss if notified promptly that a card is missing). Homeowners' policies take over where the law leaves off, paying for check forgeries your bank doesn't reimburse you for and the first $50 of loss on each credit card. The credit card coverage is especially useful for those who carry a thick collection of cards. Homeowners' policies also cover the first $1,000 of losses from counterfeit money that ends up in your pocket—assuming you had no part in printing it.

Moving-day thefts. While you're moving, burglars snatch the TV from the back of the van or from the new house. If the mover refuses to make good on belongings stolen or damaged by fire in transit, a homeowners' policy will pay—even a policy covering the house just vacated. You might still want to buy the mover's extra-priced insurance, however, to take care of things he breaks or loses.

Firemen's fees. If your cry of alarm is answered by a fire engine from a neighboring town, there's a good chance you will be charged a hefty fee for its services. Most homeowners' policies pay up to $250 of such charges.

Injuries to friends. A guest at your garden party walks into a glass door and has to be rushed to the hospital for stitches. To discourage the friend from filing a lawsuit, most homeowners' policies will pay for the ambulance and for emergency room treatment.

Borrowed tools and appliances. Your neighbor lends you his new power mower. You run it over a rock and it dies on the spot. Your policy will probably pay up to $500.

Lost luggage. In a parking lot far from home, your luggage is stolen from the locked trunk of your car. A homeowners' policy's personal property provision usually covers the loss.

Pet problems. Your dog sinks his fangs into a neighbor's leg. Most policies pay the neighbor's first aid costs and protect you if the neighbor decides to sue for negligence.

Lawn losses. A gang of neighborhood minibike racers knocks down your fence, cuts a path through the boxwood, and destroys a few saplings you've just planted. Most policies pay up to $500 for each shrub, tree, fence, and flagpole damaged by fire, vandalism, or motor vehicles.

Small-boat accidents. Homeowners' policies provide liability, fire, and theft insurance for sailboats under 26 feet long and low-powered motor-

boats (typically, under 50 hp for inboard motors, under 25 hp for outboards.)

Damaged tombstones. When your penniless Aunt Agnes died, you paid for her tombstone. A graffiti artist attacks it with a can of spray paint. Most homeowners' policies will pay $500 or more for tombstone damage caused by anything but weather, provided the policyholder bought the stone.

Source: *Money* Magazine, November 1978, pp. 111–112. Reprinted with permission.

Homeowners' Form 1 (HO-1). This type of policy is also known as the basic form. As shown in Table 12.4, the policy covers perils such as fire, lightning, explosion, riots, vandalism, and theft. Certain perils are not covered under HO-1—for example, the collapse of the house and accidental surges in electrical power that damage electrical appliances.

Homeowners' Form 2 (HO-2). This policy, more typically known as the broad form, covers a wide variety of perils, as shown in Table 12.4.

Homeowners' Form 3 (HO-3). This policy is called the special form because it combines the features of both HO-1 and HO-2. Like HO-2, it covers a broad range of perils on Coverage C—Personal property. Additionally, all risks are covered for Coverages A, B, and D. For example, an insured person who accidentally drives a car into his or her own home would be covered under HO-3 but not under HO-2. Dollar for dollar, HO-3 is considered the best homeowners' insurance buy for consumers.

Homeowners' Form 4 (HO-4). This policy, designed for renters, covers the personal property of the apartment or house renter. Additional living expenses are also covered. Any additions or improvements made to the property by the renter, even if they are permanent, are covered for up to 10 percent of the amount of personal insurance. For example, the renter paints the rented apartment, which is subsequently damaged by a fire. Under HO-4, the renter can recover his or her expenses related to painting the apartment. This is considered to be a good policy for renters.

Homeowners' Form 5 (HO-5). This policy is also called the comprehensive form because it covers all perils except those specifically excluded for Coverages A, B, C, and D. However, HO-5 is considered very expensive and therefore is not very popular.

Table 12.4 Basic Section I and II Coverages in Homeowners' Policies

Items	HO-1 Basic Form	HO-2 Broad Form	HO-3 Special Form	HO-4 Tenants' Form	HO-5 Comprehensive Form	HO-6 For Condo Owners
Coverage provided	10 perils[a]	17 perils[b]	All risk[c]	17 perils[b]	All risk[c]	17 perils[b]
Minimum coverages						
A. House	$15,000	$15,000	$20,000	Limited	$30,000	Limited
B. Detached structure	10% of A	10% of A	10% of A	No coverage	10% of A	No coverage
C. Unscheduled personal property	50% of A	50% of A	50% of A	$6,000	50% of A	$6,000
D. Additional living expenses	10% of A	20% of A	20% of A	20% of A	20% of A	40% of A
E. Personal liability	$100,000	$100,000	$100,000	$100,000	$100,000	$100,000
F. Medical payments to others	$1,000/person	$1,000/person	$1,000/person	$1,000/person	$1,000/person	$1,000/person
Special limits on liability	Unscheduled personal property at secondary residence is limited to the greater of 10% of C, or $1,000. Damage to property of others is limited to $500. Credit card and counterfeit money losses are limited to $1,000. Limitations on losses due to theft of certain unscheduled personal property are as follows: jewelry, furs, diamonds, valuable stones—$1,000; silverware—$2,500, guns—$2,000, business property on residence—$2,500.					

[a]The 10 perils are fire and lightning, windstorm or hail, explosion, riot or civil commotion, vehicles, aircraft, smoke, vandalism, glass breakage, and theft.
[b]The 17 perils include the 10 above plus falling objects, weight of ice or sleet, collapse of buildings, discharge of steam or water, damage due to steam or hot water heating system, freezing of plumbing and heating and air conditioning systems, and electrical surges damaging appliances.
[c]All risks, except those specially excluded, are covered.

Homeowners' Form 6 (HO-6). This policy is designed for condominium owners. Like the HO-4, it covers personal property and improvements made to the condominium.

Coinsurance Clause

Partial losses occur more frequently than total losses. Those people who underinsured their properties will produce more claims for the policy limit—and will therefore secure more benefits—than people who are fully insured. To counter this, insurance companies try to achieve a more equitable distribution of insurance coverage costs by maintaining a coinsurance clause in the policy. **Coinsurance** refers to the sharing of losses between the insured and the insurer. The coinsurance clause states that if the insured has insurance that is at or above a stated percentage (80 percent is the most common percent) of the replacement cost of the home, then all losses will be covered for up to the amount of the policy. If the amount of insurance is less than the specified percent of replacement cost, only a fraction of the loss will be paid, based on the following formula:

$$\text{Amount of Losses Paid} = \frac{\text{Amount of Insurance Purchased}}{\text{Stated Percent of Replacement Cost}} \times \text{Amount of Loss}$$

The ratio of amount of insurance purchased to the stated percentage of replacement cost is called the **coinsurance ratio**. Thus, the previous formula can be written as

Amount of Losses Paid = Coinsurance Ratio × Amount of Loss

The following examples illustrate the coinsurance clause. The Herrmanns have a home that has a replacement cost of $100,000. They carry $80,000 in insurance. The coinsurance clause of their policy states that the insured need insure only for 80 percent of replacement cost, so they meet the requirements of the coinsurance clause. Suppose they suffer fire-related losses of $60,000. The insurance company will pay for these losses in full. If they were to suffer losses of, say, $85,000, the insurance company would pay the full amount of insurance coverage purchased, or $80,000.

Let us now assume that the Herrmanns carry only $60,000 in insurance and so do not satisfy the coinsurance clause. The coinsurance ratio is $60,000/$80,000 = .75. The Herrmanns suffer a $60,000 loss. The insurance company would pay .75 × $60,000 = $45,000 on this loss. If the Herrmanns were to suffer a $100,000 loss, the formula gives a figure of .75 × $100,000 = $75,000. The insurance company would pay up to the amount of insurance coverage purchased, or $60,000.

Floater Policies

As Table 12.4 shows in the section "Special Limits on Liability," certain personal property is not fully insured. Thus, for example, theft of jewelry, watches, furs, and precious stones is covered for up to $1000 only. Even a half-carat diamond wedding ring can cost thousands of dollars. Aside from the sentimental value, lack of insurance coverage may make it difficult to replace certain personal properties. These personal properties can be insured through a floater, or scheduled property, policy. A **floater policy** provides all risk coverage, except for exclusions, for the item in question. Thus, an expensive fur coat can be insured against theft by buying a floater policy. The coverage would cover theft but exclude damage caused by moths.

Table 12.5 shows a sample listing of personal property that can be covered with a floater policy. The cost of the policy and exclusions are also shown in this table.

Managing Homeowners' Insurance

Some ideas for managing homeowners' insurance are provided in this section.

Table 12.5 Sample Listing of Personal Property and Floaters

Article	Cost per $100 per Year of Coverage	Exclusions
Camera	$1.65	None
Coin collection	1.60	None
Furs, mink	0.90	None
Furs, other	0.70	None
Jewelry	1.66	None
Paintings, prints	0.24	Wear and tear
Pottery	0.39	None
Silverware	0.35	None
Sports equipment	2.00	None
Stamp collection	0.60	None

Source: State Farm Insurance.

Deductibles. Most homeowners' policies have a $250 deductible that applies to Section I coverage. The $250 figure has been in use only since 1985 and is thus relatively new. Because family incomes have risen sharply in recent years, the $250 deductible is a fairly insignificant amount for most homeowners. Homeowners can lower their insurance premiums by buying a policy with a larger deductible, such as $500.

Replacement Cost Coverage. Most insurance companies offer actual cash value coverage on personal property. For instance, a ten-year-old stereo system may have an actual cash value of only $50 even though it is perfectly functional. Replacing it would require a substantial cash outlay. Some insurance companies offer replacement cost coverage on personal property. If the property is destroyed, the insured receives the replacement cost rather than the actual cash value. Before you buy coverage, you should explore the option of replacement cost coverage. The additional cost of this coverage, compared with the additional insurance proceeds that would be paid, should provide an indication of the desirability of this type of coverage.

Amount of Coverage. Because of the coinsurance clause, a homeowner should carry insurance that is no less than 80 percent of the replacement cost of the house. Usually, the basement and the foundation are not damaged even when the house is totally destroyed. Therefore, insurance for 100 percent of replacement cost might not be suitable for everyone. However, you should consider buying insurance for about 90 percent of replacement cost.

Inflation Protection Policies. Many insurance companies offer policies whose coverage is automatically adjusted for inflation. Thus, if construction costs go up 10 percent in the insured person's community, the insurance coverage amount is also increased by 10 percent. Before buying insurance, check with the insurance company to see if it offers this attractive feature.

Guaranteed Coinsurance Clause Coverage. Many insurance companies guarantee that the coinsurance clause requirement will be met. This guarantee is the same as inflation protection. In either case, the result is to see that the amount of insurance is no less than 80 percent of the replacement cost. It is desirable to deal with an insurance company offering this feature.

Other Insurance. Most insurance policies have a clause stating that if the same loss is covered by other policies as well, then only a portion of the loss will be paid. The reason for this clause is to prevent the insured person from profiting from a pure risk loss. Thus, insurance coverage should not be replicated by buying more than one policy.

Following the suggestions listed here will help with the property management portion of homeowners' insurance. You should also ask your insurance agent about other ways to save money. For instance, some insurance companies give discounts if you follow commonsense risk control measures. Installing fire and smoke detectors might result in a 2 to 5 percent discount on the insurance premiums, for example.

Spot Quiz • Homeowners' Insurance

1. Homeowners' insurance policies fully cover all personal property.
                                                        T _____   F _____

2. HO-3 provides less extensive coverage than HO-5.
                                                        T _____   F _____

3. The coinsurance clause discriminates against those homeowners who have a coinsurance ratio greater than 1.   T _____   F _____

4. A floater policy covers all personal property.   T _____   F _____

(Answers on page 398)

Managing liability risks

A **liability risk** exists when a person is in danger of losing some or all of his or her assets to pay for damages inflicted on another person. Liability risks are hereafter referred to simply as liabilities. **Tort liabilities** arise from tort laws. Thus, for example, a person driving a car creates a tort liability because he or she can cause damage to another person simply through the act of driving a car. The potential of hitting another car and causing damages creates a tort liability. Tort law would call for compensation to the driver who was hit in the accident. The payment for damages by the driver would result in a loss of assets for him or her. Our focus in the remainder of this chapter will be on tort liabilities.

Tort Liabilities

Negligence and absolute and vicarious liabilities are the three types of tort liabilities that affect consumers.

Negligence. Negligence occurs when a person fails to exercise reasonable care to prevent injury or damage to others. A person suing another for injuries or damages caused by negligence would claim that the other person did not exercise reasonable care. The term *reasonable care* implies that there is a normal way of behaving that results in a certain course of action that a reasonable person would follow. For example, after a snowfall, a person fails to clear the snow from the sidewalk on his or her property. Another person slips on the compacted snow, falls down, and breaks an arm. This injured person sues the homeowner for negligence. In this situation, the homeowner may be negligent because he or she did not exercise reasonable care in clearing the sidewalk.

Absolute Liability. Absolute liability arises when a person engages in a known dangerous act that may result in damage or injury to others. Negligence does not have to be proven in a situation involving absolute liability. For example, a person has a guard dog as a pet, and one day the dog attacks and injures a delivery person. Here, the dog owner may be subject to paying damages under absolute liability because the aggressive nature of the dog was well known.

Vicarious Liability. Vicarious liabilities arise from the actions of people under a person's control or supervision. Thus, for example, parents may be responsible for damages caused by their children. A bar owner may be responsible for overenthusiastic handling by one of his or her bouncers.

Liability Risk Identification

Liability risks arise because people own property, use property, and engage in various types of activities. For example, an uneven driveway creates liabilities for the homeowner. A person driving a rented car is using someone else's property but is still liable for causing injuries or damage. A golfer may hit someone on the head with a golf ball. A racquetball player may injure a playing partner's eye with the ball. A surgeon might put a cast too tightly on a broken leg, causing loss of blood circulation and damage to the toes. This is just a sample of liabilities—the list of ownership and use of property and personal activities that can create liabilities could go on and on.

The first step in liability risk identification is to identify all the property you own or use that could result in damage or injury to others. A stamp collection is probably harmless enough, but how about the loaded hunting rifle that could be found by a visiting child? Or the bar stool with a wobbly leg that could collapse any minute?

Some risks associated with properties are easy to identify, but others are more difficult. For example, suppose you have an apple tree in your

back yard. A neighbor's child climbs the apple tree in hopes of picking a fresh snack. However, a tree limb breaks, and the child tumbles to the ground and breaks an arm. Is the homeowner liable in this case? Maybe. The reason is a negligence liability called the **attractive nuisance principle**. Children are considered too young to be responsible for their own actions. They are, however, attracted to certain properties, such as fruit trees and swimming pools. Owners of attractive nuisances are expected to exercise special caution to protect children from these attractions.

The owner of a sports car who prefers to "run through the gears" on the open road is subject to more liabilities than the person who drives a family-oriented compact. A person with a large farm who invites weekend guests for hunting expeditions on his or her property is in a higher risk class than a studious person who resides in an apartment. The point is that risks associated with using or owning property should be fully identified.

The second step is to identify liabilities associated with your activities. These liabilities can arise from personal or professional activities. A surgeon who amputates the wrong leg is professionally liable for his or her actions. The same surgeon is personally liable if he or she hits someone on the golf course with a golf ball.

Personal liability risks may arise from a person's activities and from a person's attitude toward those activities. A weekend motocross race driver will incur certain risks because of the nature of the activity. A reckless person in the same situation will incur additional risks because of his or her attitude. You are the best person to determine which of your own activities create risk.

Liability Risk Evaluation

Liability awards reduce assets. A large award can easily wipe out all assets. A very large award may not only wipe out assets but also place a claim on future earnings. It is difficult to estimate the amount of liability that a person should carry. Courts and juries have become increasingly liberal in awarding large sums of money, and it is not rare for awards to run into the millions of dollars.

A couple of methods can be used to estimate the amount of liability exposure. One is to get a feeling for what the courts are currently awarding in tort cases. A lawyer may be helpful in estimating the size of recent awards. A car driver, for example, may be held liable for killing or maiming another person, and the accident victim or his or her estate is awarded $500,000. Because the possibility of such an accident faces a driver, he or she may decide that his or her liability exposure is around $500,000.

A second way of determining liability exposure is to consider the maximum amount of assets and earnings at risk. At worst, an award could cover net worth plus all future earnings. For example, net worth of the

car driver mentioned above is $30,000, and he or she expects to earn, on the average, $20,000 per year for the next 30 years. This person's total liability exposure is $30,000 + ($20,000 × 30) = $630,000.

Most people would consider their liability exposure to be no less than the typical liability awards and no more than their net worth and future earnings combined. By this standard, in the situation just discussed, the person's liability exposure is between $500,000 and $630,000.

Choosing a Strategy

As mentioned previously, risk can be avoided, controlled, retained, and transferred. Some people avoid risk by not owning assets or by not engaging in certain activities. Taking public transportation and not owning a car can eliminate the liability risks associated with car ownership. However, avoidance of ownership and participation in certain activities is not suitable for many people. More viable is the alternative of controlling risk.

Common sense is the best guide in controlling risks. Shoveling sidewalks after a snowfall reduces the chances of a negligence suit. A backyard swimming pool should be fenced to keep out small children. Warning signs should be posted to warn strangers of an aggressive dog on the property. Careful driving and attention to traffic signs and laws can also reduce liability risks.

Risk retention generally is not advisable. The chances of incurring a large liability are small. However, if one does occur, it can adversely affect your present and future life style. Risk should be retained only if it cannot be transferred. The best method of transferring liability risk is through insurance, which is discussed in the next two sections.

Spot Quiz • Managing Liability Risks

1. A person is negligent when she or he does not exercise reasonable care in the use of assets. T _____ F _____

2. Contract law can be related to absolute liability risks. T _____ F _____

3. Liability risks should not be retained. T _____ F _____

(Answers on page 399)

COMPREHENSIVE LIABILITY INSURANCE

Comprehensive liability insurance refers to general as well as umbrella insurance. Section I of the homeowners' insurance policy is general liability insurance. Both types of insurance coverages are discussed here.

General Liability Insurance

General liability insurance covers a wide variety of situations. **Section II** of the homeowners' insurance policy provides general liability insurance. The same coverage is available by itself and is called **comprehensive personal liability coverage**. This section will contain a discussion of Section II.

All homeowners' policies, such as HO-1, HO-2, and HO-3, have the same limits on liability coverages. Therefore, this discussion will not refer to any specific type of policy. Section II of the homeowners' policy has five major sections. **Coverage E** covers personal liability. Damages or injuries caused by the insured person are covered by this section. The standard limit is $100,000, but the limit generally can be increased with the payment of an extra premium.

Coverage F provides medical payments to others. Benefits are for persons other than the insured. The usual amount of coverage is $500, but it can be increased.

The third subsection, titled **Exclusions**, explains what is excluded. Basically, business-related liabilities are excluded, as are intentional damages or injuries caused by the insured person. Aircraft, cars, and boats are also excluded.

The fourth section lists **additional coverages**. First aid expenses are covered. Property damage by an adult insured up to $500 is covered as long as it is unintentional. Certain expenses related to liability claims are also covered. The last section, titled **Conditions**, explains the procedure for reporting an accident or incident.

The claim limits for general liability insurance require neither deductibles nor coinsurance. In general, additional coverage is available at a modest cost and should be purchased. Cars are not covered under general liability insurance. Car insurance is available separately and is discussed in the next section.

Umbrella Insurance

Umbrella insurance policies are designed to provide coverage beyond what is covered by other policies. They provide coverage for limits ranging from $1 million to $5 million. Umbrella policies extend general liability coverage as well as provide coverage for libel and slander. Umbrella policies require the insured person to carry certain levels of coverage on car and comprehensive liability insurance. These requirements vary from state to state. A check with your insurance agent will indicate what the requirements are in your

state. The cost for an umbrella policy tends to be low, around $70 per year. Many people are in a financial situation that justifies the purchase of an umbrella policy. (See "How Big an Umbrella?" below.)

Spot Quiz • Comprehensive Liability Insurance

1. HO-3 has better liability insurance coverage than HO-1.

    T _____   F _____

2. An umbrella policy provides coverage that is above and beyond that provided by auto and comprehensive liability insurance policies.

    T _____   F _____

(Answers on page 399)

How Big an Umbrella?

Danger lurks everywhere—inside your house, on the driveway, in your swimming pool, even inside the jaws of your dog. No, we aren't talking about an attack by a swarm of killer bacteria. We are talking about the liabilities created by accidents in your house and on your property, car accidents, dog bites, and so on. Multi-million-dollar judgments in liability cases, while not everyday occurrences, make the newspaper headlines often enough to make most people stop and think about liability coverage.

Many people argue in favor of taking out the maximum amount of umbrella insurance available. Even the National Insurance Consumers Organization, which is generally very critical of a variety of insurance coverages available to consumers, states that umbrella insurance is one of two types of insurance—the other being disability—that consumers should have.

Lawsuits are becoming more common, and juries are willing to grant increasingly large liability awards. Thus, umbrella insurance makes much more sense than it used to. One way to pay for umbrella insurance without increasing your total insurance costs is to increase the deductibles on your homeowners' and automobile insurance policies and to drop some unnecessary coverage. Increasing collision deductibles, for example, might expose you to minor claims but would free up the money to buy insurance that would safeguard against really big losses.

Automobile insurance

Automobile ownership creates both property and liability risks. The property risks are usually reasonably manageable. For example, an owner who completely demolishes his or her car will suffer a loss of perhaps a few thousand dollars if no insurance is carried. In the case of a used, older car, the loss would be much smaller, a few hundred dollars perhaps. However, the *liability* risks associated with car ownership can be substantial. For example, a motorist is responsible for causing an accident in which two or three people are killed. Under the tort law system, the responsible motorist could be held liable for millions of dollars. The size of the liability risk thus demonstrates the desirability of buying auto insurance.

If the motorist owns the car outright, then she or he can best decide how to manage the property risk. However, if the car is being financed and is being used as security for a loan, then the lender has a vested interest in seeing that the property risk is adequately covered by insurance. Finally, a number of states require motorists to carry a minimum amount of liability insurance. For these reasons, auto insurance is important for most consumers.

There is a variety of auto insurance policies. The **Family Auto Policy (FAP)** and the **Personal Auto Policy (PAP)** are limited strictly to personal cars. The **Basic Auto Policy (BAP)** provides coverage of both personal and business vehicles. The policies differ in what they emphasize in the coverages provided. In this section, we will look at some basic types of coverages provided in auto insurance policies.

Auto Insurance Coverages

Unlike homeowners' policies, auto insurance policies do not carry the same features from one insurance company to another. The basic type of coverage remains the same, but minor points in coverage and exclusions vary. The basic auto insurance policy can be divided into three parts, as shown in Figure 12.1. The liability part refers to bodily injury and property damage caused to others. The second part covers the insured when he or she is hit by an uninsured motorist who is at fault. The third part provides no-fault coverage. That is, the insurance company pays without trying to establish liability. These coverages are discussed in greater detail in the sections that follow.

Declarations Page

The declarations page of the auto insurance policy shows the name of the insured person, the policy number, and the policy period. The vehicle

Figure 12.1 Automobile Insurance Coverages

Type of Coverage	What Is Covered				
	Insured Car			Other Car	
	Car	Driver	Passengers	Property	Occupants
Liability					
Bodily injury			X		X
Property damage				X	
Uninsured Motorist					
Bodily injury		X	X		
No-fault					
Collision	X				
Comprehensive	X				
Medical payments		X	X		

covered is described, and the amount of the premium paid is listed. The coverages provided and the limits of liability of coverages are also mentioned.

Liability Coverages

Liability coverages provide protection from risks of causing bodily injury and property damage to others.

The Coverage. Liability coverages apply to the insured person, the spouse, and his or her immediate relatives living at home. Also covered are other drivers who drive the insured person's car with permission. Finally, coverage is extended to the use of cars belonging to others as long as the car owner has given permission for use of the car.

The vehicle described on the declarations page is covered, and some other vehicles are covered as well. For example, if the covered vehicle is being repaired or serviced, a substitute car will be covered. Newly purchased cars are also covered, but generally for no longer than 30 days.

In addition to the liability limits discussed below, the insurance company will also pay for legal expenses related to the defense of the insured and other covered persons. The cost of the defense is in addition to the liability limits.

Liability Limits.   Maximum and minimum liability limits vary from state to state. Typically, bodily injury limits are stated on a per-person and a per-accident basis. The property damage limit is stated on a per-accident basis. A policy might show that liability limits are $100,000/$300,000/$50,000. The $100,000 is the bodily injury limit per person. Thus, if a person is killed or injured in an accident, the insurance company will be willing to pay up to $100,000 to cover the insured person's liability. The $300,000 is the bodily injury limit per accident. If the insured person is at fault in an accident that injures four people, the insurance company will pay up to $300,000 to the injured people but no more than $100,000 to any one person.

The $50,000 property damage limit applies to each accident. The insured person's vehicle is not covered under this liability coverage. Only the property of others is covered. The coverage applies not just to other vehicles but to all types of properties. Covered are such items as bicycles, street signs, cars, and buildings. Liability coverages are normally abbreviated. Thus, $100,000/$300,000/$50,000 is generally mentioned as 100/300/50.

Uninsured Motorist Coverage

Bodily injury caused to the insured person and to passengers in his or her car by an uninsured motorist at fault or by a hit and run driver are covered by this coverage. The minimum coverage required varies from state to state. The coverage applies only to bodily injury and not to property damages. The liability limits are stated on a per-person and per-accident basis. Thus, limits of $15,000/$30,000 (or 15/30) mean that the insurance will pay up to $15,000 per person and up to $30,000 per accident.

No-Fault Coverages

No-fault coverage provides payment of benefits without regard to who is responsible for the loss. Often the term *no-fault insurance* is used in a narrow sense to describe a special type of automobile liability coverage. But many forms of insurance provide no-fault coverage. The most common no-fault coverages of automobile insurance are discussed below.

Collision.   Collision coverage applies to damage to the insured person's car. The damage may have been caused by an accident with another car, by the car overturning, by the car running into a lamppost or a building, or by the car getting hit while it was parked in a garage. **Collision insurance** will cover the car, whatever the reason for the damage. It will even provide coverage when the other driver is at fault. Here, the insurance company may go ahead and pay under collision coverage and then try to sue the other driver to recover its losses. The amount of coverage is equal to the lesser of the current wholesale value of the insured vehicle, or the cost of repair, less any deductible.

Comprehensive.   **Comprehensive property coverage** covers a variety of perils, such as glass breakage and losses caused by fire, theft, hail, water, flood, vandalism, and riot. Also covered are losses caused by accidents with birds and animals. Keep in mind that theft coverage applies fully to the vehicle but only partially to items stored in the vehicle. Thus, for example, luggage stored in a car would be only partially covered by comprehensive insurance. The coverage limits are the same as for collision insurance.

Medical Payments.   The coverage pays for all reasonable medical expenses caused by an accident. Surgical, medical, X-ray, dental, ambulance, hospital, nursing, funeral, and other related expenses are covered. The coverage applies to the insured person, the spouse, relatives living at home, and other passengers in the insured car. The insured person, spouse, and relatives are also covered if they are struck as pedestrians by another vehicle. The liability limits are stated on a per-person basis.

In addition to the above coverages, insurance companies provide certain minor coverages for such conveniences as car rental expense and emergency road service. The cost is generally low, and most car drivers prefer to include these coverages.

General Conditions and Exclusions

Insurance coverage applies only in the United States and its territories and in Canada. Some coverages also apply in Mexico within 50 miles of the U.S.–Mexican border. The insurance company may choose not to renew a policy at its anniversary date. The insurance company may cancel a policy if premiums are not paid when due or if the driver's license of the insured person, spouse, or a relative living at home is suspended or revoked.

Business use of vehicles is excluded for coverage purposes. Liability coverage does not apply to intentionally caused losses. Vehicles with less than four wheels (for example, motorcycles and all-terrain vehicles) are also excluded from coverage. Finally, normal wear and tear is excluded from collision and comprehensive coverage.

Spot Quiz • Automobile Insurance

1. Liability coverage will pay for damage to the insured person's car.

    T _____   F _____

2. Uninsured motorist coverage is similar to liability coverage carried by the other driver.

    T _____   F _____

3. Collision insurance loss payments are based on replacement cost.

    T _____   F _____

(Answers on page 399)

MANAGING AUTOMOBILE INSURANCE

In this section, we will consider how to manage coverages, how insurance rates are determined, how to buy insurance, and how to handle claims. The last section covers no-fault insurance. (See "How Do You Spend Your Auto Insurance Dollars?" on page 389.)

Managing Coverages

The liability coverage portion of an insurance policy is the most important part of the policy. Risks with loss of property are limited—they cannot exceed the actual cash value or replacement cost of the property. Liability, on the other hand, is open-ended, and potential losses from liabilities can be substantial. An accident in which three or four people are seriously injured can result in judgments that run into hundreds of thousands of dollars. For this reason, high levels of liability coverage should be purchased.

Second, insurance companies pay for the cost of legal defense. If the liability coverage amount is low, the insurance company may choose to go ahead and pay the liability limits and not bother with going to court. In this case the insured person will be alone in his or her legal defense. This is another reason for carrying high coverages.

The premium costs for 100/300 bodily injury coverage are somewhat higher than for, say, 25/75 coverage, but the additional cost of premiums is well worth the additional coverage provided.

How Do You Spend Your Auto Insurance Dollars?

Some of us with older cars may choose not to buy collision or comprehensive insurance. Those with new or fairly new cars may buy a lot of different types of insurance for their cars. In general, based on figures compiled by Allstate Insurance, the average American car insurance buyer spends insurance dollars as follows:

Insurance	Amount	
Liability		
Bodily injury	28%	
Property damage	16%	44%
Uninsured Motorist		
Bodily injury	5%	5%
No-fault		
Collision	27%	
Comprehensive	18%	
Medical payments	4%	
Towing	2%	51%

These percentages indicate that the largest portion of the insurance premium is spent on no-fault insurance. Currently, the accepted practice is to buy insurance with $100 deductible collision and no deductible comprehensive. Risk could probably be better managed by opting for larger deductibles—that is, $500 on collision and a $50 or $100 deductible on comprehensive.

Property damage coverage should be kept high also. Running into another car may easily cost $15,000 in damages. Running into a building may be substantially more expensive. Again, the cost of $25,000 or $50,000 coverage is reasonable when you take into consideration the amount of coverage provided. In general, most car owners should give serious consideration to carrying liability coverage in the range of 100/300/50. Anything less will save a few dollars in premiums but will substantially increase the risk from retention.

Uninsured motorist coverage is very cheap. Five dollars per year may provide 10/20 or 15/30 coverage. A reasonable level to carry for this coverage is 15/30.

Collision coverage is expensive, but higher deductible levels lower premiums sharply. For example, going from a $100 to a $200 deductible will lower premium costs by about 20 to 25 percent. Most people can easily

absorb the higher deductible. Generally, a $200 deductible is recommended. If the car is old and not being financed, serious consideration should be given to dropping collision coverage. It is difficult to justify collision coverage for a car that is more than five years old.

Costs of comprehensive coverage can also be controlled by using deductibles. Whereas collision risks can be controlled with careful driving, comprehensive risks are considered more closely related to chance events. Thus, comprehensive coverage should be carried even when collision coverage is not justified.

If people riding with the insured person are not adequately covered by health insurance, then medical payments coverage is desirable. The cost for this coverage is reasonable, perhaps around $10 per year for coverage of $5,000 per person. This coverage should be carried even if it is not required.

Buying Automobile Insurance

Insurance rates vary based on a number of factors. Additionally, rates vary from company to company. Factors that affect rates are discussed here. This section also offers guidelines for buying insurance.

Factors Affecting Auto Insurance Rates. A variety of factors affect auto insurance rates. The *type of car* covered has a big impact on rates. Rates on high-performance cars are substantially higher than rates on compact cars. Using the car for commuting to and from work will increase rates as well.

The *driving record* of the car owner affects auto insurance rates. Safe drivers pay lower rates than more risky drivers. A speeding ticket may increase insurance rates by 10 percent for three years. A safe, accident-free driving record goes a long way toward keeping rates low.

"You're a very fortunate man, sir! You were hit by one of the new down-sized cars."

Source: *Changing Times,* July 1979, p. 38.

Rates also vary from place to place. For example, car owners in Boston will pay about four times more for car insurance than people living in small rural towns. Rates for male drivers under age 25 are considerably higher than for people in other age brackets.

Some of the factors affecting rates cannot be controlled. For example, we cannot control our ages. Sometimes it is difficult to control the place of residence. However, all of us can control the type of car we drive and our driving record. Most people can easily meet their transportation needs by driving a subcompact or compact. (As discussed in Chapter 10, a small car is also less expensive to purchase and operate.) Similarly, careful, defensive driving will result in a safe driving record.

Shopping for Insurance. Many insurance companies offer discounts for different risk groups. For example, many companies offer a *two-car discount*. That is, if the car owner has two or more cars, then the premiums are discounted by 5 to 10 percent. If a young, covered driver has taken a *driver's education* course, the insurance company may give a 10 percent discount. Some companies give discounts to *academically superior* students because it has been shown that they are safer drivers than others in their age group. You should check with a number of insurance agents to find out the types of discounts available. These discounts then can be applied to your personal situation. (See "Is Bigger Better?" below.)

Is Bigger Better?

Almost every year consumer magazines, such as *Consumer Reports*, and government agencies, such as the New York State Department of Insurance, compile information from consumer surveys and complaints to judge how satisfied consumers are with their insurance companies.

In August 1985, *Consumer Reports* published the findings of its survey of 218,000 consumers on homeowners' insurance. The survey indicated that theft was the most common loss. The average claim was $650, and the average settlement was $500. On the average, claimants received 89 cents on each dollar of loss suffered. About one out of every ten claimants felt that the settlement was not fair. Those with complete or almost complete home damage were less satisfied than those with partial damage. Those claimants who had replacement cost coverage were more satisfied than those who did not.

With regard to satisfaction with insurance companies, some of the largest insurance companies had the most satisfied claimants. However, some other large insurance companies had low ratings on providing claimant satisfaction. Thus, buying insurance from the largest companies in itself does not guarantee a high degree of satisfaction when claims are filed.

Even without taking discounts into consideration, insurance rates can vary sharply from company to company. One reason is that at times different companies try to appeal to different risk groups. Thus, they charge lower premiums to preferred risk groups. Second, some insurance companies are better at managing their businesses than others. Better-managed companies can pass on their cost savings to their clients in the form of lower premiums. It is thus worthwhile to shop around for lower rates.

Finally, some insurance companies are reluctant to settle claims. Check with the insurance department in your state, which logs complaints against insurance companies, and try to avoid companies with high levels of complaints.

For a variety of reasons, some drivers are higher risks than others. They are involved in proportionally more accidents, and they commit more traffic violations. Insurance companies do not want to insure these drivers, but such drivers can buy minimum coverage through state-required **assigned-risk pools**. A driver in an assigned-risk pool will have to pay relatively high insurance premiums.

Handling Claims

Certain guidelines should be followed if you become involved in an accident. By following these guidelines, you will help your insurance company when the time comes to settle your claim.

At the Accident Scene

1. Do not discuss the accident with the other party involved.
2. Do not admit responsibility for the accident.
3. Do not discuss the type of insurance coverage you carry.
4. Obtain the name, address, and driver's license number of the other driver.
5. Jot down the make, model, description, and license plate number of the other car.
6. Give the same information to the other driver.
7. Take down the names and addresses of any passengers and witnesses.
8. If police come, write down their names, badge numbers, and station location.
9. Seek medical attention for anyone who has been injured. All states require that any accidents resulting in injury or death be reported to police.
10. File a police report if the property damage exceeds the limit for your state. (For example, the limit is $200 in Vermont, $100 in Maryland, $250 in Arkansas, $400 in Utah, and $500 in California.)

After the Accident

11. Obtain a copy of the police report and file a report with the state if necessary.

12. Notify your insurance agent about the accident. At this point, your agent will tell you how to proceed.

If you are considered to be at fault, your insurance company will negotiate a settlement with the other driver. If you are not at fault, a claims adjuster for the other company will probably contact you. The **claims adjuster** is responsible for settling a claim quickly. He or she works for the other company and is interested in obtaining the best settlement for the other company. Give the claims adjuster the same information that you would give a police officer at the accident scene. Do not discuss the accident itself. Do not provide your personal medical history. In no case should you sign a statement. If the accident results in injuries that require medical treatment, then you should meet with a lawyer to obtain advice on negotiating a settlement.

After an analysis, the claims adjuster will offer a settlement. This settlement includes payment for property damage, bodily injury, and pain and suffering. The payment for pain and suffering is normally three times the medical expenses. Thus, an accident involving $3,000 in property damage and $4,000 in bodily injury may call for a settlement of $3,000 + $4,000 + (3 × $4,000) = $19,000. If the settlement does not appear to be fair, let the insurance company know that a lawyer will be retained to handle the case. Normally, this will be sufficient to bring forth a fair settlement. However, at times it will be necessary to hire a lawyer. A lawyer will normally charge one-third of the settlement amount as his or her fee for handling the case.

No-Fault Insurance

A significant portion of insurance premiums pays for administrative and claim settlement costs. To reduce these costs and thus insurance premiums, a number of states have adopted no-fault insurance. **No-fault insurance** requires that drivers involved in accidents be paid by their own insurance companies, irrespective of who is to blame for the accident. Basically, no-fault insurance extends no-fault coverage, discussed previously, to liability coverage.

No-fault coverage has become very popular because it is considered less wasteful and more equitable than the tort liability system. However, the Association of Trial Lawyers of America is strongly opposed to no-fault insurance. They believe that no-fault insurance infringes on the right to sue for just compensation. Many other groups, especially those that are consumer-oriented, are in favor of no-fault insurance.

Although coverage varies from state to state, the major components of no-fault insurance are as follows. The insured person's insurance company must pay for the insured person's medical expenses and loss of wages. Pain and suffering claims are not allowed unless the accident results

in death or serious injury. Liability lawsuits are not allowed unless expenses exceed a certain limit.

Massachusetts was the first state to adopt no-fault insurance, in 1970. Since then almost a third of the states have adopted it. Consumers are usually more interested in a quick and fair settlement than in determining who is at fault. In the future, more and more states will probably adopt no-fault insurance.

Spot Quiz • Managing Automobile Insurance

1. Liability coverage costs can usually be reduced by using deductibles.

   T _____   F _____

2. A safe driving record generally lowers insurance premium costs.

   T _____   F _____

3. No-fault insurance is based on the tort liability system.

   T _____   F _____

(Answers on page 399)

Summary

Property owned can be either physical or personal. Both types of property involve risk of ownership. Property risks are best managed by controlling them, retaining some, and transferring the rest through insurance.

Transfer of risk is accomplished by buying homeowners' insurance. A policy called HO-3 provides very good coverage at a reasonable cost. This and other policies cover the main house, detached structures, some personal property, and additional living expenses. A coinsurance clause in the policies is designed to get homeowners to buy insurance for no less than 80 percent of their homes' replacement cost. Additional insurance on personal property can be bought through floater policies.

Tort law deals with the situation when one person causes injury, damage, or monetary loss to another person. Tort law covers tort liabilities, which include negligence, absolute liability, and vicarious liability. Use or ownership of property together with the person's activities create tort

liabilities. Liability risk identification includes identifying property owned or used and activities engaged in that can cause injury or damage to someone else. Liability risks are difficult to evaluate. They can be considered to be equal to a person's net worth plus all future earnings. Risk transfer is suggested for handling liability risks.

Comprehensive liability insurance covers both general and umbrella insurances. The latter covers large losses. Its cost is nominal, and it is recommended for most consumers.

Automotive insurance coverage can be divided into three parts. Liability coverage applies to bodily injury and property damage. Uninsured motorist coverage needs no further description. No-fault coverage applies to property damage and medical expenses.

A motorist should carry high limits on liability coverage. The cost of collision and comprehensive coverage can be managed by using deductibles. A safe driving record and a small car will produce low insurance premiums. Also, people should shop around to find the best insurance rates.

Care should be exercised when accidents occur. The accident should be reported to the police and the insurance agent. A fair settlement should be sought, with the help of a lawyer if necessary. No-fault insurance, which pays claims without establishing liability, is becoming more and more popular.

Questions

1. Is the risk associated with personal property more difficult to identify than the risk associated with physical property? Explain your answer.

2. Explain the difference between replacement cost and actual cash value. Which is better? Why?

3. Briefly explain how the risks of home ownership can be controlled.

4. What is the purpose of the declarations page of a homeowners' insurance policy? What does it include?

5. Does HO-3 or HO-5 provide better insurance coverage? Briefly explain. Which is the better buy? Why?

6. What is HO-4? Briefly explain its features.

7. What is the coinsurance clause?

8. How does a floater policy work?

9. Is it desirable to have a policy that guarantees coverage for the coinsurance clause? Why or why not?

10. Is it wise to have two insurance policies covering the same property? Explain your answer.

11. What is tort law? Give two examples of where tort law would apply.

12. Briefly explain the different types of tort liabilities.

13. What is an "attractive nuisance"? Give three examples of this concept.

14. Briefly explain two procedures that could be followed to evaluate liability risks.

15. Should liability risks be retained? Why or why not?

16. Briefly explain what general liability insurance is and what it covers.

17. How does umbrella insurance work? Would you suggest that a middle-income worker buy it? Explain your answer.

18. Briefly explain the three different types of coverage available in an auto insurance policy.

19. What is the basic difference, if any, between property damage and collision coverage?

20. Why would a driver want to carry uninsured motorist coverage if he or she is already covered for medical expenses?

21. Explain why high limits are desirable for liability coverage.

22. What factors affect auto insurance rates?

23. Explain some discounts that are available to auto insurance buyers.

24. Briefly explain what a driver should do at the scene of an accident.

25. What does a claims adjuster do? Explain how to negotiate a claims settlement from the other insurance company.

26. What is meant by no-fault insurance? How does it work?

Case Problems

1. The Wujeks have a color television set that is eight years old. Its original cost was $600, and its useful life is considered to be ten years. Replacing that television now would cost $800. Calculate the actual cash value for the television. Would the Wujeks be better off with a policy that provided replacement cost coverage? Explain your answer.

2. The Ansanas have a reasonably large collection of signed prints by Calder and Chagall, first edition collector's plates, a limited edition bronze statue by Remington, first edition novels by Faulkner, and African artifacts. They have relied on their HO-3 policy to provide insurance for their collections. What advice do you have for them?

3. The Adams have a $120,000 home on which they carry $80,000 in insurance coverage. How much would the insurance company pay if the Adams were to suffer losses of (a) $60,000; (b) $80,000, (c) $100,000? What advice do you have for the Adams?

4. Raymond and Vinnie Wu are carrying $40,000 in insurance coverage on their home. A home very similar to theirs and less than a block away recently sold for $80,000. They are concerned that they may not have adequate coverage on their home. Their insurance agent has indicated that she could appraise their property and then adjust the amount of coverage so that the policy would qualify for inclusion of the guaranteed coinsurance clause. The Wus have estimated that the guaranteed coinsurance clause would increase their premiums by about 3 percent. What advice do you have for the Wus?

5. Roy Greene is 22 years old and a recent college graduate. He has just landed his first job in Chicago. He is planning to move out of his parents' home and into an apartment. He has located a reasonably priced apartment close to work. However, the other tenants appear to be in their thirties. Roy would prefer to move out to the suburbs and live in a singles apartment complex. This would require either a 25-mile one-way drive or a 5-mile drive and a train ride daily. He has also identified a one-year old TransAm that is quite reasonably priced. From an insurance viewpoint, what advice do you have for Roy? (You should discuss both renters' and auto insurance.)

6. Nancy Guilfoyle has a six-year-old car on which she is carrying the following coverages:
   Liability, 25/75/15
   Uninsured motorist, 5/10
   Collision, $100 deductible
   Comprehensive, no deductible
   Medical payments, $5,000

   Nancy is 42 years old and is the single parent of a 12-year-old boy. She works as a data processing supervisor for a public utility company. In recent months, she has received two tickets for speeding violations. Her insurance agent has told her that her premium will go up by 15 percent at the next policy anniversary. What advice do you have for Nancy in terms of managing her auto insurance?

Bibliography

"Taking Coverage." *Changing Times* (June 1985): 75–79.

"Replacement Cost Insurance for Your Household Goods." *Changing Times* (August 1980): 16–17.

"Car Insurance: Picking the Right Policy." *Changing Times* (February 1987): 62.

"Homeowners' Insurance." *Consumer Reports* (August 1985): 473–482.

"You May Already Be Insured for That." *Money* (November 1978): 110–112.

"Insurance You Don't Need." *Money* (July 1979): 71–72.

"In Quest of the Burglarproof Buggy." *Money* (February 1987): 171–181.

Answers to Spot Quizzes

Managing Home Ownership Risks (page 369)

1. F (Items such as jewelry and diamonds may be more expensive than physical property.)

2. T (These two factors are inversely related to each other.)

3. T (Silverware, for example, depreciates very little over time.)

Homeowners' Insurance (page 378)

1. F (Certain personal property, such as furs, are not fully covered.)

2. T (HO-5 is a more comprehensive policy.)

3. F (A coinsurance ratio greater than one means that the coinsurance clause has been met.)

4. F (A floater policy covers only the properties listed.)

Managing Liability Risks (page 381)

1. T (Lack of reasonable care is negligence.)

2. F (Tort law is related to absolute liability risks.)

3. T (It can result in large losses of assets.)

Comprehensive Liability Insurance (page 383)

1. F (Both have the same coverage.)

2. T (That is the purpose of the umbrella policy.)

Automobile Insurance (page 388)

1. F (Liability coverage does not apply to the insured person's car.)

2. T (It works the same way.)

3. F (They are based on wholesale value or on the cost of repairs.)

Managing Automobile Insurance (page 394)

1. F (Deductibles are not usually available on liability coverage.)

2. T (Safe driving is rewarded with lower rates.)

3. F (Liability does not have to be proven to collect under no-fault insurance.)

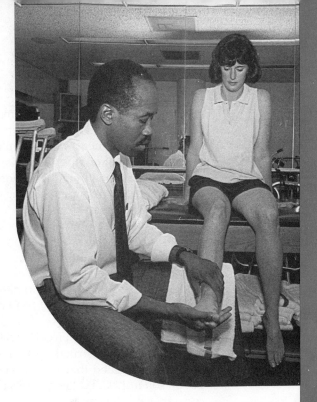

Chapter 13

Health Insurance

Objectives

After reading this chapter, you will be able to:

- Identify and evaluate health risks.
- Explain major types of health insurance policies.
- Describe procedures for managing health insurance costs.
- Explain various health insurance plans.
- State the procedures for buying disability insurance.

Members of a fraternal organization received a mail solicitation for health insurance. The sales pitch, by a major insurance company, was simple: Insure with us for hospital benefits, and we will pay directly to you $100 per day. This payment would be made irrespective of any other insurance carried. Simple enough. A good deal? Maybe yes, maybe no. It would depend on certain qualifying conditions on the policy. For example, the $100 maximum benefit requires meeting certain medical standards. Otherwise, the plan pays a maximum of $50 a day. At age 65, the daily benefits are reduced sharply. Any medical condition that had been treated in the 12 months before the insurance is bought is not covered for 12 more months.[1]

After knowing all of these qualifying conditions, it becomes obvious why this health insurance policy would not be a good deal. Health insurance and health care is a complex topic that involves big money. In the United States in 1990, about $640 billion will be spent on health-related expenses. In the past, these expenses have increased at a rate faster than the rate of inflation. When costs related to doctors, drugs, hospitals, nursing homes, and construction of medical facilities are taken into consideration, it is estimated that health-related spending will equal about $2,780 per person in 1990. Funding comes from government, insurance, and direct consumer expenditures.

The magnitude of the dollars being spent on health care requires not only an understanding of health risks but also a comprehensive plan for managing health care dollars.

Managing health risks

Chapter 11 identified three types of risks: property, liability, and personal. Personal risks are associated with premature death, sickness, and disability. The risk situations for premature death are covered in Chapter 14. In this chapter, we will cover risks associated with sickness and disability.

Health Risks

A **health risk** is said to exist when a person faces the chance of losing assets and income because of sickness or disability. A person who becomes sick and cannot work will suffer a loss of income. Treatment of the sickness will require spending money, which will decrease assets. Similarly, disabilities result in loss of both income and assets. Illnesses and disabilities can be due to natural causes, accidents, or the actions of others. In most cases, though, irrespective of what caused the sickness or disability, the

---

1. "Health Insurance Policies," *Changing Times* (December 1978): 6.

person affected ends up being responsible for the financial losses. For this reason, management of health risks takes on increased importance.

Health Risk Identification

Health risk losses are caused by nature, your own actions, and the actions of others. Many health problems occur because of natural causes. These sicknesses can cause temporary or permanent lack of ability to earn a living. Your own actions can cause health risk losses as well. For example, certain hobbies, such as motorcycling, rock climbing, and hang gliding, are associated with higher accident rates than, for example, swimming or tennis. Finally, other people may cause health risk losses. A motorist may hit a pedestrian. A thief may shoot a victim. A factory that has not been kept clean may cause lung ailments in its workers. Unsanitary conditions in a restaurant may lead to cases of food poisoning among customers.

The first step in health risk identification is to take for granted that you are exposed to all nature-caused ailments. The second step is to identify your own actions and life environment. If you engage in hazardous activities or work in a particularly hazardous environment, then higher health risks are implied. Third, you should understand your family health history. Can any health patterns in your family be identified? Fourth, you should evaluate how other people might affect your health risks. Car commuters, for example, may be exposed to greater health risk losses than train commuters. Finally, you should take into consideration your personal health history. If, for example, you are injury-prone, you might consider not only buying disability insurance but also an option to buy additional insurance without a new medical examination. The reason is that buying disability insurance requires a medical examination. If you do not pass the examination, you cannot buy additional insurance. If your health situation becomes worse, you may not be able to buy more insurance. But with the option, you can automatically buy a certain amount of additional insurance without a medical examination.

Health Risk Evaluation

Health risks are more similar to liability than to property risks. Maximum losses due to property risks can be easily established, but maximum losses due to health risks, like liability risks, are much more difficult to determine. Like liability risks, the maximum losses from health risks can easily equal your net worth and all future income. **Health risk losses** associated with sicknesses include expenses for doctors, dentists, nurses, drugs, surgery, hospitalization, X-rays, laboratory tests, and other related expenses. The average hospital stay varies from state to state but is between five and ten days. Unfortunately, protecting yourself from the costs of even a ten-day hospitalization is not enough. Hospital costs can mount very

quickly. Under the worst possible situation, you could be hospitalized for the rest of your life. For health insurance purposes, you should consider hospitalization because of sickness for a period of about one year as a reasonable evaluation of health risks. The costs for a hospitalization of this length can be substantial, running into thousands of dollars.

Disabilities can keep you from earning a living, and a severe disability could keep you from working for the rest of your life. Of course, certain expenses are reduced when you are not working. For instance, you would not incur commuting expenses. Nor would you have to pay income taxes, because you would receive no wages. With a disability, then, you could possibly live on an amount that is less than your wages. Based on your personal living and expenditure habits, this amount will probably be around 60 to 80 percent of your income. Therefore, losses due to disabilities should be considered to be potentially equal to about 60 to 80 percent of your future income.

Choosing a Strategy

Although you can avoid certain types of property and liability risks, there is no way to totally avoid health risks. You are always being exposed to sicknesses and disabilities from natural causes. Health risks can be controlled to some extent by not engaging in relatively more dangerous activities, and avoiding physical and psychological excesses can also help you lead a less stressful life, thereby reducing health risks.

Health risk losses can be very large. Therefore, total retention of these risks is not recommended. The last alternative is risk transfer. A variety of alternatives exist for transferring health risks, some of which are mandatory. For example, participation in workers' compensation and social security, which cover some health risk losses, is mandatory for many people. Other alternatives call for voluntary participation. Health and disability insurances fall into this category.

As we will see later in this chapter, an appropriate way of handling health risks is by combining retention and transfer. Retention is achieved by using deductibles, waiting periods, and maximum limits on insurance policies. Transfer, of course, is achieved by buying insurance policies to cover health risks.

Spot Quiz • Managing Health Risks

1. Health risk losses can result in partial loss of income.

                                              T _____   F _____

2. Health risk losses can be in excess of a person's assets and incomes.

                                              T _____   F _____

3. Small health risk losses can be retained.   T _____   F _____

(Answers on page 431)

Health Insurance

Occasionally, you hear people say that they can't afford to be sick. For most of us, this statement is more than a laughing matter. With 1988 average hospitalization costs estimated at around $550 to $620 per day, even a hospitalization of one week can seriously affect a person's savings. The costs of a serious ailment or a major surgery can easily wipe out a family's savings. Nobody can really afford to be sick without adequate health insurance, so a good health insurance policy is a must for everyone.

In this section we will look at different types of health insurance policies. Insurance policies, however, encompass a variety of payment plans. Therefore, we will look at payment plans before discussing different types of policies.

Payment Plans

A **payment plan** is the way in which an insurance company will pay on a claim. The three methods of payment are valued, indemnity or reimbursement, and service benefit.

Valued Plan.   Under the **valued plan**, the insurance company agrees to pay the insured a fixed sum of money if an insured event occurs. Thus, for example, if the insured is hospitalized, the insurance company may

"Exactly what is this complaint about your medical plan?"

Source: Reprinted from the *Saturday Evening Post* © 1979 the Curtis Publishing Company

pay him or her a flat sum of, say, $50 per day. The actual cost of hospitalization may vary from the amount of payment made by the insurance company.

Indemnity, or Reimbursement, Plan.   Under the **indemnity, or reimbursement, plan**, the insurance company agrees to reimburse the insured for up to a specified sum of money if an insured event occurs. For example, the insured may be covered for up to $130 per day for hospitalization. If actual hospitalization charges are $155 per day, the insurance company will pay $130 per day. However, if hospitalization charges are only $115 per day, this is the amount that the insurance company will pay.

Service Benefit Plan.   With the **service benefit plan**, the insurance company agrees to pay for medical services used by the insured. The actual cost of the services is not an issue. For example, an insurance company may pay for hospitalization. If the insured is hospitalized, his or her hospitalization bill is paid, whether the charges are $115 per day or $155 per day. The insurance pays for the services provided rather than paying a specified dollar amount for services provided. In general, during periods of steadily rising medical costs, service benefit plans provide the best type of coverage.

Types of Insurance Policies

There are two types of health insurance policies, basic and extended. Basic policies provide low levels of coverage for hospitalization, surgery, and other medical expenses. The concept of a basic policy is shown in Figure 13.1. Basic policies may or may not exclude the first few dollars on each claim. That is, some of them may have a small deductible. **Basic policies** are hospital expense insurance, surgical expense insurance, and medical expenses insurance.

The deductible amount shown in Figure 13.1 is generally small, around $25 to $100. This deductible is meant to discourage small claims and to reduce policy costs. The insurer or insurance company will pay up to the maximum policy coverage limit. Any medical expenses beyond this limit are the responsibility of the insured. For example, a person is hospitalized, and hospitalization expenses are $6,700. This person's hospitalization policy pays a maximum of $5,000 with a $100 deductible. In this situation, the insurance company pays $5,000, and the insured pays $1,700. If the insured had a $2,300 claim, the insurance company would pay $2,300 − $100 = $2,200.

Extended policies supplement basic policies. They have large deductibles and high maximum limits. They generally also require the insured to pay a portion of the medical expenses. Major medical and comprehensive insurance are the two types of extended policies. Figure 13.2 shows the concept of an extended policy.

Figure 13.1 Basic Health Insurance Policies

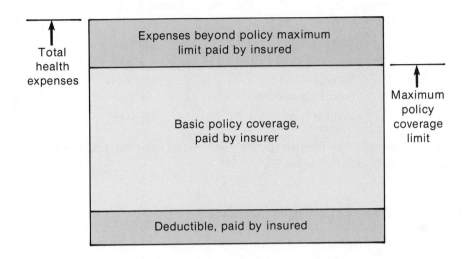

Figure 13.2 Extended Health Insurance Policies

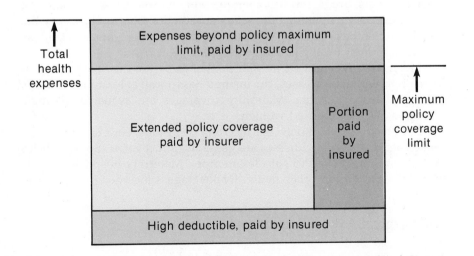

Suppose a person has a $20,500 claim on an extended policy. The policy has a $500 deductible, and the person is required to pay 20 percent of all expenses beyond the deductible. The insurer would figure its payment on the claim as follows:

Total claim	$20,500
Less deductible	500
Balance	$20,000
Insured pays 20%	4,000
Insurer pays	$16,000

In this example, the insurer would pay $16,000, and the insured would pay $20,500 − $16,000 = $4,500.

Hospital Expense Insurance

Hospital expense insurance pays for basic hospitalization expenses. The policy covers the insured, the spouse, unmarried children (the age limit varies from 18 to 23), and foster children living at home. The policy provides for room, food, nursing, and certain other hospitalization charges. Room and food coverage can be stated on a reimbursement or service benefit basis. Most policies impose a maximum limit on the number of days of hospitalization.

Nursing services are usually included if they are performed in the hospital. Private nursing services are generally available for an extra premium. Other hospitalization expenses include charges for X-rays, laboratory tests, drugs, physical therapy, and, in conjunction with surgical expense insurance, operating room and anesthetics. Some policies pay the full amount of these expenses. Others pay a certain percentage or impose a maximum limit on the coverage.

Maternity coverages are available either as part of the policy or for an extra premium. In both cases, the insured has to wait at least nine months before collecting benefits. Maternity coverages are available to single women as well as married women.

Most hospitalization policies list certain exclusions. For example, work-related accidents and sicknesses are generally not covered. Some policies exclude injuries related to suicide attempts. Maternity hospitalization is excluded unless appropriate maternity coverage is included in the policy.

Surgical Expense Insurance

Surgical expense insurance covers expenses related to surgical procedures. Coverage is generally on a reimbursement basis—that is, the policy specifies the maximum amount payable for a particular surgical procedure. The

policy is usually offered only in conjunction with hospital expense insurance. The policy covers surgery performed in a hospital and in a qualified doctor's office. The policy has certain exclusions. Work-related surgery, for example, is not covered.

Medical Expense Insurance

The coverage with **medical expense insurance** varies from policy to policy. The usual situation is that the policy will cover a portion of the charges related to a doctor's visit in a hospital. For example, the insured is hospitalized for ten days, and each day a physician checks his or her condition in the hospital. This policy will pay $5 to $10 for each daily visit by the physician. The policy generally has a maximum limit. Some policies partially pay for visits to a doctor's office. Still others pay for prescription drugs, eye examinations, and prescription eyeglasses.

Major Medical Insurance

Major medical (MM) insurance covers virtually all types of health expenses: hospitalization, room, surgery, anesthesia, recovery room, drugs, blood transfusions, artificial limbs, physical therapy, nursing care, laboratory tests, and so on. In other words, MM provides all the coverages available under hospital expense, surgical expense, and medical expenses insurance and then some.

MM differs from basic insurance in the level of coverage provided. Policy limits are generally no lower than $10,000. Quite often, the limits can be very substantial, occasionally up to $50,000 and sometimes even without limits.

One way the costs of MM policies are kept low is by using large deductibles. Typical MM policies have deductibles ranging from $500 to $1,000. Large deductibles eliminate small claims and the paperwork related to them. Another way costs of MM are kept low is by requiring the insured to pay a portion of the costs incurred. The portion paid by the insured varies from 10 to 25 percent. Some MM policies require that the insured pay his or her portion of the expenses only up to a limit. Beyond this limit, the insurer pays 100 percent of the expenses.

MM insurance coverage supplements coverage provided by basic insurance policies. That is, MM pays benefits after benefits from basic coverage have been exhausted. Table 13.1 shows how MM works. The insured incurs medical expenses of $18,900. Basic insurance coverage pays $4,400 of these expenses. The remaining balance of $18,900 − $4,400 = $14,500 is covered by MM. A $500 deductible is also applicable. The insured

Table 13.1 How Major Medical Insurance Works

Total hospitalization expenses	$18,900
Basic coverage pays	4,400
Expenses covered by MM	$14,500
MM deductible, paid by insured	500
Balance remaining	$14,000
100% over $10,000 paid by MM	4,000
80% of first $10,000 paid by MM	8,000
Amount paid by insured	$2,000
Total paid by insured ($500 + $2,000)	$2,500

has an MM policy that pays 80 percent of covered expenses for claims up to $10,000 and 100 percent of claims for amounts in excess of $10,000.

As Table 13.1 shows, deducting $500 from $14,500 leaves $14,000. MM pays all of the $4,000 in claims over $10,000. It pays .8 × $10,000 = $8,000 of the first $10,000 in claims. Altogether, MM pays $4,000 + $8,000 = $12,000. The insured pays $500 + $2,000 = $2,500.

Under the type of MM plan just discussed, the portion of MM-covered expenses paid by the insured declines as the amount of claim increases. For example, for the situation in Table 13.1, the insured pays $2,500/$14,500 = .172 (17.2 percent) of the claim. However, with a $40,500 claim, the insured would still pay only $2,500—$500 as the deductible and $2,000 for the 20 percent of the $10,000 claim. In this situation, the insured pays only $2,500/$40,500 = .062 (6.2 percent) of the total claim.

Comprehensive Medical Insurance

Comprehensive medical insurance combines basic insurance with major medical insurance. Features of this insurance coverage vary from insurer to insurer. Some insurers may have a small $25 to $100 deductible, whereas others may have no deductible. The maximum benefits vary from $10,000 to an unlimited amount. Finally, the portion of costs borne by the insured may vary from 0 to 25 percent. Comprehensive medical insurance is the most desirable form of health insurance available. It also tends to be the most expensive.

Spot Quiz • Health Insurance

1. The valued plan provides better coverage than the service benefit plan.
                                                    T _____   F _____

2. Hospital and surgical expense insurances need to be supplemented with
    MM coverage.   T _____   F _____

3. Benefits under comprehensive insurance are better than benefits under
    MM.   T _____   F _____

                                                    (Answers on page 431)

MANAGING HEALTH INSURANCE

Health insurance costs are affected by a variety of factors that generally
can be controlled by the insured. These factors as well as a discussion of
shopping for health insurance are covered in this section. (See "Pay If You
Play" on page 412.)

Managing Costs

Deductibles, coinsurance, maximum limits coverage exclusion, coverage
duplication, the waiting period, and renewability all affect the cost of health
insurance policies.

Deductibles.   Most health insurance policies contain a **deductible** that
varies from $25 to $100. The deductible allows insurers to eliminate coverage
for small claims. Also, the insurer handles less paperwork with deductibles.
Because deductibles require those who are insured to pay for a portion
of the medical expenses, it is generally believed that deductibles force insured people to control health risks better. Deductibles therefore reduce
health insurance costs. In general, the higher the deductible is, the lower
will be the cost of health insurance.

The way in which deductibles are computed varies from insurer to insurer. With some insurers, the deductible applies to all claims within a
specified time period, such as one year. All covered medical expenses are
accumulated, and the insurance begins to pay when the expenses exceed
the deductible. For example, a medical expense policy with a $30 deductible

Pay If You Play

It may only be a matter of time before people start paying health insurance premiums based on their life styles and behavior. Control Data Corporation, a major computer manufacturer, conducted a comprehensive, four-year study of 15,000 of its workers. The study showed that workers with certain life styles or behavior patterns had bigger medical bills than others. For example, health costs for obese workers were 11 percent higher than for nonobese workers. Similarly, those who did not use seat belts regularly spent 54 percent more days in the hospital than those who did use seat belts. Smokers who lit up one or more packs of cigarettes a day averaged 118 percent more in medical expenses than nonsmokers. Those who did not exercise sufficiently had medical claims that were twice those for people who exercised regularly.

Already, some state insurance regulatory agencies are considering regulations that would require insurers to take life styles and behavior patterns into consideration in setting insurance rates. Some insurance companies, such as Prudential Insurance of America, have already started to tie in group insurance rates to workers' habits and life styles. Some observers argue that these economic incentives may be sufficient to induce people to opt for healthier life styles. Others note that changes in health insurance occur slowly, and it will be quite a while before insurance premiums tied to life styles and behavior become the norm. It may be that you may not have to pay to play for the next few years.

may cover all prescription drug expenses during the year. The prescription expenses during the year are $12, $8, $8, $14, $7, and $9, and each one is for a separate illness. Total covered expenses during the year are $58, and the insurance pays $58 − $30 = $28.

Other policies apply the deductible on a per-sickness or per-incident basis. In the previous example, the insurance would not pay for any of the prescriptions because the cost of medication does not exceed $30 for any one illness.

Generally speaking, a larger deductible is recommended for people who consider their health conditions to be normal. Larger deductibles are important in reducing insurance costs.

Coinsurance. A common provision in health insurance policies is to require the insured to pay a portion of the expenses above the deductible. Typical plans call for the insurer to pay, say, 80 percent, and the insured to pay 20 percent of the costs. This sharing of costs is called **coinsurance** and is illustrated in Figure 13.2 on page 407.

Coinsurance provisions are designed to reduce insurance premiums. However, a large coinsured health insurance claim can adversely affect the insured's wealth. For example, let's assume that a person has MM with a $500 deductible and a 20 percent coinsurance clause. On a $100,500 claim, the insured would pay $500 + ($100,500 − $500) × .2 = $500 + $20,000 = $20,500. For most people, this sum of money would be quite large.

One major reason for insurance is to transfer the risk of very large losses. Coinsurance does not allow a person to do this effectively. As a result, health insurance coverage should not include a large coinsurance feature. That is, the coverage should pay for 100 percent of the claim above the deductible. Another alternative is to seek coverage in which coinsurance applies only to a portion of the claim. In other words, once expenses exceed a certain limit, the policy would pay 100 percent of expenses. Under this type of coverage, the insured's health-related expenses remain the same for any amount in excess of the coinsurance limits.

Maximum Limits.   **Maximum limits** specify the maximum amount of coverage available. With basic and MM insurances combined, or with comprehensive, the limits should be sufficiently high to provide adequate coverage for most illnesses. Typically, maximum limits of at least $100,000 are desirable.

Maximum limits are either stated on a time basis, such as one year, or on a per-illness basis. From the insured's viewpoint, limits based on a per-sickness basis provide better protection. To adequately allow for potentially large losses, it is recommended that health insurance coverage have relatively high limits.

Coverage Exclusions.   Virtually all health insurance policies contain certain types of **coverage exclusions**. These exclusions define what is not covered and place a limitation on what is covered. Many policies, for example, do not pay for routine health, eye, and dental examinations. Prescription eyeglasses may not be covered. Some policies exclude maternity expenses. Routine examinations, cosmetic and plastic surgery, oral surgery, and psychiatric care are also excluded fairly often.

Policies with many exclusions are cheaper than policies that provide more extensive coverage. Some coverage may not be important from a health maintenance viewpoint. For example, many people would not consider cosmetic surgery necessary in a good health insurance policy. On the other hand, given the day-to-day stresses of modern living, these same people might consider coverage of psychiatric care to be important. Basically, a policy that does not provide coverage that is considered desirable is not cheap enough because the insured is retaining certain health risks. Similarly, a policy providing coverage that is not needed can be considered expensive because premiums cover the costs of unnecessary coverages.

Coverage Duplication.   Most health insurance policies have a clause that requires coordination of policy benefits. This means that the insured cannot collect twice on a covered illness by **duplication of coverage**. For this reason, you should not carry multiple health insurance policies.

Waiting Period.   Insurance policies impose a **waiting period** on pre-existing medical conditions. For example, an existing bad back may not be covered until the policy has been in force one year. Similarly, maternity benefits are not payable until the policy has been in force for nine or ten months. The idea behind insurance is to cover the risks of an uncertain event occurring. However, when a medical condition is known, it is no longer an uncertain event. Insurance premiums are designed to reflect the chances of an uncertain event occurring. Waiting periods are an equitable way of preventing people from buying insurance to cover pre-existing conditions.

Renewability.   Some insurance contracts can be canceled at the insurer's option. These types of policies are not very desirable. Some policies are cancelable only if the insurer cancels all similar policies in the insured's state. Policies that can be **renewed** at the insured's option are much more desirable. They allow the insured to continue coverage on serious pre-existing sicknesses and conditions. On the other hand, if the insured has no serious conditions or sicknesses, then he or she has the option of shopping around for other, cheaper insurance programs. Policies that can be renewed by the insured are more expensive than policies that can be canceled by the insurer.

In this section we have looked at a number of features of insurance policies. Policies with desirable features, such as low deductibles, low co-insurance, high maximum limits, and renewability, are more expensive than policies with limited features. By carefully evaluating the desirability of each feature from a personal perspective, you can decide on the most suitable insurance policy for you and your family.

Buying Health Insurance

Major sources of health insurance are group insurance plans, Blue Cross/Blue Shield, private insurance companies, and health maintenance organizations (HMOs). The first three sources are discussed here. Because of their importance, HMOs are discussed in a separate section.

Group Insurance Plans.   **Group insurance plans** make insurance coverage available to group members. While "group" could refer to members of a union or social club, most often it applies to employees of the same employer. Most employers provide their employees with a group insurance plan. Some plans cover employees only, whereas others provide

coverage to employees and their families. The arrangements for sharing the insurance costs also vary. Some employers pay all insurance premiums, and other employers share these costs with their employees.

Group insurance is generally provided by Blue Cross/Blue Shield or a private insurance company. Only one master policy is issued to the employer. As a result, group insurance rates are generally lower than rates available to individuals or families. Most group insurance plans have an "open enrollment" period when even persons with preexisting conditions can join without medical examinations. These persons become eligible for benefits after a certain waiting period.

Generally, you should enroll in a group insurance plan if one is available, even if it requires making premium payments. The features of the insurance plan should be carefully evaluated. Any serious gaps in required and needed coverages should be handled by taking out additional supplementary insurance. (See "The COBRA Option" below.)

Blue Cross/Blue Shield. Blue Cross/Blue Shield (BC/BS) associations are the nation's largest providers of health insurance. The 111 BC/BS associations cover about 86 million persons nationally. These BC/BS associations receive in excess of $40 billion in insurance premiums every year. BC/BS associations are set up as nonprofit organizations, with the sole purpose of providing health insurance coverage for people. In the past, BC/BS associations have paid out about 98 cents in benefits for each dollar of premiums received.

Blue Cross (BC) provides hospital expense insurance. X-rays, laboratory fees, room, board, and so on, are covered under BC. Blue Shield (BS) provides surgical expense coverage and also pays for certain types of physicians' fees. BS coverage generally pays for usual, customary, and

The COBRA Option

You don't have to be Sly Stallone or Kojak to exercise your COBRA option. COBRA refers to the Comprehensive Omnibus Budget Reconciliation Act of 1986 and is the best buddy for someone leaving the employment of a reasonably large company. Prior to COBRA, people terminating employment at these companies had to worry about finding an alternative to the company-provided health plans. If someone had moderate or severe health problems, then finding health insurance was an impossible task. Now, COBRA requires employers with 20 or more employees to provide departing employees with the existing group health insurance for a maximum of 18 months. While the departing employee has to pay for the insurance, it gives him or her sufficient time to find a suitable replacement for the existing group health insurance benefits.

reasonable (UCR) charges. Most physicians are willing to accept BS-specified UCR fees as payment in full for their services. Those who do not accept BS fees ask their patients to pay the difference between their charges and UCR fees.

BC/BS plans are well regarded nationally. They accept people on a group as well as on an individual basis. It is worthwhile to explore health insurance with BC/BS before seeking coverage elsewhere.

Private Insurance Companies. Many private insurance companies provide health insurance plans. Some companies have excellent plans and reputations, whereas some do not have very desirable plans. Before buying insurance from a private company, you should evaluate the costs and plans of a number of different companies. First, the features of the insurance plan should be carefully evaluated. Some plans have such broad exclusions that the insurer is not really insuring very many health risks. For example, a policy that does not automatically cover newborn babies from birth should be avoided because it excludes birth defects. Each policy should be examined for features such as exclusions, preexisting conditions, waiting periods, renewability, maximum limits, and so on.

Even a good policy with desirable features may not be acceptable if its premiums are too high. One widely used measurement of the desirability of a policy is its loss ratio. The **loss ratio** is the ratio of benefits paid to premiums received. As mentioned previously, BC/BS has a loss ratio that is around 98 percent. Some private companies have loss ratios that are around 40 percent. This means that they are paying out only 40 cents in benefits for each dollar of premiums received. Other things being the same, a policy from a company with a higher loss ratio is more desirable than a policy from one with a lower loss ratio. Loss ratios can generally be obtained from the state insurance department.

Health Maintenance Organizations

A **health maintenance organization (HMO)** is a prepaid health insurance plan that provides comprehensive coverage for a fixed premium. HMOs have staff physicians and other medical personnel who work for a salary. HMOs either own a hospital or contract for delivery of hospital-related services. Most HMOs provide their members with unlimited access to their resources. Thus, a chronically sick patient can schedule a visit to a staff physician as often as needed. Most physician visits are either free or carry a nominal charge, called a **copayment**, of $2 to $5.

Under the traditional health care system, a person generally visits a physician only when he or she is sick. The focus is on curing sickness. The HMO, on the other hand, encourages its members to see physicians to prevent sickness. An HMO's focus is thus on maintaining health by preventing illness before it occurs. Perhaps because of this focus on sickness

prevention, HMO members, on the average, undergo surgery less often than persons covered by traditional health insurance plans.

Critics of HMOs frequently charge that because HMO physicians work for a salary, they do not have a strong enough incentive to provide patients with good medical care. By far and large, though, HMO physicians match private physicians in terms of training and experience.[2] There is no evidence to suggest that HMO physicians are not qualified or do not provide good medical care.

Another criticism often leveled against HMOs is that the selection of physicians available is not wide enough. This criticism does have merit. For example, in most cities, parents may be able to identify three or four pediatricians for their children. They may then check with friends and neighbors to select a suitable pediatrician. With an HMO, they may be limited to the services of the HMO's only pediatrician.

In a poll taken by a major U.S. corporation, 95 percent of its workers enrolled in an HMO plan were satisfied with the quality of care provided. Overall, HMOs provide health care benefits that are better than those provided by the traditional health insurance plans that utilize physicians in private practice.

Medicare

Among other benefits, the federal government's social security program offers retirement, survivor's, disability, and health insurance benefits to those who qualify. **Medicare**, as part of social security, provides health insurance to the categories of persons listed in Figure 13.3.

Figure 13.3 Persons Eligible for Medicare

Persons 65 years of age or older who are eligible for social security or railroad retirement benefits.

Persons who are eligible for social security disability benefits for at least 24 months.

Chronic kidney patients requiring dialysis or renal transplant, who are fully and currently insured or who are dependents of a fully and currently insured worker.

---

2. "Medical Care on a Fee Basis," *Money* (July 1978): 66.

The Medicare program has two parts. **Part A** is the basic hospital insurance program. Hospital benefits are provided for up to 90 days for each sickness. In addition, each eligible person has 60 "reserve days" of hospitalization coverage available. These reserve days are available only once. For example, if a Medicare beneficiary is hospitalized for 105 days, he or she is covered for 90 days under the basic insurance and uses up 15 of the 60 reserve days. The deductibles and benefits provided are summarized in Figure 13.4.

Figure 13.4 Part A, Medicare Basic Benefits

Coverage	Benefit Period and Deductible[a]	What Is Covered[b]
Hospital	Day 1–60: total expenses with a $492 deductible Day 61–90: total expenses with a $123 per-day deductible 60 reserve days: total expenses with a $246 per-day deductible	1. Semiprivate room 2. All meals 3. Nursing services 4. Special-care units, such as intensive care 5. Drugs 6. Blood transfusions 7. Lab tests 8. X-rays 9. Medical supplies, surgical dressings 10. Wheelchairs 11. Operating and recovery rooms 12. Physical therapy, speech therapy
Nursing facility	Day 1–100: total expenses with a $61.50 per-day deductible	1. Semiprivate room 2. All meals 3. Nursing services 4. Therapy 5. Drugs 6. Blood transfusions 7. Medical supplies 8. Wheelchairs
Home health care	100 home visits by nurse, therapist, etc.	1. Nursing services 2. Therapy

Figure 13.4 *(Continued)*

Hospice care	Two 90-day periods, one 30-day period	All except limited outpatient drugs.
Blood	All but first three pints	Blood.

Abstracted from *Your Medicare Handbook* (Baltimore, MD: U.S. Department of Health and Human Services).
[a]Deductibles are current as of January 1986.
[b]Certain conditions have to be met before coverage applies. Additionally, there are exclusions in all coverage categories.

Basic Medicare coverage also includes payments for nursing facilities and home health care. For all types of coverages, certain conditions must be met.

Part B of Medicare provides for medical insurance. Anyone who is eligible for Part A coverage can also obtain Part B coverage. Persons not eligible for Part A coverage can also obtain Part B coverage under certain conditions. Coverage provided under Part B is shown in Figure 13.5. A $75 deductible applies to all Part B claims. Thereafter, Medicare pays for 80 percent of all covered expenses. In January 1986, Part B coverage was available for $15.50 per month.

Figure 13.5 Part B, Medical Insurance

1. Doctor's services
2. Medical and surgical expenses
3. Therapy related to doctor's services
4. Supplies related to doctor's services
5. Laboratory fees
6. X-rays and other diagnostic tests
7. Outpatient hospital care
8. Home health care, unlimited visits
9. Drugs
10. Blood

Medicaid

Medicaid is a jointly funded and managed program of the state and federal governments designed to provide health care to those who cannot afford to pay for adequate health care themselves. Therefore, Medicaid coverages vary from state to state. Medicaid eligibility is based partially on income and asset requirements. Medicaid pays for a variety of services, such as hospitalization, laboratory tests, X-rays, and doctors' services. (See "Insurance You Don't Need" on page 421.)

Spot Quiz • Managing Health Insurance

1. Higher deductibles reduce insurance premiums.

   T _____   F _____

2. Coinsurance reduces insurance costs and therefore is always desirable.

   T _____   F _____

3. Group insurance plans are generally cheaper than individual insurance plans.   T _____   F _____

4. Medicare provides comprehensive insurance coverage for America's elderly.   T _____   F _____

(Answers on page 431)

DISABILITY INSURANCE

Disabilities can keep a person from working, resulting in loss of income and assets. Disabilities can be caused by accidents or sickness. The exact definition of disability varies from one insurance company to another and is discussed later in this section. Losses caused by disabilities can change a family's life style dramatically. Buying adequate protection against the effects of disabilities is a vital part of any risk management program.

Protection against losses caused by disabilities is secured by buying disability insurance. **Disability insurance** pays periodic (generally monthly) benefits when the insurer considers the insured to be disabled. How much disability insurance coverage to buy and how to buy it are the topics of this section.

Insurance You Don't Need

Some **"Medigap" policies.**   Americans over 65 cannot rely solely on Medicare for health insurance because it covers only 38 percent of their health care costs. Some companies extend their group health plans to retired employees. Otherwise, the best protection is a comprehensive "Medigap" policy costing about $300 a year. Even the finest of these won't cover 100 percent of medical expenses. But they are far superior to the limited hospital indemnity policies often advertised in Sunday newspapers and the nursing home insurance policies frequently sold door to door.

Hospital indemnity insurance pays a specified dollar amount in cash for each day the policyholder is hospitalized. But Medicare covers costs during the first 60 days of hospitalization after a $160 deductible is paid. A hospital indemnity policy might provide $30 a day for a $150 annual premium. Underwriters of hospital indemnity insurance pay out only 40 cents for every premium dollar they take in; the better Medicare supplement policies pay back at least 70 cents to the dollar. Lately, oil companies like Sunoco and Shell and department stores have started selling hospital indemnity policies.

The worst of the Medigap policies are those purporting to provide nursing home coverage. "So many people tell me 'I've got nursing home insurance, so if I ever have to go into a home, I'll be covered.' It's just not so" says Mary Bach of Access for Senior Citizens, a project of a public-interest law firm in Madison, Wisconsin. Most policies pay only when the beneficiary has been hospitalized recently and is entering the home because of that same illness. Some pay only if the home is a Medicare-certified "skilled-nursing facility." This means the residents get rehabilitative, not custodial, care. But in many parts of the country, these homes are non-existent, so the policies are worthless.

Cancer Insurance.   Anyone fearful of catastrophic illness would do better to increase his or her major medical coverage than to buy insurance against cancer or any other specific disease. Too often, the expensive continuous costs of treating cancer, such as at-home nursing care, are not covered by cancer policies. Instead, this coverage pays part of the insured's hospital costs. The average hospital stay for a cancer patient, however, is not more than two weeks.

Source: *Money* Magazine, July 1979, pp. 72, 74. Reprinted with permission.

How Much to Buy

How much disability insurance to buy depends on your living expenses and your sources of income while you are disabled. The first step is to

identify your total annual living expenses. The family budget that is prepared for managing finances (see Chapter 5) is a good start. Keep in mind that some expense categories would have to be adjusted. For example, although such expenses as food and housing might remain the same, transportation and vacation expenses might decline.

Chapter 5 gave an example of budgeting for the Dardens. We show here how the Dardens can determine their disability insurance needs. From Tables 5.2 and 5.3 on pages 140 and 142, respectively, total annual expenses are $11,950 + $9,440 = $21,390. This figure is shown as (1) in Table 13.2. The Dardens could sell their car, not go on a vacation, and stop their savings program, thereby decreasing their annual expenses by $6,920. Two expenses, cab fares and special dietary foods, would increase by $800. Total adjustments are $6,920 − $800 = $6,120. That is, if the wage earner for the Dardens was disabled, their expenses would be reduced by $6,120, to $15,260.

Table 5.1 shows the Dardens' incomes. They would continue to receive only interest and dividend income, which would be $760 annually. Additionally, the family would receive social security disability benefits of $5,160. Total incomes received would be $760 + $5,160 = $5,920. Their annual disability insurance needs are for $15,260 − $5,920 = $9,340.

The example in Table 13.2 is for one year only. Expenses keep increasing every year. If the Dardens buy only $9,340 in annual disability insurance, they will find that after one or two years, this amount is not sufficient to take care of expenses. One way of handling this problem would be to buy coverage that increases annually to keep pace with rising costs.

Buying Disability Insurance

Unlike homeowners' insurance, there is no such thing as standard disability insurance coverage. Policies by different insurers have different definitions of disabilities and different types of coverages. Some general features of disability insurance policies are explained in this section.

How Disability Is Defined. Obviously, a disability insurance policy will pay benefits only when the insured is disabled. Therefore, the policies contain a definition of the word **disability**. Two general and widely used definitions follow:

1. Disability is the inability of the insured to perform duties related to his or her present occupation.
2. Disability is the inability of the insured to perform duties of an occupation for which he or she is or may be suitable by reason of education, training, and experience.

Definition 1 is more liberal—it provides much better coverage for the insured than definition 2 because it covers a particular occupation rather

Table 13.2 Determining Disability Insurance Needs[a]

Annual living expenses (1)		$21,380
Adjustments		
Expenses that decrease		
Transportation—Installment	$1,920	
Credit card	720	
Car, registration	280	
Savings—Investment	1,800	
Savings—Vacation	1,200	
Transportation—Gas, oil	1,000	
Decreased expenses (2)	$6,920	
Expenses that increase		
Cabs	500	
Food	300	
Increased expenses (3)		$800
Total adjustments (2 − 3)		6,120
Adjusted living expenses (4 = 1 − 3)		$15,260
Incomes received		
Interest, dividend income	$ 760	
Social security	5,160	
Total incomes received (5)		5,920
Disability insurance needs (4 − 5)		$9,340

[a]This example is for the Dardens, whose budgets are shown in Tables 5.1, 5.2, and 5.3.

than just any occupation. Consider the case of the insured who is a college graduate who plays guitar in a band for a living. His annual earnings are $100,000, and he carries disability insurance for an amount of $4,000 monthly. He injures his hand in a car accident and can no longer earn a living as a guitar player. Under definition 1, he is considered to be disabled and so collects disability insurance payments. Under definition 2, the insurer tells him that he has the education to work in other occupations and so does not pay him any benefits. He starts to work as a sales representative and makes $18,000 a year.

Many insurance companies are beginning to emphasize rehabilitation in their insurance policies. They achieve this by combining and modifying

the two disability definitions just mentioned. Under this approach, the insured might be covered for the first two to five years of disability under definition 1. During this time, the insurance company may help the insured gain additional education or training for a new occupation. Another approach to encourage rehabilitation is to make partial disability payments when the insured starts a new job.

Insurance policies typically identify presumptive and partial disabilities. A **presumptive disability** is one for which the insured is automatically considered to be totally disabled. Loss of sight of both eyes or loss of two limbs are examples of presumptive disabilities. A **partial disability** is defined as one that prevents the insured from doing some but not all the duties related to his or her occupation. A salesperson who becomes deaf may be considered partially disabled. The person might be able to read lips and make sales presentations in person but would not be able to make sales presentations over the telephone.

Cause of Disability. Disabilities can be caused by accidents or sicknesses. Some policies cover only disabilities caused by accidents, whereas others cover disabilities that result from both accident and sickness.

Disability insurance policies define the types of accidents that are covered. Broader policies cover **accidental bodily injury**, which is defined as any unintended injury. Policies with more limited coverage encompass only **bodily injury by accidental means**, which requires that the injury as well as the cause of the injury be unintended.

Consider the situation in which the insured is injured while playing recreational baseball. If the insurance policy defines injury as accidental bodily injury, the insured is covered because the injury was unintended. However, if injury is defined as bodily injury by accidental means, then the insured is not covered because the cause of the injury—playing baseball—was not unintentional.

Sickness is also carefully defined in the insurance policy. Preexisting health conditions are excluded from coverage. Some policies also exclude coverage for disabilities related to cancer or mental illness.

Benefit Duration. Disability insurance policies have benefit periods that can range from a few months to the life of the insured. The longer the benefit duration is, the higher will be the policy premiums. Policies often have separate benefit durations for sickness and accident disabilities. For example, some policies pay sickness disability benefits to age 65 and accident disability benefits for the life of the insured. Generally, despite the higher costs, a policy that provides benefits to age 65 or the life of the insured person is the best type of policy.

Waiting Period. Waiting periods are similar to deductibles in health and property insurance. The **waiting period** is the time when the insured is disabled but is not receiving any benefits. Some policies have no waiting

period. Others have waiting periods of 30, 60, 90, or 180 days or longer. Insurance premiums are lower when the waiting period is longer. Waiting periods should be coordinated with other benefits that the insured might have. For example, the insured might have accumulated six months of sick leave at work. In this case, a waiting period of at least six months is appropriate. An even longer waiting period might be justified if the insured has additional financial resources to draw on.

Renewal Provisions.   The insured can terminate a health insurance contract at any time. For example, if the person is not satisfied with the disability insurance policy, then he or she need not pay the current premium due. However, what happens when the insured would like to continue with the policy? This situation is covered by the policy's renewal provisions. Some policies have **no provision**, which means that the policy expires at the end of its term.

Policies **cancelable** by the insurer do not guarantee the insured coverage for a specified length of time, because they can be canceled by the insurer at any time. Policies **cancelable on the anniversary date** can be canceled by the insurer on the date that the insurance premium is due. If premiums are paid annually, then this policy assures the insured of coverage for at least one year.

Conditionally renewable policies can be canceled by the insurer if certain conditions occur. For example, the insurer may have the option of canceling the policy if the insured changes occupations. **Guaranteed renewable** policies cannot be canceled by the insurer for a certain time period—usually to age 65—and have to be renewed at the insured's option. However, there is no guarantee that the insurance premium will not increase. Although the insurer cannot raise premiums for any one insured, it can raise premiums in a state for all the insureds in a given risk class. Thus, an arc welder may find that his or her premium rates have been increased along with the rates for all the other arc welders insured by the same company.

A **noncancelable** policy cannot be canceled by the insurer for a certain time period. Premiums cannot be increased either, except according to a schedule established at the time the policy was written. A noncancelable policy is the best type to have in terms of renewal provisions. Other things being the same, a noncancelable policy is also the most expensive policy. This policy is very desirable despite its high cost because the insured can keep it in force simply by paying contractually specified premiums on their due dates.

Other Features.   Disability insurance benefits are **coordinated** so that the insured cannot collect more than his or her salary in benefits. A **prorating** clause allows the insurer to increase the premiums if the insured changes to a more risky occupation. An insurer will limit the amount of monthly policy benefits to about 60 percent of the insured's salary. Thus,

if the insured is earning $2,000 a month, an insurer generally will not sell him or her a policy with more than $1,200 in monthly benefits.

Social Security Benefits

Social security provides disability benefits to disabled workers, to their children, and to the spouses of disabled workers. Benefits are paid after a five-month waiting period and if the disability is expected to last at least one year or to result in death. The size of the benefits is related to the worker's earnings. In general, though, these benefits are rather small and have to be supplemented with private disability insurance coverage.

Workers' Compensation

Workers' compensation pays for job-related injuries and sicknesses. Unlike social security, workers' compensation is financed by states, who raise funds by assessing employers in the state. Workers' compensation programs tend to differ from state to state, but the general features of the programs are discussed here.

Most states exclude agricultural, domestic, and casual workers from coverage. Some states also exclude persons in certain hazardous occupations from coverage. Certain injuries, such as those that are self-inflicted or a result of alcohol consumption, are also excluded from coverage.

Workers' compensation programs provide medical, income, and rehabilitation benefits. Medical benefits generally include hospital and medical care. Income benefits are generally related to the amount of wages lost because of the disability. Income benefits may be limited to a maximum of 50 to 67 percent of average salary or a fixed sum, such as $220 per week. When total disability occurs, some states pay benefits for life, whereas others limit benefits to a specific time period. Quite a few states pay special benefits to encourage disabled workers to seek rehabilitation. **Rehabilitation benefits** may include training to prepare the disabled worker for a more suitable job.

The biggest problem with workers' compensation is that not all workers are covered by it. Second, only job-related injuries and sicknesses are covered. Third, benefits may not be sufficient to allow an injured worker to properly manage living expenses. As a result, most people should consider supplementing workers' compensation benefits with disability insurance purchased from an insurance company.

Disabilities can severely affect a person's life style. A good disability insurance policy can help offset losses from disabilities. A good policy (1) should have a liberal definition of disability, (2) should provide coverage for accidental bodily injury, (3) should be noncancelable, (4) should have a waiting period that is coordinated with other disability-related benefits, and (5) should have a benefit duration that is for the life of the insured.

Spot Quiz • Disability Insurance

1. A person should buy as much disability insurance as he or she can obtain.   T _____ F _____

2. How disability is defined can affect the benefits paid by the policy.   T _____ F _____

3. In disability insurance policies, injury-caused disabilities are treated the same as sickness-caused disabilities.   T _____ F _____

4. A guaranteed renewable policy cannot be automatically renewed at a prespecified premium.   T _____ F _____

(Answers on page 431)

Summary

Sicknesses and disabilities are health risks that can cause loss of income and assets. Maximum losses due to health risks can be difficult to establish. There is really no way to avoid health risks, and because retention can result in large losses of income and assets, health risks should be transferred by buying insurance.

Health insurance policies pay benefits under the valued, reimbursement, or service benefit plans. Basic health insurance policies cover hospitalization, surgery, and other medical expenses. Extended policies extend the coverage of basic policies and include major medical and comprehensive insurance. Coverage under basic policies tends to be limited, whereas extended policies provide more extensive coverage.

Health insurance costs can be reduced by increasing the deductible and the coinsurance amount. It is generally desirable to have a policy with high maximum limits and one that is renewable at the insured's option. Many people obtain insurance from group insurance plans. Private companies, Blue Cross/Blue Shield, HMOs, and Medicare and Medicaid also provide insurance coverage.

In general, you should buy enough disability insurance so that the benefits are sufficient to cover your monthly living expenses. The disability insurance policy you select should have a liberal definition of disability.

The policy should cover disabilities due to accidental bodily injury. The benefit duration should be for the life of the insured. The waiting period for the policy should be coordinated with other sick leave benefits that the insured may have with his or her employer. The policy should be non-cancelable. Social security and workers' compensation are two other sources of disability benefits for those who qualify.

Questions

1. What is meant by a health risk? Explain how assets are affected by health risks.

2. Explain the steps that you can follow to identify health risks.

3. Briefly explain how you can evaluate health risks.

4. Is retention of health risks a good strategy? Why or why not?

5. Explain the differences, if any, between the following benefit payment plans:
   Valued plan
   Indemnity, or reimbursement, plan
   Service benefit plan

6. What is the difference between basic and extended hospital insurance policies?

7. Briefly explain the features of major medical insurance.

8. What are the pros and cons of having a relatively high coinsurance clause, say 25 percent, in an insurance policy?

9. Explain how deductibles and maximum limits on insurance policies affect costs and benefits.

10. Why do health insurance policies have a waiting period?

11. Explain why group health insurance plans are considered to be very desirable.

12. Explain what is meant by loss ratio. What does it indicate about an insurer?

13. What are HMOs? How do their benefits differ from those of extended health insurance policies?

14. Briefly explain how Medicare works.

15. Explain how you should decide how much disability insurance to buy.

16. Give two different definitions for disability. How do these definitions differ?

17. Explain what is meant by a presumptive disability.

18. Explain the difference between accidental bodily injury and bodily injury by accidental means.

19. How should you determine the appropriate waiting period for disability insurance?

20. Which disability insurance renewal provision is best? Explain your answer.

21. What is meant by workers' compensation? What are the weaknesses of the program?

Case Problems

1. Jamie Stern, a recent college graduate with a major in computer sciences, has started a new job with a firm located in "Silicon Valley" in California. Her employer has offered her two different health coverage options. The first option is a Blue Cross/Blue Shield comprehensive plan. It has a $50 deductible per hospitalization. Medical expense coverage pays for prescription drugs after a calendar year with a $30 deductible. Hospitalization expenses have a coinsurance clause that requires the insured to pay 20 percent of these expenses above $2,000. The maximum limit is $200,000. The second option is for coverage with Silicon Valley HMO. All hospital, surgical, and medical expenses are covered in full. The HMO has a $2 per visit copayment requirement. The maximum limit is $50,000. With either option, the employer pays the monthly premiums. Which option might be more suitable for Jamie? Explain your answer.

2. Rosita Chen earns $35,000 annually as a college teacher. Her monthly take-home pay is $2,000. She receives an additional $200 per month in dividends and interest income. Her monthly expenses are as follows:

Shelter	$600
Transportation	250
Food	250
Loans	200

Insurance	200
Vacation	100
Miscellaneous	200
Total	$1,800
Savings	$ 400

If she were disabled, she would be able to eliminate transportation expenses. Insurance expenses would decline by $50 per month. She would also do without a vacation. Her miscellaneous expenses would increase by $40 per month. How much disability insurance should she carry? Show your calculations.

3. Scott Hastings is 32 years old and works as a machinist. He is married and the father of two children, ages 9 and 7 years. Scott and his family are covered by an excellent comprehensive health insurance plan offered by his employer. He has accumulated the maximum of 45 days of sick leave. He is entitled to two weeks of paid vacation annually. He can and has accumulated the maximum allowed vacation time of 50 days. He is provided with some disability insurance coverage through social security and workers' compensation. Recently, however, Scott has started to feel that he is not adequately protected against a severe disability. What advice do you have for Scott? Should he buy disability insurance? Why or why not? If yes, for approximately what amount? Your discussion should also cover benefits duration, renewal provisions, and waiting period.

Bibliography

"Big Changes Ahead in How We Buy Health Care." *Changing Times* (March 1982): 60–63.

"Are You Covered if You Can't Work?" *Changing Times* (April 1982): 58–60.

"Ways to Pay What Medicare Won't." *Changing Times* (October 1985): 85–88.

"Health Insurance: Covering the Bill." *Changing Times* (February 1987): 60.

"Second Thoughts on HMOs." *Changing Times* (May 1987): 33–38.

"Two Cheers for HMOs." *Money* (May 1985): 155–160.

"Prepaid Dental Plans." *Money* (May 1985): 163.

"Weave Your Own Safety Net." *Money* (November 1986): 95–98.

''Beware the Medi-Scare Con Game.'' *Reader's Digest* (November 1981): 163, 164, 166, 168.

Your Medicare Handbook. Baltimore, MD: U.S. Department of Health and Human Services.

Answers To Spot Quizzes

Managing Health Risks (page 404)

1. T (A partial disability may result in a partial income loss.)

2. T (Assets and incomes do not define a limit for health risk losses.)

3. T (For instance, the costs of a doctor's office visits can be easily retained.)

Health Insurance (page 411)

1. F (The service benefit plan is more flexible in that it covers all reasonable expenses.)

2. T (Hospital and surgical insurances do not have high enough limits.)

3. T (Comprehensive insurance combines both basic and MM coverages.)

Managing Health Insurance (page 420)

1. T (Small claims are avoided, thus lowering premiums.)

2. F (Large claims may require the insured to pay large sums of money.)

3. T (Administrative costs tend to be lower.)

4. F (Only a portion of the health care costs are covered.)

Disability Insurance (page 427)

1. F (The amount bought should be related to financial need.)

2. T (A liberal definition is preferred.)

3. F (Sickness-caused disabilities are treated more restrictively.)

4. T (It can be renewed, but the premiums are not guaranteed.)

Chapter 14

Life Insurance

Objectives

After reading this chapter, you will be able to:

- Evaluate life risks.

- Choose a strategy for managing life risk.

- Describe the different types of life insurance policies.

- Explain the difference between term and other types of life insurance policies.

- State the major provisions of life insurance policies.

- Utilize the procedures for estimating life insurance needs.

- Discuss the procedures for comparing different life insurance policies.

Joan Halliburton is 30 years old and earns $2,500 a year as a part-time school aide. Her husband, Frank, is 33 years old and earns $28,000 annually. Their son is seven years old. Their $69,000 home has a $30,000 mortgage balance. They have $6,000 in savings. Frank has $43,000 in life insurance. What advice do you have for the Halliburton family?

James L. Athearn of the University of South Carolina, who was president of the American Risk and Insurance Association, answered the preceding question for *Changing Times* magazine. He pointed out that in the event of Frank's death, Joan would receive about $323 monthly from investing the $43,000 in life insurance proceeds and $908 from social security. Joan would need $500 in addition to the $323 + $908 = $1,231 she would be getting. Professor Athearn suggests that another $67,000 life insurance policy on Frank would provide the necessary additional income of $500 per month. The $67,000 in death benefits could be invested at 9 percent to produce income of $6,000 annually, or $500 monthly. The insurance proceeds themselves would not be spent. Frank could take out either a term or a whole life insurance policy.[1]

As the Halliburton situation illustrates, many individuals and families are not adequately prepared to handle the problems associated with premature death. This chapter deals with the topic of life risk and how to manage them through life insurance.

MANAGING LIFE RISK

Personal risks include health risks, disabilities, and premature death. The first two were covered in Chapter 13. In this chapter, our focus will be on premature death.

Life Risk

Life risk is the risk of dying prematurely, which means that a person dies before an expected age. For example, the average male in the United States can be expected to live about 70 years. If a male dies before age 70, it can be said that he died prematurely. The average life expectancy for a female is about 78 years.

In addition to the obvious emotional trauma associated with death, the premature death of the family wage earner also brings the loss of income. Whether the loss of income itself creates financial hardships for the survivors depends on the situation. If a person has no dependents, then premature death does not create a financial hardship. If a person has

---

1. "But *How Much* Life Insurance?" *Money* (May 1979): 17–18.

dependents and a sufficiently large estate to pass on, then, too, no hardship results. However, in the absence of a sizable estate, premature death does create financial hardships for a person's dependents. Evaluating life risk and developing a suitable strategy for managing it are discussed in the remainder of this chapter.

Life Risk Evaluation

A wage earner's death creates financial needs for his or her dependents. Life risk evaluation involves estimating these financial needs. Financial needs of the dependents can be divided into two categories: immediate cash needs and living expenses needs.

Immediate Cash Needs.   A variety of expenses fall into the category of **immediate cash needs.** First, there are the expenses related to the deceased's funeral, sickness and hospitalization, estate administration, and estate taxes. Even modest funerals can cost several thousand dollars. Depending on the type of medical insurance coverage carried, sickness and hospitalization expenses can range from a few hundred to several thousand dollars. Estate administrative expenses include an attorney's and an estate executor's fees. These expenses can range from $500 to several thousand dollars. Estate taxes are generally not a problem for small estates, but they can be very high for large estates.

Joe and Linda Cesari are in their early thirties. Joe works as a computer systems analyst. Linda is taking time off from her job as credit manager at a bank because the Cesaris are expecting their first child. If Joe were to die today, his funeral and estate administrative expenses and

"Expect the unexpected, Mr. Hodge.
Take a seat and we'll work out
a policy suited to your needs."

Source: *Changing Times,* May 1979, p. 19. Used
with permission.

taxes would be $5,000. They are listed in Table 14.1, which shows a worksheet for evaluating life risk.

To properly manage finances after the wage earner's death, it is generally desirable to pay off all credit and installment loans except for the mortgage loan. Planning for debt liquidation simplifies personal financial management for the dependents. The Cesaris would need $6,000 to pay off all outstanding loans. This amount is entered on line 2 in Table 14.1.

Whether mortgages and any other long-term debts should be paid off immediately depends on the lender's requirements. For example, Joe and Linda jointly own their home and are coborrowers for the mortgage. If Joe dies, Linda will assume total responsibility for paying off the mortgage. In this case, there is no need to plan for paying off the mortgage. Mortgage payments themselves are accounted for later as living expenses.

If the dependent or survivor is not a coborrower or cannot or does not want to assume the mortgage, then the loan must be repaid. A suitable alternative is to sell the home or other property that secures the loan and use the proceeds to pay off the loan. If the estate is sufficiently large, the loan can be repaid from the estate. The dependent or survivor can then make an independent judgment about whether the home or property should be kept or sold.

Finally, cash needs should include a **contingency fund** that can be used if an emergency arises. Miscellaneous and unanticipated expenses can be met from this contingency fund. The fund should equal two months' take-home salary. Line 3 in Table 14.1 shows $4,400 in a contingency fund.

Living Expenses Needs. Figure 14.1 shows how Linda's living expenses needs would vary over time. During stage 1, Linda is not working and is taking care of the child. Monthly living expenses are at a certain level. During stage 2, Linda goes back to her job. Day care or nursery costs for the child, commuting expenses, and other job-related expenses would increase living expenses needs. Note that we are talking only about living expenses needs, not how these needs are met. In stage 2, for example,

Table 14.1 Life Risk Evaluation

Immediate cash needs	
1. Funeral, estate expenses	$5,000
2. Debt liquidation	6,000
3. Contingency fund	4,400
Total cash needs	15,400
Living expenses needs	199,920
Total dollar life risk	$215,320

Linda's job is a strategy for dealing with life risk, a topic that is covered in the next section.

In stage 3 of the Cesari family life cycle, the child would go to college. College-related expenses push monthly living expenses to their highest levels. During stage 4, the child no longer lives at home, and Linda is still working. Monthly living expenses therefore drop below the level of stage 2. The final stage begins when Linda retires. Monthly living expenses are lowest during this stage.

Monthly living expense needs vary from family to family. Figure 14.1 applies to the Cesaris. However, conceptually it can apply to all families by adjusting the stages according to the family's circumstances. Actually,

Figure 14.1 Living Expenses Needs Over Life Cycle

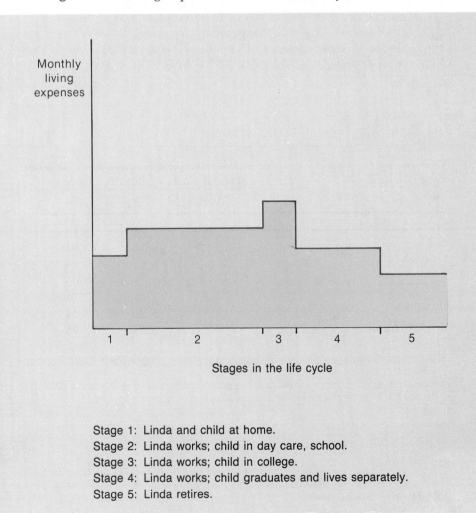

Stage 1: Linda and child at home.
Stage 2: Linda works; child in day care, school.
Stage 3: Linda works; child in college.
Stage 4: Linda works; child graduates and lives separately.
Stage 5: Linda retires.

Figure 14.1 might change even for Linda. If she remarries, for example, she and her husband would have to go through a new life risk evaluation.

Linda estimates that, on the average, she will need $2,000 per month for living expenses, which is $24,000 annually. Linda believes that she can average a 12.0 percent return on her investments. Total living expenses needs can be determined by using present value factors. Table 14.2 shows factors for various combinations of life expectancies and annual rates of return.

Suppose, for example, that Linda expects to live only two more years. **Total living expense needs** are calculated by multiplying annual living expenses by the appropriate factor. In Linda's case, the factor for two years and 12 percent is 1.89. Linda's total living expenses needs would be $24,000 × 1.89 = $45,360. Of this $45,360, she keeps $24,000 for first-year living expenses. The remainder, $43,360 − $24,000 = $21,360, is invested at 12 percent for one year. After one year, Linda has $21,360 × .12 + $21,360 = $23,923, which is what she needs to live on the second year.[2]

Linda expects to live much longer than two years, however. Let's use the factor for 30 or more years and 12 percent, which is 8.33. Linda's total living expenses needs are $24,000 × 8.33 = $199,920. On $199,920, Linda

Table 14.2 Present Value Factors*

| Years | Annual Rates of Return | | | |
	8%	10%	12%	14%
2	1.93	1.91	1.89	1.88
5	4.31	4.17	4.04	3.91
10	7.25	6.76	6.33	5.95
15	9.24	8.37	7.63	7.00
20	10.60	9.36	8.33	7.14
25	11.67	10.00	8.33	7.14
30 or more	12.25	10.00	8.33	7.14

*Payment is made at the beginning of the period. Factors for 20 and 25 years at 12% and 14% and for 30 years at all rates are present values of a perpetual annuity.

2. The amount for the second year is not exactly $24,000 because the factor in Table 14.2 is accurate only to the second decimal. A more accurate factor is 1.89286, which gives $24,000 for the second year.

would earn $199,920 \times .12 = \$23,990$ annually for her living expenses.[3] The $199,920 amount is entered in Table 14.1. **Total dollar life risk** is $215,320. That is, if Joe were to die today, given the family's present circumstances, Linda would need $215,320 to maintain herself and the child.

This example for evaluating life risk has been simplified. A more complex analysis might assume that annual living expenses increase by, say, 7 or 8 percent annually. Factors similar to those given in Table 14.2 can be calculated by using mathematical formulas to estimate total living expenses. Also, some people might prefer to have a separate category in Table 14.2 for funds for children's college education.

Choosing a Strategy

You have already discovered that there are four basic ways of dealing with risk. Risk avoidance is not applicable to life risk. Controlling life risk calls for the same type of precautionary living that was discussed in Chapter 13. Two viable alternatives for managing life risk are retention and transfer. Retention is affected by investment assets owned, by the earnings of the survivor, and by social security benefits. To a very small extent, retention is also affected by any death benefits provided by the employer.

Investment Assets Owned. The more **investment assets** you own, the more you can retain life risk. If the Cesaris owned investment assets worth $215,320, they then could afford to retain 100 percent of life risk. Actually, as we will see later, when we take into consideration social security benefits, the Cesaris could afford to retain life risk even with assets worth less than $215,320. As it turns out, the Cesaris have only about $10,000 in investment funds. At a 12 percent rate of return, Linda would earn $10,000 \times .12 = \$1,200$ annually, or $100 monthly, on these assets.

Figure 14.2 shows how the Cesaris would generate $2,000 average monthly living expenses. The $100 in earnings per month from investment assets would go toward defraying part of the living expenses.

Survivor's Earnings. The survivor or dependent may start working after the wage earner's death. Work allows the survivor or dependent not only to earn an income but also to keep busy. As Figure 14.1 shows, Linda plans to start work at the end of stage 1. When Linda goes back to work, she will average $1,100 monthly in salary. This amount is also shown in Figure 14.2. Linda will eventually retire, at the beginning of stage 5. Figure 14.2 shows this decline in Linda's salary as well.

---

3. The more accurate factor is 8.33333, which gives total living expenses of $200,000 and earnings of $24,000.

Figure 14.2 Financing Living Expenses Over Life Cycle

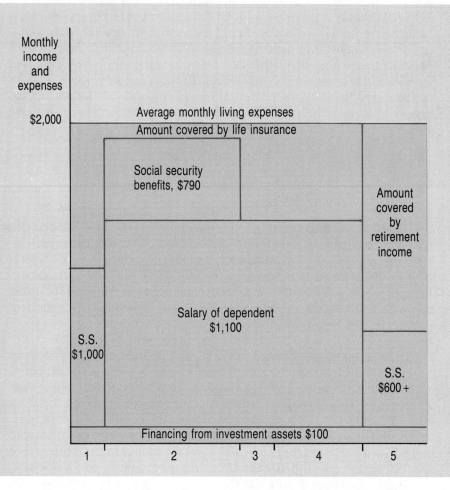

Social Security Benefits. Joe Cesari is covered by social security. His dependents, Linda and the child, will be eligible for social security survivors' benefits upon his death. Social security pays a *lump sum* death benefit to the dependent of a covered deceased worker. Currently, this lump sum benefit is $255. On Joe's death, Linda would receive this $255 payment.

Social security pays benefits to the surviving spouse if he or she is caring for one or more children who are eligible for benefits. Benefits for a surviving parent depend on the deceased worker's social security covered earnings. They will vary from about $450 per month to about $1,150 per

month. Based on Joe's covered earnings and one child, Linda will receive about $1,000 in monthly benefits during stage 1.

Social security is intended to replace earnings. If a dependent earns more than a certain exempt amount, then social security benefits are reduced by $1 for each $2 of earnings above the exempt amount. The 1987 annual exempt amount was $8,160. Linda's annual earnings in stages 2 and 3 are $1,100 × 12 = $13,200. The earnings above the exempt amount are $13,200 − $8,160 = $5,040. During stages 2 and 3, Linda will lose $5,040 × .5 = $2,520 in annual, or $2,520/12 = $210 in monthly, benefits. Thus, during this time period, she will receive $1,000 − $210 = $790 in monthly social security benefits.

Social security benefits are also paid to a surviving child under age 18 if the child is living away from home. This does not apply to the Cesari case. Social security benefits are not paid to a surviving spouse if the spouse is under age 60 and is not caring for a qualifying child. This means that Linda's social security benefits will stop at the end of stage 3.[4] Surviving spouses become eligible for social security benefits starting at age 60. Because Linda plans to work till age 65, she will not apply for social security benefits until her retirement.[5] Figure 14.2 shows the resumption of benefits starting with stage 5. Based on current rates, she will receive over $600 in monthly benefits then. Joe's employer does not provide any death benefits to its employees' dependents.

As Figure 14.2 shows, the total amount of life risk retained varies over the different stages. During stage 1, the Cesaris can retain $100 + $1,000 = $1,100 in life risk. During stages 2 and 3, they can retain $100 + $1,100 + $790 = $1,990. In stage 4, the retention amount is $1,200. In stage 5, Linda will be able to retain all of the life risk amount because she will have planned for her retirement.

Life Risk Transfer.   **Life risk transfer** is accomplished by purchasing life insurance. Figure 14.2 shows the difference between average monthly living expenses and total income from all sources. This amount of life risk cannot be retained and should be transferred by buying life insurance. The amount of life insurance needed will vary, but an average can be estimated. In the Cesaris' case, Figure 14.2 shows that life insurance coverage should be sufficient to provide, on the average, about $600 in monthly income.

The analysis in this section suggests that the Cesaris can retain about $1,400 monthly in life risk and should transfer about $600 monthly by buying a suitable amount of life insurance.

---

4. Qualifying children between the ages of 18 and 22 who were full-time students used to qualify for social security benefits. However, since 1985 college students have not been eligible to receive social security benefits.

5. While a person can retire as early as age 62, later retirements provide higher social security retirement benefits.

Spot Quiz • Managing Life Risk

1. Life risk cannot be evaluated properly.   T _____ F _____

2. It is not necessary to transfer all of life risk.   T _____ F _____

3. Social security benefits are paid for life to a surviving parent.
                                                        T _____ F _____

(Answers on page 469)

TYPES OF LIFE INSURANCE POLICIES

As mentioned in the previous section, life risk can be transferred by buying life insurance. This section discusses the various types of life insurance policies available.

A **life insurance policy** is a contract that pays the beneficiary of the insured a fixed sum of money when the insured dies. The policy owner pays fixed premiums periodically to keep the insurance in force. There are seven different types of life insurance policies: term, whole life, endowment, universal life, variable life, single premium, and annuity. Term, whole life, endowment, universal life, variable life, and single premium policies assure the insured that he or she will leave a certain size of estate in case of premature death. An annuity, however, is designed to pay a fixed amount of benefits when the insured reaches a certain age. Annuities therefore will be discussed in greater detail in Chapter 20 on retirement planning. The other six types of policies are discussed here. (See "Insurance You Don't Need" on page 443.)

Term Insurance

Unlike other types of policies, which combine insurance with savings, **term insurance** provides only pure insurance protection for a term, or specified period of time. If the insured dies during this time, his or her beneficiaries are paid a predetermined amount of insurance benefits. If the insured does not die during this time period, no benefits are paid. There are four types of term insurance policies: straight term, renewable term, decreasing term, and convertible term.

Insurance You Don't Need

Life insurance for college students. Graduating seniors are often approached by salesmen who offer special life insurance policies with low premiums and easy payment plans. A student with no dependents rarely needs life insurance, however, and buying it because the premiums are lower for young people is faulty reasoning. Though the premiums will be lower, the policyholder will be paying premiums for more years than if he waited until insurance was necessary.

Often the easy payment plans are easy only at first. A $25,000 College-Master whole life policy sold by Fidelity Union Life Insurance Co. costs a 22-year-old merely $55 the first year. A year later, though, the premium more than quadruples to $260. Fidelity Union also sells the same policy for $290 a year but lets students borrow up to $275 of the first year's premium at 8%. The loan is paid with the cash value that accumulates during the next four years. Bob Lackey, a Fidelity Union vice president, concedes, "In many cases, the need for the insurance isn't that great. But it's a good idea for the students because they get into the habit of paying for life insurance."

Children's life insurance. Unless your children are the Bee Gees all over again and are providing income to the family, the little ones do not need life insurance. But this doesn't stop insurance agents from barraging new parents with phone calls and visits after the birth announcement has appeared in the paper. Now the country's largest day-care chain is selling the insurance. Kinder-Care Learning Centers charges $21 per year for $5,000 of whole life insurance for children between the ages of one and 12. Parents who think they wouldn't have the money for burial expenses if a child were to die may have reason to buy a much smaller policy; the average cost for a child's funeral is less than $1,400.

Straight Term. A **straight term insurance** policy has a fixed amount of benefits and is issued for a fixed time period. The premiums are level and fixed on straight term. The policy has no value for the insured after its expiration date. Once the existing straight term insurance expires, you must show proof of insurability to obtain new term insurance. Insurability is demonstrated by passing the medical examination required by the insurance company.

Renewable Term. A **renewable term insurance** policy contains an option that allows the insured to renew the insurance for a specified time period a specified number of times. The typical renewal term is one to five years. For example, a five-year renewable term policy may allow the insured

to renew the policy every five years until he or she reaches age 65. Proof of insurability does not have to be presented when the policy is renewed. The insurance premiums are higher every time the policy is renewed because the insured is older and thus has a higher probability of dying.

Decreasing Term. With **decreasing term insurance**, the insurance premiums remain level over the life of the policy, but the amount of benefits declines. This type of insurance is quite popular. As the insured builds up assets over time, the need for insurance declines. Decreasing term is one way for the insured to adjust to his or her increased capacity to retain life risk. Decreasing term is also useful for paying off a mortgage loan if the insured dies prematurely. Quite often you can find decreasing term insurance whose benefits decline at about the same rate as the remaining balance on a mortgage. Decreasing term insurance is less expensive than straight term insurance.

Convertible Term. **Convertible term insurance** can be converted into ordinary life or endowment insurance at the insured's option without having to provide evidence of insurability. This is a desirable feature for people who believe that at some point they would like to switch to an insurance policy that includes a savings feature.

Many term insurance policies are both renewable and convertible. For the same amount of premium, term insurance provides more insurance protection than any other type of insurance. Therefore, it is very desirable for younger people and new families. People just starting out professionally are usually on tight budgets and generally do not have estates. Yet their insurance protection needs tend to be high. They can buy the necessary amount of term insurance at a reasonable cost. Term insurance provides vital insurance protection to many people at an affordable price.

Whole Life Insurance

Whole life insurance, unlike term insurance, remains in force for as long as the insured continues to pay the insurance premiums. The premiums for whole life remain level and fixed as long as the policy remains in force. Whole life is also called **permanent life** because the insured can keep it in force as long as he or she lives by continuing to pay the policy premiums.

The cost of a whole life policy is substantially higher than the cost of term insurance. As Table 14.3 shows, ordinary whole life rates can be three to four times higher than the rates for term insurance. The reason for the higher rates is that whole life policies build up cash values, whereas term policies do not.

Table 14.3 Sample Premiums and Cash Values*

Item	5-Year R&C** Term	Ordinary Whole Life	Paid Up at 65	Endowment at 65
Premium	$5.09	$ 17.06	$ 19.50	$ 22.29
Cash values				
After 5 years	0.00	46.00	52.00	67.00
After 10 years	0.00	127.00	139.00	173.00
After 20 years	0.00	288.00	318.00	399.00
At age 60	0.00	523.00	595.00	809.00
At age 65	0.00	601.00	700.00	1000.00

*Annual premiums are per $1,000 of insurance for a 25-year-old male. Term is renewable three times and convertible into whole life. *Best's Flitcraft Compend* (Oldwick, NJ: A. M. Best Co.) carried rates for many insurance companies.
**Renewable and convertible.

The premiums for whole life insurance go partly to pay for insurance and partly to build up savings for the insured. The savings portion of whole life insurance is called the policy's **cash value**. The insured has the right to the policy's cash value and can obtain it by surrendering his or her policy to the insurer. There are two types of whole life policies: ordinary, or straight, and limited payment.

Ordinary Life. As Table 14.3 shows, premiums for ordinary life are lower than those for paid-up life at age 65 or endowment at age 65. The lower premiums for **ordinary life** result from the assumption that the insurance premiums will be paid till the insured's death. With this policy, the cost of buying insurance is spread out over the insured's entire life. Ordinary life provides permanent protection for the least annual premium cost.

Limited Payment. With a **limited payment** plan, insurance premiums are paid only for a specified time period. Once the insured has made the payments for the specified length of time, he or she does not have to make any more payments. The insurance policy remains in force after the payment period is over. Table 14.3 lists a limited payment policy called "Paid Up at 65." The insured would make payments on this policy until age 65, after which the policy becomes **paid up**. Similarly, a 20-year pay policy would be paid up after the insured has made the required insurance

premiums for 20 years. The premiums for a limited payment policy are higher than for ordinary life because a limited payment policy builds up cash values more quickly than an ordinary life policy.

Limited payment plans typically include policies that are paid up after 10 to 30 years or at ages 50, 55, 60, or 65. In general, shorter pay periods require higher insurance premiums to pay up the policy. The main advantage of a limited payment policy is that premiums can be matched to earnings. For example, a person who plans to retire at age 60 might be better off with a paid up at 60 policy than ordinary life. With the paid up at 60 policy, no further insurance premium payments would be required, whereas with ordinary life, the person would have to continue making the premium payments after retirement.

Endowment Insurance

Endowment insurance is similar to whole life in the sense that it builds up a cash value. These policies become **endowed**, or fully paid up, after either a specified time period or when the insured attains a certain age. Typical endowment policies are endowed after 10 to 30 years or when the insured reaches age 55, 60, 65, or 70.

Endowment insurance guarantees to pay the face amount of the policy if either of two events occurs: (1) if the insured dies before the policy is endowed, the beneficiaries receive the face amount of the policy; (2) if the insured is still alive when the policy becomes endowed, he or she receives the full face amount of the policy. Notice in Table 14.3 that the endowment at 65 policy has a cash value of $1,000 at age 65.

The major advantage of endowment insurance is that payment of the face amount is guaranteed whether the insured lives or dies. Assuming that the insured survives past the endowment date, he or she can count on a fixed sum of money for planning for retirement. As Table 14.3 indicates, an endowment policy builds up a larger cash value faster than whole life policies. Because of this rapid, high buildup of cash value, an endowment policy is more expensive than whole life for most people. Also, policies with short endowment periods are more expensive than policies with longer endowment periods. That is, a policy that becomes endowed at age 60 is more expensive than one that is endowed at age 65.

Universal Life

As the name implies, **universal life insurance** is a very flexible insurance policy that allows the policy owner to periodically adjust the amount of coverage and insurance payments up or down to meet changing needs. Premiums paid are credited to the policy's **cash-value account**. Then periodically, generally every month, the insurance company deducts from the cash-value account an amount that provides the agreed-upon amount

of insurance coverage. Depending on the terms of the insurance policy, an investment management fee may also be deducted from the policy's cash-value account. The amount remaining in the cash-value account is then invested at a prestated interest rate that changes periodically. Some insurance companies adjust the interest rates as often as once a month.

The policy owner does not have to make a premium payment as long as there is sufficient money in the cash-value account to cover the cost of the insurance coverage. Thus, a policy owner who is strapped for cash could skip a payment or two. Similarly, a policy owner could make a payment large enough to cover only the cost of the insurance coverage, in which case the universal life insurance policy would behave like a term insurance policy. Or a policy owner could make all the payments due, which would make the policy look just like a whole life policy. Policy owners can also borrow against the cash-value account of the policy. Finally, universal life allows the policy owner to change the amount of insurance coverage within reasonable limits.

A universal life insurance policy provides protection against taxes. Values built up in the cash-value account accumulate tax-free until the policy owner withdraws cash from the account. Taxes are paid only on withdrawn amounts in excess of the amounts contributed by the policy owner.

Universal life has two options. Under **Option A**, beneficiaries receive the face value of the policy. Under **Option B**, beneficiaries receive the face value plus the cash value built up. Obviously, premiums for Option B are higher than premiums for Option A.

Universal life involves evaluation of three factors: (1) the interest rate paid on the cash value; (2) the cost of the insurance coverage, called the **mortality charge**; and (3) the investment management fees. From the policy owner's viewpoint, the policy should pay high interest rates and have low mortality charges and investment management fees. Insurance companies typically mix these three factors to determine premium charges that they believe will be attractive to insurance buyers. Unlike term and whole life insurances, universal life has no standard measures that can be applied to determine which policy is better. If you are interested in such a policy, it may be worthwhile to look at surveys by consumer magazines to identify highly rated universal life insurance policies.

Variable Life Insurance

With the Tax Reform Act of 1986, variable life insurance is expected to become a popular product. Variable life is similar to whole life or universal life with one major difference—the policy owner elects how the cash value will be invested. The returns earned by the investments become the returns for the policy. The policy owner can choose to have the cash value invested in stocks, bonds, mutual funds, or any combination. The cash value of the

policy will vary with the fluctuations in the underlying investments. If, for example, stocks are expected to rise, investments may be made in stock. On the other hand, if stocks are expected to decline, the policy owner may choose to invest in a money market fund whose value does not fluctuate.

The major problem with variable life is that it is possible for the cash value to decline to a low level, leaving insufficient money to keep the insurance in force. However, insurance companies are beginning to offer protection against this factor. As with any other policy, the insurance buyer should pay attention to the strength of the insurance company when considering variable life policies.

Single Premium Life Insurance

With **single premium life insurance**, the policy owner makes only one large insurance premium payment to pay up the policy. The typical premium for a policy of this type ranges from $5,000 to $1 million. The amount of the paid-up policy that a premium buys depends on the age of the buyer. For example, a $10,000 premium will buy about $52,000 in death benefits for a 35-year-old male. Single premium policies can be structured either as whole life or as variable life policies.

Generally, single premium policies do not impose any sales charges initially. As with universal life, mortality charges and investment management fees are deducted from the cash-value account of the policy. Some policies guarantee the interest rate earned on the policy. The insurance companies make their profits by earning more on the cash value than the guaranteed interest rate. The policy owner can borrow against the cash value of the policy. Cash values in the policy build up tax-free. In general, single premium policies are particularly attractive for couples over the age of 50. They can place cash in a single premium policy, build up the cash value tax-free, and then eventually borrow against the policy, also tax-free. On the death of the insured, the death benefits, less the loans and interest expense, are paid to the beneficiary free of income taxes.

Spot Quiz • Types of Life Insurance Policies

1. The major difference between straight and renewable term insurance is of insurability extending the insurance period.

    T _____   F _____

2. Whole life is more expensive than term insurance because it provides better insurance protection.   T _____   F _____

3. A fully endowed policy has a cash value equal to its face value.

T _____ F _____

4. A variable life insurance policy can be structured to look the same as a whole life policy. T _____ F _____

5. A single premium policy is paid up at the time it is purchased.

T _____ F _____

(Answers on page 469)

MAJOR PROVISIONS OF LIFE INSURANCE POLICIES

Life insurance policies have a variety of clauses, or provisions, that specify the rights and responsibilities of the insured and the insurer. A life insurance policy is a legal contract, and its clauses are binding on both parties to the contract. Thus, it is important for you to understand these provisions.

There is no such thing as a "standard" life insurance policy, but certain provisions are found in most policies. These provisions can be grouped into a number of categories: who owns the policy, who benefits from the insured's death, how the benefits are to be paid, what will cause the policy to lapse, what the terms of payment are, in what form dividends should be received, and whether it is advisable to borrow against the policy's cash value. These major provisions are discussed in this section.

Ownership of the Policy

Life insurance policies list the name of the policy owner, or policyholder. A policy owner has certain rights, including the rights to name the beneficiary, assign the policy to someone else, and cash the policy in. Normally, the insured is also the policy owner, though an individual may take out a life insurance policy on someone else as long as the individual (policy owner) has an insurable interest in the insured at the time the policy is purchased. In this chapter, though, we will assume that the insured is also the policy owner.

The Beneficiary

The **primary beneficiary** is the person who receives the death benefits from an insurance policy. The owner of the policy, usually the insured, can name

anyone to be the beneficiary. While it is usual to name one's spouse or children as beneficiaries, it is not unusual for owners to name hospitals, schools, friends, and even pets as beneficiaries.

The beneficiary has to live longer than the insured to collect on the policy. If the primary beneficiary dies before the insured and there has been no change in beneficiaries, then the death benefits go to any **contingent beneficiaries**. If primary and contingent beneficiaries die before the insured does and no new beneficiaries are named, then the death benefits become part of the insured's estate. In this case, the death benefits are distributed according to the insured's will. In the absence of a will, benefits are distributed in accordance with state laws.

Designating a beneficiary is very important from a financial viewpoint. Douglas E. Burt of Aetna Life Insurance Company states that "the single most important precaution a policyholder can take is to review his beneficiary designations periodically to make sure they are up-to-date."[6]

For example, Jay Koch designates his only child, Kay, as primary beneficiary. Subsequently, Jay has two more children, but he does not change his beneficiaries. On his death, only Kay will receive the death benefits from the insurance policy. Instead, Jay might have decided to name as beneficiary "children of the insured, Jay Koch." In this case, all children, including adopted and illegitimate children, would have shared in the benefits. Is this what Jay wanted to accomplish? Exactly how did Jay Koch want the death benefits to be distributed? Whatever he has in mind should be so reflected in the designation of his beneficiaries.

Settlement Options

The policy owner has the option of deciding how the benefits are to be distributed, either to the beneficiaries if the insured dies or to the insured if he or she survives. The nonforfeiture clause applies when the insured does not make premium payments. Settlement options related to default of premium payments are discussed later. Here our concern is with settlement options that apply when either the insured dies or has a paid up or endowed policy.

Life insurance policies have four settlement options: (1) lump sum payment, (2) interest income, (3) installment payments, and (4) annuity income.

Lump Sum Payment.   Under the **lump sum payment option**, the total policy benefits are paid to the beneficiary in cash. This option has certain advantages. Because the payment is in cash, the beneficiary can spend or invest the funds as needed. Also, the beneficiary can usually obtain a higher

---

6. "Who Will Collect on Your Life Insurance?" *Changing Times* (June 1981): 31.

"What sort of benefits?"

Source: *Changing Times*, April 1980, p. 46. Used
with permission.

rate of return on the cash benefits than with any other option offered by
the insurance company.

There are also disadvantages to this option. It places the burden of
managing the benefits on the beneficiary, and some beneficiaries may not
be able to manage the funds adequately. In some cases, beneficiaries might
spend the money rapidly and not have any source of income later. One
way to overcome this problem is for the insured to place the lump sum
payment in a trust account for the beneficiary. The trust would provide
the beneficiary with benefits while providing safety for the insurance proceeds. Trusts are discussed in Chapter 21 on estate planning. Also, insurance companies generally allow the beneficiary to choose another
settlement option.

Interest Income.   With the **interest income option**, the policy benefits
remain with the insurance company. The insurer pays interest income on
the benefits to the beneficiary. The policy owner may specify that not only
interest but also a certain amount of principal be paid to the beneficiary.
In some cases, the insured states that the beneficiary may withdraw all
of the principal at his or her option.

Some insureds use this option to pay interest income to one beneficiary,
and on this beneficiary's death, the principal is paid to another beneficiary.
For example, the insured may use this option to provide his or her spouse
with money for retirement. When the spouse also dies, the principal is
paid out to the couple's children. The major disadvantage of this option
is that insurance companies do not pay high interest income. Insurance
benefits received as a lump sum payment can earn higher returns
elsewhere.

Installment Payments.   With the **installment payments option**, the insurance company pays out the benefits in a series of installment payments. The payments may be monthly, quarterly, semiannually, or annually. There is a fixed period option and a fixed amount option. Under the **fixed period option**, the insured or the beneficiary specifies the time period over which the benefits are to be received. The payments stop when the fixed period expires. If the beneficiary dies before the end of the period, the remaining benefits either become part of the beneficiary's estate or are paid to other beneficiaries. The size of the periodic payment depends on the size of the insurance proceeds, the frequency of payment, the number of payments, and the interest rate paid by the insurance company.

The **fixed amount option** calls for payment of a fixed amount periodically until all the insurance proceeds are dissipated. Payments can be made on a monthly, quarterly, or other basis. The beneficiary selects the size of payment he or she desires to receive. The size of the insurance proceeds, the size of the periodic payments, and the interest rate paid by the insurer determine the time period for which payments will be made.

With both of these installment payment options, the insurance company guarantees a minimum rate of interest to be paid on the insurance proceeds. These minimum rates vary from 2.5 to 4.5 percent. The fixed amount option is generally more desirable because the beneficiary may be able to switch to an annuity income option, explained below.

Annuity Income.   Annuities will be discussed in greater detail in Chapter 20 on retirement planning. Therefore, only a brief mention will be made here. An **annuity** is a series of periodic payments starting at a specified date and ending at a specified date or on the death of one or more beneficiaries. Four basic types of annuity income options are available.

The **straight life**, or **pure annuity**, makes monthly payments for the life of the beneficiary. The payments stop as soon as the beneficiary dies. If the beneficiary dies prematurely, the insurance company retains the unpaid portion of the total benefits. However, if the beneficiary lives beyond his or her life expectancy, then the insurer has to continue paying benefits.

The **refund annuity** guarantees not only payments for the life of the beneficiary but also the minimum total benefits. If the beneficiary dies prematurely, then his or her estate is paid the remainder of the total benefits.

The **certain period annuity** guarantees payment for the life of the beneficiary as well as for a minimum specified period. If the beneficiary dies before the expiration of the period, payments are continued to the beneficiary's heirs until the end of the period.

The **joint and survivorship annuity** continues payment to a secondary beneficiary if the primary one dies. This annuity guarantees income for life to the surviving beneficiary.

Nonforfeiture Clause

Whole life and endowment policies build up cash values. The **nonforfeiture clause** ensures that this savings element, or cash value, will not be forfeited to the insurer under any circumstances. In practical terms, this means that the insured will not forfeit the cash value of the policy because of nonpayment of premiums. Basically, the insured has three options:

1. Take the cash value of the policy in cash.
2. Use the cash value to purchase a term policy for as many months or years as are allowed by the rates in effect at the insured person's age at the time of default.
3. Exchange the policy for a paid-up ordinary life policy.

These options are stated on all life insurance policies. If the insured does not select an option, most insurers automatically use the cash value to purchase a term policy, which is option number 2. If an insured wants to default on a cash value policy, then it is generally best to take the cash value rather than either of the optional policies.

Grace Period

Insurance policy premiums are due on a contractually specified date. A policy owner who fails to pay a premium when it is due has breached a term of the insurance contract. Contract law would permit the insurer to cancel the insurance policy under these circumstances. However, because this result was seen as unnecessarily harsh, all states have enacted laws requiring insurers to include a provision for grace periods in their life insurance policies. The **grace period** allows the insured a specified number of days in which to make a late payment and still keep the policy in force. Generally, the grace period is 30 days. That is, if payment is due on April 5, then the insured has until May 4 to make the premium payment.

The insurance policy remains in force during the grace period. If the insured dies during the grace period without making the current premium payment, the insurer will pay the beneficiary the face amount of the policy less the premium due. The policy lapses if payment is not made by the end of the grace period.

Reinstatement

The **reinstatement clause** allows the insured to reinstate a lapsed policy if certain conditions are met. The policy can be reinstated if: (1) the insured has not withdrawn the cash value of the policy; (2) the insured applies for reinstatement within a specified time after the policy lapse, generally within three to five years; (3) all unpaid premiums and related interest

expenses are paid; and (4) the insured presents evidence of insurability by passing a medical examination.

Sometimes it is more desirable to reinstate a lapsed policy than to buy a new one. Generally speaking, you can save on sales commissions by reinstating a lapsed policy. Paying the unpaid premiums immediately increases the cash value of the policy. However, if a new policy has the same options and features as a lapsed policy and is cheaper, then it is better to buy the new policy.

Incontestability Clause

Deliberate or unintentional misstatements made by the insured when she or he buys insurance can enable the insurer to void the policy, which really is a legal contract between the insurer and the insured. Problems would arise if there were no limitations on the rights of insurers to challenge information provided by the insured. For example, suppose a person takes out insurance. Thirty years later that person dies, and when the beneficiary tries to collect the policy benefits, the beneficiary is told that the insured lied about a heart condition, and therefore no benefits will be paid. The incontestability clause prevents this type of situation from occurring. The **incontestability clause** states that the insurer cannot question the validity of the information provided by the insured after the policy has been in force two years.

The insurance company thus has two years to question the validity of information provided to it by the insured. If the insurer has not contested the policy information within two years, then it cannot do so as long as the policy remains in force. For this reason, the insurer generally investigates the insurance policy applicant rather carefully.

Suicide Clause

Insurance covers chance events. Some people may seek to benefit unduly from insurance by buying insurance and then immediately committing suicide. The **suicide clause** addresses this issue. The suicide clause states that if the insured commits suicide within two years of the date the policy is issued, then the beneficiaries receive only the premiums paid, not the face amount of the policy. The insurer has to prove that death was due to suicide before it can apply this clause to any death benefits.

Installment Premium Payments

Typically, insurance premiums are due annually on the policy anniversary date. However, insurance companies make it easier for their policyholders by allowing them to make smaller monthly, quarterly, or semiannual

payments instead of a single annual payment. Such a plan is useful from a budgeting viewpoint. However, insurance companies charge a service fee of 12 to 18 percent annually on the installments due.

Dividends Clause

Insurance policies are sold on both a participating and a nonparticipating basis. **Participating policies** receive a portion of the unanticipated earnings of the insurer. These unanticipated earnings theoretically occur because the insurer had to pay on fewer claims than anticipated or earned a higher return on assets than expected or both. In practice, surplus earnings occur because the insurer overcharged on the premium. These surplus earnings, or excess premiums charged, are returned to the policy owners in the form of dividends. Dividends to participating policyholders, then, are a return of excess earnings or excess premiums charged. **Nonparticipating policyholders** are neither overcharged nor eligible for policy dividends.[7] There are five options for dividends received:

1. The insured can receive the dividends in cash.
2. The insured can apply the dividends toward premiums due and reduce the current premium due.
3. The dividends can be left with the insurer to accumulate interest. (The interest rate paid is around 3.5 to 5.5 percent.)
4. The dividends can be used to buy additional paid-up insurance.
5. The dividends can be used to buy term insurance.

In most cases, the best alternative is to receive the dividends in cash (option 1). Option 2 is similar to option 1 and is thus also a good option. Option 3 is very undesirable because of the low interest rate paid. Option 4 buys very small amounts of paid-up insurance. Option 5 is the next best alternative, because you are buying pure protection.

Loan Clause

The insured can borrow any amount up to the cash value of the insurance policy at any time, with interest rates on the loans varying between 7 and 10 percent. Excessive use of this loan clause, however, tends to negate the reason for buying insurance in the first place because benefits paid are reduced by the amount of policy loans outstanding. On the other hand, it is worthwhile to borrow against the cash value of the policy as long as the amount borrowed can be invested in safe securities that yield more

---

7. Participating policy dividends are distinct from dividends paid to stockholders of corporations. Corporate dividends are paid from earnings and are taxed as such by the IRS. Policy dividends are considered to be a return of excess premiums and are exempt from taxes.

than the loan interest rate. (See "Life Insurance and Student Loans" on page 457.)

We have considered a variety of insurance policy provisions in this section. A better understanding of these provisions will help you determine your options with an insurance policy, leading to better management of your life risk. The next section covers the management of life insurance.

Spot Quiz • Major Provisions of Life Insurance Policies

1. The primary and contingent beneficiaries participate equally in the distribution of insurance policy benefits.   T _____   F _____

2. An annuity income option is suited to providing for retirement income.
                                                                       T _____   F _____

3. A lapsed whole life policy usually has some value for the policyholder.
                                                                       T _____   F _____

(Answers on page 469)

MANAGING LIFE INSURANCE

Determining how much life insurance to buy, evaluating the cost of life insurance, and deciding among term, whole life, and endowment insurance are covered in this section.

How Much Insurance to Buy

How much insurance a person should buy depends on the person's or family's needs. One way of answering this question is to use a rule of thumb called multiples of salary. Another way is to use a life risk evaluation approach.

Multiples of Salary Method.   Using the **multiple of salary method**, a person determines insurance needs by multiplying his or her salary by some constant. An application of this method is shown in Table 14.4. The data were compiled by First National City Bank of New York. The table is based on the assumption that the surviving family has four members.

Life Insurance and Student Loans

Many insurance companies, hard-pressed to sell their products in a saturated and highly competitive market, are resorting to using student loans as a come-on to sell life insurance. An advertisement in a religious bulletin offered low-cost student loans. Parents interested in obtaining information about financing a college education for their children quickly found out that the ads were really designed to sell life insurance.

Reports in some states indicate that insurance salespeople aren't above pretending to be student loan counselors to get their feet in the door. Once they are able to talk to parents, they offer student loans if parents buy life insurance. Some try to stampede parents into signing up by indicating that banks and other financial institutions don't have enough money to lend.

Robert MacDonald, president of ITT Life Insurance Company, states that using student loans as a pretext for selling life insurance is confusing, deceptive, and at worst, immoral and illegal. Those who need student loans should seek information from financial aid advisers or counselors at schools and colleges. Those who need to buy life insurance should follow the accepted practices for buying life insurance. But don't buy life insurance just because a sales agent states that is the only way to obtain student loans.

Death benefits are considered to have been invested to yield 5 percent. It is assumed that the family's living expenses after the death of the wage earner are going to be at 60 or 75 percent of the level prevailing prior to death. It is also assumed that the family receives social security benefits. Finally, it is assumed that the family does not receive any income from any other sources, such as investment assets and pensions.

The first column of Table 14.4 lists the gross earnings of the wage earner. The remaining columns are classified by the age of the spouse and living expenses as a percent of the wage earner's earnings. We can now go back to the Cesaris and see how much insurance they need. Joe makes about $30,000 annually. Linda's age is close to 35 years, and she would need living expenses at about the 75 percent level. For age 35 years and under, at 75 percent and $30,000, the multiple is 8.0. This means that the Cesaris would need about $30,000 × 8.0 = $240,000 in insurance.

The disadvantage of this method is that the assumptions can cause the amount of insurance calculated to be overestimated. For example, as the interest earned from investments increases, the constant multiple will decline. Similarly, a family that has savings or that receives a pension will need less insurance. Despite this drawback, though, the multiples of salary method can help you quickly estimate the amount of insurance coverage needed.

Table 14.4 Multiples of Salary Approach

Your present gross earnings	Present Age of Spouse							
	25 Years		35 Years		45 Years		55 Years	
	75%	60%	75%	60%	75%	60%	75%	60%
$ 7,500	4.0	3.0	5.5	4.0	7.5	5.5	6.5	4.5
9,000	4.0	3.0	5.5	4.0	7.5	5.5	6.5	4.5
15,000	4.5	3.0	6.5	4.5	8.0	6.0	7.0	5.5
23,500	6.5	4.5	8.0	5.5	8.5	6.5	7.5	5.5
30,000	7.5	5.0	8.0	6.0	8.5	6.5	7.0	5.5
40,000	7.5	5.0	8.0	6.0	8.0	6.0	7.0	5.5
65,000	7.5	5.5	7.5	6.0	7.5	6.0	6.5	5.0

Reprinted by courtesy of *Consumer Views,* published by Citibank, July 1976.

Needs Evaluation Method. The **needs evaluation method** takes into account the evaluation of life risk and the various sources of income for the surviving family. The difference between total living expenses and incomes available is the amount of life risk that is transferred by buying insurance. In the Cesaris' case, it was stated that about $600 per month needed to be covered by life insurance. The annual income needed from life insurance is $600 × 12 = $7,200. Linda is expected to live 30 years or more. For a 12 percent annual rate of return, the present value factor from Table 14.2 is 8.33. The Cesaris will need $7,200 × 8.33 = about $60,000 in life insurance coverage on Joe. If Joe dies, Linda would receive $60,000 in benefits. This amount invested at 12 percent would give her $60,000 × .12 = $7,200 in income every year.

The multiples of salary and needs evaluation methods suggest different amounts of insurance to buy. The first suggests $240,000, whereas the second suggests $60,000. The difference is accounted for by two factors. First, Linda plans to work for quite a long time. Therefore, the needs evaluation approach shows that a lower amount of insurance is needed. Second, Table 14.4 assumes a rate of return that is different from the rate of return used in the needs evaluation approach. Adjustments made for these two factors would give similar answers with both methods.

Making Cost Comparisons

People frequently say that you do not buy insurance, you are sold insurance. There is quite a bit of truth in this statement. Many people do

not evaluate life risk and then seek suitable insurance coverage. Rather, they are solicited by insurance salespeople, who sell them insurance. This is an undesirable way of buying insurance coverage. First, sufficient analysis is not done on how much insurance to buy. Second, the consumer buys the insurance being sold by the salesperson without investigating other companies and costs. Costs for the same policy vary significantly from company to company. Therefore, it is important to make cost comparisons before buying insurance. (See "What's the Deal on No-Load Insurance?" below.)

Comparing life insurance costs can be somewhat difficult because of differences in policy clauses, options, dividends, and the pattern and timing of monies paid and received. A good evaluation method will adjust for the time value of money. That is, the method will recognize that a dollar received today has more value than a dollar received in the future. Three methods are used to make cost comparisons: (1) the net payment cost index, (2) the interest adjusted cost index, and (3) the net cost method. All of these methods assume that the policy will remain in force for a specified number of years. Typically, cost comparisons are made for 10 to 20 years. Comparisons are stated in terms of annual cost per $1,000 of insurance.

What's the Deal on No-Load Insurance?

It used to be that when you bought life insurance, the agent got to keep a hefty portion of the first year's premium. Thereafter, he or she would receive about 5 to 10 percent of the policy premium paid each year. While this arrangement still holds true for many insurance companies, some are beginning to tout "no-load" insurance. No-load, a term that originated with mutual funds, indicates that no sales commission is charged. No-load insurance, then, by definition, should mean insurance you can buy without paying any sales commission. Such is not the case, however.

Insurance is still sold by agents, and they need to receive sales commissions to survive. Here's what happens with the insurance version of "no-load." An insurance company that sells no-load insurance does not charge any commissions when the policy is sold. However, it will impose a number of other charges in place of the sales commission. For example, it may impose a surrender fee that will be charged when the policy is cashed in. Surrender charges can be up to 10 percent of the policy value. Some companies have surrender charges that decline over a number of years. No-load insurance typically includes an annual investment management fee that is taken out of the earnings associated with the policy. For example, the fee might reduce a 12 percent earnings rate to 9 percent. The deal on no-load insurance is that it's no big deal.

Net Payment Cost Index. The **net payment cost index** adjusts only premiums and dividends for the time value of money. The present value of all dividends received is netted out from the present value of all premiums paid. The net payment is divided by the number of years used for analysis to arrive at an average annual cost for the policy. Other things being the same, a policy with a lower net payment cost index is better than one with a higher index.

Interest Adjusted Cost Index. The **interest adjusted cost index**, also called the **surrender cost index**, is more comprehensive than the net payment cost index. Premiums, dividends, and cash values are adjusted for the time value of money. The present values of all dividends and the cash value are subtracted from the present value of all premiums. The resulting figure is divided by the number of years of analysis to give an average annual cost. A policy with a lower interest adjusted cost index is better than a similar policy with a higher index.

Net Cost Method. With the **net cost method**, the policy premiums for a specified number of years are added up, the expected dividends and the cash value are subtracted from that total, and the amount remaining is divided by the specified number of years to obtain an average annual net cost per $1,000 of insurance. Typically, the specified number of years is 20.

Often this method shows that the policy owner is actually making a profit by buying life insurance. Of course, the policy owner is not making a profit. A profit is shown only because the time value of money is not taken into consideration. A dollar of cash value received 20 years from today is given the same value as a dollar of premium paid today. If the rate of return is 12 percent per annum, then the present value of a dollar received 20 years from today is only 10.4 cents. Large cash values are not adjusted for the time value of money, and this method therefore understates the true cost of life insurance.

The net cost method is no longer used by insurance companies because it is not useful for making cost comparisons. However, you might encounter an insurance agent who uses it to demonstrate the low cost of the policies he or she is selling. This method has thus been mentioned so you will be aware of it.

Which Method to Use? Both the net payment cost index (NPCI) and the interest adjusted cost index (IACI) take into consideration the time value of money. However, the two methods differ; the NPCI analysis does *not* include the cash value, whereas the IACI analysis does. The NPCI analysis assumes that the insured person will die and the beneficiary will receive the face amount of the policy. In this case, the cash value is not relevant and is excluded from analysis.

The IACI analysis, on the other hand, assumes that the insured person is the beneficiary and will utilize the policy's cash value. Therefore, the IACI analysis includes the cash value. If one of the two policies being compared has lower figures for both NPCI and IACI, that is the better policy. However, the better option is not clear-cut when a policy has one higher and one lower index. Consider the following example:

	Policy A	Policy B
NPCI	$9.23	$11.59
IACI	$3.21	$ 2.16

Which policy is better? If the insured has a family history of premature deaths, then policy A is better. However, if the insured comes from a family with a history of long lives, then policy B is better because it has the lower IACI. Only the insured can determine the more suitable policy.

Two Words of Caution. Two policies can be compared only if the same rate of return is used for calculating present values. If different rates are used, then the NPCI and IACI for the policies will not be comparable. Second, insurance companies love to use low rates of return in the analysis because it lowers their cost indexes. Insist on seeing indexes that base analysis on realistic rates. An index based on a rate of 5 percent is not very useful. NPCIs and IACIs that use rates of 8 to 12 percent better reflect the true cost of insurance.

Life Insurance Riders

Riders are extra options that can be written into a policy to make it more suitable. Three important riders are waiver of premiums, double indemnity, and guaranteed insurability.

Waiver of Premium. Some insurance companies include this rider automatically, whereas others offer it as an option. With **waiver of premium**, the insurer waives premiums if the insured becomes permanently disabled. Premiums do not have to be paid for the duration of the disability, and all policy benefits remain in force during the waiver period. While this option does not provide income during the disability period, it does free up the premiums for use in meeting living expenses and is thus a desirable option.

Double Indemnity. **Double indemnity** calls for payment of twice the face amount of the policy in death benefits if the insured is killed in an accident. The option is not really useful for a person or family who has

done a proper job of life risk evaluation. If we go back to the example of the Cesari family, we note that the surviving family's expenses and life insurance needs remain the same no matter how Joe dies. Whether Joe is killed in a car accident or dies of a heart attack, his family's income needs are not affected. Despite the attraction of collecting double benefits for an accidental death, this option is not desirable.

Guaranteed Insurability. **Guaranteed insurability** gives the insured the right to buy additional specified amounts of insurance at specified intervals without providing proof of insurability. Typically, the option can be exercised every three years up to age 40. For example, at age 31, Joe Cesari buys $150,000 in insurance. He has the option of buying $20,000 in additional insurance at age 34, 37, and 40 without passing a medical examination. Shortly after buying the insurance, Joe finds out that he has developed a heart condition and is no longer insurable. However, with this option, he can eventually buy an additional $60,000 in life insurance coverage. It is nice to have this option. However, do not buy additional insurance automatically just because the insurance agent states that an option date is coming up.

Which Type of Insurance to Buy?

Which type of insurance should you buy? Keep in mind that the primary purpose of life insurance is to transfer life risk. Term insurance is thus desirable because it provides protection only. For shorter time periods— say, for periods of five to ten years—term insurance provides the best buy for your money.

One problem with term insurance is that it is generally not available after age 65 or 70. If you prefer to be insured until death, then you should buy whole life insurance. Another problem with term insurance is that premium costs rise very sharply after age 50. If you plan to carry insurance until about age 65, then it might be best to compare costs for both term and whole life before buying insurance.

If a family is just getting started, chances are that it will be on a tight budget for some time. However, this family will also have high insurance needs because it will not have much in terms of investable assets. With the limited insurance dollars available, it is better for this family to buy the maximum amount of term insurance. The other alternative—buying whole life—will result in inadequate coverage of life risk.

For the disciplined person who can save systematically year after year, term insurance will be a better buy than the other policies mentioned. Other policies combine insurance with a forced savings plan—buying a whole life policy forces a person to save systematically. A whole life policy that matures at age 65 provides the beneficiary with some funds for retirement. Such is not the case with term insurance because it has no cash value.

However, a disciplined person can buy term insurance and invest the difference between the whole life and term premiums and can end up with more money than the cash value on the whole life policy. The key word is *discipline.* If you do not have the willpower to save systematically for retirement, then whole life—or for that matter, universal or variable life—might be your best alternative.

Finally, keep in mind that whole life, endowment, variable life, universal life, and single premium policies offer certain tax advantages. For certain income and age categories, these policies may be desirable.

Shopping for Insurance

The first rule in shopping for insurance is not to buy insurance simply because your brother, sister, friend, or relative is selling it. Second, do not buy insurance without conducting a thorough needs analysis. The next step is to compare the costs of policies issued by different companies. *Consumer Reports* periodically contains information on life insurance costs. *Cost Facts on Life Insurance* (Cincinnati, OH: National Underwriter Company) also contains cost information. Both of these publications are readily available in public libraries. The final step is to select an insurance company based on the guidelines in Chapter 11.

Table 14.5 shows the NPCI and IACI for both term and whole life policies. Three columns appear under both NPCI and IACI. The first column for each index shows the lowest cost. The second column shows the median cost. (The median cost means that half of the insurance companies

Table 14.5 Life Insurance Cost Indexes*

Type of Policy	NPCI			IACI		
	Lowest	Median	Highest	Lowest	Median	Highest
Term						
Participating		NA		1.63	3.07	4.26
Nonparticipating		NA		2.44	2.96	5.43
Whole Life						
Participating	6.07	10.49	14.49	−0.14	2.62	6.63
Nonparticipating	6.58	9.84	13.75	2.10	3.59	6.54

*The costs are for a $100,000 face value policy issued to a 25-year-old male. The information was compiled from the February and March 1980 issues of *Consumer Reports.* NA = not applicable.

have indexes higher than the median, and half have indexes lower than the median.) The last column shows the highest cost.

IACI analysis covers premiums, dividends, and cash value. The IACI difference between highest and lowest costs for participating whole life is $6.63 - (-$0.14) = $6.77. This is the annual cost per $1,000 for 20 years. If you were to buy the most expensive policy, you would incur $6.77 × 100 × 20 = $13,540 more in costs for a $100,000, 20-year policy than if you bought the cheapest policy. Obviously, shopping for insurance policies can save you money.

Table 14.5 shows that whole life has a lower IACI than term insurance. This does not mean that whole life insurance is cheaper than term, however. The interest rate used in the analysis is 5 percent. If a more realistic rate of return were used, say 8 to 12 percent, then term insurance generally would be cheaper than whole life. When you buy life insurance, it is generally desirable to find an acceptable insurance company whose cost indexes are near the lower end of the cost scale.

Spot Quiz • Managing Life Insurance

1. Generally speaking, the multiples of salary and needs evaluation approaches give fairly similar estimates.   T _____   F _____

2. The net cost method is the best method for evaluating insurance policy costs.   T _____   F _____

3. The NPCI should be used when the insured person does not expect to be the policy beneficiary.   T _____   F _____

(Answers on page 469)

Summary

Life risk is the risk of dying prematurely. Evaluation of life risk covers both immediate cash needs and living expenses needs. Living expenses will vary during the survivor's lifetime, depending on the circumstances. Life risk can be retained or transferred. The amount retained depends on investment assets owned, the survivor's potential earnings, and social security

and similar benefits. The difference between living expenses and the amount of risk covered by retention should be transferred by buying life insurance.

Six major types of policies are term, whole life, endowment, universal life, variable life, and single premium. Term insurance provides pure insurance, while the other five combine insurance with savings plans. Term insurance policies are generally renewable and convertible into whole life policies. Decreasing term has level premiums with gradually declining death benefits. Term insurance policies have a fixed life.

Whole life insurance is called permanent insurance because the policy remains in force as long as the policyholder continues to pay premiums. Whole life combines insurance with savings. The savings portion of the policy is called cash value. Ordinary life policies require premium payments until the insured's death. Limited payment policies require payment for a fixed period only. Endowment insurance builds up cash value more quickly than whole life.

Universal life is a very flexible type of policy that allows the policy owner to periodically adjust the insurance premiums to suit changing needs. Variable life is similar to whole life and universal life, but it allows the policy owner to indicate how the cash value should be invested. With single premium life insurance, only one premium is paid. The cash value can be invested in fixed- or variable-return investments. With the exception of term insurance, insurance policies build up cash value tax-free.

Typically, the insured is the policy owner, but occasionally it is desirable for the beneficiary of the insured to be the policy owner. Primary and contingent beneficiaries should be carefully designated. Policy benefits can be received in a variety of ways, each with its own advantages. If the policy owner defaults on making premium payments, he or she has three options for using the cash value of the policy.

A lapsed policy can be reinstated within a specified time by meeting certain conditions. Participating policies pay dividends. The policy owner has a number of options for receiving the dividends. Policy owners can also borrow against the cash value of their policies.

Multiples of salary and needs evaluation are two methods for determining the amount of insurance a person should buy. Costs of policies can be compared by using the net payment cost index and the interest adjusted cost index. Waiver of premium and guaranteed insurability are two desirable riders to have with insurance policies.

Questions

1. Briefly explain the procedure for evaluating life risk.

2. Explain how living expenses change during the survivors' remaining life.

3. What strategies should be used for managing life risk?

4. Briefly explain the factors that affect retention of life risk.

5. What are the differences between straight and decreasing term insurances?

6. What are the advantages of owning renewable and convertible term insurance?

7. Explain the similarities and differences between ordinary life insurance and limited payment insurance.

8. What is meant by endowment insurance? How does it differ from whole life insurance?

9. Explain the major characteristics of universal life insurance. How does it differ from whole life and ordinary life insurance?

10. Why would variable life insurance be more desirable than whole life insurance?

11. Why would a single premium insurance policy have special appeal for consumers close to retirement age?

12. Explain the conditions under which it would be desirable for the beneficiary rather than the insured to be the policyholder.

13. Who would get the insurance policy death benefits in each of the following situations:
    a. The beneficiary dies before the insured.
    b. The primary beneficiary dies before the insured; there is a contingent beneficiary.
    c. The contingent beneficiary dies before the insured.

14. What are the advantages and disadvantages of a lump sum payment as a settlement option?

15. Which installment option is most desirable? Why?

16. Which annuity option is most desirable? Why?

17. What options do you have if you default on a policy premium?

18. Explain the conditions that need to be met before a policy can be reinstated.

19. What is meant by the incontestability clause? How is it advantageous for the insured?

20. How do you use the multiple of salary approach to determine the amount of insurance needed?

21. Explain how the needs evaluation approach works to determine how much insurance to buy.

22. Is the net cost method good for comparing life insurance costs? Why or why not?

23. What is the difference, if any, between the NPCI and the IACI?

24. Is the NPCI or the IACI better for comparing life insurance policy costs? Explain your answer.

25. Why is the double indemnity rider not considered desirable?

26. Generally speaking, is term or whole life insurance more desirable? Explain your answer.

Case Problems

1. Leslie Urbanski is a 29-year-old single parent with a seven-year-old daughter. For the past three years she has worked as the shoe department manager for a department store owned by a national chain. She is in line to become assistant store manager soon. Her employer provides her with term insurance equal to her salary, which is about $20,000 per year. She has become friends with an insurance agent who is in her aerobic dance class. The agent has suggested that Leslie should take out about $100,000 in term insurance, just in case. Leslie's sister has agreed to look after her daughter in the event that Leslie is disabled or dies. What advice do you have for Leslie?

2. Rex and Robin Stelson are both 35 years old, and both work as independent management consultants. Each has take-home income of about $20,000 annually. They have two children, aged five and

seven years. Their total investable assets of about $150,000 earn 12 percent annually. Their annual living expenses are about $35,000. If either spouse dies, living expenses would not decline because the surviving spouse would have to hire child and home care help. Answer the following questions, assuming that either Rex or Robin could die prematurely:
a. Perform all life risk evaluation for the surviving spouse.
b. How much life risk could the surviving spouse retain?
c. How much life insurance, if any, should each of the Stelsons buy? Assume that the surviving spouse will not receive any social security benefits and that the rate of return is 12 percent.

3. An insurance agent has offered to sell Lani Wong a $100,000 whole life nonparticipating policy. The annual premiums would be $1,700. The policy would be paid up at age 65 and would have a cash value of $70,000. A $100,000 renewable term insurance policy would cost Lani only $300 the first year. But over the next 35 years to age 65, the premiums would average about $1,450 per year. Lani has two alternatives: (a) buy the whole life policy or (b) buy the term insurance and invest the difference in premiums at a rate of return of 12 percent per year. What should Lani do? Show calculations to support your answer. (*Hint:* The present value of $1 received 35 years from today is 1.9 cents if the rate of return used is 12 percent.)

Bibliography

"The Hot Air in 'No-Load' Insurance." *Changing Times* (April 1987): 89–92.

"How to Save $500 a Year on Insurance." *Money* (September 1986): 85–92.

"Insurance and an Investment, Too." *Changing Times* (May 1986): 73–79.

"Investments That Can Save You Taxes." *Money* (February 1987): 135–154.

"It's Still Life Insurance, After All." *Money* (March 1987): 167–178.

"Life Insurance." *Consumer Reports* (June 1986): 371–402.

"Life Insurance." *Consumer Reports* (August 1986): 515–529.

"Life Insurance: Should Your Protection Double as an Investment?" *Money* (March 1987): 140–165.

Answers to Spot Quizzes

Managing Life Risk (page 442)

1. F (Life risk can be quantified and evaluated.)

2. T (Some life risk can be retained.)

3. F (Benefits stop when the child becomes 18 years old and do not resume until the parent is 62.)

Types of Life Insurance Policies (page 448)

1. T (Insurability extending the insurance period is required for straight term but not for renewable term.)

2. F (It is more expensive because of its savings component.)

3. T (This occurs on the endowment date.)

4. T (By making all the payments due and investing in bonds.)

5. T (By definition.)

Major Provisions of Life Insurance Policies (page 456)

1. F (First rights belong to the primary beneficiary.)

2. T (That is its basic purpose.)

3. T (It may have a cash value.)

Managing Life Insurance (page 464)

1. T (Both take into consideration similar factors.)

2. F (It is not adjusted for the time value of money.)

3. T (Since cash value is not included in the analysis.)

Part 5

Investments

Part 5 covers Investments, which are devices people use to build their estates. Chapter 15, "The Basics of Investing," explains why investments are necessary for personal financial planning. Methods for saving money for investments, returns, and risks are also discussed.

Chapter 16, "Information and Transactions for Securities Markets," describes securities markets and sources of information on securities. The procedures for selecting a broker and making securities transactions are also discussed. Chapter 17, "Stocks and Bonds," covers investments in common stock, preferred stock, and bonds. The advantages and disadvantages of these investments are explained.

Chapter 18, "Managing Investment Funds," explores the alternative strategies an investor can follow, such as personal management of funds, joining investments clubs, and buying mutual funds. Chapter 19, "Speculative Investments," examines convertible securities, options, real estate, commodities, coins, gold, stamps, gems, art, antiques, dolls, Americana, books, and collectibles as possible investments.

Chapter 15

The Basics of Investing

Objectives

After reading this chapter, you will be able to:

- Explain why people invest.
- Describe some ways to generate money for investing.
- List five different types of returns from investing.
- Define risk from an investing viewpoint.
- List four different types of investment risks and explain each.
- Explain the term *composite risk*.
- Discuss the relationship between risk and return in investing.
- List three different types of investment goals and explain each.
- Discuss investment alternatives and the advantages of each in meeting specific investment goals.

Craig Hall had an uncommon problem when he started college a few years
back: He had $4,000 in excess funds that he wanted to invest. While attend-
ing Eastern Michigan University in Ypsilanti, Hall started looking around
for an investment property in nearby Ann Arbor, Michigan. He bought
a run-down house for $27,250, using his $4,000 for the down payment.
During his spare hours, he painted, carpeted, and renovated the house.
Two years later he sold the house for $52,000. He cleared about $20,000
on the transaction, a 400 percent return on his $4,000 down payment. Not
bad, you say. The guy probably graduated from Eastern and moved to a
safe, comfortable job in Detroit. Right? Not quite.

Hall got hooked on investing in real estate. He continued to buy and
sell investment properties, and he wrote a book about his experiences.[1]
One final question: How well has he done? By his own estimate, Hall's
investment grew from $4,000 to over $10 million in ten years—all before
his thirtieth birthday!

Not all of us are interested in real estate investments. Besides real estate,
there are stamps, coins, comic books, lunch boxes, beer cans, dolls, jewelry,
antiques, books, prints, art objects, gizmos, and doodads. And let's not
forget stocks and bonds.

It is not very often that we hear about someone as successful at investing as Craig Hall; more familiar are tales about people who lost money
in the stock market. Every investment opportunity carries with it only a
promise of providing a return and a chance that the investment will go
down in value. That is, investments include both returns and the risk of
loss. This chapter covers the basics of the returns expected and the risks
involved in investing. The chapter also provides a brief overview of investment alternatives.

WHY INVEST?

A basic question that people face early in their careers is "Why should
I bother to invest my money?" This question can be restated as "What
should I do with my income?" Most people have two viable alternatives
for their incomes: they can spend it all or they can spend some of it and
save the rest. That is, for a given time period,

$$\text{Spending} + \text{Savings} = \text{Income}$$

---

1. Hall's amazing story is told in his book *The Real Estate Turnaround* (Englewood Cliffs,
NJ: Prentice-Hall, 1978).

All of us must make certain expenditures, such as for food, clothing, shelter, recreation, and transportation. But our incomes usually exceed what we pay for typical necessities. This excess portion of income can be either saved or spent on non-essential items. The consumer must consciously decide whether to spend or save this portion of income.

If a person decides to save a portion of his or her income, that decision raises another question: "Why save?" Savings can be viewed as postponing present consumption in favor of future consumption. A person may be willing to save if he or she believes that the satisfaction derived from savings now and consuming in the future is greater than the satisfaction derived from current consumption. For example, one person may decide to save $15 each week and use the money saved after one year to take a vacation. Another person may choose to spend the same amount on recreation each week and not save. For the first person, future consumption is more desirable than current consumption. The reverse is true for the second person.

The tradeoff between present consumption and saving for future consumption is one we all face. It is a personal decision—there is no right or wrong about it. What we are doing is maximizing our satisfaction, or welfare. Each person has a different view of how he or she can maximize his or her own welfare, and welfare is a function of both present and future consumption.

We are now in a position to go back and answer the first question we posed earlier: "What should I do with my income?" We should use our incomes to maximize our welfare. Maximizing our welfare implies maximizing our present as well as our future consumption. However, maximizing our future consumption depends on how we have invested portions of our incomes. In the previous example, a person is saving $15 a week for 52 weeks. If the person stuffs the money in a mattress, he or she will have after one year $15 × 52 = $780. Now assume that this amount is invested in a savings account that pays and compounds interest weekly. The interest rate is 5.25 percent. After one year, this person will have $800.42 in the savings account. By investing, this person has more money for future consumption than by not investing.

Now the reason for investing becomes obvious. We invest to maximize, or increase, our welfare. We invest to earn a return. Investments in savings accounts are very safe, and the returns are not risky. Other investments, such as buying stocks or antiques, do not guarantee a set return. The returns are risky. In all investments, however, there is a common issue—the investor expects the return to be positive. **Investments** can be defined as assets acquired with the expectation of earning a positive return over a certain time span.

Spot Quiz • Why Invest?

1. People invest to maximize their welfare.   T _____ F _____

2. Investing and gambling are similar.   T _____ F _____

3. Savings is a form of consumption.   T _____ F _____

(Answers on page 496)

MONEY FOR INVESTING

Craig Hall did not receive his initial investment amount of $4,000 from his parents as a "going away to college" present. He diligently accumulated the sum by doing odd jobs, starting at age ten. What alternatives exist to allow you to save for investing? Some alternatives for accumulating money for investing are discussed in this section.

Using Budgets

In Chapter 3 you learned how to prepare budgets. Using budgets effectively requires planning and discipline. Budgeting forces you to carefully consider your spending patterns and to reduce expenditures on items and services you do not really need. By controlling your expenditures, you can program savings into your budget. Budgeting for a periodic savings amount will lead to a steady accumulation of funds for investing. (See "Why Not Start Investing Now?" on page 477.)

Forced Savings

A variety of methods is available for forcing savings. A typical method is the payroll savings plan. The employer automatically withholds a specified amount from the paycheck of a participating employee and either places the money in a savings account or buys a government savings bond for the employee. This procedure allows the savings amount withheld to be thought of as "just another deduction from the paycheck."

Some people deliberately understate their exemptions for federal tax withholding purposes. This way extra taxes are withheld from their paychecks, and the people are assured of a good-sized return. Keep in mind that the extra amount withheld is really an interest-free loan to the federal government. However, if this is the only way you can save, then the use of this plan is justified. Another way of saving money is to buy a life insurance policy that builds up a cash value over time.

Why Not Start Investing Now?

Popular investments and consumer-oriented magazines such as *Money* and *Changing Times* routinely publish articles on how to invest $1,000 or $5,000 or how a certain dentist is making a bundle in the stock market between drilling molars. This doesn't mean that investing is limited to people with large chunks of money, professional degrees, or the experience of age. It is never too early to start investing, provided you follow a few simple rules. The lack of thousands of dollars for investments should not keep you from investing. If you call investment brokerage houses, you will find a broker who will be willing to accept orders for even small investment sums.

When you first start investing, you should remember four rules:

1. Investing should be done with real money rather than with "play" money. Trying to keep track of imaginary investments, even in real stocks and bonds, begins to lose appeal after a while. Investing even small amounts of real money can produce the curiosity to learn more and become more knowledgeable about current economic and business events. This accumulation of knowledge and information will prove even more beneficial when larger sums of investment monies are at your disposal.

2. Buy stocks of companies that are familiar to you. You will not only draw on your existing base of information but also continue to maintain your interest in your investments. Fast-food chains, clothing companies, and sporting goods manufacturers tend to be popular with young adults.

3. Buy stocks that pay cash dividends. Receiving periodic cash dividends tends to reinforce the reasons for investing in the first place.

4. To the extent possible, make your own investment decisions. You will learn more quickly from your own decisions, even if some of them turn out to be wrong.

Skip an Expenditure

Most people have set patterns of spending money. The expenditures are incurred almost automatically. For example, you might habitually go out for lunch every work day. One way to save might be to "brown bag" your lunch once a week, and put the lunch money saved in a jar or a piggy bank. Similarly, try periodically skipping the set expenditures involved in activities such as weekend bowling, golfing, or going to the movies.

Save the Nonroutine Incomes

Every once in a while, people receive funds that are nonroutine. A student may receive payment for painting a house during spring break or an unexpected gift from a relative. A person may sell off extra furniture or receive an excess amount from an escrow account. Rather than spending these nonroutine amounts, you should save and invest them. This can be done rather easily because the nonroutine incomes are not needed for meeting day-to-day expenses. Any one or a combination of the methods described will lead to the generation of savings, which then can be invested periodically.

Spot Quiz • Money for Investing

1. "Easy come, easy go" is a good saying as far as nonroutine income is concerned.   T _____   F _____

2. Thinking of a regular savings program as "planned expenditures" helps some people to save.   T _____   F _____

(Answers on page 496)

RETURNS FROM INVESTING

Investments involve both returns and risk. Thus, people invest with the expectation of returns and with the knowledge that these returns may not be realized. The various components of returns from an investment are discussed in this section.

Types of Returns

Interest, dividends, capital gains, rent, and retirement income are all forms of returns on investments.

Interest.   A person makes an investment by lending money to someone else. For example, opening a savings account at a bank is basically lending money to the bank. Another form of lending is buying bonds issued by the government or a corporation. One way that the federal government borrows money, for example, is by selling U.S. savings bonds. Borrowers (such as banks, corporations, and the federal government) pay interest on the loans they have received. These **interest payments** are returns to, or income for, the lenders. Annual interest income is usually expressed as a percent of the loan amount.

Dividends.   A well-managed company will generate profits. The company has two alternatives for using its profits. It can keep all or some portion of profits and reinvest them in the business. The amount of profits that the firm keeps for reinvesting is called **retained earnings**. Or the firm can return some or all of its profits to its stockholders. The portion of profits paid to stockholders is called **dividends**. Dividends are usually stated as a dollar amount per share of common stock.

Capital Gains.   When you buy certain investments, such as common stock, it is with the expectation that, besides earning dividends, the price of your stock will go up. If the stock is sold for a price that is higher than the purchase price, then the difference between the selling price and the purchase price is called **capital gains**. Capital gains are a form of return on investments. Many investments are bought with the expectation of capital gains. People invest in such items as antiques and art objects not because such objects pay dividends but because they are expected to produce capital gains. Of course, not all investments go up in price. Investments that go down in price and are sold for less than the purchase price produce **capital losses**.

Rent.   A person can buy property and then lease the use of the property to someone else. The person leasing the property pays **rent** to the owner. Most of us have lived in a rented house, trailer, or apartment at one time. Rent paid to the owner of a property is another form of return on investment.

Retirement Income.   A person who has financially planned his or her retirement will receive retirement income. This **retirement income** may be

from social security, from a pension plan, or from a life insurance policy purchased many years before. Retirement income is a form of return on investment. It's true that people have no choice about making certain types of retirement income investments, such as social security. Still, such forced payments are investments and are expected to produce returns in later years.

Some Examples of Returns

A person invests money in a savings account at a financial institution. The interest received by the person is the return on that investment. Similarly, a person who buys U.S. savings bonds will receive returns in the form of interest. People who own the common stock of Procter & Gamble or IBM, for example, are reasonably well assured of receiving periodic dividends on their holdings.

Let's assume that a person bought a house for $65,000 five years ago. Recently, this house was sold for $87,000. The difference between the selling price and the purchase price is the profit the homeowner made on the house and is a return on the $65,000 investment. Someone who buys stock for $1,000 and sells it for $1,200 one year later has earned a return of ($1,200 − $1,000)/$1,000 = .20, or 20 percent, on the investment of $1,000.

A person buys an apartment building for $100,000 and receives rent of $18,000 annually. After operating expenses of $6,000, the person is left with $12,000 every year, which is the annual return on the $100,000 investment. A person may buy an ordinary life insurance policy, which pays $500 per month after that person reaches age 65. Part of the $500 is the money originally paid for the insurance policy (the premiums). The remaining amount is the return from the policy. These are but a few examples of investment returns.

Spot Quiz • Returns from Investing

1. Returns on investments are guaranteed.   T _____   F _____

2. Some returns are received periodically, whereas others are expected but received at unspecified times.   T _____   F _____

(Answers on page 496)

Risks in Investing

The saying "There is no free lunch" is highly applicable to investments. Some investments are considered to be risk-free. U.S. savings bonds and insured deposits in savings accounts fall into this category. The returns earned on risk-free investments are the lowest possible. These returns are compensation to the investor for the use of the money invested. Investments offering higher returns carry some risk. The concept of risk is explained in this section.

What Is Risk?

An investor places $1,000 in an insured savings account for one year. The institution pays 5.5 percent interest on the investor's money. How much interest does the investor expect to receive after one year? He or she expects $55. How sure is the investor of receiving the $55 after one year? The investor is 100 percent sure. Let's assume that another investor buys $1,000 worth of stock in Xerox Corp. The investor expects that the price of the stock will be $1,100 after one year. The investor's expected return (excluding any dividends paid) is $100. How sure is the investor of receiving this $100 return? Not very sure. The actual return could be lower or higher than $100.

In the previous examples, the savings account investment is considered to be risk-free, whereas the common stock investment is considered to be risky. The differences in our expectations for realizing the returns tell us something about risk. For the savings investment, actual return will equal expected return. For the stock investment, actual return *may* equal expected return. In investment terms, **risk** is defined as the uncertainty of actual returns equaling expected returns. The higher the degree of uncertainty about the expected return is, the higher the degree of risk in the investment is.

The relationship between risk and uncertainty, or lack of knowledge, about possible future returns is shown in Figure 15.1. When there is no uncertainty about future returns, there is no risk in investing. U.S. savings bonds and insured savings accounts fall in this category. As uncertainty about realizing future returns increases, so does the risk of the investment. For example, oil and gas drilling programs are considered to be very risky because it is difficult to predict whether a new well will be productive or dry.

Types of Risks

The investor faces different types of risks when selecting an investment. These risks are explained in this section.

Figure 15.1 Uncertainty and Risk

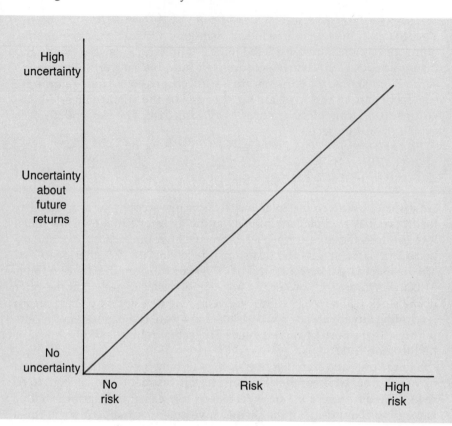

Business Risk. Different firms face different demand situations for the goods and services they offer. Some firms face steady demand for their goods and services over time. Long-distance telephone companies, for example, have very steady demand for their services. They also have a good idea of when the peak demand will occur for their services—around Mother's Day. Firms whose sales tend not to fluctuate greatly over time face low business risk. **Business risk** is the risk associated with changes in a firm's sales. The more sales fluctuate, the higher the degree of business risk will be.

Some firms—for example, those in the automotive and housing industries—face high business risk because their sales tend to fluctuate with changes in the economic environment. Figure 15.2 shows three firms with different levels of business risk. The least risky firm is firm C because its sales fluctuate very little around the trend line. Firm B is the riskiest.

Investors need to recognize business risk because fluctuations in sales lead to fluctuations in earnings, which can affect dividends. Similarly, an investor who is thinking of buying an apartment building needs to carefully

Figure 15.2 Business Risk Profiles

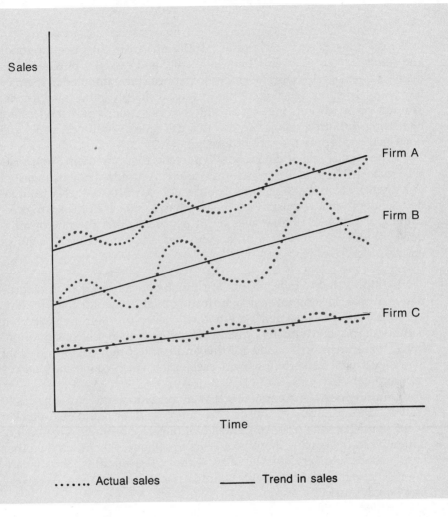

evaluate the business risk involved. If demand for the rental units fluctuates too much, the investor may not be able to generate enough rent to meet the costs of operating the building.

Market Risk.   Because of factors such as changes in business conditions, changes in interest rates, the threat of war, new government regulations, and increased competition, prices of investments tend to fluctuate over time. Under good economic conditions, for example, prices of common stocks tend to go up. Stock prices generally go down when the economy is not doing well. The fluctuations in the market value of

investments is called **market risk**. Larger fluctuations in the market values of investments produce higher levels of market risk.

Inflation Risk.   Inflation can be described best by this old saying: "A dollar is a dime, is a nickel, is gone." **Inflation** causes the prices of goods and services to go up even when the quality and quantity purchased remains the same. For example, automobile prices have doubled in the past few years. The price of a haircut has increased sharply in the past decade. The **rate of inflation** is the rate at which costs of goods and services are increasing. **Inflation risk** is the risk that the returns on investments will not equal or surpass the rate of inflation.

If the annual rate of inflation is 10 percent, then something that costs $100 today will cost $110 one year from today. A hundred dollars invested in a savings account at 6 percent would yield only $106 one year from today. Under these circumstances, the purchasing power of the savings account will diminish as time goes by. It is possible that the rate of inflation will outpace the return on savings and this possibility constitutes inflation risk.

Liquidity Risk.   Investments are purchased more for their returns potential than for any intrinsic worth they might have for the investor. To put it simply, investments are not purchased for their own sake but because they will eventually provide the ability to increase consumption. Investments are more suitable for this end result if they are **liquid**—that is, if they can be converted easily to cash, with which goods and services can be purchased.

Liquidity risk is the possibility that an investment might not be easily converted to cash. Something that cannot be sold, or liquidated, quickly suffers from liquidity risk. Apartment buildings, for example, are not very liquid; it may take many months or years to sell one. Stocks, on the other hand, can be sold very quickly, often within a few minutes. Thus, apartment buildings suffer from high liquidity risk, whereas stocks have very low liquidity risk.

Composite Risk.   Business, market, inflation, and liquidity risks combine to form **composite risk**. Composite risk is the overall risk of an investment. Different types of investments have different levels of composite risk. Insured savings accounts, for example, have no business, market, or liquidity risks. However, they do have some inflation risk. Overall, though, savings accounts have very low composite risk.

Common stocks of major industrial firms in the United States are actively traded on stock markets. Stock prices have typically kept up with inflation. In the short run, though, stock prices tend to fluctuate. Stocks therefore have low inflation and liquidity risks but some business and market risks. In general, common stocks have average composite risk.

From the investor's viewpoint, composite risk becomes important. This is the risk that the investor must bear in anticipation of earning returns. The next section will examine the tradeoffs among various levels of risks and returns.

Spot Quiz • Risks in Investing

1. Technology-oriented firms have high levels of business risk.

    T _____   F _____

2. Savings accounts have some market risk because of low interest paid on these accounts.   T _____   F _____

3. Collecting stamps as investments carries low liquidity risk.

    T _____   F _____

(Answers on page 496)

"Now I see the meaning! Renounce worldly goods on the downside, buy back on the way up!"

Source: *Changing Times*, June 1975, p. 8. Reprinted with permission from *Changing Times* magazine, © Kiplinger Washington Editors, Inc., 1975. This reprint is not to be altered in any way, except with permission from *Changing Times*.

RISK-RETURN TRADEOFFS IN INVESTING

Figure 15.3 shows six different investments: A, B, C, D, E, and F. The investments are identified in terms of both risk and return. Risk is shown on the horizontal axis, and return is shown on the vertical axis. First, would a rational person choose investment A? The answer is no. Investment A provides zero return and has some risk. Therefore, leaving the money sitting in a checking account is better than investing in A.

If you had a choice of investing in either B or C, which investment should you choose? C is the preferred alternative. B and C have the same level of risk, but C has a higher return than B. In general, for the same level of risk, investments with higher returns are more desirable than those with lower returns. The same rationale applies to a comparison between D and E. D, with a higher return, is preferred to E.

Figure 15.3 Risk-Return Tradeoffs

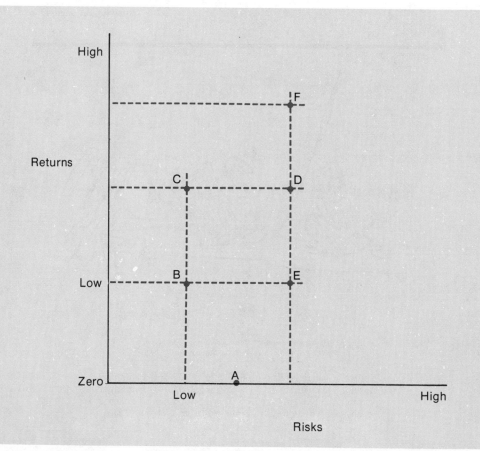

If you were given a choice of investing in either B or E, which would you choose? You are correct if you answered B. Although both investments have the same level of return, B has lower risk than E and is therefore more desirable. Similarly, if you were to compare only C and D, C would be more desirable than D. C provides the same return as D yet is less risky.

Now if you were asked to choose from A, B, C, D, and E, in which would you invest? B is preferred to A, so A can be dropped. E can also be dropped from consideration because B is better. However, we also know that C is better than both B and D. Therefore, the most preferred of the five alternatives is C. The example illustrates the fact that rational investors will choose the investment with the highest return from the same risk category or the investment with the lowest risk from the same return category.

Figure 15.3 also has a sixth investment, F. We already know that C is preferred to A, B, D, and E. Of C and F, which appears to be more desirable? Actually, both C and F are desirable. Of these two, C has a lower return and lower risk than F. Some investors would prefer C, whereas others would prefer F. When we compare C and F, we can find no preferred investment because both return and risk are different. We can, however, draw one conclusion. Investors will invest in a higher-risk project, typified by D, E, and F, only if the return is higher than for C. This means that riskier projects require proportionally higher returns to attract investors.

Spot Quiz • Risk-Return Tradeoffs in Investing

1. In Figure 15.3, F is preferred to B.   T _____   F _____

2. In Figure 15.3, F is preferred to D.   T _____   F _____

(Answers on page 496)

INVESTMENT ALTERNATIVES

The investor has a wide variety of investment alternatives. These alternatives vary both in the returns they provide and the risks they carry. Table 15.1 summarizes major types of investments and their risk and return characteristics.

Table 15.1 Investment Alternatives and Their Characteristics

Type of Investment	Business Risk	Market Risk	Inflation Risk	Liquidity Risk	Composite Risk	Expected Annual Return*
1. U.S. savings bonds	None	None	High	None	None	6.5%
2. Savings accounts	Very low	None	High	None	Negligible	5–10%
3. High-grade bonds	Low	Average	Average	Low	Very low	9–12%
4. Speculative bonds	High	High	Average	Average	Moderate	11–16%
5. Blue-chip common stocks	Very low	Average	Low	Negligible	Average	12–18%
6. Common stock mutual funds	Low	Average	Low	Negligible	Average	12–18%
7. Real estate	Low–average	Low	Low	Average–high	Above average	14–25%
8. Antiques, art objects, mineral recovery	Average–high	Average	Low–average	High	High	15–30%

*The expected annual returns mentioned here are based on long-run historical returns.

U.S. Savings Bonds and Savings Accounts

The safest types of investments are U.S. savings bonds and savings accounts. Both are highly liquid and thus are often viewed as investments where funds can be "parked" temporarily until more desirable alternatives become available. These two investments were discussed in greater detail in Chapter 6.

High-Grade Bonds

High-grade corporate bonds are issued by major, well-known corporations such as General Electric Co. and The Coca-Cola Company, that are leaders in their fields. Thus, little business risk is associated with these bonds. The market prices of these bonds tend to change with interest rate changes. The bonds can be sold readily and have low composite risk. Bonds are discussed in greater detail in Chapter 17.

Speculative Bonds

Bonds issued by lesser-known or riskier firms are considered to be speculative in nature. Speculative bonds are somewhat less safe than high-grade bonds. Because of the higher risk, these bonds provide returns that are higher than returns from high-grade bonds. Bonds issued by corporations such as American Airlines and Datapoint Corp. fall in this category.

Blue-Chip Common Stocks

Major, well-known, well-established corporations are also called **blue-chip firms**. Common stocks issued by blue-chip corporations are safe investments, but note that not all common stocks issued by various companies are safe investments. Common stocks issued by new, small companies are, in many cases, very risky investments. Common stocks, in general, tend to be riskier investments than corporate bonds. Common stocks as investments are discussed in Chapter 17.

Common Stock Mutual Funds

Common stock mutual funds are professionally managed funds whose assets are invested in common stocks. An investor can buy shares of a mutual fund. The mutual fund uses the monies received to buy common stock of various companies. The investment objectives of mutual funds vary. Mutual funds that invest in blue-chip common stock have risk and return characteristics that are very similar to the blue-chip stocks themselves. Mutual funds are discussed further in Chapter 18.

Real Estate

Typical investments in real estate include rental properties such as apartment buildings, rental homes, and professional buildings. Real estate investments have shown a steady increase in value in the past two decades. Because of these fairly steady increases in the market value of real estate investments, they are considered to have low market risk. Real estate investments provide a good hedge against inflation as well. The major problem with real estate investments is that they do not tend to be very liquid.

Unlike common stocks, real estate investments require considerable sales time and effort. Some real estate investments are on the market for a number of years before they are sold. Thus, the composite risk for real estate investments is above average. These investments are discussed briefly in Chapter 19.

Antiques, Art, Collectibles, and Minerals

Antiques, art objects, collectibles, and mineral recovery programs (such as oil drilling and mining) are all highly risky investments. For instance, collectibles go in and out of favor with collectors. Norman Rockwell prints may be in vogue at one time, only to be replaced in popularity by Alexander Calder prints. Also, collectibles are not liquid investments. The composite risk for collectibles is thus high. These investments are discussed briefly in Chapter 19.

Spot Quiz • Investment Alternatives

1. U.S. savings bonds are safe but not liquid investments.
                                                    T _____   F _____

2. Common stock mutual funds are about as desirable as blue-chip common stocks for investment purposes.   T _____   F _____

(Answers on page 497)

INVESTMENT STRATEGIES

Investing requires the establishment of definite investment strategies. Without establishing investment strategies, investing may prove to be a

tiresome, time-consuming chore without adequate return. Prior to establishing investment strategies, though, a person must set investment goals. Setting investment goals will result in certain investment criteria that are then matched with investment alternatives. In this section, setting investment goals and matching investment criteria to investment alternatives are discussed.

Setting Investment Goals

Different people have different end uses for their investment funds. In fact, one person or family might have multiple investment goals. Three basic types of investment goals can be identified: those related to precautionary, specific, and speculative funds.

Goals for Precautionary Funds. Everyone needs to set aside some funds for emergencies. Typically, three to six months of take-home salary should be placed in an emergency fund. The purpose of the **emergency fund** is obvious—to provide money during emergencies. For example, a person may be laid off suddenly from a job. The emergency fund could be used for day-to-day living expenses until a suitable job is found. Because the fund is for emergencies, it should be invested in highly liquid and very safe investments. The planning horizon for precautionary funds must be very short because emergencies can arise at any time.

Goals for Specific Funds. **Specific funds** are designed to provide funds for specific events, including retirement, leisure activities, and building an estate. These events do not occur on an emergency basis. They are highly predictable, and when they will occur can be easily estimated. For example, the typical worker knows when to expect retirement. Similarly, leisure activities, such as an extended vacation, can be planned well ahead of time. Because these activities generally occur in the future, you can consider financing them with investments that have low to average levels of risk with related returns. In meeting goals for specific funds, then, liquidity is not an important factor in the short run.

Goals for Speculative Funds. **Speculative funds** include monies that would not be missed if they were not available. In other words, you could "blow" speculative funds without changing your life style. Because speculative funds are not a required part of a person's financial plans, they can be invested in instruments that have high risks and high returns. Liquidity and the planning horizon are not important considerations in investing speculative funds.

Investment goals tend to vary with the types of funds to be invested. Liquidity and safety, risk and return, and the planning horizon all need to be carefully considered in matching investment alternatives to investment goals.

Matching Investment Goals, Criteria, and Alternatives

Proper investment management procedures require that investment alternatives be selected to ensure that investment goals are met. Precautionary funds require very safe and liquid investments. As Table 15.1 indicates, savings accounts and savings bonds are highly safe and liquid investments. For all of these investments, the principal invested cannot go down in value. The investments provide low but regular returns. Best of all, these investments can be liquidated, or sold, at any time without incurring a loss in the amount invested. Table 15.2 summarizes the alternatives that may be matched with this precautionary investment goal. Investment alternatives for specific and speculative goals are given in Table 15.2 as well.

Specific funds, by their very nature, do not need to be invested in highly safe instruments. Investors with specific long-term goals can undertake investments that have low to average levels of risk with related returns. High-grade and speculative bonds, high-grade common stock, common stock mutual funds, and some real estate provide the right combination of risk and return for meeting specific goals.

Table 15.2 Matching Investment Goals, Criteria, and Alternatives

Investment Goals	Investment Criteria	Investment Alternatives
1. Precautionary (for emergencies)	Safety and liquidity are most important	Savings accounts, savings bonds, money market mutual funds
2. Specific (retirement, estates)	Low to average risks	High-grade and speculative bonds, common stock mutual funds, some real estate
3. Speculative (luxury items)	High-risk investments	Risky stocks, real estate, collectibles, mineral recovery, tax shelter programs

Speculative investment goals allow the investor to "take a flier" on an investment that has the potential of providing high returns. Risky stocks, real estate, collectibles, and mineral recovery programs are highly risky investments that hold the promise of high returns.

This section has shown how investment goals can be met by selecting the appropriate investment alternatives. Later chapters in this part of the book will provide a more detailed view of the investment alternatives mentioned here.

Spot Quiz • Investment Strategies

1. Precautionary funds can be used to buy good deals in real estate.

   T _____ F _____

2. Goals for specific funds are typically long-term in nature.

   T _____ F _____

3. Speculative funds should be invested in government bonds.

   T _____ F _____

(Answers on page 497)

Summary

This chapter provides a brief overview of some of the basic concepts in investing. Investment planning allows a person to maximize his or her well-being—that is, investing allows a person to enjoy life more. Money for investing can be generated by using budgets, forcing yourself to save, and skipping expenditures from time to time.

Investments have two important aspects. People invest with the expectation of returns and are willing to undertake reasonable risks to earn these returns. Returns from investing come in the form of interest, dividends, capital gains, rent, and pensions. The risk in investing is that the expected return may not be obtained. Investing exposes you to business, market, inflation, and liquidity risks. In general, riskier investments have higher expected returns.

The investor has a variety of investment alternatives. Stated in order of increasing risk, some of these investments are savings accounts, savings bonds, high-grade bonds, speculative bonds, blue-chip common stocks, common stock mutual funds, real estate, collectibles, and mineral recovery programs.

The first step in investing is to define your investment goals. These goals produce certain investment criteria that can be matched with proper investment strategies.

Questions

1. Give two examples to show why you should defer present consumption for future consumption.

2. What is meant by "maximizing your welfare?"

3. Why do people invest?

4. Explain some ways you could use to generate money for investing.

5. Give an example of a method of forced savings for investing.

6. Explain briefly four different types of returns from investing.

7. Define risk from an investing viewpoint.

8. Explain briefly the following terms:
   a. Business risk
   b. Market risk
   c. Composite risk

9. What is liquidity risk? Why is it important from the investor's viewpoint?

10. Is it possible to obtain high returns from low-risk investments? Explain your answer.

11. What is the relationship between risk and return in investing? Explain.

12. Explain the types of investment goals a person could have.

13. Is it possible to have more than one investment goal at the same time? Provide a brief explanation for your answer.

14. Can you think of any investment alternative that could meet all three investment goals at once? Explain your answer.

Case Problems

1. Mr. and Mrs. Hamid Rashad are both 24 years old. Both are working in management capacities with industrial firms in the St. Louis metropolitan area. Their combined earnings are about $50,000 per year. They are planning to start a family in two or three years. They have $47,000 in their savings account and are currently renting a duplex apartment.
    a. Establish suitable investment goals for the Rashads. Your plan should include specific dollar amounts for each goal.
    b. What investment alternatives would you recommend to the Rashads? Explain.
    c. What financial advice would you give the Rashads?

2. Thomas and Betty Polonus are in their mid-fifties. Mr. Polonus is an executive with a bank who earns about $55,000 a year. Mrs. Polonus is involved with volunteer work. They plan to retire in ten years. They have $3,000 in a savings account. Their house is worth $140,000 and is paid for. They also own $150,000 in real estate and $7,000 in corporate bonds.
    a. Which investment goals should be of primary importance to the Polonuses? Explain.
    b. Are the present investments proper for Mr. and Mrs. Polonus? Explain.
    c. The total assets of this couple are $300,000. Show how you would distribute this amount over various investment alternatives so that the couple can better meet the investment goal explained in part (a) above.

Bibliography

"How Safe Are Your Investments?" *Money* (January 1982): 36–37.

"How to Protect Yourself from Investment Scams." *Changing Times* (July 1986): 26–31.

"The Secrets of Backyard Investors." *Money* (March 1985): 62–77.

"A Strategy for All Seasons." *Money* (January 1982): 38–44.

"Why Dumb Things Happen to Smart People." *Money* (April 1985): 112–118.

Answers to Spot Quizzes

Why Invest? (page 476)

1. T (Investing is done with the expectation of increasing the amount available for future consumption.)

2. F (Gambling does not carry an expectation of positive returns.)

3. T (Savings leads to future consumption.)

Money for Investing (page 478)

1. F (Nonroutine income can be saved easily.)

2. T ("Spending money on savings" is a useful idea for maintaining a savings program.)

Returns from Investing (page 480)

1. F (For example, no one guarantees returns on common stock investments.)

2. T (Interest income from bonds, for example, is received periodically, whereas returns in the form of capital gains on stock are expected and dependent on price fluctuations.)

Risks in Investing (page 485)

1. T (Rapid changes in technology greatly affect sales.)

2. F (The principal on deposit remains fixed.)

3. F (Stamps cannot be sold readily.)

Risk-Return Tradeoffs in Investing (page 487)

1. F (Because both risk and return are different, B and F cannot be compared directly.)

2. T (For the same risk level, F provides a higher return.)

Investment Alternatives (page 490)

1. F (U.S. bonds are highly liquid investments.)

2. T (Common stock mutual funds and blue-chip common stock offer about the same returns for the same risks.)

Investment Strategies (page 493)

1. F (Precautionary funds should be invested only in highly liquid assets.)

2. T (Goals for specific funds are generally related to retirement or estate planning.)

3. F (Government bonds are not risky enough to provide potential for high returns.)

Chapter 16

Information and Transactions for Securities Markets

Objectives

After reading this chapter, you will be able to:

- Define *securities markets* and describe their function in an industrialized society.

- Name four classifications of securities markets and describe each.

- Identify the government agency that regulates securities markets.

- Name at least five sources of securities information.

- Explain what is meant by *buying on margin* and *selling short*.

- Discuss the difference between market and limit orders.

- Explain what is meant by a *stop-loss* order.

Yves Hentic earned a master of business administration degree from Harvard University and now leads a busy, hectic life. He starts his day early in the morning and can relax only somewhat after four in the afternoon. Mr. Hentic's day is spent in the noisy, crowded room of a brokerage firm in New York, where he trades stocks and does very well. *Changing Times* magazine asked him about his expected profits in each transaction he undertakes. His response was, "I won't try a deal for under 100 percent annualized. Many work out to 400 percent annualized." Mr. Hentic is an example of a person who makes a comfortable living by buying and selling stocks.[1]

Where does an investor or trader, such as Mr. Hentic, make transactions? What is a brokerage firm? Where are the stocks bought and sold? How do you obtain information about securities? What are the mechanics of making securities transactions? Answers to these questions are provided in this chapter.

Securities markets

A scanning of any newspaper published in a major city or of a national newspaper will provide you with information on the trading prices of a wide variety of investments. In addition to prices, the newspapers also carry information about the volume of transactions and short commentaries on the overall trends in the market. In financial circles, the word *market* refers to a **securities market**—a place where stocks, bonds, and other financial instruments are traded.

Efficient securities markets are very important to society. Securities markets, when working properly, allow businesses to raise money, grow, provide jobs, and produce more goods for consumers. Highly developed countries, such as the United States, Japan, France, and Canada, have very good securities markets. Developing countries, such as Kenya, Malaysia, and Bolivia, generally do not have good securities markets. Securities markets are good for society because they serve a very important function: They provide an efficient flow of money from those who have funds to invest to those who want to use funds.

Securities markets can be classified as either primary or secondary. In **primary securities markets**, corporations sell stocks and bonds, generally through brokers, to investors. The funds go from investors to corporations. The working of primary markets is shown in Figure 16.1.

Once corporations sell stocks and bonds, investors trade these securities among themselves. **Secondary securities markets** involve transactions and funds between investors and brokers only, as shown in Figure 16.1. The

---

1. See "Three Successful Speculators—How They Do It," *Money* (December 1980): 50.

Figure 16.1 Primary and Secondary Markets

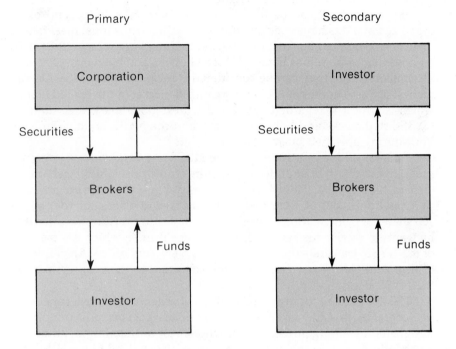

vast majority of securities transactions take place in the secondary markets. The securities transactions reported in newspapers are, in most cases, secondary market transactions.

Securities markets can also be classified as **organized** or **over-the-counter**. From an investor's viewpoint, an understanding of this classification is very important.

Organized Markets

Organized securities markets have physical buildings where securities are traded. These markets have formal requirements for governing their affairs and allowing stocks and bonds of companies to be traded on them. The best-known organized market is the **New York Stock Exchange (NYSE)**, which is also known among investors as the **Big Board**. The American Stock Exchange, the Pacific Stock Exchange, the Midwest Stock Exchange, and the Cincinnati Stock Exchange are all examples of organized markets.

The New York Stock Exchange is the most prestigious organized market. Major corporations, such as General Motors, Procter & Gamble,

Monsanto, IBM, and Xerox, are listed on the NYSE. A **listed firm** has its securities traded in an organized market. Only members of the NYSE can buy and sell stock on this exchange.

Not every stock can be traded on the NYSE. The NYSE and other organized markets have special requirements that firms must meet before their stock becomes eligible for listing and trading. For example, the NYSE requires that corporations have 2,000 stockholders and net worth of at least $16 million before they can be considered for listing.[2] The NYSE has the highest listing requirements of any organized market in the United States, which is why it is regarded as the most prestigious market. Trading in NYSE-listed stocks and bonds takes place in the NYSE building in New York during specified business hours.

Let's take a look at trading on the NYSE. At 11:17 A.M., New York time, investor A in Boston decides that he wants to sell his 100 shares of General Motors stock. He calls brokerage firm A (a **brokerage firm** arranges purchases and sales of securities for investors) and places an order to sell 100 shares of General Motors stock. Investor A also specifies the price that he wants to receive for his shares.[3] Brokerage firm A, which is a member of the NYSE, transmits the sell order to its New York office. An employee of firm A in New York telephones the sell order to the firm's broker on the NYSE floor.

The floor broker for firm A takes this sell order to the market specialist in General Motors and asks for a quote. The **market specialist** is a person designated by an organized market who is responsible for ensuring that an orderly market is maintained in a given stock. The General Motors specialist quotes 68¼–½. The 68¼ is the "bid" price and means that the specialist is willing to buy 100 shares of GM at $68.25 per share. The ½ refers to 68½ and means that the specialist will sell 100 GM shares at $68.50 per share. Figure 16.2 shows how the order flows from one party to the next.

At 11:18 A.M., New York time, investor B in Phoenix has decided that she wants to buy 100 GM shares. She calls her broker in Phoenix, who transmits her buy order to the firm's New York office. The floor broker for firm B arrives just when the market specialist is giving floor broker A a quote for GM. Brokers A and B quickly establish that A is selling and B is buying. They negotiate a price of 68⅜ for the transaction and report it to their respective New York offices. The 68⅜ means that A sold and B bought 100 GM shares at $68.375 per share. New York office A transmits this information to broker A in Boston. Broker A calls investor A and informs him that he "got out" of GM at 68⅜. This whole procedure takes about two to five minutes. Had floor broker B not shown up, floor broker A would have sold the 100 GM shares to the market specialist at the bid

---

2. The NYSE has additional listing requirements that are not mentioned here.
3. Buy and sell orders can be either market or limit orders. These terms are explained in a later section of this chapter.

Figure 16.2 Order Flows on Organized Markets

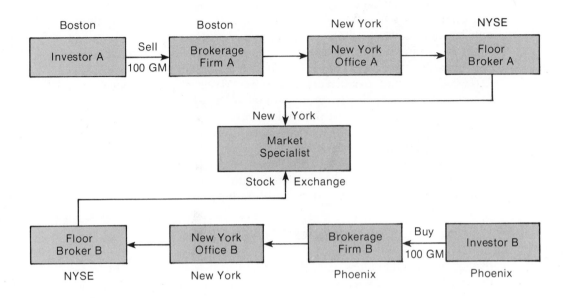

price of 68¼. If the market specialist had bought the GM stock for his own account, he would have served his responsibility for maintaining an orderly market in GM.

As this example indicates, organized markets are nothing more than auction places where stocks and bonds are constantly bought and sold. Active organized markets provide investors with liquidity—they can buy and sell relatively easily. Stocks of more than 4,000 companies are listed and traded on the organized markets in the United States.

Over-the-Counter Market

The second form of securities market is called the **over-the-counter (OTC) market**. Stocks that are not traded on organized markets are called **unlisted stocks**. Unlisted stocks trade in the OTC market. The OTC market does not have a central building or place where unlisted stocks can be bought and sold. Rather, the OTC is composed of dealers who maintain an inventory of unlisted stocks for buying and selling. A large OTC dealer may maintain an inventory of many OTC stocks. Similarly, inventory of stock of a large OTC company may be maintained by many dealers.

OTC stocks are bought and sold in a manner somewhat similar to that for listed stocks. Let's assume that investor XYZ wants to sell 100 shares of an OTC stock. XYZ would call broker ABC, who would, in turn, call ABC's New York office. At the New York office, the OTC trader would

call dealers maintaining the desired OTC stock. After obtaining bid and ask prices from four or five dealers, the trader will be able to sell the OTC stock to the dealer who quoted the highest bid price.

Companies whose stocks trade in the OTC market are, in general, smaller and less stable than companies whose stocks trade in organized markets. Typically, as companies grow larger and are able to meet listing requirements, they will apply to be listed on an exchange. Prices for some OTC stocks are hard to obtain at times. Some OTC stocks do not have much in terms of buy and sell activity. In general, for a beginning investor, OTC stocks may not be the most desirable investments initially.

In recent years, OTC stock dealers have attempted to provide investors with better price data on the OTC stocks in their inventories. Stock brokers can obtain instant bid and ask price quotations on the larger and more actively traded OTC stocks. Buying and selling these OTC stocks is easier than buying and selling less frequently traded OTC stocks.

Regulation of Securities Markets

In 1929, the market values of stocks declined very dramatically. This rapid decline became known as the "stock market crash of 1929." Fraud, misrepresentation, and unethical behavior on the part of brokers, dealers, investors, and corporate officers were partially responsible for the 1929 crash. As a result of the 1929 crash, the federal government started to regulate the behavior of brokers, dealers, investors, firms, and securities markets. These government regulations were designed to curb fraud and unethical behavior. The Securities Acts of 1933 and 1934 specified the rules and regulations applicable to securities trading. These acts created the **Securities and Exchange Commission (SEC)** to oversee securities trading. A brief description of the regulations is provided below.

Filing Company Reports.   The SEC requires that larger companies (those with more than $3 million total assets and 500 or more stockholders) that issue securities traded in interstate commerce periodically file financial statements with the SEC. These companies are referred to as **reporting companies**. It is believed that disclosure of timely information through periodic filings provides investors with relevant information about the financial condition of these firms.

Insider Trading.   Company officers, directors, and perhaps large stockholders may possess information that is not available to the general investors. These persons with access to special information are called **insiders**. It is illegal for insiders to profit from the special information they possess. They are required to file with the SEC monthly stockholding reports. In recent years, a number of people with insider information have been successfully prosecuted by the government for violating insider trading regulations.

Dissemination of Information. SEC regulations require that all information to be released by a company be given widespread publicity. The idea is to give every investor equal access to company information.

Trading Regulations. Trading regulations are designed to prevent manipulation of stock prices by small groups of investors. The Federal Reserve System regulates the use of credit in the buying and selling of securities. Credit rules are designed to discourage speculation in securities.

Government regulations are designed to provide equality for all investors. Regulations require sufficient information disclosure so that investors can make reasonable evaluations for their buy and sell decisions. The regulations are not designed to prevent investors from making unwise decisions or from losing money. All investors have an equal right to profits and losses in the securities markets. (See "Monday, Bloody Monday" below.)

Monday, Bloody Monday

It was early in the morning, around 5:45 a.m., and the jogger had carefully chosen a new path to avoid the encounter with the mixed breed dog who so enjoyed snapping at his heels. Yes, October 19, 1987, was going to be different for the jogger. No dogs and no cars to worry about and a beautiful path through the woods to enjoy. And yet, the jogger felt something was strange. Out of the corner of his eye he saw a strange phenomenon. A small sparrow, three ounces of fury, was attacking a hawk. "Nah. Can't be," he thought.

The jogger arrived at his desk in the office of a major brokerage firm to find a stack of orders to sell stock. "Bunch of fools," he told himself. "They'll be begging to get back in at these prices."

For an hour the flood to sell orders continued to pour in uninterrupted. The jogger thought about the feeding frenzy behavior of sharks. The sell orders kept rolling in.

Investors in Hong Kong were dazed. Their stock market had seen the largest decline in history. The London market had never quite encountered a sell day like this one. Perhaps the end of the world was near.

Later in the day, the jogger heard a White House emissary state that "the underlying economy remains sound." The chairman of the NYSE, John Phelan, stated that this was the "nearest thing to a financial meltdown that I ever want to see." The DJIA had closed down 508 points, or 23 percent, for the day. Investors had suffered a loss of $500 billion in one day. The jogger's thoughts turned to the sparrow attacking the hawk.

Spot Quiz • Securities Markets

1. Unlisted stocks can be bought and sold on the New York Stock Exchange.   T _____   F _____

2. A person selling some stock directly to his next-door neighbor is operating in the OTC market.   T _____   F _____

3. Unlisted stocks should not be bought.   T _____   F _____

4. Securities and Exchange Commission regulations prevent investors from losing money on investments.   T _____   F _____

(Answers on page 525)

SOURCES OF SECURITIES INFORMATION

Good investment decisions require that investors take into consideration all relevant information. Before an investment decision about buying or selling securities can be made, investors need to get a feel for what the overall market as well as individual securities are going to do. The investors' need for information thus extends to both general market and specific firm information. These topics are covered here.

Current Market Information

At most social get-togethers, you will hear remarks about the securities markets, such as, "Well, the market was up today. Did you make any money?" How do you know if the market is up, down, or sideways today? Since the word *market* here refers to securities markets, when people say the "market is up," they mean that generally prices of individual securities moved up. The trend of the market is measured by a variety of indices, some of which are explained in the sections that follow.

Dow Jones Industrial Average.   The **Dow Jones Industrial Average (DJIA)** is the most popular measure of the market. The DJIA is an index that is based on the prices of 30 substantial U.S. industrial manufacturing firms. Included in the DJIA are such firms as E.I. du Pont de Nemours & Co., Eastman Kodak Co., Exxon Corporation, General Electric Co., and

Sears, Roebuck and Co.. Because of the significant nature of the firms included in computing this index, the DJIA is considered to be fully representative of the overall performance of all stocks.

Besides the DJIA, the Dow Jones Company has three other indices: one based on 20 transportation stocks, one based on 15 utility stocks, and a composite index based on all 65 stocks in the other indices. All four Dow Jones indices are widely recognized as measures of market movements. The Dow Jones averages are widely reported in most newspapers and television news reports.

Standard & Poor's Averages. Like the Dow Jones indices, **Standard & Poor's (S&P)** also has multiple indices. One is based on 400 industrial firms, the second on 40 financial stocks, the third on 40 utilities, the fourth on 20 transportation stocks, and the fifth on all 500 stocks mentioned. The S&P averages are also widely quoted in the news media. Investors consider S&P indices to be somewhat more reliable than the Dow Jones indices because S&P indices include more stocks in the computations.

NYSE Indices. The **NYSE indices** are some of the most comprehensive market indices available. Their computation includes every relevant stock listed on the NYSE. The five NYSE indices are industrial, transportation, finance, utilities, and composite. The NYSE indices, generally considered to be the most precise indicators of overall trends in the market, are widely reported in the news media as well.

Other Indices. In addition to the indices already mentioned, you may see some other indices. One set of indices is reported by the Financial News Network, with the main index being the **Financial News Composite Index (FNCI)**, or ''Fancy.'' The NASDAQ system, which deals with OTC securities, reports six indices, the most common one being the NASDAQ 500 Index. Two other indices that are reported in *The Wall Street Journal* are the Value Line and the Wilshire 5,000 indices.

Current Information on Firms

Most newspapers carry daily price information on securities. Newspapers with very large circulations, such as the *New York Times* and *The Wall Street Journal*, carry price information on a very large number of securities.

Reading Price Quotations. A typical price quotation for a stock is shown in Table 16.1. The first two columns show the highest and the lowest price for the stock during the past 52 weeks. The highest price was 17⅜, or $17.38 per share. Sometime during the past 52 weeks, the stock sold at a price of 12¼, or $12.25 per share. The next column shows the name of the stock. Newspapers usually abbreviate the full name of the company.

"Jason I." stands for Jason Industries Incorporated. The abbreviations are designed so that most investors can easily recognize the name of the stock.

The fourth column, titled "Div.," indicates the dollar amount of annualized cash dividends per share that the firm is currently paying. The newspaper shows that the annual dividend payment for Jason Industries is $0.60. The annualized dividend is calculated by taking the most recent quarterly cash dividend and multiplying it by 4. As the quarterly dividend changes, the annualized dividend changes proportionally.

The fifth column is titled "Yld. %," and it is calculated by multiplying the dividend by 100 and dividing by the closing price. For Jason Industries, the dividend yield is .60 × 100/15.88 = 3.8%. This column indicates that, based on today's closing price and the annual dividend, Jason Industries is paying dividends at a 3.8% rate.

The next column is titled "P/E Ratio." P/E ratio means the ratio of today's closing price to the firm's earnings for the 12 most recent months. The value of 7 shown means that Jason Industries is currently selling for seven times its earnings.

The column titled "Sales 100s" shows the number of shares traded in the stock today. For Jason Industries, 174 × 100 = 17,400 shares exchanged ownership today.

The "High," "Low," and "Close" columns report the high price, the low price, and the closing price for the stock for today. Today, Jason Industries traded as high as 16⅜, or $16.38 per share. Its low price for the day was 15¾, or $15.75 per share. The last trade in the stock was at a price of 15⅞, or $15.88 per share. These columns provide a measure of the price activity in the stock.

The last column, titled "Net Chg.," shows the dollar amount of change between yesterday's closing price and today's closing price. Jason Industries declined ¼, or $0.25 per share, from yesterday's close.

Not all newspapers report price information in the format shown in Table 16.1. Some papers omit certain columns to conserve space. At times, additional data about firms are indicated through footnotes. These footnotes are explained at the end of the price quotations. For example, the letter *u* appearing before the price listed in the column marked "High" would indicate that the price was the highest price recorded in the past 52 weeks.

Table 16.1 Typical Price Quotation

52 Weeks		Stock	Div.	Yld. %	P/E Ratio	Sales 100s	High	Low	Close	Net Chg.
High	Low									
17⅜	12¼	Jason I.	.60	3.8	7	174	16⅜	15¾	15⅞	−¼

The Wall Street Journal. *The Wall Street Journal (WSJ)*, published Monday through Friday, is considered to be the foremost daily financial newspaper. Besides price information, it contains current information on interest rates, dividends and earnings reports, corporate news, market commentaries, and news and analysis on economic conditions. Serious investors should read the *WSJ* daily to stay abreast of news about the economy and about firms.

Barron's. *Barron's* is a weekly financial newspaper carrying weekly price information. A section titled "Market Laboratory" carries a wealth of information about securities markets and the economy. In addition, each issue of *Barron's* contains a number of detailed reports on firms.

Forbes. *Forbes* is a semimonthly financial magazine providing reports on firms and commentaries on market trends. Price information on stocks is not provided in *Forbes*.

Historical Information on Firms

Historical information on firms, which allows us to look at the trends in the firm's financial performance, is useful for gauging the progress of the firm. Two principal sources of historical information are the firm itself and investment manuals.

Company-Prepared Reports. Every year corporations issue **annual reports** to their stockholders and to other interested parties. Annual reports typically contain a letter from the chief officer of the firm to the stockholders, a review of the firm's sales and financial performance for the year ended, detailed financial statements, and a summary of the firm's financial records for the past 8 to 12 years. Annual reports are useful not only for understanding the firm's history but also for gauging its future performance.

As mentioned previously, firms are required to file quarterly and annual reports with the SEC. These reports, called 8-Q and 10-K reports, contain more detailed information than is found in the annual report. In most cases, 8-Q and 10-K reports are available from the SEC as well as from the firm itself.

Investment Manuals. **Investment manuals**, such as *Moody's Manuals* and *Standard & Poor's Manuals*, provide a wide variety of information on firms. The manuals are classified into such categories as industrial, OTC, utilities, finance, and transportation. Manuals provide historical financial data as well as a description of the firm's business. The manuals list manufacturing plant locations, names of senior officials of the firm, major divisions of the firm, and a description of the types of securities issued by the firm.

Advisory Information on Firms

The sources of information just listed provide investors with factual information about firms. Many investors consider it useful to read reports that are not only factual but also analytical and judgmental. That is, investors seek information that tells them what to do with their investment funds.

There are a number of different investment advisory services. An example is *Value Line Investment Surveys*, which provides a brief financial picture of a firm and in addition offers ranking for the firm's expected performance and safety for the next 12 months. A page of a *Value Line* report is shown in Figure 16.3. Sears, Roebuck & Company is rated 3 for timeliness (expected performance over the next 12 months) and 3 for safety. The ratings range from 1 (highest) to 5 (lowest).

In addition to their manuals, Standard & Poor's and Moody's also publish advisory information. For example, S&P publishes *Stock Guide* and *Corporate Reports*. Articles in *Corporate Reports* are periodically updated and make recommendations about a firm's short- and long-term prospects. An example of an *S&P Corporate Report* is shown in Figure 16.4.

Also available to investors, for a fee, is a large number of **investment advisory letters**. Investment advisory letters are written by individuals who believe that they have a feel for the pulse of the market. These letters advise investors about market trends and make recommendations for buying and selling securities.

Not much hard data are available on the merits of advisory services. Some analysts claim that, in the long run, advisory services do not provide real benefits. Others claim that advisory services are worth the subscription money. Whether spending money on advisory services is worthwhile is something that investors need to determine for themselves.

Spot Quiz • Sources of Securities Information

1. According to Table 16.1, yesterday's closing price for Jason Industries was 15⅝.   T _____   F _____

2. If Jason Industries paid $0.20 per share in dividends this quarter, the "Div." column would list an amount of $0.80.   T _____   F _____

3. Every investor should use investment advisory services.
                                                                                          T _____   F _____

(Answers on page 525)

Figure 16.3 A Value Line Investment Survey

SEARS, ROEBUCK NYSE-S	RECENT PRICE 35	P/E RATIO 7.7 (Trailing: 8.1 Median: 9.0)	RELATIVE P/E RATIO 0.67	DIV'D YLD 5.9 %	VALUE LINE 1660

High	61.6	45.2	37.2	39.6	34.6	28.1	21.9	20.8	32.0	45.1	40.4	41.1	50.4	59.5				160
Low	39.1	20.8	24.2	30.8	27.0	19.8	17.8	14.9	15.8	27.0	29.5	30.9	35.9	26.0				120

Insider Decisions 1987

	J	J	A	S	O	N	D	J	F	M	A	M	J	J	A
to Buy	3	2	0	4	1	1	2	1	2	0	2	0	1	1	
to Sell	1	1	0	2	0	1	1	5	1	1	0	0	0	0	

9.0 × "Cash Flow" p sh

Options Trade On CBO

2-for-1 split

Target Price Range

Institutional Decisions

	2Q'86	3Q'86	4Q'86	1Q'87	2Q'87
to Buy	166	176	162	202	167
to Sell	178	172	154	139	180
Hld'g (000)	179777	183980	185724	194327	198772

Relative Price Strength

3.0 Percent
2.0 shares
1.0 traded

December 4, 1987 Value Line
TIMELINESS 3 Average
(Relative Price Perform-
ance Next 12 Mos.)
SAFETY 3 Average
(Scale: 1 Highest to 5 Lowest)
BETA 1.30 (1.00 = Market)

1990-92 PROJECTIONS
	Price	Gain	Ann'l Total Return
High	95	(+170%)	31%
Low	70	(+100%)	23%

© VALUE LINE, INC. 90-92E

1972	1973	1974	1975	1976	1977	1978	1979	1980	1981	1982	1983	1984	1985	1986	1987	1988	1989		
35.00	39.12	41.50	43.02	46.86	53.51	55.63	55.19	79.89	78.64	85.43	101.20	107.38	112.13	117.58	127.00	140.20		Sales per sh (A)	179.00
2.34	2.57	2.09	2.17	2.71	3.21	3.51	3.24	2.81	2.72	3.41	4.84	5.12	4.76	4.92	5.90	6.70		"Cash Flow" per sh	9.00
1.97	2.16	1.62	1.65	2.19	2.62	2.86	2.54	1.92	2.06	2.46	3.80	4.01	3.53	3.62	4.50	5.00		Earnings per sh (B)	6.75
.81	.88	.93	.93	.80	1.08	1.27	1.28	1.36	1.36	1.36	1.52	1.76	1.76	1.76	2.00	2.08		Div'ds Decl'd per sh (c)	2.40
14.38	15.87	16.60	16.72	18.61	20.27	21.98	23.53	24.38	23.77	25.08	27.60	29.48	31.79	33.98	37.00	40.00		Book Value per sh	50.00
314.02	314.56	315.65	317.09	319.01	321.87	322.63	317.33	315.36	347.89	351.41	354.57	361.61	363.10	376.60	378.00	378.00		Common Shs Outst'g	380.00
28.5	22.1	20.8	20.1	15.5	11.2	8.0	7.6	8.6	8.4	8.8	9.9	8.3	10.0	12.0	Bold figures are			Avg Ann'l P/E Ratio	12.0
1.96	2.18	2.91	2.68	1.98	1.47	1.09	1.10	1.14	1.02	.97	.84	.77	.81	.81	Value Line estimates			Relative P/E Ratio	1.00
1.4%	1.8%	2.7%	2.8%	2.4%	3.7%	5.5%	6.7%	8.2%	7.8%	6.3%	4.1%	5.3%	5.0%	4.0%				Avg Ann'l Div'd Yield	3.0%

CAPITAL STRUCTURE as of 12/31/86
Total Debt $14871.3 mill.
Due in 5 Yrs $6260.3 mill.
LT Debt $10066.7 mill.
LT Interest $1000.0 mill.
Incl. $221.2 mill. capitalized leases.
(LT interest earned: 2.8x; total interest coverage: 1.7x)
(44% of Cap'l)

Leases, Uncapitalized Annual rentals $396.8 mill.
Pension Liability None vs. None in '85

Pfd Stock $250.0 mill. Pfd Div'd $22.6 mill.
2.5 mill. shs. adj. rate pfd. Callable 5/14/87 at 103
(Called) (1% of Cap'l)
Common Stock 376,598,755 shs. (55% of Cap'l)

17946	17514	25195	27357	30020	35883	38828	40715	44282	48000	53000		Sales ($mill) (A)	68000
3727	3680	3062	3239	3991	3383	3450	3450	3404	3450	3500		Number of Stores	4100
921.5	810.1	606.0	650.1	861.2	1342.2	1454.8	1303.3	1351.3	1700	1900		Net Profit ($mill)	2550
49.1%	43.8%	12.6%	1.6%	21.4%	30.2%	24.1%	19.6%	25.2%	26.0%	28.0%		Income Tax Rate	30.0%
5.1%	4.6%	2.4%	2.4%	2.9%	3.7%	3.8%	3.2%	3.1%	3.5%	3.6%		Net Profit Margin	3.8%
2533.4	2651.5	2721.6	3103.1	3146.1	3620.5	4530.0	4115.2	4013.0	4350	4600		Inventories ($mill) (D)	6000
7.1	6.6	7.2	6.8	6.6	6.9	5.9	6.6	6.7	6.5	6.5		Inventory Turnover (D)	6.5
3750.0	3994.8	1174.3	(E)NMF	(E)NMF	6581.9	9828.0	10152	11978	11500	12000		Working Cap'l ($mill)(D)	14000
2040.2	2473.5	2961.9	4779.3	5816.1	7116.2	8997.0	9906.6	10067	10500	11000		Long-Term Debt ($mill)	11500
7091.6	7467.2	7688.8	8268.9	8812.4	9786.9	10911	11794	13047	14000	15100		Net Worth ($mill)	19000
11.0%	9.2%	7.0%	7.4%	9.1%	10.9%	9.8%	8.3%	8.0%	9.0%	9.0%		% Earned Total Cap'l	10.0%
13.0%	10.9%	7.9%	7.9%	9.8%	13.7%	13.3%	11.1%	10.4%	12.0%	12.5%		% Earned Net Worth	13.5%
7.2%	5.4%	2.4%	2.9%	4.6%	8.6%	7.6%	5.6%	5.4%	6.5%	7.5%		% Retained to Comm Eq	8.5%
44%	50%	70%	63%	53%	37%	45%	51%	49%	44%	41%		% All Div'ds to Net Prof	36%

CURRENT POSITION (D) (Smill)

	1984	1985	12/31/86
Cash Assets	168.5	405.6	593.4
Receivables	12317.9	12260.1	12408.4
Inventory(LIFO)	4521.8	4092.5	4013.0
Other	1222.2	1426.5	1697.3
Current Assets	18230.4	18184.7	18712.1
Accts Payable	2185.1	2278.9	2363.9
Debt Due	2136.9	1781.2	2188.6
Other	3007.1	3086.5	3198.7
Current Liab.	7329.1	7146.6	7751.2

ANNUAL RATES of change (per sh)
	Past 10 Yrs	Past 5 Yrs	Est'd '84-'86 to '90-'92
Sales	10.0%	9.5%	7.5%
"Cash Flow"	8.0%	11.0%	11.5%
Earnings	7.5%	11.5%	12.0%
Dividends	7.0%	5.5%	5.5%
Book Value	6.5%	6.0%	8.0%

QUARTERLY SALES ($ mill.) (A) Full
Cal-endar	Mar. 31	June 30	Sept. 30	Dec. 31	Year
1984	8372	9439	9648	11369	38828
1985	8769	9835	10043	12068	40715
1986	9390	10750	11171	12971	44282
1987	10480	11718	12193	13609	48000
1988	11500	13000	13500	15000	53000

EARNINGS PER SHARE (A) Full
Cal-endar	Mar. 31	June 30	Sept. 30	Dec. 31	Year
1984	.60	.99	.88	1.54	4.01
1985	.60	.72	.71	1.50	3.53
1986	.52	.77	.88	1.45	3.62
1987	.75	1.03	1.08	1.64	4.50
1988	.80	1.15	1.15	1.90	5.00

QUARTERLY DIVIDENDS PAID (C) Full
Cal-endar	Mar. 31	June 30	Sept. 30	Dec. 31	Year
1983	.34	.38	.38	.38	1.48
1984	.38	.44	.44	.44	1.70
1985	.44	.44	.44	.44	1.76
1986	.44	.44	.44	.44	1.76
1987	.44	.50	.50		

BUSINESS: Sears, Roebuck & Company, the world's largest retailer of general merchandise, sells through retail stores, catalog, telephone sales offices, and independent catalog merchants. Credit sales over half of total. Also owns Allstate Insurance Company, a major underwriter. Equity in undistributed earnings of subsidiaries, principally Allstate Insurance, accounts for 56% of income. Acquired Coldwell Banker and Dean Witter in '81. Has 311,800 employees, 320,000 stockholders. Payroll costs: estimated 23% of sales. Employee pension fund owns 16% of stock; insiders, under 1%. Chairman & Chief Executive Officer: E.A Brennan. Incorporated: New York. Address: Sears Tower, Chicago, Illinois 60684. Tel.: 312-875-2500.

We expect Sears will end the year on a firm note. Merchandise sales appear to be responding to the company's greater emphasis on soft goods and a more aggressive pricing policy. The Allstate Insurance operation should continue to benefit from higher volume, rates, and investment income. **There will be some negatives in the 1988 picture...** We think sales of hard goods, which account for nearly half of Sears' merchandise sales, will be lackluster next year (see Industry Analysis). The earnings of the insurance company may be hurt, first, by a much lower level of capital gains and, second, by the smaller tax credits arising from the new tax law that boosted insurance earnings in 1987. Corporate results in 1987 were also aided by one-time credits for a change in pension accounting. **...as well as some positives.** The company's greater emphasis on soft goods and competitive pricing might partly offset the weakness we envision for hard goods. The principal favorable development we envision at Sears is a much smaller loss from the company's new credit card, *Discover*. **Total return prospects will interest many investors**, especially in view of the

stock's good Safety rating. Following the market crash, Sears' relative price earnings ratio is the lowest in many years. Moreover, the estimated yield is much above the average of all stocks and the payout is well covered, both by estimated earnings and the company's strong finances. More significantly, we think earnings will make good progress to 1990-92, suggesting an average price in those years much above the current. Changes in retailing strategies and reductions in distribution costs might result in good progress in that area. We expect Allstate will remain a strong performer, perhaps aided by additional services. The greatest swing might come from the *Discover* credit card. Sears has made some heavy outlays on this venture, on which it may be receiving a handsome return 3 to 5 years hence.

Milton Schlein

Restated Sales (and Net Profit Margins) by Business Line
	1984	1985	1986	1987
Merchandise	26386(3.1%)	26385(2.5%)	27095(2.3%)	28000(2.5%)
Insurance	8948(7.1%)	10318(5.5%)	12634(5.5%)	14700(6.0%)
Real Estate	822(8.9%)	943(8.7%)	1152(7.7%)	1300(8.0%)
Fin'l Svcs.	2485(d1.6%)	2639(0.1%)	3401(d1.5%)	4000(1.5%)
World Trade	187(d13.5%)	230(d5.0%)	-(-.-)	-(-.-)
Company Total	38828(3.8%)	40715(3.2%)	44282 (3.1%)	48000(3.2%)

(A) Fiscal year ends Jan. 31st of following calendar year through '80. Calendar year thereafter. Incl. unconsolidated subsidiaries from '80. Incl. Coldwell Banker & Dean Witter from 12/31/81. 100% of Simpson-Sears from '83. (B) Average shares. Next earnings report due mid-Feb. (C) Next dividend meeting about Jan. 20. Goes ex about Feb. 2. Dividend payment dates: Jan. 3, Apr. 1, July 1, Oct. 1. ■ Dividend reinvestment plan available. (D) Retail operations only. (E) No meaningful comparison; accounting changed.

Company's Financial Strength A
Stock's Price Stability 70
Price Growth Persistence 50
Earnings Predictability 80

Figure 16.4 A Standard & Poor's Corporate Report

McDonald's Corp.   1447K

NYSE Symbol MCD   Options on CBOE (Mar-Jun-Sep-Dec)   In S&P 500

Price	Range	P-E Ratio	Dividend	Yield	S&P Ranking	Beta
Nov. 9'87	1987					
42⅛	61⅛–31⅜	15	0.50	1.2%	A+	1.05

Summary

Aggressive expansion and creative merchandising over the years have enabled McDonald's to maintain its position as the dominant force in the fast-food industry. Continuation of these strategies, plus increasing penetration of international markets and selective menu additions, should permit further earnings growth. A weaker dollar relative to foreign currencies has aided sales growth in recent periods.

Current Outlook

Earnings for 1988 are estimated at $3.45 a share, up from the $2.87 expected in 1987.

The $0.12½ quarterly dividend is the minimum expected.

Revenues for 1988 are expected to increase about 14%, aided by restaurant openings and new products. MCD is expected to maintain its leadership position in the fast-food industry, and profitability is likely to remain strong. A substantially lower tax rate is expected in 1988.

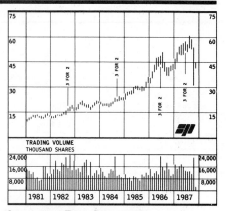

Total Revenues (Million $)

Quarter:	1988	1987	1986	1985
Mar.	---	1,068	941	809
Jun.	---	1,246	1,077	956
Sep.	---	1,314	1,134	1,015
Dec.	---	---	1,088	982
	---	---	4,240	3,761

Total revenues for the nine months ended September 30, 1987, increased 15%, year to year. Pretax income was up 13%, and after taxes at 43.3%, versus 43.4%, net income rose 14%, to $415.8 million ($2.18 a share) from $366.2 million ($1.89, adjusted for the June, 1987 3-for-2 split).

Common Share Earnings ($)

Quarter:	1988	1987	1986	1985
Mar.	E0.68	0.56	0.48	0.43
Jun.	E0.93	0.77	0.67	0.60
Sep.	E1.03	0.86	0.74	0.66
Dec.	E0.81	E0.68	0.59	0.53
	E3.45	E2.87	2.48	2.22

Important Developments

Oct. '87—In the nine months ended September 30, 1987, MCD's systemwide sales totaled $10.65 billion, up 15% from a year-earlier. This included an 11% rise for U.S. sales and a 28% increase in foreign sales (17% if currency exchange rates had remained at 1986 levels. Of the systemwide total, 66% of sales were by franchised units, 25% by company-operated restaurants, and 8% by affiliate-operated units. MCD said that in the first nine months of 1987, the operating margin for company-operated units improved, year to year, despite a 13% rise in beef costs. In May MCD nationally introduced prepackaged salads. At September 30, 1987 MCD had 9,678 restaurants, up 5.4% year to year. Of the total, 7,441 (77%) were in the U.S. Franchisees operated 6,624 (68%) of the worldwide total.

Next earnings report expected in late January.

Per Share Data ($)

Yr. End Dec. 31	1986	1985	1984	1983	1982	1981	1980	1979	1978	1977
Book Value	11.67	10.49	9.19	8.05	7.02	6.33	5.27	4.33	3.67	2.93
Earnings	¹2.48	¹2.22	1.95	1.70	1.48	1.29	1.09	0.93	0.79	0.67
Dividends	0.43	0.39⅛	0.33¾	0.28¾	0.23⅜	0.18¾	0.14⅝	0.10⅛	0.06⅜	0.03½
Payout Ratio	17%	18%	17%	17%	16%	14%	13%	11%	8%	5%
Prices—High	51⅛	36⅜	24⅞	22⅛	19½	14⅜	10⅜	10¼	11⅞	10½
Low	32½	22¾	18⅛	16¼	11½	9½	7⅛	7¾	8¾	7½
P/E Ratio—	21–13	16–10	13–9	13–10	13–8	11–7	9–7	11–8	15–11	16–11

Data as orig. reptd. Adj. for stk. div(s). of 50% Jun. 1987, 50% Jun. 1986, 50% Sep. 1984, 50% Oct. 1982. **1.** Fully diluted: 2.45 in 1986, 2.18 in 1985. E-Estimated.

Figure 16.4 *(Continued)*

1447K

McDonald's Corporation

Income Data (Million $)

Year Ended Dec. 31	Revs.	Oper. Inc.	% Oper. Inc. of Revs.	Cap. Exp.	Depr.	Int. Exp.	Net Bef. Taxes	Eff. Tax Rate	Net Inc.	% Net Inc. of Revs.
1986	4,144	1,173	28.3%	965	248	189	848	43.4%	480	11.6%
1985	3,695	1,065	28.8%	830	208	157	782	44.6%	433	11.7%
1984	3,366	966	28.7%	672	185	135	707	45.0%	389	11.6%
1983	3,001	840	28.0%	682	165	123	628	45.4%	343	11.4%
1982	2,715	724	26.7%	532	143	109	546	44.9%	301	11.1%
1981	2,477	667	26.9%	427	133	104	482	45.0%	265	10.7%
1980	2,184	575	26.3%	410	113	102	403	45.1%	221	10.1%
1979	1,912	483	25.2%	459	92	83	345	45.3%	189	9.9%
1978	1,644	423	25.7%	357	75	69	313	48.0%	163	9.9%
1977	1,384	363	26.2%	309	62	59	267	48.8%	137	9.9%

Balance Sheet Data (Million $)

Dec. 31	Cash	Current Assets	Current Liab.	Ratio	Total Assets	Ret. on Assets	Long Term Debt	Common Equity	Total Cap.	% LT Debt of Cap.	Ret. on Equity
1986	205	473	799	0.6	5,968	8.8%	2,131	2,448	5,089	41.9%	20.7%
1985	155	369	663	0.6	5,043	9.4%	1,638	2,187	4,297	38.1%	21.0%
1984	75	255	514	0.5	4,230	9.9%	1,268	1,943	3,638	34.9%	21.1%
1983	66	231	430	0.5	3,727	9.8%	1,171	1,755	3,225	36.3%	21.0%
1982	44	200	378	0.5	3,263	9.8%	1,056	1,529	2,817	37.5%	20.8%
1981	40	176	353	0.5	2,899	9.5%	926	1,371	2,483	37.3%	21.1%
1980	113	234	333	0.7	2,643	8.8%	970	1,141	2,251	43.1%	21.1%
1979	141	247	274	0.9	2,354	8.8%	966	952	2,025	47.7%	21.6%
1978	157	243	252	1.0	1,953	9.0%	783	796	1,651	47.4%	22.6%
1977	132	208	215	1.0	1,645	9.3%	688	643	1,385	49.7%	23.4%

Data as orig. reptd. **1.** Reflects merger or acquisition.

Business Summary

McDonald's Corp. operates, licenses and services the world's largest chain of fast-food restaurants. At December 31, 1986 there were 7,272 units in the U.S. and 2,138 units in other countries, mostly in Canada, Japan, Australia, the United Kingdom and West Germany. Contributions by geographic segment in 1986:

	Revs.	Profits
United States	73%	79%
Canada	10%	8%
Other	17%	13%

Units in operation at year- end:

Operated by:	1986	1985	1984	1983
Company	2,301	2,165	2,053	1,949
Franchisees	6,406	6,150	5,724	5,371
Affiliates	703	586	527	458
Total	9,410	8,901	8,304	7,778

The restaurants offer a substantially uniform menu including hamburgers, fries, chicken, fish, specialty sandwiches, beverages and desserts; most also serve breakfast.

Franchise fees under domestic arrangements executed between 1970 and 1986 are generally 11.5% of sales, including 8.5% for rent and a 3.0% service fee. Licensees also make sizable investments in start-up costs.

Dividend Data

Dividends were initiated in 1976. A dividend reinvestment plan is available. A "poison pill" stock purchase right was adopted in 1985.

Amt. of Divd. $	Date Decl.	Ex-divd. Date	Stock of Record	Payment Date
0.16½	Jan. 14	Jan. 22	Jan. 28	Feb. 6'87
0.18¾	May 15	May 20	May 27	Jun. 5'87
3-for-2	May 15	Jun. 23	Jun. 8	Jun. 22'87
0.12½	Jul. 15	Jul. 23	Jul. 29	Aug. 7'87
0.12½	Oct. 8	Oct. 20	Oct. 26	Nov. 6'87

Next dividend meeting: mid-January '88.

Capitalization

Long Term Debt: $2,349,274,000, incl. capital lease obligations.

Common Stock: 189,631,138 shs. (no par). Institutions hold some 61%. Shareholders of record: 41,000.

Office—McDonald's Plaza, Oak Brook, Ill. 60521. **Tel**—(312) 575-3000. **Chrmn**—F. L. Turner. **Pres & CEO**—M. R. Quinlan. **EVP-Secy**—D. P. Horwitz. **VP-Treas**—R. B. Ryan. **Investor Contact**—S. Vuinovich. **Dirs**—R. M. Beavers, Jr., R. J. Boylan, J. R. Cantalupo, G. C. Gray, J. M. Greenberg, D. P. Horwitz, D. G. Lubin, G. Newman, M. R. Quinlan, E. H. Rensi, B. F. Smith, A. P. Stults, R. N. Thurston, F. L. Turner, E. C. Walker, D. B. Wallerstein. **Transfer Agent & Registrar**—The First National Bank of Chicago. **Incorporated** in Delaware in 1965.

Information has been obtained from sources believed to be reliable, but its accuracy and completeness are not guaranteed. Tom Graves, CFA

Selecting a Broker

A **stockbroker** is a person licensed by the SEC to process buy and sell securities orders for clients. The broker is an important source of market information and is the link between investment decisions and actual securities transactions. Lack of harmony between investor and broker can lead to frustrating investment experiences, so selecting the right stockbroker is important. The selection process has two steps: selecting a brokerage house and then selecting a broker.

Selecting a Brokerage House

Brokerage houses are businesses that employ stockbrokers. Brokerage houses vary sharply in size, the services they provide, and the commissions they charge for their services. Some brokerage houses are local firms, some are regional, and some have nationwide operations. Irrespective of size, investors need to take into consideration the services provided by and the commissions charged by various brokerage houses.

Brokerage House Services.   All brokerage houses have one thing in common—they all handle securities transactions. Beyond that, their services vary widely. Many large regional and national brokerage houses, such as Merrill Lynch, Pierce, Fenner & Smith Incorporated and PaineWebber, provide monthly account statements to their customers. These monthly statements can be useful for record-keeping purposes.

Many brokerage houses periodically conduct seminars for their customers, where guest lecturers speak about such topics as the economy, market trends, and investment strategies. Brokerage houses also often make available to their customers extensive written reports on companies. Some brokerage houses have daily, weekly, or monthly newsletters and bulletins alerting their clients to changing market conditions.

Some brokerage houses have good-sized investment libraries in their local offices. These libraries include *S&P* and/or *Moody's Manuals, S&P Corporate Reports, The Wall Street Journal,* and other investments-related printed materials. Stock quotation machines, news wire services, and price ticker-tapes are other common fixtures in brokerage offices.

Brokerage houses will hold their clients' securities for safekeeping. An investor can buy securities in his or her own name or in a **street name**. A security is bought in street name when the brokerage house buys the

security in its own name on behalf of the investor and keeps it in its safe for the investor. Holding securities in street names is generally much safer than keeping securities at home in your own name. Many brokerage houses provide this service without cost, whereas others charge a fee for it.

Accounts of brokerage house customers are insured by the **Securities Investor Protection Corporation (SIPC)**, a federal government agency. Assets in these accounts are insured for up to $500,000, of which no more than $100,000 may be in cash. This insurance protects the investor's assets in the case that the brokerage house goes bankrupt. Some brokerage houses carry additional non-SIPC insurance and protect their customers' accounts for up to $5,000,000 worth of securities. An investor with over $500,000 of investable funds might consider maintaining an account with a brokerage firm that offers insurance in excess of SIPC limits.

Brokerage House Commissions.   Brokerage house commissions vary sharply from one house to the next. A special type of brokerage house called a **discount broker** has grown rapidly in recent years. Discount brokers, in general, do not provide any investment advice or information. Rather, they focus heavily on taking and processing securities transactions. As the name implies, discount brokers have relatively low commissions. In general, commissions are related to services provided by brokerage houses. General brokerage houses offer more services than discount brokers and charge more in commissions. Even within the general and discount categories, though, commissions can vary quite a bit.

When you select a brokerage house, you must recognize the tradeoffs between types of services offered and commissions charged. A beginning investor should maintain an account at a general brokerage house. A more seasoned investor should consider opening an account with a discount broker. (See "Computer Trading From Home" on page 516.)

Selecting a Broker

Once you have selected a brokerage house that has an office in your town, visit the office and meet a number of the stockbrokers. The brokers generally are referred to as account executives or registered representatives. You should feel at ease talking with the potential broker, and the broker should show an interest in your investment goals. A broker who immediately begins to recommend stock purchases may not have your best interests in mind.

You should determine the broker's investment philosophy. When investor and broker philosophies are at odds, chances are that the investor

will not be well served. A beginning investor should deal with a broker who is more oriented toward lower-risk, stable firms and long-term profits.

Once the choice has been narrowed down to two or three brokers, you should check with friends and other sources and try to obtain recommendations. In a pinch, brokers can be asked to provide references. These references should be contacted before you select a broker.

Opening an Account

After a brokerage house and a broker have been selected, you can open an account. Accounts can be either cash or margin accounts. **Cash accounts** are those customers who buy their securities with cash. The purchase price plus commissions usually have to be paid within five business days of the transaction date.

Margin accounts are for investors who borrow a portion of the purchase price to pay for their securities. In addition, brokers engaged in specialized trading techniques (explained later) also need to maintain a margin account. Securities are purchased in a street name for margin account customers.

Computer Trading From Home

You don't have to call up your broker and ask for a quote on Digital Widgets, wait to receive the bid and ask prices, then place an order and wait for it to be processed and reported back to you. Nowadays, you can trade securities from your home with the help of an appropriately equipped personal computer (PC). In terms of equipment, you will need a PC with a good amount of memory, generally two disk drives, a modem, and an appropriate software package.

A number of discount brokers offer computerized trading services for their clients with PCs. The brokers can generally provide clients with software that allows the clients to obtain quotes automatically and to enter buy and sell orders through their computers. This is where the modem comes in. It is a device that permits the PC to hook up via the telephone lines to the broker's computer. Market information on stocks and other securities is constantly fed into the broker's computer; this information is then transmitted to the client's PC. The investor can check bid and ask prices and enter orders to buy and sell securities from the PC. The software program, which typically costs $150 to $300, can also be used to check on your account with the broker. Now, if only the PC could give investment advice. Or does it?

"Forget pride, Emerson. For the sake of the firm I suggest you get in line and find out what she knows."

Source: *Changing Times*, April 1979, p. 9.
Reprinted with permission.

Spot Quiz • Selecting a Broker

1. It is always wise to select a general brokerage house.

   T _____ F _____

2. SIPC insurance protects the investor from the theft of securities kept in the investor's house.

   T _____ F _____

3. Compatibility between broker and investor is an important consideration in the selection of a broker.

   T _____ F _____

(Answers on page 526)

MAKING SECURITIES TRANSACTIONS

Making securities transactions requires opening and maintaining an account, specifying the type of order to be placed, and utilizing a specific trading technique. Opening an account was discussed earlier; in this section, we will discuss placing an order and utilizing a specific trading technique.

Placing an Order

For both cash and margin accounts, the investor needs to specify the type of order to be placed. Securities orders to buy and sell can be market, limit, or stop-loss orders. The number of shares bought or sold, or the size of the order, also needs to be considered.

Market Order.   A **market order** is one for which the investor instructs the broker to obtain the best price deal possible when the order is filled. For a buy market order, the broker will negotiate the lowest price possible. For a sell market order, the highest price is negotiated. Typically, a market order is filled at a price very close to the price prevailing at the time the order was placed, though this may not be the case for a stock that does not trade actively. In any event, if the stock is trading and there is sufficient time before the markets close for the day, a market order will be executed on the day that it is placed with the broker.

Limit Order.   In a **limit order**, the maximum buying price or the minimum selling price is specified by the investor. Table 16.1 showed that Jason Industries closed at 15⅞. If an investor likes the stock and wants to buy it but believes that the price will come down from 15⅞, that investor can place a limit order to buy, say, 100 shares at 15½. This limit order is transmitted to the market specialist making the market in Jason Industries. The specialist enters the buy order at 15½ in his or her book. If the price of Jason Industries stock drops to 15½ and no other buyer is in a limit order buy queue ahead of our investor, then our investor will have acquired his or her 100 shares at 15½. The 15½ specifies the maximum price. At times, a lower buy price is obtained.

A sell limit order works in a similar way. The investor specifies the minimum price that he or she is willing to take for the stock. The order is entered in the specialist's book and is generally executed if the market price reaches the limit order and is always executed if the price rises above the sell limit order. Placing a limit order does not mean that the order will be filled. If, for example, the price of Jason Industries does not fall to 15½, then the buy limit order will not be filled. Limit orders should be used with either infrequently traded securities or with securities whose prices fluctuate widely.

Stop-Loss Order.   A **stop-loss order** is an order to sell stock at the market price when the price of the stock declines to a specified level. Let's assume that an investor owns 100 shares of Jason Industries (JI), purchased at 12½. The current price for JI is 15⅞. The investor is afraid the stock will decline further. Therefore, the investor places a stop-loss order for JI at 15½. This means that if the JI price declines to 15½, the investor's order will become a market order to sell. The investor's stock will be sold at 15½ or a lower price.

If the stock price does not reach the specified trigger price, the order is not executed. If, for example, the price for JI starts to move up, the investor's stop-loss order will not be filled. Stop-loss orders can be used to protect gains already made or to limit potential losses. In the example just cited, the investor is using a stop-loss order to protect his or her profits. If the stock price starts to move up, the investor can raise the specified price on the stop-loss order to continue to protect profits.

Size of Order. Transactions involving multiples of 100 shares are called **round lot** orders. Orders for 100, 200, 700, and 1,900 shares are round lot orders. Transactions involving fewer than 100 shares are **odd lot** orders. Stock transactions are completed in round lot orders. Orders processed on, for example, the NYSE are in multiples of 100. Odd lot orders are executed through the services of a special broker called the **odd lot broker**. Odd lot brokers charge a commission of 1/8 per share in addition to the regular brokerage commissions charged. The odd lot broker charges the price that prevails for the first round lot order filled after the odd lot order is received. Someone wants to sell 57 shares of a stock. A round lot in the stock trades for $29¾ immediately after the odd lot order is received. The odd lot order is filled at $29¾ + 1/8 = $29⅞ per share. As you can see, it is cheaper to transact in round lot orders.

Utilizing Trading Techniques

Two common trading techniques utilized by investors are buying on margin and short selling.

Buying on Margin. **Buying on margin** means that the investor borrows some funds from the brokerage house to make purchases. Buying on margin is also referred to as **buying long.** Buying on margin requires that the investor have a margin account. Opening a margin account requires a minimum of $2,000 in cash, and some brokerage houses impose higher limits.

The **margin** refers to the minimum percentage of the purchase price put up by the investor. Margin requirements are set by the Federal Reserve Board and are changed periodically. When the margin requirement is 100 percent, it means that the investor has to put up 100 percent of the purchase price of the stock. If the margin requirement is, say, 60 percent, the investor has to put up at least 60 percent of the purchase price. Margin borrowing carries an interest rate that is about 1 to 1.5 percent higher than the prime lending rate, which is the lending rate that banks charge their most creditworthy clients, such as General Motors and IBM.

Margin buying is used to magnify expected profits. A disadvantage is that losses are also magnified with margin buying. An example follows. Investor Harris has $9,000 to invest. Harris is interested in buying XYZ

stock at $30 per share. Current margin requirements are 60 percent. Harris can buy either 300 shares in a cash account for $30 × 300 = $9,000 or 500 shares for $30 × 500 = $15,000. Harris would put up $15,000 × .6 = $9,000 and borrow $6,000 from the broker to pay for the purchase. (Commissions are ignored in this example.) Table 16.2 shows the transactions.

One year later Harris sells the stock at $40 per share, making a profit. Total selling price with margin is $40 × 500 = $20,000. Interest on the $6,000 loan is paid at 15 percent. After loan repayment and interest payment, Harris has $12,000 in net proceeds without margin and $13,100 with margin.

Table 16.2   Magnification of Profits and Losses With Margin Buying

Transaction	Without Margin	With Margin
Purchase of Stock		
Shares purchased at $30	300	500
Total purchase price	$9,000	$15,000
Amount put up	9,000	9,000
Amount borrowed	0	6,000
Stock Sold at Profit		
Shares sold at $40	300	500
Total selling price	$12,000	$20,000
Less amount borrowed	0	6,000
Less interest paid at 15%	0	900
Net proceeds from sale	$12,000	$13,100
Less amount put up	9,000	9,000
Profits (or loss)	$ 3,000	$ 4,100
Profits (or loss) in percent	33.3%	45.6%
Stock Sold at Loss		
Shares sold at $20	300	500
Total selling price	$6,000	$10,000
Less amount borrowed	0	6,000
Less interest paid at 15%	0	900
Net proceeds from sale	$6,000	$ 3,100
Less amount put up	9,000	9,000
Profits (or loss)	($3,000)	($ 5,900)
Profits (or loss) in percent	(33.3%)	(65.6%)

Profits are $12,000 − $9,000 = $3,000 without margin buying and $4,100 with margin buying. Percentage profits are higher for margin buying at $4,100 × 100/$9,000 = 45.6 percent. Margin buying has magnified the profits for Harris.

Margin buying also magnifies losses, as the last part of Table 16.2 illustrates. Let's assume that one year from now Harris sells the stock for a loss at $20 per share. Without margin buying, Harris loses $3,000 of $9,000, or 33.3 percent. However, with margin buying, Harris loses $5,900 of $9,000, or 65.6 percent.

As the example illustrates, margin buying is a two-edged sword. In general, beginning investors would do well to avoid margin buying when they first start investing.[4]

Selling Short.   Just as buying on margin is referred to as buying long, a **short sale** is one in which the investor sells borrowed securities with the expectation of buying them back later at a lower price. Let's assume that investor Harris expects market prices to decline in the near future. Harris wants to sell short 100 shares of a stock selling for $20 a share. Harris borrows the shares from his or her broker and sells them. After a few weeks, the price of the stock has declined to $15 a share. Harris now buys 100 shares of the stock at $15 a share and replaces the borrowed stock. Harris has made a profit of ($20 × 100) − ($15 × 100) = $500 on this transaction.

As the example illustrates, investors can sell stocks short in anticipation of a price decline. However, the short seller loses money if the price of the shorted stock goes up. In the example, let's assume that the price of the stock goes up to $25 a share. Harris buys the stock at $25 a share and replaces the borrowed stock. Harris bought the 100 shares for $2,500 and sold them for $2,000, thereby suffering a $500 loss on the transaction.

In the example, notice that for a short sale, the stock selling takes place first and the buying is done later, which is the reverse of a normal buy and sell transaction. Otherwise, the mechanics of computing profits and losses remain the same. Short sales can take place only if the investor has a margin account. A short sale requires the investor to put up minimum cash equal to the margin percentage applied to the selling proceeds. In our example, 100 shares were sold short for $20 × 100 = $2,000. If the margin requirements are 60 percent, Harris will have to put up $2,000 × .6 = $1,200 in cash. In addition, Harris is responsible for paying to the stock owner any dividends declared on the stock. Short selling is a risky trading technique suitable only for seasoned investors.[5]

---

4. Some additional restrictions not detailed here are imposed on margin accounts.

5. Special requirements for short selling are not mentioned here.

Spot Quiz • Making Securities Transactions

1. A limit order assures the person that the order will be executed at the specified price.   T _____   F _____

2. Margin buying magnifies profits and losses because of the use of borrowed funds.   T _____   F _____

3. Selling short is riskier than buying long.   T _____   F _____

(Answers on page 526)

Summary

Securities transactions take place on securities markets. Organized securities markets, such as the NYSE, have a physical building and governing rules. The over-the-counter market is a network of securities dealers engaged in buying and selling securities. Securities markets, brokers, dealers, investors, and corporate officers are governed by SEC regulations designed to prevent fraud, misrepresentation, and unethical behavior.

The overall performance of securities markets is represented by indices such as the Dow Jones averages, the Standard & Poor's averages, and the NYSE indices. Current information on firms is available through major daily and weekly newspapers and magazines such as *The Wall Street Journal, Barron's,* and *Forbes*. Historical information about firms is contained in annual reports issued by firms and in investment manuals. Advisory information on firms is available through services such as *Value Line* and *S&P Corporate Reports*.

Selecting a broker is a two-step process requiring selection of a brokerage house as well as a broker. Brokerage houses vary in services offered and commissions charged. General brokerage houses have more services and higher commissions than discount brokerage houses. Selecting a broker at the desired brokerage house should depend on compatibility

between broker and investor. Either cash or margin accounts can be opened by investors.

Orders for securities can be market or limit orders. Investors can protect their investments by placing stop-loss orders that are triggered when prices of securities decline to a certain specified level. Orders placed can be either round lot or odd lot orders.

Investors can magnify their expected profits by borrowing limited sums of money to finance securities purchases. This is called buying on margin, or buying long. Investors can profit from expected market declines by borrowing stock, selling it, and then buying it back later at a lower price. This procedure is called selling short. Selling short is riskier than buying long.

Questions

1. What functions do securities markets have in society?

2. Briefly explain how an organized market is used for executing an order.

3. Explain the difference, if any, between a primary and a secondary market.

4. What are the differences between organized and OTC markets? Are there any similarities? Explain briefly.

5. What are the basic reasons for regulating securities markets?

6. Obtain a recent issue of *The Wall Street Journal*. Select a stock and explain the price quotation provided for it.

7. Read the information provided on a corporation listed in either the *S&P* or the *Moody's Industrial Manual*.

8. Write to a company whose address is obtainable from an investment manual and request a copy of an annual report. Write a brief report on the information provided in the annual report.

9. What is the relationship between brokerage house services and commissions? Why does this relationship exist?

10. What are some important criteria for selecting a broker? Explain briefly.

11. What is the major difference between market and limit orders? Explain situations where market orders should be used. When should limit orders be used?

12. What is a stop-loss order? How does it work?

13. Explain the differences between round lot and odd lot orders.

14. What is meant by buying on margin?

15. What is a short sale? Why is it riskier than buying on margin?

Case Problems

1. Michael Oliveira is 22 years old and is working as a sales representative for a large consumer goods manufacturing company. His district sales director, John Ferguson, is 35 years old. John has two children, aged 7 and 9, and his wife works as an account executive for a large nationwide brokerage firm. Mike and John are driving together to call on a client. Mike asks John if he would be able to obtain some investment information from his wife. John says, ''Well, as a matter of fact, we are just a couple of blocks from Joanne's office. We will stop by her office so you can open an account and start putting your money to work.''
   a. Discuss the situation from Mike's viewpoint.
   b. What should he have done about the needed investment information?
   c. What advice do you have for Mike?

2. Herman and Sue Yip are in their late forties. Sue is a vice president with a large bank, and Herman is a university professor. The last of their three children has recently graduated from college. Herman and Sue are considering selling their home and moving into an apartment that would be closer to work and recreation for both of them. The sale of their house will free up sizable funds that they want to invest. When they visited a local brokerage firm, they met a broker who believed that by buying on margin and selling short they would be able to accumulate sufficient funds for their retirement. Rather than opening an account with the brokerage firm, they decided to think over the broker's advice.
   a. Did the Yips make the right decision in not opening an account? Explain your answer.
   b. What advice do you have for the Yips?

Bibliography

"Canned Plans Get Canned." *Money* (September 1987): 117–128.
"An Inside Guide to Stock Market Guides." *Money* (April 1981): 55–62.
"The Tempting Case for Foreign Stocks." *Money* (April 1985): 141–148.
"When Brokers Go Broke." *Money* (January 1982): 57–58.
"Where to Get Great Investment Advice for Free." *Money* (September 1987): 131–138.
"Who Makes the Most Investing." *Money* (December 1986): 68–70.

Answers to Spot Quizzes

Securities Markets (page 506)

1. F   (Unlisted stocks cannot be traded on the NYSE.)

2. T   (Transactions that do not take place on an organized market are OTC transactions.)

3. F   (Careful decisions about OTC stocks are no different from decisions about listed stocks.)

4. F   (SEC regulations do not provide protection against losses.)

Sources of Securities Information (page 510)

1. F   (Yesterday's closing price was $15\frac{7}{8} + \frac{1}{4} = 16\frac{1}{8}$.)

2. T   (The annualized dividend rate is $0.20 \times 4 = $0.80.)

3. F   (Some investors may believe that these services do not provide information of any value.)

Selecting a Broker (page 517)

1. F   (The seasoned investor may select a discount broker.)

2. F   (SIPC insurance applies only to assets held in brokerage house accounts.)

3. T   (Lack of compatibility will not benefit the investor.)

Making Securities Transactions (page 522)

1. F   (Limit orders may not be executed at times.)

2. T   (Use of borrowed funds magnifies profits and losses.)

3. T   (The potential for losses in selling short are higher than for buying long.)

Chapter 17

Stock and Bond Investments

Objectives

After reading this chapter, you will be able to:

- Describe the returns from common stocks.

- Explain the rights of common stockholders.

- Know the advantages and disadvantages of owning common stock.

- Differentiate various values for common stock.

- Discuss earnings and dividend terms related to common stock.

- Explain the difference between stock dividends and stock splits.

- Describe the different types of common stocks.

- Know the advantages and disadvantages of preferred stock ownership.

- Describe types of bonds and their features.

- Explain why bond prices change.

- Compare the advantages of bond ownership with the disadvantages.

For most Americans, thinking back to the mid-seventies will not bring back a lot of fond memories. The United States economy was headed into a recession, and a lot of people were out of work. Gasoline and heating oil costs were about to skyrocket out of sight. Interest rates were on their way to high levels, and stock markets were on their way down. Around this time, Leonard Edelman paid special attention to common stocks that were sensitive to changes in interest rates. He correctly anticipated that higher interest rates would force down the profits of utility companies engaged in generating and distributing electricity. He believed that declines in profits would lead to declines in the prices of utility stocks. He therefore proceeded to sell short utility stocks. His strategy proved to be successful. Prices of utility stocks did drop sharply. He was able to buy back utility stocks at low prices to replace the stocks that he had borrowed and sold short. As interest rates started to move down, Edelman bought shares of utility companies. He was able to sell these shares at a profit as the stock markets recovered. His strategy for selling short and then buying long doubled his $100,000 investment in stocks.[1]

As the example of Leonard Edelman illustrates, investments in securities can be profitable. The purposes of this chapter are to discuss popular investment securities—namely, common stock, bonds, and preferred stock—and to suggest investment strategies.

Common stock

Corporations issue two basic types of securities. One type represents borrowing by the corporation and is called **debt issues**, or **bonds**. The second type represents ownership and is called **equity securities**. Equity securities include both preferred stock and common stock. Common stock, discussed in this section, is evidence of ownership in a company. The owners of common stock in a company are called **stockholders**. Investors buy and sell stock in companies because they expect to receive returns from their stock holdings. Stockholders also have certain rights that go along with their shares of common stock. From an investment viewpoint, common stock ownership has both advantages and disadvantages.

Returns From Common Stock

Returns to common stockholders take the form of cash dividends and capital gains.

---

1. See "The Silver Lining for Stocks," *Money* (September 1979): 53–54.

Cash Dividends. Corporations are in the business of earning profits for their stockholders. A portion of these profits is retained within the firm for expansion, such as buying new equipment and buildings. The remaining earnings are not needed by corporations for use within the company and are paid out in the form of **cash dividends** to stockholders. Typically, cash dividends are paid quarterly and reported on an annualized basis. For example, a company has indicated that it is going to pay $1.20 in cash dividends this quarter. Its annual dividend rate would be reported as $1.20 × 4 = $4.80. Annualized cash dividends are reported in the investments section of most major newspapers, *The Wall Street Journal*, and other financial publications.

Capital Gains. Shares of major corporations are bought and sold in large quantities daily. Stocks of General Motors Corp. and Xerox Corp., for example, are actively traded on the New York Stock Exchange. The market prices of shares of corporations change daily. Most stockholders believe that their stock holdings will increase in value, and in general, common shares go up in value over time as corporations increase their earnings. Besides changes in earnings, other factors, such as the economic environment and interest rates, affect market prices. Because of these factors, market prices of common shares change over time. These changes produce profits—and sometimes losses—for stockholders. For example, an investor buys one share of a stock for $60 ($P0$). After one year, the share is selling for $65 ($P1$). The investor's gain is $65 − $60 = $5. This gain is called a **capital gain**. However, if the share price had declined to, say, $52 after one year, the investor would have suffered a **capital loss** of $60 − $52 = $8.

Total Return From Common Stocks. The total return from common stocks is the sum of cash dividends and capital gains. Total return, in percentage terms, can be expressed as

$$R = \frac{D + P1 - P0}{P0} \times 100$$

where

R = Total return
D = Cash dividend paid during the year
$P1$ = Price of a share at the end of the year
$P0$ = Price of a share at the beginning of the year
In our example, D = $4.80, $P1$ = $65, and $P0$ = $60. Total return is

$$R = \frac{\$4.80 + \$65 - \$60}{\$60} \times 100 = 16.33 \text{ percent}$$

Total returns can be negative as well as positive. In the example where
$P1$ is $52, total return is

$$R = \frac{\$4.80 + \$52 - \$60}{\$60} \times 100 = -5.33 \text{ percent}$$

From an investment viewpoint, total returns on common stock investments
are more important than either cash dividends or capital gains.

Rights of Common Stockholders

Investors in common stocks have a variety of rights that are explained in
this section.

Right of Ownership.   Investors own a proportional share of the corporation through their stock holdings. As an example, an investor owning 10 shares out of 100 shares issued by a corporation would own 10/100,
or one-tenth of the corporation. In practice, corporations typically have
millions of shares outstanding. Owning 100 or 200 shares out of millions
of shares gives the average investor very, very small proportional ownership of the corporation.

Right to Limit on Loss.   A corporation is a special type of legal entity.
A corporation can enter into legal contracts on its own behalf. For example, a corporation can borrow money. If the corporation ultimately is unable
to repay the borrowed money, the lenders cannot collect from the owners
of the corporation. The liability of the owners is limited to what they have
invested in the corporation. Investors' losses on stock holdings are limited
to the amount of money they spent to purchase the shares of stock.

Right to Establish Major Policies.   Stockholders establish major
policies of the firm, elect the board of directors, and vote on changing the
firm's documents of incorporation. Stockholders make their desires known
on various corporate matters by voting. Obviously, an investor owning
100 or 200 shares of common stock out of millions is not going to influence
corporate policies if his or her opinions are different from those of the majority of the stockholders.

Right to Vote.   Stockholders have the right to vote on corporate matters subject to a stockholder vote. As stated earlier, for the average investor,
the right to vote has little meaning. In general, investors give corporate
managers the right to vote on their behalf through a device called a proxy.
Proxies will be explained later.

Right to Share in the Distribution of Assets. Two types of assets can be distributed to stockholders. The more common type of asset distributed to stockholders is cash, in the form of cash dividends. Every owner of shares of a firm is entitled to receive dividends if and when they are declared. A **declaration of dividends** is a formal announcement by the board of directors that dividends will be paid to stockholders. Investors, in general, have no legal rights to the earnings of a corporation. Stockholders can expect to receive dividends only when they are declared. Typically, growth firms pay a relatively low portion of their earnings in dividends. They prefer to plough their earnings back into their businesses. Slow-growth firms tend to pay out a higher proportion of their earnings.

The second type of assets distributed to stockholders is residual assets after liquidation. Sometimes firms find it difficult to carry on their businesses. Some of these firms decide to go out of business by filing for bankruptcy. A bankrupt firm is **liquidated**. That is, its assets are sold, its creditors are paid off, and any assets left over—**the residual assets**—are distributed to stockholders.

Under normal circumstances, healthy firms do not go through liquidation. However, some firms go through bankruptcy and liquidation, and stockholders have a legal right to the residual assets of the firm. As a practical matter, very rarely do stockholders get anything when a firm is liquidated because the liquidated value of its assets typically does not cover all of the firm's liabilities.

Other Rights. Stockholders have the right to hold onto their stocks for as long as they wish. They can freely transfer their shares to other investors.

Stockholders have the right to examine the firm's financial records. This right forces firms to provide periodic information to their stockholders through news releases, annual reports, and quarterly and annual income statements and balance sheets.

Advantages and Disadvantages of Common Stock Ownership

Common stock ownership has certain advantages that makes it attractive for investors. However, you should carefully evaluate some disadvantages before you invest in common stocks.

Advantages of Common Stock Ownership. As was explained in the previous section, stockholders have *limited liability*. This feature is attractive from an investment viewpoint, because the maximum amount the investor can lose is what he or she has invested. The limited liability feature is particularly attractive to investors who would prefer to invest in the shares of high-risk, high-return firms.

Investors in common stocks typically have good liquidity. **Liquidity** for securities means the ability to buy and sell securities relatively easily and quickly. Stocks listed on the New York Stock Exchange, for example, can be bought and sold in minutes. The same type of liquidity does not exist with some investments, such as real estate and antiques.

Profits made on investments are considered to be income and are taxed accordingly. As explained in Chapter 3, profits on sales of investments owned for more than one year are called long-term capital gains. Long-term capital gains qualified for preferential tax treatment before the Tax Reform Act of 1986 repealed this preferential treatment. It is possible, though, that the importance of preferential tax treatment in helping businesses raise money may eventually result in its reinstatement.

Some investments require large sums of money. Such is not the case with common stock. Investors can invest in common stock even with small sums of money. The investor who has only a small amount, such as $50 per month, to invest can start a systematic program of investing in stocks.

As mentioned in Chapter 15, common stocks have proven to be good protection against inflation. Firms that are able to pass on inflation-related cost increases to their customers can show steadily increasing profits. These increases in profits allow for higher dividends as well as for the potential of higher stock prices. Investors, who obtain a combined return from dividends and capital gains, are provided with inflation protection through their stock holdings.

Investment in common stocks provides the investor with the opportunity for making a "big score." A **"big score"** occurs when unexpected news about a corporation produces abnormally high returns for its stockholders. Frequently, merger announcements produce large profits for the stockholders of the firm that is being bought out. Sometimes, a firm announces unexpected good news, and its stockholders benefit. Some time ago, a mining company announced the discovery of a large amount of copper ore. The price for its shares more than doubled immediately after the announcement. The big score does not occur very often; but with common stock investments, the potential is there.

Disadvantages of Common Stock Ownership. The major disadvantage of common stock ownership is that, in any given year, there is no guarantee that the expected return will be realized. In general, over the long run, investors can expect to obtain the expected return from common stock investing. In the short run, however, returns can vary dramatically. This is less of a disadvantage for stocks in industries such as public utilities, automotive, and energy. In these industries, dividends are more important than capital gains. Dividends remain relatively stable, and therefore

total returns are fairly stable. In growth-oriented industries, such as electronics, investors expect a large portion of their returns in the form of capital gains. The returns on these stocks can be very unstable for short periods.

Investment in stocks requires a healthy time commitment from investors. Rarely can an investor expect to buy stocks, put them away for a while, and obtain reasonable returns. More typical is the situation where an investor buys stocks and constantly evaluates his or her portfolio in light of new information about the economy, stock market trends, and specific stocks. Investment in stocks implies a time commitment for gathering, analyzing, and using information for managing a portfolio.

Another disadvantage of investment in common stock is that there is no guarantee that an investor will be able to sell the security at a profit. For the investor who is buying for the long run, short-term price changes are generally not important. However, if a financial emergency arises during a period when stock prices are down, selling the stock may not be desirable. The potential for losses during emergency sales of investments can be a severe problem with stock investing. (See ''Program Trading'' below.)

Program Trading

No, this isn't a write-up about two computer science majors. *Program trading* is the term for computerized securities trading decisions. In some firms, tremendously large buy and sell decisions are made by computers. A firm using program trading may have its computers monitor prices in a number of different markets, and, when the prices and timing are right, the computer will execute buy orders in one market and sell orders in another market. Sometimes, the program trading orders of a number of firms reach the trading floors at about the same time because the firms are using similar trading rules. The result can be temporary chaos in securities markets. Thus, large changes in the Dow Jones Industrial Average and other market indicators sometimes occur because of program trading. There is little that the average investor can do in reaction to the price swings caused by program trading. However, some consolation can be found in the fact that these dramatic price changes generally last for a short time and do not seem to affect the returns on securities bought for investment purposes.

Spot Quiz • Common Stock

1. A stock that pays $3 per year in dividends and sells for $40 a share will provide a total return of 12 percent if it goes up to $45 a share after one year.   T _____   F _____

2. In practice, the right to vote and the right to establish major policies for the firm are of little value to the average stockholder.
   T _____   F _____

3. Profitable firms are required to pay a portion of earnings in dividends.
   T _____   F _____

4. While common stock investments are expected to have positive returns, there is no guarantee of a return for the investor.
   T _____   F _____

(Answers on page 559)

COMMON STOCK TERMS

The discussion of common stock in financial publications and elsewhere frequently involves the use of specialized terms. For instance, special terms are used to refer to the number of shares a firm has, to the value of stocks, to earnings and dividends, and to stock price adjustments. This section contains an explanation of some common terms.

"I found that stock of yours that wasn't listed. It's here in the obituaries."

Source: *Changing Times*, April 1981, p. 46. Reprinted with permission.

Number of Shares

Firms classify their shares as authorized, issued, treasury, and outstanding.

Authorized Shares. The term **authorized shares** refers to the maximum number of shares that a firm can issue. Table 17.1 shows a corporate balance sheet. Associated Electronics Corp. (AEC) can issue a maximum of 10,000 shares.

Issued Shares. The term **issued shares** refers to the number of shares actually issued and sold to investors. AEC has issued 3,200 shares.

Treasury Shares. From time to time, a firm may decide to repurchase its shares from investors. Shares repurchased by the firm are called **treasury shares**, or treasury stock. Firms can eventually either resell treasury shares or retire them. AEC has 200 treasury shares on its balance sheet. If AEC were to retire these 200 treasury shares, its issued shares would decline to 3,200 − 200 = 3,000.

Table 17.1 Corporate Balance Sheet for AEC

Associated Electronic Corporation			
Balance Sheet, August 31, 19—			
Assets		*Liabilities and Equity*	
Current Assets		Liabilities	
Cash	$ 5,000	Current	$10,000
Receivables	10,000	Long-term	20,000
Inventory	10,000	Total liabilities	$30,000
Total current assets	$25,000		
		Equity	
Fixed Assets		Common stock, $10 par,	
Equipment	$20,000	10,000 authorized,	
Plant	30,000	3,200 issued	$32,000
Total assets	$75,000	Retained earnings	18,000
		Less: Treasury stock	
		200 shares at cost[1]	(5,000)
		Total liabilities and equity	
			$75,000

[1]The two hundred treasury shares were purchased for $5,000. The cost of the purchase is shown as an offset in the equity section.

Outstanding Shares.   The number of **outstanding shares** equals shares issued less treasury shares. AEC has 3,000 shares outstanding. Outstanding shares are important for the investor because they are a measure of the potential supply of shares for a firm.

Value

There are three different measures of the value of stock: book, par, and market.

Book Value.   The **book value** of a firm is equal to its total assets minus total liabilities. Chapter 2 explained the concept of net worth. Net worth and book value have the same meaning. The book value of a company is based on historical accounting information. For AEC, book value is $75,000 − $30,000 = $45,000. This figure is also obtained by adding all entries in the equity section. For AEC, this is $32,000 + $18,000 − $5,000 = $45,000.

Book value generally depends on the size of the firm. Larger firms generally have higher book values than smaller firms. From an investment viewpoint, book value is not important for the average investor. More important is **book value per share**, which is total book value divided by the number of shares outstanding. Book value per share for AEC is $45,000/3,000 = $15.00 per share.

Par Value.   **Par value** is the nominal value of a share. Many years ago it represented the minimum price at which a firm could issue shares. Now it has no practical relevance. Today, most firms issue common stock that has no stated par value or a very small par value. Table 17.1 shows that shares of AEC have a par value of $10.

Market Value.   **Market value** is the going price for a share. Market value is the price that investors would pay for buying shares or receive for selling shares. Market value is important for the investor, because it is the price associated with buying and selling securities.

Earnings and Dividends

An abbreviated income statement for AEC is shown in Table 17.2.

Net Income.   **Net income** is the difference between sales and all expenses, including taxes. AEC has net income of $2,000. In general, larger firms have larger net incomes than smaller firms do. If expenses and taxes are in excess of sales, the firm will show a **net loss**. In recent years, some major corporations, such as General Motors Corp. and Ford Motor Co., have suffered annual net losses of hundreds of millions of dollars.

Table 17.2 Abbreviated Income Statement for AEC

Associated Electronic Corporation

Income Statement

For Year Ending August 31, 19—

Sales	$200,000
Expenses	
(including taxes)	198,000
Net income	$ 2,000
Dividends	1,500
To retained	
earnings	$ 500

Earnings per Share.   **Earnings per share (EPS)** are net income divided by the number of shares outstanding. AEC's EPS is $2,000/3,000 = $0.67 per share. EPS is important because it represents each share's proportional claim on earnings. EPS is widely reported in the financial press.

Price to Earnings Ratio.   The **price to earnings ratio (P/E ratio)** is obtained by dividing market value of a share by its EPS. Say that AEC shares are selling for $10 each. The P/E ratio for AEC would be $10/$0.67 = 15. The P/E ratio tells the investor how much he or she would have to pay to "buy" one dollar of earnings. Growth-oriented firms have high P/E ratios. Firms that are not in favor with investors have low P/E ratios. P/E ratios allow investors to compare firms.

Cash Dividends.   The portion of net income paid out in cash to investors is called **cash dividends**. AEC has paid out $1,500 in dividends for the year ending August 31, 19____. Of more importance is **dividends per share**, calculated by dividing dividends by the number of shares outstanding. Dividends per share for AEC were $1,500/3,000 = $0.50 per share. Cash dividends per share provide a portion of the dollar returns that investors obtain from investing.

Dividend Payout Ratio.   The **dividend payout ratio** is obtained by dividing dividends per share by earnings per share. For AEC, the payout ratio is $0.50/$0.67 = .75, or 75 percent. This ratio indicates the percentage of earnings that is paid out in dividends every year. Growth stocks have low payout ratios.

Dividend Yield.   Dividends per share times 100 divided by current market value per share gives the **dividend yield**. For AEC, the dividend yield is $0.50 × 100/$10.00 = 5 percent. Dividend yield is a portion of the total return from investing.

Retained Earnings.   Tables 17.1 and 17.2 both show entries labeled "Retained earnings." The two entries have different meanings. **Retained earnings** on an income statement equal net income less dividends for the year. Table 17.2 shows retained earnings for AEC of $500. The entry from the income statement is transferred to the balance sheet and added to the entry there. AEC shows retained earnings of $18,000 on its balance sheet. The balance sheet retained earnings is a cumulative figure going back to the beginning of the corporation. The $18,000 includes the $500 from the income statement.

Price Adjustments

Often firms will adjust the price of their shares through one of two methods: stock dividends and stock splits. The reason behind adjusting the price is to move the stock into a more popular price range. For example, a firm's shares may be selling for $100 each. The firm's managers may believe that the stock would be more desirable to investors if it sold for $25 a share. Price adjustment methods would allow them to lower the price to $25.

Stock Dividends.   A **stock dividend** is the payment of stock as dividends. After a stock dividend, each investor owns more shares in the firm. However, the investor's proportional ownership in the firm remains unchanged. For example, investor A owns 100 shares of ABC company. ABC has 1,000 shares outstanding. Investor A owns 100 × 100/1,000 = 10 percent of ABC. Then ABC declares a 20 percent stock dividend. This means that ABC is going to distribute 1,000 × .2 = 200 new shares to its stockholders. Stockholders will receive one-fifth of a new share for each share they own. Investor A, who owns 100 shares, will receive 20 new shares.

In most cases, the total market value of an investor's holdings in a firm does not increase or decrease after a stock dividend. Because more shares are outstanding after the dividend, earnings per share will decline. If the P/E ratio remains the same, the price of the stock will decline to reflect the increased number of shares outstanding.

Table 17.3 shows how this would work for investor A. ABC's EPS would decline from $6 to $5 after the dividend. Assuming that the P/E ratio

remains the same, the price would decline from $60 to $50 a share. Total market value for investor A will remain unchanged at $6,000. Investor A has neither gained nor lost because of the stock dividend.

Stock Split.   A stock split has basically the same result as a stock dividend. By accepted usage, any stock dividend of 25 percent or more is called a stock split. A **stock split** takes place when the par value of a firm is reduced in proportion to the number of new shares being issued. A two-for-one stock split means that one new share will be issued for each old share outstanding. In a two-for-one split, for example, the par value of the share is halved. A two-for-one stock split would be equivalent to a 100 percent stock dividend.

With both stock dividends and stock splits, the firm's goal is to lower the price per share of its stock. As Table 17.3 shows, there are no real benefits in stock dividends and splits for the investors. Why, then, do firms go through these actions? One major reason might be that this is how managers signal investors that all is going well with the firm. The message may be that continued growth in earnings will soon carry the price back up to previous levels. In any case, stock dividends and splits are quite popular with managers of firms.

Table 17.3   Effect of Stock Dividend on Market Value

Item	Before 20% Stock Dividend	After 20% Stock Dividend
ABC Company		
Shares outstanding	1,000	1,200
Net income	$6,000	$6,000
Earnings per share	$6	$5
Price to earnings ratio	10	10
Price per share	$60	$50
Investor A		
Number of shares owned	100	120
Market value	$60 × 100 = $6,000	$50 × 120 = $6,000
Ownership in ABC	10%	10%

$\mathbf{S}$pot Quiz • Common Stock Terms

1. For a firm with no treasury shares, issued shares will be more than outstanding shares.   T _____   F _____

2. Market values are related to par values for common stock.
   T _____   F _____

3. Dividing the dividend payout ratio by the price to earnings ratio gives dividend yield.   T _____   F _____

4. A three-for-two stock split would be the same as a 50 percent stock dividend.   T _____   F _____

(Answers on page 559)

$\mathbf{I}$NVESTING IN COMMON STOCKS

Common stocks can be divided into four major categories. Investors will select stocks from these categories based on their risk and return preferences. However, investments in common stocks imply an understanding of the environment for investing as well as of those factors affecting the timing of investments. In this section, a discussion of types of common stocks is followed by an explanation of the analyses needed for investing.

Types of Common Stocks

Four types of common stocks available for investments are blue-chip, growth, income, and speculative.

Blue-Chip Stocks.   The term *blue chip* is related to poker, where the blue chips have the highest values. Firms whose stocks are **blue-chip** are highly stable and financially strong. Blue-chip firms are generally the industry leaders in their product or service markets. They have a long, established history of earnings and dividend payments. The firms have wise managements who do not subject the firm to unnecessary risks.

Because of their stability in earnings, blue-chip firms are looked upon to provide their stockholders with fairly stable returns. That is, blue-chip

stocks have a history of consistent annual dividend payments. Because investors have very high confidence in blue-chip firms, their stocks sell at P/E ratios that are higher than other firms in their industries. Examples of blue-chip firms are Exxon, General Electric, IBM, and Procter & Gamble. Blue-chip stocks are characterized by low risk, average dividend yields, and average potential for capital gains.

Growth Stocks. Firms whose sales and earnings have grown rapidly for several years in a row and who are expected to sustain the high growth rates are called **growth firms**. Their growth rates have to be higher than that of the economy as well as that of their industries. Growth companies typically are in high-technology areas, but there are exceptions to this rule. Fast-food retailing and general merchandising, for example, are not technology-dependent, yet growth-oriented McDonald's and Wal-Mart come from these industries.

Growth firms have a great need for money to finance their expansions. Consequently, growth firms choose to retain most of their earnings and have low dividend payout ratios. Thus, dividend yields on growth stocks are low, but the potential for capital gains is very high. The prices of growth stocks tend to fluctuate a lot, making them relatively high risk investments. Examples of growth stocks are Wal-Mart, McDonald's, Genentech, Microsoft, and Ashton-Tate.

Income Stocks. **Income stocks**, as the name implies, are characterized by high dividend yields. However, not all high-dividend-yielding stocks are income stocks. Income stocks are generally very safe investments, which makes them attractive for persons who seek a steady income with low levels of risk. Some stocks have high yields because their prices are low due to possible future bad news. For example, the price may be low and the yield high for stock of an oil company whose overseas assets may be nationalized. The high yield in this case would reflect the very high risk for the investor.

Income stocks are also called **mature stocks**. Mature firms typically are in low-growth industries. Their potential for growth in sales and earnings is low. As a result, they have high dividend payout ratios. Income stocks have high yields, low potential for capital gains, and relatively low risk. Examples of income stocks are American Telephone & Telegraph Co. (AT&T), and other public utilities.

Speculative stocks. **Speculative stocks** are characterized by the potential for very high returns. Speculative stocks are also very risky. Many speculative stocks are "glamour" stocks—that is, investors believe that there is something special about the firms. Some years ago, firms with the syllable *tronics* in their names were considered to be glamour stocks. One firm with the word *electronics* in its name was selling for a high P/E ratio even though it only manufactured gutters and downspouts.

Sometimes firms working on a technological breakthrough attract investors. Some firms may be desirable because investors speculate that these firms will be taken over by other firms. Sometimes investors are attracted to firms whose assets are expected to appreciate in value. Some gold and silver mining stocks fall in this category. A variety of reasons may attract investors to speculative stocks. The driving force for investments in speculative stocks is the potential for very high gains. Speculative stocks seem to go in and out of investor favor and thus tend to be high-risk investments.

Besides the categories of stocks already discussed, investors occasionally mention cyclic and defensive stocks. **Cyclic** firms are those whose sales and earnings fluctuate with the economy. Many of the blue-chip stocks fall in this category. **Defensive stocks** belong to firms whose earnings do not change with changes in economic activity. Many income stocks fall in this category.

Analysis for Investing

There are probably as many different investment philosophies as there are investors, but all of the available advice can be boiled down to one simple truism: "Buy low and sell high." Half of this objective can be accomplished by identifying and purchasing **undervalued securities**. These "bargain" securities are those selling for less than other securities with similar earnings records, growth potential, and risk characteristics.

In buying undervalued securities, it is the investor's expectation that ultimately other investors will recognize these bargains and start buying them. Buying by investors will force the prices of these undervalued securities upward, thereby producing healthy profits for those investors who correctly identified the undervaluation.

Another important aspect of analysis is the correct identification of the investment climate. For example, an investor may identify the undervalued nature of a particular stock and buy shares. Other investors may recognize the undervalued nature, but they may not be feeling confident enough to invest money. In this case, the undervalued security will continue to remain undervalued. (See "Like the Stuff? Buy the Stock!" on page 543.)

Analysis for investing is a three-step process. First, the investment climate needs to be analyzed. Next, the right industries should be identified. Last, undervalued securities in the right industries should be selected for investing.

The Investment Climate. Individual stocks as well as the stock markets in general react to the economic environment. News about inflation, war, unemployment, taxes, economic growth, and so on affects stock prices. Investors' perceptions or feelings about the economic environment make them optimistic or pessimistic about investing. The economic environment and the mood of investors in general form the **investment climate**.

Like the Stuff? Buy the Stock!

Did you know that right at this moment you might be wearing, using, or looking at a product made by a company that is destined to make rich investors out of those willing to buy its stock now? Sound farfetched? Not really.

Patricia Schwyn, an aerobics teacher in Chicago, really liked her Reeboks. When Reebok International initially sold its stock to the public in 1985, Patricia and husband, Michael, bought some stock at $22 a share. Hardly a year later they cashed in by selling their Reebok stock for around $110 a share. Because of their interest and expertise, a number of personal computer users got into Compaq Computer stock early and have seen their money quadruple in two years. In 1984, an investor noticed his children's friends wearing sharp-looking clothes made by Oshkosh B'Gosh. He wrote for the company's annual report, liked what he read, and bought Oshkosh stock for $5 a share. By early 1987, Oshkosh stock was selling for $75 a share, b'gosh.

The above examples aren't meant to imply that stock in anything that catches your fancy is going to be a highflier. Rather, they suggest that taking an investments-oriented interest in products and services you see in your daily life can at times hold the potential for providing extraordinary profits. So keep your eyes peeled for things that intrigue you. Check out the financial numbers in annual reports. Who knows, you may have the next Compaq on your hands. By the way, did you hear about this restaurant that specializes in barbecued goat and is about to go public?

Investors should have a feel for the investment climate before making investment decisions. Business and financial publications such as *The Wall Street Journal, Barron's,* and *Business Week* are excellent sources of information on economic and investment trends. These periodicals frequently carry comments and analyses by top-level economists and report on interviews with financial and stock market analysts. Reading these periodicals can help you make wise judgments about investing.

The Leading Industries. The second step is to identify the **leading industries**—those industries whose prospects for profits and growth are outstanding. For example, in recent years the mineral extraction, or mining, industry has done very well. The reason is that oil companies, in efforts to diversify, have been seeking out mining firms to buy. Similarly, at one time the electronics industry was considered to be very desirable for investing. The leading industries change over time, and business periodicals and investment advisory services are excellent sources for identifying leading industries.

Undervalued Securities.   Once the leading industries have been identified, the next step is to find **undervalued securities** in these industries. Undervalued securities have the potential for providing high returns on investments. There are two approaches to identifying undervalued securities: fundamental and technical.

In the **fundamental approach**, the investor is concerned primarily with the financial performance of the firm. The investor should look at the firm's pattern of growth in sales and earnings and note whether the firm has a large share of the total market for some of its major products. Does the firm have a consistent history of paying dividends? Does the firm have a financially strong balance sheet? How does its P/E ratio compare with those of other firms in the industry? Answers to these questions help you determine the basic strengths of a firm. This type of fundamental analysis can lead to identifying undervalued securities.

Some years ago a small airline called Allegheny Airlines used to fly in and out of Pittsburgh. The only problem was that Allegheny was neither small nor flying in and out of just Pittsburgh. Management changed the name of the airline to U.S. Air and advertised itself as a major airline. Investors found U.S. Air to be a very desirable investment, and their purchases increased the price of its stock. Those investors who had recognized Allegheny as an undervalued stock obtained very high returns on their investments in Allegheny.

In the **technical approach**, the primary concern is with identifying patterns of demand and supply for the stock of a firm. A technical analyst believes that all fundamental factors about a firm are reflected in the demand and supply patterns. With the technical approach, the analyst is not at all concerned with sales, earnings, prices, P/E ratios, or anything else along these lines. The price movements, volume, short selling, odd lot trading, stock buying and selling by corporate officers, and similar indicators are carefully analyzed. The technical analyst then tries to predict price movements.

Many technical analysts use charts to predict price movements. An example of a chart is given in Figure 17.1. Chartists talk of pennants, flags, gaps, wedges, reversals, uptrends, and a whole lot more. References at the end of the chapter can be used for additional readings on the topic.

Another approach to investing can be called the random walk approach. The **random walk**, or **efficient markets, hypothesis** states that all information about a stock is widely known and fully accounted for in market prices. Investors, all of whom have equal access to information, process information and make decisions based on their knowledge. Any expected good or bad news is acted on by investors. Their actions keep stock prices at levels appropriate to the information about the firm. If, as the random walk theory holds, the market does efficiently process all relevant information, then market price is always an accurate measure of "true" value and there is no such thing as an undervalued stock.

Figure 17.1 Example of Chart for Technical Analysis

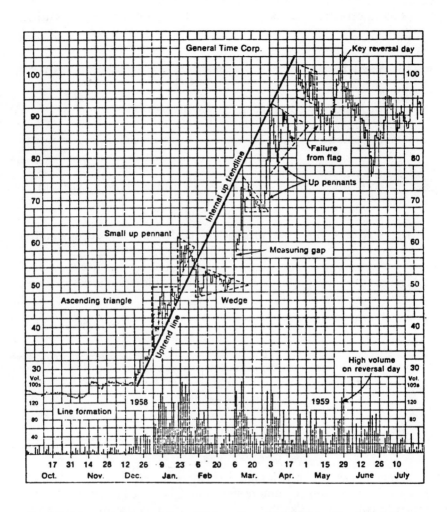

Reprinted by permission of the publisher. Copyright 1982 by Standard & Poor's Corporation.

The random walk approach states that fundamental and technical analysis of stocks is useless because all information about the stock is already reflected in its price. An investor using the random walk approach simply would not seek out any information about the firm. In the random walk approach, the only analysis needed is identification of the firm's risk level. This information is used to construct a select set of stocks, called a **portfolio**, that provides the investor with the highest return for a given level of risk.

In this section, we have looked at the types of stocks available for investment and the analyses needed for investing. Chapter 18 will explain how this information can be used for building a portfolio of securities.

Spot Quiz • Investing in Common Stocks

1. Blue-chip stocks are characterized by high levels of growth in earnings.   T _____ F _____

2. Blue-chip stocks are so safe that they can be bought without any analysis.   T _____ F _____

3. The analyst is concerned primarily with demand and supply patterns in fundamental analysis for selecting stocks.   T _____ F _____

4. The random walk approach to analysis requires the investor to read investment periodicals.   T _____ F _____

(Answers on page 560)

PREFERRED STOCK

Preferred stocks are considered hybrid securities because they have characteristics of both common stocks and bonds. Preferred stocks are similar to common stocks in that both pay dividends and have no fixed maturity date. They are similar to bonds in that their dividends generally remain fixed.

Returns From Preferred Stock

The only return investors can expect from preferred stocks in the long run is dividend income. Typically, the dividends on preferred stocks remain fixed. In the short run, preferred stock investors also have the potential for capital gains or losses because preferred stock prices fluctuate with changes in the interest rate.

Advantages and Disadvantages of Preferred Stock Ownership

Like any other investment vehicle, preferred stocks have advantages and disadvantages for the investor.

Advantages of Preferred Stock Ownership. Preferred stocks provide investors with a stable dollar return over time. In bankruptcy or liquidation of the firm, preferred stock has preference over common stock for distribution of assets.

Disadvantages of Preferred Stock Ownership. The dividends on preferred stocks generally remain fixed. Therefore, preferred stock investors cannot participate in the growth of the firm. Preferred stocks in general have no voting rights, so preferred stock investors cannot assert their voices through voting as common stockholders can. Preferred stocks also do not afford the type of protection provided to owners of bonds.

Types of Preferred Stocks

Preferred stocks can be classified by their features, or properties. Two important features are the cumulation and the participation clauses.

Cumulative Preferred Stock. **Cumulative preferred stocks** require that any dividends missed must be paid before dividends can be paid on common stock. For example, a firm has a cumulative preferred stock issue outstanding that pays $10 in dividends in every year. The firm suffers from non-profitability one year and misses all of its dividend payments in the year. Next year, the firm returns to profitability. The firm now has to pay $20 in dividends on preferred stock before dividends can be paid on common stock. The cumulative feature provides some safety for the investors. In some cases, extended periods of losses have led some firms to cumulate large sums of dividends on its preferred stock.

Participating Preferred Stock. **Participating preferred stocks** allow the investor to participate in the growth of the firm. Typical participation clauses allow dividends on preferred stock to go up when the firm's earnings go up. Another variation is for preferred stock dividends to keep up with common stock dividends when the latter become larger than the former. Participation clauses are very desirable from the investors' viewpoint.

Some preferred stocks have a **call provision** that allows firms to call in the preferred stock at their convenience. The firm can retire a preferred

stock by calling it. Another feature is the conversion clause, which will be discussed in Chapter 19.

Preferred stocks, in general, are not considered to be good investments. Other types of investment vehicles tend to have more desirable risk and return characteristics.

Spot Quiz • Preferred Stock

1. Preferred stocks are so named because they are preferred by many investors.   T _____   F _____

2. The best type of preferred stock would be a cumulative, participating preferred.   T _____   F _____

(Answers on page 560)

Bonds

An institution, such as a corporation, that desires to raise funds can issue bonds as well as common and preferred stocks. A bond represents indebtedness by the issuing institution to the investor. By buying a bond, the investor is lending money to the bond issuer. Bonds are issued by firms, municipalities, counties, states, turnpike authorities, school districts, and the federal government.

In this section, we discuss types of industrial bonds, terms associated with bonds, returns from bonds, factors affecting bond prices, and the advantages and disadvantages of bond ownership.

Types of Bonds

A **bond** is a promissory note issued by the firm to the bond buyer. Bonds are generally issued in denominations of $1,000. Firms need to raise millions of dollars at a time. Therefore, thousands of bonds are issued at a time by the firm. Each debt issue containing these bonds is governed by a contract, called an **indenture**, between the selling firm and the buyer. The indenture agreement contains the terms of the borrowing. Some of these terms, or features, are discussed later.

Bonds can be either registered or bearer. A **registered bond** is registered in the name of the bond buyer. A **bearer bond** is not registered in the name

of any specific person. The person who possesses a bearer bond is considered by the firm to be the owner of the bond. Mortgage bonds, debenture bonds, and subordinated debenture bonds are three popular types of bonds.

Mortgage Bond. A **mortgage bond** is the safest type of industrial bond an investor can buy. Mortgage bonds are secured by the physical assets of the firm. If a firm is liquidated, the proceeds from selling the pledged physical assets are used to satisfy the claims of mortgage bondholders before the claims of other creditors. **Senior mortgage bonds** have first claim over proceeds from liquidating pledged assets. **Junior mortgage bonds** claim satisfaction priority that is lower than that of senior mortgage bonds. Although mortgage bonds are not completely risk-free, they are the least risky of the investment instruments issued by firms.

Debenture. A bond not secured by liens against specific assets of the firm is called a **debenture**. In liquidation, debenture holders have claims satisfied along with the claims of the general creditors from the assets remaining after the secured creditors have been paid. The fact that debentures are unsecured bonds does not mean that they are unsafe. Debentures issued by blue-chip firms, such as American Telephone & Telegraph and General Electric, are very safe investments.

Subordinated Debenture. A **subordinated debenture** is one that subordinates its claims to the specified debts. That is, a subordinated debenture gives other specific creditors of the firm a priority in satisfying claims on liquidation. A bank that provides credit to a firm may insist that any new debt be subordinated to the bank's lending. In this case, subordination provides more security for the bank and less for the subordinated debentures. This greater risk generally means that subordinated debentures pay a higher interest rate than more secured bonds issued by the same company.

Bond Terms and Features

Some common terms and features associated with bonds are explained in the paragraphs which follow.

Trustee. Bond buyers generally do not have the resources to monitor the firm and see whether the indenture agreements are being met. The **trustee** acts on behalf of bondholders and sees to it that the firm complies with the indenture agreements.

Sinking Fund. A **sinking fund** is a fund set up to help the firm retire its bonds eventually. The firm makes periodic payments into the bond

sinking fund. The trustee uses the monies in the sinking fund to buy back and retire a portion of the firm's bonds outstanding. A sinking fund forces the firm to reduce its indebtedness. Therefore, it is generally viewed favorably by investors.

Call.   A **call provision** in the indenture agreement allows the firm to call in its bonds before they are due. Call provisions are advantageous to the firm because the firm can call in bonds when interest rates become relatively low. A bond with a call provision is not considered very desirable by investors.

Maturity.   Bonds have limited life, or **fixed maturity**, which means that bonds have to be bought back by the issuing firm on or before maturity date. Bond maturities are in the 15-to-30-year range.

Bond Values.   The price at which the firm buys back its bonds at maturity is called **face value**, redemption value, or value at maturity. Generally, face value is $1,000. Usually, bonds are sold by firms at face value. The current price of bonds is called **market value**.

When firms call their bonds for redemption prior to maturity they generally pay a price that is higher than the face value. The price paid for redeeming bonds outstanding is known as the **call value**.

Returns From Bonds

Bonds provide investors with a fixed dollar return in the form of interest income. Three different returns are associated with bonds; coupon rate, current yield, and yield to maturity.

Coupon Rate.   The **coupon rate** for a bond is its annual interest divided by its face value. A $1,000 bond paying $120 in interest annually will have a 12 percent coupon rate. The coupon rate for a bond remains fixed from the time the bond is issued until it matures.

Current Yield.   The **current yield** for a bond is its annual interest divided by its current market price. For example, a bond paying $120 in interest and selling for $850 has a current yield of $120 \times 100/\$850 = 14.12$ percent. An investor who bought this bond for $850 would receive $120, or 14.12 percent, in current income annually.

Yield to Maturity.   The **yield to maturity** is the total return provided by a bond held to maturity. Let's assume that a $1,000 bond with a coupon rate of 12 percent is selling for $850. As shown above, its current yield is $14.12 percent. Assume that the bond matures in ten years. The investor purchasing the bond for $850 will receive $120 in interest annually for ten

years. In addition, the investor will receive $1,000 for the bond on its maturity. The face value is $150 higher than the current market price for the bond. This $150 is also a profit, or return, for the bond buyer. This $150, allocated over the ten years by using a complex formula, and the interest income combine to give the yield to maturity. The approximate yield to maturity is calculated by using the formula

$$\text{Yield to Maturity} = \frac{\text{Annual Interest Payment} + \dfrac{\text{Face Value} - \text{Purchase Price}}{\text{Number of Years to Maturity}}}{\tfrac{1}{2}(\text{Face Value} + \text{Purchase Price})}$$

For the bond above

$$\text{Yield to Maturity} = \frac{\$120 + \dfrac{\$1,000 - \$850}{10}}{\tfrac{1}{2}(\$1,000 + \$850)} = \frac{\$120 + \$15}{\$925} = .146$$

The approximate yield to maturity on this bond is 14.6 percent. Bonds selling for more than their face values have yields to maturity that are lower than their coupon rates. The yield to maturity equals the coupon rate when a bond is selling at its face value. The yield to maturity is important for the investor because this is the actual yield provided by the bond. In other words, buying a $1,000, 12 percent coupon rate bond for $850 provides the investor with the same return as a $1,000, 14.6 percent bond bought at face value.

Factors Affecting Bond Prices

Bond prices are affected mainly by changes in the interest rates and in the riskiness of the firm issuing the bonds.

Interest Rates and Bond Prices.   As the previous discussion indicated, investors are most interested in the yield to maturity. Changes in the economy and in business conditions produce changes in interest rates. Prices of bonds already outstanding move up or down to bring yields to maturity in balance with the prevailing interest rates. Let's say that a firm issued $1,000, 12 percent bonds at face value one year ago. Interest rates have gone up to 14.6 percent now. Any firm issuing a similar bond would be able to sell a $1,000, 14.6 percent bond for $1,000. No investor would be willing to pay $1,000 for the 12 percent bond because it would only yield 12 percent. Because the prevailing yield is 14.6 percent, the price of the 12 percent bond would have to decline to $850 before investors would buy it. The reason is that at a price of $850, the 12 percent bond provides a 14.6 percent yield to maturity. Similarly, bond prices go up as interest rates decline.

Firm Risk and Bond Prices.   Even if interest rates do not change, bond prices may change because of changes in the riskiness of the bond-issuing firm. As far as bondholders are concerned, the risk they face is that firms may not be able to pay interest on bonds. The quality of bonds and the associated risks are evaluated by two bond rating services. Moody's and Standard & Poor's both rate bonds. Figure 17.2 shows bond ratings by these two services.

Aaa or AAA rated bonds are of the highest quality, have the lowest risk, and carry the relatively lowest interest rates. As you move down the scale from Aaa (AAA) to C(D), bond quality decreases and riskiness increases. If the bond rating for a firm changes, the prices of its already outstanding bonds will change correspondingly. If, for example, a firm's rating changes from Aaa to Aa, the firm will be perceived as being slightly riskier than before. Investors will require a higher yield for Aa than for Aaa bonds. Because the coupon rate remains fixed, the price of the bonds will decline slightly to provide investors with a higher yield.

Other Factors.   Two other factors also affect bond prices. Callable bonds tend not to rise much above face value in price when interest rates decline. The reason is that when interest rates decline, the firm is more apt to call high-interest-rate bonds. The investor recognizes this and is unwilling to pay a price much higher than the call value of the bond.

Figure 17.2   Quality of Bond Ratings

Moody's		Standard & Poor's	
Rating	Meaning	Rating	Meaning
Aaa	Highest quality	AAA	Highest grade
Aa	High quality	AA	High grade
A	Upper medium quality	A	Upper medium grade
Baa	Medium quality	BBB	Medium grade
Ba	Somewhat speculative	BB	Somewhat speculative
B	Speculative	B	Speculative
Caa	Very speculative	CCC	Very speculative
Ca	Near default	CC	Near default
C	In default	C	In default; ratings
		DDD	vary with expected
		DD	salvage value
		D	

Years remaining to maturity also affect bond prices. The prices of bonds with long lives fluctuate more than prices of short-lived bonds. The difference between face value and market value of bonds has a smaller influence on the prices of long-lived bonds because this difference is allocated over more years. For short-lived bonds, the difference between face value and market value becomes more important in providing investors with a return. Because the bond matures in a short time and investors receive face value for the bond, the market value deviates little from the face value.

Spot Quiz • Bonds

1. A bearer bond provides more safety than a registered bond.
   T _____ F _____

2. Subordinated debentures provide less security than mortgage bonds.
   T _____ F _____

3. A call provision is attractive for bondholders.   T _____ F _____

4. Current yield equals the coupon rate when the market value of a bond equals its face value.   T _____ F _____

5. Interest rates are the sole factor affecting bond prices.
   T _____ F _____

(Answers on page 560)

MUNICIPAL BONDS

Many states, cities, municipalities, turnpike authorities, school districts, hospitals, and similar institutions also issue bonds. These bonds are generally called **municipal bonds**. The major advantage of municipal bonds is that interest income from them is exempt from federal income taxes. Further, interest income from municipal bonds is also exempt from state income taxes in the state of issue. Thus, a Pennsylvania resident buying bonds issued by Philadelphia would be exempt from paying either federal or state income taxes on interest income from these bonds.

Municipal bonds can be divided into two categories. **General obligation bonds** (or GOs) are secured by a state's or city's power to tax. Many

states and cities have GOs outstanding. As with industrial bonds, municipal bonds are rated by Moody's and by Standard & Poor's.

The second category of municipal bonds is called **revenue bonds** (or revs). Revs are backed by special sources of income. For example, turnpike, bridge, and tunnel revs are secured by toll income. Airport revs are secured by airline leases. Housing revs, such as by university dormitories, are secured by rental income. Revs are also rated by Moody's and Standard & Poor's.

For an investor in the 28 percent tax bracket, a 10 percent yield on a municipal bond is equivalent to a 13.9 percent yield on a non-tax-exempt bond. Therefore, municipal bonds are attractive investments for people in the high income tax bracket. The major disadvantages of municipal bonds are infrequent trading and trading in volume of $5,000 or more. The small investor can overcome both of these disadvantages by buying tax-exempt or municipal bond funds. Bond funds can be bought and sold readily. In addition, most bond funds have minimum investment requirements of $1,000–$2,500.

Spot Quiz • Municipal Bonds

1. Municipal bonds are exempt from all types of income taxes.

   T _____   F _____

2. GOs are safer than revs.   T _____   F _____

(Answers on page 560)

BOND INVESTMENT CONSIDERATIONS

Bond investments have certain advantages and disadvantages for the investor.

Advantages of Bond Investments

Bond investments tend to be suited to individuals who have already acquired a substantial fund to invest and who depend on the income from that fund to meet living expenses. People nearing retirement age are a prime example.

Lower Risk.   Bonds are less risky than either common or preferred stocks of the same company. For example, AT&T's bonds have lower risk for the investor than either AT&T preferred or common stock.

Stable Return.   Bonds generally provide investors with a stable return in the form of interest income. Those who count on investment income for living expenses find this stability of bond returns very desirable. If you are willing to hold the bond until maturity, then the return on the bond is completely known. Further, the yield on bond investments tends to be higher than yields on savings accounts or certificates of deposit.

Information Processing.   Buying common stocks requires a lot of information processing by the investor. Such is not the case with bond investments. Bonds are rated for quality. Once an investor has decided on bond quality and maturity date, it is a simple matter to identify bonds that meet the investor's requirements.

Disadvantages of Bond Investments

Bond investments are generally not well suited to young adults or other individuals who have not acquired large amounts to invest, do not depend on investment income to meet living expenses, and can afford to assume more risk in return for greater long-term returns.

Low Returns.   Historically, returns on bonds have been lower than returns on either preferred or common stock investments. This, of course, is not surprising. For any investment, if risks are low, then returns will also be comparatively low. As Chapter 15 pointed out, bonds in general are low-risk, low-return investments.

High Cost Per Unit.   Bonds typically have $1,000 face values. Their market values fluctuate around face value. For the average investor, it becomes difficult to buy three or four bonds at a time. Buying into bond mutual funds is a way of getting around this problem. Mutual funds are discussed in Chapter 18.

Other Considerations

The first four bond ratings are generally called **investment grade** quality. Bonds with ratings other than investment grade are called, in Wall Street language, **junk bonds**. That is, any bond with a rating of Ba/BB or lower is called a junk bond. Some investors specialize in buying junk bonds selectively. Junk bonds have higher yields and at times appear to have

reasonable levels of risk. More knowledgeable investors should carefully explore the feasibility of buying some junk bonds.[2]

Spot Quiz • Bond Investment Considerations

1. Bond investing is not time-consuming for the investor.

   T _____   F _____

2. A bond rated Baa can be called a junk bond.   T _____   F _____

(Answers on page 560)

Summary

Corporations issue two basic types of securities: debt issues called bonds and equity issues called common and preferred stocks. Common stock represents ownership in the firm. Cash dividends and capital gains combine to provide returns on common stock investments. Common stockholders, besides owning the corporations, have limited exposure to loss, can establish the firm's major policies, can vote, and own a proportional share of the firm. Investments in common stocks provide for lower taxes on capital gains as well as some protection against inflation. However, common stock returns can vary sharply.

Four types of common stocks for investing are blue-chip, growth, income, and speculative. The risk and return characteristics on these types of stocks vary. The idea behind investing is to find undervalued securities. Identification of undervalued securities requires analyses of the investment climate, the right industries, and, finally, the undervalued securities.

Preferred stocks provide investors with relatively fixed dollar dividend returns. In general, they are not good investment vehicles.

Bonds such as mortgage bonds and debentures represent indebtedness by firms. Bond returns tend to be fairly stable. Bond prices are affected by changes in interest rates and in the risk of the bond-issuing firm. The riskiness of a bond is determined by its quality rating. Municipal bonds provide income that is exempt from federal income taxes.

---

2. See "Why Investors Bet on Junk Bonds," *Money* (May 1981): 31–33.

Questions

1. Briefly explain the returns you would obtain from investing in common stocks.

2. Explain the concept of total returns from common stock investments.

3. Explain three major rights of common stockholders.

4. Which stockholder right is most important? Why?

5. What are some of the advantages of common stock ownership?

6. Briefly explain some of the disadvantages of common stock ownership.

7. Explain the following terms:
   a. Authorized shares
   b. Issued shares
   c. Treasury shares
   d. Outstanding shares

8. Briefly explain the difference, if any, among book, par, and market values for common stocks.

9. Why is the P/E ratio important for investors?

10. What are the differences, if any, between stock splits and stock dividends?

11. What are the risk and return differences among the four types of common stocks?

12. Briefly explain the steps involved in common stock analysis.

13. What are the differences between the fundamental and the technical approaches to common stock analysis?

14. What is a preferred stock? Would you buy preferred stock? Explain your answer.

15. Briefly explain the major types of bonds.

16. Would you prefer to buy a bearer or a registered bond? Explain your answer.

17. Explain the following terms:
   a. Coupon rate
   b. Current yield
   c. Yield to maturity

18. If you were considering buying a bond, would current yield or yield to maturity be more important to you? Explain.

19. Why are bond prices affected by interest rates and riskiness?

20. What are municipal bonds? What is the one major difference between municipal and industrial bonds?

21. What factors would you consider in buying bonds?

Case Problems

1. John Amayo is considering buying stock in American Industries Corporation (AIC). AIC's EPS is $4.00, and the stock is selling at a P/E ratio of 7. The dividend payout ratio for AIC is 60 percent. Mr. Amayo expects the price of AIC to go to $35 a share after one year. What is Mr. Amayo's expected total percent return from buying AIC?

2. Debbie Cheng believes that General Solar Corporation (GSC) may be a good stock to buy. GSC is currently selling for 8 times earnings and has a dividend yield of 4.0 percent. GSC is paying $1.60, or 32 percent of its earnings, in dividends. A stock similar to GSC has an expected total return of 14 percent. If GSC's price is expected to go to $45 a share, is Miss Cheng's optimism about the stock justified? Provide full numerical support for your answer.

3. Pi Keowan owns 100 shares of Tiger Corporation (TC). TC has 1,500 shares outstanding, and its EPS is $4.50. Its stock sells at 6 times earnings. TC declares a 50 percent stock dividend. How many shares will Mr. Keowan have after the dividend? How will his ownership of the firm be affected? Will the dividend lower the EPS for TC? If so, what impact, if any, will it have on the P/E ratio for TC and on Mr. Keowan's wealth?

4. Sue Tomko wants to buy one of two bonds with the higher yield to maturity. Bond A has a coupon rate of 8 percent and is going to mature in 11 years. It can be purchased for $780 and has a face value of $1,000. Bond B is selling for $950 and will mature in 15 years. Its face value is $1,000. Bond B pays $160 per year in interest. Which bond should Ms. Tomko buy? Why?

5. Jamie Rutherford is thinking of buying a new bond to be issued soon. Mr. Rutherford knows that prevailing yields to maturity are 16 percent. The bond will be a 30-year bond with a coupon rate of 17 percent.

The bond will have a $1,000 face value. What price should Mr. Rutherford be willing to pay for the bond? Explain your answer.

Bibliography

"The Best Ways to Invest $1,000, $10,000 and $25,000." *Money* (May 1985): 60–63.

"A Bull Market Bonanza." *Money* (July 1986): 113–118.

"Calling All Bonds." *Changing Times* (November 1986): 45–48.

"A Day in the Life of the Stock Market." *Money* (June 1986): 106–148.

"How a Technician Spots a Trend." *Money* (April 1986): 131–138.

"How to Start Investing." *Changing Times* (April 1987): 23–28.

"A Plan for All Seasons." *Changing Times* (April 1987): 31–32.

"Stock Market Basics for Beginners." *Changing Times* (June 1981): 41–46.

"Why Investors Bet on Junk Bonds." *Changing Times* (May 1981): 31–33.

Answers to Spot Quizzes

Common Stock (page 534)

1. F (The total return will be ($3 + $45 − $40) × 100/$40 = 20 percent.)

2. T (For the average investor, these rights are meaningless.)

3. T (Firms are not required to pay dividends.)

4. T (Returns on common stock investments are not guaranteed.)

Common Stock Terms (page 540)

1. F (They would be the same.)

2. F (Par values are nominal values for common stock.)

3. T (Definitional.)

4. T (In each case, one new share is issued for two old ones.)

Investing in Common Stocks (page 546)

1. F (Blue-chip stocks show average growth.)

2. F (While they are safe, investors still need to analyze the investment climate.)

3. F (The fundamental analyst is concerned mainly with the firm's financial performance.)

4. F (The random walk approach does not require any information processing.)

Preferred Stock (page 548)

1. F (They are called preferred because of the priority of their claims over those of common stock.)

2. T (These two features are desirable from the investor's viewpoint.)

Bonds (page 553)

1. F (A bearer bond, if it is lost or stolen, may be difficult to replace.)

2. T (Mortgage bonds are the safest.)

3. F (Call provisions are advantageous for the bond-issuing firm.)

4. T (This is the only time when it happens.)

5. F (Changes in risk, age, and callability all affect prices.)

Municipal Bonds (page 554)

1. F (They are exempt only from federal income taxes.)

2. T (GOs are backed by the authority to tax.)

Bond Investment Considerations (page 556)

1. T (Bond quality ratings simplify the task of finding suitable bond investments.)

2. F (The top four ratings are investment grade.)

Chapter 18

Managing Investment Funds

Objectives

After reading this chapter, you will be able to:

- Compare various methods for personally managing investment funds.

- Explain how investment clubs operate.

- Describe the various types of mutual funds.

- Differentiate between load and no-load funds.

- List the different types of returns from investing in mutual funds.

- Explain the advantages and disadvantages of buying mutual funds.

- Select a mutual fund.

Jason Harris is proud of the way he has handled his personal investment funds over the past ten years. He started out by buying $300 worth of stock of a large manufacturing firm. He also began subscribing to *The Wall Street Journal* and *Barron's*. Based on his studies and analyses of economic and financial information in various newspapers and periodicals as well as in *Value Line, Standard & Poor's,* and *Moody's,* he has systematically invested $200 each month in stocks and bonds. He is quick to point out that his investment portfolio is currently worth $33,400. He believes that his portfolio returns justify the 10 to 15 hours he invests weekly in processing information about stocks and bonds.

Ann Sanchez is a market researcher for a consumer products company in San Francisco. She and seven of her friends from the company have formed a partnership called Lombard Street Investment Club. Each partner pays $200 every month to the club. The partners meet once a month to decide how to invest the $1,600 received for the month. Occasionally they invite people associated with investments to address their club. Ann's return on her portion of the investment club has averaged about 18 percent annually for the past five years.

The Juswaiks consider themselves too busy to spend time on investment analysis. They periodically buy shares of a no-load common stock mutual fund. In three years, their investment in the mutual fund has doubled.

What do Jason Harris, Ann Sanchez, and the Juswaiks have in common? All four want to obtain the maximum out of their investment dollars. Harris is trying to accomplish this by managing his funds personally. Sanchez believes that managing funds through an investment club is most desirable. The Juswaiks have opted for professional management of their funds by buying into a mutual fund. Each person is following a different strategy for managing investment funds.

Three basic issues are involved in managing investment funds. The first is selecting the right investments—that is, identifying and buying those investments that have the desired risk and return characteristics. (Stock and bond categories and selection procedures were outlined in Chapter 17.)

The second step is selecting the *right time* to make investments. This topic was discussed briefly in Chapter 17, and additional pointers will be offered in this chapter. The third step is selecting investments to achieve *proper portfolio diversification*. This last step is something like not putting all your eggs in one basket. It is generally not considered a good investment strategy to place all your investment funds in just one or two securities. If something adverse happens to the stock or stocks, the impact on your net worth can be substantial. Buying too many stocks is not desirable either because investment funds would then be spread too thinly over too many securities. Proper **portfolio diversification** means holding a suitable number of securities. Investment experts have determined that a properly diversified portfolio will contain about 10 to 20 stocks.

The purpose of this chapter is to explain methods of managing personal investment funds. The first part deals with personal management of funds; investment clubs are discussed in the next part; and the last part of the chapter is devoted to a discussion of professional management of investment funds.

Personal management of investment funds

Investors who wish to manage their own funds should follow the information-processing procedures outlined in Chapter 17. Once suitable stocks have been identified, investors must time the purchase of the stocks and ensure proper diversification. Timing is the more problematic issue. In this section, two procedures that address the timing issue and one that handles the diversification issue are discussed.

Dollar Cost Averaging

As mentioned in Chapter 17, the first object in investing in securities is to buy low. Unfortunately, few investors can predict unfailingly just what a low price is. Stock prices rarely move up (or down) in regular increments. More often, a month-long uptrend will include many days when the price actually falls as investors sell shares to capture profits (commonly called **profit taking**).

Because it is difficult to identify low prices without the benefit of hindsight and because it is psychologically easier to buy securities when prices are rising, investors need a system that helps them purchase securities when prices are low. **Dollar cost averaging** is a system for regular investing that automatically ensures that more securities are purchased at low prices than at high prices.

The principle of this method is to invest approximately the same dollar amount in the same stock at regular intervals over a long time period. In dollar cost averaging, it is important that none of the four parts of the principle be violated. That is, the investor must (1) invest approximately the same amount each period, (2) make investments each period (the period may be a month, three months, or whatever), (3) purchase the same stock each time, and (4) do this for a long time period, say, three to five years.

An example of dollar cost averaging is shown in Table 18.1. We have assumed that the investor has approximately $300 available for investing

every four months. In time period 1, the investor selects a stock selling for $15 per share and purchases 20 shares for $300. In time period 2, the stock price has moved up to $16 a share, so 19 shares are bought for $304. The investor now owns 20 + 19 = 39 shares at a cost of $300 + $304 = $604. The total value of these shares is $39 × 16 = $624. The average cost per share is $604/39 = $15.49.

The investor continues this process for nine periods, after which the investor owns 174 shares that cost $2,707 and are worth $3,480. As Table 18.1 indicates, the investor's total value was in excess of total cost for every period except periods 3 and 4. Even in period 5, when the price of the stock was less than the beginning price of $15 a share, the investor was showing a profit.

The dollar cost averaging method is advantageous for small investors because it forces the investor to buy stock when prices are declining and low and when the investor may not be psychologically prepared to buy stocks. We emphasize that investors should continue dollar cost averaging for at least three to five years. This time span usually covers one business cycle, and the investor will probably encounter a stock price cycle with both high and low prices. If the price of a stock declines continuously, however, the dollar cost averaging method will not work.

Table 18.1 Dollar Cost Averaging Example[a]

Period	Price of Stock	Shares Bought	Cost[b]	Total Shares	Total Cost[c]	Total Value[d]	Average Cost per Share[e]
1	$15	20	$300	20	$ 300	$ 300	$15.00
2	16	19	304	39	604	624	15.49
3	13	23	299	62	903	806	14.56
4	12	25	300	87	1,203	1,044	13.83
5	14	21	294	108	1,497	1,512	13.86
6	16	19	304	127	1,801	2,032	14.18
7	18	17	306	144	2,107	2,592	14.63
8	20	15	300	159	2,407	3,180	15.14
9	20	15	300	174	2,707	3,480	15.56

[a]It is assumed that approximately $300 can be invested each time period.
[b]Obtained by multiplying columns 2 and 3.
[c]Costs are cumulated from column 4.
[d]Obtained by multiplying columns 2 and 5.
[e]Obtained by dividing column 6 by column 5.

Ratio Planning

Ratio planning is a method of diversifying a portfolio that is suitable for the investor who already has an established portfolio. Ratio planning requires managing two portfolios—an **aggressive portfolio** composed of common stocks and a **defensive portfolio** composed of bonds. Typically, during recessions business activity declines, and interest rates and prices of common stocks fall. Interest rates and bond prices are inversely related. That is, bond prices go up when interest rates fall and vice versa. Therefore, there are times when prices of common stocks fall and bond prices rise. The idea behind ratio planning is to move funds from the aggressive to the defensive portfolio during an economic recession and from the defensive to the aggressive portfolio when the economy expands.

The moving of funds between the two portfolios is relatively easy. This is where the *ratio* in ratio planning comes in. The investor selects a ratio for dividing funds between the two portfolios. Typically, this ratio is 50-50. That is, initially, half of the investment funds are placed in the aggressive portfolio and the other half in the defensive portfolio. This 50-50 ratio of investment dollars in the two portfolios is always maintained. Periodically, perhaps every three months, the investor calculates the total value of the securities in each portfolio. If the value of the aggressive portfolio is higher than the value of the defensive portfolio, enough stocks are sold and the proceeds invested in the defensive portfolio to maintain the 50-50 ratio. The same procedure is followed if the value of the defensive portfolio is higher than that of the aggressive portfolio.

In ratio planning, if stock prices rise or if bond prices fall, bonds become better buys than stocks. Therefore, funds are moved from the aggressive to the defensive portfolio. If stock prices fall or if bond prices rise, stocks are relatively better buys. Therefore, bonds are sold and stocks are purchased. Ratio planning is relatively simple and may be useful for the investor who has accumulated investment funds.

Systematic Investment Plan

Systematic or **monthly investment plans** (**SIP** or **MIP**) are similar to dollar cost averaging and are offered by most brokerage houses. An SIP is useful for the investor who can invest only small amounts every month. An investor with an SIP makes periodic payments to a brokerage house. The brokerage house then buys shares for the investor. With an SIP, the investor can buy fractional shares. Let's say that an investor is putting $50 into an SIP every month. He or she buys stock selling for $20 a share. The investor would be able to buy $50/$20 = 2.5 shares of the stock.

SIPs are advantageous for the investor because small amounts can be invested periodically. SIPs also offer the same investment advantages as dollar averaging. In addition, most participating brokerage houses will

automatically reinvest dividends for the investor. The major disadvantage of SIPs is that brokerage commissions can be from 5 to 10 percent of the investment funds.

In this section, three plans for investors handling their own investment portfolios were discussed. Dollar cost averaging and SIPs help the investor with the timing of stock purchases. Ratio planning, which provides investors with needed diversification, is designed for the investor who has an investment portfolio.

Spot Quiz • Personal Management of Investment Funds

1. Dollar cost averaging does not work if stock prices are constantly rising.
   T _____ F _____

2. In some recessions, both stock and bond prices decline, and ratio planning will not lead to much switching of funds.   T _____ F _____

3. SIPs provide stock accumulation at a low cost.   T _____ F _____

(Answers on page 584)

INVESTMENT CLUBS

Investment clubs are a compromise between handling your own fund and investing in mutual funds. **Investment clubs** are started by small groups of people who pool their investment funds to buy stocks and bonds. Typical investment clubs have from 5 to 15 members. To start an investment club, a few persons get together and form a partnership for investing money. Club members select club officers and draw up the rules and regulations for operating the club. Every member makes a monthly dollar contribution. This pool of money is available for investment. One or more club members make recommendations for buying securities. These recommendations are voted on, and appropriate action is taken. Securities are sold in the same way.

Investment clubs offer the investor many advantages. Club members are generally friends, neighbors, coworkers, and other people that the investor knows. Club members can manage pooled funds without giving up control over what is bought and sold. Because of the requirements for

stock analyses and recommendations, club members learn more about the economy and the stock market. Because of the pooling of funds, members save on commissions compared with SIPs. Investment clubs allow members to make small monthly investments. Periodic buying provides the benefits of dollar cost averaging. Different recommendations on and purchases of stocks lead to diversification after a few months of club operation. Club members benefit from the presentation of viewpoints and analyses during club meetings. Finally, some club members become involved with the record-keeping chores for the club and gain valuable experience in preparing balance sheets and income statements. (See "What's Your Bag?" below.)

The **National Association of Investment Clubs (NAIC)** helps investors start investment clubs. At a modest cost, NAIC will provide record-keeping forms and forms for performing stock analyses. Information about NAIC's fees and services can be obtained by writing to it at 1515 E. Eleven Mile Road, Royal Oak, Michigan 48067. Many stockbrokers are also willing to provide assistance to people who are starting an investment club.

What's Your Bag?

Moneybags—that's the name of an investment club in Marin County, California. Fifteen people meet monthly to discuss and analyze stocks and to manage the portfolio of their investment club.

The National Association of Investment Clubs (NAIC) reports that there are about 25,000 investment clubs across the country, with about 6,400 belonging to NAIC. The portfolio of the average NAIC member club has outperformed the S&P Index in seven of the last ten years, a remarkable record when you consider that many of the clubs are relatively new and inexperienced.

The average NAIC-affiliated club has 15 members; the average portfolio, with an average of 15 stocks, had a market value of $84,000 in late 1985. The average member contributes $25–$30 per month. Most club members have personal investments that are about three times the size of their share in the investment club. While 35 percent have both male and female members, 31 percent of clubs are all male, and 34 percent are all female. NAIC points out that the important ingredients for a successful club are a stable investment philosophy, capability and willingness to research stocks, common interests among members, and the ability to wait for results. It may be difficult to get into an existing club, but it's relatively easy to start a new one (you should make sure that the treasurer is bonded). Who knows? A few years from now, this page might be describing your successful club.

Spot Quiz • Investment Clubs

1. Investment clubs are similar to mutual funds.   T _____   F _____

2. Investment clubs are ideally suited to persons with large sums of investable funds.   T _____   F _____

(Answers on page 584)

Mutual funds

A **mutual fund**, as the name implies, is a pool of investment funds contributed by investors and managed by professional money managers. Investors buy shares of the mutual fund. The funds thus raised are invested by the mutual fund manager. Mutual funds can be classified by (1) how they are organized, (2) their sales commissions, and (3) their investment objectives. These classifications are discussed in this section, along with returns from mutual fund ownership.

Types of Mutual Funds by Organization

Organizationally, mutual funds are of two types: closed-end and open-end. Closed-end mutual funds are generally called investment companies. Open-end mutual funds are simply called mutual funds.

Closed-End Investment Companies.   Organizationally, **closed-end investment companies** are corporations. Closed-end companies issue only a fixed number of shares initially to investors. Thereafter, these shares are traded on the stock exchanges and the OTC market. Investors who want to buy shares in an investment company would have to buy them from another investor.

After raising funds initially from investors by selling new stock, investment companies invest these funds in securities issued by other companies. The prices of shares in an investment company are determined by the supply and demand for these shares. Thus, price may vary from the market value of the assets of the investment companies. Investors buying and selling shares in investment companies pay brokerage commissions, explained in Chapter 16.

Open-End Mutual Funds. Open-end mutual funds do not have a fixed number of shares outstanding. The number of shares outstanding for mutual funds varies from day to day. Investors desiring to buy into a mutual fund buy their shares directly from the mutual fund. Similarly, those wishing to sell their mutual fund holdings sell their shares back to the fund.

Like investment companies, mutual funds invest their money in the securities of corporations. Unlike investment companies, the price of mutual fund shares is directly related to the value of the assets the funds own. The price of a share of a mutual fund is equal to the fund's **net asset value (NAV)**. NAV for a fund equals the total market value of the fund's assets less its liabilities divided by the number of fund shares outstanding. Table 18.2 gives an example of calculating NAV. The mutual fund in question has $32,000 in total assets and $7,000 in liabilities. Net assets are $25,000, and with 4,000 shares outstanding, NAV is $6.25. Investors buying and selling mutual funds may or may not pay a sales commission, a topic discussed in the next section.

Types of Mutual Funds by Sales Commissions

Depending on their sales commissions, mutual funds are either no-load or load funds.

No-Load Mutual Funds. No-load mutual funds do not charge any sales commissions for selling their shares to the investor, although a few no-load funds charge a 1 to 2 percent **redemption fee** when buying back their shares from investors. No-load funds do not have a sales force to sell

Table 18.2 Calculating Net Asset Value for a Mutual Fund

Assets owned	
500 shares of ABC Co. at $30/share	$15,000
300 shares of LMN Co. at $20/share	6,000
600 shares of XYZ Co. at $15/share	9,000
Cash	2,000
Total assets	$32,000
Liabilities	7,000
Net assets	$25,000
Number of shares outstanding	4,000
Net asset value ($25,000/4,000)	$6.25

their shares. Investors must contact the no-load funds directly about buying into the funds.

Load Mutual Funds. **Load funds** charge commissions on sales of their shares. Load funds employ a sales force to sell their shares. These sales personnel are paid a commission for their selling efforts. The commissions charged by load funds typically range from 7 percent to 8.5 percent. The commission, or load, is subtracted from the money contributed by the investor. For example, an investor pays $1,000 to a load fund that charges an 8 percent commission. The investor's investment in the fund would be $1,000 − ($1,000 × .08) = $920. (See "Mutual Fund Charges" below.)

Mutual Fund Charges

Load mutual funds charge a sales commission on their mutual fund shares transactions. Loads, or sales commissions, are typically front-ended, meaning that the commissions are paid when the shares are initially sold to the investor. But some funds have back-end loads, which means that they charge their commissions when investors redeem their shares. Some mutual fund managers argue that the reason for back-end loads is to discourage frequent switching of money in and out of mutual funds. Back-end loads are also called deferred sales charges. Some deferred sales charges are structured so that they decrease each year that the monies remain with the mutual fund, and, in some cases, the charges disappear totally after five or six years. Thus, for example, the deferred sales charge may be 6 percent if funds are withdrawn in the first year, 5 percent if the funds are withdrawn in the second year, and so on.

In addition to loads, all funds charge management and expense fees to cover bookkeeping, mailing, management, and other expenses. The fees are charged directly against the fund and not to individual investors. Annual management and expense fees of .5 to 1.25 percent are reasonable. Fees above these levels are cause for concern and perhaps a reason for switching to another fund.

Both load and no-load funds will often charge a fee called the 12b-1 fee, which allows a fund to cover marketing costs. In recent years, funds have used 12b-1 fees, which can range from .5 to 1.5 percent of funds' assets annually, as a substitute for sales commissions. A 1 percent annual 12b-1 fee over 10 years will generally be greater than an 8 percent front load. Thus, funds charging 12b-1 fees should be considered load funds even if they are listed as no-load funds. If a fund's management and expense fees and any 12b-1 fees combined exceed 1.25 percent of net assets annually, then a closer look at the fund's performance is warranted. If the performance is not there, then consider switching funds.

Reading Mutual Fund Quotations. Share prices for mutual funds are quoted every business day in *The Wall Street Journal* as well as in most large daily newspapers. The quotations differ for no-load and load funds. An example is shown in Figure 18.1. The first column lists the name of the mutual fund. The second column lists the NAV. For Flex, NAV is $7.60 per share. The third column shows either "N.L." or a price. "N.L." means that the fund is no-load. Investors can buy and sell shares of Flex for $7.60 per share. The last column lists the change in NAV from the previous trading day. Flex was up 1 cent per share.

If the column titled "Offer Price" lists a price, then the fund in question is a load fund. Clax, for example, is a load fund. Its NAV is $8.03. That is, an investor selling shares back to Clax would receive $8.03 per share. An investor buying Clax would pay $8.73 per share. The commission paid is $8.73 − $8.03 = $0.70 per share. The load for Clax is $0.70 × 100/$8.73 = 8.0 percent. Notice that the load is calculated on the offering price and not on NAV.

Types of Mutual Funds by Investment Objectives

Mutual funds establish their investment objectives, which then dictate the type of securities bought by the mutual funds. These objectives provide another way of classifying mutual funds. This classification is important for the investor because it provides an indication of the risk and return associated with the mutual fund. Based on investment objectives, mutual funds can be classified into common stock, balanced, income, bond, specialty, money market, and tax-exempt categories.

Common Stock Mutual Funds. **Common stock mutual funds** are the most prevalent type of funds. These funds invest in the common shares of companies. Chapter 17 explained the different types of common stock. Investing in different types of common stocks creates different levels of

Figure 18.1 Mutual Fund Quotations

Name	NAV	Offer Price	NAV Change
Flex	7.60	N.L.	+.01
Burke	11.32	N.L.	+.03
Clax	8.03	8.73	+.02
Dran	10.28	11.23	+.02

risk and return for mutual funds. As a result, the common stock category can be further broken down into a number of subcategories. **Speculative common stock mutual funds** seek very high returns on their investments and are willing to bear high risks. These funds are relatively small in size, usually less than $100 million in assets. They seek out obscure companies for investing. They also engage in speculative short-term trading and short selling.

Growth-oriented mutual funds invest their funds in reasonably well known growth companies. These funds aim for high long-term capital gains and are less risky than speculative funds. **Growth and income mutual funds** place equal emphasis on returns through capital gains and dividend income. Returns from these funds tend to be lower but more stable than returns from growth and speculative funds. A fourth category, specialized funds, is discussed separately below.

Balanced Mutual Funds.   **Balanced mutual funds** are also called stock and bond funds. Their objective is to minimize fluctuations in NAV. Balanced funds provide relatively stable income because of bonds in their portfolios and hold the potential for capital gains because of their common stock investments. Balanced funds tend to be relatively safer than common stock funds.

Income Mutual Funds.   **Income mutual funds** try to give investors the highest possible current income. Generally, income funds invest in bonds and preferred stocks, but on occasion they invest in common stocks also.

Bond Mutual Funds.   **Bond mutual funds** emphasize safety of the principal. They limit their investment to quality bonds and preferred stocks. These funds are safe, provide high current income, and hold little potential for capital gains.

Specialty Mutual Funds.   **Specialty mutual funds**, also called **sector funds**, limit their investments to specialized stocks, selected industries, certain geographic regions, or special commodities. Some funds, for example, specialize in gold. They buy shares of gold bullion or of gold mining companies. Funds specializing in energy buy only shares of energy-related companies. Certain funds specialize in investments in foreign companies.

Money Market Mutual Funds.   **Money market mutual funds** invest in securities that mature in one week to one year. The average time to maturity for money market fund investments ranges from three weeks to six months. These short maturities provide very high liquidity for money market funds.

Money market funds have promoted themselves as alternatives to savings and checking accounts. Whereas savings and checking accounts pay 5.25 to 5.5 percent in interest, money market funds pay interest that is considerably higher than 5.5 percent. During periods of high interest rates, money market funds have paid 18–20 percent interest. Established money market funds tend to be safe investments. Because money market funds can be considered alternatives to checking and savings accounts, they were discussed in Chapter 6.

Tax-Exempt Bond Mutual Funds. **Tax-exempt funds** invest in high-grade bonds issued by state and local governments. All interest income from these bonds is exempt from federal income taxes. Some funds buy securities issued only in one state. Investors from that particular state who buy shares in the funds are also exempted from paying state income taxes. These funds appeal to investors in high income tax brackets.

Returns From Mutual Funds

Investors obtain returns from mutual funds in the form of dividends, capital gains distributions, and capital gains.

Dividends. Mutual funds are exempt from taxes if they distribute at least 95 percent of all income received by them to their shareholders. Therefore, either annually or more frequently, mutual funds pay to their investors 95 percent or more of the dividends received by the fund during the year. These are the dividends received by the funds from securities they own. For tax purposes, investors treat these dividends exactly the same as dividends received directly from corporations.

Capital Gains Distributions. Mutual funds generate capital gains by selling securities for more than they paid for the securities. These capital gains are distributed to investors as well. The tax treatment for capital gains distribution is the same as for capital gains from direct investment in corporations.

Capital Gains. The price of shares of mutual funds changes, depending on changes in their NAVs. Investors who sell their shares for a price higher than the purchase price realize capital gains. If the shares are held for longer than one year, the gains are long-term and qualify for preferential tax treatment. Gains on shares held for less than one year are treated as ordinary income.

Spot Quiz • Mutual Funds

1. Mutual fund owners are directly involved with the day-to-day management of fund assets.   T _____   F _____

2. Shares of closed-end mutual funds sell at net asset value.
   T _____   F _____

3. The major difference between load and no-load mutual funds is commissions.   T _____   F _____

4. Balanced mutual funds are generally riskier than bond mutual funds.
   T _____   F _____

5. Tax-exempt mutual funds are generally exempt from all taxes.
   T _____   F _____

(Answers on page 584)

ADVANTAGES AND DISADVANTAGES OF MUTUAL FUNDS

Investing in mutual funds provides investors with many advantages and a few disadvantages, discussed in this section.

Advantages of Mutual Funds

Mutual funds provide such advantages as diversification, liquidity, professional management, convenience, and financial flexibility.

Diversification. The biggest advantage of mutual funds is that they provide diversification. For proper diversification, the investor needs to invest in 10 to 20 stocks, which may not be easy for the average investor. Even investing only $500 in each security would require a total investment of $5,000 to $10,000. Mutual funds invest in anywhere from 50 to 200 stocks. By buying shares of a mutual fund, the investor automatically obtains the benefits of diversification.

An investor investing on his or her own would pay normal brokerage commissions. A mutual fund, because it buys large numbers of shares at

a time, is able to secure a lower commission per share. A fringe benefit of buying mutual funds, then, is that the investor indirectly saves on brokerage commissions.

Liquidity.   Open-end mutual funds are committed to redeeming, or buying back, their shares at net asset value. The prices of mutual funds are reported daily in most major newspapers, so investors can follow the progress of their mutual fund. If they are dissatisfied with the fund's performance, they can promptly cash in their holdings. Listed closed-end funds can also be readily sold. Thus, mutual funds provide investors with more liquidity than holding stocks and bonds directly.

Professional Management.   Mutual funds are professionally managed. Thus, most investors (with the exception of those who have invested in very speculative mutual funds) do not have to worry about losing their investments in mutual funds. An investor who buys into an established mutual fund can be reasonably certain that the fund managers will do a diligent job of meeting the fund objectives. This type of professional management is desirable even for veteran investors, who might disregard stated investment objectives occasionally.

Convenience.   Mutual funds are very convenient for the average investor. The investor who does not own mutual funds has to keep track of dividends and interest income received, prices and dates of stock purchase and sale, stock splits and dividends, and corporate correspondence such as proxies. These chores are done away with for investors in mutual funds. Mutual funds keep track of all dividends, interest income, and capital gains distributed. The periodic financial statements from mutual funds summarize all relevant information for investors.

Financial Flexibility.   Mutual funds provide investors with considerable financial flexibility. On instruction, mutual funds will automatically reinvest dividends and capital gains for investors. This is a great advantage for the average investor, because he or she would receive a small sum in dividends, and investing this small amount would carry relatively high commissions. This feature is especially desirable for investors who do not seek a current return on their investments.

Mutual funds also offer **systematic withdrawal plans**. Such a plan allows the investor to receive a check for a certain amount automatically every period from the mutual funds. For example, an elderly person might invest $100,000 in an income fund and sign up for systematic withdrawal. The mutual fund then would send this investor a check for, say, $1,000, every month. The income to be received by the investor should be sufficient to cover the amount of the check. However, if it is not, the fund will sell off some of the investor's holdings to make up the difference. Generally, systematic withdrawal plans are set up so that, over the long run, withdrawals equal the returns to be distributed to the fund investor.

Disadvantages of Mutual Funds

There are really no major disadvantages to purchasing mutual funds. Load funds charge a sales commission, but this disadvantage can be overcome by buying a comparable no-load fund. Another potential disadvantage is that some investors do not want diversification. They want to concentrate their holdings in just one or two stocks for speculative purposes. Mutual funds are not desirable for these investors.

Spot Quiz • Advantages and Disadvantages of Mutual Funds

1. The investor should buy 10 to 15 mutual funds for proper diversification.   T _____   F _____

2. A bond fund is a more liquid investment than buying a few bonds.
                                                    T _____   F _____

3. Systematic withdrawal is useful only for elderly persons.
                                                    T _____   F _____

(Answers on page 584)

SELECTING A MUTUAL FUND

Selecting a mutual fund for investment is a four-step procedure: (1) matching fund objectives to personal investment goals, (2) identifying open-end funds, (3) identifying no-load funds, and (4) evaluating fund performance. These steps are discussed in detail in this section.

Match Fund Objective to Investment Goals

The first step is to match the stated investment objective of the mutual fund to your personal investment goals. As explained earlier in the chapter, mutual funds have different investment objectives. An investor interested in high safety of the principal would consider bond mutual funds. A person interested in high liquidity would consider money market funds.

Identify Open-End Funds

Mutual funds can be either closed-end or open-end. The price behavior of closed-end funds is similar to that of corporate stocks. In buying a closed-end fund, an investor contends not only with changes in net asset value but also with changes in the difference between net asset value and market price for the fund's shares. For this reason, it is recommended that an investor consider only open-end mutual funds.

Identify No-Load Funds

Some mutual funds charge a sales commission. Others (no-load funds) buy and sell their shares at net asset value. All research to date indicates that there is no difference between the performance of load and no-load funds. Within a certain investment objective category, a no-load fund can be expected to do as well as a load fund. Therefore, the search for a suitable mutual fund should be limited to no-load funds.

Evaluate Mutual Fund Performance

Different funds within an investment objective category have different levels of performance. For example, within the income category, some funds will have better performance than others. The law requires a mutual fund to provide potential investors with a **prospectus** that contains, among other information, a summary of the fund's performance for the past few years and a statement of its investment objectives. Brochures and periodic financial statements provided by a mutual fund also give an indication of the fund's performance. However, these materials are not very helpful because they do not provide performance comparisons with other funds.

One good source for mutual fund performance ratings is *Forbes* magazine, which publishes ratings on mutual funds each fall. An example is shown in Figure 18.2. *Forbes* rates mutual funds in both up markets and down markets. (An up market occurs when stock prices in general are moving up; the opposite holds true in a down market.) In the example shown, Nicholas Fund is rated B in up markets and A+ in down markets.

Another important consideration is annual expenses. The last column in Figure 18.2 shows annual expenses per $100 for mutual funds. Annual expenses can increase if a mutual fund is actively involved in buying and selling securities. In general, if performance ratings are fairly similar, then a fund with lower expenses is preferable to one with higher expenses. Nicholas Fund has annual expenses per $100 of $0.86.

The asset size of the mutual fund is generally a less important consideration. In general, a fund with assets in excess of $500 million should be given more consideration. At this asset size, the fund can be properly

Figure 18.2 Sample of 1987 Fund Ratings*

Performance in UP markets	Performance in DOWN markets	Fund/distributor	Investment results — Average annual total return 1976–87	Latest 12 months total return	return from income dividends	Total assets 6/30/87 (millions)	% change '87 vs '86	Maximum sales charge	Annual expenses per $100
		Standard & Poor's 500 stock average	15.7%	25.1%	3.2%				
		Forbes stock fund composite	16.9%	19.8%	1.7%				
D	D	National Industries Fund/National Inds	10.6%	11.5%	0.9%	$ 32	2%	none	$1.68
		National Real Estate-Stock Fund/National Secs	—*	3.5	3.5	20	68	7.75%	1.50p‡
D	C	National Stock Fund/National Secs	14.8	14.6	5.2	229	-19	7.25	0.98
		National Telecommunications & Technology/AFA	—*	14.9	1.1	59	-19	4.75	1.75
D	B	Nationwide Fund/Nationwide	13.0	20.4	2.2	467	26	7.50	0.62
C	B	Nationwide Growth Fund/Nationwide	17.6	18.9	2.9	235	41	7.50	0.65
		Nautilus Fund/Eaton Vance	—*	9.6	none	21	1	4.75	1.78
B	F	Neuwirth Fund/National Finl	14.4	3.4	none	31	-2	none	1.78‡
		New Beginning Growth Fund/Sit	—*	17.6	0.2	56	38	none	1.24
		New Beginning Income & Growth Fund/Sit	—*	18.4	2.2	10	110	none	1.50
		New Economy Fund/American Funds	—*	17.1	1.6	970	27	8.50	0.68
D	A	New England Equity Inc Fund[1]/New England	15.9	12.6	2.8	48	54	6.50	1.19‡
A	B	New England Growth Fund[2]/New England	23.9	25.2	0.4	472	51	6.50	0.84‡
B	B	New England Retirement Equity/New England	18.1	22.2	0.3	153	50	6.50	0.90‡
B	B	New Perspective Fund/American Funds	19.4	39.2	1.8	1,119	29	8.50	0.66
A	C	New York Venture Fund/Venture	21.8	18.7	0.9	230	38	8.50	0.96
B	C	Newton Growth Fund/Newton	17.5	26.6	1.3	48	37	none	1.23‡
A	F	Niagara Share Corp/closed end	15.5	23.3	2.0	218	16	NA	1.04
		Nicholas Applegate Fund/closed end	—*	—*	—*	97	—	NA	NA
B	A+	Nicholas Fund/Nicholas	23.7	11.8	2.9	1,294	19	none	0.86

Figure 18.2 (Continued)

		Fund							
		Nicholas II/Nicholas	—*	16.9	2.0	407	20	none	0.78
		Nicholas Limited Edition/Nicholas	—*	—*	—*	7	—	none	NA
		Noddings Convertible Strategies/Noddings	—*	7.6	3.6	12	75	none	1.70
		Nomura Pacific Basin Fund/Nomura	—*	61.6	none	103	130	none	1.45
•B	•C	Northeast Investors Growth/Northeast Inv	—*	16.1	0.2	30	90	none	1.80
•C	•C	Nova Fund/Nova	—*	25.2	none	33	25	8.50r	1.70
D	B	Old Dominion Investors' Trust/Investors Secs	14.3	20.6	4.7	7	17	8.50	1.25
B		Olympic Trust-Series B/Olympic Trust	—*	6.5	0.2	9	93	none	1.00p
B	D	Omega Fund/International	14.8	23.2	1.4	38	3	5.50	1.47‡
C	D	One Hundred Fund/Berger	14.3	10.4	none	12	-3	none	1.71‡
D	B	One Hundred One Fund/Berger	14.0	10.2	3.3	4	68	none	NA
		Oppenheimer Blue Chip Fund/Oppenheimer Inv	—*	—*	1.2	17	—	4.75	1.50‡
		Oppenheimer Capl Appreciation/Oppenheimer Inv	—*	0.1	0.9	9	93	none	0.75
		Oppenheimer Challenger Fund/Oppenheimer Inv	—*	6.1	none	14	-8	2.50	3.33
•C	•D	Oppenheimer Directors Fund/Oppenheimer Inv	—*	11.4	2.0	200	-30	8.50	1.07
C	B	Oppenheimer Eq Income Fund/Oppenheimer Inv	17.6	20.6	4.9	731	92	8.50	0.92
B	F	Oppenheimer Fund/Oppenheimer Inv	11.7	8.7	0.2	274	-4	8.50	1.00

Total return is for 9/30/76 to 6/30/87. Funds are added to this section when assets exceed $5 million and deleted when assets drop below $2 million. Stock funds rated only if in operation since 11/30/80. *Fund rated for two periods only: maximum allowable grade A. *Fund not in operation for full period. ‡Fund has shareholder paid 12b-1 plan exceeding 0.1% (hidden load) pending or in force. p: Net of partial absorption of expenses by fund sponsor. r: Includes back end load that reverts to distributor. NA: Not applicable or not available. ¹Formerly NEL Equity Fund. ²Formerly NEL Growth Fund. ³Formerly NEL Retirement Equity Fund.

diversified while still investing reasonably large sums of money in each stock it owns. In Figure 18.2, Nicholas Fund has assets of $1,294,000,000.

Buying the Fund

If the fund selected is a no-load fund, the investor has to contact the fund directly for purchases. Many no-load funds advertise regularly in financial newspapers. Also, *Wiesenberger's Investment Companies,* available in many libraries, contains addresses of mutual funds. The investor should contact the mutual fund selected and request a prospectus before investing. The prospectus should be read carefully to make sure that the fund has not changed its investment objectives.

Spot Quiz • Selecting a Mutual Fund

1. Mutual funds can be selected at random since they are all similar.
                                        T _____ F _____

2. Under some circumstances, the purchase of load funds is justifiable.
                                        T _____ F _____

3. Reading a fund prospectus helps the investor match investment goals with fund investment objectives.   T _____ F _____

(Answers on page 584)

Summary

This chapter covers the handling of personal investment funds. Investors have several choices. They can make their own investments directly. In this case, investors need to make sure that their timing is appropriate and that their portfolios are adequately diversified. Dollar cost averaging, ratio planning, and systematic investment plans can help investors with timing and diversification.

A group of investors can form an investment club in which members pool their financial resources for investing. Members also benefit from sharing investment advice.

Another option is to have investment funds professionally managed by buying mutual funds. Mutual funds can be either closed-end or open-end. Prices of open-end mutual fund shares are directly related to the net asset value of the fund. Some funds charge a sales commission and are called load funds. No-load funds do not charge a sales commission.

Mutual funds can be classified by their investment objectives. Common stock mutual funds can be speculative, growth, or growth and income oriented. Other types of mutual funds are balanced, income, bond, specialty, money market, and tax-exempt bond. The risks and returns from different types of funds vary. Returns from mutual funds are in the form of dividends and capital gains.

Investing in mutual funds has many advantages, such as diversification, liquidity, professional management, convenience, and financial flexibility. Selecting the right mutual fund is a three-step process: mutual fund investment objectives are matched to personal investment goals; consideration is limited to open-end, no-load mutual funds; and mutual fund performance is evaluated.

Questions

1. Explain the three basic steps involved in managing personal investment funds.

2. What is meant by "timing an investment purchase"? Why is timing important for the investor?

3. Why is diversification important for the investor?

4. Explain how dollar cost averaging works.

5. What is meant by ratio planning? How can it be used by the investor for investment management?

6. What are systematic investment plans (SIPs)? How can they aid investors in personal investment management?

7. What are the major advantages of joining an investment club?

8. What are the differences between closed-end and open-end mutual funds? Which one would you prefer to buy? Why?

9. Explain the different types of investment objectives that could be followed by a common stock mutual fund.

10. Explain the differences among the following types of mutual funds:
    a. Balanced
    b. Income
    c. Bond

11. Why would an investor want to invest in a money market mutual fund?

12. Can you see yourself buying tax-exempt mutual funds ten years from now? Why or why not?

13. What is the difference, if any, between capital gains and capital gain distributions from mutual funds?

14. What are the major advantages of investing in mutual funds?

15. Briefly explain the steps in selecting an appropriate mutual fund for investing.

16. How would you evaluate the performance of a mutual fund?

Case Problems

1. P. Valenzuela, 25 years old, is working as an assistant manager for a retail chain store in New Mexico. Her parents left her $12,000 in a trust fund; which she will receive in cash at age 27. On her current job, Ms. Valenzuela can save about $300 per month. Her academic training is in retailing, and she has very little familiarity with stocks, bonds, and investing. She is thinking about "getting into the market." A local stockbroker has suggested some stocks for her to buy. Some of her friends have invited her to join an investment club. Local newspapers have recently carried advertisements about mutual funds. Discuss an investment strategy that Ms. Valenzuela might want to follow. Provide explanations.

2. Jamie Bjorg is following the dollar cost averaging method of investing. He has been buying $300 of XYZ Company stock every three months. In the last two years, stock prices for XYZ at purchase times were $20, $30, $20, $15, $25, $30, $25, and $37.50, respectively. Show in tabular

form the number of shares bought each period, the total number of shares, the total cost, and the average cost per share (as in Table 18.1). How much total profit or loss does Jamie have?

3. Brockton Mutual Fund is a no-load fund. Its assets are shown below:

1,000 shares of ABC Co.	$40,000
1,000 shares of BX Co.	$80,000
3,000 shares of LM Co.	$1,900,000
Cash	$60,000

    Brockton's total liabilities equal $27,000. Brockton has 23,000 shares outstanding. What is its net asset value?

4. Claire Mutual Funds charges an 8.5 percent load. Its total assets equal $350,000, and total liabilities equal $11,000. It has 19,000 shares outstanding. What is its net asset value? What would be the offer price for one share of Claire?

Bibliography

"Find a Fund to Match Your Goals." *Changing Times* (September 1986): 63–67.

"Fixed Income Mutual Funds." *Consumer Reports* (September 1987): 570–576.

"How Hidden Charges Snatch Away Profits." *Money* (November 1986): 231–232.

"How Zeros Add Up." *Changing Times* (September 1985): 53–55.

"Join the Club." *Changing Times* (October 1986): 103–106.

"Unzipping the Zeros." *Money* (April 1985): 103–110.

"When a Load Becomes a Burden." *Money* (July 1985): 135–138.

"When the House Always Wins." *Money* (July 1987): 97–100.

"When to Take the Money and Run." *Money* (November 1986): 237–240.

"Winners One and All." *Money* (December 1986): 173–180.

Answers to Spot Quizzes

Personal Management of Investment Funds (page 566)

1. F (Dollar cost averaging does not work if stock prices are constantly declining.)

2. T (Declines in both stock and bond prices will generally leave the ratio intact.)

3. F (Brokerage costs associated with SIPs tend to be high.)

Investment Clubs (page 568)

1. T (Club members pool their investment funds.)

2. F (Investment clubs are more suitable for investors with small amounts of investable funds.)

Mutual Funds (page 574)

1. F (Mutual funds are professionally managed.)

2. F (Generally, closed-end funds do not sell at net asset value.)

3. T (The "load" is the commission.)

4. T (Bond funds are safer.)

5. F (They are generally not exempt from state income taxes.)

Advantages and Disadvantages of Mutual Funds (page 576)

1. F (Buying one mutual fund provides diversification.)

2. T (Mutual funds are more liquid than individual investment securities.)

3. F (For example, a college student can also benefit from a systematic withdrawal plan.)

Selecting a Mutual Fund (page 580)

1. F (Mutual funds have different investment objectives.)

2. T (A load fund should be bought if it has superior performance in its class.)

3. T (Investment objectives are stated in the prospectus.)

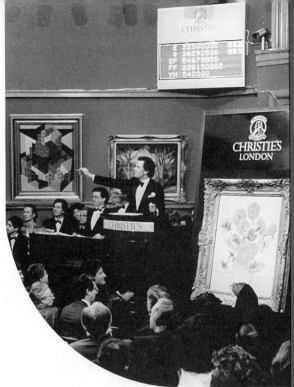

Chapter 19

Speculative Investments

Objectives

After reading this chapter, you will be able to:

- Explain the advantages and disadvantages of buying convertible securities and options.

- Discuss the pros and cons of investing in various types of real estate projects.

- Recognize the difference between cash and futures markets for commodities.

- Describe how commodities can be traded.

- Explain how and why people invest in gold, coins, stamps, art, and collectibles.

Jay Lamont used to report on the fortunes or misfortunes of the Phillies, Eagles, Flyers, the 76ers, and other odd and sundry teams and individuals engaged in sporting activities in and around Philadelphia. In other words, Mr. Lamont was a sports writer, earning $110 a week in 1968. At that time, he decided to buy a house in Ocean City, New Jersey, for $15,300. His down payment was $300. Ocean City became popular as a summer resort as well as a year-round commuter community. Mr. Lamont's fortunes grew with Ocean City's. As the price of his property increased, his equity increased. Using this increased equity, he purchased additional real estate properties. Now his net worth is around $1 million, and he has investment interests in well over one hundred rental units.[1]

The earliest stamp issued by the United States, a 5-cent Ben Franklin, cost $285 in 1970. Now it is worth over $6,000. The 1964 Migratory Bird Hunting stamp, issued by the United States Department of the Interior and featuring the nene goose, cost $6 in 1970. Today the stamp has a purchase price of about $130.[2] A 1.5-carat, white, round-cut diamond purchased in 1975 for about $9,400 more than tripled in value in five years.[3]

So you say that real estate, stamps, and gems don't turn you on? How about a nice lithograph by Calder? Or perhaps an oriental rug, a Chippendale armchair, an original Barbie doll, or Paul Revere's signature? Still not interested? How about a crash course on speculative investments? That's the topic of this chapter. Discussed in the following pages are the dos and don'ts of investing in convertible securities, options, real estate, commodities, gold, coins, stamps, gems, art, and miscellaneous other collectibles.

CONVERTIBLE SECURITIES

Convertible bonds and **convertible preferred stocks** give the stockholder the right to convert the securities into common stock. The terms of conversion are specified in the indenture agreement covering the initial sale of the securities to investors.

Conversion Price and Ratio

Generally, conversion must occur during a specified period. Two important conversion terms are the conversion price and the conversion ratio. The price of common stock at which the bond can be converted is called

---

1. See "Waiting Out Profits in Rental Property," *Money* (January 1978): 36.
2. See "Stamps for Licking Inflation," *Money* (June 1981): 82–83.
3. See "The Siren Song of Gems as Investments," *Money* (May, 1980): 119.

the **conversion price**. The **conversion ratio** is the number of common shares received by the investor on conversion of a convertible bond.

Convertible bonds, which are more common than convertible preferred stocks, are the subject of the following discussion. However, the points made are equally applicable to convertible preferred stocks.

Xmax Corporation issued convertible bonds a couple of years ago. The bonds were issued at their face value of $1,000. The bonds carry a coupon rate of 10.5 percent, paying $105 per year in interest. The bonds are convertible into 20 common shares at $50 a share. At time of issue, Xmax common was selling for $40 a share. The conversion price is $50 and the conversion ratio is 20.

You may have noticed that for the Xmax bonds, conversion price times conversion ratio equals face value. This rule holds true in general. That is,

$$\text{Conversion Ratio} \times \text{Conversion Price} = \text{Face Value}$$

In general, prices of convertible securities depend on the price of the underlying common stock. Thus, if the price of Xmax common goes to, say, $80 a share, the price of the convertible bond will be at least $80 \times 20 = $1,600. If the price were less than $1,600, investors would buy the bonds, convert them, and sell the common shares received at $80 per share to make an instant profit.

All convertible securities contain a **call provision**, which enables the issuing firm to force conversion when the market value of the common shares that can be acquired in conversion exceeds the call price. This provision lessens the potential attractiveness of the convertible security because the investor cannot plan on owning the security for a specified time period.

Advantages and Disadvantages of Convertible Securities

Convertible securities offer investors distinct advantages. They provide a fixed dollar return as well as the opportunity to participate in the price appreciation of the firm's common stock. If the price of the common stock does not appreciate above the conversion price, the convertible security tends to act as a regular bond or preferred stock, limiting the downside price movement of the security. The major disadvantage is that the dividend, or coupon rate, on convertible securities is lower than on equivalent nonconvertible securities. Thus, for example, if Xmax had chosen to issue nonconvertible bonds, it would have had to pay around 13 percent in interest.

For the investor considering convertible securities, the tradeoff is accepting a lower fixed dollar return in return for the potential of price appreciation and capital gains. Convertible securities tend to be speculative

investments because they provide a fixed return, while their prices fluctuate based on the performance of the common stock. Overall, convertible securities can be attractive investments.

Spot Quiz • Convertible Securities

1. In general, by knowing the conversion ratio, you can calculate the conversion price.   T _____   F _____

2. Investors buy convertible securities in the expectation of receiving fixed returns.   T _____   F _____

(Answers on page 617)

OPTIONS

J. Abrams plans to profit from a recent stock purchase whether the stock goes down or up. It is easy to see how he will profit when the stock goes up. But how can a person profit when a stock goes down? At the same time Abrams buys the stock, he sells a "call" on the stock. This way, Abrams makes money if the stock goes up. If the stock does not go up, Abrams will have reduced the purchase price by the amount received from selling the "call."

A call is an example of an option. An **option** is a contract that gives the option buyer the right to buy from or sell to the option seller a fixed number of common shares of a specified company at a certain price during a specified time period. A **call** is an option to buy the shares. That is, a call gives the option buyer the right to "call" the stock. A **put** is an option to sell shares.

How Options Work

Let's assume that Abrams has bought 100 shares of Xmax Corporation at $40 a share, or $4,000.[4] Abrams also sells a 90-day call on 100 shares of Xmax for $300. The exercise, or **striking price**, for the call is $40. By selling

---

4. To simplify our example, we are ignoring the broker's commissions on the stock and option transactions. In actual investing, you would need to take into consideration the transaction costs as well.

the call option, Abrams has given the call option buyer the right to buy 100 shares of Xmax at $40 within the next 90 days. The call buyer will exercise the call only if the price of Xmax common goes above $40 a share. Let's assume further that Xmax goes up to $45 within the 90-day period. The call buyer exercises the call, and Abrams sells the stock at $40 a share. His profit on this transaction is $300, the amount received for the call. Of course, if Abrams had not sold the option, the stock could have been sold for $45 a share, giving Abrams a $500 profit.

Now let's assume that Xmax price declines to $38 a share. The call is not exercised, so Abrams sells the stock for $38 a share. The transaction does not result in a loss, however. Abrams sold 100 shares for $3,800; $3,800 plus the $300 for the call less the purchase price of $4,000 gives Abrams a $100 profit. At any price below $37 a share, Abrams's loss will be $300 less than the loss he would have incurred if the call had not been written.

Let's take a look at options from the viewpoint of the Xmax call buyer. If Xmax goes to $45 a share, the call is exercised, and the 100 shares are sold immediately for $4,500. The buyer's profit on this transaction is $4,500 − $4,000 − $300 = $200. The buyer's return on the $300 investment is $200 × 100/$300 = 66.67 percent. Had the buyer bought the stock at $40 a share, the return would have been $500 × 100/$4,000 = 12.5 percent. Buying a call increased the buyer's return.

How would the call buyer have fared if Xmax's stock price had gone down? At $38 a share, the buyer would have lost $300, or 100 percent of the investment.

Using Options

Options, both puts and calls, on stocks of many companies are traded on the Chicago Board Options Exchange and other exchanges. Options can be used in a variety of ways to meet investment strategies. First, options can be traded purely for their potential for providing large returns. Let's assume that an investor feels that the price of XYZ stock will increase from its current price of $50 to $70 within the next five months. A five-month call for 100 shares of XYZ with a striking price of $50 might cost $500. Purchase of the 100 shares at $50 and sale at $70 would produce a profit of $7,000 − $5,000 = $2,000. The return would be $2,000 × 100/$5,000 = 40 percent. The profit from buying and exercising the call would be $7,000 − $5,000 − $500 = $1,500. The return would be $1,500 × 100/$500 = 300 percent.

Buying puts also enhances profit potential. If XYZ stock goes from $50 to $40 a share, a short sale of 100 shares at $50 a share would produce profit of 20 percent. A put would produce profits of $5,000 − $4,000 − $500 = $500. That is, selling a put would result in a 100 percent return.

As the examples show, buying options can provide better returns than buying or selling the underlying securities. If stock prices do not behave

as expected, however, option trading can result in 100 percent losses. In the XYZ stock example, if the price remains at $50, neither buying nor selling short will produce any gains or losses. But in both cases the options will produce 100 percent losses because neither the call nor the put would be exercised.

Options can also be used to limit your maximum losses. Let's assume that an investor buys XYZ stock at $50 and also buys a put on XYZ at $50. If the XYZ price declines, the investor exercises the put and limits the loss to the price paid for the put. If the price goes up, profits are reduced by the cost of the put. Similarly, the potential loss in selling XYZ short can be limited by buying a call on XYZ at the short selling price. Thus, using options in these ways limits losses but also reduces potential profits. (See ''Index Options'' on page 591.)

In the previous example, Abrams owned 100 shares of XYZ, and the call written is a covered call. A **covered option** is one in which the option writer either has the security to sell on a call or the money to buy the security on a put. If Abrams had sold a call on XYZ without owning XYZ, it would have been an **uncovered,** or **naked, call**. Naked option writing is very risky. If, for example, Abrams had written a naked call, the call would have been honored only by purchasing XYZ at the going price.

Only a few of the methods of using options have been discussed here. Options can be used to seek high-percentage returns and to limit potential losses on buying long or selling short.

Spot Quiz • Options

1. An investor who believes that the price of a stock is going to fluctuate wildly should buy both a put and a call on the stock.

    T _____   F _____

2. Naked options should be sold only by experienced investors.

    T _____   F _____

(Answers on page 618)

Real estate

Doyle McGowan, Jr., was arrested and spent almost seven years in jail for possession of marijuana. He left jail with an intense desire to make

Index Options

William Tedrow, vice president of Integon Property and Casualty Corporation in Winston-Salem, North Carolina, likes to speculate on movements of the stock market as measured by stock indices such as the S&P 100 Stock Index or the DJIA. However, rather than buying all the stocks included in an index, he simply buys or sells options on these indices. Options on the S&P 100 Stock Index trade on the Chicago Board Options Exchange, including puts and calls, reach a daily trading volume of about 400,000 contracts. As mentioned in Chapter 16, the S&P 100 Stock Index is a weighted average of the current market value of 100 stocks. The S&P 100 Stock Index option has a value of $100 times the S&P 100 Index. Thus, when the index is at 300, the S&P 100 option has a market value of $100 × 300 = $30,000.

Index options, both put and call, are priced relative to the index itself. Let's say that the current S&P 100 Index is at 300. An S&P Index call at 290 that expires one month from now would have a value of at least 10, reflecting the spread between the index and the call price. Because the index has a life of one month and holds the potential for gains, it will sell for more than 10, perhaps 13. This call price of 13 is equal to a market price of $100 × 13 = $1,300. A put at 290 expiring one month from now, when the index is at 300, has a negative spread of 10 and would probably sell for 1/8 or 1/4. That is, you would be able to buy this put for about $100 × 1/8 = $12.50 to $100 × 1/4 = $25. As with stock options, an index option that expires results in a 100 percent loss.

The attraction of index options is that you can speculate on your instincts or knowledge about how the market is going to perform over the near term. If you are bullish, you could buy calls, and if you are bearish, you could buy puts. If you are right, your returns can be substantial compared to the movement in the index itself. If you are wrong, you will generally lose 100 percent of your investment in the option. Mr. Tedrow uses only a small portion of his investment funds for trading index options. He states that even if his whole option trading amount is lost, "my children will still go to college and they're still going to eat."

up for lost time. In 1969, he put $2,000 down on two houses that he had purchased for $21,000 in San Francisco. The houses were run-down and were not located in what was considered a desirable neighborhood. He renovated the houses and rented them out. He sold one of them for $28,500 in 1974. The second was worth $95,000 by 1979.[5]

---

5. See "Recessionproof Real Estate," *Money* (September 1979): 50.

McGowan's story is not one of good luck. Rather, it reflects careful planning and investing in an area where a little bit of elbow grease can provide healthy returns. This section deals with four approaches to investing in real estate: buying mortgages and deeds of trust, direct property ownership, joining a real estate syndicate, and buying shares of a real estate investment trust.

Mortgages and Deeds of Trust

Mortgages were explained in Chapter 9. In some states, a **deed of trust** is used in place of a mortgage and is similar to a mortgage except that the deed is held by a trustee (usually a bank) until the loan is fully repaid. Both devices are used to secure loans. The amount of protection provided depends on priority. A **first mortgage**, for example, has first priority against the pledged property if the borrower defaults on the loan. The priority of a **second mortgage** is next to the first mortgage. That is, if a borrower defaults, the property in question is foreclosed through legal proceedings initiated by the lenders. Proceeds from the sale of the property are used to pay off the first mortgage or deed of trust. The funds left over are used to satisfy the claim of the second mortgage holder. Any surplus still remaining is paid to the borrower.

First Mortgages. First mortgages and deeds are rather uncommon investments because financial institutions such as savings and loan associations and banks generally write them. Occasionally, though, financial institutions and loan brokers will aid in identifying sources for writing first mortgages. Yields on first mortgages are high. Since these mortgages generally are for no more than 80 percent of the value of the property, they tend to be safe investments.

Second Mortgages. Second mortgages and deeds are more generally associated with providing a partial down payment for the property buyer. For example, the buyer may be able to secure an 80 percent first mortgage from a bank. The property seller may then provide a 10 percent second mortgage to the buyer. Second mortgages typically are written with maturities ranging from three to eight years. Second mortgages are riskier than first mortgages. However, they also provide higher yields.

Unit Trusts and Mutual Funds. The **Government National Mortgage Association (GNMA)** and the **Federal Home Loan Mortgage Corporation (FHLMC)** issue mortgage-backed securities that investors refer to as Ginnie Maes and Freddie Macs, respectively. Ginnie Maes and Freddie Macs are traded in the open market. However, they are of large denomination and are generally priced beyond the reach of the average investor.

Two alternatives to direct investing in Ginnie Maes and Freddie Macs are unit trusts and specialized mutual funds. Both unit trusts and specialized mutual funds buy these large-denomination, mortgage-backed securities and then sell small-denomination shares to the investing public.

A **unit trust** is a fixed collection of Ginnie Maes and Freddie Macs. For example, a unit trust sells 1,000 shares or units for $1,000 each. The total proceeds of $1,000 × 1,000 = $1,000,000 are immediately invested in Ginnie Maes and Freddie Macs. This portfolio of securities remains fixed for the life of the unit trust. All incomes received from the securities purchased are distributed proportionally to the unit buyers. Unit trusts can be purchased from many brokerage houses for a sales charge of 3 to 4 percent. Unit trusts can be resold to other investors only.

The specialized mutual funds investing in mortgage-backed securities are very similar to unit trusts in terms of their investment strategy and the returns they provide to investors. They are different from unit trusts in two respects. First, these funds do not maintain a fixed collection of securities. Rather, they constantly buy and sell securities in the open market. Second, investors can sell their shares back to the fund.

Unit trusts and specialized mutual funds do not provide yields as high as those from direct investment in mortgages. However, they do provide the average investor with the opportunity to invest in mortgage-backed securities.

Advantages of Mortgages.   The major advantage of investing in mortgages and deeds of trust is the high yield obtained by the investor. With mortgage prepayment penalties and late payment charges factored in, the effective yield for the investor can be one percentage point higher than the stated mortgage rate. Because loan brokers can handle the mortgages or deeds, the investor's time involvement is minimal.

Disadvantages of Mortgages.   The investor should be able to invest fairly large sums of money. Buying a 10 percent second mortgage on a $100,000 house requires investing $10,000 for three to eight years. The buyer of second mortgages and deeds also needs to be sure that the property is properly appraised. Let's assume that an $80,000 property already has a $64,000 first mortgage. The property is incorrectly appraised at $100,000, and a loan broker sells a $20,000 second mortgage on the property. The buyer of the second mortgage is not going to recover his or her full investment if the borrower defaults on the loans and the property is foreclosed. Dealing with a reputable loan broker provides some safeguards against incurring losses of this type.

Property Ownership

Buying mortgages provides steady but not spectacular current returns. In contrast, direct property ownership provides not only current income but

also future income when the property is sold at a profit, plus certain tax benefits. In direct property ownership, the buyer gets the benefit of price appreciation for the property.

There are numerous alternatives for direct property ownership, including houses, duplexes, small apartment buildings, small shopping centers, commercial buildings, office buildings, condominiums, and farms. In this section, our focus will be on houses, duplexes, and small commercial properties.

Houses, Duplexes, Small Apartment Complexes. The basic principle for anyone considering investing in real estate is to start with buying your own home. It does not matter whether the home is a conventional single-family house, a condo, a co-op, or a mobile home. The important thing is to start by investing in your own home. Owning a home provides the advantages of investing in real estate and allows you to become familiar with various aspects of real estate investing, discussed later. (See Chapter 9 for a discussion of owning a home.)

A **duplex** contains two apartment units. Many first-time investors get started with duplexes, living in one unit and renting out the second unit. Small apartment complexes contain six to ten units. Again, the investor can live in one unit and rent the other units.

Buying Desirable Properties. Desirable rental properties are those that have been properly maintained, are neat and clean, contain appliances that are in good working condition, and have good tenants. First-time investors typically try to buy desirable properties. As a result, the prices of desirable properties tend to be high. One benchmark to use in determining whether you can afford to buy a particular property is whether the purchase leaves you able to "shake hands with yourself." An investor's cash inflow from investing is rental income. Cash outflows include mortgage payments, real estate taxes, insurance, maintenance, and some utilities. **Shaking hands** means breaking even on a cash flow basis—in other words, when cash inflows equal cash outflows.

Many desirable properties actually produce a negative cash flow: cash outflows are higher than cash inflows. At times some investors do not worry about negative cash flows because they believe that price appreciation for the properties and depreciation charges provide them with a healthy return.

Buying desirable rental houses for prices in excess of $40,000 generally is not recommended. Tenants resist paying rent in excess of $600 for houses, and a house bought for $40,000 will have about $600 per month in cash outflows associated with it.

Buying Turnaround Properties. **Turnaround properties** are those that have not been properly maintained. Such properties are relatively cheap to buy. However, they require "sweat equity." The investor has to be

willing to put in time and effort to improve, or turn around, the property. Before buying a turnaround, you should ask some questions: Can improvements be made so that rents can be raised? Is the property in an acceptable location? Is the building structurally sound? If the answer to any of these questions is no, you should not buy the property. (See "Elbow Grease and Sweat Equity" below.)

After purchasing a turnaround, the buyer should begin making repairs. Find out if there are services to tenants that can be upgraded at reasonable costs. Improving dim lighting in hallways and keeping the property clean can increase the rental value of the property. Most of these improvements will be appreciated by the tenants, and they will not mind paying higher rents. You can expect some turnover, however, especially as rents are raised.

Some Don'ts to Remember. Jay Lamont suggests that investors remember the following items:[6]

1. Don't buy property all over the place; try to stay in one geographical location.
2. Don't buy property in cities that have or are considering rent control.
3. Don't buy in a city where the population is declining.
4. Don't buy in a "one-employer" city.

Elbow Grease and Sweat Equity

Gene Simons and Jane Honda, fishing enthusiasts, were casting around for investment opportunities. However, this dynamic duo could not find anything that was reasonably priced and held the promise of large profits until they saw a television program extolling the virtues of turnarounds. That's when they decided to buy a run-down property, put in elbow grease, turn it around, build up sweat equity, and sell it for a large profit.

After looking around, they bought a run-down building for a song and decided to convert it into—what else?—an aerobic and weight training gym. They cleaned the premises, remodeled the interior, installed equipment, constructed locker rooms and showers, and then performed routine maintenance after opening the gym. After successfully operating the gym for one year, they sold it for a very large return on their original investment and invested the money in exercise videos. The moral of the story is that elbow grease combined with real sweat can result in improved health for your equity.

---

6. See "Waiting Out Profits in Rental Property," *Money* (January 1978): 36–37.

5. Don't sign a purchase agreement without the help of a lawyer.
6. Don't allow pets: it can be difficult to get rid of animal odors and fleas.

Advantages and Disadvantages of Property Ownership.   The major advantage of buying houses and smaller complexes is the potential for price appreciation. Real estate investments can be expected to outperform inflation. For investors in high income tax brackets, real estate investments can also provide tax advantages.

The major disadvantage of owning rental property is that the investor generally is required to be a property manager, a collector, a rental agent, a repairer, and a decorator. Many experienced landlords suggest that a new investor estimate the time it will take to manage the property and multiply that number by three to get a better estimate of the time that actually will be required. An alternative to managing the property yourself is to hire a property management firm. However, such firms will charge about 5 to 8 percent of gross rentals as property management fees, charges that might well cause outflows to exceed inflows. Moreover, many people argue that the best property manager is the one whose investment is at stake. Weighing the potential for profits against the hassles of property management requires careful consideration.

Commercial Properties.   The mention of commercial properties brings to mind visions of the Empire State Building, Sears Tower, and the Transamerica Building. However, Ma and Pa grocery stores, laundromats, stores, small shopping centers, office buildings, warehouses, closed-down schools, even parking lots are all commercial properties suitable for investing by investors of modest means.

In 1976, Mike di Paolo, an artist, found a nice house in a prime location in downtown Philadelphia. The house had been for sale since 1973. No one had tried to purchase it because with its chandeliers, fireplaces, and other fancy decorations, no one knew what to do with the place. Mike believed that the house would be an ideal location for a men's store. He bought the building for $135,000, with a $20,000 down payment. Mortgage payments are $10,000 annually. The tenant, a clothing company, pays $20,000 annually in rent plus taxes, insurance, utilities, and repair costs. On his $20,000 investment, Mike makes an annual $10,000 profit. In addition, he has depreciation and mortgage interest tax benefits.[7] As this example indicates, commercial properties can provide substantial returns.

Considerations in Buying Commercial Property.   Look for *alternative uses* for properties that are for sale. A warehouse might be turned into a nightclub or a restaurant. A school could be converted into an office building. An old house could be made into doctors' offices.

---

7. See "Waiting Out Profits in Rental Property," *Money* (January 1978): 42.

Review the leases of current tenants and review the lease alternatives for future tenants. For instance, look for *shorter leases* for existing tenants— long-term leases can keep you from negotiating higher rents. **Escalator clauses** tie rent increases to inflation rates. **Triple net leases** require the tenant to pay all utilities, insurance, taxes, and maintenance costs. **Percentage leases** allow the owner to collect extra rent when the tenant's sales are higher.

Advantages and Disadvantages. Commercial properties are free from most rent control laws, so rents can be raised as the owner sees fit. The cost of moving a business is high; therefore, tenants tend to stay at the same location for long time periods. Maintenance of commercial properties is easier than of residential properties because tenants generally vacate the premises around five p.m. Leases tend to be for longer time periods. Irresponsible or uncooperative tenants are easier to evict. A tenant may be locked out of the property if rent is late by a few days. Finally, renovation of commercial property that is at least 20 years old may provide special tax benefits.

One disadvantage is that commercial properties are not as cheap as houses or duplexes. The investor generally needs around $25,000 to start investing in commercial property. Also, leases for commercial properties are very complex. A lawyer should review the lease before it is signed. In addition, obtaining financing for commercial properties can be very challenging.

Real Estate Syndicates

For the investor who would like to buy into a multimillion-dollar hotel in downtown Houston or own a piece of the action in an 80-story building, a real estate syndicate is the answer. A **real estate syndicate** is a group of investors who pool their investment resources to buy high-priced real estate. The person who organizes the syndicate is called the **general partner** or **syndicator**. The people who contribute their capital are **limited partners**. The general partner identifies desirable investments, puts the syndicate together, manages the syndicate real estate portfolio, and manages the partnership. He or she is paid a percentage of the gross rental income in fees. Limited partners contribute investment funds and have no direct voice in managing the properties or the partnership.

In August 1974, Craig Hall bought an apartment complex in Westland, Michigan, for $9.46 million. He financed the down payment and improvements by forming a real estate syndicate. He sold 44 limited partnerships for $25,000 each. In December 1976, he sold the property for $11.84 million. Each limited partner received $92,000 in cash. In addition,

the partners also received significant tax benefits for the time that they owned the property.[8]

Returns from Syndicates.   Real estate syndicates provide returns in three different ways. First, the net cash flows—the difference between cash inflows and cash outflows—are distributed to the limited partners. Second, the properties owned are depreciated, and the depreciation charges are passed along to the limited partners. The partners can deduct these charges, and, since they are noncash charges, they increase the after-tax income for the partners. (Chapter 3 provides a more extensive explanation of the tax advantages of depreciation.) Third, properties generally grow in value. When the properties are sold for a price higher than their cost, limited partners receive capital gains returns.

Considerations in Joining a Syndicate.   The costs of selling the syndicate partnerships should be low, around 6 to 8 percent of funds being raised. Check to see whether the general partner is providing services such as maintenance and insurance. If so, he or she may be in a position to overcharge the limited partners. The general partner should not receive more than 6 to 8 percent of gross rentals for property and partnership management.

The limited partner should have a lawyer check the syndicate agreement and make sure that liability is limited. Syndicates that invest in a number of properties are better than those that invest in just one property. If possible, the performance record of the syndicator should be verified.

Advantages and Disadvantages.   An important advantage is that investors with small sums of money—around $2,500 to $5,000—can buy into major properties. A carefully chosen syndicate provides very good returns without the problems associated with direct ownership. The investor has limited liability and does not have to manage the properties. A limited partnership in a large syndicate provides partial ownership claims to a variety of properties.

On the negative side, syndicates can involve initial high costs in the form of sales commissions and partnership formation costs. Unlike property owned directly, it is very difficult, if not impossible, to sell a limited partnership to another investor. Limited partners can generally expect to sell their partnership only when the syndicate is dissolved. Buying into a syndicate therefore tends to be a long-range proposition.

---

8. See ''Running Up Profits From Run-down Buildings,'' *Money* (March 1979): 52.

Real Estate Investment Trusts

A **real estate investment trust** (or **REIT**) is similar to a closed-end mutual fund. REITs raise equity funds by selling common stock to the public. Funds are then used to buy properties. REITs are exempt from paying federal income taxes if they pay out at least 90 percent of their income to their stockholders. The income paid out is taxable to the stockholders.

Three types of REITs are available to investors. A C&D trust makes short-term loans for construction and development. In 1974–75, high interest rates combined with a recession produced many bad loans for C&D trusts, and some of these trusts went bankrupt. Others were supported to some extent by banks. Many trusts have not provided their investors with much in the form of returns, so C&D trusts are not desirable investments at this time.

Long-term mortgage REITs invest their funds in long-term bonds. Those mortgage REITs that are sponsored by life insurance companies are generally desirable investments. Equity REITs own the properties and are generally the safest of the REITs. Their returns tend to be lower than returns on mortgage REITS, however.

Currently, about 60 REITs trade on the major stock exchanges, and another 100 sell in the OTC market. REITs can be bought and sold like any other corporation. Equity REITs are desirable real estate investments.

Spot Quiz • Real Estate

1. The buyer of the property has possession of the deed in a deed of trust transaction.   T _____ F _____

2. Direct property ownership is desirable for the busy investor.
   T _____ F _____

3. Commercial property should be bought based on the financial data provided by the seller.   T _____ F _____

4. A real estate syndicate can have unlimited liability.
   T _____ F _____

5. Common shares of REITs will generally sell at their asset value.
   T _____ F _____

(Answers on page 618)

COMMODITIES

Commodities include farm products such as wheat, corn, and soybeans; cattle; metals such as silver, copper, and gold; forest products; and financial items such as foreign currency and interest rate instruments. The one underlying characteristic of a commodity is that the item is homogeneous. That is, the quality and grade of the commodity can be precisely specified. Thus, investors buying or selling silver, for example, automatically know the purity of silver being sold or bought. The same applies to other commodities. Even grains being traded, such as wheat, are homogeneous in quality and grade. In this section, we will discuss commodities trading, the mechanics of trading, and the relative merits of commodities trading.

Commodities Trading

Commodities can be traded in both cash and futures markets.

Cash Markets. In a cash market, the commodity physically changes hands. Most of us are familiar with one aspect of commodities trading: the local farmers' market. Perhaps you have had the pleasure of going to a farmers' market on a Saturday morning to buy a dozen ears of corn, some fresh red tomatoes, and a quart of juicy, sweet strawberries. The quantities involved are, of course, small. If you were to buy and sell much larger quantities, say 5,000 bushels of soybeans or 112,000 pounds of sugar, you would be dealing with the cash commodities markets. Because most investors are neither direct producers nor consumers of commodities, cash markets are not relevant.

Futures Markets. For most commodities, demand tends to remain relatively steady from one year to the next. That is, American consumers are not going to change their coffee-drinking habits dramatically from year to year. The supply of commodities, on the other hand, generally depends on the weather, insects, government controls, strikes, and a host of other factors. Expected changes in the supply of commodities led some users of commodities to start contracting for delivery of commodities long before the harvest was in. Thus, for example, a bread baker would contract for delivery of specified quantities of flour long before the wheat was harvested. The buying of commodities for future delivery led to the development of the futures market, where futures contracts are traded. A **futures contract** calls for delivery of a specific quantity of a commodity at a certain price, place, and date. The contract spells out the quality or grade, quantity, and place of delivery of the commodity as well as certain other formalities.

Unlike the cash market, a commodity is not physically needed for trading in the futures market. For example, an investor could sell a futures contract to deliver one unit of sugar (which is 112,000 pounds) one year

from today. The contract seller does not have to need the sugar on hand to sell the contract. This particular aspect of the futures market makes the market very desirable for the investor.

Mechanics of Commodities Trading

Trading commodities to earn profits consistently is a difficult and demanding task that requires an understanding of commodities, futures markets, margin requirements, open positions, and maximum price variations.

Major Markets and Commodities.   Figure 19.1 lists the major futures markets and the commodities that are traded on these markets. On the Chicago Board of Trade, for example, you can trade futures in corn, soybeans, silver, and United States Treasury bonds.

Futures trading requires a standardized contract. The quality and grade of the commodity is specified. In addition, a unit of trade, or one contract, involves a fixed quantity of the commodity. Thus, for example, a gold contract is for 100 troy ounces. Figure 19.2 provides a sampling of commodities and the sizes of contracts.

Margin Requirements.   In commodities trading, margin requirements tend to be very low. Thus, investors are attracted to commodities trading because they can buy contracts for large quantities of commodities with small sums of money. Margin requirements for common stocks were explained in Chapter 16. Margin requirements for commodities provide

Figure 19.1 Major Markets and Commodities

Futures Market	Commodities Traded
Chicago Board of Trade	Wheat, soybeans, corn, cotton, cattle, silver, U.S. Treasury bonds, GNMA certificates
Chicago Mercantile Exchange	Cattle, eggs, pork bellies, lumber
New York Mercantile Exchange	Metals, potatoes, plywood
Commodity Exchange	Copper, gold, silver
International Monetary Market	British, Canadian, Japanese, Swiss, German currencies; U.S. Treasury bills

Figure 19.2 Trading Information on Commodities

Commodity	Exchange Trading	Size of Contract	Minimum Margin per Contract[a]	Minimum Commission per Round Turn[a]
Cattle (live)	Chicago Mercantile	40,000 pounds	$ 900	$40.00
Corn	Chicago Board of Trade, MidAmerica Commodity	5,000 bushels	1,000	30.00
Ginnie Mae certificates	Chicago Board of Trade	$100,000 principal amount (8% certificates)	1,500	60.00
Gold	Commodity Exchange, Chicago Mercantile, Chicago Board of Trade, MidAmerica Commodity, New York Mercantile	100 troy ounces	300	45.00
Pork bellies (frozen)	Chicago Mercantile	36,000 pounds	1,500	45.00
Silver	Commodity Exchange, Chicago Board of Trade, MidAmerica Commodity	5,000 troy ounces	1,000	22.50
Soybeans	Chicago Board of Trade, MidAmerica Commodity	5,000 bushels	3,000	30.00
Sugar #11	New York Coffee & Sugar	112,000 pounds	2,000	62.00
Treasury bills (90-day)	Chicago Mercantile	$1 million (face value at maturity)	1,500	60.00
Wheat	Chicago Board of Trade Kansas City, MidAmerica Commodity, Minneapolis	5,000 bushels	1,250	30.00

[a]Minimum margins and commissions are established by the exchange.

investors with the same two-edged sword. The major difference is that margin requirements for common stocks are in the 50 to 100 percent range. In commodities, margin requirements are around 5 to 15 percent.

Figure 19.2 shows minimum margin requirements for some commodities. For example, for silver, the minimum margin requirement is

$1,000. If silver is selling for $12 per ounce, a 5,000-ounce contract is worth $12 × 5,000 = $60,000. Thus, an investor can gain or lose on $60,000 of silver by putting up only $1,000 in margin. A rise in the price of silver of $1 per ounce will give the investor a $5,000 profit on a $1,000 investment. The reverse also holds true.

Round Turn.   Most investors neither deliver nor take delivery of the contracted commodity. The normal way of trading in commodities is called **round turning**. An investor buying or selling a contract is said to have an **open position**. The investor completes the transaction by selling the contract bought earlier or buying back the contract sold earlier to **close out** the open position. The process of opening a position and then eventually closing it is called a **round turn**. A commodity producer generally closes out an open position by delivering the commodity on the contract sold previously. Similarly, a commodity user may close out a position by accepting delivery of the commodity.

Maximum Price Variation.   Whereas stock prices can fluctuate up or down without limits, such is not the case with some commodities. Some commodities have maximum price variations that cannot be exceeded. Maximum price variation regulations are established by the exchanges and are designed to prevent dramatic fluctuations in commodities prices.

Advantages of Commodities

Trading in commodities has a number of advantages that attract investors. The potential for profits in commodities trading is very high because of the low margin requirements. The commodities market is one of the few places where investors with small sums of money can become millionaires quickly—if luck is with them.

Contracts in many commodities are actively traded on the markets. Thus, the investor has great marketability for contracts bought and sold. A few commodities, though, are not actively traded.

The last column in Figure 19.2 shows typical round turn transaction costs for trading commodities. The costs of trading commodities tend to be low compared to the costs of trading other speculative investments.

Disadvantages of Commodities

The major disadvantage is that the potential for losses is very high in commodities trading. Low margin requirements mean that minor errors in predicting the direction of the price changes can rapidly wipe out the investor's margin, or equity. Thus, trading in commodities is appropriate only for people who can afford to lose all of their investment funds. In other words, you should not invest any more in commodities trading than you can afford to lose.

Also, many investors are professional traders in commodities who spend many hours a day analyzing information and price trends in commodities. Thus, commodities trading requires a much larger time commitment than investing in stocks to compete with these professionals.

Spot Quiz • Commodities

1. Commodities trading is of interest only to producers and users of commodities.   T _____   F _____

2. A drop in the price of silver of 20 cents per ounce will produce a 100 percent loss for a silver contract buyer.   T _____   F _____

3. Raising margin requirements for trading commodities would raise the profit potential.   T _____   F _____

(Answers on page 618)

GOLD, COINS, STAMPS

Investments in gold, coins, and stamps can serve as a hedge against declining purchasing power during inflations because these investments are tangible and have relatively fixed supplies. Thus, investors tend to think of them as relatively safe investments, especially when compared with the pieces of paper that represent a futures contract or share of common stock. However, the truth is that several risks are associated with these investments. The markets for gold, coins, and stamps are not subject to the same degree of regulation that exists in securities markets, and investors are often at the mercy of dealers with superior knowledge and experience. In addition, these investments tend not to be liquid, and they do not pay interest or dividends while they are being held.

Gold

In 1971, gold was selling for under $40 an ounce. By 1974, the price had risen to $200 per ounce. The price peaked at over $800 per ounce and by late 1987 had fallen to about $470 an ounce. Gold investors—or gold bugs,

as they are more popularly known—who bought early saw their investments double and quadruple. More recent investors have not fared as well. Still, gold holds a certain charm and attracts many investors. There are five ways of investing in gold: bullion, coins, jewelry, stocks, and futures. Investments in stocks of gold mining companies and futures in gold are similar to investments in other stocks and futures and should be evaluated on the same basis.

Gold Bullion. Americans have been able to own gold legally only since December 1974. **Gold bullion** is bars of gold. Buying gold bullion can be a problem. First, the buyer has to verify that the bar is, in fact, all gold and not gold bars with lead cores. Then the buyer will need to prove that the bar is all gold when he or she tries to sell it. Overall, gold bullion is not the best way to buy gold.

Gold Coins. Gold coins are of three types: bullion, monetary, and numismatic. **Bullion coins** are sold basically for their gold content and are probably the best form of gold investment. Among the more popular ones are the American Eagle, the South African Krugerrand, and the Canadian Maple Leaf. Each of these coins contains exactly one troy ounce of gold. Bullion coins generally sell for 2 to 4 percent over their precious metal content. When you buy bullion coins, you should not pay more than the 2 to 4 percent premium, sales taxes, if any, and shipping charges. Avoid dealers who tack on commissions, storage charges, and other fees.

Monetary coins commemorate special events in foreign countries. New Guinea, the Philippines, and Hong Kong are some of the countries that issue monetary gold coins. Such coins are sold through newspaper advertisements. Unfortunately, the face value of these coins is nowhere near their precious metal content. Generally, the gold content of the coins is about one-third of the face value. The coins do not become collectors' items, and from an investment viewpoint, they do not hold much appeal.

Numismatic gold coins are collected as coins and will be discussed in the section on coins.

Jewelry. Gold jewelry is not a desirable method of investing in gold because a significant portion of the cost of the jewelry is associated with the quality of the workmanship. When resold, jewelry will fetch a price based on the gold content, not the workmanship, and thus will result in a loss.

If you want to invest in gold, bullion gold coins are the best method. Remember, though, to purchase the coins only from a reputable firm. Finally, keep in mind that your gold will produce neither interest income nor dividends. (See "Croesus' Siglos" on page 606.)

Croesus' Siglos

Ole King Croesus of Lydia (merry ole soul that he was and not knowing quite how to pay for purchases with his gold and silver) decided to convert his gold and silver into stamped pieces that we now call coins. A small silver siglos from his time (560–546 B.C.) goes for about $600, while a similar gold coin from that era sells for about $3,000. Coins are generally classified as ancient, classic foreign, early United States, and modern.

The American Numismatic Association has developed a coin grading system that ranges from MS-70 (for mint state) to AC-3 (for about good). The top ratings go to uncirculated, specially minted coins called proofs. Nicks, scratches, and wear reduce the value of coins. Markups on coin purchases may be up to 30 percent of wholesale prices and imply a patient wait before an investor can sell a coin for profit.

Coins

Coins have become popular as investment vehicles in recent years. Two factors affect the value of coins: scarcity and condition. Bullion coins, for example, are not scarce and will sell for only a small premium above the value of their precious metal content. Rare coins, however, have shown price increases far greater than the increases in the value of their metal content. The other important factor in determining a coin's price is its condition: an uncirculated coin will sell for three to five times the price of the same coin that shows some signs of handling.

Three journals, *Coin World, Coin Dealers Newsletter,* and *Numismatic News*, contain important information for coin collectors. Another source of information is the American Numismatic Association.[9]

Many coin dealers sell silver coins in a bag containing $1,000 of face value in dimes, quarters, and halves. These bags contain about 715 to 725 troy ounces of silver. A good price to pay for a bag is 720 times the current price of silver plus a 6 percent premium. With silver at, say, $12 per ounce, a bag would be sold for about (720 × $12) X 1.06 = $9,158.40. Remember that coins stored at home should be insured against theft.

Stamps

Stamp collecting has grown rapidly as a hobby in the past 20 years. However, investing in stamps does not require you to be a stamp hobbyist

---

9. 818 North Cascade, Colorado Springs, CO 80903.

(or **philatelist**). In fact, a collector's biases may get in the way of good investment decisions about stamps. Currently, about 25 million Americans buy stamps. About 90 percent of these are hobbyists, and the remaining 10 percent are serious investors.

Rarity, authenticity, and quality are important factors in determining stamp prices. In general, stamps issued after 1930 are not rare enough to merit significant price appreciation. Even some 60- and 70-year-old stamps have not appreciated much in value because they are in abundant supply.

Authenticity means that a stamp is what it appears to be. At one auction, a stamp expert noticed that 12 of 13 stamps to be auctioned were either forgeries or had been altered.[10] Nonauthenticated stamps can lose their value quickly when the investor offers them for sale.

The quality of a stamp is hard to establish. Used stamps sell for about half the price of unused stamps. An 1851 United States 1-cent stamp in mint condition may be worth $100,000. Another stamp that shows wear may be worth only $8,000.

Sources of Information. Local stamp dealers may be helpful in providing information about stamps. However, keep in mind that they are in the business of selling stamps. Their recommendations will be based on the stamps in their inventory.

Independent advisers offer investment recommendations for a fee. They do not sell stamps and do not direct their clients to trade with any particular dealer. Advisers will accept clients with as little as $1,000 to invest. They typically charge 5 to 15 percent of the stamp price for their investment advice.

The American Philatelic Society[11] can provide information about local stamp clubs. Joining a stamp club and talking with other collectors is an important source of information. The American Stamp Dealers' Association[12] can provide a list of dealers, advisers, and auction houses in your area.

Scott's Specialized Catalogues of stamps list estimated retail values of foreign and U.S. stamps. Certain weekly magazines, such as Linn's Stamp News,[13] provide current information on the buying and selling prices of stamps. Stamp Market Update[14] carries investment-oriented articles and commentaries on market trends. These and other publications provide historical and current information on stamp prices, and they should be consulted before you buy stamps.

---

10. "Stamps for Licking Inflation," Money (June 1981): 84.
11. P.O. Box 800, State College, PA 16803.
12. 840 Willis Avenue, Albertson, NY 11507.
13. P.O. Box 29, Sidney, OH 45365.
14. 3 East 57th Street, New York, NY 10222.

Buying Stamps.   A collector is most interested in collecting sets of stamps. An investor seeks to build a diversified portfolio of stamps. An investor should start a stamp collection with 10 to 20 stamps. Good stamps for the beginning investor, such as the 1901 Pan American Exposition set or the 1915 Panama-Pacific Exposition issue, provide reasonably priced stamps with good potential for price appreciation. (See ''Stamp It Investment'' on page 609.)

A stamp investor should be willing to keep the stamps for at least five to ten years because holding stamps for shorter time periods will not provide adequate returns. Note, too, that stamps can be easily ruined—two stamps stuck together are practically worthless. Thus, they should be stored in silicone-treated glassine envelopes. Buy only from reputable dealers, and never purchase any stamp worth over $200 without a guarantee of authenticity. Reputable dealers and auction houses should be willing to refund the purchase price and certification costs if you purchase stamps that turn out to be forgeries or to have been altered. (Dealers should provide a written refund guarantee.) The American Philatelic Society and the Philatelic Foundation[15] certify stamps for a fee of about 3 percent of the value of the stamps.

The popularity of investing in stamps has been growing rapidly and should continue to grow. The stamp market is also spreading geographically, with investors from many foreign countries actively buying and selling stamps.

Spot Quiz • Gold, Coins, Stamps

1. Gold monetary coins are good investments.   T _____   F _____

2. Silver coins of recent years are priced based on their silver content.
                                                     T _____   F _____

3. Stamps are good short-term investments.   T _____   F _____

(Answers on page 618)

---

15. 270 Madison Avenue, New York, NY 10016.

Stamp It Investment

David Lineman, noted philatelist and author of *The World of Stamps* and *Stamp Collecting*, on stamp collecting: "It can be practiced any hour of the day or night, it causes no traffic jams, and it can be as cheap or expensive a hobby as the collector wants." Interest in stamp collecting in the United States has been growing rapidly. Most collectors start out by specializing in a particular area. Birds, animals, space, aircraft, and flowers are some popular specializations.

The United States Postal Service is particularly helpful if you are interested in collecting U.S. stamps. One of its publications, *Introduction to Stamp Collecting*, is free. Another, *The Postal Service Guide to U.S. Stamps*, costs $5 and shows every stamp the United States has ever issued. A free copy of another guide, called *Stamp Collecting Made Easy*, is available from *Linn's Stamp News*. Even though experts state that understanding the intricacies of stamp collecting requires considerable time, stamp collecting may be a good investment area to get into as a continuation of a childhood hobby.

GEMS, ART, COLLECTIBLES

Gems, art, and collectibles can serve investors' aesthetic interests as well as meeting certain investment goals. In order for these forms of investment to meet investment goals, special care must be taken in their selection and authentication.

Gems

Currently, United States investors buy about $2 billion in gems annually for investment purposes. Since 1977, some pension funds have also begun to invest in gems. As with other types of speculative investments, such as stamps and art, the gem investor generally buys gems at retail prices and sells them at wholesale prices. Therefore, an investor must hold the gems for five to ten years to realize significant profits.

About 90 percent of investment funds in gems go toward buying diamonds. De Beers Consolidated Mines of South Africa is a major force in the mining and pricing of diamonds. Diamond prices have usually increased steadily from year to year. However, in recent years, De Beers has been less effective in controlling market prices for diamonds. As a result, diamond prices have fluctuated more.

Diamonds are graded on carats, color, clarity, and cut—the four Cs. Clarity refers to flaws within the diamond. Investment-grade diamonds

should weigh at least one carat, be white in color, have only minor flaws, and have excellent sparkle. Diamonds and other gems should be purchased only from reputable dealers who are willing to provide a **GIA grading**—a numerical grading scale for diamonds, developed by the Gemological Institute of America, that most dealers use to grade stones. Diamonds should not be purchased from "diamond investment firms," who do most of their business by phone.

Gems can be risky investments. As mentioned previously, they generally can be sold only at or below wholesale prices. Also, diamonds can be easily stolen, so insurance against theft is a must. Despite these risks, diamonds can be worthwhile investments for people with investment funds and the patience to wait for price appreciation.

Art

Investing in art has become immensely popular in the past two decades. Our discussion will focus on prints as investments, primarily because investment-grade paintings are too expensive for the average investor. A number of factors affect art prices.

The Artist. The reputation of an artist is the major factor in determining art prices. A print by Miró will fetch a much higher price than a print by Friedlander. Even prints by old masters, such as Dürer, Rembrandt, and Goya, are still available at reasonable prices and hold high potential for appreciation.

Number Available. A rare print will cost much more than a common print. Prints that are numbered and signed by the artist will sell for 10 to 20 times the price of an unsigned print by the same artist. Prints labeled "signed in stone" are not investment-grade prints. Prints carry a number, such as 37/150, which means that the print in question is 37th out of 150 prints.

Authenticity. Art forgeries abound. Even experts are occasionally fooled into identifying a forgery as authentic. Reputable dealers and auction houses thus issue "certificates of authenticity" and will refund the purchase price if a print they sold turns out to be a fake.

Condition. Recent prints by such artists as Miró, Calder, Vasarely, and Klee do not suffer from printing plate deterioration. That is, print number 150 will look the same as print number 1. However, prints by old masters do suffer from plate deterioration. For instance, in 1973, a fine print of Rembrandt's *The Agony in the Garden* sold for $70,000. A similar print showing some deterioration sold for only $3,600.

Buying Art.   You must have a knowledge of art to invest in art. Visits to museums and art institutes are good learning experiences. Visiting auction houses can help you develop a feel for prices. The *Print Collectors Newsletter*[16] provides a good indication of current prices. Primary sources of prints are art auction houses and galleries. Although neither source will offer prints at wholesale prices, they generally can provide authentication and should refund your money if a print turns out to be a fake.

Another important consideration in print buying is to specialize in the works of a particular artist. A California print collector specialized in prints by Whistler. His collection of over 150 prints was considered to be one of the finest Whistler collections. Another collector specialized in works by American artists. If you have limited funds, as is the case for most of us, specialization is one way to develop "clout." Remember that investment in art is a long-term proposition—the art investor must be willing to wait a few years for his or her investments to produce high profits.

Collectibles

Collectibles include antiques, rugs, rare books, photographs, beer cans, dolls, autographs, nostalgic items such as clothes worn by movie actors and actresses, and anything else people might want to buy and sell. If you are interested in collectibles, you should try to join a suitable club. The *Encyclopedia of Associations* lists many groups involved with collectibles. In this section, we take a brief look at some popular types of collectibles suitable for average investors.

Buying at Auctions.   You can purchase collectibles in stores, through the mail, and at shows, fairs, flea markets, and auctions. Auctions are important sources for buying collectibles for several reasons. Auctions offer a wide variety and large volume of merchandise. Investors who buy at auctions avoid paying a dealer's profit. As a result, generally speaking, prices of collectibles are lower at auctions. Figure 19.3 provides some tips on bidding at auctions.

Antiques.   Paul Revere made his famous journey through the streets of Boston long ago. However, his handiwork, such as spoons, forks, and silverware, lives on, bringing prices that he would not have believed. Escalating prices and decreasing supplies have encouraged the production of fake antiques. One expert suggests that fakes flood the market whenever production costs for fakes become lower than the prices of the authentic items. Some fakes defy detection even by experts. A Rhode Island cabinetmaker became tired of hearing about the quality of the craftsmanship of antiques. Therefore, he proceeded to create a "seventeenth century" chair,

---

16. 205 East 78th Street, New York, NY 10021

Figure 19.3 Tips for Bidding at Auctions

1. Don't be afraid of big and important auctions. While the dealers and rich collectors are focusing their attention on a few expensive items, you can often pick up lesser pieces cheaply.
2. Although an auction may be advertised as involving French or English antiques, there are almost always a few lots that don't fit into the category—making them excellent targets for bargain hunters.
3. Study the catalog and visit the presale exhibit, note pad and tape measure in hand. Look for flaws, signs of reworking, and identifying marks. Take or check measurements to ensure that the pieces you're interested in will fit where you want them.
4. Read the conditions of sale and terms of guarantee, if any, in the catalog before you buy.
5. Post a refundable deposit before the sale. If you wait till after you've made a successful bid, you can miss an upcoming lot that you want to bid on while you're securing your purchase with the required deposit.
6. Try to sit or stand on the side so you can spot the dealers; they're usually in a group. From this vantage point you can see where the bidding is coming from and gauge your competition.
7. There's no need to sit or stand all day to bid on just one lot; the attendants at the presale exhibit can estimate when a lot should come up. Stay alert during the auction for lots that are slightly out of order.
8. If you can't attend the auction, send or drop off an "order bid" to be executed by the auction house. This means that you are entitled to buy at a price one step above the last bid from the floor, up to the price specified in the order. Of course, you won't be able to raise your maximum if bidding gets intense.
9. No single bidding technique is always best. If your competition appears to be a dealer, psychology is of little value. Against other collectors you can either bid aggressively from the beginning, trying to scare them off, or stay out until almost the end, hoping your new bid will discourage the survivors.
10. To avoid damage, remove your purchases without delay.
11. If you change your mind you won't be able to get a refund, but naturally the house will resell a piece for a commission.
12. To sharpen your price judgments, get a list of sale prices afterward and compare it with the catalog.

Reprinted with permission from "Investments You Can Love," *Money* (August 1978): 40–41.

which was eventually bought by a prominent museum. Only then did the craftsman admit that he had constructed the ''antique.''

Like the art investor, the serious investor in antiques needs extensive knowledge. You can learn about antiques by reading, by visiting museums, and by talking with dealers. A reputable dealer will stand behind his or her merchandise.

Chippendale furniture, Early American chests, Federal settees and breakfast tables, clocks from around 1785, pewter lamps from 1815 to 1825, and silver items from around 1750 are some of the antiques that are currently popular. English and French furniture from the eighteenth century are considered to be good buys these days. No matter what you buy, though, establish the item's authenticity prior to purchase.

Dolls.   Dolls have gained popularity as collectibles recently. Nineteenth century china dolls and early twentieth century cloth dolls are good investments. The head of the doll should be in nearly perfect condition, and dolls with closed mouths are better investments than are open-mouthed dolls.

Americana.   Pewter, quilts, rugs, and hunting decoys have gone up in value about 20 percent a year for the past 25 years. These items are attractive because of the quality of the workmanship. Early twentieth century quilts made by the Amish are also considered to be good investments.

*"You can't throw it in
the ocean . . . it's a collectible."*

Source: *Changing Times*, August 1978, p. 30. Reprinted
with permission.

Books. It is best to invest in books by one author or on one subject. Only first or limited edition books should be bought. Generally, old books have good appreciation potential, but some newer books do also. For example, Heller's *Catch-22* sold for $5.95 in 1961 and is worth about $200 now. Church bazaars and garage sales are worth scouting for bargains.

Nostalgia. At a 1981 auction at the Sotheby Parke Bernet Gallery in London, a handbag, a pair of evening gloves, and a brassiere that belonged to Marilyn Monroe were auctioned for $1,015. What's the big deal, you say? The items were listed in the auction catalog with a suggested sale price of $60! Action Comics No. 1, the June 1938 issue, cost 10 cents new. Its current price is over $5,000. Items related to Disney characters are excellent investments. Elvis Presley dolls, that cost $5 in 1959 now sell for about $2,000 each. Toys that can be wound up, metal mechanical toys, metal soldiers, posters, autographs, old photographs, and old clocks are all items worth investment consideration.

For all collectibles, keep in mind that you are generally buying at retail and selling at wholesale, so you must hold the items for several years to earn a profit. Remember, too, that you must be able to store your collection safely.

Spot Quiz • Gems, Art, Collectibles

1. In general, the reputation of the artist determines the price of the art print.   T _____ F _____

2. Art and collectibles can be liquid investments.   T _____ F _____

3. Authenticity is important in buying collectibles.
                                                              T _____ F _____

(Answers on page 618)

Summary

Speculative investments, which are characterized by high risk and high return, are discussed in this chapter. Convertible securities give the investor the right to convert his or her holdings into common stock. Con-

vertible securities provide fixed dollar returns while holding the promise of price appreciation. Options are rights to buy or sell common stock. Options can provide investors with high returns as well as large losses. Options can also be used in conjunction with buying long or selling short to limit the amount of potential losses.

Real estate investments are of four types: buying mortgages, buying property, joining a syndicate, and buying shares in REITs. Mortgages provide fixed but high yields. Property that an investor can buy includes single homes, duplexes, small apartment buildings, and commercial property. Buying turnaround properties carries a higher potential for capital gains. A real estate syndicate is a group of investors who pool their resources to buy larger properties. Returns from joining a syndicate are not as high as returns from direct property ownership. REITs are similar to closed-end mutual funds in that both invest in real estate. Equity REITs are desirable investments.

Commodities include farm products, forest products, cattle, metals, and financial instruments. Most investors buy and sell commodity futures rather than the actual commodities. The margin requirements for trading commodities are low, thereby providing investors with high leverage, which holds the potential for very high profits.

Gold, coins, stamps, gems, art, and collectibles have become increasingly popular as investments in recent years. With most of these items, you buy at retail and sell at wholesale. As a result, you must be willing to wait a few years before expecting profits. Rarity, quality, and authenticity are very important in the purchase of any of these items.

Questions

1. What is meant by the term *speculative investment*? Explain the risk and return characteristics for speculative investments.

2. What is the relationship between conversion price and conversion ratio for a convertible security?

3. What are the advantages and disadvantages of convertible securities?

4. What is an option? How does an option differ from a convertible security?

5. How can options be used with short selling? With buying long?

6. What are the different ways of investing in real estate? Explain briefly.

7. What are the major differences between buying desirable properties and buying turnaround properties?

8. Explain the following concepts related to buying commercial property:
    a. Triple net leases.
    b. Percentage leases.
    c. Escalator clauses.

9. How does a real estate syndicate work?

10. What is an REIT? Explain briefly.

11. List ten types of commodities for which futures trading is available.

12. What is the major difference between cash and futures markets?

13. Explain how margin requirements make commodities trading speculative.

14. What is meant by maximum price variation in commodities trading?

15. From an investment viewpoint, explain the risk, return, and liquidity characteristics of gold, coins, stamps, art, and collectibles.

16. When you buy stamps, coins, art, and collectibles, what are the important things to remember?

17. Explain the pros and cons of using dealers versus buying at auctions.

Case Problems

1. J. Majors is considering buying a convertible bond that is paying 13 percent in annual interest. The face value of the bond is $1,000, and it is convertible into 40 shares of common stock. In one year, the price of common stock is expected to be $30 a share. What is the conversion price for the bond? Majors buys the bond at face value. Calculate his minimum expected percentage return.

2. Sarah Lividini is selling short 100 shares of Winston Company at $30 a share. Ms. Lividini buys a six-month call on 100 shares of Winston at $30. Her option costs $300.
    a. After six months Sarah covers her short at $20 per share. How much profit did Sarah make?
    b. How much profit would Sarah have made if she had not bought the call and had covered her short at $20 per share?
    c. How much money would Sarah have lost if she had covered her short when the price of Winston was $40 per share? Explain your answer.

3. Frank Mitterrand bought 100 shares of Adam Industries at $40 a share. A six-month put for 100 shares at $38 a share cost him $250. After six months, the price of Adams has dropped to $32 a share. Frank has to make a decision whether to exercise his put. What advice do you have for Frank? What would his gain or loss be from his stock transactions if he were to exercise his put?

Bibliography

"Coveting the Coin of the Realm." *Money* (March 1985): 157–164.

"Elvis' Great Career Move." *Money* (August 1987): 30–31.

"The Explosion in Options." *Money* (May 1981): 122–128.

"Figuring the Real Return on Real Estate." *Changing Times* (February 1986): 85–87.

"How Not to Take a Licking in Stamps." *Money* (November 1986): 77–82.

"How to Play the Markets Without Buying Stocks." *Money* (March 1985): 91–98.

"Investing in Condomania." *Money* (May 1981): 59–62.

"The Right and Wrong Ways to Buy Gold." *Money* (August 1987): 47–54.

"Ten Tips on Getting Top Dollars." *Money* (April 1986): 113–114.

Answers to Spot Quizzes

1. T (Face value divided by conversion ratio gives the conversion price.)

2. F (Investors expect both fixed returns and capital gains from convertible securities.)

Options (page 590)

1. T (This way the investor can profit both ways. A put and a call together is called a straddle.)

2. T (Naked options are very risky.)

Real Estate (page 599)

1. F (The deed is kept by the trustee.)

2. F (Direct property ownership takes up time.)

3. F (Alternative uses for the property may require you to generate new financial data.)

4. T (Liability is not automatically limited in a syndicate.)

5. F (They will be priced based on demand and supply; asset values are not directly involved.)

Commodities (page 604)

1. F (Commodities futures are investments for speculative investors.)

2. T (The drop will produce a $.20 \times 5{,}000 = \$1{,}000$ loss, wiping out the $1,000 margin.)

3. F (The profit potential would decline.)

Gold, Coins, Stamps (page 608)

1. F (Monetary coins are generally overpriced.)

2. T (Their prices fluctuate with the price of silver.)

3. F (Stamps are long-term investments.)

Gems, Art, Collectibles (page 614)

1. T (The artist is the major determinant of the price.)

2. F (They tend not to be very liquid.)

3. T (Without authenticity, it will be difficult to recover even the purchase price.)

Part 6

Retirement and Estate Planning

Part 6 covers planning strategies for retirement and the transfer of your estate. Chapter 20, "Planning for Retirement," explains why retirement planning is important. The discussion of retirement income includes social security, employer pension plans, annuities, and individual retirement plans. A section also covers leisure and recreation planning.

Chapter 21, "Estate Planning," covers the importance and goals of estate planning. The need for and typical provisions of a will are explained, the mechanics of calculating estate and gift taxes are shown, and a variety of trust arrangements are explained. The last section deals with specific estate planning strategies.

Chapter 20

Planning for Retirement

Objectives

After reading this chapter, you will be able to:

- Discuss the importance of retirement planning.
- Explain the factors affecting retirement life style.
- Understand how the social security system works.
- Define the terms associated with pensions.
- State the safeguards provided by the Employment Retirement Income Security Act.
- Explain how annuities work.
- Define the different types of annuities.
- Explain the types of individual retirement plans.
- Describe leisure and recreation planning for retirees.

Money magazine asked a number of business leaders and other people with substantial professional achievement to answer this question: "What was the wisest thing you did in preparing for retirement?" Don Budge, the retired professional tennis player, stated that he placed his money in paid-up annuities for safety and blue-chip common stocks for growth. Richard C. Gerstenberg, retired chairman of General Motors, stated that he and his wife put considerable effort into finding a desirable second home for retirement. After retiring from the Senate in his eighties, Sam Ervin returned to his law practice in North Carolina. He had never really planned to retire because, as he put it, "I figured I'd rust out before I wore out."[1]

Must you really invest in annuities and stocks to retire? Do you need to find a suitable home? How about working until you are all rusted out? This chapter discusses some of the answers.

INTRODUCTION TO RETIREMENT PLANNING

Sam Ervin was 82 years old at the time *Money* magazine conducted its survey on preparing for retirement, and he was not quite ready to be considered "rusted out" by retirement time. Rather than retiring, he chose to return to his law practice. Is it really necessary for everyone to retire at a certain age? The answer is a strong no! Colonel Sanders was at the ripe "retirement" age of 66 when he started his highly successful chain of Kentucky Fried Chicken stores. Rachel Carson wrote *Silent Spring* when she was what some people would label "retirement age."

There is no physical or psychological reason why we should consider age 65 or 60 or 62 or any other age as "retirement age." Adults of all ages, including those of "retirement age," are perfectly capable of contributing to their own well-being and that of their families and society in general. And they can have a good time doing it.

Whether an older individual elects to retire or not, that individual's life style will probably change, however. With children no longer at home, the five-bedroom house is too large. Conversely, the need for financial security is greater. In this section, we will consider the need for retirement planning, the factors affecting retirement life style, ways of determining retirement income needs, and sources of retirement income.

Need For Retirement Planning

Most young people do not think seriously about planning for retirement. For someone who is 22 years old, retirement may be 40 or more years away.

---

1. "The Smartest Thing I Ever Did Was . . .," *Money* (July 1979): 44–45.

So why worry about it? The principal reason is financial security. Government statistics and various studies indicate that perhaps as many as one out of every five retirees has an income that may be considered to be below the poverty level. Furthermore, when income patterns of retirees above and below the poverty levels are analyzed, it becomes apparent that many more retirees above the poverty level receive a good portion of their income from sources other than social security than do their counterparts below the poverty level. What does this mean? Simply that retirees above the poverty level have done a better job of planning for retirement than those below the poverty level. Their planning has resulted in investments and savings that are providing them with income to supplement their social security income. Such is not the case with many retirees below the poverty level.

Figure 20.1 further illustrates the need for financial planning for retirement. During the college years, expenses generally exceed income. This deficit is financed by borrowing from parents and financial institutions and by scholarships and grants-in-aid. Expenses increase during the working years. Income, however, is in excess of expenses. During the early working years, people have to pay off the loans accumulated during the college years. Often people also incur expenses associated with forming a new household and parenting. As a result, savings are relatively low during the early working years.

During the later working years, children generally have left home. Housing expenses remain relatively fixed. Other expenses increase but not very rapidly. Meanwhile, earnings keep increasing. The net result is that savings are relatively high during this stage. Increased emphasis should be placed on retirement financial planning during this time.

During retirement years, expenses decline to between 60 and 70 percent of preretirement levels, and earnings decline completely. During this period, income can come from a variety of sources, including social security and pensions. However, social security and pension income is usually not sufficient to meet living expenses. As Figure 20.1 shows, the difference between living expenses and social security and pension income is made up by income provided by retirement funds. Thus, planning for retirement is important if you want to cover all of your living expenses during your retirement years.

Many of us do not fully realize the effect of inflation on living expenses. Let's assume, for example, that a couple is earning $3,000 per month now. These earnings are sufficient to meet the couple's living expenses. If they were to retire today, they would need about 70 percent of their earnings, or $3,000 × .7 = $2,100 per month in retirement income. However, they are not retiring today. They are planning to retire 40 years from today. Let's assume that, because of inflation, their retirement expenses will increase at a 5 percent annual rate. Based on the current retirement income needs of $2,100 per month, how much monthly income will they need 40 years from today? $2,800? $3,500? How about $14,784 per month?

Figure 20.1 Lifetime Income and Expenditure Patterns

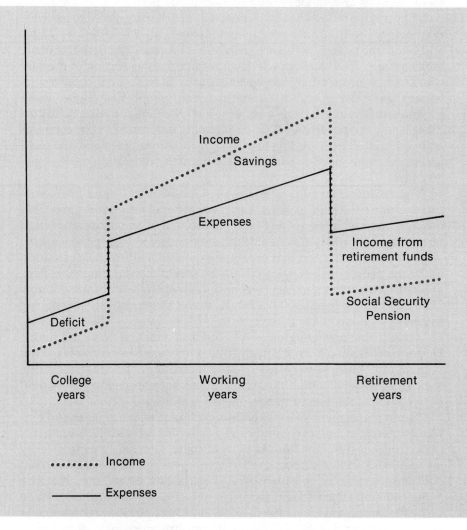

If $2,100 per month in retirement income is adequate today, then with a 5 percent inflation rate, $14,784 per month in retirement income will be needed 40 years from today just to maintain today's standard of living. Obviously, $14,784 is a large sum of money. Perhaps 40 years from now social security will pay $8,000 per month in retirement income. Perhaps a pension might provide another $3,000 to $5,000 per month. Perhaps. But the best way to ensure sufficient retirement income is to plan for it now.

Retirement is not just a period when you stop working. Rather, it is a period when the way you spend your time changes. A retiree has more time to enjoy hobbies, take vacations, participate in sports, meet new

people, and provide services. Planning for retirement also calls for planning for leisure and recreation. Although you do not need to start this planning as early as retirement income planning, you do need to begin planning a few years before retirement age. Actively planning for leisure and recreation leads to more enjoyable retirement years.

Factors Affecting Retirement Life Style

Factors affecting life style—career choice and income—were discussed in Chapter 1. Two additional factors are involved in determining a person's life style during retirement years. One is age at retirement, and the other is financial assets accumulated.

Age at Retirement. Many firms and institutions allow their employees to take early retirement, which gives a person more leisure and recreation time. From a financial planning viewpoint, though, early retirement has certain disadvantages. First, with early retirement, there are more retirement years. Therefore, benefits from social security and pensions are lower for those who retire early. Second, there are fewer working years, which means that there is less time to save for retirement. These two factors combine to make it more difficult financially to retire early. To maintain a suitable life style with early retirement, you need to save relatively more during your working years.

Financial Assets Accumulated. Retirement life style is affected by the financial assets you have accumulated during your working years. Higher levels of accumulated financial assets allow a better life style. A systematic savings plan combined with a good investment strategy will provide the financial assets needed to thoroughly enjoy your retirement years.

Determining Retirement Income Needs

For most people, living expenses are reduced after retirement. As we have mentioned, retirement income needs generally are about 60 to 70 percent of income earned just prior to retiring. If a family's income before retirement is $3,000 per month, then the family will need about $1,800 to $2,100 per month in retirement income.

If living expenses were not constantly rising because of inflation, it would be relatively easy to calculate retirement income needs. However, such is not the case. Inflation places unrelenting upward pressures on costs and living expenses. As mentioned earlier in the chapter, $2,100 per month today would equate to $14,784 per month 40 years from today, assuming a 5 percent annual inflation rate. Minor changes in assumptions about inflation rates can dramatically change retirement income needs. Nobody can forecast what inflation rates are going to do far into the future.

Therefore, it becomes very difficult to determine retirement income needs 15 or 20 or 30 years from now.

One approach to determining retirement needs is to assume that living expenses will not change over time. With this approach, the couple that lives on $3,000 per month now will need between $1,800 and $2,100 per month when they retire 40 years from now. It is important to note that your estimation of retirement needs should be revised fairly often, about once every other year, to adjust for rising salaries and the impact of inflation. Otherwise, your assumption can lead to a gross understatement of retirement needs. With the new retirement income estimates, you would also need to evaluate your plans for financing this income. This requires evaluation of the current social security and pension benefits as well as an examination of investment strategies and level of annual funding related to retirement planning. An example will be shown later in this chapter.

Sources of Income

Retirement income can come from a variety of sources. Social security and employer pension plans provide retirement income for a significant number of retirees. Many people plan for their retirement by setting up retirement-oriented savings and investment plans. One of the most popular plans for accumulating retirement funds is an individual retirement plan. Another investment plan that provides retirement income is annuities, which were briefly mentioned in Chapter 14. Social security, employer pension plans, individual retirement plans, and annuities will be discussed in greater detail in the following sections.

Spot Quiz • Introduction to Retirement Planning

1. Retirement savings are generated by postponing current consumption.
                                        T _____   F _____

2. Early retirement results in lower retirement benefits.
                                        T _____   F _____

3. Retirement income needs could be estimated easily if there were no inflation.   T _____   F _____

(Answers on page 657)

Social security

Social security is a social welfare program administered by the federal government that provides four types of benefits: Medicare health insurance, disability insurance, survivors' benefits, and retirement benefits. Medicare and disability benefits were covered in Chapter 13, Health Insurance. Survivors' benefits were covered in Chapter 14, Life Insurance. Retirement benefits provided by social security are covered in this section.

How the Social Security System Works

The social security system has been in effect since 1935. Initially, it covered only half the workers in the United States. However, in recent years the program has expanded and now covers nine out of ten workers. The system is designed to meet only a portion of the retirement income needs of retirees. Recipients of social security retirement benefits are expected to have planned for other sources of income to supplement these benefits.

Funding of social security is governed by the **Federal Insurance Contributions Act (FICA)**. Paycheck withholdings for FICA are social security taxes paid by the employee. Social security is funded by equal contributions from employers and employees. The current social security tax rate is shown in Table 20.1. The rate applies only to wages up to a specified limit. Wages in excess of the limit are not subject to social security taxes. Maximum taxable wages in recent years were as follows:

1978	$17,700
1979	22,900
1980	25,900
1981	29,700
1982	32,400
1983	35,700
1984	37,800
1985	39,600
1986	42,000
1987	43,800
1988	45,000

Maximum taxable wages in future years will rise automatically each year to reflect the average earnings increases. It is estimated that maximum taxable wages will increase to $52,000 by 1993.

With increases in both the tax rates and the maximum taxable wages, social security taxes have increased sharply in recent years. In 1982, for example, maximum taxes were .0620 × $32,400 = $2,008.80. By 1987, maximum taxes had risen to .0715 × $43,800 = $3,131.70. By 1993, they are

Table 20.1 Social Security Tax Rates*

1974	5.85%	1985	7.05%
1975	5.85	1986	7.15
1976	5.85	1987	7.15
1977	5.85	1988	7.15
1978	6.05	1989	7.15
1979	6.13	1990	7.65
1980	6.13	1991	7.65
1981	6.65	1992	7.65
1982	6.70	1993	7.65
1983	6.70	1994	7.65
1984	6.70		

*Tax rate schedule applicable to both employers and employees. Self-employed people follow a different tax rate schedule

expected to be .0765 × $52,000 = $3,978. These dollar amounts need to be doubled to take into consideration the matching contributions paid by employers on behalf of their employees.

Many people try to equate social security with an insurance program, but social security is not funded on the same basis as insurance benefits. Rather, one generation of workers provides retirement benefits to the previous generation and will be provided with benefits by the next generation.

A question that arises frequently is whether those who have higher incomes, and thus pay maximum taxes, ever get back all of their contributions. The answer is no. The social security system is a welfare system. Thus, benefits as a proportion of income are higher for those with relatively low incomes and lower for those with relatively high incomes.

The social security system is a hotly debated subject. Some people assert that benefits from social security should be expanded to include a wide variety of social welfare programs. Others say that the system should be scaled back. Expanding the program would create additional funding needs that would have to be met by further increasing social security taxes. The average taxpayer may be unwilling to pay higher taxes. On the other hand, the same taxpayer may be counting on receiving the present level of benefits, making it politically undesirable to reduce benefits. Thus, it appears that at least for the foreseeable future, the present funding and benefit features of social security will not change. (See ''Keeping Track of Social Security Records'' on page 629.)

Keeping Track of Social Security Records

Remember those little computer cards that said "Do not fold, staple, spindle, bend, or mutilate"? The reason you weren't supposed to do all of that is because Uncle Sam had a specially designed machine that did it all for you. (Some students tell me that retired machines are now housed in the bursar's office on campus.) Anyway, because of folding, spindling, mutilating, and various electronic glitches, sometimes your social security records are not properly posted to your account. There is also the matter of volume: at any one time, the Social Security Administration will be dealing with anywhere from 10 to 15 million *incorrect* social security numbers or names. This is another reason that your earnings are not always correctly credited to your account.

What should you do to find out if your earnings are correctly recorded? The Social Security Administration will give you a statement showing the earnings credited to your account. The statement shows annual earnings for the last three years and lumps together the earnings for years prior to the last three. By looking at this statement, you can tell whether your account had been credited with the correct earnings for the past three years. Contact your nearest Social Security Administration office not only to request this earnings statement but also to correct any mistakes. Because only the last three years of earnings are reported separately, you should request this statement every three years.

Who Is Covered by Social Security

All workers and all self-employed people in the United States, with a few exceptions, are covered by social security. The exceptions are

1. Federal civil employees.
2. State and local employees who vote as a group not to join.
3. Ministers, clergy, priests, and others who are opposed to social security on religious grounds.

Federal employees have their own retirement system. Most state and local employees do choose to join social security, although some exceptions, such as state employees in Illinois, do exist. As mentioned previously, nine out of ten workers in the United States are covered by social security.

Qualifying for Benefits

A worker who is eligible for retirement benefits can start receiving benefits at age 62 or 65. The following people related to a retired worker who receives benefits are also eligible to receive benefits:

1. Unmarried children under 18.
2. Unmarried children over 18 who were disabled before age 22 and are still disabled.
3. A spouse 62 years old or older.
4. A spouse under 62 years old who is caring for a child under 16 who is receiving benefits.

As mentioned in Chapter 14, surviving spouses are eligible for benefits at age 60 or older. For the Cesari case mentioned in Chapter 14, Linda Cesari would be eligible for retirement benefits related to her job as well as those she would receive because she is Joe's widow. Social security will pay her the higher of the two monthly benefits. In other words, she will not receive social security benefits both as a worker and as a widow.

In order to qualify for social security benefits, a worker must accumulate **quarters of coverage**. For 1987, each $460 of covered annual earnings produced one quarter of coverage. The dollar amount of covered earnings needed for one quarter of coverage increases each year. Wages and self-employment income are included in covered earnings. Dividends, interest income, rents, capital gains, and income from trusts are excluded from covered earnings. A person cannot earn more than four quarters of coverage each year. Thus, if you had at least $460 \times 4 = $1,840 covered earnings in 1987, you would have earned four quarters of coverage. Coverage is accumulated as earnings are received. Thus, in 1987, a person earning, say, $1,900 per month would have received credit for four quarters of coverage at the end of January.

In general, you are fully covered and eligible for social security benefits if you have accumulated at least 40 quarters of coverage (there are certain exceptions to this general rule). The Social Security Administration produces many pamphlets that explain retirement benefits and qualification requirements.[2]

Applying for Benefits.   An eligible person does not automatically start receiving social security benefits. You must apply for benefits at the nearest Social Security Administration office at least two months before your planned retirement date. The application can be made in person or over the telephone. The social security office will ask for the following documents:

1. A social security card or number.
2. Proof of date of birth.
3. W-2 (Wage and Tax Statement) forms or self-employment tax return forms for the previous two years.

---

2. A sample of these pamphlets includes *Your Social Security, Thinking About Retiring? Estimating Your Social Security Retirement Check, Social Security Information for Young Families,* and *Your Social Security Rights and Responsibilities.*

A spouse applying for benefits will need to submit similar documents. Eligible children need to submit only items 1 and 2. In some situations, additional documents may be required. Once the Social Security Administration has verified the eligibility of the applicant, it will start issuing monthly benefit checks.

Amount of Benefits. The amount of benefits a retiree receives depends on the person's age at retirement and the amount of covered earnings during the person's working years. Full retirement benefits are paid at age 65. Reduced benefits are paid for early retirement at age 62. The percentages of benefits for early retirement are shown in Table 20.2. The table also shows that benefits increase if late retirement is chosen.

Benefits are also affected by a person's covered earnings. Higher earnings result in higher benefits. Covered earnings in past working years are averaged to determine the amount of benefits. There is no fixed minimum level of benefits. For 1987, the maximum monthly benefits for a worker retiring at age 65 were $789. The maximum benefits for eligible dependents of a deceased worker could be as much as $1,807 per month for 1987. Social security benefit checks increase automatically to keep up with inflation. Benefits are increased if the cost of living has increased by 3 percent or more in the past year.

Factors That Affect Benefits

A variety of factors can result in a reduction in benefits. The major cause for reduced benefits is that the worker continues to work after retirement.

Table 20.2 Age and Benefit Amounts*

Age	Percent	Age	Percent
62	80	68	109
63	87	69	112
64	93	70	115
65	100	71	118
66	103	72	121
67	106		

*Benefits are stated as a percent of benefits a person would receive if he or she retired at age 65.

Annual Limits on Earnings. Social security benefits are meant to replace earnings lost because of disability, death, or retirement. Benefits therefore are reduced or eliminated when a retired person works for wages. As mentioned previously, dividends, interest income, pensions, and so on are not considered earnings for social security purposes. Wages and self-employment income are considered wages. If a retiree's wages exceed a certain limit, then benefits are reduced by $1 for every $2 of earnings above the limit. The limits are increased every year. For 1987, the limits were $6,000 for workers under age 65 and $8,160 for workers over age 65. No limits apply to workers over age 70. Thus, if a 64-year-old retiree earned $12,000 from a job, he or she would have lost ($12,000 − $6,000)/2 = $3,000 in retirement benefits for 1987.

If a covered worker is affected by the annual income limit rule, and if the worker's family is also receiving benefits, then the family benefits will also be reduced. Starting in 1990, $1 in benefits will be withheld for each $3 in earnings above the limit for people 65 and over.

Taxation of Benefits. In 1984, the federal government began taxing social security benefits under certain conditions. You are required to pay taxes on a portion of your social security benefits if the benefits exceed the following base amounts: $25,000 if you are a single taxpayer; $32,000 if you are married and file a joint return; $0 if you are married, live with your spouse at any time during the year, and file a separate return. The amount of benefits subject to taxes is the smaller of half of your benefits or half of your adjusted gross income plus tax-exempt interest plus half of your social security benefits minus the base amount mentioned above.

Other Factors. A retired worker's spouse will lose any benefits if he or she is divorced. However, if the marriage lasted more than 10 years, benefits will continue to be paid to the divorced spouse. Benefits are interrupted if a person visits certain countries, such as Cuba or Vietnam. However, the retiree receives all back checks once he or she leaves that country.

Spot Quiz • Social Security

1. The social security system provides a pension to all covered retired workers.   T _____ F _____

2. Only covered workers are eligible for social security retirement benefits.
                                                                T _____ F _____

3. The amount of benefits received is not dependent solely on the worker's earnings.   T _____ F _____

(Answers on page 657)

Employer pension plans

Many employers offer retirement income plans to their workers. These plans are designed to provide workers with a pension to supplement social security benefits. **Pensions** are regular, periodic payments that employers pay to their qualifying retired workers. Pension funds differ in terms of eligibility requirements, how they are financed, and how retirement benefits are paid. These topics are covered in this section.

Eligibility

Employees generally must fulfill eligibility requirements before joining their employer's pension plans. That is, for a variety of reasons, not every employee can join a pension plan at work. Some employers view pension plans as a special benefit for employees. Thus, only selected employees are allowed to join the pension plan. Many employers believe that new employees may not remain on the job very long. Therefore, often an employee must wait at least one year before becoming eligible to join his or her employer's pension plan. Some employers require that workers earn at least a certain minimum wage to qualify for a pension plan. Others require that only workers over a certain age (usually 25 years) can join. Many of these eligibility requirements are designed to keep out of the pension plan those workers who might leave the firm after a short time. (See "Job Changes Kill Pension Benefits" on page 634.)

Funding

By agreeing to pay a worker a pension, an employer creates a liability for itself. The liability is that at some future point in time, the worker will no longer be working but will have to be paid a pension. Funding refers to the way in which the firm plans to meet its future pension liabilities. One way to fund these liabilities is on a "pay-as-you-go" basis. Under this method, the firm pays its retired workers from its current operating budget. This method of funding pension liabilities is not desirable from the workers' viewpoint. If the firm goes bankrupt, it will not be able to pay pensions. Pay-as-you-go pension plans are called **unfunded pension plans**. Social

Job Changes Kill Pension Benefits

Many people try to get ahead by changing jobs frequently. It is not unusual for "fast-track" managers to change jobs every two or three years. New jobs bring new assignments, new challenges, and, perhaps more importantly, higher salaries than if you had stayed with the old job. Sounds like a good deal, you say. Generally, yes, but job hopping does have a negative side effect. It hits you hard in your pension benefits.

Let's consider a simple example. You get 1 percent retirement credit for each year that you work for a company. The percentage applies to your highest annual salary on the job. You stay on the job for 40 years, and the last year you earn $100,000, which is your highest annual salary at the company. Since you accumulate 1 percent for each year of service and you worked 40 years, you have accumulated a retirement credit of 40 percent. Thus, at retirement you receive $100,000 × 0.40 = $40,000 in annual pension.

Let's consider a situation in which you change jobs every 10 years and receive a final year's salary of $130,000. Your earnings and pension benefits might be as follows:

	Worked	Percent Credit	High Salary	Pension
Job 1	10 years	10	$ 20,000	$ 2,000
Job 2	10 years	10	40,000	4,000
Job 3	10 years	10	80,000	8,000
Job 4	10 years	10	130,000	13,000
			Total Pension:	$27,000

Instead of receiving a pension of $40,000, you end up with a pension of $27,000. One way of capturing this lost pension is to negotiate at each new job an additional fringe benefit that adjusts for the loss of the pension benefits.

security, as well as many state and local government retirement plans, are unfunded.

A firm can also estimate its future pension liabilities and then make current payments to these future liabilities. A **funded pension plan** is one in which future pensions earned in the current year are funded currently. In a **fully funded plan**, the firm has funded the plan for every worker for each year of his or her employment. In other words, the firm has no future pension liabilities. Funding a pension plan requires a firm to estimate the mortality rate for its workers, labor turnover, covered wages, and rates

of return on its invested assets. A safe pension fund is based on accurate estimates of these factors. From the workers' viewpoint, a funded plan is much more desirable than an unfunded plan.

Pension Contributions

Pension funds are financed by contributions from either the employer or both the employer and the employee. A **noncontributory plan** is one to which the employee does not make any contributions. Such a plan is funded only by payments made by the employer. The contributions are tax-deductible for the employer but are not taxed to the employee until he or she begins to receive benefits. Most corporate pension plans are noncontributory.

A **contributory plan** is one to which both the employer and the employee make periodic contributions. Employees generally contribute between 2 and 20 percent of their earnings to such a plan. Employers usually contribute a matching or a higher amount to the fund. Some corporate and most government pension plans are of the contributory type.

Vesting

A worker is entitled to all pension plan contributions that he or she has made. If a worker decides to leave the present job, he or she can withdraw all pension contributions he or she has made. **Vesting** is the gaining of rights by the worker to the pension contributions made by an employer on the worker's behalf. Thus, a vested worker has the rights to all contributions made to a pension plan on his or her behalf. A nonvested worker has rights only to his or her contributions to a pension plan. Employers have different policies regarding vesting. Some employers vest their employees immediately. Some do not allow any vesting for the first five years. Others provide for a gradual vesting over a period of five to fifteen years. Minimum vesting requirements are established by law and are explained later in this section.

Employers also follow different policies with regard to the vested funds of a worker who no longer works for the employer. Some employers permit their former employees to withdraw their vested funds in cash. Others do not allow withdrawal of vested funds. Rather, they provide retirement benefits, generally starting at age 65, that are based on the dollar amount of the ex-worker's vested funds.

Retirement Age

Most pension plans specify the age at which a person can retire and start receiving a pension. Usually, this retirement age is 65. Some plans allow workers to retire early and receive lower benefits. Some pension plans base

their retirement on the number of years of service rather than on the age of the worker. For example, police departments often allow their workers to retire after 20 or 30 years of service, even if the workers are not 65. With increases in average life expectancy, there is some movement toward letting workers stay on the job longer and delay retirement until age 68 or 70. A decision to retire early should be made only after a complete analysis of your financial situation at retirement time. (See "Early Retirement = More Leisure Time?" below.)

Retirement Benefits

Pension plans specify the manner in which retirement benefits will be computed and paid. A **defined-contribution plan** specifies the minimum contribution that an employer and an employee would have to make annually. These contributions are invested and managed by a pension fund manager. At retirement, the worker is paid a pension that is based on the size of the accumulated pension funds. A well-managed pension fund will provide workers with a higher pension than one that has not been properly managed. Pensions from a defined-contribution plan depend not only on the level of the periodic contributions by the employer and the employee but also on how well the funds have been managed.

Early Retirement = More Leisure Time?

You bet. More and more people are retiring early nowadays. The normal retirement age is considered to be 65 years. However, about three out of every five workers quit their jobs before age 65. Why? For one thing, retirement benefits are much better now than they used to be. Consider, for example, social security. If you retire at age 62, you will receive 20 percent less in benefits than if you retire at age 65. At first this looks like a bad deal until you figure out that in three years you will receive 3 X 80 percent = 240 percent of your benefits at age 65. Now, if you wait until age 65, you will get 100 percent of your benefits, but it will take 240%/20% = 12 years to recover what you would lose by retiring at age 62.

Another reason given by many retirees is that early retirement allows them to enjoy life. Russell H. Hubbard, formerly an executive at General Electric, states, "My days are so full of interesting things to do, I don't know how I ever had time to work." A third reason is that many corporations continue to provide medical benefits to their retirees even if they retire early. Early retirement does equal more leisure time. Those over age 50 who are planning retirement should consider joining the American Association of Retired Persons, 1909 K Street NW, Washington, DC 20049. For a $5 annual membership fee, you will receive retirement brochures and tips.

A **defined-benefit plan** specifies a method for computing retirement benefits and guarantees the worker a certain pension. Most defined-benefit plans are based on both wages and number of years of service. For example, a plan might pay 2 percent of the last five years' average salary for every year of service. Say that a person has earned, on the average, $24,000 every year for the last five years. She has worked at the firm for 30 years. Her annual pension would be .02 × $24,000 × 30 = $14,400.

Some defined-benefit plans pay benefits based only on income or numbers of years of service. Still other plans pay a fixed dollar amount of benefits each month provided the retiree has worked for the employer for a minimum number of years. A few plans tie their benefits to social security benefits. Such plans might guarantee that pension and social security benefits combined will equal a certain percentage of the person's average salary before retirement. These plans are not desirable because higher social security benefits reduce the amount of pension benefits provided by the employer.

A few pension plans pay out benefits in lump sums. Most, however, prefer to pay monthly pension benefits. These periodic benefits are paid from the accumulated pension assets. A few pension plans simply use the money in a particular worker's account to buy that worker an insurance annuity. Whatever the method used to compute retirement benefits, a good pension plan will pay enough pension so that the retiree can live comfortably on the pension and social security benefits combined.

Employee Retirement Income Security Act

Until 1974, no federal laws regulated the management of pension funds. Some state laws existed, but they did not provide the average worker with a great deal of protection. As a result, workers had to rely on the fairness of their employers and their labor unions to protect their pension funds and provide them with a pension on retirement. Such reliance was often not justified. Employers occasionally found ways of denying pensions to retiring workers or pension funds were mismanaged, thereby earning very low returns and providing very small pensions. The **Employee Retirement Income Security Act (ERISA)** was passed in 1974 to curb abuses and bad business practices related to pension funds.

ERISA provides some safeguards against mismanagement of pension funds. For example, fund managers cannot sell their personal property to the funds they manage. Pension fund investments in the employing firm cannot exceed a specified maximum. Pension funds must file annual reports with the Secretary of Labor. ERISA also established the **Public Pension Benefit Guarantee Corporation (PPBGC).** PPBGC is financed by an annual contribution of $1 per worker by employers. PPBGC pays covered workers up to $750 per month in pension benefits if a covered pension benefits fund cannot meet its obligations.

The major benefit of ERISA is its vesting and funding requirements. The act specifies a variety of vesting options, and employers must choose one of these methods for their employees. One method requires full vesting after 10 years of work. Another requires 25 percent vesting after 5 years of work, 50 percent after 10 years, and full vesting after 15 years. A third vesting method is based on a combination of age and number of years worked. These vesting procedures are designed to safeguard workers' rights to their pension funds.

ERISA imposes minimum funding standards on employers. This assures workers that some funds will be available for pensions in case their employers go bankrupt. Finally, ERISA specifies that full-time workers over age 25 become eligible to join their employers' pension plan after a maximum wait of one year. This requirement prevents employers from excluding their permanent employees from pension plans for an unduly long time. Overall, ERISA provides workers with some measure of security regarding their pension funds.

Spot Quiz • Employer Pension Plans

1. Pay-as-you-go plans, because they pay pensions as they come due, are safer than funded plans.   T _____ F _____

2. A noncontributory plan may not be better than a contributory plan.
                                   T _____ F _____

3. A defined-contribution plan does not guarantee a fixed pension.
                                   T _____ F _____

(Answers on page 657)

Annuities

An **annuity** is a series of periodic payments beginning on a specified date and ending on a specified date or on the death of one or more beneficiaries. Annuities provide retirement income. They are based on principles of risk transfer and therefore are sold by insurance companies. Some basics of annuities were covered briefly in Chapter 14, Life Insurance. How annuities work, the types of annuities, and how they are priced are discussed in this section.

How Annuities Work

Life insurance is meant to cover the risk of dying prematurely. Annuities, on the other hand, are designed to cover the risk of living too long. From strictly a risk and insurance viewpoint, a person who lives beyond his or her life expectancy can be said to have lived too long. Dying prematurely creates financial hardships for the person's dependents. Living too long creates financial hardships for the person because he or she may not have accumulated enough retirement funds to cover the situation of living too long. A well-designed annuity plan transfers the risk of living too long to the insurer who provided the annuity.

Two alternatives are explained here to illustrate how annuities work. In the first alternative, we assume that a traditional investment is made. The second alternative is an annuity. Let's assume that Jane Wallace has $100,000 in cash. Her life expectancy is three years; however, she may die before the three years are over or she may live more than three years. She can earn a 12 percent rate of return on her assets by investing the $100,000 in a money market certificate. Because she does not know for sure how long she will live, she decides not to touch the $100,000 principal. Therefore, she lives on the $100,000 × .12 = $12,000 annual income from investing the $100,000. This approach guarantees her a retirement income for as long as she lives because her principal is never spent. The disadvantage of this method for ensuring retirement income is that she does not receive as much in retirement income as she could with an annuity.

Her second alternative is to buy an annuity with the $100,000. To simplify the example, we assume that an insurance company can provide Jane with a 12 percent return on her $100,000 as well. Furthermore, we ignore the administrative costs and profits of the life insurance company. The life insurance company, or insurer, will provide Jane with a rate of return that is based on probability and the law of large numbers, concepts discussed in Chapter 11. The insurer is insuring many people in the same life situation as Jane. Some will die prematurely, and some will live longer than expected. But on the average, they will live three years. Therefore, the insurer can base the size of the annuity on Jane's life expectancy of three years.

The insurer will be able to provide Jane with annual annuity payments of $37,174.[3] The average person in Jane's situation will live three years. Therefore, this average person will receive three annual payments. Each payment will be made at the beginning of the contract year. An example is shown in Table 20.3. At the beginning of contract year 1, Jane pays the insurer $100,000. The insurer pays her $37,174 as the first annuity payment immediately. The balance of $62,826 is invested for one year at 12

---

3. Present value factors of the type shown in Table 14.2 can be used to calculate the amount of an annuity.

Table 20.3 How an Annuity Works*

Period	Beginning of Period Balance	Payment	Balance	Return	End of Period Balance
1	$100,000	$37,174	$62,826	$7,539	$70,365
2	70,365	37,174	33,191	3,983	37,174
3	37,174	37,174	0	0	0

*Principal amount = $100,000; rate of return = 12% on the balance amount; payment made at beginning of period; present value factor = 2.69. $100,000 / 2.69 = $37,174.

percent. First year interest income is $62,826 × .12 = $7,539, and the year-end balance is $62,826 + $7,539 = $70,365.

At the beginning of year 2, the insurer pays Jane the second annuity payment of $37,174. The insurer now has $70,365 − $37,174 = $33,191. This amount invested at 12 percent yields $33,191 × .12 = $3,983 in income. The second year-end balance is $33,191 + $3,983 = $37,174. The insurer pays Jane $37,174 at the beginning of year 3, leaving a balance of zero dollars. From an insurance viewpoint, some annuitants in Jane's age group will live longer than three years and will receive more than three payments. Others will live less than three years and will receive fewer than three payments. On the average, though, the insurer will pay out three annuity payments to each annuitant.

As the example shows, an annuity will provide a person with retirement income that is higher than income earned by buying a safe investment. The disadvantage of an annuity generally is that no assets will be left for the person's estate. For example, if Jane lives off the income of the $100,000 money market investment, her estate will receive $100,000 on her death. However, with the annuity just explained, her estate will receive nothing. This is a decision that each person must make to suit his or her personal needs for retirement income and desires for leaving an estate.

Types of Annuities

Annuities can be classified by the methods used to distribute the annuity benefits and by the methods used by the insurer to invest the principal sums on behalf of the annuitants.

Classification by Method of Benefit Distribution. The factors involved in this classification method are the beneficiaries, the amount of

the annuity, and the length of time over which the benefits are to be paid. The **straight life annuity** is the type explained in Table 20.3. The **refund annuity** guarantees minimum total benefits, whereas the **certain period annuity** guarantees a minimum benefit period. A **joint and survivorship annuity** provides payments throughout the entire lives of two persons. If one of the two persons dies, benefits continue to be paid to the surviving person. However, typically, the payments to the surviving person are less than those made to both together. The reduction in payments ranges from 25 to 50 percent. The reduction feature allows insurers to offer joint and survivorship annuities at a somewhat lower cost. The annuities mentioned thus far were also discussed in Chapter 14.

The **annuity certain** does not involve any life contingencies. Instead, the insurer guarantees payments for a fixed time period. Benefits for this time period are paid to either the insured person or to the insured person's beneficiaries. The annuity stops when the time period is up. This annuity is useful if you need income only for a specified time period. For example, an annuity of this type may provide benefits to a surviving spouse for a few years until he or she becomes eligible for retirement income from another source, such as social security.

The straight life annuity provides the highest income for a given sum of money. In other words, straight life is the cheapest annuity for providing a given sum of retirement income. This annuity, however, is not popular because it does not provide for payments to beneficiaries. The refund and certain period annuities hold the potential for providing some benefits to survivors. However, they are more expensive than the straight life annuity. This is also the case with the joint and survivorship annuity. If you do not plan to leave an estate, then the straight life annuity is considered best. The desirability of other annuities depends on the purchaser's need to provide survivors with some benefits.

Classification by Investment Objectives. The second classification scheme for annuities is related to how the insurer invests the principal sums on behalf of the annuitants. Where these funds are invested affects the returns earned and therefore the dollar amount of benefits paid to annuitants.

Fixed Annuities. In a **fixed annuity**, the dollar amount of periodic benefits remains fixed. The insurer invests the principal sums received in very safe bonds and mortgages. The interest rate earned on these investments is known and fixed. Therefore, based on life expectancy, the insurer can guarantee the annuitant a fixed, periodic sum of money. The example for Jane Wallace is a fixed annuity. The principal advantage of a fixed annuity is that the retiree is assured of a fixed sum of money every month, every quarter, or every year. The major disadvantage is that fixed annuities do not provide protection against the effects of inflation. Thus, for Jane Wallace, the annual payment remains fixed at $37,174 even if her living expenses increase every year.

Variable Annuities.   In a **variable annuity**, the dollar amount of the period benefit varies from payment to payment. Variable annuities are meant to provide the annuitant with some protection against inflation. The principal sum or the premium payments made to buy the annuity are invested in common stocks rather than bonds and mortgages. Historically, common stocks prices have tended to increase steadily. A simple example will illustrate how a variable annuity works.

Let's assume that Jane Wallace, from our previous example, uses her $100,000 to buy a variable annuity instead of a fixed straight life annuity. Based on our earlier assumptions, a fixed straight life annuity would pay her $37,174 annually. For the variable annuity, the insurer invests the annuity payments in a portfolio of common stocks. A small portion of this portfolio is called an **accumulation unit**. Say that each unit has a market value of $10.[4] Jane's annuity payment is $37,174, which is the equivalent of 3,717.4 units. All of her annuity payments will be equal to the market value of the 3,717.4 units. The first payment is 3,717.4 × $10 = $37,174. At the beginning of year 2, the units have a market value of $11 each. Jane's second annuity benefit will be for 3,717.4 × $11 = $40,891.4. At the beginning of the third year, the units have a value of $11.60 each, and Jane receives 3,717.4 × $11.60 = $43,121.84.

As the example illustrates, the principal advantage of a variable annuity is that benefits can be expected to increase over time. The major disadvantage is that there is no guarantee that unit prices will keep rising or that some minimum amount of benefit will be paid. For example, if the unit value were to decline to $8 each by the beginning of year 2, Jane would receive only 3,717.4 × $8 = $29,739.20. Despite this disadvantage, many retirees choose variable annuities for retirement income.

One strategy for retirement planning is to invest half of the principal sum in a fixed annuity and the other half in a variable annuity. The fixed annuity provides for a minimum level of benefits, and the variable annuity provides some protection against increasing living expenses.

Cost of Annuities

Annuity costs depend on a variety of factors. One is the age of the annuitant at the time the annuity starts. Older persons have lower life expectancies. For a given level of benefits, annuities are cheaper when payments begin later in life. Annuity costs also depend on the size of the monthly benefits desired. Other things being the same, an annuity with larger benefits will be more expensive. As mentioned previously, the type of annuity makes a cost difference as well. A straight life annuity will be cheaper than other types of annuities. Another influencing factor is the sex of the

---

4. Each accumulation unit can be thought of as a share of a mutual fund, and its value is equivalent to the net asset value of a mutual fund share.

annuitant. Women have longer life expectancies than men. Other things being the same, an annuity for a woman will be more expensive than one for a man.[5] Finally, annuity costs will be lower with relatively well managed insurance companies. Chapter 11 contains a discussion on selecting an insurance company.

Spot Quiz • Annuities

1. Annuities provide protection against outliving your retirement assets.

   T _____ F _____

2. A refund annuity guarantees an estate if premature death occurs.

   T _____ F _____

3. A variable annuity provides steadily increasing periodic benefits.

   T _____ F _____

(Answers on page 657)

INDIVIDUAL RETIREMENT PLANS

Besides social security and corporate retirement plans, individuals can set up a variety of other retirement plans for themselves. The principal ones are the Keogh plan, the individual retirement account, and a tax-deferred savings plan.

Keogh Plan

A **Keogh retirement plan** is limited to self-employed individuals. With a defined-contribution plan, any self-employed person, whether a plumber or a doctor, can place up to $30,000 annually in a retirement account. However, the amount cannot exceed 25 percent of the person's income. That is, self-employed persons earning less than $120,000 annually can place up to 25 percent of their income in a Keogh retirement plan. Those earning $120,000 or more annually can place up to $30,000 in a Keogh plan.

---

5. By the same token, life insurance premiums for women are lower than for men of the same age.

The defined-benefit Keogh plan is more complex and requires that you contribute an amount that is needed to fund the defined benefits, based on your life expectancy. A ceiling is placed on the maximum benefits that can be paid.

The individual's Keogh plan has to be administered by a trustee. A bank, insurance company, brokerage house, mutual fund, or other institution dealing with money management can act as trustee. The individual places the money in the Keogh account, where it is invested and earns tax-free returns until the individual retires. Keogh contributions are tax-free also. For example, a self-employed person earning $40,000 this year can contribute up to $40,000 × .25 = $10,000 to a Keogh plan. If this person makes the maximum contribution of $10,000, he or she would have a current-year taxable income of $40,000 − $10,000 = $30,000. Neither this $10,000 nor any returns earned on it are taxable until the contributor retires and starts drawing benefits.

A person cannot withdraw any funds from a Keogh plan until age 59½ years without paying a penalty. If a Keogh contributor dies, his or her estate can withdraw the money from the plan without paying a penalty. The person must start withdrawing funds from a Keogh plan by age 70½ years. All withdrawals of principal, interest, dividends, and profits from a Keogh plan are taxable as ordinary income during the year that the funds were withdrawn. Keogh funds can be transferred from one trustee to another. Each year, a person can either make the current payment into an existing Keogh plan or into a newly opened plan with a new trustee.

Individual Retirement Account

The 1981 tax law permits all workers, whether self-employed or working for someone else, whether covered by a pension plan or not, to open an **individual retirement account (IRA)**. As the name implies, an IRA is a retirement plan that an individual establishes for himself or herself. Under current regulations, a worker can contribute up to $2,000 each year to an IRA as long as the contribution is not in excess of 100 percent of wages earned. A worker can also open an IRA for a nonworking spouse, provided that no more than $2,250 is contributed to both IRAs combined. If both spouses are working, each can contribute up to $2,000 to an IRA.

The 1986 Tax Reform Act has changed the requirements for tax deductibility of IRA contributions. Prior to 1987, all IRA contributions were fully tax-deductible. However, starting with 1987, the tax deductibility of IRA contributions is assured only if you are not covered by a retirement plan at work. If you are covered by a retirement plan at work, then your IRA contribution will be tax-deductible only if you meet the following adjusted gross income (AGI) limits:

1. If you are single and your AGI is less than $25,000, your IRA contribution is fully tax-deductible. For every $50 increase in AGI above

$25,000, the amount of tax-deductible contribution that you can make decreases by $10. That is, an AGI of $26,000 is $1,000 over $25,000, and you lose ($1,000/$50) × $10 = $200 in tax deductible IRA contributions. Only $2,000 − $200 = $1,800 will be tax-deductible. For AGIs above $35,000, none of the IRA contribution is tax-deductible.

2. If you are married, filing jointly, and your AGI is less than $40,000, your IRA contribution is fully tax-deductible. For AGI above $50,000, the tax deductibility is lost. For AGI amounts between $40,000 and $50,000, the deductibility declines by $10 for every $50 increase in AGI.

IRAs are governed by the same general rules as Keogh plans. Money from IRAs cannot be withdrawn before age 59½ years without paying a penalty. Withdrawals from IRA accounts on retirement, with the exception of after-tax contributions, are taxable at normal income tax rates. Custodial or trustee IRA accounts can be opened with an institution that is involved with money management. Each year's IRA contribution can be made to an existing account or to a newly opened account. Funds can be easily transferred from one IRA custodian to another.

Tax-Deferred Savings Plans

The tax law changes of 1978 created a new tax-deferred plan for workers. The plan, often called a **salary-reduction plan (SRP)** or a **401(K)** plan, allows a worker to place a certain portion of his or her salary in investment accounts selected by the company. Only those workers whose employers offer SRPs are eligible to participate. The employer generally limits the maximum amount that can be contributed to an SRP—usually around 10 percent. SRPs allow workers to defer taxes on their SRP contributions and earnings until the funds are withdrawn.

IRAs and SRPs are similar in that both provide tax deferral on contributions and earnings. One difference is that, whereas IRA contributions can be invested in any eligible investment, SRP contributions can be invested only in employer-selected investments.

SRPs offer certain distinct advantages over IRAs. With an SRP, funds can be withdrawn from the plan when the worker leaves the employer, becomes disabled, or suffers a financial hardship. A lump sum SRP withdrawal after age 59½ is given more favorable tax treatment than one from an IRA. A worker can borrow from an SRP but not from an IRA. In summary, an SRP is worth exploring if your employer offers it.

Investing Keogh/IRA Funds

Keogh and IRA accounts can be opened with a financial institution or a brokerage house. Most financial planners suggest that Keogh/IRA funds be invested in income-producing investments rather than in investments

that emphasize capital gains. The main reason is that these plans do not recognize capital gains. All incomes are taxed at normal income tax rates. For this reason, tax-exempt bonds should not be purchased. Collectibles such as precious gems, art, and coins are not eligible for purchase in Keogh/IRA plans. Debt financing cannot be used with these plans, thus excluding margin accounts. Commodities futures are not eligible for these plans either.

Common stocks, mutual funds, money market funds, bonds, certificates of deposit, limited real estate partnerships, and a few other investments are eligible for Keogh/IRA plans. The primary focus for investing Keogh/IRA funds should be on the safety of the principal. Therefore, certificates of deposit are very desirable investments for Keogh/IRA plans. Many financial institutions pay good rates on their CDs. Usually, they charge a small fee of $5 to $10 for setting up a Keogh/IRA plan.

No-load mutual funds are also desirable for Keogh/IRA plans. Perhaps the best ones are the mutual fund "families." A **family mutual fund** allows the saver to move funds among a variety of mutual funds, including money market, income, and common stock. Charges for setting up a Keogh/IRA plan with a mutual fund are very low, about $5 to $10. However, be careful not to open an account with a load mutual fund.

Self-Directed Plans

Many institutions where Keogh/IRA plans can be established are willing to act as fund custodian and let the contributor direct the plan's investment strategy. A **self-directed brokerage account** allows the investor/saver to manage his or her own Keogh/IRA funds. Discount brokerage houses charge about $25 to set up a Keogh/IRA plan and another $25 per year to perform the custodial services for the plan. The saver can buy or sell eligible securities as he or she desires. The usual commissions apply to Keogh/IRA plan transactions. For sophisticated investors/savers, self-directed plans place them in control of their own investment funds and allow them to try to earn high returns. A well-managed portfolio in a self-directed Keogh/IRA plan could produce higher returns than those obtained by investing in CDs or mutual funds. A general rule to remember is that you should have at least $10,000 in Keogh/IRA funds before opening a self-directed brokerage account.

Spot Quiz • Individual Retirement Plans

1. Any worker can open a Keogh plan.   T _____ F _____

2. Keogh/IRA funds can be withdrawn prematurely if the worker has financial problems.   T _____ F _____

3. IRA funds can be managed only by a trustee.   T _____   F _____

(Answers on page 658)

LEISURE AND RECREATION PLANNING

The most important thing you can do to plan for leisure and recreation during your retirement years is to plan for sufficient funds for living expenses. Previous sections on social security, pensions, annuities, and individual retirement plans explained how this could be done. To enjoy your retirement years fully, though, you also need to do some nonfinancial planning.

You need not start preparing for retirement leisure and recreation as early as you begin planning for retirement income. However, you do need to make some concrete plans. The following discussion will suggest some of the issues you will want to consider.

Where to Live

The choice of a place to live after retiring depends a lot on your interests. Many retirees move to the sunbelt for sun and surf, but a few actually move to New York or other large cities to catch up on the plays, operas, concerts, and restaurants they missed during their working years. Many retirees simply stay where they have worked and lived to be close to old friends, business acquaintances, and relatives. Those who want to move should take into consideration health facilities, such as hospitals and trauma centers; financial service institutions, such as banks and brokerage houses; recreational facilities, such as golf courses and swimming pools; leisure activities, such as workshops and clubs; public transportation, housing, restaurants, and security.

The cost of such budget items as housing, food, transportation, clothing, and medical care should be carefully evaluated. The Bureau of Labor Statistics[6] annually compiles information on living costs in various cities and sections of the United States. Copies of its studies are available free of charge. Books on retirement planning are another source of information about places to consider for retirement. Some of these books are listed in this chapter's reading list.

---

6. Office of Information, Room 1539, GAO Building, 441 G Street NW, Washington, DC 20212.

Leisure Activities

Planning leisure activities may seem unimportant or unnecessary. But many people who fail to plan find that they become lonely and depressed when they stop working. One way to plan is to cultivate interests now that you will pursue in greater depth when you retire. Another way is to keep track of all those things you want to do but never seem to have time for. Some retirees are even successful at turning their leisure activities into money-making ventures. A vice president of a major Detroit corporation had for many years wanted to spend time working with wood. After retirement, he combined his woodworking and business skills to produce and sell small, handmade wooden toys and game sets. A retired auto mechanic repairs lawn mowers to ''keep himself in chips.'' The *Craftmaster's Market*,[7] which costs about $12, lists places where finished goods can be sold.

New activities can lead to new friends as well as absorbing new interests. Have you always wanted to know more about birds? The National Audubon Society maintains many wildlife sanctuaries nationwide. A good pair of binoculars, a guide book, and an adventuresome spirit can lead to many enjoyable—and perhaps companionable—hours of bird watching.[8]

Many colleges and universities offer a variety of courses during the summer months. Generally, these courses are not meant for academic credit. You might learn about such subjects as French cooking, tracing your roots, the philosophy of sports, the psychology of cars, and, of course, the traditional basket weaving. Dorm rooms and cafeteria meals are usually very reasonably priced. The continuing education division of a nearby college can provide information on these courses. Your local library also has many books that provide information on leisure activities.

Traveling

Retirement brings the freedom to travel and explore other places, cultures, and countries. A little time spent planning a vacation can reduce travel costs and place the seemingly unaffordable trip within your means. In addition, planning ahead can make the vacation more enjoyable. Some pointers on planning vacations, particularly overseas vacations, are provided in this section.

Where to Go.   Many countries maintain **national tourist offices** in the United States. Large amounts of information about the countries are available from these offices, whose addresses are readily available in public libraries. Travel guides—available from libraries and bookstores—and travel

---

7. Writer's Digest Books, 9933 Alliance Road, Cincinnati, OH 45242.
8. Membership information is available from National Audubon Development, 950 Third Avenue, New York, NY 10022.

*"I just assumed that a 'Cruise to Nowhere'
would at least leave the dock."*

Source: *Changing Times*, February 1979, p. 2. Reprinted with permission from *Changing Times* magazine, © Kiplinger Washington Editors, Inc., 1979. This reprint is not to be altered in any way, except with permission from *Changing Times*.

agents also provide useful information about vacation spots. Typically, the first-time overseas traveler vacations in Northern Europe. One reason is that English is widely spoken there, so the first time traveler can feel comfortable.

Travel Documents.   A valid **passport** is needed to travel to most countries. Information on applying for a passport is available from travel agents, local post offices, local court clerks, and local offices of the "U.S. Government, State Department." Information on passports and a brochure titled *Your Trip Abroad* are available free of charge from the Office of Passport Service.[9] It generally takes about six weeks for a passport to be issued.

Many countries require that visitors be immunized against certain diseases. A call to the local public health department will provide information on the inoculations needed for travel to various countries.

Some countries require visitors to have a visa. A **visa** is an endorsement made by a foreign country in the traveler's passport, that allows the traveler to visit the country. A travel agent can tell you whether a visa is needed for travel to a particular country. Information on visas can be obtained from the consulate of the countries to be visited. Allow about three weeks for each visa needed.

---

9. Department of State, Washington, DC 20524.

Medical Care. Travelers should make sure that they are covered by health insurance for overseas travel. If your current policy does not apply in other countries, then it is worthwhile to buy a short-term health insurance policy to cover medical bills incurred during overseas travel. Check with a travel agent about buying this short-term coverage.

The traveler should carry a first aid kit that includes bandages, first aid cream for cuts, disinfectant, aspirin or substitute, vitamins, decongestants, motion sickness pills, and Lomotil. (The last-mentioned item is a must for travel.) Travelers with vision impairments should carry an extra pair of glasses.

If you become ill while you are abroad, try to contact the U.S., Canadian, or British consulate for referrals to local English-speaking physicians. A list of English-speaking doctors is available from the International Association for Medical Assistance to Travelers.[10] Travelers with special medical problems should consider obtaining a **Medic Alert Identification Tag**. This widely recognized tag provides essential information for physicians attending during an emergency situation.[11]

Travel Funds. Traveler's checks issued by American Express, Citicorp, Thomas Cook, and Barclay's Bank are readily available at financial institutions. Financial institutions often provide these checks free of charge to their customers. Call local financial institutions to find out which ones offer free traveler's checks. It may even be worthwhile to open a new account to buy free traveler's checks. When you are abroad, cash these checks only at banks, which usually give the best exchange rates. Hotels, shops, and restaurants will also cash traveler's checks, but they will give a relatively low exchange rate.

Packing. The key to enjoying traveling is to travel light. Clothes should be permanent press and wrinkle resistant. Heavy-duty shoes will stand up to wear and tear, and remember to pack a good supply of absorbent cotton socks. Other useful items include a lightweight raincoat with hood, a flashlight, a sewing kit, a notebook, an alarm clock or a wristwatch with an alarm, and premoistened disposable towelettes. Travelers should seriously consider buying a money belt or a zippered pouch that can be worn underneath a shirt or blouse. A voltage converter will enable you to operate hair dryers and other small appliances overseas.

A good, well-built camera is a must. Film is very expensive overseas, so you should carry a good supply. Special lead-lined bags, available at film shops, will protect film from airport X-ray machines.

---

10. 350 Fifth Avenue, Suite 5620, New York, NY 10001.
11. Information about the tag is available from Medic Alert Foundation International, P.O. Box 1009, Turlock, CA 95381.

Transportation. Travel overseas by air is relatively cheap. Fares are constantly changing, so a travel agent is the best source of information. In general, charter, group, and special excursion fares called APEX fares are cheaper than regular fares. However, all carry certain restrictions regarding travel dates and impose cancelation penalties. It is generally worthwhile to read the travel section of the Sunday *New York Times* or another major newspaper to learn more about charter, group, and APEX fares. It is also advisable to confirm the information provided by the travel agent with the charter or group organizer or the airline itself. Remember that off-season fares tend to be considerably lower than peak-season fares. (See "Travel Abroad Without Hassles" on page 652.)

If you are traveling with a group tour, overseas local land transportation is generally provided. Otherwise, you must plan on using local transportation. The **Eurailpass**, which must be purchased in North America, allows unlimited rail travel in most European countries. Buses, airlines, and boats also provide transportation abroad. Driving in most foreign countries tends to be much more hectic and dangerous than in the United States and thus should be avoided if possible.

Places to Stay. Living accommodations abroad can range from very bad to excellent, depending on how much you pay. Most foreign countries operate hotel booking agencies whose offices are conveniently located in airports, train stations, and town centers. For a small service fee, they will find accommodations for you in a given price range in a particular area of town. It is generally worthwhile to book hotel rooms through these agencies, because it saves considerable time and is very convenient.

Time Sharing. A relatively new type of vacation accommodation is called **time sharing**. For instance, you might buy a one-week time share in a two-bedroom luxury apartment facing the ocean in the Florida Keys for $3,500 to $5,000, depending on the season you choose. Purchasing this one-week time slot would allow you to use the apartment for one week at the same time every year. In addition to the purchase price, you would also pay about $100 annually in maintenance fees as well as a proportional share of real estate taxes and utilities.

Many people believe that buying a time share is an inexpensive way of vacationing. Time sharing has its problems, though. Maintenance expenses can increase over time. There is insufficient consumer protection legislation related to time sharing. Another problem is that you may not want to return to the same place year after year. In general, although the concept of time sharing is good, you should seek legal advice before buying a time share unit.

Home Swapping. The high cost of vacationing has convinced some people that swapping homes during vacation time is the way to go. The usual procedure for swapping is to list your home with a home swapping

Travel Abroad Without Hassles

One of the biggest hassles of traveling abroad is health care. Thousands of Americans become ill or are involved in accidents and need medical care while traveling overseas. The problem of finding a doctor who can provide competent health care can be a major horror story. Fortunately, a number of overseas medical assistance programs, such as HealthCare Abroad, NEAR, Europe Assistance Worldwide Services, Travel/Net, Access America, and WorldCare Travel Assistance Association, provide members or subscribers with varying levels of health care. Services range from providing medical consultation services by an English-speaking doctor to hospitalization benefits. Costs and limitations vary sharply from plan to plan. Check with your travel agent to find a plan that supplements whatever other coverage you have and that suits your needs.

Other problems besetting travelers are loss of luggage, money, credit cards, tickets, and other travel documents. A few suggestions will help you reduce your risk. First, leave expensive items, such as jewelry and furs, at home to avoid tempting thieves. Second, always lock your luggage when traveling.

Insurance is available for lost, stolen, or damaged baggage and for trip cancelation and interruption. The latter will pay if the tour operator or airline goes bankrupt or if a nonrefundable ticket cannot be used because of accident or sickness.

Third, remember that pickpockets thrive in busy airports. Despite the warning signs in all international airports, every year thousands of travelers have their wallets and purses stolen in airports. To prevent such a problem, don't carry all your money, credit cards, and travel documents in one bag or purse. Instead, spread them around in different pockets. When you are in a hotel, check to make sure doors are properly locked. Also, don't hesitate to use the hotel safe deposit box for storing your passport and other important documents. Finally, make photocopies of your credit cards, tickets, and other travel documents so you have a record of serial numbers in case they are lost. Also, carry extra pictures of yourself and at least one identification card separately from everything else. These will come in handy if your passport needs to be replaced.

service.[12] The listing may cost $15 to $50. Once the home is listed, you can contact owners of listed homes in a suitable area and negotiate a swap. Home swapping can also have problems. For instance, first-time swappers

---

12. Vacation Exchange Club (350 Broadway, New York, NY 10013), Holiday Exchanges (Box 878, Belen, NM 87002), Inquiline (35 Adams Street, Bedford Hills, NY 10507), and Interservice Home Exchange (Box 87, Glen Echo, MD 20768) are some of the listing services.

may wonder whether their home will be cared for properly. In general, though, swappers report good experiences.

Spot Quiz • Leisure and Recreation Planning

1. A hobby can become a money-making venture.

    T _____ F _____

2. Time sharing and home swapping reduce vacationing costs.

    T _____ F _____

(Answers on page 658)

Summary

Financial security is the main reason for retirement planning. Social security and pension benefits generally are not enough to cover all living expenses during retirement. Therefore, other sources of retirement income need to be planned. Because of inflation and constant changes in the social security system, it is difficult to estimate retirement income needs. As a general rule, though, these needs will be about 60 to 70 percent of your earnings just prior to retirement.

The social security system provides retirement benefits. The system is financed through tax withholdings. You must accumulate 40 quarters of coverage to qualify for social security retirement benefits. Receipt of these benefits is not automatic—they must be applied for at a Social Security Administration office. You can start receiving benefits as early as age 62. Retirees can earn a small amount of money annually without losing social security benefits.

Many employers have pension plans for their workers. Pension plans can be operated either on a "pay-as-you-go" basis or on a funded basis. The latter method is more desirable from the employee's viewpoint. Some pension plans require employees to contribute money, whereas others do not. A worker is vested if he or she has rights to the employer's pension contributions made on his or her behalf. Pension benefits are usually geared to a person's income, age, and length of service to the employer. Pension fund practices are governed by ERISA.

Annuities are a way of transferring to an insurer the risk of living too long. Annuities provide the covered person with periodic payments that can be used for living expenses. Straight life, refund, certain period, joint and survivorship, and annuity certain are the major types of annuities. They have different features, benefits, and costs. Fixed annuities provide fixed periodic benefits, whereas variable annuities provide variable benefits that may keep pace with inflation.

A Keogh plan for a self-employed person is an example of an individual retirement plan. This plan allows you to shelter some of your income annually from taxes. The sheltered income is placed in a retirement fund, where all earnings are also sheltered from taxes. Funds in the plan are taxed only when they are withdrawn. An IRA is similar to a Keogh plan except that all workers are eligible to open IRAs. CDs and mutual fund families are good places for investing Keogh/IRA funds.

Retirement planning also includes planning for a place to live, leisure activities, and vacationing. There is virtually no limit to what you can do in these areas to make your retirement years more enjoyable.

Questions

1. Why is retirement planning important?

2. Explain how inflation and social security complicate retirement planning.

3. How do age at retirement and financial assets accumulated affect retirement life style?

4. Briefly explain the various sources of retirement income.

5. Briefly explain how the social security system works.

6. Should social security benefits be expanded or contracted? Explain your answer.

7. How does a person qualify for receiving social security benefits?

8. What factors affect the amount of social security benefits a person receives?

9. Explain how working after retirement can reduce your social security benefits.

10. What, if any, is the difference between pay-as-you-go and funded pension plans? Which one is better for the employee? Why?

11. Explain the difference between a contributory and a noncontributory plan. Is one better than the other? Explain your answer.

12. What is meant by vesting? What advantage does vesting have for the employee?

13. Briefly explain the defined-contribution plan and the defined-benefit plan. Which one is better for the employee? Explain your answer.

14. What benefits does ERISA have for workers?

15. What is an annuity? What protection does it provide?

16. What are the major differences between fixed and variable annuities?

17. Who can set up a Keogh plan? Explain the major features of such plans.

18. How does an IRA differ from a Keogh plan? How are they similar?

19. Explain where Keogh/IRA funds can be invested.

20. What does a self-directed Keogh/IRA plan allow a person to do?

21. Briefly explain how hobbies can generate retirement income.

22. What are the advantages and disadvantages of time share vacation homes and home swapping?

Case Problems

1. Jonah Sikes is almost 62 years old. Based on his social security contributions, if he were to retire at age 65, he would receive $570 in monthly benefits. He would prefer to continue working on a part-time basis after retirement, earning about $9,000 annually. Assume that these earnings are tax-free. Using 1987 figures provided in the book, what would Jonah's social security benefits be if he were to retire at age 65? Recalculate Jonah's retirement benefits by assuming that Jonah retires at age 62. What advice do you have for Jonah about retiring at age 62 or 65?

2. Sharon Ober has $160,000 with which to cover her retirement living expenses. She is evaluating two options. She can invest the money in money market mutual funds that will pay her 16 percent annually or she can buy a straight life fixed annuity. The insurer, based on her

life expectancy of five years and a rate of return of 13 percent, will pay her an annuity of $40,257 each year.

   a. Prepare a table similar to Table 20.3 to show that this annuity amount of $40,257 is correct.

   b. What advice do you have for Ms. Ober? Explain your answer.

3. Gordon Bilinsky has recently started working for a company that has a defined-benefit retirement plan. Gordon's contribution to the retirement plan of 8 percent of his salary is matched by his employer. The retirement benefits are 2 percent of Gordon's average salary for the five years prior to retirement for each year of service. Gordon has 30 more years to work before retiring. Thus, this plan would pay him 60 percent of his average salary for the five years before retiring. His friend, Julie Jensen, is enrolled in a defined-contribution retirement plan. She also contributes 8 percent of her salary to the plan, and her employer matches this contribution. Although her retirement benefits cannot be guaranteed, her employer believes that the plan will pay about $11 in monthly retirement benefits for each $1,000 of retirement *principal* contributed. Julie is also eligible for retirement after 30 years. Gordon and Julie are discussing which plan is better. What is your analysis? Explain your answer. Would your answer be different if both people were to retire after only ten years? Explain. (*Hint*: Assume that earnings remain constant.)

Bibliography

"Building a Cycle-Proof IRA." *Money* (March 1987): 66–74.

"The Compelling Case for Keoghs." *Money* (December 1985): 171–180.

"Five IRAs That Are Working Harder." *Money* (March 1986): 74–84.

"The Foreign Retirement." *Money* (February 1985): 86–94.

"Here's Another Excuse to Retire Early." *Changing Times* (March 1986): 83–87.

"The IRA Lives! New Moves for a New Era." *Money* (March 1987): 58–67.

"IRAs: Shake, Rattle and Rollovers." *Money* (November 1985): 251–262.

"Making Hay With Your 401(K)." *Money* (January 1985): 103–108.

"Making the Most of Your IRA Now." *Money* (October 1986): 63–70.

"Smart Ways to Swap Your Dollars." *Changing Times* (April 1985): 33–55.

"Stalking the Ideal IRA." *Money* (February 1985): 72–77.

"Tips for Trouble-free Travel Abroad." *Changing Times* (May 1986): 45–46.

"Tips on Picking a Tour." *Changing Times* (March 1987): 76.

"Your IRA: Still a Good Deal?" *Consumer Reports* (January 1987): 12–15.

"Your Pension Plan." *Changing Times* (May 1983): 26–30.

Answers to Spot Quizzes

Introduction to Retirement Planning (page 626)

1. T (Postponing current consumption means savings.)

2. T (Lower benefits are provided to early retirees because they contribute less and draw benefits for a longer period.)

3. T (With inflation, this estimation becomes difficult.)

Social Security (page 632)

1. F (A covered retired worker who earns more than the annual limit on earnings will not receive any pension.)

2. F (Certain other persons are also eligible.)

3. T (Age is also a factor.)

Employer Pension Plans (page 638)

1. F (Pay-as-you-go plans are riskier because the money is not there to cover future pension payments.)

2. T (It depends on the level of benefits provided.)

3. T (The pension depends on how well the pension funds have been managed.)

Annuities (page 643)

1. T (That is the idea behind annuities.)

2. T (Minimum total benefits are guaranteed.)

3. F (Benefits are variable and can decrease as well as increase.)

Individual Retirement Plans (page 646)

1. F   (Only self-employed persons can open Keogh plans.)

2. T   (If funds are withdrawn prematurely, however, the person must pay a penalty and income taxes.)

3. F   (They can be self-directed as well as managed by a trustee.)

Leisure and Recreation Planning (page 653)

1. T   (Many people with crafts skills do make money from their hobbies.)

2. T   (Large hotel bills are not incurred.)

Chapter 21

Estate Planning

Objectives

After reading this chapter, you will be able to:

- Explain what is meant by estate planning.
- Discuss the importance of estate planning.
- State the goals of estate planning.
- Discuss how a valid will can be written.
- List the major features of wills.
- Explain how a will is probated.
- Define the responsibilities of an executor/executrix.
- Explain how gift and estate taxes are computed.
- List the various types of trusts.
- Discuss estate-planning strategies.

June Barkley was only 42 years old when her husband died at age 43 of a heart attack. She had not played an active role in managing the family's finances. Nor had her husband done a very good job of planning his estate. After her husband's death, she was not able to find his will, his safe deposit box, or any record of his real estate investments in the Southwest. Says Mrs. Barkley, "For all I know, he had another checking account. He may even have had a couple of insurance policies that I don't know about." After her husband's death, she discovered that a former wife was the beneficiary of an insurance policy for which Mrs. Barkley was paying the premiums. Mr. Barkley was in the process of changing beneficiaries on this policy when he died. Based on this fact, June Barkley sued in court and received a small portion of the policy benefits.[1]

This situation demonstrates the problems that can occur when a person does a poor job of estate planning. The basics of estate planning, wills, estate and gift taxes, and trusts are covered in this chapter.

THE BASICS OF ESTATE PLANNING

Many people consider death and dying too depressing to talk about, so they ignore the subject. Unfortunately, death can create many severe financial problems for the survivors. Had Mr. Barkley made financial plans in anticipation of his death, his widow would not have suffered all the financial problems that she did. Estate planning, its importance, and its goals are discussed in this section.

Estate Planning

A person's **estate** includes all of his or her assets. Thus, cash, stocks, bonds, real estate, houses, cars, books, furniture, clothes, and other property are all part of a person's estate. An estate also includes assets that might not be immediately recognizable as assets. For example, life insurance, even if it is term insurance without any cash value, is part of a person's estate. Retirement plans, such as pensions and Keogh/IRA accounts, are also part of the estate. Social security pays survivor's benefits; therefore, expected social security payments are also included in the estate.

The assets in your estate need not be held solely in your name. The appropriate portion of jointly owned property is also part of your estate.

Estate planning is the systematic accumulation, management, and transfer of a person's estate. The accumulation of assets was the topic of many of this book's chapters. Career planning, setting financial goals, tax

---

1. "Saving Widows From Still More Losses," *Money* (May 1981): 90.

planning, consumerism, budgeting, credit management, buying a home, and risk management all dealt with increasing earnings and managing expenses so that more assets could be accumulated. Other chapters, such as those on insurance and investments, discussed ways of protecting assets and making them grow. The final part of estate planning is the planning related to the transfer of the estate.

Transfer of Estate

Some people are very good at accumulating and managing assets but not so good at planning for the transfer of the estate. Perhaps they feel that this aspect of estate planning is automatically provided for them by the judicial system. In a sense, they are right. If an estate transfer plan does not exist, state laws specify how the estate is to be distributed to the survivors. The only problem is that the distribution of the estate according to state laws may not coincide with the way the **decedent**, or deceased person, would prefer to have the estate distributed.

Another problem with the nonsystematic transfer of the estate is that often the beneficiaries do not receive as much as they would have received if the decedent had planned for the transfer. A systematic transfer of the estate can take place only if a person utilizes standard methods of estate planning. One way of ensuring a systematic transfer of the estate is through the use of a will. The **will** is a legal document that specifies how the decedent wants his or her estate to be distributed after his or her death.

The government levies **estate taxes** on the transfer of estates that are larger than a certain specified sum. Thus, management of estate taxes is also an important part of estate planning. Trusts are one way the impact of estate taxes can be minimized. A **trust** is a legal procedure whereby one person manages assets for the benefit of another person. Another way to lessen the impact of estate taxes is by giving gifts. A **gift** is the transfer of assets from one person to another, and certain amounts of assets can be transferred in this way without incurring taxes.

Because most of this book has been concerned with asset accumulation and management, our focus in this chapter will be on the transfer of the estate, including wills, trusts, gifts, and the management of estate taxes.

Importance of Estate Planning

Previous chapters on asset accumulation and management have emphasized the positive aspects of estate planning. Consequently, in this section we will mention some typical problems that arise if proper estate planning has *not* taken place.

Meeting Immediate Cash Needs. Chapter 14, Life Insurance, showed how immediate cash needs can be estimated. Lack of planning for these

cash needs can mean that estate assets have to be sold under distress conditions, at distress prices, to raise cash. For instance, a widow or widower might have to sell the home or family farm to raise cash. Proper estate planning can prevent these situations.

Meeting Estate-Related Costs. Costs related to the transfer of an estate can be substantial. Fees of attorneys, accountants, and appraisers, and other legal expenses, must be paid. For large estates, federal estate taxes and state estate or inheritance taxes must also be paid. These costs can add up, but careful estate planning can help prevent a situation in which, for example, the family-run business has to be sold to pay estate taxes.

Beneficiaries. Unsystematic estate planning can result in the transfer of estate assets to the wrong beneficiary or in the transfer of assets at the wrong time. For example, assets meant for the children may, through incorrect planning, pass on to the surviving spouse. These types of problems can be avoided by planning systematically for the transfer of the estate.

Economic Factors. Economic conditions constantly change, and their impact on an estate can be severe. Inflation and other economic factors can produce unanticipated results. For example, the block of automotive company stock willed to parents to provide them with a steady income may no longer be paying dividends. The bonds left to the spouse may still be paying interest; however, because of inflation, the purchasing power of the interest income may not be sufficient. And the shares of high-technology stock left to the cute little niece or nephew may now be worth over a million dollars. An ongoing review of assets and their ultimate disposition minimizes the impact of economic factors on a suitable transfer of the estate.

Good estate planning provides for the transfer of the estate in keeping with the decedent's wishes, thus ensuring that the right amounts of assets are passed on to the right beneficiaries. Finally, good estate planning provides more benefits to the beneficiaries. (See "Ignorance Is Bliss?" on page 663.)

Goals of Estate Planning

The estate should be transferred in such a way that benefits for the beneficiaries are maximized. This can be accomplished by meeting the four goals of systematic transfer of the estate, timely transfer of the estate, minimization of administrative costs, and minimization of estate taxes.

Systematic Transfer. A systematic transfer of the estate requires a listing and classification of all of a person's assets; liabilities; insurance; pension, veterans', employment, and survivors' benefits; income;

Ignorance Is Bliss?

It took Edna Shaver, wife of a Columbus, Ohio, physician, five years to settle her husband's estate after his death. Why so long? Because her husband, wishing to spare her the details associated with managing investments, did not keep her fully informed about the family's investment decisions. This lack of information resulted in delays in appraising the estate and delayed payments to the beneficiaries. Another woman received a notice from a bank indicating that the bank was going to foreclose on a property because of delinquent mortgage payments. Only then did she find out that her recently deceased husband owned an investment property on which mortgage payments had not been made after his death.

Knowing the details of your spouse's finances can help you avoid the types of problems encountered by these two beneficiaries. At the minimum, spouses should be fully aware of all family assets. It is desirable to prepare a list of assets, including information on real estate holdings, life insurance policies, bank accounts, brokerage and mutual fund accounts, safe deposit boxes, collectibles (such as precious gems, coins, stamps, and paintings), and other assets of value. It is particularly important to list assets that may not be readily identifiable. Forgetting to list a car may not be a problem, because the spouse is aware of its existence. But forgetting to list a brokerage account may be a problem if stocks and bonds are held in street name. The list should also include the names of the stockbroker, insurance agent, accountant, bankers, and others who know of assets that are part of the estate.

Your work history is a very special type of asset. Generally, you accumulate pension benefits on the job. Keeping a record of your work history allows your surviving spouse to file for pension benefits related to the jobs. The Retirement Equity Act of 1984 specifies that all corporate pensions must be of the joint and survivor type. This means that the surviving spouse can collect pension benefits from the jobs of the deceased spouse. The only exception to this rule is if both spouses agree in writing to waive the joint and survivor provision. A listing of jobs held in the past would be valuable in helping the surviving spouse to collect pension benefits.

Those who have served in the U.S. armed forces often have provided for a variety of benefits for their spouses. For example, spouses of veterans are often eligible for a pension and burial expenses. Finally, some surviving spouses fail to check with the Social Security Administration for survivors' benefits. Most surviving spouses, especially those with dependent children, are eligible for benefits. Overall, ignorance is not bliss when it comes to settling estates. Keeping your spouse or your major beneficiary informed about your estate items greatly eases the burden of settling an estate.

beneficiaries; and key documents and their locations. A listing of this information is shown in Figure 21.1. A systematic transfer also takes into consideration alternative methods of transferring the estate so that other goals of estate planning are met. A careful estate planner will use a will, trusts, and gifts appropriately.

Timely Transfer.   The transfer of the estate should be timely. In other words, the appropriate portion of the estate should pass on to the designated beneficiary without undue delay. Nor should the estate pass on to a beneficiary before the appropriate time. In the most obvious case, a person would not want to distribute his or her total estate prior to death, which might happen if gifts were the only estate planning device used. However, the rule also applies in not so obvious cases. For example, a decedent may prefer not to pass on an inheritance to a spendthrift offspring

Figure 21.1   Information Useful for Expediting an Estate Transfer

Assets

1. Type	2. Brief description	4. Purchase price	5. Date of purchase	6. Current price
	3. Account number			

Liabilities

1. Lender's name	2. Loan purpose	3. Amount	4. Payment date	5. Current balance

Insurace

1. Type	2. Insurer	3. Policy number	4. Amount	5. Beneficiary

Benefits

1. Type	2. Company	3. Administrator	4. Amount	5. Beneficiary

Income

1. Type	2. Source	3. Amount

Beneficiaries

1. Name	2. Address	3. Relationship

Key Documents

1. Name	2. Location

immediately. In this case, a trust could provide the offspring with a reasonable income until he or she reaches a specified age reflecting, hopefully, a higher level of financial prudence.[2]

Minimization of Administrative Costs. Administrative costs for an estate transfer can easily exceed 10 percent of the value of the estate. A well-thought-out estate plan can substantially reduce this cost.

Minimization of Estate Taxes. Without proper planning, estate taxes can consume a substantial portion of an estate. There is nothing wrong with using gifts, charities, and trusts to minimize estate taxes.

We have established the rationale for proper estate planning in this section. In later sections in this chapter, we will consider how certain strategies can implement the goals of estate planning.

Spot Quiz • The Basics of Estate Planning

1. In general, estate accumulation is more important than estate transfer.

   T _____   F _____

2. Estate planning helps the beneficiaries cope with inflation.

   T _____   F _____

3. The estate assets should be made available to the beneficiaries as soon as possible.   T _____   F _____

(Answers on page 690)

WILLS

A will expresses the way a person wishes his or her property to be disposed of after his or her death. A man who makes out a will is called a **testator**, whereas a woman is referred to as a **testatrix**. Wills range from very simple to very complex. In most cases, though, they are simple enough to be prepared at a reasonably low cost—$100 to $300—and complex enough

---

2. A trust is an arrangement whereby property is transferred by one party, the settlor, to another party, the trustee, to be used according to the terms of the trust agreement for the benefit of a third party. As estate-planning devices, trusts can be used to reduce taxes and to control the use of property both before and after a person's death.

to require preparation by an attorney. Hiring an experienced attorney to prepare a will can help you avoid the pitfall of writing a will that may not be considered valid.

Writing a valid will is important for a variety of reasons. It allows a person to dispose of his or her assets in a suitable manner. In the absence of a will, state laws govern the disposal of the estate. A will allows a testator/testatrix to appoint a suitable and acceptable individual (called an **executor**) to oversee the distribution of the estate. Finally, a will makes life more pleasant for the survivors by removing the unduly expensive and involved legal process of a transfer associated with the absence of a will.

A well-written will accomplishes four major objectives. First, it ensures that a person's estate is disposed of in accordance with his or her wishes. Second, the will reflects the needs of the beneficiaries. Third, taxes and administrative costs of estate transfer are held to a minimum. Fourth, the will recognizes potential changes that may occur after the death of the testator/testatrix. Careful consideration by a person to these objectives can result in a will that is acceptable to all parties involved.

Writing a Valid Will

To be considered valid in courts, a will must meet certain legal requirements of testamentary intention and formality in execution.

Testamentary Intention. Testamentary intention means that the testator/testatrix intended to write a will that would be effective on his or her death and stated so in writing in the will. Only a person with testamentary capacity can write a valid will. **Testamentary capacity** exists when a person can decide reasonably well on the distribution of his or her estate. Testamentary capacity thus refers to soundness of mind as well as to undue influence. A person writing a will is considered to be of sound mind if he or she (1) knows the assets in the estate and (2) understands how the assets should be disposed. Courts generally consider a testator to be of sound mind unless proven otherwise. The second requirement for a will to be valid is that the testator must not be under the undue influence of another person when the will is being written.

Formality in Execution. **Formality in execution** means that certain formal or legal procedures must be observed when the will is drawn up. The will must contain a statement to meet the testamentary intention requirement. The will must be signed by the testator, usually at the physical end of the will. The testator's signature must be witnessed by a specified minimum number of witnesses. For example, some states require three witnesses for a valid will, and some states specify that a beneficiary cannot witness a will.

Some states recognize wills that have not been formally executed and witnessed if they are written entirely in the testator's own handwriting. Such wills are called **holographic wills**, and even in states that recognize them, they must meet certain minimal requirements of form. Holographic wills are quite often challenged in courts by survivors who are excluded as beneficiaries. A few states even recognize oral wills (**nuncupative wills**) under certain, very limited, circumstances.

Major Features of Wills

Although the exact language varies, most wills have major features in common. Wills are generally titled "Last Will and Testament of [Name of Testator]" and include the following clauses or features.

Preface and Testamentary Intention.   This clause states the domicile of the testator and the testamentary intentions and revokes all previous wills. It might read:

> I, [Name of Testator], of [County, State], being of sound and disposing mind, do hereby make this my last will and testament, and revoke all prior wills.[3]

Payment of Debt and Final Expenses.   This clause specifies that debts and medical and funeral expenses be paid out of the estate:

> I direct that all my just debts and funeral expenses be paid out of my estate as they become due.

Appointing an Executor.   An **executor** is a person or institution responsible for administering the testator's estate. The executor is appointed by a clause that might begin:

> I appoint [Name of Executor] to be the executor of my last will and testament. If said executor does not survive me, I appoint [Name of Alternate Executor] as executor.

In practice, this clause tends to be lengthy and complex. Because of the importance of the role of an executor is settling an estate, we will discuss the topic in greater detail later.

---

3. The language in these clauses has been simplified to make them easier to read and understand. In many cases, more complex language might be necessary in order to avoid ambiguity or the possibility of misinterpretation. In some cases, complex language is used because prior court decisions have ensured its legal effect. However, there is a trend toward eliminating unnecessarily complex legal language, or legalese.

Appointing a Guardian.   It is desirable to name a guardian for any minor children of the testator. Normally, the surviving spouse would be named in the following fashion:

> I hereby appoint my wife [Name] as guardian of the person and property of my children [Names]. If my wife does not survive me, I appoint my sister/brother [Name] as guardian.

This appointment clause also tends to be complex and lengthy. Note that the guardianship applies not only to minor children but also to the property of the minor child. Some states prohibit the surviving spouse from being the sole guardian of a minor child's estate. (See "Contingent Benevolence" below.)

Disposition of Property.   The dispositive clauses in a will can range from simple to complex. In a simple will, the executor is usually given the

Contingent Benevolence

For contingent benevolence take two aspirin and call the doctor in the morning. However, you will find out that the doctor cannot cure a case of contingent benevolence. The phrase often refers to a phenomenon that is becoming quite popular, in which a testator will specify the conditions under which a beneficiary will receive his or her inheritance. Typically, a parent will specify the conditions that must be met for a child to receive either a portion of an estate or monies from a trust fund. For example, some parents may specify that a child will receive income from a trust fund as long as he or she remains drug-free.

Some of these contingencies do not hold up to court challenges. For example, a parent who dislikes an in-law may specify that a child will inherit only if he or she divorces his or her spouse. The New York courts have ruled this contingency invalid because it forces divorce. On the other hand, courts have generally ruled as valid contingencies that require a child to remain married or to marry a person of a particular faith.

This increase in contingent benevolence seems to indicate that parents are becoming increasingly concerned about regulating their children's behavior through the use of wills and trusts. Sociologists argue that if parents feel that they cannot control their children's behavior while they are alive, they might use contingencies to either control behavior after their deaths or, in some cases, to seek revenge. Whatever the motives, most children choose not to challenge these contingencies, viewing them as their parents' last wishes. In the meantime, some lawyers and sociologists advise, only partially in jest, that you be nice to your parents.

discretion to distribute the **personal effects** of the testator (items such as clothing, furniture, and books) among certain named beneficiaries in roughly equal proportions. The **residue**, or remaining assets (real property, cash, stocks, and so on), might then be distributed in similar fashion or certain items might be earmarked for certain individuals. The dispositive clauses in a simple will might read as follows:

> All of my furniture, household goods, jewelry, and personal effects shall be distributed among my children [Names] in approximately equal shares as my executor shall determine.

> To the individuals and institutions listed below, I give the following:

> To my husband [Name], I give my diamond engagement ring.
> To my son [Name], I give the sum of $20,000.
> To my daughter [Name], I give my Mercedes-Benz.
> To my alma mater [Name], I give 1,000 shares of IBM common stock.
> All the rest of my estate I bequeath to my husband [Name].

A bequest for religious, educational, political, or general social interest accomplishments (such as a bequest to a testator's college) is called a **charitable bequest**. A bequest of specific property (such as a Mercedes-Benz) is called a **specific bequest** or **specific legacy**. A bequest of money, on the other hand, is called a **general bequest** or **general legacy** because the money comes out of the general assets of the estate.

"He left each of you one million out of an estate worth $360.47."

Common Disaster Clause. Wills should contain a clause that covers the situation in which both spouses die simultaneously or the identity of the spouse who died first cannot be determined. This may happen, for example, in an airplane crash or a car accident. The common disaster clause prevents litigation to establish which spouse died first and prevents the assets from being taken through probate twice—once for transfer from the estate of one spouse to the estate of the second to die and once for transfer to the other survivors. Such a clause might read as follows:

If my husband [Name] and I shall die under such circumstances that it is not possible to determine the order of our deaths or if he shall die within a period of six months after the date of my death, then all gifts to him shall be void and my estate shall be administered as if he had not survived me.

Attestation Clause. The testator's attestation is contained in this clause:

In witness whereof, I have affixed my signature to this, my last will and testament, on [Date].

[Signature of Testator]

Often this clause is lengthy and also includes the names of the attesting witnesses. It may also mention the total length in pages of the will.

Witness Clause. The witnesses certify that they have witnessed the testator signing the will:

Signed by [Name of Testator], the testator as his last will and testament, in our presence, who at his request and in his presence, and in the presence of each other, sign our names as attesting witnesses.

[Signature of Witnesses]

It is generally desirable to have at least three witnesses attest the testator's signature. A beneficiary should not be a witness. The witnesses do not have to read the will. In some states, an attorney might suggest that the signatures of the testator and the witnesses be notarized.

What is stated in a will varies, depending on the testator's situation. However, most wills contain the clauses just described. Writing a will should be considered an important part of estate planning. It is also important to let the beneficiaries know how the will is going to affect them after the testator's death so that feelings of resentment among beneficiaries are minimized.

Changing a Will

Changes in the testator's personal situation or beneficiaries' situations, such as births, deaths, marriages, and changes in finances, might require changes to an existing will. A **codicil**, or addition to a will, is one way of making appropriate changes. It requires the same formality in execution as the will itself. However, using a codicil to change a will may produce litigation that could turn out to be costly. Thus, it is usually desirable to prepare a new will rather than change an existing one.

Storing a Will

A will that cannot be found is assumed to have been destroyed by the testator. Therefore, it is important to keep the will in a safe yet accessible location. The most desirable place to keep a will is with the attorney who drew it. The attorney may keep the will in his or her office or place it in a safe deposit box in a bank. Alternatively, the will can be left with a financial institution if the institution is the executor or if it provides such a custodial service. As a last resort, a will could be kept in a person's own safe deposit box. Keep in mind, though, that the executor will not be able to retrieve the will until the state has inventoried the contents of the box. The will should not be kept at home because it can be easily lost or stolen.

Probating a Will

After the death of the testator/testatrix, his or her will must be probated before the estate can be distributed. **Probate** is the legal process of proving to a court that the will is valid and of carrying out the will's terms. The first part of probating is proving the validity of a will. The executor presents the will to the appropriate court. Many states require that witnesses testify in court on the validity of the testator's signature. However, if the signatures on the will are notarized, courts in some states accept the signature as valid without testimony from the attesting witnesses. If the will is valid, the court issues the executor the authority to carry out the terms of the will. The executor/executrix can now fulfill his or her legal role, which is explained in detail in the next section.

The cost of probating a will can be high. In general, probating costs, including court costs and an attorney's and an executor's fees, can be between 5 and 10 percent of the value of the estate. The high cost of probating is a very strong argument for avoiding probate to some extent through the appropriate use of gifts and trusts.

Role of the Executor/Executrix

The executor (a woman executor is called an executrix) is responsible for carrying out the wishes of the testator. This person reports periodically to the probate court and must file a final accounting report with the court before he or she is discharged from responsibilities. The executor is responsible for the reading of the will and will also help with the funeral arrangements.

On the testator's death, the executor takes immediate steps to protect the testator's estate. This may involve maintaining business interests, safeguarding valuables, caring for personal property, and managing real property. The executor also petitions the court for probating the will.

Next, the executor prepares an inventory of all assets in the estate. The inventory includes cash, securities, real estate, life insurance, cars, personal property, and other property owned by the decedent. He or she also inventories all debt outstanding. Some assets, such as cash, life insurance, and most securities, have an established market value. Other assets, such as real estate, cars, and personal property, do not have a currently established market value. The executor arranges for appraisals of these assets.

The executor next settles all claims against the decedent. These may include funeral expenses and other liabilities. If the decedent has income taxes due, the executor will prepare the proper income tax returns and file them. The executor is also responsible for filing forms for paying estate income taxes, gift taxes, and estate taxes.

Now the executor is ready to distribute the estate according to the wishes of the testator. All legacies, bequests, and other payments are distributed. After the estate distribution, the executor prepares an accounting of the estate for the probate court. If creditors, beneficiaries, tax authorities, or others are not satisfied with the distribution and have filed claims against the decedent's estate, then the executor has to help the estate attorney prepare a suitable defense against the charges.

As the discussion indicates, the executor/executrix has an important role in the transfer of the decedent's estate. The role requires an understanding of the law and of accounting and management practices. An executor should be knowledgeable and experienced with estate transfers. He or she should be financially responsible. The executor should be objective and impartial in making decisions regarding the estate.

All of these factors argue against appointing a friend or a relative as an executor. Appointment of a professional executor or a suitable financial institution can prevent many problems. Although professional executors charge a fee for their services, they may actually keep the estate settlement costs low because of their experience. A competent attorney who prepares the will can help you identify a suitable executor for the estate. (See "Executor of an Estate?" on page 673.)

Letter of Last Instructions

A **letter of last instructions** contains instructions by the testator as well as certain other information that the testator might wish to convey to the executor and beneficiaries. Several copies of the letter should be made and left in prominent, accessible places. At the minimum, the letter should include the following information:

1. The location of the will and other important documents.
2. Funeral instructions.
3. All the information shown in Figure 21.1.
4. A list of memberships in unions, clubs, and associations.

In addition to this information, the letter of last instructions may also contain suggestions for the executor about management of the estate. The executor, of course, is not bound by these instructions. At times, though, they can help preserve the estate until its final disposition. The letter may also contain an explanation of the legacies and bequests contained in the

Executor of an Estate?

Two days after the death of your best friend, you are informed that she has named you the executor of her estate. What should you do? If you are like most people who are named executors, you will feel flattered by your friend's confidence in your abilities and will take on the job. However, unless you have specialized skills related to estates or have intimate knowledge about the estate, you would be better off not accepting the executorship.

The compensation paid to executors is generally determined by the probate judge, and in many cases it is simply not worth the trouble involved in settling the estate. Executors have to worry about preserving the estate through prudent investment decisions, defending the estate against improper claims, filing timely tax returns, distributing the estate's assets, and so on. Besides the stress created from handling these estate matters, executors may also become liable for losses related to mishandling the estate. For example, an executor who does not recognize antiques as such and sells them as used furniture may have to compensate the estate for the true value of the antiques.

So when you find out that you have been named an executor, perhaps the best thing to do would be to not accept the appointment. However, if you decide to accept the appointment, then you should insist that the probate court appoint either a lawyer or a bank as coexecutor to provide the professional assistance needed in settling the estate.

will. Note that a letter of last instructions is not a substitute for a will; it merely provides supplementary information.

Estate Transfer Without a Will

A decedent without a will dies intestate. **Intestacy** is the situation that is created when a person dies without leaving a valid will. State laws govern the transfer of the decedent's estate when he or she dies intestate. These laws vary from state to state. In general, though, spouses and children are given preference over other relatives.

Intestate Distribution. Generally, the surviving spouse will receive at least a share of the decedent's estate. The surviving spouse receives the total estate if the decedent has no children, grandchildren, or other immediate relatives. The surviving spouse will receive from one-third to one-half of the estate if the decedent has one or more children and grandchildren. The rest of the estate would go to the children and grandchildren. The spouse will receive about one-half of the estate if the decedent has no children but does have immediate relatives, such as parents, brothers, and sisters.

The children would receive the total estate if the decedent does not have a spouse. If the decedent has neither a spouse nor children, the estate would go to the decedent's parents. In the absence of parents, the estate would be distributed among brothers and sisters and so on. The court will appoint an administrator for an intestate decedent's estate. The role of the estate administrator is basically the same as that of an estate executor. The difference is that the intestate decedent has no choice over who ultimately administers the estate.

Nonprobate Property Transfer. Sometimes the form of ownership can determine how property is transferred from the decedent to a beneficiary. It is possible to transfer property ownership without a will and without going through probate.

There are three forms of property ownership. **Separate property** is property that belongs to only one individual. Property acquired by a person before marriage is an example of separate property. **Community property** is property acquired by either of the spouses during their marriage, irrespective of the wage-earning status of either spouse. Arizona, California, Idaho, Louisiana, Nevada, New Mexico, Texas, and Washington are community property states. All property acquired by a married couple is assumed to be jointly owned.

The third form of ownership is **joint ownership**, which means that two or more persons jointly own the property in question. Joint ownership is of three forms. With **joint tenancy**, each of two or more owners owns a nonspecific fraction of the property. If one owner dies, his or her share

passes to the remaining owners. Each owner can dispose of his or her share without permission from the other owners. In **tenancy in common**, the deceased owner's share goes to his or her heirs. **Tenancy by the entirety**, available only to married persons, is the same as joint tenancy except that one spouse cannot dispose of his or her share without the permission of the other spouse.

If property is held in joint tenancy or in tenancy by the entirety, the decedent spouse's share automatically passes to the surviving spouse. The legal requirements for these forms of ownership are that both tenants become owners of the same property at the same time with identical ownership rights. An attorney can help in converting separate property to joint tenancy or to tenancy by the entirety for estate-planning purposes.

Spot Quiz • Wills

1. An unwitnessed will probably will not be considered valid by a court.
   T _____ F _____

2. A general legacy might require selling estate assets.
   T _____ F _____

3. The executor can distribute the estate assets immediately upon the testator's death.
   T _____ F _____

4. Intestate distribution provides money to the decedent's chosen charities.
   T _____ F _____

(Answers on page 690)

GIFT AND ESTATE TAXES

Three types of taxes are imposed on a decedent's estate: an estate tax, a gift tax, and an inheritance tax. The **estate tax** is imposed by the federal government on the decedent's estate. One possible way of avoiding the estate tax might be to give away one's estate. That is, a person facing death might give all assets to someone else. The person would then own no assets, no estate would be left, and therefore no estate taxes would have

to be paid when the person dies. Actually, taxes cannot be avoided by giving away assets. Anticipating this tax-avoidance strategy, Congress imposed a gift tax as well. A **gift tax** is a federal tax that is imposed on the gift giver, not the receiver. As we will see later in this section, the gift and estate taxes are combined.

Some states also impose an estate tax, and other states place an **inheritance tax** on the beneficiary rather than a tax on the estate. The net result is the same in both cases. In general, though, state estate and inheritance taxes are lower than federal estate taxes.

The **Economic Recovery Tax Act (ERTA)** of 1981 made some substantial changes in the way in which gifts and estates are taxed. With a little planning, most people can pass their estates on to their beneficiaries without having to pay any estate taxes at all. Before we explain how gift and estate taxes are computed, however, an explanation of the gift tax exclusion, the marital deduction, and joint ownership is needed.

Gift Tax Exclusion

Since 1982, a person can give away up to $10,000 every year to each gift recipient without incurring any tax liability. If both spouses concur in making a gift, a person can give away up to $20,000 every year to each recipient tax-free. There is no limit on the number of gift recipients. A person with substantial assets could give, with the spouse's consent, $20,000 to each of his or her children every year for a few years as a method of reducing the size of the taxable estate.

A person can give an unlimited gift to his or her spouse either prior to death or by a bequest in a will. In other words, if a person wants to give all of the estate to his or her spouse, it can be done without paying any estate taxes at all.

Prior to 1982, gifts made within three years of death were automatically included in the decedent's estate. This law was changed effective 1982. Now gifts made anytime up to death are not included in the estate. These gifts are tax-free to the giver as long as the $10,000 or $20,000 annual limit mentioned previously is not violated. As we will see later, however, from a tax viewpoint, it is not always desirable to give your children certain gifts.

Marital Deduction

The **marital deduction** is an estate tax exemption for the bequest that the testator makes to his or her spouse. If the marital deduction is equal to the estate, no estate taxes are paid. This rule, effective since 1982, is a substantial change from the rule that prevailed until 1981. Before 1982, the maximum marital deduction for a large estate was 50 percent of the estate's value. The new law makes it easy for wealthy individuals to transfer their estates to their spouses free of estate taxes.

Joint Ownership

Prior to 1982, the total value of all property held in joint tenancy or tenancy by the entirety was included in the decedent's estate unless the surviving spouse could prove that he or she actually paid for his or her share of the property out of personal funds. ERTA changed this rule. Only half of the jointly owned property goes into the decedent's estate now. The other half of the property is considered to be owned by the surviving spouse and is not included in the decedent's estate. The benefit of this change is that property held in joint tenancy or in tenancy by the entirety can now pass to the surviving spouse free of probate, as mentioned previously, and free of gift and estate taxes.

Although this change is generally desirable because it reduces the size of the decedent's estate, it is not always desirable. For example, consider the situation that would arise when the surviving spouse dies and leaves a substantial estate. There is no marital deduction now, so the estate would be hit with a heavy tax. Such a situation could be avoided by using a trust to provide income to the surviving spouse and then, on his or her death, passing on the estate tax-free to other beneficiaries. This solution is discussed in more detail in the section on trusts.

Computing Gift and Estate Taxes

The procedure for computing gift and estate taxes is explained in the following sections.

Gross Estate. The first step is to compute the gross estate. All real and personal property owned by the decedent is included in the **gross estate**. This includes all cash, stocks, bonds, shares of all jointly owned property, cars, jewelry, tools, appliances, clothes, and everything else owned by the decedent. Any life insurance owned by the decedent is also included in his or her estate. Annuities and any other assets that could be transferred to beneficiaries are included in the gross estate. In Table 21.1, which shows a simplified method for computing gift and estate taxes, the gross estate is $1,202,000.

Taxable Estate. Certain expenses and bequests are deducted from the gross estate to determine **taxable estate**. Such expenses as funeral and estate administration expenses and debts can be deducted from the gross estate. The marital deduction, all bequests to qualified charities and public institutions, and orphan's deductions are also deducted from the gross estate. (An orphan's deduction is a bequest left to a sole parent's surviving children under age 21; there is a legal limit on the amount that can be deducted in this category.) Deducting all these items from the gross estate gives the taxable estate. Table 21.1 shows that total deductions are $617,000.

Table 21.1   Computing Gift and Estate Taxes*

Gross estate		$1,202,000
Less: Funeral expenses	$ 10,000	
Administrative expenses	25,000	
Debts	32,000	
Marital deduction	500,000	
Charitable deduction	50,000	
Orphan's deduction	0	
Total deductions		617,000
Taxable estate		$ 585,000
Plus: Adjusted taxable gifts		120,000
Tentative tax base		$ 705,000
Tentative tax		$ 231,650
Less: Credit for gift taxes	$ 21,600	
Unified credit*	192,800	
State tax credit	5,000	
Total credits		219,400
Net gift and estate tax payable		$ 12,250

*It is assumed that death occurred in 1988.

Deducting this amount from the gross estate of $1,202,000 gives a taxable estate of $585,000.

Tentative Tax.   Adjusted taxable gifts are added to the taxable estate to give the **tentative tax base**. Adjusted taxable gifts are gifts made in excess of the limits mentioned previously. Table 21.1 shows the adjusted taxable gifts of $120,000, giving a tentative tax base of $705,000.

The 1981 tax law substantially reduced gift and estate taxes. In 1981, the maximum tax rate was 70 percent. This rate has now been reduced to 50 percent. Table 21.2 shows the tentative gift and estate tax rates.

The estate and gift tax for a tentative tax base of over $500,000 but not over $750,000 is $155,800 plus 37 percent of the excess over $500,000. On a tentative tax base of $705,000, the tentative tax would be $155,800 + .37($705,000 − $500,000) = $231,650.

Credits.   Actual taxes paid are affected by credits against the tentative tax. The decedent's estate can claim credit for all gift taxes paid. Table 21.1 shows a credit of $21,600 for gift taxes. Federal rules also allow for a **unified credit**, which is a credit that may be used to reduce the amount of estate

Table 21.2 Tentative Unified Gift and Estate Tax Rates

If The Amount Is		Tentative Tax Is			
Over	But Not Over	Tax	+	%	Over
$ 0	$ 10,000	$ 0	18	$ 0
10,000	20,000	1,800	20	10,000
20,000	40,000	3,800	22	20,000
40,000	60,000	8,200	24	40,000
60,000	80,000	13,000	26	60,000
80,000	100,000	18,200	28	80,000
100,000	150,000	23,800	30	100,000
150,000	250,000	38,800	32	150,000
250,000	500,000	70,800	34	250,000
500,000	750,000	155,800	37	500,000
750,000	1,000,000	248,300	39	750,000
1,000,000	1,250,000	345,800	41	1,000,000
1,250,000	1,500,000	448,300	43	1,250,000
1,500,000	2,000,000	555,800	45	1,500,000
2,000,000	2,500,000	780,000	49	2,000,000
2,500,000		1,025,800	50	2,500,000

taxes that have to be paid. The middle column of Table 21.3 shows this unified credit, which increased from $47,000 in 1981 to $192,800 in 1987 and later years. Table 21.1 assumes that death occurred in 1988. Thus, the unified credit is $192,800.

The unified credit can also be translated into the dollar amount of an estate that would be exempt from taxes. For 1988, the right column of Table 21.3 shows an equivalent exemption of $600,000. We can verify this amount by calculating the taxes payable on it. This amount falls in the 37 percent marginal tax bracket discussed previously. Taxes payable are $155,800 + .37($600,000 − $500,000) = $192,800. This means that in 1988, any taxable estate not over $600,000 would not have to pay any estate taxes.

The last credit shown in Table 21.1 is for $5,000 for state estate tax credit. Total credits equal $219,400. **Net estate taxes** equal tentative taxes less total credits. This estate would pay $12,250 in federal net gift and estate taxes.

Strategies for managing gift and estate taxes will be considered after a discussion of trusts, in the next section.

Table 21.3 Unified Credit for Estate and Gift Taxes

Year	Amount of Credit	Equivalent Exemption
1981	$ 47,000	$175,625
1982	62,800	225,000
1983	79,300	275,000
1984	96,300	325,000
1985	121,800	400,000
1986	155,800	500,000
1987 on	192,800	600,000

Spot Quiz • Gift and Estate Taxes

1. Unlimited gifts and bequests can be made to all members of a person's family.   T _____ F _____

2. The gross estate includes all of jointly owned real property and all personal property.   T _____ F _____

3. From 1987 on, taxable estates under $600,000 will not have to pay any estate taxes.   T _____ F _____

(Answers on page 691)

TRUSTS

Earlier in this chapter, trusts were mentioned as an alternative estate-transfer tool. A trust is a device for transferring property from one person to another person, who manages the property for the benefit of a third person. The one who provides the assets for the trust is called the **grantor**, **settlor**, or **trustor**. The individual or institution that manages the assets is called the **trustee**. The person who receives the benefits is called the **beneficiary**. The assets given to trust are called **corpus** or **principal**. A trust,

then, is a legal procedure that allows the trustee to manage the principal given by the grantor, in accordance with his or her instructions, for the benefit of the beneficiary.

Trusts are an important tool in estate planning. They are useful for meeting the estate-planning goals of systematic and timely transfer of the estate and minimization of administrative costs and estate taxes. Different types of trusts are designed to accomplish slightly different objectives. The most important trusts are explained in this section, after the need for appointing a good trustee has been explained.

Appointing a Trustee

The grantor has the right to name a trustee. A trustee's actions are governed by law. In general, the trustee is held accountable for prudent management of the trust principal. A trustee therefore must have a good understanding of management and investments. The trustee should also understand the needs of the beneficiaries. Finally, the trustee is charged with handling any accounting or tax-related duties, as well as legal disputes affecting the trust.

An individual can be named as a trustee. Trust management fees, however, tend not to be very large. The annual management fees are usually around 1 percent of the trust principal. For this small fee, individuals generally do not want to act as trustees. Most trusts therefore are managed by the trust departments of financial institutions. These trust departments provide very good trust management services for very reasonable fees.

Living Trusts

Living trusts are also called **inter vivos** trusts. A **living trust** is created while the grantor is still alive. It can be either irrevocable or revocable.

Irrevocable Trust. An **irrevocable trust** is one where the grantor has no control over the trust principal or its income. The grantor cannot revoke or alter any of the terms of the trust. The trust income is taxed either to the trust or to the beneficiary if it is distributed. The trust can be used to accomplish three things. First, income taxes can be reduced through the use of an irrevocable trust. Second, this trust can be used to pass inheritances to beneficiaries without going through probate. Third, the trust can be set up to provide funds for a specific purpose. For example, parents could set up an irrevocable trust for a child with the stipulation that income from the trust be distributed only as long as the beneficiary stays enrolled in college. The trust might also state that the principal not be paid to the beneficiary until he or she graduates from college.

Revocable Trust. A **revocable trust** is controlled by the grantor and can be revoked by him or her. For tax purposes, the government assumes that no trust was created because the grantor controls the trust assets. Therefore, no gift taxes are paid when this trust is created, and trust income is taxed to the grantor. The advantage of this trust lies in the grantor's ability to change the terms of the trust. This trust allows the grantor to bypass probate for the principal placed in trust.

Testamentary Trust

A **testamentary trust** is created by placing an appropriately worded clause in one's will. The trust principal comes under the trustee's control on the testator's death. The main advantage of a testamentary trust is that it provides prudent management for the trust principal. For a minor or an inexperienced beneficiary who may not be able to properly manage his or her inheritance, this trust provides the necessary management until the principal is paid out at some designated appropriate time. In some cases, a testamentary trust is set up to provide income to the surviving spouse, and, on his or her death, the principal is distributed to the children or other heirs.

Family Trust

A **family trust**, also known as a **bypass trust**, is a special type of testamentary trust designed to take advantage of both the marital deduction and the unified credit for gift and estate taxes to provide the largest estate possible to children. We will use a simplified example, ignoring expenses and adjustments, to illustrate how a family trust works. ABC has a gross estate of $1.0 million. ABC takes a marital deduction of $1.0 million, and ABC's estate passes tax-free to the spouse, XYZ. On XYZ's death, the tentative tax on $1.0 million is $345,000. The unified credit is $192,800, resulting in an estate tax of $345,800 − $192,800 = $153,000. Thus, $1,000,000 − $153,000 = $847,000 is passed on to the heirs.

With a family trust, ABC would take a marital deduction of $600,000 and place the other $400,000 in a testamentary trust for the heirs. ABC would specify that the income from the trust would go to XYZ, and the principal would go to the heirs on XYZ's death. Because XYZ does not have control over the trust, it is excluded from his or her estate. On XYZ's death, the $400,000 passes tax-free to the heirs, because it is less than $600,000. Also, XYZ's estate of $600,000 passes tax-free to the heirs. Thus, with the use of a family trust, ABC and XYZ have been able to reduce estate taxes by $153,000. Family trusts are effective for estates over $600,000; up to $1.2 million can be passed on to children tax-free.

Life Insurance Trust

A trust can be set up and named the beneficiary of the grantor's life insurance policies. On the grantor's death, life insurance benefits are paid to the trust. The trustee manages the principal in accordance with the terms of the trust. This arrangement places insurance benefits in the hands of prudent management. A similar result could be achieved by selecting an appropriate settlement option for the life insurance policy. But often a trust arrangement can produce a higher income than that provided by the life insurance company. The estate derives estate tax savings if this trust is irrevocable.

Custodianship Account for Minors

A custodianship account of minor children can be easily established under the **Uniform Gifts to Minors Act**. The gifts to this account cannot exceed $30,000. The minor child needs a social security number before this account can be opened. Most financial institutions and brokerage offices are equipped to open this account. Someone other than the grantor, usually the other spouse or a close relative, is named custodian of the account.

The major advantage of a custodian account is that income from the fund is taxed to the minor, who is in a much lower tax bracket than the parents. Thus, after-tax income is built up at a faster rate than if the parents retained the money. Let's assume that a parent sets up a custodian account for $30,000 for a minor child of eight years. The child is expected to attend college in ten years. The account earns 9 percent every year after taxes for the next ten years. All earnings are accumulated and reinvested. When the child is ready to start college ten years from now, the custodian account will contain $71,021. This amount might be just enough to pay for four years of college by then.

But what if the child does not want to go to college? Here lies the major disadvantage of a minority custodian account. The money in the account is legally the minor's. The account must be turned over to the minor when he or she reaches legal age, which ranges from 18 to 21 years of age, depending on the state. Despite this weakness, the minority custodian account is a worthwhile device for lowering taxes and accumulating money for college expenses.

Other Trusts

Minority trusts created under Internal Revenue Code Sections 2503 (b) and (c) allow for setting up trusts similar to a custodianship account except that more than $30,000 can be placed in them. These trusts are more expensive to set up than a custodian account, and they must be managed by a trustee rather than a custodian.

The Tax Reform Act of 1986 repealed two popular trusts for estate management. They are mentioned here because similar trusts may be introduced eventually. A **Clifford trust** was irrevocable for ten years and one day, after which the trust principal automatically reverted to the grantor. The trust was also revoked if the beneficiary died. The trust was used primarily to provide income for elderly parents and children in college. Income paid out to beneficiaries was taxed at their lower rates.

A variation on a Clifford trust was a device called a **Crown loan** or **interest-free demand loan**. A Crown loan allowed the grantors to take back their contribution at any time rather than waiting for ten years, as was the case with the Clifford trust. A Crown loan was set up by making an interest-free loan to the trust, with the loan being callable at any time.

Spot Quiz • Trusts

1. All trusts are useful for minimizing taxes.   T _____   F _____

2. A testamentary trust cannot be changed after the testator's death.
                                                     T _____   F _____

3. The principal in a family trust reverts to the decedent's estate after the death of his or her spouse.   T _____   F _____

(Answers on page 691)

ESTATE-PLANNING STRATEGIES

The goals of estate planning were discussed earlier in the chapter. Some additional strategies for achieving these goals are suggested in this section.

Charitable Donations

Estate taxes can be lowered by donating to a qualified institution. Religious, educational, and veterans' organizations, volunteer fire companies, public libraries, and the YMCA are all examples of institutions to whom tax-exempt donations can be made. Under the right circumstances, giving away assets to charities can be less painful than you would think. An example will clarify the situation.

Let's assume that a person bought stock for $10,000 in 1982. In 1988, on this person's death, the stock was worth $30,000. The stock will be part of the decedent's taxable estate. Estate taxes on this $30,000 stock may equal as much as $15,000.

If this stock is donated by a will to charity, the decedent takes an income tax deduction on her income tax return (which would be prepared by the estate executor). Also, the taxable estate is reduced by $30,000, resulting in estate tax savings of up to $15,000. Under the right conditions, the income tax deduction and the taxable estate reduction, combined with the pleasures of giving, can make charitable donations desirable.

Gift Giving

By making maximum annual tax-free gifts of $10,000 (or $20,000 under certain conditions) each year to his or her children, a parent can substantially reduce the size of the taxable estate. One obvious danger is that the donor loses control over the assets. Another problem also has to do with the tax treatment of inherited assets. The cost basis for gifted assets is the donor's original cost. The cost basis for assets transferred through the estate is the value at the time of the testator's death (or the value six months after death, whichever is more advantageous).

Let's assume that the person mentioned in the previous example makes a gift of the stock to her son. When the son sells the stock, he will have to compute capital gains based on the original cost of $10,000. Instead of gifting the stock to her son, the person could have willed it to him. Her tentative tax base is less than $600,000 and thus not subject to taxes, according to Table 21.3. The stock would have passed tax-free to her son, and his cost basis would have been $30,000 instead of $10,000 when the stock was a gift.

As the example shows, the choice between giving and bequesting is affected by the type of assets involved, the size of the tentative tax base, and the tax-exempt equivalent amount. Theoretically, decisions about giving or bequesting can be made right up to death. An analysis of the factors mentioned here can result in more for the beneficiaries.

Marital Deduction and Trust

With the 1981 tax laws, it is natural to believe that one way of avoiding gift and estate taxes is to take a marital deduction large enough to leave the tentative tax base smaller than the tax-exempt equivalent amount. This, of course, is correct. Taking an appropriately large marital deduction can reduce estate taxes to zero. However, the surviving spouse, assuming no remarriage, does not have a marital deduction to use, and thus the estate may be subject to large estate taxes.

One way of getting around this problem, which exists only for estates larger than the tax-exempt equivalent amount, is to use the family trust. As the previous example illustrated, a family trust can be used effectively to reduce estate taxes. Careful planning can result in substantial savings of estate taxes.

Life Insurance

As mentioned previously, life insurance proceeds are added to the decedent's taxable estate. If the size of the estate is large, significant amounts of estate taxes may have to be paid on the life insurance proceeds. One strategy for removing the life insurance proceeds from the estate is to transfer ownership of the policy to the beneficiary—for example, the spouse. The beneficiary now owns the policy and has the right to cancel or surrender the policy or borrow on its cash value. However, the beneficiary also can receive the death benefits without having the policy go through probate or the insured person's estate paying any taxes. This is an especially desirable strategy if a person has large amounts of life insurance. With the 1981 tax law, the strategy works equally well for ordinary life and term insurance.

Power of Invasion

One reason for establishing a trust is to provide benefits to a beneficiary. Yet no one can forecast economic events with a high degree of certainty. A trust that might have satisfied a beneficiary's wants under one set of economic circumstances may not do so under a different set of economic conditions. Flexibility in establishing a trust may be desirable if the objective of the trust is to provide the best possible benefits to the beneficiary. One way of creating flexibility is to give either the trustee or the beneficiary the power of invasion.

Power of invasion gives a person the right to partially liquidate the estate principal and pay out the proceeds to the beneficiary. Let's assume that a trust has been set up to provide a college-bound child with tuition money. The earnings from the trust remain the same, but college tuition keeps going up. The trustee or the beneficiary so empowered may "invade" the trust and use a portion of the estate principal to help with tuition payments. The grantor may build a safeguard into the trust by specifying that, say, no more than 5 or 10 percent of the estate can be invaded in any given year. Allowing power of invasion for a trust allows the trustee more flexibility in meeting the grantor's desires for providing benefits to the beneficiary.

Spot Quiz • Estate-Planning Strategies

1. Giving a gift reduces the taxable estate but may not be desirable.

    T _____   F _____

2. The estate cannot avoid estate taxes by using a very large marital deduction.   T _____   F _____

(Answers on page 691)

Summary

Estate planning calls for systematically accumulating, managing, and transferring your estate. Estate transfer costs, the needs of beneficiaries, and changes in the economic environment make estate planning essential. A good plan for the estate calls for systematic and timely transfer of the estate with minimum costs and taxes related to the transfer.

A will provides for systematic transfer of a person's estate. To be considered valid, a will has to meet the requirements of testamentary intention and formality in execution. A will has a variety of major sections that need to be carefully expressed. Changes to a will can be made by a codicil, although it is preferable to write a new will. The will is probated after the testator's death, and the estate is disposed in keeping with the terms of the will. An executor for a will must handle many duties and should be carefully chosen. In the absence of a will, the estate is transferred according to the state intestacy laws.

Federal gift and estate taxes as well as state estate and inheritance taxes are imposed when an estate is transferred. When you calculate the gift and estate taxes due, you must take into consideration the gift tax exclusion, the marital deduction, and the unified tax credit.

Trusts can help save income taxes and estate taxes, provide funds for beneficiaries, and allow an orderly transfer of a person's estate. Major types of trusts are the minor custodian account, the irrevocable living trust, the testamentary trust, and the family trust.

Donations to charitable institutions and gift giving decrease the estate, and both can be used for estate planning. In some cases, though, where the estate is not large enough, the transfer of assets through a will might

be more desirable than a transfer through gift giving. By carefully combining the marital deduction and a trust, it is possible to avoid paying some estate taxes.

Questions

1. What is meant by estate planning? What is included in a person's estate?

2. Why is a systematic transfer of your estate important?

3. Briefly explain the four goals of estate planning.

4. What is a will? Why is it important to write a valid will?

5. Briefly explain the legal requirements for writing a valid will.

6. Explain the difference between a general and a specific legacy.

7. What is a codicil? Explain why some experts believe that writing a new will is more desirable than changing an existing one with a codicil.

8. Briefly explain the responsibilities of an executor/executrix.

9. What does a letter of last instructions contain? What is its purpose?

10. Explain intestacy. Briefly explain how an intestacy distribution takes place.

11. Explain the differences among:
    a. Joint tenancy.
    b. Tenancy in common.
    c. Tenancy by the entirety.

12. Explain why gift and estate taxes have been combined.

13. Explain the role of the marital deduction in the transfer of an estate.

14. What are the responsibilities of a trustee?

15. Briefly explain how a minor's custodian account works.

16. What are the advantages and disadvantages of an irrevocable trust?

17. Is a testamentary trust more desirable than an irrevocable trust? Explain your answer.

18. What is a family trust? What are its advantages?

19. How can gift giving help with estate transfer? Explain a situation where gift giving may not be desirable for transferring portions of the estate.

20. Explain power of invasion. Should power of invasion be included in a trust set up to provide income to parents? Explain your answer.

Case Problems

1. Barkley Sanders died in 1988 and left a gross estate of $2,600,000. His expenses paid from the estate were as follows: funeral, $30,000; administrative, $50,000; debt, $290,000; marital deduction, $1,400,000; charitable, $200,000; other, $0. He gave away $250,000 in taxable gifts. His estate received $46,800 in credit for gift taxes. State estate tax credit was $23,000. Show your calculations for his net gift and estate taxes payable.

2. Suppose that Barkley Sanders's widow, Ruth Sanders, dies in 1989. She leaves an estate that has a tentative tax base of $1,100,000 (Mrs. Sanders cannot use a marital deduction because she did not remarry). Her estate receives a state estate tax credit of $33,000. How much will her estate have to pay in net gift and estate taxes payable? Show your calculations. Use the information in Problem 1.

3. Mr. Castell's properties and their values and forms of ownership as of January 1989 are shown below:
   Stock, $300,000, separate
   House, $100,000, joint
   Business, $500,000, separate
   Other, $100,000, joint
   Only his portions of the joint properties are listed above. The Castells have two children who recently graduated from college. Mr. Castell does not have a will, neither has he done any planning for transferring his estate. What advice do you have for him? Your discussion should include a reasonable plan for transferring Mr. Castell's estate.

Bibliography

"Creative Ways to Save for College." *Money* (October 1986): 101–102.

"How to Avoid Estate Taxes." *Money* (December 1985): 60–66.

"If There's a Will, There's a Way." *Money* (December 1985): 70–74.

"The New ABCs of Asset Shifting." *Money* (October 1987): 91–96.

"Planning a Hassle-Free Legacy." *Money* (October 1987): 82–88

"A Short Course in Estate Planning." *Money* (October 1987): 74–80.

"Take Care of Your Heirs." *Changing Times* (September 1986): 32–38.

"Trusts That Make Your Family Secure." *Money* (December 1985): 52–58.

"Trusts You Can Change at Will." *Changing Times* (November 1987): 141–144.

"What Every Spouse Should Know." *Money* (December 1985): 99–104.

"Who Should You Name as Trustee?" *Changing Times* (June 1985): 85–86.

Answers to Spot Quizzes

The Basics of Estate Planning (page 665)

1. F (Both are equally important.)
2. T (That is one of the important aspects of estate planning.)
3. F (Sometimes it is useful to delay distribution of assets.)

Wills (page 675)

1. T (Chances are it will be declared invalid.)
2. T (Some assets may have to be sold to raise cash.)
3. F (The executor needs to probate the will in court first.)

4. F (A person who dies intestate has no say on how his or her estate is distributed.)

Gift and Estate Taxes (page 680)

1. F (Unlimited gifts and bequests can be made only to one's spouse.)

2. F (Only the appropriate portion of jointly owned property is included.)

3. T (The equivalent exemption amount is $600,000.)

Trusts (page 684)

1. F (Revocable trusts do not minimize taxes.)

2. T (The testator cannot change the will after his death.)

3. F (The principal is distributed to the specified beneficiaries.)

Estate-Planning Strategies (page 687)

1. T (A variety of factors affect the decision to make a gift.)

2. F (You can use a very large marital deduction to avoid estate taxes.)

Glossary

A

Acceleration clause. Causes the total loan to become due immediately if the borrower misses a payment. Allows the lender to repossess the security if the borrower defaults on a payment.

Accounting method. The way in which a taxpayer keeps financial records, on either a cash or an accrual basis.

Accrual basis accounting method. Income earned and expenses incurred are recognized as they occur, irrespective of whether any money is received or paid.

Accumulation unit. A small portion of a portfolio of common stocks in which the annuity payments have been invested by the insurer.

Activity checking account. Service fees are charged on this account.

Add-on clause. Allows the lender to maintain a security interest in all items financed by the lender until all items are repaid.

Adjustable rate mortgage (ARM). The applicable rate is periodically adjusted.

Adjusted balance method. Interest is charged on the balance outstanding after it has been adjusted for payments and credits.

Annual depreciation charge. The decline in value of a property due to normal wear and tear.

Annual percentage rate (APR). The effective interest rate applicable to a loan:

$$APR = \frac{200 \times I \times n}{L \times T}$$

where I = total dollar amount of interest, n = number of payments per year, L = loan amount, and T = total number of payments plus one. This formula is limited to payments that are regular and constant.

Annual reports. Issued annually by the corporation to its stockholders and to other interested parties.

Annuities. Savings or investment plans that provide for monthly income at a later stage in life.

Annuity certain. Does not involve any life contingencies. Payments are guaranteed for a fixed time period and are paid to either the insured or the insured's beneficiaries.

Assets. Everything that a person owns, whether the items are paid for or not.

Assigned-risk pool. A driver in this will have to pay relatively high insurance premiums because, due to a variety of reasons, he or she tends to be more risky than other drivers.

Assumption clause. Allows the owner of a house to transfer the mortgage to a buyer.

Attestation clause. The testator's or testatrix's attestation is contained in this clause. It is usually lengthy and also includes the names of the attesting witnesses.

Audit. A close examination of financial records.

Authorized shares. The maximum number of shares that a firm can issue.

Automatic teller machine (ATM). An electronic terminal for handling banking transactions.

Average daily balance method. Interest is charged on the average daily balance outstanding. The average balance is calculated by adding the balances outstanding each day and dividing the total by the number of days in the billing month. Payments made during the billing month reduce the average balance outstanding.

B

Bait and switch. An illegal method of advertising and selling in which the consumer, initially interested in the advertised product, is persuaded to buy an alternative item.

Balanced mutual fund. One that invests in both stocks and bonds.

Balance sheet. A listing of what a family or person owns and owes at a certain point in a certain time period. It has three categories: assets, liabilities, and net worth.

Balloon payment clause. Installment loan payments that are too small to fully pay off the loan at maturity result in the borrower facing a relatively large final payment when the loan matures.

Bank credit cards. Credit cards issued by banks. The most widely used ones are MasterCard and Visa.

Bankruptcy. A legal procedure that allows a person to give up certain assets in return for release from certain financial obligations.

Basic auto policy (BAP). Provides coverage to both personal and business vehicles.

Basic health insurance policy. Provides low levels of coverage for hospitalization, surgery, and other medical expenses.

Bearer bond. Not registered in any specific name.

Beneficiary. A person named to receive money or property under a will, trust, or life insurance policy.

Bequest. Anything left to another in a person's will.

Big board. The New York Stock Exchange is the biggest organized market.

Binder. A temporary contract that allows the agent to provide coverage from the time the application is received.

Blank endorsement. The payee's signing of only his or her name to the back of a check.

Blue chip stocks. Highly stable and financially strong firms.

Blue Cross/Blue Shield Association. The nation's largest providers of health insurance. They are a set of nonprofit organizations with the sole purpose of providing health insurance coverage.

Bond. Represents indebtedness by the issuing institution to the investor.

Bond mutual fund. One that emphasizes safety and invests in high-grade bonds.

Book value. Total assets minus total liabilities.

"Bounced" check. A check that has been returned for insufficient funds.

Budgeting. A system of record keeping involving detailed planning to account for all incomes and expenses.

Bullion coins. Coins that are sold basically for their precious metal content.

Business risk. Risk associated with changes in the firm's sales.

Buying long. Buying securities on margin with the expectation of selling them in the future at a higher price.

Buying on margin. The investor borrows a portion of funds from the brokerage house to buy securities.

Bypass trust. See Family trust.

C

Call provision. A provision in a security issue that gives the firm the right to call, or redeem, the security outstanding before maturity.

Call value. The value at which a security is called for redemption prior to maturity.

Capital assets. For tax purposes, property that is owned for personal use or investment purposes. Property used in operating a business is not a capital asset.

Capital gains. The gains that result when an investment is sold for more than its cost.

Capital loss. The loss that results when an investment is sold for less than its cost.

Cash basis accounting method. All income actually received and all tax-deductible expenses actually incurred are reported for the year.

Cash dividends. Portion of earnings paid out in cash.

Cashier's check. A check that the bank writes on itself.

Cash inflow. All income, including fees, scholarships, grants, gifts, loans, etc.

Cash value. The savings portion of a whole life insurance policy.

"Caveat emptor." "Let the buyer beware."

Certain period annuity. Guarantees payment for the life of the beneficiary as well as for a minimum specified period. If the beneficiary dies before the expiration of the period, payments are continued to the beneficiary's heirs until the end of the period.

Certificate of title. A lawyer's certification that no claims appear to be outstanding against the property.

Certified check. The bank has already deducted the check amount from the account and is guaranteeing payment on the check.

Check. A written order to a bank to pay a sum of money from a demand deposit account.

Checking account. See Demand deposit account.

Clifford trust. A trust that is irrevocable for ten years and one day, after which the trust principal automatically reverts to the grantor. It is also revoked if the beneficiary dies. Repealed by the 1986 Tax Reform Act.

Closed-end investment company. A corporation that invests in the shares of other companies.

Codicil. An addition to a will; used to change or modify an existing will.

Coinsurance clause in health insurance policies. Requires the insured to pay a portion of the expenses above the deductible.

Coinsurance clause in homeowners' insurance policies. Provides that the insurance coverage must be at or above a stated percentage (usually 80 percent) of the replacement cost of the home before partial losses will be covered to the policy limit.

Collateral. Designation of or security given as a pledge for the repayment of a loan.

Collision (no-fault) coverage. Applies to damage to the insured's car. It will cover the car whatever the reason for the damage, even when the other driver is at fault. The amount of coverage is equal to the lesser of the current wholesale value of the insured vehicle or the cost of repair, less any deductible.

Commercial banks. Institutions that offer a full range of services to the consumer, including demand deposit accounts, savings accounts, special accounts, etc.

Common stock. Evidence of ownership in a company.

Common stock mutual fund. One that invests in the common shares of companies.

Community property. Acquired by both spouses during their marriage, irrespective of the wage-earning status of either spouse.

Composite risk. Business, market, inflation, and liquidity risks combined.

Comprehensive homeowners' liability insurance. General as well as umbrella insurance.

Comprehensive medical insurance. Combines basic insurance with major medical insurance. Features covered vary among insurers.

Comprehensive (no-fault) coverage. Covers a variety of perils, such as glass breakage and losses caused by fire, theft, hail, water, flood, vandalism, riot, and accidents with birds and animals. Coverage limits are the same as for collision insurance.

Conditional sales contract. Title to the goods remains with the lender, while the buyer has physical possession of them. The title goes to the buyer when the loan is repaid. This type of contract is often used with items such as appliances and furniture.

Condominium (condo). An individually owned unit in an apartment complex. There are two types: new construction and conversion of rental units.

Consumer finance companies. Also called small loan or finance companies. They have higher APRs than banks have, reflecting the risky nature of their loans.

Consumerism. Getting the most for one's money.

Consumption goods. Includes food, groceries, gasoline, eating in restaurants, and clothing.

Contingency fund. A fund included in cash needs that provides cash to be used if an emergency arises.

Contingent beneficiary. The policyholder's second choice as beneficiary, dependent on the standing of the primary beneficiary.

Contract for deed. The property seller provides financing for the property.

Conversion price. The price of common stock at which a convertible security can be converted.

Conversion ratio. The number of common shares received by the investor converting a convertible security.

Convertible preferred stock. One that can be converted into common stock.

Convertible term life insurance. Can be converted into ordinary life or endowment insurance at the insured's option without the insured's having to prove evidence of insurability.

Cooperative apartments. The owners buy a proportional share of the total complex rather than just their units.

Corporate bonds. Debt securities issued by corporations.

Coupon rate. For a bond, its annual interest divided by its face value.

Covered option. One in which the option seller had the security to sell on a call by the option buyer or the money to buy on a put by the option buyer.

Credit. All money borrowed, other than home financing.

Credit life insurance. Term insurance designed to pay off the remaining balance on the loan in case of the borrower's death.

Credit union. An institution whose depositors are also its owners. It lends money only to its owners.

Crown loan. An interest-free loan made to a trust by grantors, with the loan being callable

at any time rather than after ten years. Repealed by the 1986 Tax Reform Act.

Cumulative preferred stocks. These require that any dividends missed be paid before dividends can be paid on common stock.

Current yield. For a bond, its annual interest divided by its current market price.

Custodianship account for minors. An account set up for a child in the form of gifts, which cannot exceed $30,000. It is managed by a custodian.

D

Day-of-deposit to day-of-withdrawal (DD/DW) method of computing interest. Interest is paid on the actual balance on deposit.

Debenture. A bond not secured by liens against specific assets of the firm.

Debt consolidation loan. A new loan that is taken out to repay the loans outstanding. One debt payment is substituted for many debt payments.

Deceptive practice legislation. Laws enacted to prohibit deceptive trade practices. They cover door-to-door as well as mail order selling.

Declarations section of an insurance policy. Contains the basic identifying details of the policy. It consists of the name of the policyholder, what is insured, the amount of insurance, the cost of the policy, and the time period covered by the insurance.

Decreasing term life insurance. Has insurance premiums that remain level over the life of the policy, but the amount of benefits keeps declining.

Deductible clause. Allows the insured to retain the loss equal to the deductible amount.

Deductible of an insurance policy. The amount of loss retained.

Deed. A legal document transferring title from owner to buyer, typically recorded with

the clerk of the county in which the property is located.

Deed of trust. A mortgage held by a trustee during the period in which the mortgage loan is outstanding.

Defined benefit plan. Specifies a certain method for computing retirement benefits and guarantees the worker a certain pension.

Defined contribution plan. Specifies the minimum periodic contribution that an employer and an employee are to make annually toward the employee's retirement benefits.

Delinquency charges clause. Installment lender will impose a late payment charge if the payment is not made within a specified time period.

Demand deposit account. Account from which the account owner can withdraw funds on demand. No interest is received on this account.

Deposit or "earnest money." Money that the buyer pays to indicate his willingness to follow through with the purchase agreement.

Depreciation. Expensing the wear and tear of long-lived assets used in business.

Disability. Two general and fairly widely used definitions are as follows: (1) the inability of the insured to perform duties related to his or her present occupation; (2) the inability of the insured to perform duties of an occupation for which he or she is or may be suitable by reason of education, training, and experience.

Disclosure legislation. Laws enacted to require manufacturers and sellers to provide more information to consumers.

Discount broker. One who processes securities transactions for relatively low commissions.

Dividend clause. Included in a participating life insurance policy, allowing insurer to pay dividends to the policyholder.

Dividend payout ratio. Dividends per share divided by earnings per share.

Dividends. Portion of earnings paid out to a firm's stockholders; reported on a per-share basis.

Dividend yield. Dividends per share times 100, divided by the market value of a share.

Dollar cost averaging. A method for buying stocks that requires that the same dollar amount be invested in the same stock during each time period over a long time.

Double indemnity. With this option, payment of twice the face amount of the policy in death benefits is made if the insured is killed in an accident.

Dow Jones industrial average (DJIA). The most popular measure of the stock market's performance.

Down payment. Money that the buyer puts up toward the purchase of a house, car, or other asset.

E

Earnings per share (EPS). Net income divided by shares outstanding.

"Easy" credit. Very few credit applicants are rejected by the lender.

Economic factors. Economic conditions that can change and have an impact on an estate.

Effective interest rate. The interest rate actually received by the account owner.

Efficient markets hypothesis. See Random walk hypothesis.

Electronic terminals. Automatic teller machines (ATMs) installed by many banks to handle routine customer transactions.

Employee Retirement Income Security Act (ERISA). A federal law passed in 1974 to curb abuses and bad business practices related to pension funds.

Endorsement (insurance). A statement attached to an insurance policy changing the terms of the policy.

Endorsement of payee. The payee's signing of his or her name to the back of a check.

Endowment life insurance. Either after a specified time period or when the insured attains a certain age, the policy becomes endowed, or fully paid up.

Equal Credit Opportunity Act of 1975. Prohibits credit discrimination on the basis of sex or marital status.

Equity. Net worth.

Escrow account clause. Most lenders require that borrowers make monthly insurance payments equal to one-twelfth of anticipated real estate taxes and insurance into this account. This assures the lender that there are funds from which the taxes and insurance can be paid.

Estate. Includes all of a person's assets. Also included is the appropriate portion of any jointly owned property.

Estate building. The accumulation or saving of money.

Estate planning. The systematic accumulation, management, and transfer of a person's estate.

Estate-related costs. Costs related to the transfer of an estate.

Estate taxes. Taxes levied on the transfer of estates that are larger than a certain specified sum.

Executor or executrix. A person or an institution responsible for administering the testator's estate.

Exemption. Release from tax payments that the IRS allows. Reduced taxable income by $1,950 for 1988 for each dependent.

Expense items. Categories of different ways in which money is spent.

Expense record book. Separate pages for expense categories are found here for recording.

Extended health insurance policy. Supplements the basic policy. It has large deductibles and high maximum limits. It generally also requires the insured to pay a portion of the medical expenses.

Extended warranty (automobile). Excludes routine maintenance and focuses on major repairs to the engine and the drive train.

F

Face value. The value at which a firm buys back its bonds.

Fair Credit Reporting Act of 1971. Designed to force credit bureaus to keep only correct information about borrowers on file.

Family auto policy (FAP). Limited strictly to personal cars.

Family trust. A trust that takes advantage of both the marital deduction and the unified credit for gift and estate taxes to provide a larger estate to one's children.

Federal Deposit Insurance Corporation (FDIC). A government agency that provides insurance for accounts held at banks; most banks carry FDIC insurance.

Federal Housing Authority (FHA). A government agency that provides mortgage loan insurance to financial institutions.

Federal Savings and Loan Insurance Corporation (FSLIC). A government agency that provides insurance for accounts held at savings and loan associations.

Financial assets. Assets that are readily convertible into cash.

Financial goals. Goals established for maximizing income and getting the most out of the income received.

Financial management records. Records used for short-term as well as long-term management of financial resources.

Financial planning. Planning related to income and expenses.

Financial statements. Income statements, balance sheets, forecasts of inflows and expenses, budgets, and Budget Control Sheets.

First-in, first-out (FIFO) method of computing interest. Withdrawals are deducted from the beginning balance before computation.

First mortgage. A mortgage with the highest priority against pledged property.

Fixed annuity. An annuity in which the dollar amount of periodic benefits remains fixed.

Fixed-rate mortgage. A mortgage loan that is at a set specified interest rate for a specific time period.

Flexible budgeting. A system of budgeting that allows for adjustments.

Floater policy. Provides all risk coverage, except for exclusions, for the personal property item in question.

Forecasted budget. The combination of forecasting cash inflows and forecasting expenses.

Fortuitous loss. A loss associated with chance events only.

Free checking account. Has no service charges at all and no minimum balance.

"Full" warranty. Provides the consumer with extended coverage on the product.

Funded pension plan. In this pension plan, future pensions earned in the current year are funded currently.

Funding. The way in which a firm plans to meet its future pension liabilities.

Futures contract. Requires delivery of a specific quantity of a commodity at a certain price, place, and date.

Futures markets. Where futures contracts are traded.

G

Garnishment of wages. See Wage assignment or garnishment clause.

General legacy. A bequest of money that comes out of the estate in general.

General liability insurance. Coverage for a large variety of situations.

General obligation bonds. Secured by a state's or city's power to tax.

Gift. The transfer of assets from one person to another.

Gift giving. A method of transferring a person's estate, while the person is still living, through gifts to specified beneficiaries.

Gift tax exclusion. A lawful method by which a person can give a gift without incurring any tax liability.

Gold bugs. Investors who have a very strong preference for buying gold.

Gold bullion. A bar of gold.

Grace period. Allows the insured a certain number of days in which to make a late payment and still keep the policy in force.

Graduated payment mortgage (GPM). For the first few years, GPM payments are lower than payments for a conventional mortgage. In later years, GPM payments are higher than conventional mortgage payments.

Grantor. A person who gives the assets for the trust.

Group insurance plan. Insurance coverage made available to group members, usually employees of the same employer but sometimes social club members.

Growth stocks. Firms that are expected to sustain high growth rates.

Guaranteed insurability. With this option, the insured has the right to buy additional specified amounts of insurance at specified intervals without providing proof of insurability.

H

Hazard insurance clause. Lenders require borrowers to carry this in order to protect the lender's financial stake in a house.

Health maintenance organization (HMO). A health insurance association that provides comprehensive coverage for a fixed, prepaid premium.

Health risk. Exists when a person faces the chance of losing assets and income due to sickness and disability.

High-grade bonds. Very safe and low-risk bonds.

Holding cost of a house. The cost of a house plus any expenses related to the final settlement that are not tax deductible plus any expenses related to permanent house or property improvements.

Holographic will. One in which all the formal requirements of a valid will are not met.

Homeowners' Form 1 (HO-1). Also known as the basic form. It covers certain perils such as fire, lightning, explosion, riot, vandalism, and theft.

Homeowners' Form 2 (HO-2). Also known as the broad form. It covers a wide variety of perils.

Homeowners' Form 3 (HO-3). Also known as the special form. It combines the features of both HO-1 and HO-2.

Homeowners' Form 4 (HO-4). Designed for renters.

Homeowners' Form 5 (HO-5). Also known as the comprehensive form. It covers all perils except those specifically excluded from Coverages A, B, C, and D.

Homeowners' Form 6 (HO-6). Designed for condominium owners. It is like HO-4.

Home Owners Warranty (HOW) Program. Builders in this program guarantee that their workmanship, materials, and construction are up to established standards.

''House poor.'' Buying more house than one can afford.

Housing records. All records related to purchase, sale, or rental of housing as well as records of permanent home improvements.

I

Implied warranty. Means that a product is capable of doing what it is supposed to do.

Impulse buying. Unplanned spending of money.

Income. Money earned or received from any and all sources.

Income deficit. The resulting figure when expenses are in excess of income.

Income statement. A listing of incomes including wages or salaries; bonuses and sales commissions; interest from accounts, funds, and bonds; dividends; and gifts and profits from item sales. These are added up to obtain total income on cash inflow, from which is subtracted the sum of listed expenses. This determines an income surplus or deficit that the family or person has incurred for a certain time period.

Income stocks. Firms with high dividend yields.

Income surplus. The difference between a greater total of incomes and a lesser total of expenses.

Incontestability clause. States that the insurer cannot question the validity of the information provided by the insured after the policy has been in force for two years.

Incremental tax rate. The tax rate that applies to increased or incremental earnings.

Indemnity or reimbursement payment plan. Under this type of plan, the insurance company agrees to reimburse the insured for up to a specified sum of money if an insured event occurs.

Indentures. A contract between a bond seller and a bond buyer.

Individual retirement account (IRA). A retirement plan that an individual establishes for himself or herself.

Inflation. A steady, sustained increase in the prices of goods and services.

Inflation risk. The risk that the value of investments will not increase at least as rapidly as the rate of inflation.

Inheritance taxes. Some states place this on the beneficiary rather than taxing the estate.

Insiders. Those investors who have knowledge about a company that is not available to other investors.

Installment loans. Loans that must be repaid by making a series of payments. These are associated with the purchase of durable goods and services such as cars, appliances, and home remodeling. The loan amount as well as the payments are fixed.

Installment sales contract. The most common form of installment loan. It is for the lender's benefit. It is designed to allow the lender to recover its loan in case the borrower is not willing or able to repay the loan as scheduled.

Insurable interest. The person buying this has to have a direct interest in having the object insured; if not, he or she will be ineligible for the insurance.

Insurance. A legal contract that transfers the risk of incurring the insured loss to the insurance company.

Insurance records. Records containing all insurance policies; photographs of expensive items, and appraisals of those items.

Interest. Return that the lender earns for loaning money to the borrower.

Interest-adjusted cost index. Premiums, dividends, and cash values are considered on a time-value-adjusted basis. The formula for this method is as follows: (present value of all premiums − present value of all dividends and cash value) ÷ (number of years of analysis) = average annual cost.

Internal Revenue Service (IRS). A division of the U.S. Department of the Treasury. It is the agency in charge of administering and enforcing the Internal Revenue Code and collecting taxes.

Internal Revenue Service ruling. The IRS's interpretation of a law applied to a special situation.

Inter vivos trust. See Living trust.

Intestacy. The situation created when a person dies without leaving a valid will.

Intestate decedent. A person who dies without leaving a valid will.

Intestate distribution. The distribution of the decedent's estate according to state law when intestacy occurs.

Investment asset. An asset owned for its investment value.

Investment climate. The economic environment and the mood of investors in general.

Investment clubs. A club whose members pool their investment funds to buy and sell securities.

Investments. Assets acquired with the expectation of earning a positive return over time.

Irrevocable trust. A trust in which the grantor has no control over the trust principal or its income.

Issued shares. Shares that are actually issued and sold to investors.

J

Joint account. A checking or savings account in the names of two or more persons. There are two types of joint accounts. One type allows any owner to withdraw funds; the other type requires the permission of all owners before funds can be withdrawn.

Joint and survivorship annuity. Continues payment to a secondary beneficiary if the primary one dies. This annuity guarantees income for life to the surviving beneficiary.

Joint ownership. Two or more persons jointly own a property. It is in three forms: (1) joint tenancy; (2) tenancy in common; and (3) tenancy by the entirety.

Joint savings account. In the name of more than one individual.

Joint tenancy. Each of the two or more owners owns a nonspecific fraction of the property.

Junior mortgage bond. Priority of claims is lower than that of senior mortgage bonds.

Junk bonds. Risky bonds.

K

Keogh plan. A retirement plan limited to self-employed individuals.

L

Land contract. A financing method in which the deed is held in escrow until the mortgage is paid off.

Last-in, first-out (LIFO) method of computing interest. Withdrawals are deducted from

the last deposit first, then from the most recent ones.

Law of large numbers. When the same event is repeated many times, actual outcomes are numerically close to expected outcomes.

Lease. Rental agreement.

Letter of last instructions. Contains instructions by the testator as well as certain other information that the testator might wish to convey to the executor and beneficiaries.

Liabilities. Money owed by a family or person.

Liability risk. Risk of causing and paying for damages to someone else.

Life insurance policy. A legal contract that pays the survivor of the insured a fixed sum of money when the insured dies.

Life insurance rider. Extra options that the policyholder can have written into the policy to make it more suitable.

Life insurance trust. A trust that is set up and names the beneficiary of the grantor's life insurance policies.

Life style. The manner of living of an individual or family.

Limited-payment whole life insurance. Has insurance premiums paid only for a specific time period. It remains in force after the payment period is over.

Limited warranty. Much more restrictive than a full warranty.

Limit order. The investor specifies a maximum buying price or a minimum selling price for a security.

Liquid assets. Includes cash, money in checking and savings accounts, certificates of deposit, and other investments that can be readily converted into cash.

Listed firm. One whose securities trade on organized markets.

Living trust. Created while the grantor is still alive.

Load mutual fund. One that charges a commission on the sales of its stock.

Loan amortization. The systematic repayment of the loan principal and interest.

Loan sharks. Lenders who operate outside the legal limits imposed by state and federal laws.

Long-term gains and losses. Occur when properties are held for more than one year.

Long-term goals. Goals with a planning horizon of more than one year.

Long-term planning. Planning associated with managing housing, insurance, and investment funds.

Loss ratio. The ratio of benefits paid to premiums received by an insurance company.

Low-balance method of computing interest. Interest is paid on the lowest balance on deposit in the account during the interest period.

M

Magnetic ink character recognition (MICR). A process for expediting check clearing.

Major medical insurance (MM). Covers virtually all types of health expenses—hospital expenses, surgical expenses, medical expenses, and then some.

Margin. Minimum percentage of the purchase price put up by the investor.

Margin account. A special type of account in which the investor has to put up only a portion of the security's purchase price.

Marginal tax rate. Given a base taxable income, this is the rate that applies only to the last dollar of taxable income.

Marital deduction. A bequest that a testator makes to his or her spouse.

Market order. The investor instructs the broker to obtain the best price possible on a securities transaction.

Markets. See Securities markets.

Market specialist. A person who is designated by an exchange and is responsible for maintaining an orderly market in a given stock.

Market value. The current price for a share.

Maturity. The length of time over which a loan is repaid.

Medicaid. Part of the federal government's social security provision of health insurance benefits. It pays for a variety of health care services. Persons eligible for this are those who cannot afford to pay for adequate health care themselves—eligibility is partially based on income and asset requirements.

Medical expense insurance. Medical expenses covered in this type of policy vary from policy to policy. It usually covers a portion of the charges related to a doctor's visit in a hospital.

Medical payments coverage of auto insurance. Pays for all reasonable medical expenses caused by an accident, such as surgical, medical, X-ray, dental, ambulance, hospital, nursing, funeral, and other related expenses. It applies to the insured, the spouse, relatives living at home, and other passengers in the insured car. The insured, spouse, and relatives are also covered if they are struck as pedestrians by another vehicle. Liability limits are stated on a per-person basis.

Medicare. Part of the federal government's social security provision of health insurance benefits. Those eligible for this are: (1) persons 65 years of age or older who are eligible for social security benefits; (2) widows 51 years of age or older who are eligible for mother's and disability social security benefits; (3) persons who are eligible for social security disability benefits for at least 24 months.

Medicare, Part A. The basic hospital and medical insurance program, which also includes payments for nursing facilities and home health care.

Medicare, Part B. The provision for supplementary medical benefits.

Minimum balance checking account. A specified dollar amount or a minimum balance must be maintained in this account at all times.

Minimum savings balance checking account. The checking account owner must maintain a minimum balance in a savings account, on which interest is received.

Minority trust. Similar to a custodianship account except that more than $30,000 can be placed in it. It is managed by a trustee.

Minor's savings account. A minor can own an account with the permission of his or her legal guardian.

Mobile homes. Prefabricated shelter units that are built in a factory, then moved to their permanent location.

Monetary coins. Issued to commemorate certain events in some foreign countries.

Money market mutual funds. A mutual fund that has invested its assets in short-term government and private securities. There are two types: taxable money funds and tax-free money funds.

Money order. A guaranteed payment order that is readily accepted and easily negotiable; it is widely used in making payments through the mail.

Monthly investment plan. See Systematic investment plan.

Mortgage. Borrowing to finance a house purchase.

Mortgage bonds. Bonds secured by physical assets of the issuing firm. There are two types: senior mortgage bonds, which have first claim over proceeds from liquidating pledged assets, and junior mortgage bonds.

Mortgage REITs. Real estate investment trusts that invest in long-term mortgage bonds.

Municipal bonds. Bonds issued by states, cities, school districts, and other public institutions.

Mutual fund. Pool of investment funds contributed by investors and professionally managed.

Mutual insurance company. Owned by its policyholders. It can be expected to neither earn profits nor lose money.

N

Naked option. See Uncovered option.

National credit cards. Examples are American Express, Diners Club, and Carte Blanche. They are very similar to bank credit cards in use, except that (1) while bank cards are usually free, national cards charge an annual fee; (2) national cards do not offer revolving credit as bank cards do; (3) bank cards are accepted by substantially more businesses than are national cards.

National Credit Union Administration (NCUA). Insures accounts at credit unions.

Negative cash flow. Cash inflows are less than cash outflows.

Net asset value of a mutual fund. The price of one share of a mutual fund. It is equal to the fund's total market value less its liabilities, divided by the number of its shares outstanding.

Net cost method. The formula for this method is as follows: (a certain chosen number of years of policy premiums) − (expected dividends to be paid plus the policy cash value) − (comparison period) = average annual net cost per $1,000 of insurance.

Net income. The difference between sales and all expenses.

Net long-term gain. (Long-term gain) − (long-term loss) = net long-term gain.

Net short-term gain. (Short-term gain) − (short-term loss) = net short-term gain.

Net or closed-end car lease. The lessee's financial responsibilities end with the last lease payment, providing the car has lower mileage than that specified in the lease and shows only normal wear and tear.

Net payment cost index. This method adjusts only premiums and dividends for the time value of money. The formula for this method is as follows: (present value of all premiums paid − present value of all dividends received) ÷ (number of years used for analysis) = average annual cost for the policy.

Net worth. What a family or person would own after paying off all liabilities. (Assets) − (liabilities) = net worth.

No-fault auto insurance. Requires that drivers involved in accidents be paid by their own insurance companies, irrespective of who is to blame for the accident. Basically, it extends no-fault coverage to liability coverage.

No-fault coverages of auto insurance. Apply to the insured; losses are covered without regard to who is at fault. They include collision, comprehensive, and medical payments.

No-load mutual fund. One that does not charge a sales commission on the sale of its stock.

Nominal interest rate. The stated or advertised interest rate.

Noncontributory pension plan. In this pension plan, the employee does not make any contributions.

Noneconomic spending. Expenses that cannot be related to quality, price, or family consumption needs.

Nonfinancial assets. Assets in the form of physical property, such as real estate, cars, boats, and personal property.

Nonforfeiture clause. Contains the insured's settlement options if he or she defaults on premium payments.

Nonparticipating life insurance policy. Does not pay a portion of the unanticipated earnings of the insurer to the policyholder.

Nonprobate property transfers. Transferring property ownership without a will and without probate. This occurs through the conversion of separate property and/or community property to joint tenancy, tenancy in common, or tenancy by the entirety for estate planning purposes.

Note. A legal document in which the borrower promises to repay the loan under agreed-on terms.

NOW account. Equivalent to checking accounts paying interest on the funds on deposit.

Numismatic coins. Collected for their uniqueness and their value as antiques.

NYSE indices. The most comprehensive set of measures of market performance.

O

Odd lot orders. Orders involving less than 100 shares.

Open-end car lease. The lessor specifies a wholesale value for the car at the end of the lease period. Lease payments are based on the difference between the new car price and the end-of-lease wholesale value. When the lease is over, the lessee is responsible for any difference between the actual and agreed-on wholesale prices.

Open-ended credit. Charge accounts and credit cards issued by stores, oil companies, banks, and other companies.

Open-end mutual fund. Mutual funds without a fixed number of shares outstanding.

Option. A contract that gives the option buyer the right to buy from or sell to the option seller a fixed number of common shares of a specified company at a certain price during a specified time period.

Organized markets. Buildings where securities are traded.

Overdraft. Occurs when a check is presented to a bank for an amount that is greater than the checking account balance.

Outstanding shares. Issued shares less Treasury shares.

Overextension. Spending more through credit than one can afford to spend.

Over-the-counter (OTC) market. A group of securities dealers who maintain an inventory of unlisted stocks.

P

"Paid-up" limited-payment whole life insurance. A policy for which payments are made until the policyholder turns 65, after which the policy becomes "paid up."

Partial disability. One that prevents the insured from doing some, but not all, of the duties related to his or her occupation.

Participating life insurance policy. Pays a portion of the unanticipated earnings of the insurer to the policyholder.

Participating preferred stocks. Dividends increase with increases in the firm's earnings.

Par value. A nominal value for a share.

Pawnbroker. Lender of money that is secured by the borrower's goods.

"Pay as you go" pension plan. The firm pays its retired workers their pensions from its current operating budget.

Payee. The person to whom a check is made out.

P/E ratio. Ratio of closing stock price to the firm's earnings for the 12 most recent months.

Pension. Regular, periodic payments that employers pay to their qualifying retired workers.

Permanent life insurance. See Whole life insurance.

Personal assets. A person's attitude, personality, skills, and value system.

Personal Auto Policy (PAP). Limited strictly to personal cars.

Personal identification number (PIN). A number used by a customer to identify himself or herself to an ATM.

Personal property. Includes furniture, appliances, clothing, and other personal belongings. Also known as household property.

Points. A loan service fee; each point equals 1 percent of the amount of the loan.

Postdated check. A check dated later than the date on which it was written.

Power of invasion. A clause in a trust allowing either the trustee or the beneficiary the right to partially liquidate the estate principal and pay out the proceeds to the beneficiary.

Preferred stock. Hybrid security without maturity and generally paying a fixed dividend.

Prepayment. A loan repaid before it matures.

Prepayment of loan clause. Allows lenders to charge the borrower a penalty for repaying a loan before its due date (prepaying).

Presumptive disability. One for which the insured is automatically considered to be disabled.

Price adjustments. Adjustments made in the price of the stock through stock dividends and stock splits.

Primary beneficiary. The policyholder's first choice of beneficiary.

Primary markets. Corporations sell securities, generally through brokers, to investors.

Probability. The numerical measurement of the chance that an uncertain event will occur.

Probate. The legal process of proving to a court that a will is valid and of carrying out the will's terms.

Progressive tax rates. Taxes increase as taxable income increases.

Proportional tax rate structure. The percentage of taxable income paid in taxes remains the same irrespective of the level of taxable income.

Prorating clause of disability insurance. Allows the insurer to increase the premiums if the insured changes to a more risky occupation.

Put. An option to sell.

Q

Quality-of-products legislation. Laws enacted to ensure that products sold to consumers are wholesome.

Quarters of coverage for social security. A certain amount of covered income earned produces one-quarter of coverage for qualifying for social security benefits.

Quitclaim deed. Allows title grantor to relinquish his or her interest in the property.

R

Random walk hypothesis. All information about a stock is widely known and fully accounted for in market prices.

Rational investment choice. The highest return in the same risk category or the lowest risk in the same return category.

Ratio planning. A fund management technique that requires transferring funds between a defensive and an aggressive portfolio.

Real estate brokers or agents. The sales personnel at a realty company.

Real estate investment trust (REIT). Similar to a closed-end investment company; specializes in buying real estate properties.

Real estate syndicate. A group of investors who pool their money to buy high-priced real estate.

Real property. Land and all property attached to land, such as buildings, trees, fences, etc.

"Red bread." Deficit spending category.

Refund annuity. Guarantees not only payments for the life of the beneficiary but also minimum total benefits. If the beneficiary dies prematurely, his or her estate is paid the remainder of the total benefits.

Registered bond. Registered in the name of the bond buyer.

Regressive taxes. The percentage of income paid out in taxes decreases with increases in income.

Renewable term life insurance. Has an option that allows the insured to renew the insurance for a specified time period a specified number of times.

Rent. Payment for use of someone else's property.

Repossession. The lender usually has the legal right to physically take back goods if they have been used as collateral for a loan that is in default.

Restrictive endorsement. The payee's signing of his or her name to the back of a check,

together with words that limit the manner in which the check can be negotiated.

Resume. A brief summary of one's job requirements, experience, education, and background.

Retained earnings. On an income statement, this equals net income minus dividends paid for the year. On a balance sheet, this is cumulated from year to year.

Retirement. To give up one's work, business, etc., especially because of age.

Revenue bonds. Backed by special sources of income.

Reverse annuity mortgage. The homeowner can take out a loan on the equity of the house.

Revocable trust. A trust that is controlled by the grantor and can be revoked by him or her.

Revolving charge accounts. A charged purchase can be paid for with partial payments. The customer also has the option of placing additional purchases on the charge account as long as a specific credit limit is not exceeded.

Rider. See Endorsement (insurance).

Risk. The possibility that actual returns may not equal expected returns.

Risk management. The identification of a desirable combination of control, retention, and transfer of risk.

Rollover mortgage. The interest rate and other loan terms are renegotiable after a fixed time period.

Round lot orders. Orders in multiples of 100 shares.

Round turn. The usual way of trading commodities; involves opening, then closing a position.

"Rubber" check. See "Bounced" check.

Rule of "78." The method most often used to calculate the amount of finance charges to be rebated when a loan is repaid before its maturity date.

S

Safe deposit box. A locked metal box in a bank's vault in which a renter stores items that are hard to replace.

Savings. Amount of income not spent.

Savings banks. These provide services very similar to services provided by commercial banks.

Savings and loan associations. Institutions that specialize in offering savings accounts and in providing mortgage funds.

Secondary markets. Buying and selling of securities takes place between investors.

Second mortgage. One that is next in priority to a first mortgage.

Secured installment loans. Loans for cars, home improvements, boats, furniture, appliances, and other durable goods. These loans are backed by collateral.

Securities and Exchange Commission (SEC). A federal agency that oversees securities trading.

Securities Investor Protection Corporation (SIPC). A federal agency that insures investors' accounts at brokerage houses.

Securities markets. Places where stocks, bonds, and other financial instruments are traded.

Selling short. Selling borrowed stock.

Senior mortgage bond. Has first claims over proceeds from liquidation of pledged assets.

Series EE bonds. U.S. savings bonds. Interest on these is received only on redemption.

Series HH bonds. U.S. savings bonds. Can be redeemed after six months and have a maturity period of 10 years.

Service contract. Agreement purchased by an appliance owner to keep his or her appliance in working order.

Shared appreciation mortgage (SAM). The lender charges a lower interest rate on the mortgage, in return for a portion of the price appreciation on the project.

Short-term capital gains and losses. Occur when the property is held for one year or less.

Single-premium life insurance. Requires only one premium payment.

Sinking fund. A fund set up to help a firm to eventually retire its bonds.

Special endorsement. A payee's signing of his or her name to the back of a check, together with words specifying the person to whom the payee is making the check payable.

Special warranty deed. Guarantees only that the owner has attached no claims or restrictions to the property.

Specific legacy. A bequest of a specific item.

Speculative bonds. Bonds that investment advisers believe have a high degree of investment risk.

Standard deduction. A specified amount claimed as a deduction on each tax return.

Standard & Poor's averages. A set of very popular measures of securities market performance.

Stockbroker. A person licensed by the Securities and Exchange Commission to process buy and sell securities orders for clients.

Stock dividends. Payment of stock as dividends.

Stockholders. Owners of common stock in a company.

Stock insurance company. Similar to any other corporation. It sells its services to its customers or policyholders; it raises capital from its stockholders, and all profits and losses go to them.

Stock split. The par value of shares is reduced in proportion to the new shares being issued.

Stop-loss order. An order to sell stock at the market when the price has declined to a specified level.

Stop-payment order. An order by a depositor to a financial institution to refuse to pay a check when presented for payment.

Straight life annuity. Pays monthly payments until the beneficiary dies. The insurance company retains the unpaid portion of the total benefits should the beneficiary die prematurely.

Straight term life insurance. Has a fixed amount of benefits and is issued for a fixed time period.

Street name. Securities are purchased by a brokerage house in its own name on behalf of a client.

Striking price. The exercise price for an option.

Subordinated debenture. Subordinates its claim to certain specified debts.

Surrender cost index. See Interest-adjusted cost index.

Systematic investment plan. Also known as monthly investment plan. Requires systematic payments for periodic stock purchases.

T

Tax. A compulsory payment of a percentage of income, property value, etc., to support a government.

Tax bracket. Tax rate that applies to the last dollar of taxable income.

Tax-deferred savings plan (TDSP). A retirement plan that allows workers at qualified companies to defer taxes on as much as 10 percent of their salaries.

Tax evasion. Payment of less in taxes than the law requires. It is illegal. It is caused by understatement of earnings and/or overstatement of expenses.

Tax-exempt bonds. Bonds issued by state and local governments.

Tax rate schedules. Schedules used in determining taxes if the taxpayer uses income averaging, if the maximum tax on personal service income is applicable, or if income or

exemption limits stated in Tax Table A are exceeded.

Tenancy by the entirety. Available only to married persons. It is the same as joint tenancy, except that one spouse cannot dispose of his or her share without permission of the other spouse.

Tenancy in common. The deceased owner's share goes to his or her heirs.

Tenant. A person renting housing.

Term life insurance. Provides insurance protection only, covering the insured for a specified period of time.

Testamentary capacity. Only a person with this can write a valid will. It exists when a person can reasonably well decide on the distribution of his or her estate. It refers to soundness of mind as well as absence of undue influence.

Testamentary intention. The testator or testatrix intended to write a will that would be effective on his or her death and stated so in writing in the will.

Testamentary trust. A trust created by placing an appropriately worded clause in the testator's will. The clause places the trust principal under the trustee's control on the testator's death.

Testator. A male making out a will.

Testatrix. A female making out a will.

Thirty-day or regular charge account. Charged purchases must be paid for in 30 days.

Time deposit account. The account owner receives interest on deposits, and withdrawals are low in number.

Time-share homes. The buyer buys the use of the house for a short time period, which varies from one week to six months.

Title. The right to ownership of a property.

Title abstract. A history of the ownership of the property.

Title insurance. Provides the home buyer with insurance against any claims arising from a defective title. It can be purchased through a title insurance company.

Traveler's checks. Checks that are readily accepted as guaranteed payment because the person must buy them in order to use them. They are safer to carry than cash, as they can be easily replaced if stolen.

Treasury shares. Shares repurchased by a firm.

Triple net leases. Require tenants to pay all utilities, insurance, taxes, and maintenance costs.

Trust. A legal procedure in which a trustee manages the principal given by the grantor, in accordance with his or her instructions, for the benefit of the beneficiary.

Trustee. An individual or institution that manages the assets for a trust.

Trust savings account. Owned by one person on behalf of another.

Truth-in-Lending Act. A federal law requiring lenders of consumer credit to disclose to borrowers certain facts about the loan they are making.

Turnaround property. A run-down property that can be fixed up and sold for a profit.

U

Umbrella insurance. Provides coverage beyond that provided by other policies. It extends general liability coverage and provides coverage for libel and slander.

Uncovered option. One in which the option seller does not have the security to sell on a call.

Unfunded pension plan. Same as a "pay as you go" pension plan.

Unit pricing. Information provided on price per unit for products sold.

Unit trust. A special type of mutual fund.

Universal life insurance. The insured can periodically adjust the amount of coverage up or down to meet changing needs.

Unlisted stock. One that is not listed on an organized exchange.

U.S. savings bonds. Bonds that are issued and fully backed by the U.S. government.

V

Valued payment plan. Under this type of plan, the insurance company agrees to pay the insured a fixed sum of money if an insured event occurs.

Variable annuity. An annuity in which the dollar amount of periodic benefits varies from payment to payment.

Variable life insurance. Similar to whole life insurance, except that the policyholder can specify how the premiums are to be invested.

Variable rate mortgage (VRM). A mortgage for which interest rates are not fixed. The rate applicable to the mortgage goes up or down as interest rates in general go up or down.

Vesting. The gaining of rights by a worker to the pension contributions made by an employer on the worker's behalf.

W

Wage assignment or garnishment clause. A lender can collect a portion of the borrower's wages if the borrower has defaulted on a loan.

Waiver of premium. With this option, the insurer waives premiums if the insured becomes permanently disabled. All policy benefits remain in force during the waiver period.

Warranty. The consumer's assurance that a product will work as it is supposed to. A guarantee issued by a manufacturer or supplier of goods and services explaining its obligation and, generally, the user's or buyer's responsibilities also.

Warranty deed. The safest deed for the buyer, since it guarantees that the title is free of any legal claims.

Whole life insurance. Remains in force as long as the insured continues to pay the insurance premiums. The premiums remain level and fixed as long as the policy remains in force.

Will. A legal document that specifies how a person wants his or her estate to be distributed.

"Window sticker" price. Lists the manufacturer's suggested list price for a car and the itemized prices of the options.

Worker's compensation. State-financed benefits payable to a worker disabled by a job-related injury or sickness. It varies from state to state. Benefits include medical, income, and rehabilitation.

Y

Yield. Calculated by dividing dividend times 100 by the closing stock price.

Yield to maturity. Total return provided by a bond held to maturity.

Z

Zoning laws. Laws of cities or municipalities that regulate what types of building can occur in certain areas of the city.

Index

G

H

Q

R

S